LONDON
A HISTORY

Francis Sheppard, author of *London 1808–1870: the Infernal Wen*, and of *The Treasury of London's Past*, was from 1954 to 1982 General Editor of the multi-volume *Survey of London*, now part of the Royal Commission on the Historical Monuments of England.

LONDON
A HISTORY

Francis Sheppard

OXFORD
UNIVERSITY PRESS

OXFORD

UNIVERSITY PRESS

Great Clarendon Street, Oxford OX2 6DP

Oxford University Press is a department of the University of Oxford.
It furthers the University's objective of excellence in research, scholarship,
and education by publishing worldwide in

Oxford   New York

Athens Auckland Bangkok Bogotá Buenos Aires Calcutta
Cape Town Chennai Dar es Salaam Delhi Florence Hong Kong Istanbul
Karachi Kuala Lumpur Madrid Melbourne Mexico City Mumbai
Nairobi Paris São Paulo Singapore Taipei Tokyo Toronto Warsaw

with associated companies in Berlin Ibadan

Oxford is a registered trade mark of Oxford University Press
in the UK and in certain other countries

Published in the United States
by Oxford University Press Inc., New York

© Francis Sheppard 1998

The moral rights of the author have been asserted
Database right Oxford University Press (maker)

First published 1998
First issued as an Oxford University Press paperback 2000

British Library Cataloguing in Publication Data

Data available

Library of Congress Cataloging in Publication Data

Sheppard, F. H. W. (Francis Henry Wollaston), 1921–
London: a history / Francis Sheppard.
p.   cm.
Includes bibliographical references and index.
1. London (England)—History. I. Title.
DA677.S54   1998
942.1—dc21   98–7999

ISBN 0-19-285369-4

1 3 5 7 9 10 8 6 4 2

Typeset by Pure Tech India Ltd, Pondicherry
Printed in Hong Kong

For Sue and Christopher Hibbert
with respect and love

PREFACE

This work attempts to describe the history of London from Julius Caesar to the present day. It also attempts to show that London is not a parasite dependant on the labours of the provinces, but has in fact been for centuries the mainspring of the cultural, economic, financial, and political life of the nation, as well as for a long period its largest manufacturing centre. So if the era of the nation state is now drawing to an end and regionalization is to become the new order of the day, London might well benefit, and cease to underpin the rest of the United Kingdom.

I am most grateful to Oxford University Press for so patiently and uncomplainingly awaiting the completion of the book, and in particular I wish to thank Ivon Asquith, Tony Morris, Ruth Parr, and Anna Illingworth. The numerous anonymous readers who were consulted by the Press made most valuable suggestions from which I hope the book has benefited; and so too did the copy editor, Rowena Anketell. I am especially indebted to Professor Christopher Brooke, who read the first drafts of the medieval chapters, and to Professor Theo Barker, whose cheerful suggestions about the later chapters were of immense value.

This is not a work of original research, and so it is based on the labours of innumerable scholars who have worked in the inexhaustible and perennially fascinating field of the history of London. To all of them, I tender my respectful thanks. First and foremost, of course, are numerous members of the staff of the Museum of London, where I have spent so many happy hours, and in particular John Clark, Valerie Cumming, Mireille Galinou, Max Hebditch, Gavin Morgan, Alex Werner, and Oona Wills. In the finding of illustrations I am especially grateful to His Honour Owen Stable, QC, and Mrs Stable for allowing me to reproduce a picture in their possession, and for providing me with a photograph of it. At the Prints, Maps and Drawings Department of the Guildhall Library there has always been a warm welcome and enormous knowledge freely available from Ralph Hyde and John Fisher; and at the City of Newcastle Central Library Mrs Patricia Sheldon provided highly valued help about the Tyneside coal trade.

Finally, I am most grateful to Bruce Hunter for his reassuring interest; to Christopher Hibbert for the frequent use of his photocopying machine; and to the staff of the London Library for so patiently entering up on my behalf the loan of so very many books and periodicals; and above all, to my wife, who expects so little and gives so much.

F. H. W. S.

CONTENTS

LIST OF PLATES

MOL = Museum of London

MoLAS = Museum of London Archaeology Service

Between pages 78 and 79

1. Bird's-eye view from the south-east c.AD 120 (drawn by Peter Froste for MOL)
2. Bird's-eye view from the north-west c.AD 250 (drawn by Peter Froste for MOL)
3. Model of north end of the bridge (MOL)
4. Late first-century quay near Fish Street Hill, with base of bridge pier (MoLAS photograph)
5. Model of second-century basilica and forum (MOL)
6. Defensive wall at The Crescent (MoLAS photograph)
7. Saxon brooch found at Mitcham (MOL)
8. Penny of King Alfred (MOL)
9. Part of the Bayeux Tapestry (by special permission of the City of Bayeux)
10. Penny of William the Conqueror (MOL)
11. City seal, St Thomas Becket enthroned (Corporation of London Records Office)
12. William the Conqueror's charter to London (Corporation of London Records Office)
13. John Ball preaching outside London, 1381 (British Library, MS Royal 18 E 1, fo. 165v)
14. Westminster in 1647; engraving by Hollar (MOL)
15. London from Southwark: oil on wood, c.1630 (MOL)
16. St Paul's Cathedral: engraving by Hollar (MOL)
17. The Tower, aerial view (MOL photograph)
18. The Great Plague: engraving, 1665 (MOL)
19. The Great Fire: oil, 1666 (MOL)

Between pages 174 and 175

20. Braun and Hogenberg's map-view of London, 1574 edn. of *Civitates Orbis, Terrarum*
21. London in 1720, from Strype's edition of Stow's *Survey of London*
22. London in 1831, surveyed by John Outhett (Guildhall Library, Corporation of London)
23. Railways and underground railways, 1913 (London Transport Museum)
24. Underground railways in 1933 (London Transport Museum)

LIST OF FIGURES

DEFINITIONS

London, or the city, or the capital, means the whole metropolitan urban area as built up at the time to which these terms wherever used refer.

The City, with a capital C, has either a geographical or a functional meaning. Geographically, 'the City' means the City of London, i.e. the area (sometimes also referred to as the Square Mile) governed by the City Corporation, or more correctly the Corporation of London, which is situated mostly but not wholly within the ancient defensive walls—hence the distinction between the intramural and extramural areas of the City. Functionally, 'the City' is a collective term denoting either the municipal authorities (i.e. usually the Corporation or its forebears) or the business and financial operations conducted mostly within the area of the City, but which in recent years have spread out to other parts of London and the South-East. It is hoped that the distinction between these meanings will be clear from the context in which the term 'the City' has been used.

The County of London is the Administrative County of London as defined by the Local Government Act, 1888.

Greater London is the Greater London Council area as defined in the Local Government Act, 1963.

The Home Counties are Hertfordshire, Essex, Kent, Surrey, and Middlesex.

The South-East Region consists of Bedfordshire, Berkshire, Buckinghamshire, East Sussex, Essex, Greater London, Hampshire, Hertfordshire, Isle of Wight, Kent, Middlesex, Oxfordshire, Surrey, and West Sussex.

Among the noble cities of the world that are celebrated by Fame, the City of London, seat of the Monarchy of England, is one that spreads its fame wider, sends its wealth further, and lifts its head higher than all others.

William FitzStephen's *Descriptio Londoniae*, 1170s

London is the common country of all England, from which is derived to all parts of this realm all good and ill occurrent here.

Thomas Bedyll, Archdeacon of London, to Thomas Cromwell, 14 June 1537

All our Creeks seek to one River, all our Rivers run to one Port, all our Ports join to one Town, all our Towns make but one City, and all our Cities and Suburbs to one vast, unwieldy and disorderly Babel of buildings, which the world calls London.

Thomas Milles, Customer for Sandwich, 1604

I looked on it [the City] as the master wheel, by whose motion the successive rotations of all the lesser must follow.

Lord Mordaunt to King Charles II, 26 January 1660

The happiness of London is not to be conceived but by those who have been in it. I will venture to say that there is more learning and science within the circumference of ten miles from where we now sit than in all the rest of the kingdom.

Dr Samuel Johnson, 1769

'Doesn't the best of everything come to London?' he would ask, 'and doesn't it follow as a nattaral consequence, that the best 'unting is to be had from it?'

Mr Jorrocks, in *Handley Cross* by Robert Surtees, 1845

London...takes a lot of understanding. It's a great place. Immense. The richest town in the world, the biggest port, the greatest manufacturing town, the Imperial city—the centre of civilisation, the heart of the world.

H. G. Wells, *Tono-Bungay*, 1909

More than ever, London is the omnipotent, all-knowing, unassailable hub of the nation.

Raymond Seitz, US Ambassador to London 1991–1994. (From his memoir, *Over Here*, published by Weidenfeld & Nicholson, London, 1998)

Introduction

In the parish church of St Mary at Taunton in Somerset there stands a full-length effigy of Robert Gray, a native of that town and a Citizen and Merchant Taylor of London, where he died in 1638, possessed of a considerable fortune. At his shop in Bread Street in the City he had built up a retail and wholesale trade chiefly in cloth, and for many years he had ridden around to the great provincial fairs buying cloths which he finished and dyed. Much of his business between distant places like Exeter, Bristol, or Beverley and London was transacted by means of inland credit transfers known as bills of exchange, and by 1635 it was profitable enough to enable him to build a substantial range of almshouses in Taunton for the benefit of the aged poor there. These almshouses, decorated with Gray's own coat of arms and that of the Merchant Taylors' Company of London, still stand in East Street, Taunton, still, after the lapse of more than three and a half centuries, fulfilling Gray's original intentions. And round the corner in St Mary's church, Robert Gray himself is commemorated by the inscription beneath his effigy:

> Taunton bore him, London bred him,
> Piety train'd him, virtue led him;
> Earth enrich'd him, heaven carest him,
> Taunton blest him, London blest him.
> This thankful town, that mindful city,
> Share his piety and his pity.
> What he gave, and how he gave it,
> Ask the poor, and you shall have it.

Robert Gray's career is just a small single strand in the ancient and ever-changing web of relationships between London and the rest of England. This book, besides following the long history of London from prehistoric times to the present day, also attempts to trace the warp and weft of some of the bonds which have linked metropolis and provinces. Sometimes London's role has been presented much like that of a spider, hungry to gobble up any living creature within its web; or sometimes London has been seen in a more favourable light, as the sun at the centre of its universe. Either way, it is certain on the one hand that London has always depended upon the country not only for the nourishment of food and fuel but also, until about a century ago, for the lifeblood of a continuous supply of immigrants (such as Robert Gray); and that on the other hand the economy, culture, and demographic structure of the provinces were and still are, in

constantly changing ways and degrees, powerfully affected or sometimes dominated by the metropolis.

In comparison with other great cities of the world London has moreover for
centuries had a uniquely ascendant position. In the later sixteenth century (the
earliest period for which reasonably reliable figures of population are available)
London was thirteen times larger than the second biggest city in England (Norwich), and even in 1901 the new County of London was still over six times larger in
population than its nearest rival, Liverpool. In no other Western country (except
perhaps in the case of Amsterdam in the seventeenth century) was a single city so
demographically dominant—in the 1930s over one in five of the whole population
of England and Wales lived in Greater London—and nowhere else were the roles of
political capital, chief port, chief financial, commercial, manufacturing, and cultural centre all concentrated within one metropolis. London was and still is indeed
altogether unique.

This long ascendancy within the island of Britain was in considerable measure
the result of favourable geographical position. London's site was chosen by the
founding Romans because it was the lowest bridgeable point across the island's
principal river, the estuary of which was opposite to the great waterway of the
Rhine, leading into the heart of Europe. After the Norman Conquest and the
establishment in England of a highly centralized and territorially compact unitary
state, its boundaries for the most part sharply defined by the immutable frontier of
the sea, London emerged in the fourteenth century as its natural and permanent
political capital. This position has never since been seriously challenged; and at
critical moments in the nation's history, such as during the Henrician Reformation
or the Civil War or the Blitz of 1940, its behaviour had a probably decisive
influence on the course of national events. Even the Industrial Revolution can be
thought of not only in terms of the coal, steam, machinery, and factories generally
associated with the great new cities of the North, but also in some degree as a
response to the vast demand for food, fuel, clothes, and goods of all kinds created
by London, which was by far the greatest centre of consumption anywhere in the
Western world; and through the *circulation* of capital London certainly provided a
crucial metropolitan link in the virtuous circle of the evolving national economy
during the age of industrialization.

Then later London became the hub and capital of the British Empire as well as of
Britain itself, and the pound sterling, efficiently managed from London by the
gentlemanly capitalists of Westminster and the City, became in Victorian times the
principal vehicle of international trade throughout the world. In many fields of
activity, whether financial, commercial, political, professional, cultural, or fashionable, London was the place to be—the national centre of wealth and power,
each of its numerous functions buttressing the others.

This concentration of functions and of wealth in the metropolis is the principal
ingredient in the drift to the South-East which (interrupted for only a while by the
rise of the industrial towns of the North) has been going on for centuries, recently
reinforced by the changing economic posture of the nation brought about by

membership of the European Union. But London itself has exploded outwards, new means of travel, transport, and electronic communications having all greatly extended the range of metropolitan influence. For the statisticians and demographers, always in need of geographical units that correspond with contemporary realities, the South-East Region, of which London is the core, extends from Southampton to Harwich, and over a third of all the population of England and Wales lives within it. So despite its relative decline in the hierarchy of the great cities of the world, and despite its own internal problems, London within Britain is perhaps as paramount as ever. On the other hand Fax, the Internet, and the electronic revolution work both ways, and much metropolitan business nowadays can be conducted just as well from outside London as within it; and at the time of writing (1997) devolution of some political affairs to Scotland, Wales, and perhaps the English regions is impending. It seems, in fact, that for better or worse, the age-old ascendancy of the capital city is under more serious threat than for almost a thousand years.

PART I

Londinium

INTRODUCTION

London was founded by the Romans. When Julius Caesar and his expeditionary force reached the River Thames for the first time in the year 54 B C they found no town or even any permanent settlement there. In his account of his two expeditions to Britain (the first one, a quick reconnaissance raid in the previous year, had not penetrated as far as the Thames) Caesar only mentions one town, the capital of the British chief, Cassivellaunus, which, so some scholars now think, was at Wheathampstead in Hertfordshire. In Caesar's day it was, in his own words, 'a natural stronghold of the surrounding forest and swamps, into which large numbers of both cattle and men had already flocked'. Though the Britons call it a town [*oppidum*], he continues, 'it was so only in the British acceptation of the term, by which is meant no more than a central rallying-point from hostile incursion, formed of some inaccessible piece of woodland that has been fortified by a high rampart and ditch'. There were, in fact, no towns in the modern sense of the word in Britain before the Romans; and if London had existed even in the old British sense, Caesar would certainly have tried to capture it (as he did indeed capture Cassivellaunus' citadel) and would therefore have mentioned it.[1]

The Romans were great town builders. For them the city state of the classical world was the natural form of social organization, and city life was regarded as the norm throughout the Mediterranean basin. Along the coastal belt of North Africa there were over three hundred *municipia*, and in Provence and Languedoc in Southern Gaul the numerous *colonia* established for retired army veterans included such towns later known as Arles, Orange, and Nîmes. In these regions the process of urbanization had already made substantial headway in pre-Roman times under Greek auspices, but further away from the Mediterranean pre-Roman centres were much fewer. Under the Romans those which had natural advantages of situation soon became flourishing towns. Lyons, for instance, at the confluence of the Rhône and the Saône, became the Roman capital city of all the Gauls; and Paris had existed for several centuries as a riverside settlement of the Parissi tribe on the Île de la Cité. But in Britain such centres as existed in pre-Roman times were for the most part not situated at the topographically nodal points later favoured by the imperial administrators; and by their names such ancient cities as Gloucester, Lincoln, or Cirencester, testify to their specifically Roman foundation.

By contrast the name London — or Londinium, to give it its standard Roman form — proclaims no clear message about origins. According to Geoffrey of Monmouth, writing in the twelfth century AD, the city had been founded in the year 1108 B C by Brute, a god or demigod descended from Venus and Jupiter. Some thousand years later King Lud, supposedly a near relative of Cassivellaunus, had improved the place by constructing 'faire buildings, Towers and Walles', and named it Caire-Lud, or Ludstown, in honour of himself. John Stow, the Elizabethan historian whose *Survey of London* was first published in 1598, did not believe a word of all this, but he was not convinced by any alternative explanation either.[2] The Celtic root 'Lond' has more recently been sometimes explained as 'town of Londinos', a personal name based on *londo*, 'fierce'; but it might also refer to a local topographical feature. Many modern scholars profess a cheerful agnosticism on the matter.[3]

Archaeological excavations in and near the historic core of London (i.e. the City) have revealed a number of scattered artefacts dating from pre-Roman times. In Southwark traces of Iron Age occupation have been discovered, an Iron Age grave has been found within the Tower, and at Bermondsey farming was evidently taking place in the period 2000–1000 BC;[4] but no evidence of any permanent prehistoric settlement in the City has been found. What is certain, however, is that the Romans often made use of native names and Latinized them, and that within a very few years of the conquest in AD 43 the place was known as Londinium.

1

Urban Origins

The Roman invasion of Britain took place under the auspices of the Emperor Claudius, who ruled from AD 41 to 54. His reason for undertaking this hazardous project seems to have been more concerned with his own insecure position in Rome than with any inducements that Britain could offer. He had unexpectedly been elevated to the throne by the praetorian guard, the *corps d'élite* of the Roman army, members of which had been involved in the murder of his nephew and predecessor, Caligula. So what Claudius needed, if he was to avoid a similar fate, was military glory — the only means by which this hitherto awkward and retiring man could hope to keep the loyalty and respect of his formidable guardians.

The Britain to which Claudius' army came had changed considerably since Caesar's day. Like large parts of the continent of Europe it had for centuries been inhabited by Celtic Iron Age peoples, the relatively recently arrived Belgic branch of which was already in Caesar's time, as he himself noted, firmly settled in the south-eastern part of the island. A century later the ascendant tribal kingdom here was that of the Catuvellauni, whose famous King Cunobelinus (Shakespeare's Cymbeline) was minting coins at both Verulamium (St Albans) and Camulodunum (Colchester), and whose influence also extended into Kent. After Caesar's conquest of Gaul and the ensuing Romanization of that new province trade between Britain and the Continent, which had hitherto been concentrated at the port of Hengistbury Head (near Christchurch, in Hampshire), was evidently conducted on a much larger scale. Strabo, the Greek geographer who wrote about midway between Caesar's and Claudius' incursions, says that the British chiefs had submitted to the payment of Roman duties on both imports and exports to and from Britain. Much of this trade was in luxury goods, imports consisting of oil, ivory, amber, glass, 'and other petty wares of that sort', and exports including gold, silver, and hunting dogs, as well as the slaves for which Britain was long famous. There were also more workaday British products — grain, iron, and hides, all of which would have been needed in large quantities by the Roman armies stationed in the region of the Rhine in the early years of the first century AD. For commerce of this kind the harbours and inlets of the Kent and Essex coasts, and above all of the Thames Estuary, rather than distant Hengistbury

Head, provided the natural location. In this transference of the principal scene of commercial activity, which took place during the century or so between 54 BC and AD 43, may be seen the first faint assertion of the geographical power of what was to become Britain's economic centre of gravity.[1]

Aulus Plautius, who had previously been governor of the frontier province of Pannonia (Hungary) on the Danube, was the commander of the Claudian army. This is thought to have amounted to some 40,000 men, half of them being legionaries of predominantly Italian birth and the other half being auxiliaries recruited from more recently conquered territories. Despite the enormous strength of the force the expedition got off to a bad start, for, as Cassius Dio, our main source for these momentous events, relates, the soldiers refused to embark in a campaign 'outside the limits of the known world'. After some delay, however — which made their departure very late in the season — they agreed to go, and the fleet of transports set sail across the Channel in three divisions. The place or places of landing are not known, though it seems likely that Richborough, near Sandwich in Kent, was one of them, and no opposition was at first encountered. However, a stiff two-day battle somewhere along the River Medway (perhaps near Rochester) soon ensued, in which Aulus Plautius won the initiative by sending across a detachment of German auxiliaries specially trained to swim in full armour. Thereafter the Britons retreated westwards to the River Thames, which with their knowledge of the country they had no difficulty in crossing; and soon afterwards the Roman army arrived in the London area for the first time.[2]

The Thames was then very much wider and shallower than it is now. Around the site of the later London Bridge the river was tidal, and at high tide it was some five times as wide as it is now (some 1,000 metres compared with the present c.200 metres). The general scene confronting Aulus Plautius and his men was probably very similar to the great expanses of marshy flats or saltings still to be seen in many of the inlets along the coasts of East Anglia, to which wind and rain and sometimes tide still bring flood waters. On the south side of the river this alluvial strip, broken up by numerous muddy creeks, was about 1 kilometre wide opposite to the future site of the City, narrowing to about 200 metres opposite that of the Palace of Westminster. There, on the north side, the topography was much the same as on the south side, but further downstream at the future City site were several squat low hills or plateaux, with steep descents to the swampy ill-defined margin of the river.[3]

Cassius Dio says that

'the Britons retired to the river Thames at a point where it empties into the ocean and at flood-tide forms a lake. This they easily crossed because they knew where the firm ground and the easy passages in this region were to be found; but the Romans in attempting to follow them were not so successful. However, the Germans swam across again and some others got over by a bridge a little way upstream, after which they assailed the barbarians from several sides at once and cut down many of them. In pursuing the remainder incautiously, they got into swamps from which it was difficult to make their way out, and so lost a number of men.'[4]

Where these various events took place is not known. Fords used in the Iron Age probably existed at Brentford, Fulham, Battersea, and Westminster, and the retreating Britons may have used any or all of these. It is extremely unlikely, however, that any bridge, such as that mentioned by Cassius Dio, existed before the Romans' arrival. He may, of course, have meant that some detachments of the Roman army had got across by a temporary pontoon bridge which they had themselves built — Julius Caesar is known to have built a bridge across the Rhine in ten days;[5] but it is perhaps more likely that Dio, who was writing a century and a half after the event, confused this supposed native bridge with the London Bridge later built by the Romans.

Dio goes on to record that because of the continuing resistance of the Britons 'and because of the difficulties he had encountered at the Thames, Plautius became afraid, and instead of advancing any further, proceeded to guard what he had already won, and sent for [the Emperor] Claudius', as he had been instructed to do 'in case he met with any particularly stubborn resistance'.[6]

Claudius was at that time in Rome, and at least six weeks must have elapsed before he arrived in Britain to take personal command. During this enforced wait Aulus Plautius would probably have consolidated his bridgehead by a fort on the north side of the river, and started to secure his communications with Gaul by a road to his base at Richborough. In order to protect these communications from being cut by the Britons, the natural point for such a fort would be at the lowest place where the Thames could in normal conditions be forded. This was almost certainly at Westminster, where it seems the river was not then tidal. There, surrounded by the adjacent swampy alluvial plain and by the Tyburn stream, rose the little island of Thorney, on the flood plain gravel of which now stand the Palace of Westminster and Westminster Abbey — a natural site for a somewhat beleaguered Roman commander to entrench himself; and there traces of Roman occupation, particularly beneath the Abbey and in Parliament Square, have indeed been found, though their significance is not yet clear.[7]

So when Claudius arrived to take charge he may have found detachments of his army entrenched on Thorney Island. More reliable evidence of fortified and apparently short-lived enclosures of very early date has also been found on the site of St Bride's church, Fleet Street, and near Aldgate,[8] and it seems likely that by the time of the Emperor's arrival one or more bridgeheads existed somewhere on the north side of the river. At all events Claudius had no difficulty in advancing northward and capturing the chief centre of the Catuvellauni at Camulodunum (Colchester). Numerous tribes thereupon capitulated, and Claudius sailed away after a stay of only sixteen days, leaving Aulus Plautius with orders to subjugate the rest of the island. The first stage of the conquest was over.[9]

Neither Cassius Dio nor Suetonius nor Josephus, the authors of the only surviving written accounts of these events, mention London either by name or implication during the Claudian invasion; and despite the vast enlargement of knowledge made by the archaeological discoveries of recent years, the circumstances of the origin of Londinium are still far from clear. There are, however, good reasons for thinking that the foundation of the city did not take place until five or ten years after the arrival of the Romans in AD 43.

Important evidence for this relates to the alignment of the roads built by the Romans in the area, and to the position of the first river-crossing. Two of the earliest of these highways were those from the port of Richborough to London and from near London to Verulamium (St Albans). The former was built to provide a direct line of communication between Plautius' army beside the Thames and his Channel base, and the latter to provide a route forward to the interior of the island and to the nearest large native centre, exceeded in importance only by Camulo-dunum. Both these roads are called Watling Street, though this may not be of any significance. Of much greater interest is the fact that the alignment of both of them points towards the supposed ford at Westminster and not to the London Bridge area. The Kentish Watling Street extends westwards towards Westminster virtually

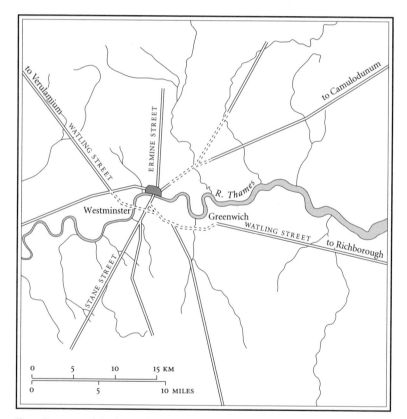

Fig. 1. Roman roads in the London area, showing the alignment of the two arms of Watling Street on Westminster

straight for 12 miles as far as Greenwich, where it is within sight of the ford. From Greenwich its westward continuation becomes unclear. Some deviation would certainly have been necessary to avoid the swampy ground around Deptford. Traces of a road have been found in Peckham, and eighteenth-century antiquaries mention a Roman road leading across St George's Fields (then unbuilt upon) to the significantly named Stangate Ferry opposite to the Palace of Westminster and the Abbey.[10] On the north side of the river the modern Edgware Road follows the course of the other Roman Watling Street, but no trace of any Roman road has been found south of the south end of Edgware Road at Marble Arch. The alignment of the highway does, however, point to the supposed ford at Westminster, not to the London Bridge area. It is unthinkable that either of these two highways would have been aligned on the Westminster ford if a better crossing or even perhaps a bridge already existed a couple of miles lower down the river; so it seems certain that they were built before any crossing around London Bridge had come into use. The recent discovery of a first-century road near the south end of the later bridge and evidently leading towards the Westminster crossing would, if confirmed, provide corroborative evidence for the existence of a ford there and of a strong Roman presence in its vicinity before the foundation of Londinium.[11]

From all this it follows that that foundation must have been the result of deliberate Roman policy. A considerable body of modern archaeological evidence shows that the decision was made in about AD 50–5. By that time the invading army had overrun most of southern Britain and established a 'frontier' just beyond the Fosse Way, which extends diagonally across the country from Ilchester in Somerset to Lincoln. The financial and economic exploitation of this newly pacified area could therefore begin, and Camulodunum, Verulamium, and Canterbury all trace their origins as Roman cities to the mid-century years. But at Londinium the task was different. It was a 'green field' site, and so there was no native settlement on which Roman institutions could be grafted, as was the usual practice elsewhere in Britain. At Londinium the task was also made much more formidable by the overriding need for an effective river crossing. Such a crossing was, indeed, Londinium's *raison d'être*, but the formidable engineering works needed to provide it can only have been carried out through the active direction of the Roman authorities and perhaps of the governor, who in about AD 50 was Publius Ostorius Scapula.[12]

Perspectives

Of all the hundreds of towns founded by the Romans throughout their Empire, or reconstituted from earlier settlements, none has had a greater influence on the course of human affairs than London. In Britain, other cities of Roman origin like Colchester, Cirencester, or York are not of the same order as London. Nor, when viewed across the perspective of nearly two thousand years, are even such great

Roman centres as Cologne, Lyons, or Cordoba. Only Paris, Constantinople, and Rome itself can stand comparison with London.

At all these cities, and, indeed, at all towns and cities everywhere, the physical landscape of the earth provides a basic ingredient in the shaping of each individual history; and at London as elsewhere the geological strata, the location in relation to the sea and to other lands, and the nature of the site itself have all been powerful agents in the formation of the city. Millions of years ago, when the surface of the earth ceased to heave and bulge, what is now the London Basin of the Thames Valley began to take something like its present shape — that of an arrowhead, pointing westward to the Goring Gap. There, some 45 miles west of London, the Thames flows through a narrow cleft flanked on either side by two long low ranges of chalk hills: the Chilterns, extending north-eastwards towards Cambridgeshire, and the western tip of the North Downs, extending (with breaks) eastwards through Surrey and Kent. The V-shaped declivity between these two chalk escarpments was for an immeasurable period covered by a shallow sea. On the bottom of this was deposited the sediment now called London Clay, which varies in thickness from 15 to 500 feet in different parts of London. But clay drains badly, and such land as existed was swampy, covered with tropical trees and plants, and frequented by crocodiles and what the Geological Survey describes as 'very odd-looking creatures from a present-day point of view'.[13]

In the London Clay fragments of fossilized plants washed down from the land have been found. This indicates that this muddy sea or lagoon was really the estuary of a large river, the course of which varied greatly over the ages in response to climatic changes. During the Ice Ages much of the northern hemisphere, including most of Britain, was intermittently covered with sheets of ice. As less

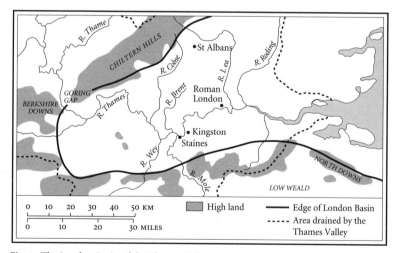

Fig. 2. The London Basin of the Thames Valley

water reached the sea through either rivers or rainfall, the level of the ocean fell. It has been estimated that during one such glacial period the sea was at least 330 feet (100 metres) lower than it is today, and Britain still formed part of the Continental land mass. But interspersed between these great freeze-ups, when the mean annual temperature was perhaps 10°C colder than it is now, there were warm periods of some fifty thousand or more years. The ice melted and the rivers produced torrential discharges which, in the case of the Thames, deposited a layer of gravel and sand up to 100 feet in thickness upon the clay bottom of the sea. In northern Europe there were several such climatic oscillations, and at each thaw the force of the river scooped out a fresh trough in the gravel brought down on the previous postglacial flood, most of which remained undisturbed. Eventually, however, after some half-million years, the Thames settled into a more or less stable course, flanked on either side by a belt of alluvium and peat deposited in more recent but still prehistoric times. These flat and marshy areas, now such districts of London as Rotherhithe, Pimlico, or the Isle of Dogs, were in their turn flanked by a series of ascending terraces of gravel, each one marking a major glacial episode of the faraway Pleistocene age. The width of these terraces varied greatly in different parts of the course of the river, the alluvial plain, for instance, being anything from

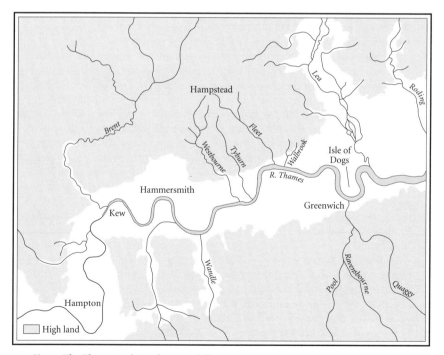

Fig. 3. The Thames and its tributaries: hill contours in the London area

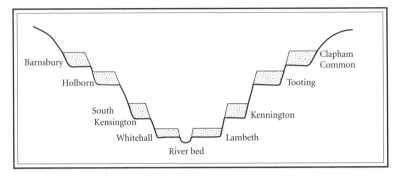

Fig. 4. Gravel terraces of London: cross-section

a few hundred feet to a mile in extent. The numerous tributaries of the Thames, such as the Wandle or the Lea or the Westbourne, carved out their own little valleys at right angles, cutting across the terraces of the main river to form a geological pattern of great complexity. Yet even when obscured by modern streets and buildings and engineering works it is still sometimes possible to detect the gradient between one main terrace and another, as, for instance, in the Haymarket or in South Kensington at Exhibition Road, which slopes upwards past the Science Museum to Hyde Park through three different terrace levels.[14]

The gravel deposits drained better than the remaining clay areas further away from the river, where the heavy wet soil encouraged the growth of dense impenetrable forest. So it is in the gravel areas, often near the river where fish provided abundant food, that man first settled in the London Basin. At Swanscombe, near Gravesend in Kent, pieces of a human skull not dissimilar to *Homo sapiens* have been found. They are thought to date from the last-but-one interglacial warm period, some 250,000 years ago, and are the earliest known fossilized human remains in Britain. At Acton and Stoke Newington there are traces of early toolmaking, extending over long periods of time; and the numerous finds of prehistoric weapons and tools which have been made in many parts of the London area, notably at Hampstead, Putney, and above all at Brentford, indicate a sizeable though scattered human presence for thousands of years before the Roman invasion. On the future site of Londinium itself, however, no settlement has been found.[15]

Most of this human activity took place after the final retreat of the glaciers, which at their maximum extent are thought to have reached what are now the northern outskirts of London. After the end of the Ice Ages — in perhaps around c.11,000 BC — the climate improved, the level of the ocean therefore rose, and in about 5,000–7,000 BC the sea cut through the bridge of land to continental Europe, and Britain became an island.[16]

After the coming of man this was the most important single event in the history of Britain, and the modern geographical forms which then took shape determined the course of much of London's history. The Thames estuary is situated opposite to the mouth of the greatest inland waterway into continental Europe — the Rhine, from which it is separated only by a narrow strip of sea. During all the centuries before the ages of steam and of motor and airborne transport the Rhine was the principal commercial highway of the Western world, along which passed ceaselessly up and down the goods of Northern Europe, the Mediterranean, and even of the East; and as the facts of geography usually change relatively little, the Rhine is still, despite the successive transport revolutions of recent times, the jugular vein of modern European trade, its importance still increasing. On or near to its northern outlets in the Low Countries there grew up many of the richest cities (in their day) of the Continent — Bruges, Ghent, Brussels, Antwerp — all easily accessible from the Thames estuary; and through the Narrow Seas was funnelled all the ocean-going trade of the Baltic and the towns of the Hanseatic League.

Inland, the Thames provided access deep into southern England, which has always been the richest part of Britain. For centuries this concentration of wealth was in some part due to the natural system of internal communication provided by such waterways as the Severn, the Bristol Avon, and the winding rivers of East Anglia; while the Thames and its numerous tributaries, notably the Kennet and the Lea, extended its commercial catchment area into some half-dozen of the more prosperous counties of England.

So London's situation at the head of the Thames estuary is a natural focal point of commerce. Internally it has always been the gateway to a rich hinterland which since the development of mass land transport has extended far beyond the confines of the Thames Basin. Externally it adjoins the world's busiest shipping lanes, and is located at the head of the long line of commercial and industrial centres which extends from North Italy, along the Rhine and through the Low Countries to London. Paris, by contrast, or Lutetia, to use its Roman name, has enjoyed different natural advantages. Although it was far from the sea and not even the lowest crossing point of the Seine and so not a magnet for trade, it was always nevertheless a strategically vital centre of communication, from which roads radiated out to all four points of the compass. Even before the Roman conquest there had been a Celtic *oppidum* on the Île de la Cité, unlike in Londinium, where there had been no pre-Roman settlement; and in the fourth century two Roman emperors made their base headquarters at Lutetia during the conduct of expeditions against the Germans.[17]

For London the influence exerted by geographical circumstances has almost always been beneficial; but this has not always been the case elsewhere. In England at the once flourishing ports of Richborough, Rye, and Winchilsea the sea has receded; at Bruges the river has silted up, and at Venice the discovery of the New World jolted world trade routes into new courses, much to the benefit of the ports of Northern Europe, including London, where there has never been any such physical calamity. Even the recent shifting of the docks downstream to Tilbury has brought renewed vigour to an obsolescent area of the metropolis. The fact that the principal roads laid down by the Romans, the principal railways built by the

Victorians, and the principal motorways and air routes of more modern times all radiate out from London provides striking evidence of the largely unchanging power of geographical forces. So it comes as no surprise that London's Heathrow is the busiest international airport in the world, while the runner-up in this league is London's second airport, Gatwick. Moreover the happy chance of great distance from and hence great difference of time from both New York and Tokyo has allowed London (at any rate at the time of writing) to remain one of the three principal financial centres of the world. Location has certainly favoured London throughout the ages.

London has also been blessed in other ways. War, religious strife, and politics have all contributed to the relative decline of other great cities. Cases in point include Venice, menaced by the Turks' advances in the Mediterranean in the sixteenth century; Antwerp, in the same century the first commercial city of the emerging new Atlantic economy, ravaged by religious tumult and the Spanish army; Cologne, where the expulsion of the Jews, the exclusion of Protestants from citizenship, and frequent wars all induced a long slow decline; or Vienna, an imperial city suddenly deprived in 1919 of its empire. London, however, has hardly suffered from such untoward events except during the Dark Ages, when it probably ceased to exist as a city, before re-emerging as a trading centre and frontier town fought over by rival regional kingdoms. The re-establishment of central power and order brought better times for London; and when authority broke down again during the Civil War in the seventeenth century London, far from experiencing a setback, had a crucial role in resolving the conflict and emerged more authoritative within the realm than ever before.

London has indeed always prospered within the political framework provided by a powerful unitary state. In England such a state has existed continuously for longer than anywhere else in the world; and one of the reasons for this — in fact probably the principal reason — is that the sea has provided Britain with fixed frontiers unviolated from outside for almost a thousand years. Thus geography and politics are intertwined. Britain is, and has been for centuries, a small compact island, its rich southern regions endowed with good natural internal communications uninterrupted by mountains or other physical obstacles, and its security protected by the sea and a strong system of government. These, and favourable location to other lands, are the basic ingredients in the making of London, first into the political capital of the realm and the head of the national commercial market, and then (for a while) into the principal centre of trade throughout the whole world.

2

Early Londinium

During the last fifty years or so, and particularly since the early 1970s, there has been a huge extension of knowledge about Roman London. The first great archaeological discoveries — the fort (1949) and the temple of Mithras (1954) — were made by Professor W. F. Grimes, whose work was heavily handicapped by lack of money. But after years of neglect of its archaeological responsibilities the Corporation of the City of London was in 1973 prodded by sustained public criticisms into setting up a Department of Urban Archaeology. Within a few years this became the largest archaeological research unit in Europe, a part of the new Museum of London, and, during the ensuing boom years of City office building, financed by property developers as well as by public funds. The riverside wall (1976), the bridge and harbour (1981), the basilica (1986), and the amphitheatre (1987) were among the most famous of the discoveries made during hundreds of excavations conducted by the Department. However, this brief golden age of City archaeology came to an end with the collapse of the property boom in 1990–1, when the Department was superseded by the smaller Museum of London Archaeology Service (MoLAS), which excavates on a reduced scale and analyses the results of previous digs. Meanwhile the value of all this work had been immeasurably enhanced by new scientific techniques, notably by dendrochronology — the application of tree-ring studies to the dating of timber, which in London was first used in 1973 — and by the computerization of pottery studies. Archaeological work in the City during the last half-century had itself been a notable episode in the long history of London, and this and several other chapters of the present book would have been very different without it.[1]

We have already seen that after the Claudian invasion in AD 43 the ford at Westminster continued for some little time to be the principal crossing point of the Thames, for the two arms of Watling Street would not have been laid out in alignment with it if it were no longer being used. Soon after AD 50, however, roads in Southwark were in existence the alignment of which only makes sense if they are presumed to have led to a crossing on or very near to the site of the later medieval bridge. The mere existence of these approach roads implies a firm decision to move the main crossing point of the Thames downstream from Westminster.[2]

There were several reasons for this decision. In its very earliest years Londinium seems to have been primarily a staging point and supply base between the Channel ports at Richborough or Dover and Camulodunum (which was then still the principal city of the province) and the military frontier to the north. So the further downstream that the Thames could be crossed the shorter would be the overland journey. Secondly, there was an important advantage for water-borne traffic, for the Thames was undoubtedly tidal at the site of Londinium during the first century AD, but the tidal head may not have extended as far upstream as West-minster. The difference in level between high and low water was evidently around 1.5 to 2.5 metres, and this degree of fluctuation would have been invaluable in sweeping sailing vessels up the Thames against both the current of the river and the

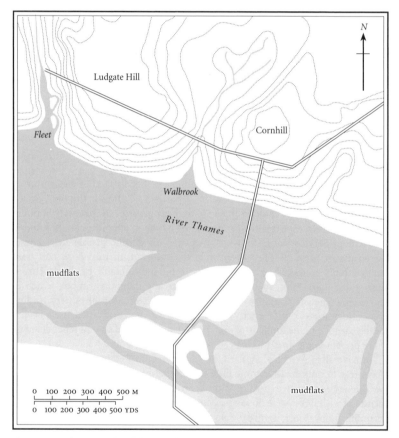

Fig. 5. Natural topography of the site of London in the first century AD, with the Thames at low tide

prevailing westerly wind. Thirdly, the terrain on at any rate the north side was much more favourable for a permanent settlement than at marshy Westminster. At the site of Londinium there were two extensive plateaux (Ludgate Hill and Cornhill) some 12 metres in height above modern ordnance datum, part of slabs of gravel and clay deposited millions of years previously and subsequently cut through by two small tributary streams, the Fleet and the Walbrook, which would provide additional supplies of running water.[3]

This advantage was, however, offset by difficult conditions on the south side of the river, where in Southwark the approach roads, which were built soon after AD 50, had to cross marshy unstable ground and several minor inlets of the Thames. At one recently excavated site three layers of oak logs supported the rammed gravel surface, which was some 6 or 8 metres in width; and elsewhere the road was founded on a timber raft stabilized by a line of vertical stakes.[4] Near to the main channel of the river a single road or causeway led either to a pontoon bridge — no archaeological trace of a bridge at this early date has yet been found — or to a ferry crossing to the embryo settlement on the north side of the river. There the main north–south street leading down from the Cornhill plateau to the river followed the alignment of Gracechurch Street and Fish Street Hill, where traces of a bridge built in later Roman times have been recorded.[5]

This earliest Londinium contained the elements of a layout plan, with metalled streets and drainage ditches. It was not a major military base, the army having moved up to Wales and the North, nor did it have any significant public buildings, for it seems to have sprung up quickly around the realigned road system with, presumably, at least the tacit approval of the governor of the province.[6]

The main east–west street was built along the plateau parallel with the river, its course now overlaid by the eastern part of Lombard Street and the western part of Fenchurch Street. About halfway between it and the riverbank a parallel street was also laid out, its course still marked by the eastern portion of Cannon Street and by Eastcheap. Both roads were between 5 and 9 metres wide and consisted of hard gravel rammed and cambered. To the north of the main east–west street, and east of Gracechurch Street, was a large open gravelled area or courtyard some 1,320 square metres (or a third of an acre) in extent, perhaps used as a market place.[7]

By about AD 60 the built-up area is thought to have extended over some 30 or more acres — quite small, and less than half the area of contemporary Camulodunum — mostly to the east of the Walbrook stream. There was also a scattering to the west of the Walbrook along the line of Poultry, where a 60-metre length of road has recently been discovered,[8] and Newgate Street. The buildings were in general timber-framed, with wooden post foundations, wattle-and-daub walls (plastered internally), clay floors, and thatched roofs. A range of shops in Fenchurch Street had both piped water and a drainage system. Many of the first Londoners were probably enterprising immigrant Roman citizens and traders, supported by the substantial labour force which their domestic and commercial activities generated.

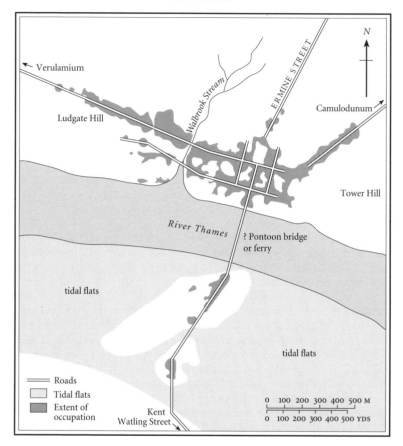

Fig. 6. Extent of London in c.AD 60; the first permanent bridge was built later in the first century

According to the Roman writer Tacitus Londinium was already a place 'greatly renowned for the number of its traders and supplies', the traders no doubt attracted by the prospects for making money in an undeveloped new colony. Objects which businessmen of this kind imported in the early years included pottery and wine from southern Gaul, olive oil from Spain, and fine glass from Italy and Syria; and one of the shops in Fenchurch Street contained a bulky consignment of grain brought all the way from somewhere in the eastern Mediterranean. This first Londinium must, indeed, have had something in common with the Wild West 'cowboys towns' of the North American frontier in the nineteenth century.[9]

The Boudiccan Revolt

Like many such places, Londinium unexpectedly proved to be extremely unsafe. In AD 60, when the governor of Britannia, Suetonius Paulinus, was far away in Anglesey with the XIVth legion, busily subduing that island's turbulent inhabitants, the Iceni, a tribal client-kingdom in East Anglia, suddenly rebelled. Outraged by the exactions of the officers of Decianus Catus, the Roman procurator or financial officer in Britain, and enfuriated by the brutal and humiliating treatment meted out to their queen, Boudicca, and to her two daughters, the Iceni rose in revolt. They were soon joined by their powerful neighbours, the Trinovantes, on the site of whose pre-Claudian headquarters the Romans had begun to construct the city of Camulodunum. There the huge temple built (at native expense) in honour of Claudius had become the symbol of the Trinovantes' subjection; and latterly, when Camulodunum had been officially declared a *colonia*, many of them had had their lands confiscated for the use of incoming Roman army veterans who were to be settled there. Boudicca and her allies quickly overran the whole of East Anglia and defeated a detachment of the IXth legion. And after the capture of Camulodunum most of the inhabitants were massacred.[10]

By this time the procurator had fled overseas, but Suetonius had arrived posthaste at Londinium from North Wales with a small force, probably of cavalry. There, so Tacitus tells us, he decided in the interests of the province as a whole to abandon the town to the enemy. 'Undeflected by the prayers and tears of those who begged for his help he gave the signal to move, taking into his column any who could join it. Those who were unfit for war because of their sex, or too aged to go or too fond of the place to leave, were butchered by the enemy.' After the Roman evacuation a terrible and most brutal massacre ensued; and although Tacitus' statement that a total of 70,000 people were slaughtered at Camulodunum, Londinium, and Verulamium (St Albans, which was also sacked) may be an exaggeration, the casualties during the Boudiccan revolt must have been very large indeed.[11]

Traces of this traumatic event in London's history still exist in the form of a readily recognizable layer of soil, generally about 0.5 metre in thickness and found at a depth of about 4 metres beneath the modern street level, bright red in colour from the oxidized iron in the burnt clay. These traces have been seen on a score of sites, mostly in the town centre to the north of London Bridge but also further out at Aldgate, to the west of the Walbrook, and even in Southwark. It is now thought that many of the inhabitants had left Londinium with their belongings before the arrival of the Boudiccan horde, for modern archaeological excavations have found relatively few artefacts in the abandoned buildings; but some things were too bulky to remove, and in the granary in Fenchurch Street the pile of grain left behind was up to 1 metre thick. The intensity of the holocaust has been gauged from modern tests which have shown that a temperature of over 1,000°C is needed to blacken and fuse pottery of the kind found in that condition on several Boudiccan sites.[12]

After abandoning Londinium to its fate Suetonius retired north-westward to rejoin the main body of his XIVth legion, and eventually assembled a force of some 10,000 men. At a great battle (perhaps at Mancetter in Warwickshire) he defeated the numerically much superior British hosts, and to avoid capture Boudicca committed suicide by poison. The rebellion was over, but there was widespread famine, and any Britons suspected of opposition were (in Tacitus' words) 'subjected to devastation by fire and sword' by Suetonius and his legionaries, now reinforced from Germany. However the new procurator, Julius Classicianus, who had succeeded Decianus Catus, advocated less savage treatment of the indigenous population; and after Suetonius had been suspended as governor peaceful conditions began to return to the much-bruised province.[13]

The Transformation of Londinium *c.*AD 61–*c.*AD 122

After the disaster of the Boudiccan revolt Londinium's recovery was at first slow; there were no survivors, in outlying parts of the ruined settlement subsistence farming prevailed, and for some years there seems to have been little building activity except on the river foreshore, where a massive quay was built as early as AD 63.[14] Around AD 80 a modest start was made, with the building of the first forum (perhaps associated with a move towards some form of self-governing status for the settlement), and a small temple nearby. In the last two decades of the first century there began a period of spectacular growth which lasted until around AD 120. This evidently reflected a deliberate new policy initiated in high places during the reign of the Emperor Domitian (AD 81–96), and was perhaps the result of a review of the administration of the whole province in the aftermath of the Battle of Mons Graupius in Scotland (AD 84).[15] The little forum was rebuilt on a greatly enlarged scale, and soon Londinium, as the chief city in the province, was endowed with the principal physical attributes of Roman urban civilization — a palatial pile perhaps for the governor of Britannia, a fort for the garrison, an amphitheatre, and public bathhouses. Most importantly of all, it possessed a bridge across the Thames — the sine qua non for its regeneration (Plate 1).

The Bridge and the Harbour

The Boudiccan sack of the city had extended across the river to Southwark, and it is therefore inconceivable that if a pre-Boudiccan bridge had indeed existed it would have been left intact. In 1981 archaeological excavations on the north side of Thames Street disclosed a wooden pier of what can only have been the northern end of a Roman bridge (Plates 3–4). Modern dendrochronological tests for the dating of wood have shown that the timbers used in the pier were felled between the years 78 and 118, with the years 85 to 90 being the most likely for its construction.[16]

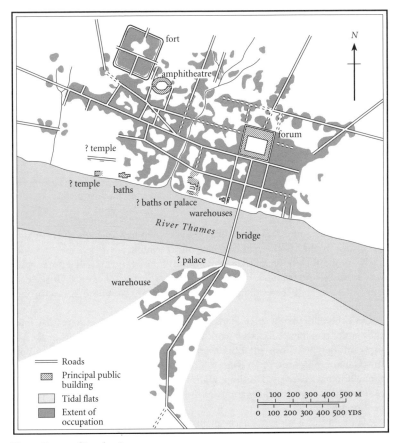

Fig. 7. Extent of London in c.AD 120

The pier revealed by the archaeologists was a box-like structure measuring 7 metres by 5 metres and consisted of massive squared oak timbers laid horizontally on what was in the first century AD the foreshore of the open tidal river, but is now more than 100 metres north of the modern waterfront, so great have been the changes over two thousand years in the course and level of the river. It stood just east of the foot of Fish Street Hill on a line similar to that of the medieval London Bridge, at the narrowest point of the river hereabouts and opposite to the road in Southwark aligned upon the presumed bridgehead there. The bridge itself is thought to have been over 320 metres in length and entirely wooden in construction, the decking being carried on timber pier bases in the shallow water and on piled trestles in midstream. The roadway on the bridge was probably about 4 or 5 metres in width, considerably less than the recorded width of the roads which led

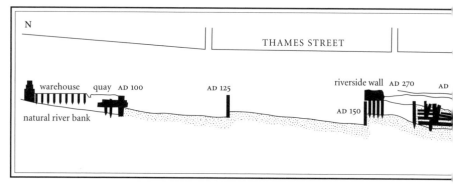

Fig. 8. Advances *c.*100 metres in London's waterfront from the first century AD to the present day; north–south section

to it. At low tide quite large ships of a type known to have plied on the river above the bridge would have been able to pass underneath it.[17]

By around the middle of the second century (i.e. *c.*AD 150) half a dozen major roads radiated out from Londinium, the hub of which was the bridge. In later ages this pattern has not changed. London is still the hub of communications throughout Britain.

On either side of the pier of the bridge the archaeologists have also found substantial remains of harbour works, the earliest of which date from the later first century. They consisted of timber-faced waterfront quays projecting out over the tidal foreshore, and upon them stood masonry or timber buildings which are thought to have been used as shops and/or warehouses for the short-term storage of imports or exports. Upstream from the bridge there was also some residential development (Plate 3).

Major advances of the waterfront further out over the bed of the river had already been made by the end of the first century, and at numerous later times. Works of this kind, which in varying forms extended some way east–west on either side of the bridge, eventually advanced the Roman waterfront in the vicinity of the bridge into the original course of the river by some 50 metres; and by the fifteenth century by some 100 metres. The Roman works are seen as having created a recognizable pattern of development consisting of buildings parallel with the river alternating with others extending north–south across the artificial terraces which were constructed along the steeply sloping hillside above the river. The motives for these great works are thought to have been the need to provide deep-water berths for shipping, to counteract the silting up of the foreshore, and to win more land below the hill. Whatever the motives, the sheer scale of the operations — involving, for instance, the procurement and manhandling of hundreds of massive baulks of oak, some nearly 9 metres in length — implies some form of official auspices, perhaps that of the town council previously predicated.[18] For the principal port of an outlying province like Britain, London's harbour was certainly

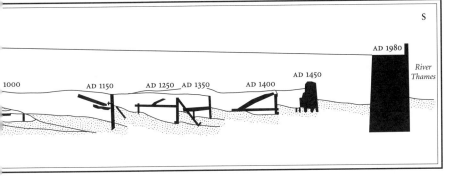

large, but in comparison with the huge Roman works discovered at some Mediterranean ports, it was of course inconsiderable.

Public Works and Buildings

Up on the more easterly of Londinium's two hills other public works of comparable importance were also going on, for in the latter part of the first century the first forum and basilica were constructed on a site later straddled by Gracechurch Street. A Roman forum was a rectangular or square enclosure lined with official or commercial buildings, the most important of which was usually the basilica, a large aisled hall often occupying the whole of one side of the forum and housing the legal and administrative centre of the town. In Londinium the first basilica stood on the high ground at the north end of the rectangular forum and looked down across the courtyard and through the entrance on the south side of the forum to the street leading down to the bridge. It was 44 metres long and 22.7 metres wide, but by contemporary British standards London's first basilica and forum were quite small, those at Verulamium, for instance, being over three times as great in area. The archaeological evidence points to their having been built in about AD 80; and this is supported by Tacitus, who states that Agricola, the governor of the province from 78 to 84, encouraged the Britons to build 'public squares with public buildings [*fora*]'.[19]

The presence of a forum and basilica usually denotes the existence of a self-governing community, so by this time Londinium may have achieved the status of a *municipium*. However, within a very few years — c.85–90 — site works began for the building of a much larger complex, which gradually arose around the modest original basilica and forum. The new basilica was no less than 167 metres long (about the length of St Paul's Cathedral) and in addition to its two aisles there were ranges of rooms on the north side of the hall (Plate 5). The buildings on the east and west sides of the forum were each flanked on either side by arcades, as also was the range on the south side, which faced outwards to the main east–west street of

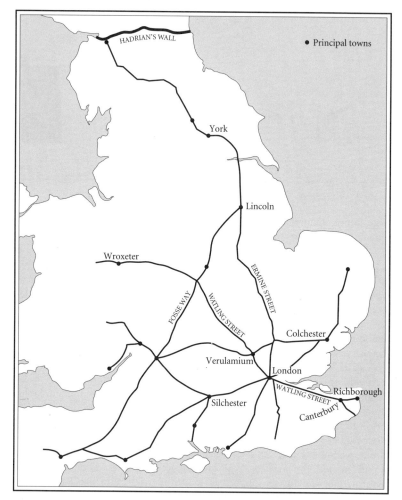

Fig. 9. London as the hub of communications throughout Britain

the town (now Lombard Street and Fenchurch Street); and in the centre of the courtyard there was perhaps a colonnaded promenade or a shallow pool of ornamental water. This second basilica and forum, which took some thirty years to complete, was some five times larger than its predecessor, and the new complex was not only by far the biggest building of its kind in Britain but also one of the largest in the whole Roman world. Raising and levelling the surface of the whole site involved, so it has been calculated, the dumping of soil equivalent to 2,800 loads of a 7-cubic-metre modern tipper lorry. Building work of this magnitude suggests that political motives must have inspired it; and just as the first basilica and forum may have celebrated a new status for Londinium, perhaps of *munici-pium*, so the second may have marked the establishment of the permanent residence of the provincial governor in his 'capital', and possibly its promotion to the status of *colonia*.[20]

By the end of the first century the conquest of virtually the whole of Britain was complete, and the governor no longer had to be out on campaign with his army for much of each year. Londinium was probably already the largest town in the province, certainly the centre of the new road network, and of course by sea readily accessible from Gaul and other western parts of the Empire. Although no direct evidence for the presence of the governor there has yet been found, Londinium was nevertheless the natural place for him to have his fixed base; and traces of what at any rate until recently were thought to have been his official palace have been found in the vicinity of Cannon Street Station on numerous occasions since the 1840s. More recently, however, the discovery of a large sophisticated building on the south side of the river in Southwark has provided another possible location.[21]

Whatever its purpose may have been, the site, scale, and layout of the great pile in Cannon Street, which was apparently built within a decade or so of the year AD 100, are similar to those of governors' palaces in other provinces of the Roman Empire, notably at Cologne on the Rhine. It extended over more than 3 acres of ground and was laid out on three different levels or artificial terraces between the Roman street beneath Cannon Street and the river waterfront. The main entrance, leading into a courtyard, was on the south side of the modern Cannon Street,* and there were splendidly decorated state rooms and a large enclosed garden with an ornamental pool.[23]

Another smaller but still substantial mansion has been found a few yards to the east of the 'palace', and it has been suggested that this may have been the residence of either the *legatus iuridicus* (the head of the legal system in the province) or of the procurator.[24]

Wherever his headquarters in Londinium may have been, the governor had a staff, perhaps some two hundred in number, which was drawn from all of the four legions stationed in Britain around the year AD 100; and amongst the rare surviving funerary monuments of Roman soldiers who died in Londinium there are two which attest to the administrative duties performed by the officers commemorated. The governor also had a guard of some thousand men; and the need to provide quarters for these substantial military establishments evidently explains the building, in peacetime in the early second century, of a twelve-acre stone-walled fort on the outskirts of Londinium — a discovery made by Professor

---

* The revelation of this complex has also enabled the archaeologists to suggest an explanation for the hitherto puzzling 'London Stone', a massive monolith which since at least medieval times has been regarded as the very hub of the City of London. Until 1742 this stood on the south side of Cannon Street, almost exactly on the line of the central axis of the supposed palace and on the probable site of the principal entrance to it, where may well have stood a monument or milestone from which distances throughout the province were to be measured. The surviving top part of London Stone is now recessed in the wall of a modern building on the north side of Cannon Street.[22]

W. F. Grimes in 1949. It stood on high ground away to the north-west of the city and had the rectangular shape, rounded corners, and cruciform internal street plan standard in the layout of Roman forts. Traces of the barrack blocks which it contained have been found more recently, and a substantial stretch of its western walls may still be seen in Noble Street, near Cripplegate.[25]

An equally important discovery made in 1987 revealed the existence of Londinium's amphitheatre, built roughly contemporaneously with the fort, underneath Guildhall Yard. The oval arena, enclosed by masonry walls, earthen embankments, and wooden seats, lay beneath what has probably always remained an open space and place of public assembly throughout London's history. A thousand years later, in the thirteenth century, the first Guildhall was built over the centre of the northern side of the arena, the very place which important dignitaries would have occupied in Roman times. The existence of the amphitheatre here provides an extraordinary example of continuity at and around the Guildhall site; and its oval shape is still apparent hereabouts in the curving course of Aldermanbury, Gresham Street, and Basinghall Street.[26]

Other buildings erected under some form of official auspices included two sets of public baths, one on the north side of Cheapside, and the other (much larger) at Huggin Hill, deeply terraced into the steep slope down to the river. Both are thought to date from the late first century, and to have been enlarged within a few years, those at Cheapside perhaps for the use of the soldiers quartered at the nearby Cripplegate fort. There were also several sacred edifices. A small first-century temple to the west of Gracechurch Street formed part of the short-lived first forum complex, and a larger one dedicated to the divinity of the emperor certainly existed, though its position is not known. Public sponsorship was evidently involved in the building of both of these, but probably not in that of the temple of Isis, known only from a first-century flagon roughly inscribed 'Londini ad fanum Isidis'.[27] Across the river in Southwark, where the built-up area extending along the waterfront and the roads to the south occupied some 45 acres (18 hectares), about one-seventh of the size of Londinium itself, the large masonry building previously mentioned as perhaps the governor's palace was, if not the palace itself, at least probably related in some way to the provincial administration.[28] Meanwhile over in Gaul Lutetia was acquiring similar municipal status symbols — a forum, basilica, amphitheatre, and public baths, but no fort, for Lutetia was always an open city, only the island being in later Roman times defended with a wall.[29]

So when the Emperor Hadrian visited Britain in the year 122 he found in Londinium a city where the authorities had in one way or another made or caused to be made a very considerable investment of money, materials, and labour; and all of this had been done within the short space of a mere fifty years or so. Londinium had become the administrative nerve centre of the province, and its grand public edifices must have dominated the buildings of the rest of the city, most of which were still only timber-framed, with wattle and daub or mud brick infilling. Official expectations for the future of Londinium must have been very great.

Second- and Third-Generation Londinium and Londinienses

Of all the many thousands of people who lived in Londinium throughout the three or four hundred years of the Roman period, only a few hundred are known to posterity by name. Of this select band only Julius Classicianus, the procurator of Britain shortly after the Boudiccan revolt, is known from both an archaeological source — the inscription on his tombstone, parts of which were found near Tower Hill in 1852 and 1935 and are now in the British Museum — and a literary source — Tacitus. The inscription records that he was procurator of the province, that he was of northern Gaulish extraction, and that his wife, Julia Pacata Indiana, also of Gaulish origin, had caused the monument to be erected. From the discovery of the tombstone in London it may also be inferred that he died there. Tacitus relates little more about Classicianus than that after Boudicca's revolt he favoured humane methods of management of the conquered Britons.[30]

Yet despite the existence of these two independent sources, nothing is known about what Classicianus actually did in Britain. As procurator he was responsible directly to the emperor, not to the governor. It was his duty to collect the taxes, pay the troops, and generally have charge of the interests of the imperial treasury throughout the province. Like his predecessor, Decianus Catus, he almost certainly had his official base in Londinium. The legal status of Londinium throughout most of the Roman period is, however (like that of many other Roman towns), obscure. Although Camulodunum was in the early years the leading town in the province, Londinium soon became the focal point of the road network and therefore the natural centre of financial administration. The earliest known building in Londinium constructed of stone, part of which has been found in the pre-Boudiccan town centre (on the north side of Lombard Street and west of Gracechurch Street), may, so the archaeologists suggest, have been Classicianus' headquarters. But despite its solid official-looking character this building only had a short life, for after Boudicca's rebellion it was superseded during the transformation of Londinium which was just beginning. Whether this process was initiated by Classicianus himself is not known, for the date of his death is not recorded.[31]

As the transformation of Londinium did not begin until some years after the rebellion, it may be that Agricola (governor of Britain from 78 to 84) was its progenitor. It was his policy, so his son-in-law Tacitus relates, 'to encourage rough men who lived in scattered settlements (and were thus only too ready to fall to fighting) to live in a peaceful and inactive manner by offering them the pleasures of life'. Accordingly, he 'urged them privately and helped them officially to build temples, public squares with public buildings [*fora*] and private houses [*domus*]'. The children of leading Britons were educated 'in the civilized arts', use of Latin became more prevalent (though Celtic languages persisted among the indigenous population), and 'Roman dress, too, became popular and the toga was frequently seen'. Romanization, in fact, became the order of the day under Agricola and his successors, and 'little by little there was a slide towards the allurements of degeneracy: assembly-rooms [*porticus*], bathing establishments and smart dinner parties'.[32]

The half-century or so between the mid-70s and the mid-120s was a time of rapid urban growth throughout all the settled parts of the province. Such great Roman centres as Lincoln, Gloucester, Cirencester, and Dorchester were all established or greatly enlarged during these years. At Londinium the programme of public building works was on such a massive scale that it must have reflected at least de facto recognition in Rome that Londinium had either become or should be made into the principal city and 'capital' of the province. Such recognition would in turn have entailed some change in the city's legal and administrative status. Neither the date nor the nature of this change is known, and throughout the whole period of the Roman occupation the constitutional status of Londinium is, indeed, far from clear; but a charter granting self-government through the establishment of a nominated town council was the normal method used for effecting such municipal promotions.[33]

By Hadrian's time Londinium had also become a considerable industrial centre. Much of this activity was concentrated in the valley of the Walbrook, which in early Roman times was a sizeable stream, up to a hundred metres in width. Here pottery, tanning, and leatherwork, particularly shoemaking, seem to have been the main manufactures, and there were also water-powered mills for grinding grain. Londinium's size by the early second century was indeed such that the supply of its everyday needs must have generated a substantial volume of trade. The early cemeteries (which Roman law required to be situated outside the bounds of all towns) had already ceased to be used, and their replacements were much further out, at Warwick Square (over half a mile west of the Walbrook) and Haydon Square in the east; and industrial sites have been found north of Newgate Street, in the vicinity of St Paul's Cathedral, and in Southwark.[34] So the traders or merchants referred to by Tacitus, and for whom Londinium was already famous, had evidently been as busy in commerce and manufacturing as had been their counterparts in the official domains. Often, no doubt, the personnel of the two fields overlapped, venturers like Aulus Alfidius Olussa, who was born in Athens and died in Londinium before the year AD 100, very possibly being involved in the development of the forum as well as of their own private fortunes.[35]

Many of these pioneer entrepreneurs came from nearby parts of the Empire, but others were of Mediterranean origin, carrying on the ancient habit of many Mediterranean cities of fostering new outposts in distant lands; and they brought with them Mediterranean modes of living and thought. Remains of a few of their stone-built houses have been found, the floors sometimes laid with mosaics, the interior walls lined with plaster and adorned with decorative painted motifs, and generally reflecting the opulent lifestyle of the occupants. A temple for the worship of Isis, a cult of Egyptian origin which had spread throughout much of the Mediterranean world and the existence of which in Londinium is attested by the famous Isis flagon, demonstrates the powerful influence of even faraway cultures.[36]

Modern archaeology has been able to provide some indication of both the scale and variety of Londinium's early import trade. (Exports are of necessity more difficult to trace, but they probably included leather, oysters, and minerals such as lead, silver, and gold; and trade in slaves certainly existed). Bulk commodities like olive oil and wine could of course only be produced in a more southerly climate (though some wine was produced in Roman Britain), and their import generated an elaborate commercial organization. Samian pottery cups and plates were brought in on a large scale from Gaul, which was also the principal source of supply for lamps (pottery vessels fuelled by olive oil). Fish sauces, much favoured in the Roman cuisine, came from Spain, as well as being produced locally, mill-stones for grinding corn came from the Rhineland, bronze tableware and glass from Italy, marbles from Greece and the Pyrenees, and emeralds from Egypt.[37] These last provide certain evidence for the presence of rich ladies in Londinium, and no doubt they also created a demand for correspondingly sophisticated articles of dress, which only very rarely survive for the modern archaeologist to find. All in all Londinium was in the early years of the second century being absorbed into the Mediterranean commercial orbit; and already it was becoming a centre of conspicuous consumption, as it continued to be throughout most of its history.

3

Change and Decay

Within a few years of Hadrian's visit to Britain in AD 122 much of Londinium was destroyed by fire. There is no contemporary reference to this conflagration, or possibly succession of local fires, but archaeological evidence leaves no doubt that such a disaster or disasters did occur between AD 120 and 130. Over 100 acres of the City were devastated, extending from Newgate Street in the west almost to the Tower in the east. Traces of fire have frequently been found within this large area — itself a measure of the extent of the outward growth of Londinium during the previous half-century. Fire did not, however, touch the Cripplegate fort, nor, seemingly, the basilica and forum, all of which were built of stone. Nor did it extend to Southwark; so presumably the bridge survived.[1]

Second-Century Recession

The Hadrianic fire marks the onset of a profound change, and in some respects of a decline, in the nature of Roman London. At a number of recently excavated sites there was no evidence of renewed occupation until after the end of the second century, and in some cases no traces of any subsequent Roman activity at all. Elsewhere such rebuilding as did take place sometimes soon fell into disuse. In Southwark most of the buildings which had sprung up alongside the approach roads to the bridge had been abandoned soon after the mid-second century. There too an important water channel was allowed to silt up, as also was the ditch surrounding the Cripplegate fort. The embankments beside the Walbrook stream, hitherto an industrial area, collapsed; and by around the end of the second century some buildings, including the forum and basilica, had been deliberately demolished: even such very substantial buildings as the Cheapside and Huggin Hill baths had been dismantled. So also, at an unknown date in the Roman period, had been the staterooms of the supposed governor's palace.[2]

The archaeologists have also noted other equally puzzling changes. Veins of featureless dark earth or silt, overlaying (and hence, of course, later than) first- and second-century remains, have been found in many parts of the City and South-wark (and in some other Romano-British towns), sometimes up to 1.5 metres thick. It seems that the first stage in the formation of this dark earth was either through horticultural activity or other reuse of the sites of deserted brick-earth or wooden buildings, and/or through the dumping of waste and rubbish there. By whatever means the loam was produced, thin maggot-like worms and earthworms then got to work, sometimes assisted by the roots of scrub and trees, and over the course of time broke down all organic matter including remains of timber and even brick-earth buildings. So only masonry foundations withstood the long-term effects of worms and roots, while many traces of less durable buildings were destroyed. Archaeological evidence therefore becomes much less abundant for the period after the mid-second century, and the meaning of some of it is not clear. Taken as a whole however, it does, nevertheless, suggest a substantial fall in the population of Londinium after about AD 150.[3]

At its greatest extent in the early second century the population of Londinium may have been in the region of 30,000 — greater, perhaps, than it would be again for over 1,000 years. Recent estimates of the population of Roman Britain as a whole, i.e. of England and Wales, range between almost three and up to six million. All such estimates must necessarily be uncertain and partly speculative, but they do at least give some idea of the scale of the matter.[4] The population of Londinium, it may be noted, amounted to at most only 1 per cent (or 0.5 per cent if the figure of six million is used) of that of Britain as a whole, far below the ratio of later times — in 1550, for instance, 2.5 per cent of the population of all England, and in 1700 11 per cent. In terms at any rate of the likely numbers of its inhabitants it seems therefore that even in its heyday London's position in relation to the provinces was in Roman times less important than it was later to become.

Despite the extent of the damage which it caused, the Hadrianic fire of AD 120–30 cannot have been the main cause of the recession of Londinium. Nor can the frequent military operations in North Wales and Southern Scotland which took place during the Antonine period (138–92) account for it, although they may have drained limited resources away from the southern part of the province and may even, by often requiring the governor's presence on the northern frontiers, explain the contraction of his palace in Londinium. Other cities in the western part of the Empire were also beginning to contract, at any rate in the third century — Amiens, Lyons, and Milan, for instance — and in Britain in particular the favourable commercial opportunities provided during the years of the early Empire, when the potential of the new markets which existed there could most easily be exploited, were by the mid-second century over. As the Romanization of the province advanced, so this 'colonial' nature of its trade declined. The first frenetic phase of the Romano-British economy had passed, and things were settling down. Most trade was becoming local, centred on the tribal capital of each region. Home-produced goods began to take the place of imports; and Londinium's function as the principal centre of trade both within the province and with the rest of the Empire began to diminish.[5]

However, this changing pattern of trade does not by itself provide a complete explanation for the great fall in the population of Londinium after around AD 150, perhaps by some two-thirds. Still less does it explain the virtual termination of production in about AD 160 at the potteries at Brockley Hill (at Stanmore) and Highgate which had hitherto commanded a large market in Londinium, or the abandonment of the area beside the Walbrook. Demographic decline is nevertheless well attested by the numerous deserted buildings, by the deposits of dark earth, which often imply the practice of gardening or farming, and by the much smaller quantities found by modern archaeologists of building remains and general domestic bits and pieces relating to the years after c.150. The third quarter of the second century, when the depopulation of Londinium seems to have been at its height coincides with the Plague of Galen, an epidemic brought back by soldiers returning from service in the East and which swept across Europe in AD 166–7. This was perhaps bubonic plague, a frequent carrier of which was the black rat, a species undoubtedly present in Londinium from at least the third century, and very probably earlier too. Whatever the precise nature of the disease may have been it is certain that pestilences were often prevalent in many parts of the Empire in the later second century. Londinium, with its frequent contacts with Gaul and Germany, would have been the natural point of first entry for any epidemic, and the fall in population which began there seems to have been followed in the early third century by a similar decline in other parts of south-east Britain.[6]

Public Building: Harbour, Wall, and Official Embellishments

Despite this setback, the large-scale public or semi-public investment which had been made during the years c.AD 70–125 still continued in Londinium. On the waterfront, in the central part of the harbour around the bridgehead, the line of the riverside quay was advanced twice during the second century. Traces of the first advance are accompanied by fire-damaged debris which may associate it with the aftermath of the Hadrianic conflagration of c.120–30. After another advance early in the third century a broad level terrace some 50 metres in width and perhaps over 500 metres in length had been formed, bringing the waterfront in terms of the modern layout well south of Thames Street.[7]

The most striking evidence for the importance with which Londinium continued to be regarded by the rulers of both Britain and the Empire at large is provided by the great defensive landward wall which was built around the City at some time between AD 190 and 225 (Plate 2). It was 3.2 kilometres (2 miles) in length, extending from the site later occupied by the Tower in the east round to Blackfriars in the west. The principal material was Kentish ragstone (Plate 6), some 86,000 tonnes (85,000 tons) of it, so it has been calculated, being transported in around 1,300 barge-loads down the Medway from the quarries near Maidstone and up the Thames to the quays at Londinium. The wall was 2.74 metres (9 feet) thick at ground level and some 6.4 metres (21 feet) high, including the crenellated parapet. Outside it there was a V-shaped ditch generally some 4.2 metres (14 feet) wide and

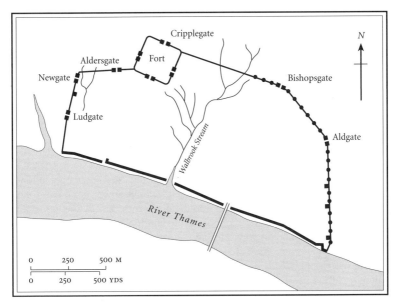

Fig. 10. London's defences: the fort, city and riverside walls, and bastions

1.6 metres (5.5 feet) deep, the earth from which was heaped up in a bank against the inner side of the wall. Originally there were four main gates, at Aldgate, Bishopsgate, Newgate, and Ludgate, which provided access for the four principal roads radiating out from the City. Aldersgate seems to have been added at a later date in the Roman period, and Cripplegate was the entrance to the fort.

The wall enclosed an area of some 133 hectares (330 acres). This was a far larger area than that of any other Roman town in Britain, the second in size being Cirencester, with only 97 hectares (240 acres); and though it was never one of the biggest cities of the ancient world the enceinte of Londinium was nevertheless exceeded in size by only four towns in the whole of Gaul and Germany. Much of it, particularly in the western part, was, however, never built upon in Roman times, or even until well into the Middle Ages. This was not uncommon in other towns in the Empire, for the Romans walled areas primarily in order to be able to defend them; and the nature of the natural topography was therefore an important reason for the great size of Londinium's enclosure. The forum area, on Cornhill directly above the bridgehead, was, of course, the nucleus of the town; but this was not so easily defensible on its west side, where the Walbrook stream flowed, as was the adjacent plateau, where St Paul's Cathedral now stands at the top of Ludgate Hill. This, on its western side, sloped steeply down to the much deeper valley of the Fleet River; and if Ludgate Hill were included, the nearby and pre-existing Cripplegate fort, containing the garrison's quarters, could not sensibly have been left out. So the walls of the north and west sides of the fort became the north-west corner of the new city wall, their slightly different alignment forming a small kink in the northern side of the latter, noticeable on countless maps of London produced in later centuries. The fort walls were only half as wide as the new town wall, so the thickness of the fort's northern and western stretches was doubled; and the gate on the north side of the fort was retained as an auxiliary passage, later known as Cripplegate. It may be noted that the inclusion of a fort within the enceinte of a walled city was very unusual in the Roman Empire, and at Londinium it does perhaps emphasize the importance of the local topographical features in the planning of the wall.[8]

The wall has left an ineffaceable mark on London's development. For over fourteen centuries it provided the City's principal defence against attack. Its enceinte was never enlarged, as often happened during the Middle Ages in many large Continental towns and cities (Paris or Vienna, for instance), nor was its course ever significantly changed. Until well into the nineteenth century it continued to exert a powerful influence over the street layout and topography of the City.

Who built the wall, and why? During the earlier part of the period 190–225, within which it is certain from archaeological evidence that the wall was built, the Empire was riven by rival claimants to the throne, one of the most formidable of whom was Clodius Albinus, the governor of Britain. He had proclaimed himself emperor after the assassination of Commodus in 192, and after no doubt con-solidating his power in Britain he had taken his army across to Gaul, where in 197 he was defeated and killed at Lugdunum (Lyons) by his still more formidable adversary, Septimius Severus, hitherto governor of Pannonia (Hungary). In the aftermath of this civil war there was widespread retribution, confiscation, and bloodshed in Britain, aggravated by disorders in the north which necessitated extensive military operations in the frontier region there throughout much of Severus' reign. This lasted until his death in 211 in Britain, the problems of this lately rebellious province having demanded his personal presence there during the last three years of his life. So both he and his defeated rival Albinus had needed a secure strategic base in Britain from which to exert their authority, and either of them might therefore have built Londinium's wall. As subsequent events were to show on several occasions, Londinium's chief importance in later Roman times was strategic rather than commercial — a base from which to exert authority, whether legitimate or usurped. The building of the wall added greatly to the strength of this base; but at present the archaeological evidence is still not precise enough to make an accurate judgement about the date of its construction.[9]

There is no sign that the wall was put up in haste to meet some short-term emergency, and this perhaps makes it more likely that it was built by Severus than during the short and hectic time of Albinus. It was also very probably during Severus' reign that a monumental stone arch some 8 metres (26 feet) high, and a decorative stone screen over 6.2 metres (20 feet) wide, both ornamented with figures of traditional Roman deities, were erected somewhere in the south-western part of the walled area, where hitherto little building had taken place. During archaeological excavations in 1975 nearly fifty large blocks of stone which had originally been part of these two monuments and which were later reused to strengthen the defensive wall along the riverside were found at Blackfriars. Two stone altars were also found there, with inscriptions recording the rebuilding of decayed temples, and a carved relief depicting four mother goddesses. These discoveries suggest the building during and/or soon after the Severan period of a religious enclosure or park not far from Blackfriars. (The existence of such a park would also help to explain the absence, so far as is at present known, of a Roman street grid in the south-western part of the walled area.) Severus himself and his immediate successors had a penchant for architectural splendour. During much of his time on campaign in the north his wife, Julia Domna, and their younger son, the future Emperor Geta, are thought to have resided in southern Britain, very probably in Londinium. This powerful lady is known to have had a particular interest in religion; and the presence of the imperial court in the province may well have instigated a large programme of embellishments in the City. Substantial alterations to the governor's supposed palace at the Cannon Street site were certainly made at about this time; and taken with the harbour works, the building of the wall, and the embellishments in the south-west quarter of the City, it seems that after the later second-century decline there was around AD 200 a substantial measure of outward revival in Londinium, sponsored evidently by powerful public authority.[10]

Third-Century Disorders

All this energetic activity throughout Britain on the part of the imperial family (including Severus' elder son and immediate successor, Caracella, who accompanied his father on the northern campaigns) may be seen as part of the imperial determination to take a firm grip on this potentially unreliable frontier province. So too may the division of Britain in the early third century into two separate entities, Britannia Superior, containing the south and west, with its capital presumably still at Londinium, and Britannia Inferior (so called because further from Rome), centred on York.[11]

For nearly a century after this subdivision of the province there were no more over-mighty governors in Britain, which became almost a backwater. But although the status of Londinium was clearly diminished by the partition, the City was nevertheless still a rich place in the third century, as the remains of large houses — perhaps a hundred of them — clearly attest. They were usually built of Kentish ragstone and were laid out around a courtyard. Sometimes they had mosaic floors, and one, at Billingsgate, had its own bathhouse and was perhaps an inn. Along the Walbrook valley, where reoccupation was beginning again in the third century, there were several such fine buildings, one of which was associated with a temple built in the 240s for the practice of the eastern cult of Mithras and furnished with the magnificent sculptures (now in the Museum of London) which were discovered by Professor Grimes in 1954. In Southwark similar substantial buildings mostly date from the later third century. This type of structure implies a much less dense pattern of occupation than in earlier centuries — almost a 'garden city' kind of layout; and so too does the frequent presence of layers of dark earth. It also implies the presence of considerable wealth in third-century Londinium, but it seems that the possessors of this wealth were more probably bureaucrats or army officers than men of commerce; and so such urban revival as occurred was of political rather than economic origin.[12]

At the riverside the advance of the waterfront which was made in the early third century proved to be the last one during the Roman period, for the growing insecurity of the times evidently did not favour trade. There was frequent inter-necine strife within the Empire and in 259 Posthumus, an enterprising officer from Germany, declared himself emperor of an independent state comprising Germany, Gaul, Spain, and Britain. This 'Gallic Empire' survived for some fifteen years, until it was reconquered by Aurelian in 274; but by then Saxon raiders were frequently threatening the coasts and inlets of Britain. Many of the forts for the defence of these coasts, which became known as the Saxon Shore, date from the troubled later years of the third century, the impetus for much of the work being perhaps provided by the Emperor Probus (276–82).[13] At Londinium the City's defensive enclosure was completed by the building, mainly between c.255 and 275, of a great wall extending along the riverside from the Tower in the east to Blackfriars in the west, approximately on the line of Lower and Upper Thames Street; and the temples at the religious 'precinct' may have been restored at about the same time.[14] A late third-century signal tower recently discovered at Shadwell, some 1.2 kilo-metres (0.75 mile) east of the City and commanding a view over the river as far as Woolwich Reach, was evidently one of a chain of such posts extending down the estuary to the forts which guarded the open sea.[15]

The slow deterioration of the western part of the Empire could not, however, be halted for long, and for a short while at the end of the third century Britain became an independent state under Carausius. The Emperor Maximian had put this self-made and energetic officer in command of the sea and land forces in the vicinity of the Channel, with orders to suppress the bands of Saxon pirates and brigands still infesting the coasts there. However, Carausius was soon suspected of being in league with the enemy, and Maximian ordered his execution. So to save himself Carausius resorted to Britain and in 286 set himself up as emperor. There he successfully ruled his island realm for some six years, in the course of which he established London's first mint. This produced coins of much better quality than that of their debased predecessors, and it continued to operate under his successors until about 324. But in 293 Carausius was murdered by one of his ministers, Allectus, who during his brief reign started to raise a palatial pile at Peter's Hill (to the south of the later St Paul's Cathedral), substantial remains of which have recently been discovered and very accurately dated by dendrochronology. Three years later Allectus was himself defeated and killed in a battle somewhere near Silchester by an invading Roman army from Gaul. The remnants of Allectus' forces, mostly barbarian mercenaries of Frankish origin or recruited from the natives living near the northern frontier, retreated to Londinium, which they proceeded to plunder. Total disaster was prevented by the timely arrival of a seaborne force commanded by Constantius Chlorus. He and his men landed, slew the marauding rabble in the streets, and (so we are told by a contemporary) gave the citizens 'the pleasure of witnessing the slaughter, as if it were a public show'. The rescue of Londinium — probably the bloodiest event in the City's history since the Boudiccan pillage in AD 60 — was celebrated by a splendid gold medallion (found in France) depicting the triumphant Constantius, armed and mounted, and a war galley full of men, all advancing towards Londinium, which is represented by a suppliant female figure outside the City's gates. An inscription describes Constantius as 'Redditor Lucis Aeternae' (the restorer of eternal light).[16]

At that time Constantius was one of the two Caesars appointed by the two joint emperors or Augusti, Diocletian and Maximian, in whose reign the Empire began to polarize gradually towards east and west. Under Diocletian, who ruled from 284 to 305, the administration of the cumbersome Empire was being decentralized. He had delegated much of his authority in the west to Maximian, and later the two Augusti had appointed junior colleagues or Caesars, who were also their successors-designate. Beneath this tetrarchy were the praetorian prefects, each of whom managed a large tract of the Empire. Britain now became part of the praetorian prefecture of the Gauls, which also included Spain, the German Rhineland, and of course Gaul itself, and the permanent headquarters of which was at Trier — not at Paris, it may be noted, which was relatively unimportant in Roman times. Below the prefects came the *vicarii*, each of whom was in charge of a group of provinces known as a diocese. Britain itself was subdivided again, as it had been a century earlier by Severus or his son, but this time into four small provinces. Together they formed a diocese, the headquarters of whose *vicarius* was almost certainly in Londinium.[17]

Little is known about the workings of this new system — indeed, even the areas covered by the four provinces are uncertain — and their effect on Londinium is obscure. It may, however, be inferred that while the *vicarius* of Britain no longer wielded the supreme authority directly under the emperor which first- and second-century governors of the undivided province had possessed, he must on the other hand have had something of the same supervisory relationship with the four provincial governors and their staffs as a modern Whitehall department has with the provincial local authorities. Diocletian's administrative reforms are certainly known to have entailed a massive increase in the cost and the number of officials employed in the imperial service; and in Britain many of them were no doubt based in Londinium.[18]

Towards Disintegration

In 306 Constantius (by that time joint emperor with Galerius) died at York, where, like Severus a century earlier, he had been on campaign against the Picts. His son

Constantine (Constantine the Great) was immediately proclaimed Augustus by the army in Britain, and by 312 he had gained complete mastery of western Europe, to which in 324 he added the sovereignty of the east as well. His long reign lasted until 337, and brought revived prosperity to Britain, which despite all his other labours (including the refoundation of Byzantium as Constantinople) he revisited on at least two occasions. Even such a distant frontier province as Britain could not safely be ignored for long, and although the north probably commanded most of his attention, Londinium no doubt also experienced his powerful presence.[19]

For Londinium and for the whole of the Roman world the single most important event in Constantine's reign was the Edict of Milan of 313, by which Christianity secured toleration. Personal belief in an exclusive religion was now accepted. Very soon the emperor himself was assuming such new duties as the suppression of heresy and the promotion of unity within the Christian Church; and these new components were to dominate the evolving equation of European thought and behaviour for over a thousand years.[20]

One of their first consequences was the Council of the Church held at Arles in 314, which from Britain was attended by the bishops of York, London, and Lincoln and by two priests probably representing the bishop of the fourth of the provinces into which Britain had been divided.[21] The existence in Londinium at this date of a recognized Christian community is therefore certain. There is little evidence, however, for its earlier history, nor for the tradition that the church of St Peter-upon-Cornhill was founded in AD 179. Nevertheless St Peter's (of course rebuilt on several occasions) stands in the centre of the site formerly occupied by the Roman basilica, and religious rites of some sort may have been practised there at an early date.* At all events, by Constantine's time the Christians in Londinium were evidently strong enough to ransack the temple of Mithras in Walbrook.[22]

For Britain Constantine's reign was something of an Indian summer before the lengthening shadows of winter closed in, for conflict both within and on the frontiers of the Empire was becoming almost endemic. Only three years after Constantine's death in 337 one of his three sons, Constantine II, Augustus of Britain, Gaul, and Spain, had been killed in battle in Italy by one of his brothers. In 353 the army of Britain was again on the losing side when the usurper Magnentius, de facto ruler for three years of most of the west, killed himself after defeat in battle in Gaul (AD 353); and, in the fearful reprisals and confiscations which ensued, the *vicarius* of Britain also committed suicide.[23] Only seven years later an incursion on the northern frontier by the Picts and Scots required the dispatch from Gaul of a special expeditionary force commanded by the Roman general Lupicinus. In the disastrous year 367 large parts of the whole island, including the hitherto virtually unviolated south-east, but apparently not Londinium itself, were overrun by barbarian hordes, and the restoration of order demanded another task

* Archaeological excavations by MoLAS made in 1995 partly beneath Trinity House to the north of Tower Hill revealed the foundations of a large late Roman building which may have been a Christian basilica. At the time of writing (1997) the purpose of this building has not yet been determined, and there is a possibility that it was never finished.

force and the attention of its great commander, Theodosius, for at least two years.[24]

Both Lupicinus and Theodosius landed at Richborough, and both of them at once made for Londinium, Lupicinus doing so (in the words of a contemporary account) 'that he might there take such decision as the aspect of affairs demanded'. Theodosius also 'marched towards Londinium', but on the way he 'attacked the predatory and straggling bands of the enemy', loaded with plunder. Thereafter, 'amid scenes of jubilation which recalled a Roman triumph, he made his entry into the City which just before had been overwhelmed by troubles, but was now suddenly re-established almost before it could have hoped for deliverance'.[25]

It was apparently in connexion with these events that Londinium was renamed Augusta, presumably in recognition of the citizens' laudable conduct during such traumatic times; but the new name seems only to have been used for official purposes.[26] More enduring monuments were provided by the hurried improvements made to the fortifications of Londinium (and to other towns in Britain), probably by Theodosius. The great stone arch and decorative screen erected in the Severan period of the early third century were demolished and their materials used to strengthen the western end of the riverside wall.[27] On the eastern side of Londinium a range of projecting semicircular bastions was built along the outer side of the City wall in order to provide an improved field of defensive fire. Some of these bastions also contained reused blocks of stone, taken from the funerary monuments in the adjacent cemeteries. This quarrying of the nearest available materials demonstrates the urgency with which the defences of Londinium now had to be reinforced; and the failure (during the Roman era) to continue the series of bastions along the whole length of the wall may suggest that there was not enough time for the completion of such extensive works.[28]

The repeated efforts made by successive emperors in the second half of the fourth century to defend Britain demonstrate the importance which Rome still attached to the island — the Empire's only island possession outside the Mediterranean, situated on the very edge of the known world, and so perhaps possessing an alluring mystique not enjoyed by any other province. As for Londinium, the fact that it was the immediate destination of both Lupicinus and Theodosius is proof of the continuing value placed upon the City as Britain's principal centre of administration, intelligence, and rapid communication; and so too are the hasty measures taken for its defence, even at the cost of the destruction of hitherto venerated monuments.

Nevertheless the main scene of events in later fourth-century Britain had in some sense shifted to the north, and in particular to York, the military headquarters of the army of the northern frontier. From its mostly northern stations much of the army of Britain had twice, in AD 340 and 353, crossed to the Continent in support of the ambitions of imperial aspirants (both unsuccessful). It was to do so twice more: in 383, led by Magnus Maximus, an usurper set up by the army of Britain after a successful campaign against the Picts and Scots, and in 407 when it elevated Constantine III, who quickly took ship for Gaul.[29]

These Continental forays had greatly reduced the strength of the defensive garrisons in the island, and done so in times when Britain was under increasing attack from north and east, and even from the Irish to the west. Around the year 399 the last serious attempt to reassert imperial control was made under the auspices of Stilicho, the Vandal general of the Emperor Honorius. In Londinium what seems to have been a defensive stronghold within the site of the later Tower of London was probably built by this final expeditionary force.[30] Soon, however, the imperial forces were being withdrawn again, the Visigothic chieftain Alaric was in Italy itself, and in 406 barbarian hordes crossed the frozen Rhine and invaded Gaul. After Constantine III had left Britain in 407 few troops were still left there. Soon afterwards there was a particularly strong barbarian onslaught on Britain and Gaul which Constantine was unable to resist; and it was this situation which (in the words of Zosimus, writing less than a century later) 'brought the people of Britain and some of the nations of Gaul to the point where they revolted from Roman rule and lived by themselves, no longer obeying Roman laws'.[31]

Londinium is not explicitly mentioned in this account, but Zosimus goes on to say that 'The Britons took up arms and, fighting for themselves, freed the cities from the barbarian pressure'; and many of the provinces of Gaul, 'in imitation of the Britons, freed themselves in the same manner, expelling the Roman officials and setting up their own administration as well as they could'. In 410 the famous 'Rescript' of the Emperor Honorius to the cities of Britain instructed them to undertake their own defence. It was addressed to the cities because, presumably, there were no longer any imperial officials to whom such orders would otherwise have been sent. Londinium as the administrative centre of Roman Britain had ceased to exist.[32]

Economic Affairs

However, Londinium was also the principal commercial centre of Britain. The evidence for what happened in the City in this sphere in the third, fourth, and early fifth centuries is almost entirely archaeological, for Roman writers seldom bothered much about trade; and despite all the recent advances in both the quantity and the scientific interpretation of archaeological discoveries, the window which that evidence opens still has only a limited view over this part of the landscape of the ancient world. The scale of Roman commerce is also particularly hard to assess; and so too is the role of Londinium in that commerce.

We have already seen that as the Romanization of Britain proceeded the 'colonial' type of commerce of the early years of the imperial occupation, based largely on imports, began to decline; and that internal trade became more local. Communications within Britain were good; nearly fifty coastal Roman harbours have been identified south of Hadrian's Wall, there were numerous navigable rivers (of which the Thames was the most important), and the road network had brought cohesion to the whole country. So in the building of Londinium, for instance, there were no problems of transport in bringing even such a cumbersome commodity as stone from such distant places as Purbeck, Bath, Northampton-shire, or Lincolnshire (the latter for the monumental arch), as well, of course, as from Kent; and tiles came in some quantity from Bedfordshire.[33]

In the third and fourth centuries home-produced goods were often superseding imports. The pottery made in the Alice Holt–Farnham area and in the Oxfordshire region of the Thames Valley, which captured much of the Londinium market, provides a case in point. Overseas trade, primarily in such commodities as olive oil which could not be produced internally, and wine, continued for a while; but in the third century the trade in oil was being disrupted by the repeated disturbances in Gaul, which also reduced other commercial contacts between Britain and the Mediterranean world. With the establishment of Diocletian's praetorian prefecture of the Gauls, the headquarters of which were at Trier, the centre of gravity of Britain's overseas trade shifted from the Mediterranean to northern Gaul and Germany. The Rhineland (including the Moselle) became Britain's main supplier of wine;[34] and it was probably to the nearby Roman garrisons there that many of Britain's famous woollen garments — one of the province's most important exports — were sold. Certainly it was to the Rhineland that in AD 359 the Emperor Julian, on campaign on the frontier there, sent a fleet of no fewer than six hundred ships carrying corn from Britain.[35]

In the later Roman years Britain seems, indeed, to have been used as a con-venient source of supplies for the troops on the constantly threatened Rhine frontier. This and all other trade with the Rhineland was no doubt good for business at the port of Londinium, but there is nevertheless evidence suggesting that the volume of trade there was declining in the third and fourth centuries.[36] Such a decline would of course reflect the decline which is thought to have taken place in the population of Londinium at this time, and supports the idea that many of the imported goods landed there were for consumption in Londinium itself rather than for distribution elsewhere in Britain. The harbour installations, which had always been small in comparison with those of such other Roman ports as Trier, and which had always been concentrated near to the bridge, do not seem to have been renewed or enlarged after the middle of the third century. Nor, from about the same time, was the line of the waterfront ever advanced again in Roman times. The riverside defensive wall, which we have seen was built in the mid-third century, may have obstructed the movement of goods along some of the quays, but its overall effect on the commerce of the port is not clear. A change in the level of the river would have been much more significant. Recent research has indicated that in later Roman times the level of the river may have actually been falling;[37] and this idea is supported by the fact that each successive advancement of the water-front quays was built at a lower level than the previous one, the difference in the levels of the earliest first-century quays and those of the last of c.250 being perhaps as much as 1.5 metres (5 feet).[38] If the tidal head did indeed move below Londinium the adverse effect on the overseas trade of the port would of course have been very considerable. The establishment in the 270s of a new roadside settlement at Old Ford on the River Lea, a tributary of the Thames and some 3 miles downstream from Londinium, and its survival into the early fifth century, may be related to such upstream tidal changes.[39] Lastly there is always the most obvious explanation for commercial contraction in later Roman times: the mounting disorder and dislocation of trade routes caused by barbarian irruptions, particularly into Gaul in the third century, and by Saxon seaborne incursions into Britain.

Despite this evidence of declining overseas trade, another line of research suggests that until the early fifth century trade was still substantial in scale, and that Londinium had a large share of it. The archaeological evidence for late Roman trade is comparable with that for late thirteenth-and fourteenth-century trade because the same types of object — pottery, and to a lesser extent glass, coins, and metalwork — survive in approximately similar quantities. Given such a general level of quantitative comparability, information contained in medieval documentary sources can be applied to the later Roman commercial landscape, which is virtually unilluminated by any written evidence. The archival sources show that the bulk of medieval England's overseas exports consisted of wool or later of cloth, while the principal import was wine. These commodities have left little or no archaeological trace of their existence, nor have many other less important items of medieval foreign commerce such as foodstuffs or furs. However, the written records show that the medieval trade in them — and hence perhaps also, so it has been inferred, that of later Roman times — represented every year the voyages to and from the ports of Britain of hundreds of small ships.[40] If this comparison is taken one stage further it may be that London's supremacy in the medieval export trade, which is so amply demonstrated in the customs accounts, may also have prevailed in the later Roman years.

Whatever its scale, however, trade depends heavily on a ready supply of money; and by the 420s the use of coins in Britain had virtually ceased. Coins had been struck in Londinium at various times during the Roman period — between 287 and 324, and again under Magnus Maximus (383–8) — but at other times they had been brought in in bulk from Continental mints, chiefly for the payment of the troops and civilian administrators stationed in the island. Shortage of coins nevertheless often prevailed, and may explain the readiness of the army in Britain to back usurpers such as Carausius (286–93), who (as we have already seen) set up his own mint in Londinium. The last Roman coins found in Britain in any numbers are those of the Emperors Arcadius and Honorius struck down to AD 402. The discontinuation of the supply thereafter may simply have been because the emperors had no money to pay their troops, or because they were no longer able to deliver money to outlying parts of their war-torn Empire, or because there were no longer any troops or officials in Britain to be paid. Whatever the reason, the result was the same: the collapse of the money economy in the early fifth century.[41]

Londinium had been a Roman foundation, and for nearly four centuries it had lived as a bough of the mighty oak tree of the Empire. When the sap ceased to flow and the limbs began to crack, the City withered, for it had always been more

Roman than British. The process of regression has left little trace; but archaeo-logical excavations in Billingsgate, in one of the great houses built in the third century, have exposed something of it. Stratigraphical evidence associated with the wood-ash of the heating system shows that Romans were probably still living there early in the fifth century, but soon afterwards the house was in decay. A hidden hoard of coins, unrecovered by its owner, fell to the floor, and the roof collapsed. Gradually silt and rubbish swamped many of the rooms, and it was in this silt covering the floor of one of them — the *frigidarium* or cold room — that modern excavators found a Saxon saucer brooch thought to be of the mid-fifth century.[42] A new epoch in the history of London had opened.

PART II

From Londinium to the Chartered City of London *c.*400–*c.*1530

INTRODUCTION

The period of Western European history which followed the decay of classical culture around the fifth century used to be known as the Dark Ages; but in recent years this term has fallen out of favour with historians, partly, no doubt, because modern archaeological and other research has thrown so much new light on these hitherto obscure times. What happened in London in the five centuries of fundamental change which took place there between *c.*400 and *c.*900 is certainly a great deal clearer now than was the case even as recently as twenty years ago, but many obscurities remain.

These are particularly impenetrable in the fifth and sixth centuries, for it is still not certain whether the walled city was ever completely deserted or whether there was unbroken vestigial habitation of small parts of it, and possibly even survival during at least part of the period of some form of urban authority there. The archaeological evidence for these two centuries is minimal, and the first hard fact about early Saxon London comes from a documentary source — Bede's Ecclesiastical History, which describes the appointment in 604 of a bishop of the East Saxons, with his see in London, and the building of the church of St Paul there.

When he was writing in the 730s Bede described London as a 'metropolis...a mart [*emporium*] of many peoples coming by land and sea'. Until recently, however, archaeology had been unable to substantiate the existence of such a busy commercial centre; and it was not until 1984 that it was realized that the Middle Saxon settlement referred to by documents in Old English as Lundenwic — *wic* meaning a port or trading town — and by Bede, writing in Latin, as an *emporium*, was in the seventh to ninth centuries situated outside and west of the walled Roman city, in the area of Fleet Street and the Strand — a conclusion which has now been confirmed by archaeological excavations there.

For over two centuries, from approximately the first half of the seventh to approximately the mid-ninth century, there were thus two components of London: within the walls an ecclesiastical centre around St Paul's (and possibly a royal one nearby, around Aldermanbury), and outside the walls to the west an undefended trading settlement. However, as a result of the Viking attacks of the mid-ninth century the *wic* was abandoned, and soon after Alfred, King of Wessex, had expelled the Vikings and occupied London in 886 the fortified city was re-established — the *burh* or borough of Lundenburg. Thereafter the whole of the walled area was very gradually recolonized; but when Edward the Confessor built a new royal palace at Westminster beside his newly rebuilt abbey there, London as a whole again assumed a dual nature which it has never wholly lost, with the seat of royal power and government geographically distinct from the burgeoning economic centre. In the later Middle Ages London emerged as the undisputed capital of the realm, its municipal authority buttressed by a succession of royal charters and its industrial, commercial, and demographic influence spreading outward ever further afield.

4

Londinium and Lundenwic
c.400–c.886

Urban life in Britain had been a specifically Roman creation. We have already seen that in 54 BC Julius Caesar had noted that the Britons' idea of a town consisted of 'no more than a central rallying-point from hostile incursion, formed of some inaccessible piece of woodland that has been fortified by a high rampart and ditch.' But when, some four centuries later, his successors began to abandon the province, they left scores of urban centres which they had planted throughout the land. In the disorders which ensued the Britons proved unable to support these centres, at least in the manner in which the Romans had supported them; and the Germanic invaders, unlike the Roman conquerors of the first century AD, were unaccustomed to urban life. Also unlike the Romans, they never went away. In the course of time the Anglo-Saxons became the ascendant element in the population of what became England, and the language spoken there was fundamentally changed. So the towns which ultimately emerged, while of course resembling their Roman predecessors in being responses to the unchanging facts of geography, differed greatly from them in being wholly indigenous artefacts.

Uncertain Times c.400–c.600

Three types of evidence partially illuminate the obscurity of the fifth and sixth centuries: literary, archaeological, and linguistic, the last particularly through the study of place names. The only surviving written account of events in fifth-century Britain is by Gildas, a priest living in or near North Wales in the mid-sixth century. His dates, events, and places are all often obscure or even perhaps mythical; and he makes no mention of London, which he probably never visited and of whose very existence he may well have been ignorant.[1] There are references to Britain in the Gallic Chronicles and in Constantius' Life of St Germanus, who twice visited the island, in 429 and in about 448. Much later comes the

Anglo-Saxon Chronicle, which took its present form in the late ninth century but parts of which draw on earlier material. In the eighth century there is the great Ecclesiastical History written by Bede, but he, like Gildas, lived far from London, of which he probably had no first-hand knowledge. Likewise the archaeological material, to be reviewed later, is scanty in the extreme — far more so than for either the preceding or later times; and the evidence of place names presents many puzzles. In the case of London itself the Roman form 'Londinium' has changed less than that of any other important Roman town in Britain, evolving only to Old English 'Lunden' or 'Lundenwic', and soon settling into such forms as 'Lundonia' or 'Londonia', in marked contrast with the much less readily apparent journey of, for instance, Eboracum to York, or, in many other cases, with the total loss of the Roman name. But whether the survival of the name in relatively unchanged form may imply unbroken habitation is far from clear.[2]

It is, however, certain that by the early fifth century there was already a strong Germanic presence in the island, assimilated in varying degrees to Roman ways. German troops had formed part of the Romans' army of invasion in AD 43, and many of their increasingly numerous successors had settled in Britain. From the early third century there had been Germanic incursions along the east coast north of the Thames estuary; and in the fourth century these attacks had required the creation of a new military command post known as the comes Litoris Saxonici (the count of the Saxon Shore), who had charge of the coastal areas from Norfolk to the Isle of Wight. For a while the fortresses built along the Straits of Dover may have reduced Saxon irruptions further west into the Channel, and Germanic settlements along the coast of Kent and Sussex were therefore later and less intensive than those further north, and were made by different peoples, notably (in Kent) by the Jutes.[3]

After the withdrawal of Roman authority internal disorder seems to have prevailed for several decades, and ultimately some of the old Roman *civitates* (tribal or cantonal administrative areas) began to re-emerge as small independent native kingdoms.[4] During this confused period of what Gildas calls 'bella civilia' at least one hard-pressed petty king engaged the support of Germanic chieftains against warring bands coming down from the north; and in exchange they and their followers were rewarded with land — an extension, evidently, of the old Roman custom of settling barbarian soldiery as *foederati* or allies within the Empire. But now there was no longer any imperial authority to control such fearsome immigrants, of whom Hengist and Horsa, invited in by a British warlord named Vortigern, are the most famous to posterity. So within a few years they had themselves become conquerors; and at the battle of Crecganford (probably Crayford) in 457 Hengist, according to the Anglo-Saxon Chronicle, defeated the Britons of Kent, who fled in great terror to London.[5]

This is the last literary reference to London as a Roman (or at least quasi-Roman) city, and it suggests that London still existed as a place of refuge for the Romano-British population. The archaeological evidence for the fifth century is also extremely scanty, and almost non-existent for the sixth. Two hoards of gold coins of the late fourth century and a silver ingot found in the Tower are thought to have been deposited there in the early fifth century, and to have been used to buy the services of troops, probably barbarian mercenaries. They also indicate that this part of London was at least worth defending; and so too does the remodelling at about this time of the riverside wall at the south-east corner of the walled area. Two late Roman belt buckles found in the Walbrook and in the cemetery in West Smithfield also suggest a continuing military presence. Shards of Mediterranean pottery, found mainly near the riverfront, may have been in use in the early fifth century, and imply the continued existence of trade.[6] Nevertheless, the discoveries made at the Billingsgate house (mentioned in Chapter 3) point to the mid-fifth century as a time of rapidly advancing decay, and the Saxon brooch found there suggests a Germanic presence in the City soon afterwards. So what may have happened to London?

A ring of pagan and therefore early Saxon cemeteries around the southern sides of London at such places as Mitcham, Croydon, Ham, and Northfleet has been taken as evidence of early fifth-century Teutonic penetration along the Thames Valley and its southern tributaries to around the area of Reading, unimpeded by any London *territorium* or sphere of influence. The early immigrants seem, indeed, to have circumvented London, which they were evidently wary of approaching, for no trace of them closer than 6 kilometres (4 miles) has been found (at Greenwich); and it may be significant that on the north side of the river, which could more easily be defended by any surviving power in London, the nearest early Saxon cemetery is at Hanwell, some 15 kilometres (over 9 miles) away. But whether such settlers lived and died near London by permission of and as quasi-mercenary defenders of such a Romano-British power in London, or whether their settlements represented a halt in the advance of a hostile northward or westward migration from the south or east coasts is uncertain. Either supposition does, however, imply the survival of London as some sort of inhabited place for some time after the collapse of Roman rule.[7]

So too may the evidence from Mucking, where archaeological excavation has proved continuity of Saxon occupation from around AD 400 into the seventh century. This settlement in south-east Essex was made on high ground overlooking the Thames estuary some 32 kilometres (20 miles) downstream from London. The site was ideal as a lookout post from which warning of the approach of hostile vessels could be transmitted back to the City, perhaps by means of signal towers such as the one recently discovered at Shadwell. But although this may have been the original function of the settlement, its purpose may well have changed over the course of time, and its existence spanning the fifth to the seventh centuries cannot necessarily be taken as evidence for a corresponding continuity in London itself.[8]

A powerful case for the survival of London as a kind of 'sub-Roman slum' with 'a continuing, if unexalted, civic consciousness' was put in the 1930s by (Sir) Mortimer Wheeler. He pointed out that London was at the centre of the most intensely Romanized part of Britain, flanked to the north of the Thames by the large walled cities of Colchester and Verulamium and to the south by those of Rochester, Canterbury, and the fortified port of Richborough. This area extended westward up the great artery of entry into southern England as far as the neighbourhood of the Goring Gap, and was designated by Wheeler as the 'Sub-Roman Triangle' of Britain. Within this area archaeological traces of early Saxon settlement are rare when compared with those in the adjoining areas; and this may suggest that the less advanced culture brought from the third century onwards by the Germanic immigrants was absorbed into the sophisticated and firmly founded Romano-British civilization which they encountered there.[9] Similarly the distribution of place names shows a more dense retention of Romano-British names in a wide swath which extends across central southern England and which includes the whole of Wheeler's 'Sub-Roman Triangle', than in any other part of Britain. The survival of such place names, much rarer in many other areas of the country, indicates some measure of continuous occupation, however flimsy.[10]

There is also some enigmatic evidence, eloquently set forth by Wheeler, for the survival of some sort of forceful but probably declining authority within this postulated Romano-British enclave. This takes the form of the earthworks known as Grim's Ditches, the longest line of which extends intermittently along the brow of the Chiltern Hills to the north-west of London from near Berkhampstead in Hertfordshire to the Thames in the neighbourhood of Nuffield. Not far from Bushey, in Middlesex and much nearer to London, there is another roughly parallel stretch; and there is a third on the diagonally opposite or south-east side of London at Bexley in Kent, on the side of the valley of the River Cray. All these works consist of a massive ditch and bank, those at Bushey thought by the archaeologists to be no earlier than the fourth century. The name Grim, however, indicates an origin in the pagan Saxon times of the fifth of sixth centuries. The most

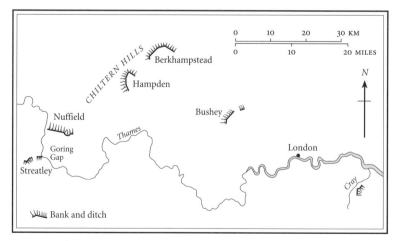

Fig. 11. Grim's Ditches

remarkable feature of these earthworks is that in all three cases the ditch is on the side nearer to London. They were therefore built by the Teutonic peoples dwelling outside the dykes, evidently as lines of political demarcation to define both the limits of their conquest and the outermost extent of the *territorium* of a still vigourous power within. The relative dates of the dykes on the Chilterns and near Bushey are not known, but scholarly opinion favours the view that the stretch in Middlesex is the later, and that it therefore marks a contraction of the territory of the authority inside.[11]

That authority can only have been that of London; and that such an authority did at one time extend over a very large area is attested by early medieval documentary evidence. The famous charter of Henry I (1100–35) to the citizens of London* confirms their right to 'have their chaces to hunt, as well and fully as their ancestors had, that is to say, in Chiltre, and in Middlesex and Surrey'. William FitzStephen, writing a few years later, almost certainly in the 1170s, refers to the Londoners' hunting rights as extending over Middlesex, Hertfordshire, and all Chiltern, and Kent 'as far as the waters of Cray'. These rights, already an ancient survival in the early twelfth century, must certainly have existed back in Saxon times, though whether as far back as early Saxon times cannot be known; and the striking similarity of their extent with the area adumbrated by Grim's Ditches may be more than just coincidence.[13] At all events no other plausible explanation of these ancient rights or of those very solid and indestructible earthworks has yet presented itself.

Most of the evidence so far considered relates to the environs of London. For the City itself the first firm fact (provided by Bede) relating to Saxon London is the establishment of a bishopric there in 604. In 596–7 Pope Gregory the Great had sent a mission to convert the people of England, and its leader, the Benedictine monk Augustine, had established himself at Canterbury, where King Ethelbert of Kent had a Christian queen. In 601 a second band of Benedictine missionaries had arrived from Rome, with instructions for the establishment of two provinces, one in London and the other in York, corresponding with the division of Britain made by the Emperor Severus in c.AD 200. Soon afterwards Augustine sent the leader of these reinforcements, Mellitus, forward to preach in the province of the East Saxons (i.e. Essex), whose king, Saeberht, was the nephew of Ethelbert and subject to him. By 604 the work of conversion had advanced far enough for Ethelbert to build the church of St Paul in London, of which Mellitus became bishop.[14]

These well-authenticated events are generally held to provide good reason for thinking that urban civilization had not survived in London during the sixth century. There is no hint of the previous existence of any Christian community there, still less of the episcopal see which (as mentioned in Chapter 3) had undoubtedly existed in London at the time of the Council of Arles in 314;[15] and Pope Gregory's designation of London as one of the two provincial centres from

---

* The recently questioned but still more recently reasserted authenticity of this charter does not diminish its value as a genuine statement of the citizens' privileges in the 1130s and 1140s.[12]

which the conversion of Saxon England was to be organized was more probably due to the survival of a tradition of London's former greatness in Roman times than to any more recent eminence. In many of the cities of Gaul it was primarily the local episcopate which had provided a measure of social continuity after the collapse of Roman authority. In Britain, however, the break was much sharper than in Gaul, and it is therefore hard to imagine that London retained a 'continuing civic consciousness' without any such ecclesiastical leadership.[16] Moreover the absence of any surviving sub-Roman presence in London is confirmed by the precarious nature of Mellitus' sojourn there; for in 616 he was expelled by Saeberht's pagan sons, and the bishopric was not restored to London until the middle of the seventh century.[17]

In the fifth and sixth centuries the walled area must have been full of crumbling ruins of Roman buildings, and the bridge was probably no longer usable. Some components of the Roman street layout did, it is true, survive into medieval times, notably the line of Fleet Street, Ludgate Hill, Watling Street, the eastern part of Cannon Street, and Eastcheap; and if any organized community or garrison existed after about 450 it was probably at the Cripplegate fort, where the Roman street pattern also endured, or at the south-east corner of the walled area within the site later occupied by the Tower.[18] But in the anarchic fifth and sixth centuries trade had dwindled, and the route along the Thames Valley had broken down.[19] Without either settled government or trade London had lost most of its *raison d'être*; and at a more general level the change of language from British or Latin to 'Old English' also implies a fundamental change of population and culture. So Londinium seems to have slowly wilted away, the process reinforced perhaps by the virulent outbreaks of plague known to have devastated parts of the ancient world in the mid-fifth century.[20]

Revival c.600–886: Lundenwic

In England the nadir of post-Roman civilization was reached earlier than anywhere else in Western Europe — perhaps around the year 500 — and the change of language and people was more fundamental than elsewhere. The process of change was also drawn out over a longer period, for through the obstacle of the sea the immigrants came in relatively small bands, unlike the mass hordes which periodically overran continental Europe. Changes of political power were violent, and the immigrants — or conquerors — never became so Romanized as many of their counterparts on the Continent. So Britain was diverging, fundamentally because it was an island; and it was in some measure due to this insularity that the permanent political unification of England was achieved at such an early period — in the confused times of the seventh to the eleventh centuries, when the supposed seven kingdoms of the Saxon heptarchy were gradually assimilated into a single realm.

Throughout much of these times — certainly until the early tenth century — London was often at the territorial extremity of one of these kingdoms, whose main centres of power were elsewhere. Their shifting territories and allegiances were seldom defined with precision, and are certainly not accurately known now. It seems, however, that the homelands of the Middle Saxons may originally have embraced a much larger area than that later known as Middlesex, and may even perhaps have included the area south of the Thames later known as Surrey — an idea consistent with Wheeler's theory of some surviving political authority in post-Roman London. But by the seventh century the extent of the Middle Saxons' territories had been much reduced by encroachments from the East and West Saxons of Essex and Wessex, and perhaps too from the powerful kings of Kent. So London found itself in a marginal location on the frontiers of prolonged Saxon contentions.[21]

At the time of Augustine's Christian mission (*c*.597–604) London was under the sway of the East Saxon monarchy. The diocese which came into being in the early seventh century with St Paul's as its cathedral extended in medieval times over Essex, Middlesex, and much of Hertfordshire as well as London, and (as often happened with diocesan boundaries) was probably coterminous with the local kingdom. The East Saxon monarchy was, however, in its turn for some time subordinate to that of Kent, but by around 670 effective control of London was passing to the kings of Mercia, in whose hands it remained for well over a hundred and fifty years. South of the Thames the growing kingdom of Wessex eventually enlarged its sway all over Surrey, as testified by the boundaries of the diocese of Wessex's principal city, Winchester, which extended right up to the Thames at Southwark, and continued to do so for some thousand years, until 1877.[22]

So the territories of Saxon kings and bishops were often coterminous with each other. In London there may also have been physical contiguity between the two authorities, for there is reason to believe that (until its removal to Westminster by Edward the Confessor in the mid-eleventh century) the seat of royal secular authority was situated on the City's western hill, within or close to the Roman fort and amphitheatre and not far from the bishop's church of St Paul. As early as the 670s the Kentish kings are known to have had a 'hall' in London where their merchants were to record their transactions. And according to thirteenth-century tradition Offa, King of Mercia (757–96), had his palace next to the church of St Alban, Wood Street, which perhaps served as a royal chapel, and which recent excavation has shown to have probably originated in the eighth or ninth century.[23] Such a palace or residence, if indeed it did exist there, would have been within the curtilege of the Roman fort at Cripplegate — a natural place for a Saxon king to use as a fortified base within the ruins of Londinium. Immediately to the east is Aldermanbury, the defended enclosure or *burh* of the *ealdorman* (or leading city magnate), at the south-east corner of the confines of the erstwhile fort. Nearby were the earliest recorded *hagas* (small enclosures of property belonging to a community or important individual based outside the City) such as those of Bassishaw (the *haga* of the men of Basingstoke) or Staining (Staines),[24] clustered

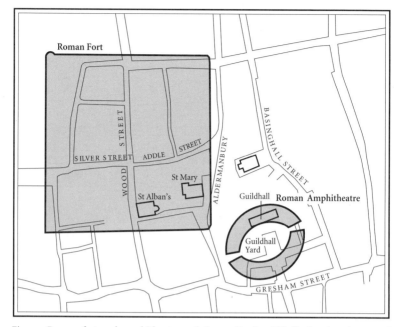

Fig. 12. Roman fort and amphitheatre and the medieval guildhall, showing the curved alignments of Gresham Street, Aldermanbury, and Basinghall Street

in this same royal area, much as in later centuries the town houses of great nobles clustered in the West End near the royal palaces at Westminster, Whitehall, and St James's.

So there is reason to think that by the end of the mid-Saxon period (c.650–850) the centre of government was established on the western hill, far away from the site in Roman times of the forum and basilica on the eastern hill, and from the governor's palace on the waterfront. This concentration of secular authority on the western hill has continued down to the present time, for (as previously mentioned in Chapter 2) since at least the thirteenth century the City's Guildhall has stood upon part of the site of the Roman amphitheatre, close to the fort; and this superimposition of one place of public assembly upon another is, to quote Professor Martin Biddle, 'unlikely to be the result merely of chance'; and nor is the position of the Saxon enclave of Aldermanbury and the *hagas* of Bassishaw and Staining, huddled round the site of the amphitheatre. Professor Biddle has also suggested the possibility that the folkmoot — probably the City's oldest court or assembly — may have met 'from time immemorial' in the amphitheatre before its displacement to Paul's Cross, where it was meeting in the thirteenth century. A hypothesis of this kind would, of course, be untenable if there were reason to suppose that the amphitheatre had not survived the Roman period. The topographical evidence, however, suggests that it did survive (doubtless in ruinous form), for the curving courses of Gresham Street, Aldermanbury, and Basinghall Street can be convincingly explained by the continued existence of the amphitheatre, the exterior of which they closely encompass. So the superimposition of Guildhall in medieval times upon the site of the amphitheatre implies a continuity in the exercise of public functions in this part of the City which extends back into remotest and largely unrecorded times.[25]

Elsewhere within the Roman walls there is very little archaeological evidence of human occupation in the seventh to mid-ninth centuries, though at the opposite extremity from the fort part of the church of All Hallows, Barking (so called from its connexion with Barking Abbey, founded in the seventh century) probably dates from the mid-Saxon period.[26] Documentary evidence, on the other hand, demonstrates that commercial revival had certainly begun in London in the later seventh century. A charter of 672–4 refers to land 'by the port of London, where ships come to land'. In 679 a prisoner was sold as a slave to a Frisian merchant 'at London'; and (as previously mentioned) at around the same time the kings of Kent had a royal hall there, at which in the presence of the king's reeve or agent the merchants of Kent could have their purchases warranted.[27] It was from London, too, that St Boniface twice (in 716 and 718) embarked for his Continental journeys; and in the 730s and 740s the king of Mercia was granting to various religious institutions exemptions from payment of tolls on ships there, one of his charters specifically mentioning the existence of taxcollectors, which implies the existence of trade on some scale. There is, in fact, ample documentary material to support Bede's well-known description of London, written in about 730, as a 'metropolis . . . a mart of many peoples coming by land and sea'.[28]

Coins tell much the same story. Gold coins with the legend 'LONDUNIV' perhaps date from the 630s; a century later King Aethelbald of Mercia was issuing pennies 'DE LUNDONIA', and in 829 King Egbert of Wessex's coins were inscribed 'LUNDONIA CIVIT[AS]'. Production seems indeed to have been almost continuous, and sometimes on a huge scale, as for instance around 870, when some fifteen moneyers were working at London for the king of Mercia to supply enough coins for the payment of the Danegeld exacted by the Viking army of occupation.[29]

The fact of London's commercial revival from the seventh century onwards cannot therefore be doubted; but the extreme scarcity within the walled area of early or even mid-Saxon archaeological evidence for this economic activity has until recently greatly puzzled successive generations of scholars. In 1984, however, Professor Martin Biddle and Dr Alan Vince convincingly demonstrated that 'Lundenwic' — the name-form often used in seventh-century documents — was situated outside and to the west of the walled Roman city, on the gravel terrace which extends along the north bank of the Thames from the River Fleet to Charing Cross.[30] *Wic*, derived from the Latin *vicus* (meaning a village, or quarter of a city), was commonly used to denote mid-Saxon trading settlements, as, for instance, at Norwich, Ipswich, or Sandwich. Sometimes these settlements were made near an old Roman walled site — Hamwic (Southampton) near Clausentium, or

Fordwich, outside Canterbury — and always they were situated on a sheltered shore or on a navigable river.[31]

At Lundenwic the uncluttered gravel foreshore provided a much better place for the beaching of ships than did the ruinous old Roman waterfront, the dangerous waters of which no doubt concealed submerged piles and fallen stonework. Remains of primitive Saxon harbour-works, consisting of a brushwood platform covered with rubble and ragstone, have been found a little to the east of Charing Cross Station, 160 metres north of the present line of the Thames,[32] which was only formed in 1864–70 by the building of the Victoria Embankment. Along the brow of the plateau stretched the great thoroughfare of Fleet Street and the Strand — the latter meaning in Old English 'land at the edge of a piece of water, especially the sea, a shore, a bank'. Scattered archaeological evidence (not all of it very precise) from a score of finds made between Whitehall and the Fleet River suggests the existence there of a large settlement between the seventh and the mid-ninth century. More recent scientific excavations have discovered timber buildings, wells, pits, and pottery imported from the Continent. At the site of the Jubilee Hall in Covent Garden there was industrial activity, attested by iron and bronze furnace slag, millstones imported from the Rhine Valley, and loom weights used in weaving.[33] The evidence of bones of animals suggests that cattle, sheep (needed for wool as well as meat), and pigs may not have been raised within the settlement in sufficient numbers to feed the population, and were therefore brought in from the nearby countryside.[34] All in all Lundenwic seems to have been the largest mid-Saxon settlement in England, a focal point in a trading network extending along the Thames from Mercia to Kent and across the sea to such great Continental centres of exchange as Quentovic (near Boulogne) and Dorestadt on the Rhine in the Netherlands.[35]

The first post-Roman documentary reference to the port of London dates from c.672–4, and it is therefore possible that the new *wic* had been established by a Kentish king in the mid-seventh century, or perhaps by an earlier ruler of the East Saxons, whose metropolis was said by Bede to have been at London.[36] Like all early Saxon trading settlements, Lundenwic had no defensive walls, and was therefore very vulnerable to the Viking incursions of the ninth century. Soon after Offa's death in 796 the British Isles had entered a long period of renewed violence caused largely by the Norse or Viking attacks from Scandinavia. The kingdom of Northumbria, which with that of Kent had been one of the earliest missionary centres of Christianity in England, was devastated, and Mercia much weakened. In 842 raiders came up the Thames for the first recorded time and caused 'great slaughter' at London and Rochester; and in 851 the crews of a huge force of 350 Viking ships stormed London and Canterbury. Twenty years later London was sacked for a third time, but after wintering there the wandering Viking horde moved off to disrupt the kingdom of Mercia. In 878 another Viking force, described as 'a body of pirates', was back in the region of London, where it 'drew together and sat down at Fulham on the Thames'. By that time there had been much fighting to and fro between the Danes and King Alfred of Wessex, who now ruled the only Saxon kingdom to have survived the Viking onslaughts largely undiminished. After his great victory over the Danes at Edington in Wiltshire, also in 878, Alfred had pressed steadily forward north and east against them. At last in 886 he occupied the ruins of London, and, in the words of the Anglo-Saxon Chronicle, 'all the English people that were not under subjection to the Danes submitted to him'.[37]

The mid-ninth-century Viking depradations led to the abandonment of Lundenwic, in circumstances not at present known, and to the gradual reoccupation of the walled city—Lundenburg. The first traces of this reoccupation can be dated archaeologically to the decade 870–80, while in the Strand area virtually no archaeological material of the tenth century has been found. So after some two hundred years the site of Lundenwic was deserted for a while; but the memory of the settlement has survived to this day in the name Aldwych, 'the old *wic*', the first known use of which in reference to the central area of the Saxon settlement (where the Strand and Fleet Street meet) dates from the year 1211.[38]

5

From Lundenburg to the Birth of a Municipal Commune c.886–1215

During the three and a quarter centuries 886–1216 London was regenerated on its original Roman site and grew to become the embryonic capital of a politically united England. In the mid-eleventh century Edward the Confessor moved his principal residence and seat of royal authority from the walled city to Westminster, which was to become the political headquarters of the nation; while through the growing strength of its internal institutions and of its economic clout the City acquired a substantial measure of civic autonomy which was confirmed by Magna Charta in 1215.

The sources for this long period are more profuse and varied than for earlier times, but still extremely limited. Topographical evidence, coins, the dedication of churches, and the names of streets and wards can all be brought to bear, and in recent years the archaeologists' spades have been used on a scale and with scientific aids previously undreamt of. Written documents of title or record — charters, accounts, surveys — survive, not yet abundantly but nevertheless in growing numbers; there are chronicles and histories — narratives of near-contemporary events or of more distant past times; and there is the first long description of 'The Most Noble City of London'. This was written in the 1170s by William FitzStephen as a prologue to his Life of Archbishop Thomas Becket, whose secretary he had been and of whose murder in Canterbury Cathedral in 1170 he had been an eyewitness. He was clearly an enthusiastic devotee of London, and although his historical facts cannot always be relied upon — he thought that London had been founded before Rome — his vivid picture of the city of his own day provides the colour which other more prosaic sources lack.

London and the Invaders

Alfred's occupation of London was the first great landmark in the political unification of England. That unification was not to be completed for over another century, but because he had made himself the acknowledged leader in the wars against the Vikings Alfred also became the first Saxon king to command real authority outside his own realm. Thus he was able to commit the government of London, still a Mercian town, to his son-in-law Aethelred, *ealdorman* of the remnant of Mercia, who married Alfred's daughter, Aethelflaed. In the continuing wars against the Danes Aethelred (d. 911) proved the loyal coadjutor of Alfred and of Alfred's son and successor. This was Edward the Elder of Wessex, who after the death of his sister, the Lady Aetheflaed, in 918, became king of Mercia as well as of Wessex, thereby uniting the two Saxon monarchies.[1]

London, of course, was never the 'capital' of either Mercia or Wessex — in the days of constantly peregrinating monarchs capital cities were still far away in the future. But London was situated at the hub of the prevailing frontier system, where the newly united kingdoms of Mercia and Wessex and the Vikings' Danelaw (which extended over East Anglia and the eastern Midlands) all converged. At its southern end the boundary between Mercia and the Danelaw which was agreed by Alfred and Guthrum the Dane in 886 followed the course of the River Lea, at its southern end less than 3 miles east of London; and when another Danish army established itself along the coastlands of the Thames estuary in the mid-890s and raided up the Lea, London and its citizens were once again in the front line of battle. It was this unrivalled strategic situation, in relation not only to the interior of England but also of course to continental Europe, which inexorably drew successive Saxon and Danish kings and chieftains disputing for the supremacy of England towards London.[2]

London's revival under Alfred's successors was made possible by the interlude of peace which prevailed throughout the second and third quarters of the tenth century. It seems to have been towards the end of this period, in the reign of Edgar the Peaceable (959–75), that a shadowy body known as the *cnihtengild* was formed. This was an association of prominent English citizens charged in some way with the defence of the eastern side of the City and endowed with extensive lands and rights of soke (i.e. of private jurisdiction) around Aldgate and Portsoken, the latter being a large area adjoining Aldgate.[3] The *cnihtengild* may well have been a product of the Scandinavian (chiefly Danish) attacks along the east and south coasts of England which were resumed in the 980s. Throughout the ensuing forty years of battle and devastation, which at one time or other extended across most parts of the country, London often mounted formidable opposition to the Danes. Also throughout much of this confused period London (rather than Winchester, the traditional headquarters of the kings of Wessex) was the principal stronghold of Ethelred the Unready, great-great-great-nephew of Alfred and king of England 978–1016, who without London's resources would probably have been unable to maintain such prolonged opposition to his redoubtable adversary, Swein, King of the Danes.

At first the marauders seem to have avoided London, probably because after 994 they knew how strong the City was. In that year Swein and his allies 'came to London . . . with 94 ships, and they proceeded to attack the city stoutly and wished also to set it on fire; but there they suffered more harm and injury than they ever thought any citizen would do to them'. After this reversal successive Viking armies gave London a wide berth for some years, and in 1009 the City repulsed another attack. 'Praise be to God', recorded a Saxon chronicler of the time, 'that it yet standeth sound.' In 1013, when Swein returned intent on conquering the whole country and making himself king of all England, he was able to overrun the whole of the Danelaw and most of Mercia and Wessex; but when he turned on London 'the citizens would not yield, but resisted with full battle, because King Ethelred was inside'. Many of Swein's men were drowned in the river, and soon afterwards he marched away to complete the reduction of the West Country.[4]

Eventually, however, when 'the whole nation regarded him as King in all respects', London did submit to Swein. A Danish garrison was at once planted in the City, and King Ethelred fled to the Continent. But within a few weeks the whole situation was transformed by the death of Swein, on 3 February 1014. He was succeeded by his son Cnut, but by April Ethelred was back in Lincolnshire with a force strong enough to reject the youthful Cnut, whose turn it now became to withdraw from the country. London was, however, still held by the Danish garrison, and so Ethelred had to assault his former stronghold, which he did with his new ally, Olaf, later king of Norway and canonized as St Olaf. If the Norse sagas, which are the source for many vivid particulars of the Anglo-Danish wars, may be relied upon, Ethelred's first attack was made on the 'large trading town which is called Southwark'. This failed, the place being protected by 'walls of wood, stones and turf'; and so too at first did a ship-borne assault on the recently rebuilt bridge, which was manned by the Danish army. But some of Olaf's ships did manage to attach ropes to the bridge and pull part of it down. Southwark was in due course captured, and soon afterwards London itself capitulated and became Ethelred's headquarters once more.[5]

In the summer of 1015 Cnut returned, and within a few months had made himself master of Wessex, Mercia, and even Northumbria. Ethelred's son Edmund (generally known as Edmund Ironside) had assembled an army, but it refused to move without 'the assistance of the citizens of London'; and so in the spring of 1016 Edmund joined his father in London for what was to be the decisive contest for possession of the whole kingdom.[6]

But at the very moment when the struggle was about to begin, and Cnut's ships were about to enter the Thames, King Ethelred died, on 23 April 1016. He was buried in St Paul's Cathedral, having 'held his kingdom with great toil and difficulties as long as his life lasted'. At once, we are told, 'all the councillors who were in London and the citizens chose Edmund as king'; but a more widely based assembly met at Southampton and swore fealty to Cnut.[7]

So the war continued, with Edmund reasserting Saxon authority in Wessex while Cnut moved towards London. By mid-May 1016 Cnut's fleet was at Greenwich, and in order to make the investment of the City complete his men were soon afterwards cutting a channel along which some of his ships were hauled round the southern end of the bridge and relaunched into the upper waters of the river. Then 'they ditched the city around, so that no one could go either in or out'. At this point Edmund returned, attacked the Danish lines in the rear, and drove the besiegers off; but his losses were so heavy that he had to retire to Wessex to raise reinforcements, and the siege was resumed. However, Cnut too was having problems of supply, and after the failure of a last tremendous attack on the City by both land and river he and his fleet and army withdrew to the coasts of East Anglia to reprovision.[8]

In October 1016 the two armies met at Ashington, near the coast of south-east Essex in what was to be the final battle of the long war. The Danes were victorious, but not decisively so; and soon afterwards the two kings met and agreed to divide the country, Edmund taking Wessex and Cnut all the territories north of the Thames, including London. But the agreement had hardly been made before Edmund died, on 30 November of that fateful year 1016; and within a few months Cnut was in control of all England.[9]

The men of London had to make their own terms, and when Cnut's ships came up the river they had no choice but to 'make a truce with the army and buy themselves a peace'. The price was the enormous sum of £10,500 — nearly 5 tons of silver pennies — which amounted to 13 per cent of the total Danegeld payment levied by Cnut on the whole of England.[10]

The Danish dynasty established by Cnut did not last long, for after his death in 1035 and those of both his sons within another seven years, the ancient Saxon line was restored in the person of Edward (the Confessor, 1042–66), son of Ethelred the Unready. 'All the people', so the Anglo-Saxon Chronicle records, 'chose Edward as King, in London.' But the new monarch knew little of England, for he had had to spend much of his previous life in Normandy, safely outside Cnut's reach, and the early years of his reign were dominated by his over-mighty father-in-law, Godwine, Earl of Wessex. In 1051, however, there was a showdown; Godwine was summoned to appear at a meeting of the *witan* or king's council in London to answer various charges, and after a trial of strength Godwine and his entourage were banished.[11]

This extreme step produced a reaction, for in 1052 Godwine and his son Harold returned at the head of a powerful fleet. After preliminary skirmishes along the south coast they turned inevitably to London. There Edward's smaller fleet was moored along the north bank of the river above the bridge, through which Godwine's ships were able to pass on the incoming tide, backed by more of his followers on the Southwark side. The royal fleet was surrounded, Godwine and Harold, who now enjoyed the support of the principal citizens of London, were able to land on the north bank, and at a meeting of the *witan* held outside the City, the king capitulated. Thereafter Edward ruled in the shadow of all-powerful Godwine (who died in 1053) and his son Harold, who was to be Edward's eventual successor in 1066.[12]

This episode, sometimes referred to as the English Revolution of 1051, was soon followed by the removal of the royal court from within the walls of the City to the then desolate Island of Thorney, some 1.5 miles away, and the rebuilding of the little monastery soon to become known as Westminster Abbey — an event of cardinal importance in the history of London, to be discussed more fully later. Edward might well, of course, have performed this act of piety even if the humiliations of 1052 had never taken place, for he is said to have had a special devotion to St Peter, to whom Westminster Abbey is dedicated. But in the building of the adjacent first royal palace at Westminster fear as well as piety may have been the motive — fear of the rumbustious citizens of London who lived at such close quarters to the royal palace at Aldermanbury. At all events, Edward's abbey was consecrated on 28 December 1065, during the celebration of Christmas; but the king was too ill to be present, and he died in his palace nearby a few days later. On 6 January 1066 he was buried in the abbey (Plate 9), and his successor, Harold, was crowned there on the same day. Since then the coronation of every sovereign (except Edward V and Edward VIII, who were not crowned) has taken place at Westminster Abbey.[13]

The ensuing events in the year 1066 are the best known in English history. But William the Conqueror's victory and the death of Harold at the Battle of Hastings, which took place on 14 October, were not the end of the story, for London had still to be reckoned with. Guy, bishop of Amiens, the supposed author of one of several accounts of events, had no doubt about the crucial importance of London's posture after Hastings. It was, he says, 'a great city, overflowing with froward inhabitants and richer in treasure than the rest of the kingdom. Protected on the left side by walls, on the right side by the river, it neither fears enemies nor dreads being taken by storm.' There the remnants of Harold's forces had rallied under the leadership of Ansgar the Staller, who had been severely wounded at Hastings. There the *witan* had hastily elected a new king — Edgar the Atheling, great-nephew of Edward the Confessor; and 'the flying rumour that London had a King spread abroad, and what remained of the English nation rejoiced'.[14]

So after a few weeks' respite, in which he received a number of submissions including that of Winchester, William 'directed his march to where populous London gleamed'. Other accounts describe how after an inconclusive fight at the southern end of London Bridge William circled slowly round the beleaguered city, crossing the Thames at Wallingford and devastating the countryside along his path. After thus terrorizing and isolating the people of London Bishop Guy says that William took up residence in the Confessor's palace at Westminster and ordered the investment of the City. 'He built siege-engines and made moles and the iron horns of battering rams for the destruction of the city; then he thundered forth menaces and threatened war and vengeance, swearing that, given time, he would destroy the walls, raze the bastions to the ground, and bring down the proud tower in rubble.'[15]

'When they heard such things, dread wore down the citizens of London' and their leaders submitted, perhaps after secret negotiations in which William promised to be a good lord to them. The Anglo-Saxon Chronicle relates that the decisive meeting between the English leaders as well as the leading men of London took place at Berkhamstead, some 26 miles north-west of the City; but Guy states that the leaders of the *witan* and of the people of London processed 'with downcast bearing' to Westminster, where they surrendered the City and appeased William's wrath 'by a gift offered with homage'. The precise circumstances and whereabouts of London's surrender are unclear — there may have been acts of submission at both Berkhamstead and Westminster — but certainly the capitulation was the decisive incident in the Norman Conquest after Hastings; and it quickly led on to the coronation of William in Westminster Abbey on Christmas Day — the only occasion on which there have been two such ceremonies within a single year.[16]

Thus ended the long succession of foreign invasions to which England had been periodically subjected for over half a millennium. Political unification of the country had been finally and permanently achieved, and possession of London had often been a vital element governing the outcome of these internecine struggles.

The Regeneration of London

When extensive resettlements in Lundenburg began at the end of the ninth century nearly five hundred years had elapsed since the Romans had left Londinium. What sort of scene may the Saxons have found?

Much of the Romans' great stone buildings — the forum and basilica, the governor's supposed palace, the fort, the baths and larger houses, and above all the walls — must still have been standing, ruinous, decayed, and desolate, no doubt, but still substantially intact, for the long process of robbing for later building purposes had hardly yet begun. There must too have been traces of some of the principal roads, now perhaps only tracks covered with soil and debris. But little of the Romans' wooden and wattle-and-daub buildings can have survived, and substantial parts of the walled area had never been developed at all. So a good deal of the site had perhaps reverted to scrub, much as it had been in pre-Roman times.

We have already seen that ever since the building of the first church of St Paul in London in 604, such early Saxon activity as there was had mainly been in the western half of the walled area, part of which had become the centre of ecclesiastical and royal authority. To the east of the Walbrook the situation is, however, more obscure. This area had been the original hub of Roman London, but the bridge across the Thames had almost certainly been washed away or deliberately broken down in the fifth or sixth centuries, and so the settlement had lost its *raison d'être*. It was isolated from the the Saxon *cité* by the Walbrook, which could readily be crossed at only two points, at Cannon Street and beside the Mansion House; and it has been suggested that, if the correct interpretation of the meaning of the name Walbrook is 'brook of the Welsh [i.e. Britons]', the stream may even have been for a while the dividing line between the ascendant Saxons to the west and the denizens of a surviving Romano-British slum to the east. All Hallows, Barking by the Tower, dates from the late seventh or early eighth century; and the intriguing tradition of great antiquity of St Peter's-upon-Cornhill, standing on the crest of its hill above the bridge upon part of the site of the Roman basilica, provides a puzzle which has already been mentioned.[17]

After his occupation of London in 886 Alfred repaired the walls and established a garrison within them; and towards the end of his long reign he held a council at Chelsea (where King Offa of Mercia had had a hall or palace), to discuss the 'restoration' of the City. Urban renewal had been a vital ingredient in his success against the Vikings, and continued to be so during the general Saxon recovery which took place during the first quarter of the tenth century.[18] As well as being fortresses of resistance to Viking incursions, the Alfredian *burhs* were intended to be market towns, where people lived, worked, and traded, and where the king could raise money by the levying of tolls. Their expression of a deliberate royal policy is often reflected in their internal planning; and in London the origins of parts of the medieval street layout may be traced back to the Alfredian rehabilitation of the City.[19]

This layout was conditioned by the natural topography of the site and by the Roman walls and gates — two factors which still exert their influence on the modern City, though (after Victorian street improvements, the damage caused by bombing in 1940–5 and still more by postwar redevelopments) with diminishing force. Modern main roads still enter the walled area at the same points as their Roman precursors — at Ludgate, Newgate, Aldersgate, Bishopsgate, and Aldgate, for instance. Within the walls they still extend at a few points along Roman highways, as in Bishopsgate, in part of Cannon Street, and in Newgate Street and the western extremity of Cheapside, where an early Roman boundary may provide the explanation for the kink which still exists in the alignment of the latter two streets.[20] The Cripplegate fort, too, still makes its impress upon the streets in that area. But in general the Roman layout of even the main thoroughfares had been lost or greatly modified by Alfredian times, as also happened in varying degrees in other towns of Roman Britain. In the eastern half of the City in particular the curving course of several of the principal streets (Threadneedle Street, for instance), and the jumble east of the Mansion House bear little relation to any earlier layout; and this is also the case with the network of minor streets which began to appear in the late ninth century.[21]

Most of this development was at first along the waterfront, where the ruinous Roman wall was both a quarry for building materials and a hazard for ships. Here the earliest developments were near the haven of Queenhithe. This was then known as 'Aetheredes hyd' — the landing place of Aethelred, Alfred's son-in-law and *ealdorman* in London, who was one of the magnates present at the royal council held at Chelsea to discuss the restoration of London. Two awards made by Alfred in 889 and 898–9, one to the bishop of Worcester and the other to the same bishop and to the archbishop of Canterbury, relate to tolls and market and mooring rights in two adjacent rectangular plots near Queenhithe. These plots extended up the hill from the ruinous Roman riverside wall, and in the 890s several north–south lanes came into being on or near them, two (Bread Street Hill–Bread Street, and Garlick Hill–Bow Lane) extending as far as Cheapside, the great food market which probably dates from this time. Despite their obscurity these grants provide solid evidence for Alfred's policy of urban renewal and for his commercial as well as military intentions in London.[22]

Queenhithe was probably the only harbour in Alfredian times, but another haven, lower down the river at Billingsgate, is known from written sources to have been in existence by c.1000, while a third, at Dowgate at the mouth of the Walbrook, is probably a little later. Activity at Billingsgate may have been prompted by the rebuilding of the bridge, which would have been an obstacle to downstream traffic from Queenhithe. The bridge itself, which probably stood on or close to the alignment of its Roman predecessor, was built of wood in the late tenth or early eleventh century. At its south end there was evidently a fortified Saxon enclosure, the *burh* of Southwark, and by blocking the upstream movement of hostile ships the bridge soon became a key element in the defence of London.[23]

The rebuilding of the bridge symbolized London's reviving fortunes. Along the waterfront a series of narrow lanes began to spread northwards, of which a few, such as Laurence Pountney Lane or Lovat Lane, may still be seen even after the recent formation of the Thames Street dual carriageway. Two great food markets, West Cheap (Cheapside) and East Cheap, grew up, one on each of the City's two hills.[24] Both markets were wide thoroughfares extending east and west and, as neither of them follows Roman alignments closely, they may have been laid out as part of the Saxon street grid established by the north–south lanes extending up from the river. Gracechurch Street is also of early medieval origin and may well have been formed at the same time as the bridge was rebuilt, for its northern part, on its way down to the riverside, cuts right through the centre of the Roman basilica.[25] At the waterfront new jetties and embankments projected ever further out into the river outside the Roman wall, in places pushing back the waterline as much as 35 metres — so far that by the second half of the eleventh century an east–west road, Thames Street (the southern kerb of which was situated at various points on the disintegrating Roman wall), was needed to provide this new ground with adequate access to the rest of the City. By the early twelfth century the reclaimed land was solid enough for new churches — St Magnus and St Botolph — to be built on it.[26]

Churches and Religious Foundations

These were just two of the hundred or so tiny churches which were built within the walls between about 900 and 1200. Although substantial remains of very few of them now survive, many of them, and of the dozen or so religious communities which were founded in and around the City in the later eleventh and twelfth centuries, have nevertheless made enduring marks on modern London.

Most of the churches were originally proprietory — built in wood or stone either by a great man on his own property for the use of himself and his followers or by a

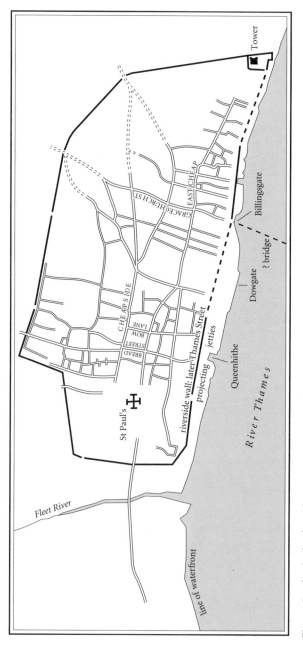

Fig. 13. London in the eleventh century

group of residents acting together.[27] In either case the worshippers at the
church would pay offerings of various kinds for its upkeep and for that of a
priest, and so the area which each church served would become fixed — a process
largely completed by around 1200. The size of these areas, or parishes, varied
considerably, most of the smallest being in the southern parts of the City in the
riverside or near-riverside areas of earliest resettlement, where the population was
most dense.[28]

Further out, either within the City walls or in the nearby countryside, there was
a ring of religious communities founded chiefly in the twelfth century. Just inside
Aldgate was the Augustinian Priory of Holy Trinity, founded by Queen Matilda,
wife of Henry I. Nearby stood the Benedictine nunnery of St Helen's in Bishopsgate Street, the church of which survived both the Dissolution of the Monasteries
by Henry VIII (when it became a parish church) and the Great Fire of 1666 and the
Blitz of 1940–1. Not far from Aldersgate was the secular college or royal free chapel
(its status was unique) of St Martin's le Grand, founded late in the reign of Edward
the Confessor, the canons of which were often active in royal service and the
privileged precinct of which provided sanctuary for fugitives.[29]

Outside the walls between Fleet Street and the river were the Knights Templar
(their full name was Knights of the Temple of Solomon of Jerusalem), a religious
order formed for the protection of travellers on pilgrimage to the Holy Land, and
experts in the transmission of men and money across Europe — the formidable
couriers and travel agents of medieval times, and the guardians of one of the chief
treasuries of Henry II. Their twelfth-century round church, its shape modelled on
the Dome of the Rock of Jerusalem, still stands, much restored, as the Temple
Church; but the Knights Templar were suppressed by the Pope in 1312 and their
London house passed to the kindred Order of Knights Hospitallers, who granted
part of the site to the lawyers for use as a hostel. The Hospitallers were in their turn
suppressed in 1539, and ultimately ownership of the enlarged riverside site, including the Temple Church, was granted by the Crown to the Benchers of the two Inns
of Court of the Inner and Middle Temple.[30]

The Temple precincts formed the western end of a ring of twelfth-century
religious foundations which encircled the City. To the north-west were two great
houses — the Augustinian Priory of St Bartholomew, the Norman choir of which
survived the Henrician Dissolution of the Monasteries to become a parish church;
and the Priory of St John of Jerusalem, the original London headquarters of the
Knights Hospitallers, the gatehouse of which still stands astride St John's Lane in
Clerkenwell. A little further away was the nunnery of St Mary, Clerkenwell, one of
three nunneries in the northern outskirts, the others being at Holiwell in Shoreditch and at Stratford-atte-Bow. Outside Bishopsgate was the hospital of Augustinian canons known as St Mary Spital, which at the time of the Dissolution had
over a hundred beds. The eastern end of the ring was formed by Queen Matilda's
hospital (for the aged poor) of St Katharine by the Tower, which after its demolition in the 1820s for the building of St Katharine's Dock, removed to its present
location beside Regent's Park.

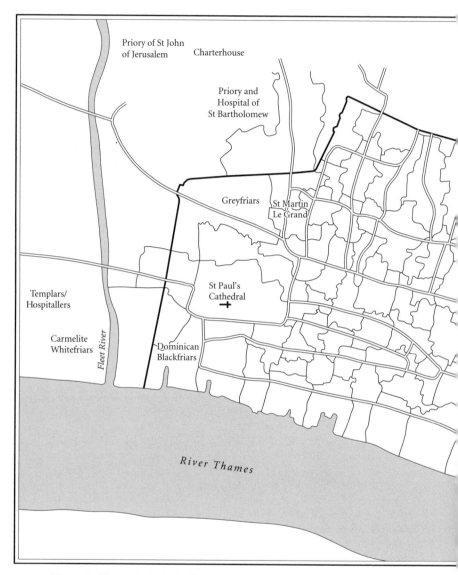

Fig. 14. Parishes and principal religious houses

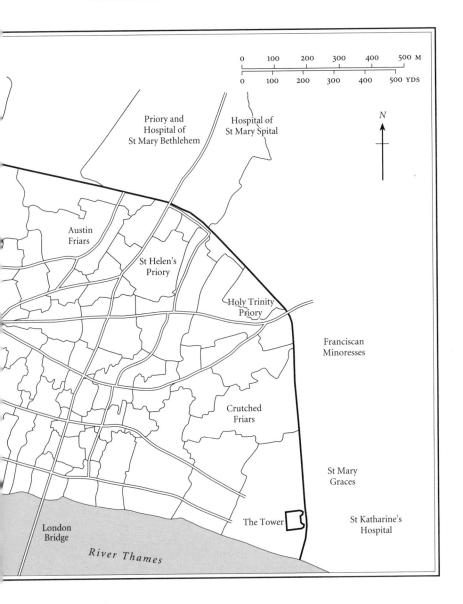

0   100   200   300   400   500 M

0   100   200   300   400   500 YDS

N

Priory and
Hospital of
St Mary Bethlehem

Hospital of
St Mary Spital

Austin
Friars

St Helen's
Priory

Holy Trinity
Priory

Franciscan
Minoresses

Crutched
Friars

St Mary
Graces

London
Bridge

The Tower

St Katharine's
Hospital

River Thames

South of the river was the Benedictine Abbey of Bermondsey and the Augustinian Priory of St Mary Overie, part of which became after the Dissolution the parish church of St Saviour, Southwark, and is now, after changes in diocesan boundaries, the cathedral of the see of Southwark. Nor should this catalogue of twelfth-century London monasticism omit two great hospitals which despite being run by or connected with religious houses survived the Dissolution and are now national institutions — St Bartholomew's (still after eight hundred years on its original site in Smithfield, though its future is now uncertain), and St Thomas's (part of the Priory of St Mary Overie), which removed in Victorian times from Southwark to Lambeth.[31]

Lastly in this tremendous concentration of religious foundations — by far the largest in the country, and in the later medieval centuries to be enlarged by yet more communities — were London's two most famous minsters — the abbey church of St Peter's, Westminster, built by Edward the Confessor, and the cathedral church of St Paul's. There had probably been a minster church at Westminster since the days of King Offa of the East Saxons in the early eighth century; and in c.960 St Dunstan had founded a Benedictine abbey there on the extensive lands which had been granted to the monks by King Edgar the Peaceable. Edward the Confessor's new church (Plate 9), of which nothing now survives above ground, was hardly shorter in length than the present abbey (which dates from the thirteenth and later centuries) and was the first major church to be built in England in the new Romanesque manner.[32] At St Paul's the Saxon church was destroyed in 1087 by a fire — a very common hazard in medieval London — and its successor dated largely from later Norman times and the twelfth century. It was the largest church in England ('Once it was a Metropolitan See', wrote FitzStephen in the 1170s, 'and it is thought that it will be so again'), 560 feet long, intended perhaps to out-do the new cathedral at Winchester (begun in 1079); and its steeple was nearly 100 feet higher than that of Salisbury.[33]

Tower, Bridge, and Palaces

The Tower of London also had its origins in the late eleventh century, for soon after the Conquest William caused 'certain strongholds' to be made in the City against what a writer of the time described as 'the fickleness of the vast and fierce population'. The main stronghold, consisting of a mound surrounded by a moat and surmounted by a wooden palisade, marked the first stage in the building of what was to become the most powerful fortress in Britain: the Tower of London, a 'Palatine Citadel, exceeding great and strong', according to William FitzStephen. Strategically placed just inside the south-east angle of the City walls, it was no doubt primarily intended to overawe the citizens, but it also served as a defence for the City from seaborne attack, Norse incursions not yet being altogether things of the past. Later in his reign William began the building of the great near-square keep known as the White Tower, its walls 90 feet in height and 15 feet thick at the base, its sole entrance some 15 feet above ground and approached by wooden stairs which could be removed in dangerous times. Caen stone, brought all the way from Normandy, was the principal material used — in itself a remarkable testimony to the power and resources at William's command, for even such mighty builders as the Romans had been quite content to use Kentish ragstone for the walls of Londinium. At the south-west corner of the City there were two other forts dating from early Norman times — Castle Baynard, just inside the City wall on the eastern side of the Fleet River, which was held by one of William's tenants-in-chief, Ralph Bainard; and Montfichet's Castle, a little to the north of Castle Baynard, but of which little is known.[34]

Like the building of the Tower, the rebuilding of the Saxon bridge (or perhaps of its Saxon-Norman successor, for there is evidence of a mid-eleventh-century rebuilding at some time after 1056), was a monument to the strategic and economic importance of London. The new bridge, built of stone between 1176 and 1209 to replace its wooden predecessor, was one of the wonders of the medieval world, for stone had not been used in Europe in any sizeable bridge since Roman times. There were nineteen stone arches, supported by piers which were protected from the force of the current and tide by giant wooden platforms known as starlings. These starlings reduced the width of the waterway from some 900 feet to less than 200 feet, and caused enormous lateral pressure to build up. Nevertheless the bridge stood until 1831, covered for much of these six centuries with houses, shops (no less than 129 tenements are listed in a rental of 1460), and two chapels. Its never-ending repair was managed by the City's Bridge House Trust and financed by voluntary offerings from its citizens and the Crown, from tolls, bridge rents, and the income from the numerous properties bequeathed over the years for its upkeep. Like the Tower, the bridge was an integral part of the defences of London and of the whole realm, a barrier to ship-borne invasion up the river and a fortified gateway equipped with its own drawbridge — powerful enough to withstand landward assault, as, for instance, in 1471 from Thomas Fauconberg and in 1554 from Sir Thomas Wyatt and his rebels.[35]

The Tower and the new bridge testify to the wealth which existed in London in the century and a half after the Norman Conquest. So too do the great houses or palaces kept in London even so early as the 1170s by, so FitzStephen tells us, 'almost all' the bishops, abbots, and great men of England. The greatest of these was built by the king himself, William Rufus, in 1097 as an extension of Edward the Confessor's palace — Westminster Hall, 240 feet long, its walls over 6 feet thick, and for FitzStephen 'a building beyond compare'. Most of the early great houses were of courtyard plan and were within the still unsuburbanized walled City.[36] But the bishops of Winchester had their palace in Southwark, which was within their own diocese, while by the very early thirteenth century the archbishop of Canterbury had a house at Lambeth, conveniently close to the royal palace at Westminster.

The Origins of Municipal Organization

The modern Corporation of the City of London can trace its lineage further back into the mists of time than any other secular institution in the land except the monarchy. It is unique amongst local authorities and municipal corporations in not deriving its modern form from Acts of Parliament, and in having the power to reform its own constitution; but throughout its 1,000-year history successive generations of the City's ruling magnates have had to struggle with Crown or Parliament for the enlargement or defence of its special position.

The origin of this lineage may be found in the folkmoot, the ancient open-air assembly of the citizens, which met three times a year, possibly in the Roman amphitheatre.[37] At the time of the Alfredian revival of London's fortunes the City was evidently governed for the king by his reeves or portreeves through these assemblies, or through smaller indoor versions of them from which a bench of *judices* or magistrates composed of the principal local citizens was drawn. In the first half of the tenth century bishops were evidently also involved in some way, but it was the king's reeves who presided over daily justice and administration, and in whom may perhaps be seen the origin of the sheriffs (or 'shire reeves') of London and Middlesex, later to emerge more clearly in the eleventh and twelfth centuries.[38]

Similarly the aldermen — who like the sheriffs are still today an integral part of the City's constitution — may trace their pedigree to the headmen of the wards which appear to have developed early in the eleventh century, though their origin may have been still earlier. At first, in the times of the Danish attacks, the functions of the wards (twenty-four in number, and even nowadays only twenty-six) were probably defensive — the keeping of watch and ward — and fiscal — the raising of taxes for the payment of Danegeld; and each ward had its own court or wardmote, presided over by its alderman or headman.[39] The size of the wards differed greatly and reflected the differing densities of settlement within the walls in late Saxon times, for the outer wards were much larger than those in the more thickly repopulated inner areas. At Bishopsgate, Cripplegate, and Aldersgate each ward included a large area outside as well as inside its particular gate, the protection of which was its main function; and within the ward of Farringdon, which originally embraced areas on both sides of the wall and in size was the largest ward of all, there were two City gates — Newgate and Ludgate.[40]

After Cnut's occupation of London in 1016 it seems likely that the Saxon kings' man in the City, the reeve or sheriff, was replaced by a Viking *staller* — the Scandinavian name for the principal officer in the royal household, who also had important military functions. After the restoration of the Saxon royal line in 1042 Edward the Confessor used English *stallers* to support his power; and the *stallers* in their turn acted through the bench of principal local citizens, whose court seems to have become known in the Danish period as the court of husting (another Scandinavian word, meaning an indoor assembly), an all-purpose governing

Plate 1. View from the south-east *c.*AD 120

Plate 2. View from the north-west *c.*AD 250

Plate 3.
Model of the north end
of the bridge

Plate 4.
Late first-century quay
near Fish Street Hill, with
(right foreground) base of
north pier of bridge

Plate 5.
Model of second-century
basilica and forum,
looking north

Plate 6.
The defensive wall at
6–7 The Crescent

Plate 7. Sixth-century gilded-silver brooch found in Saxon cemetery at Mitcham

Plate 8. Silver penny of King Alfred minted in London, with monogram of letters *Londonia*

Plate 9. Consecration of Westminster Abbey and funeral of Edward the Confessor, 1065–6, from the Bayeux Tapestry, by special permission of the City of Bayeux

Plate 10. Silver penny of William
the Conqueror

Plate 11.
The City's thirteenth-century seal,
with St Thomas Becket enthroned
over the London skyline

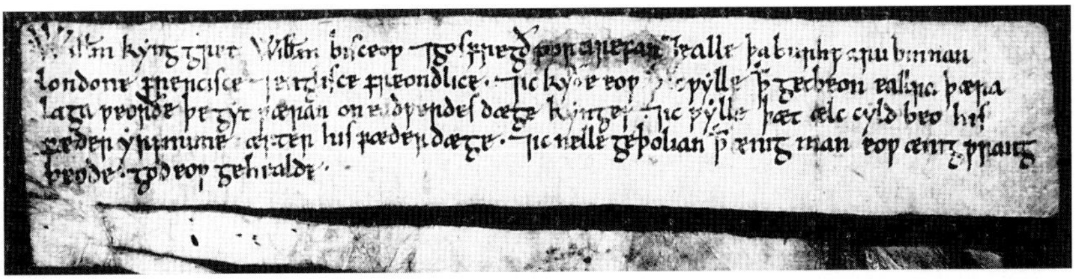

Plate 12.
William the Conqueror's
charter to the citizens of
London

Plate 13.
John Ball preaching to
Wat Tyler (left) and the
rebels outside London
during the Peasants'
Revolt, 1381

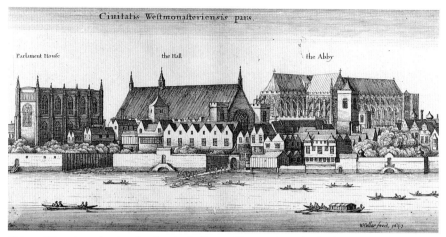

Plate 14. Westminster in 1647, showing the Parliament House at St Stephen's Chapel (left), the Hall (centre), and the Abbey (right)

Plate 15. London from Southwark *c.*1630

Plate 16. St Paul's Cathedral

Plate 17. The Tower, showing the Norman keep and the inner and outer curtain walls of Henry III and Edward I

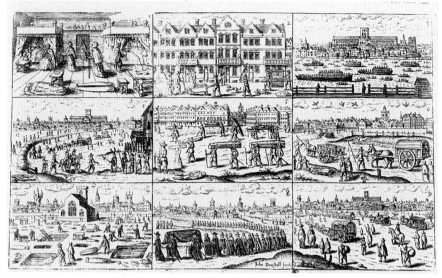

Plate 18. The Great Plague, 1665, showing a deathbed, houses shut up, mass exodus, burials, and return of population

Plate 19. The Great Fire, 1666

body, very possibly of pre-Danish origin, which managed general administrative and judicial business.[41]

The Emergence of the Chartered Community 1066–1215

By the middle of the eleventh century London was still under the direct and powerful dominion of the Crown, but the citizens were beginning to devise their own ways of managing their public concerns. After the Norman Conquest it became the custom for successive kings to confirm the citizens in the enjoyment of their existing customs and to grant them special privileges in return for financial concessions. It was thus a mutually advantageous process — the City needed protection from over-mighty barons, and the Crown needed money; but the stages whereby the City obtained a substantial measure of independence from royal interference were often uncertain, wobbly, and easily reversible. Nevertheless, after the lapse of a century and a half London's communal identity, embodied (together with other privileges) in the citizens' right to elect their own mayor, had been purchased in a succession of royal charters, and specifically confirmed in 1215 by Magna Charta.

Shortly after his coronation William issued a charter to the bishop, portreeve, and citizens of London. In this little document (Plate 12), which still survives in the Corporation of London Records Office, the king sent greetings 'in friendly fashion' and declared his will that the laws and customs of the City should 'be preserved as they were in King Edward's day'. This probably unique sign of William's regard — so far as is known he never accorded such a mark to any other English city or town — reflects the wariness with which the Conqueror deemed it politic to handle London. This was so even after his overwhelming victory at Hastings had added right of conquest to his other claims to the Crown of England. The whole country had become his personal property, and within a few years he had established there a hereditary monarchy more powerful and efficient than any other of its time in Europe. Yet even he felt the need to be cautious in his dealings with London; and he certainly took no chances, as his great fortresses at the Tower, Castle Baynard, and Montfichet testify.[42]

Little is known about the government of London's 'vast and fierce populace' in early Norman times. By the twelfth century the court of *husting* was meeting weekly and had largely superseded the folkmoot, while aldermen were probably presiding over the courts of the twenty-four wards.[43] But the office of *staller* had disappeared, and the bishops were no longer so prominent as leaders in the City's secular affairs. At the same time new positions of power were coming into being: castellan of the Tower, in 1100 in the hands of one of the great tenants in chief, William De Mandeville, and the lordship of Castle Baynard, bestowed by Henry I on a member of the Clare family, powerful in eastern England, the holders of which later became hereditary commanders of the City militia. The presence of these great feudal magnates in the City may explain the demise of that ancient body, the *cnihtengild*.[44]

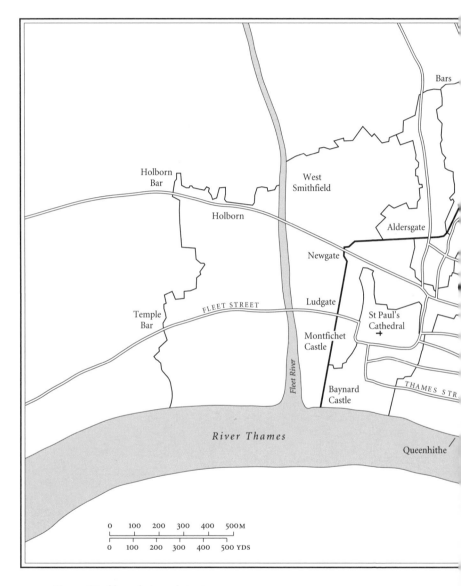

Fig. 15. Ward boundaries and streets

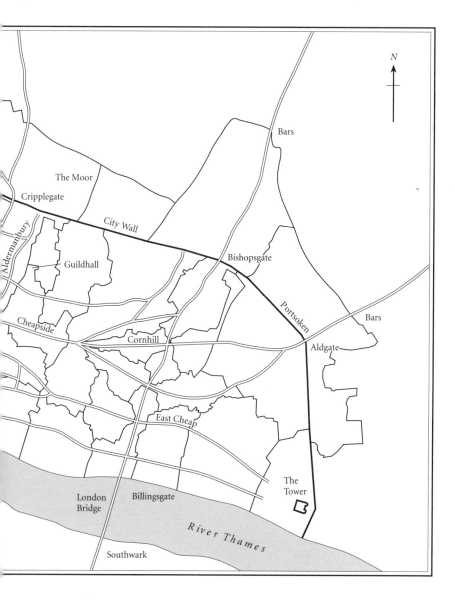

N

Bars

The Moor

Cripplegate

Aldermanbury

City Wall

Guildhall

Bishopsgate

Portsoken

Cheapside

Bars

Cornhill

Aldgate

East Cheap

The Tower

London Bridge

Billingsgate

River Thames

Southwark

The principal royal officials in the City in the eleventh and early twelfth centuries were the portreeves. The portreeve was the reeve of a trading place or town, while the sheriff was the reeve of a shire, and both officers were the king's local agents for all manner of purposes, but particularly for the collection of royal revenues. The relationship between the portreeve of London and the sheriff of adjacent Middlesex is impenetrably obscure. At around the time of the Conquest the two offices of portreeve and sheriff may have been held by the same man. By 1128 they had certainly merged, but by the end of the twelfth century it had become customary for two sheriffs to be appointed or elected annually to have charge of the King's business in both London and Middlesex. This peculiar circumstance is perhaps an echo of the situation previously postulated for fifth- and sixth-century London, in which the City may have been the centre of a political power extending over the surrounding territory. Some such idea certainly reappeared for a brief while, though only as an administrative experiment, in the early years of Henry I (1100–35) and again in the disorderly times of Stephen (1135–54), when from 1141 to 1144 Geoffrey De Mandeville held the earldom of Essex, the custody of the Tower of London, the shrievalties of London and Middlesex and of Essex and Hertfordshire, plus in all three shires the office of justice. Such concentrations of power in the Home Counties around London did not survive under Henry II (1154–89), and local justiciarships faded away altogether. However, the arrangement whereby two sheriffs acted jointly for London and Middlesex proved extremely durable, lasting until 1888, when the shrievalty of Middlesex was separated from that of London. Even now two sheriffs are still elected every year to act in the City only.[45]

By the end of the eleventh century urban growth in Western Europe had advanced far enough to produce marked differences of custom and occupation between town and surrounding country. In the Low Countries and parts of Italy and Germany these growing differences led ultimately to the formation of autonomous city states, but in England townsmen's ambitions to control their own affairs were limited by the existence of a strong monarchy. In the process by which London nevertheless obtained a considerable degree of self-government, taxation, and hence the shrievalty, had a central role.

During the early years of Norman rule the king's revenues in London arose principally from court fees and market and harbour tolls and were collected by his officers, the portreeves or sheriffs. In the Conqueror's time it is thought that these revenues may have been commuted into a fixed sum or farm of £300 per annum, and thereafter there were long contentions between the Crown and the City about the amount of the farm and about how the sheriffs who collected it should be appointed. By a charter (whose authenticity has been questioned and more recently reasserted)[46] Henry I granted the citizens the right to choose their own sheriff and their own justiciar to keep the pleas of the Crown, together with exemptions from certain fiscal burdens; and (as mentioned in Chapter 4) he also confirmed their hunting rights in Middlesex, Surrey, and the Chilterns.[47] During the civil wars of the reign of King Stephen (1135–54) London backed the king — an enormous force went out to be mustered, FitzStephen tells us — but the citizens' right to choose the sheriffs seems to have been lost (if it had existed), and the charter which Henry II granted in 1155 makes no reference to the matter. However, it did enumerate many of the citizens' judicial privileges such as exemption from attendance at courts outside the City and sustained the City's own laws of property and the citizens' freedom from local tolls throughout England.[48]

With the death of Henry II in 1189 London's civic evolution entered a new and crucial phase which was to last for some twenty-five years. The new king, Richard I (1189–99), was in England for less than six months of his entire reign, the rest of which was spent in crusading in the Holy Land, or as the emperor's prisoner in Germany, or in warfare in France — all expensive activities which required a great deal of money. When he had gone off on crusade in December 1189 William De Longchamp, bishop of Ely, chancellor and justiciar of England, had been left in charge. After quickly provoking widespread animosities among the barons he needed the support of the City, and the annual farm of London and Middlesex was reduced, its payment at the Exchequer being made by two sheriffs who had evidently been chosen by the citizens.[49] Matters came to a head in the autumn of 1191, when the baronial malcontents and Richard's brother and future successor, John, the centre of opposition to the chancellor, converged on London, where Longchamp had taken refuge in the Tower. The citizens now had to choose whether to support the king's chancellor or the king's brother in the struggle for control of the realm. At a great meeting of bishops and magnates of the realm as well as citizens held in St Paul's on 8 October Longchamp was deposed in favour of King Richard's new emissary, Walter of Coutances, archbishop of Rouen; and in the culmination of at least half a century of civic aspiration the citizens were rewarded for their support with the grant of the 'commune'.[50]

Communes were sworn associations, generally of townsfolk, which were formed in the twelfth century in Italy and Northern France in response to some crisis in the affairs of some particular town; and these embryonic forms of civic self-government were often accompanied by a new municipal magistrate: the mayor. London had first declared a short-lived commune during the critical year of civil war in 1141, but it was not until 1191 that the combination of an absent and expensive king, an ambitious heir apparent, and a hated chancellor had presented another opportunity to achieve the civic independence of a commune. In return for the recognition of their commune by John and Walter of Coutances the citizens swore to accept John as king if Richard should die childless, and to bear them faithful service.[51]

The mayor of London first appears in 1193 (though the office may have originated four years earlier) in the person of Henry FitzAilwin, who had been an alderman for over twenty years and was to continue as mayor until his death in 1212. In that difficult year, 1193, FitzAilwin was involving himself in the collection of money to ransom King Richard, then imprisoned in Germany, and the citizens were taking an oath that saving their allegiance to the king they would 'keep the commune and be obedient to the Mayor of the City of London and to the *echevins* of the same commune'. The *echevins* — a French word pointing to French influence, and particularly to that of the City of Rouen, on London's evolution at this time — may probably be identified with the twenty-four aldermen, whose ancient court emerged in the thirteenth century as the City's principal ruling body, the mayor always being chosen from one of its number.[52]

However, although the lineaments of the City's medieval constitution were beginning to appear, some two centuries were still to elapse before its permanent existence was fully accepted by the monarchy. On his last brief visit to England in 1194 Richard had no truck with the infant commune, and the charter which he did grant to London, in exchange for a fine of 1,500 marks, merely confirmed the privileges contained in the charter granted by Henry II in 1155; mayor, commune, elective sheriff, farm at £300 — none of these was even mentioned.[53]

Five years later newly crowned King John also ignored the mayoralty and the commune in his new charter, although this did grant the citizens the right to choose their own sheriffs and pay the farm at only £300. But like Richard before him, John had perforce to accept tacitly the continued existence of the mayor and commune, for London was too important a source of revenue to antagonize. The concession of the shrievalty and farm cost the citizens 3,000 marks, and throughout the rest of the reign London was subjected to numerous arbitrary levies of one kind or another — aids, 'gifts', and tallages, the last being particularly resented as a servile tax imposed on the king's demesne tenants. The mayoralty — the right to elect a mayor every year — was not conceded until May 1215, when John granted it by another charter in a last desperate (and unsuccessful) attempt to detach London from the baronial insurgency which culminated a month later in the grant of Magna Charta. By the Great Charter itself London's ancient liberties were confirmed but not defined: the levying of aids was, indeed, limited, but there was no reference at all to tallage.[54]

So the troublous quarter-century which had begun with Richard's accession in 1189 ended with London having achieved the status of a chartered self-governing community with its own communal seal and its own elected head, independent of the sheriffs, who were by now also chosen by the City.[55]

Work and Life

How big was the City which was able to achieve such privileged status? For Saxon, Viking, and Norman times only informed guesses can be made about the size of London. In Cnut's day (1014–35) the population may have been about 10,000 to 12,000.[56] By the time of William the Conqueror (1066–87) it may have been between 10,000 and 20,000 or more, and Dr Derek Keene has suggested that it more than doubled in the twelfth century, and again in the thirteenth century, leading to a population of 80,000 to 100,000 in 1300; but other estimates prepare a figure of only 60,000. Whatever the true figures may have been, it seems certain that in the twelfth century London was probably twice as big as the next largest city in England (York), and three times as rich; and that until about 1200 (when Paris became a rival) it was even the largest city north of the Alps. Yet despite its unique urban stature, perhaps only one in every hundred of the peoples of England lived in London in 1100 and England remained an overwhelmingly rural kingdom.[57]

Most Londoners in Norman times were of Saxon origin. The Vikings had not settled permanently in London in large numbers, they left little trace in the City's street names, and although six churches were dedicated to St Olaf their strategic locations suggest that they may have been garrison chapels for the Danish occupying forces.[58] Even after the Norman Conquest London seems to have continued to be a predominantly English city. William's charter to the bishop and portreeve was written in Old English, and the continuing Englishness of the City is attested by the popularity of the Saxon St Botolph, to whom three churches of apparently post-Saxon origin were dedicated.[59] In early Norman times many of the canons of St Paul's had English names, as in the second quarter of the twelfth century had nearly half the recorded moneyers of London and well over half the aldermen known by name. But after a century or so the two peoples were assimilating, Archbishop Thomas Becket (d. 1170), a Londoner by birth and soon to become one of London's favourite saints (Plate 11), both of whose parents were of Norman origin, providing a case in point.[60]

There were also small colonies of foreign merchants, who were in theory not permitted to stay for more than forty days. However, in the twelfth century Danes and Norwegians could stay for a year, and the men of Cologne had a permanent warehouse and fortress at Dowgate, which later became the headquarters of the Hanseatic League in London, the Steelyard. The merchants of Rouen and Flanders — the most numerous of all the aliens — being less far from their home ports, did not need fixed stations in London. The Jews, on the other hand, who were probably brought over by William the Conqueror, were tightly concentrated around St Lawrence Jewry and the street still known as Old Jewry.[61]

Work

In the twelfth and preceding centuries most work was still concerned with food, drink, or clothing, and many of the craftsmen involved with these basic necessities of life clustered alongside or near to the great West Cheap, now Cheapside. Just beyond its western extremity in what is now Newgate Street, were the butchers' stalls and shambles, conveniently close to the cattle market at Smithfield. Eastward from the shambles were (and still are) Friday Street (the fish market), Bread Street, Milk Street, and Ironmonger Lane, while the cordwainers congregated nearby in the area still known as Cordwainer Ward. Likewise the vintners gave their name to Vintry Ward, which extended down to the riverside. Hardly less essential to the economy were the saddlers and lorimers, who made horse-harness, and the goldsmiths, all adjacent to Cheapside; and near Eastcheap were the candlemakers (Candlewick Ward) and another fish market near Billingsgate (Fish Street).[62]

Little is known about how work was organized prior to the twelfth century — and not much was known even then — but it was certainly small in scale, much of it was done at or near the home, and regulation of it was less pervasive than it was later to become. In earlier times it seems likely that all resident householders had the right to work and trade in the City, and the duty to perform certain services. The status of citizenship was, in fact, still vague and ill-defined. But the collection of taxes, the testamentary and trading privileges granted by royal charters (such as that of freedom from tolls throughout the kingdom), and the continuous arrival of more migrants (or 'foreigners', as outsiders from other parts of England were called) gradually made precision necessary. So craftsmen in various trades or mysteries began to form fraternities or associations (as workers in all fields and at all times generally do), their purposes being religious, charitable, and convivial as well as economic. In London the first known example of such an association or guild is that of the weavers, which was in existence in 1130; and fifty years later there were nineteen such clubs.[63]

These early guilds were often ephemeral, just as modern voluntary committees often are; and they were not necessarily centred on a particular trade. Of those which existed in 1179–80, the guild of St Lazarus doubtless supported the sick, while five, described as 'of Bridge', concerned themselves with the rebuilding of London Bridge, then in progress. Others included the goldsmiths, the pepperers (mainly concerned with the spice trade), the butchers, the weavers, and some clothworkers. Apart from the goldsmiths' and pepperers' guilds, these associations were probably not the direct forefathers of any of the guilds and livery companies which later regulated trade and industry; but they pointed the way in that direction.[64]

Money and Trade

An adequate money supply — enough coins in circulation to raise trade above the level of barter — was an essential ingredient in the medieval economy, and under its Saxon kings England in the tenth century had evolved the most advanced currency in Northern Europe.[65] London's inland trade in such basic commodities as cattle, fish, grain, and timber depended on readily available coin, as did that of England as a whole. So it was the richness of Saxon England that had attracted the marauding Viking bands, and (as we have already seen) London's share of the tribute exacted by Cnut in 1018 amounted to 13 per cent of the total for England — probably well above the average rate per head of population, and an indication of London's great wealth.

Most of the bullion from which the millions of silver pennies in circulation in England at the time of Ethelred II (the Unready, 978–1016) had originated in the German silver mines in the Hartz Mountains. In the first half of the eleventh century a quarter of these pennies were struck in London,[66] where minting probably had a continuous history from the days of Alfred until the removal of the Royal Mint to Wales in 1968–75; and by the time of the Norman Conquest

London possessed a monopoly of the crucial operation of engraving the dies from which all coins there and at the provincial mints were made (Plates 8 and 10).[67]

The German silver bullion needed to maintain the currency had to be paid for through foreign trade, of which London was generally the principal centre. In Viking times it seems that exports consisted chiefly of slaves and, increasingly, of wool.[68] The Viking commercial sphere, in which furs as well as slaves were a crucial commodity, extended in a crescent from Britain across Scandinavia and Russia to Byzantium and the frontiers of the East. In the eleventh and twelfth centuries, however, the axis of English overseas trade was moving towards Germany, Flanders, and France. Foreign merchants were making their presence sufficiently felt in London for King Ethelred to regulate the tolls to be paid by merchants from the Rhineland, Flanders, and Normandy, and (as previously mentioned) in the twelfth century the men of Cologne had a permanent depot at Dowgate. Between about 1000 and 1150 the Flemish cloth industry grew with such speed that the supply of wool had to be augmented from abroad, so wool became and remained for several centuries England's principal export and source of wealth, much of the trade passing through London.[69]

London's advance as a centre of international trade was not, however, continuous. Through the succession of Danegelds and *hergelds* (the latter imposed annually for the payment of the Danish fleet and army) the country was steadily drained of its liquid capital; and this loss continued under the Norman conquistadors, aggravated for a while by falling output from the German silver mines. English merchants no longer penetrated to the Mediterranean, as they had in the tenth century, while at home their shortage of currency opened the way for itinerant Flemings to buy and pay in coin for wool at the regional fairs which by the twelfth century were challenging London's supremacy in foreign and distributive trade.[70]

This recession in London's economic fortunes was reversed in the later twelfth century when the flow of silver from new mines in Germany was followed by an expansion of the coinage and hence of purchasing power in England. Demand for wine increased, chiefly from Rouen, La Rochelle, and Bordeaux; English merchants returned to the Mediterranean in search of spices; and in the 1170s, according to FitzStephen, foreign merchants in London were dealing in such exotic commodities as silks, olive oil, precious stones, and gold, as well as wines and furs. There was, in fact, renewed wealth, and this provided London with the financial muscle needed to bargain successfully with the Crown between 1189 and 1215 (as we have already seen) for substantial privileges of self-government.[71]

Everyday Life

Londoners were tough in early medieval times. Dwellings, warmth, clothing, sanitation, food and drink—all were primitive by the standards of many other ages. Life itself was often 'nasty, brutish and short', and according to a grumpy contemporary, Richard of Devizes, Londoners themselves were equally unpleasant. He did 'not at all like that city', and after expatiating on the vices of its citizens he concluded that 'if you do not want to dwell with evil-doers, do not live in London'. Despite all this William FitzStephen, who knew London well, thought it was one of 'the noble cities of the world ... blessed by a wholesome climate, blessed too in Christ's religion, in the strength of its fortifications, in the nature of its site, the repute of its citizens, the honour of its matrons; happy in its sports, prolific in noble men'.[72]

In the tenth and eleventh centuries most Londoners lived in sunken-floored huts or slightly more substantial buildings with cellars and timber-framed structures at ground level, all generally roofed with thatch. Stone was not used for dwellings until half a century after the Norman Conquest. Heating and cooking was from open hearths with smoke outlets in the roof, and so accidental outbreaks of fire were frequent, a huge one in 1136 causing devastation all the way between the Bridge and St Clement Danes. Water came either from the Thames, Fleet, or Walbrook or from shallow wells, which were often adjacent to the cesspits, lined with board or wattle, and the rubbish pits generally used for the disposal of ordure and refuse. The streets were narrow, frequently unpaved, undrained, and obstructed by evil-smelling laystalls.[73]

However, during the mayoralty of Henry FitzAilwin (1192/3- 1212) London's first code of building regulation, known as the Assize of Buildings, began to improve matters. The regulations covered such things as the ownership of party walls and their materials and thickness, the provision of gutters, the positioning of cesspits, and after another fire in 1212 thatch of all kinds was banned in favour of tiles, shingles, or boards. Enforcement was through the aldermen and the wardmotes of each particular ward, and evidently had some effect, for there were no more widespread fires until 1666.[74]

There were also numerous pleasures to be enjoyed. Although the range of food and drink available may have been narrow by later standards, the menu described by FitzStephen at a public 'cook-shop' or 'take-away' near the Vintry offered, according to the season, 'Viands, dishes roast, fried and boiled, fish great [including sturgeon] and small, the coarser flesh for the poor, the more delicate for the rich, such as venison and birds both big and little [including Guinea fowl and partridge]'. The art of cooking, he concluded, was 'part of the art of civic life'. Out of doors, too, there were vigourous pursuits — racing every Saturday at Smithfield horse market, mass joustings on Sundays in Lent, aquatic tourneys on the river at Easter, hawking, hunting, and in winter, skating on the marshes at Moorfields. Schoolboys went in for cock-fighting, and out in the fields they practised a form of ball game which attracted large crowds of after-dinner spectators.[75]

Many of these activities took place on the numerous feast days of the Church, for religious beliefs and practices penetrated into every nook and cranny of daily life. With a hundred or so parish churches, a dozen or more religious houses, and the biggest cathedral in the land, the Church's outward and visible presence manifested itself everywhere throughout London. Through its priests and nuns it enjoyed a virtual monopoly of learning, for although primitive literacy was beginning to germinate among the laity, few laymen and even fewer laywomen could as yet read or write. Through the sacraments and the liturgy, even if they were often celebrated in a slovenly and perfunctory manner, the Church commanded the still universal and unquestioning assent of the population; and through Archbishop Thomas Becket the Church manifested Londoners' sense of identity. He was their own special saint and popular hero: canonized within three years of his martyrdom (in 1170) and a Londoner born and bred on whose birthplace in Cheapside a church and religious house (St Thomas of Acon) was soon established, to whom the chapel on London's new stone bridge was dedicated and whose image was displayed on one side of the common seal of London in the early thirteenth century (Plate 11). FitzStephen (if he was still living) must certainly have approved, for to him there was no city

deserving greater approval for its customs in respect of church-going, honour paid to the ordinances of God, keeping of feast-days, giving of alms, entertainment of strangers, ratifying of betrothals, contracts of marriage, celebration of nuptials, furnishing of banquets, cheering of guests, and likewise for... care in regard to the rites of funeral and the burial of the dead.

Indeed, 'the only plagues of London', he thought, were 'the immoderate drinking of fools and the frequency of fires'.[76]

London and the Kingdom

Under Alfred's successors in the early tenth century London, hitherto a Mercian city, had been fully incorporated into the Kingdom of Wessex and at once became central in the affairs of the two newly united kingdoms. Three hundred years later it had developed into an embryonic capital city, its unique status within the much larger Kingdom of England having received royal recognition at Runnymede in 1215.

The Danish wars were an important stage in this evolution. Through its prolonged defiance of the invaders London acquired the prestige which enabled it to claim to elect the king, as happened in 1016 after the death of Ethelred the Unready, when 'all the councillors who were in London and the citizens chose Edmund as king', and again in 1042 after the death of Cnut, when 'all the people chose Edward [the Confessor] as king, in London'.[77] Cnut himself had well understood that through its wealth and strategic location London was the best base for his naval and military garrisons — much preferable to Winchester, hitherto a long-standing focal point for the Anglo-Saxon kings.[78]

Besides London's growing role within the kingdom there was also a crucial change within the structural framework of London itself — the removal of the royal residence from the City to Westminster after the crisis of 1052. Since Edward the Confessor's time no reigning monarch has lived for more than a short time within the walls of the City, and Westminster has been the seat of royal power. In later centuries the greatly enlarged royal palace at Westminster (Edward's palace was probably only built of wood) became the normal place of meeting of Parliament whenever it was summoned, and successive monarchs, beginning with Henry VIII, moved on to nearby palaces at Whitehall, St James's, and Buckingham House. Just as Westminster became the seat of the legislature, so too Whitehall became the hub of the administration of the realm, and in and after the seventeenth century the surrounding areas became the natural place of metropolitan residence for the rich, the powerful, and all manner of men who had business at court, public office, or Parliament: the 'West End'. London, in fact, had bifurcated — a fundamental division still writ large on the face of the modern metropolis, the first stage of which was inaugurated not far short of a thousand years ago.

For William I and his immediate successors London required special treatment, manifested on one hand by the Conqueror's charter confirming the citizens' laws and customs and on the other by his building three castles within the City's walls. Through the (almost continuous) union of England and Normandy between 1066 and 1204 Winchester may have enjoyed renewed importance in the geography of royal power. But while kings and their households were still constantly on the move, royal government was nevertheless becoming more complex and sophisticated, and therefore less mobile; and it was at Westminster that the embryonic fiscal and legal departments of state began to settle.[79]

This long process had begun in the reign of Henry II with the transference of the king's chief treasury (i.e. storehouse of treasure and records) from Winchester, the old royal city of the West Saxons, to the London 'Temple', the riverside headquarters of the religious Order of Knights Templar, and in the thirteenth century to the royal palace at Westminster.[80] This had already been enlarged by the building of William Rufus's Great Hall, and it was there at the palace that the king's sheriffs attended twice yearly at the Court of Exchequer to pay in the royal revenues and have their accounts examined and recorded on the pipe rolls. Soon afterwards the king's court for hearing ordinary suits (or common pleas) between man and man ceased to follow the king around in his constant peregrinations, and settled in a fixed place, as King John was forced to acknowledge in clause 17 of Magna Charta; and this place was Westminster. By that time, too, the archbishops of Canterbury, so often leading men in medieval affairs of state, had made their headquarters not in Canterbury, but at Lambeth, opposite to the royal Palace of Westminster.[81]

London's growing role in the development of the nation is also apparent in the fundamental national matters of the succession to the Crown and the struggles for the constriction of its power. London's claim in determining the succession reached its fullest extent in 1135, when in the dispute between Henry I's daughter the Empress Matilda and his nephew Stephen the citizens of London asserted 'their right and privilege' to elect the sovereign, and chose Stephen. This claim was evidently based on precedents established in Saxon times when the succession had been in doubt, as in 1016 and 1042; and after the Battle of Hastings London had been very much involved in the abortive election of Edgar the Atheling as Harold's successor. The claim made in 1135 was therefore an extension of earlier exemplars; but it differed from them in containing for the first time something in the nature of a bargain or *pactio* between City and King.[82]

This bargain did not amount to much, for in return for London's support Stephen only swore to do his utmost to restore peace throughout the realm. (The importance of this support became apparent in 1141 when Matilda, having captured Stephen and entered London for her coronation, was summarily ejected by the citizens, who had formed themselves into a short-lived commune — a repulse from which her fortunes never recovered.) However, the idea of a bargain persisted, and was next apparent in the crisis of 1191, when in exchange for the grant of the commune the citizens recognized John as heir presumptive.[83]

In the events of 1215 surrounding Magna Charta possession of London was the decisive bargaining counter between the king and the insurgent barons. The mayor of London, William Hardel, was one of the twenty-five barons appointed to execute the terms of the Great Charter, and so too was Robert FitzWalter, Lord of Baynard's Castle and commander of the City militia. However, although the City *per se* was not a principal party in the crisis of 1215, its secondary role was momentous, for the capture of London by the barons by stealth on 17 May 1215 marked the turning point of events. The barons' possession of London compelled John to accept their demands at Runnymede a month later,[84] and the value which he placed on London was demonstrated by the charter of 9 May by which, in a desparate attempt to retain London's allegiance, he had granted the citizens the right to elect their own mayor every year. The subsequent enforcement of the terms of Magna Charta was moreover specifically made dependent on possession of London and the Tower, which until 15 August were to continue to be held by the barons and the archbishop of Canterbury respectively as a guarantee of the king's good faith in implementing the promised concessions. After the expiry of the deadline, and the king's failure (according to his adversaries) to put the Charter into effect, the barons continued in possession of the City; and it was to London that Prince Louis of France (to whom the barons had subsequently offered the Crown) immediately resorted after his arrival in England. There the citizens, led by FitzWalter and the mayor, did him homage, and but for the death of John in October 1216 their old claim to elect the sovereign would no doubt have been revived.[85]

More generally, London's influence over the events of 1215–16 is also apparent in the barons' organization of themselves into a sworn company or *conjuratio* — a sort of national commune — and in the establishment of the 'committee' of Twenty-Five to enforce the Charter, devices which may well have been derived from London's commune of 1191 and from the councils of *echevins* or aldermen of the ensuing years.[86]

So already London's weight was being exerted at times of great political crisis in several different ways: as shaper of events, as place for the acclamation of a new king, as supreme political and economic prize, and as exemplar of urban constitutional innovation.

6

The Emergence of the Medieval Capital
c.1216–c.1530

During the thirteenth century the population of London is thought to have doubled, and by 1300 there were probably between 60,000 and 100,000 inhabitants — far fewer than in Paris, which by then contained over 200,000 people. But during the epidemic of the Black Death in 1348–9 the population of London was decimated, and it was not until around 1500–50 that pre-plague levels were reached again.[1] During much of those two hundred years the City was a relatively uncrowded place, and for the most part prosperous and stable — at any rate after the spasm of hiccups which occurred in the erratic reign of Richard II. Throughout the fourteenth century Westminster and London were becoming more and more the political capital of the realm, while in the City itself a series of constitutional innovations and experiments (mostly in the reigns of Edward II and Richard II) constructed the unique system of municipal government which still exists there in fundamentally unchanged form today. And through the mounting strength of its commercial and financial clout as the economic centre of England the City's leaders were generally able to take a detached and self-interested stance in times of political commotions, secure in the knowledge that London's support would be crucial in determining the ultimate outcome.

City, Crown, and Capital

King John's recognition of the London commune and the general confirmation of the City's liberties in Magna Charta were important landmarks in the evolution of London's unique status within the realm. But the City was still far from secure, for in the last resort it was defenceless against a powerful or obstinate king. Conversely, the Crown needed the City's resources — particularly its financial resources; so complementary needs and mutual suspiciousness became the hallmarks of the relationship between City and State, as they still are today.

At first the balance of advantage lay with the Crown. During the long reign of Henry III (1216–72) there were frequent disputes, often revolving round the City's liability to tallage without consent, and between 1239 and 1257 the liberties of the City were suspended and its government taken back into the king's hands on at least ten occasions — often for quite short periods, terminated by payment of a fine. In 1263 London's leading aldermanic clique was overthrown by the *populares* led by a cluster of rich merchants of the newly organized crafts and committed to unequivocal support for Simon De Montfort and his baronial confederates. But they were themselves quickly ousted after De Montfort's death at the Battle of Evesham in 1265, and London was subjected to loss of liberty and a huge fine. In 1285 Edward I (1272–1307) used popular unrest as the reason to take the City into his own hands and rule it through his warden for thirteen years, the mayoralty not being resumed until 1298.[2]

By this time, however, the nature of the relationship between Crown and City was beginning to change, for the tallage of towns was being replaced by new taxes sanctioned by Parliament, to which representatives from the boroughs, including London, were summoned. The relationship was also becoming more confused, for social dissensions were emerging within the City itself, particularly during the times of national discontent which coincided with the reigns of such ineffective kings as Edward II (1307–27) and Richard II (1377–99). In 1319 London's popular radical movement (then at one of the climaxes of its fortunes), was able to extract from the king (then at a low point) a charter which greatly enlarged the power of the citizen commonalty, notably in its control over the City's growing administration and judicial bureaucracy, and over the aldermen, who were to be elected annually – a practice which was, however, disregarded except in the years 1376–94. Two years later (in 1321) Edward's virtual suspension of the City's liberties ensured that London would provide crucial support for his deposition in 1327; and for this the City was rewarded by Edward III (while still under the tutelage of Isabella and Mortimer) with the confirmation of all its ancient liberties, the resolution of numerous other matters of dissension during the previous century, and the additional grant of the bailiwick of Southwark and a monopoly of all markets within 7 miles of the City.[3]

The grants of 1327 virtually ended London's long struggle with the Crown for royal recognition of the City's unique degree of autonomy within the kingdom. In 1392 Richard II did, it is true, arbitrarily dismiss and imprison the mayor and the sheriffs for a few months, but the resentment evoked by this outmoded behaviour helps to explain London's acceptance of Henry IV in 1399; and thereafter no sovereign was unwise enough to treat the City with such contumely until Charles II did so during the charter crisis of 1683. So by the end of the fourteenth century London had acquired almost the whole array of rights sought after from the Crown by many towns throughout the previous three centuries;[*] and one of the

---

* But legal incorporation (the right granted to many boroughs in the later Middle Ages to have perpetual succession and a common seal, to sue and be sued, and to hold lands etc.) was not formally granted to London until as late as 1608, doubtless because such rights had long been assumed to have already been in existence.[4]

last of these acquisitions proved in the long run to be one of the most valuable. This was the right granted in charters of 1341, 1377, and 1383 for the mayor, aldermen, and commonalty to amend the City's own constitution. Despite its oligarchic nature the City Corporation never became a close corporation as happened in many provincial towns and cities; and it was this power of self-reform which saved it, alone of all the old incorporated cities and boroughs, from reform by the Municipal Corporations Act of 1835.[5]

Guilds and Civic Constitution

While the City's privileged position was being built up by this succession of royal charters, the guilds and the civic authorities and their relationship with each other were also evolving. In the thirteenth and fourteenth centuries the number of craft guilds proliferated, and gradually they took over the regulation of their respective callings. Ownership of property no longer of itself conferred citizenship, and the freedom to work and trade there could only be obtained by birth from a freeman father (patrimony), by purchase (redemption), or by apprenticeship to a freeman.[6] Apprenticeship being the commonest method of entry to the freedom, citizenship became closely related to membership of a guild, of which by the early fifteenth century there were over a hundred.

Dissensions of one kind or another were frequent — between kings and guilds, between the City authorities and the guilds, and above all between individual guilds. These last were often over lines of demarcation between one craft and another, but by the fourteenth century the leaders of about a dozen guilds were getting much richer than most of the others. Many members of such greater guilds as the mercers, grocers, drapers, fishmongers, clothworkers, or vintners, were becoming mainly wholesale traders dealing extensively in the provinces and (particularly if they dealt in wool, cloth, or wine) in foreign commerce. The economic interests of merchants of this kind differed markedly from those of the members of the more numerous lesser guilds such as the cordwainers, glovers, or weavers, who were primarily producers rather than traders; and these differences provided an important source of internal conflict.[7]

By the early fourteenth century the guild leaders, and especially those of the great mercantile trades, were becoming indisputably the men of power, and the way was open for them to elbow themselves into a share in the City's government. This proved to be a rough journey, for in the unstable times of Edward II the politics of the City were constantly intertwined with highly volatile national events. In the climax of popular aspiration of 1310–11, when London sided with the reforming magnates known as the Ordainers against the king, a citizen 'commonalty' gained brief control of the City's powerful new professional bureaucracy (said to have amounted to some thirty-five clerks in 1300) and a recognized association with the aldermen in the municipal government. But when the crafts attempted at mass assemblies to take over the role of this still inchoate commonalty, reaction set in, and it was only after the crises of 1319 and 1327 that the inviolable position of the crafts in the City's affairs was permanently accepted. By a charter of 1319 they were granted control of admission to the freedom of the City and hence to important economic advantages which included the exclusive right to trade retail there; and in 1327 four of the principal guilds obtained charters of their own giving them rights of search for defective workmanship not just in London but throughout the whole kingdom.[8]

Meanwhile the development of the City's municipal institutions was following a course in some respects parallel with that of the nascent parliamentary institutions of the realm. In both cases a new 'lower house' was emerging: the House of Commons at Westminster and the Court of Common Council in the City, the members of both of which were the elected representatives of a wider constituency. The analogy cannot, however, be pressed too far, for whereas the Commons were in some sense an extension of the Lords, from which (so it is now generally accepted) they divided into a separate House in the 1330s, the Common Council evolved not from the Court of Aldermen but from the Great Congregation or mass assembly of the citizen commonalty, which was the lineal descendant of the old folkmoot.[9] In the troubled times of Edward II these unwieldy great concourses or congregations had claimed a share in the government of the City, but at one such meeting in 1322 of 'a very great commonalty' it had been agreed that two persons should be elected by the freemen of each ward to make ordinances for the whole commonalty. From this precedent of election by the wards there gradually emerged the Court of Common Council, which by the end of the fourteenth century had acquired considerable legislative, administrative, and financial powers, and which some four hundred years later superseded the Court of Aldermen as the main instrument of the City's government.[10]

In the fifteenth century attendance at meetings of the Great Congregation apparently became so large that in 1475 membership was restricted to the guild 'liverymen' — the more prosperous members of the mysteries, who were entitled to wear a special livery — and to the members of the Common Council. The main function of the Great Congregation — or Common Hall, as it has been called since about the seventeenth century — was to elect the Lord Mayor and one of the sheriffs every year; and from the sixteenth century until 1918 it also elected the City's Members of Parliament, usually (until 1885) four in number.[11] Thus the craft guilds, or livery companies, as they became known in the fifteenth century, were assimilated into the City's system of government, of which they became an integral part, unlike any of their counterparts in the other ancient cities of the realm. So by the end of the fifteenth century all the main components of the City's complicated constitution had emerged; and to an extraordinary extent they still survive to this day, little changed.

Civic and Royal Contentions 1376–1400

This development was only completed after a series of internal convulsions in the last quarter of the fourteenth century. As in the days of Edward II London's internal conflicts during the reign of Richard II were closely related to national events. Now they were complicated by interguild conflicts, the growing ascendance of the greater guilds, the interests of whose rich leaders were mainly mercantile rather than industrial, being resisted by the more numerous handicraft guilds. There was also dissension between the victualling trades which wanted to retain their monopolies in the supply of food and the crafts which wanted to keep prices down; and within the greater guilds there was competition between groups of merchant capitalists with conflicting interests in the wool and cloth trades. The yeast in this potent brew was supplied by the erratic policies of the Crown, endemically short of money, whose capricious changes in the location of the wool staple towns and its manipulation of the City's trading privileges, often favouring alien merchants at the expense of indigenous Londoners, kept the whole concoction bubbling with dangerous vigour.[12]

The cauldron boiled over in the final year of the now senile Edward III. The ructions of the Good Parliament of 1376 led to crucial though short-lived changes in the way London was governed: the Common Council was to be elected by the guilds or mysteries instead of from the wards (where the aldermen's influence was greatest), and the aldermen themselves were to hold office for only one year (as the royal charter of 1319 had unsuccessfully required) instead of for life. In this sudden overthrow of the merchant oligarchy the prime mover was John of Northampton, an alderman and agitator skilled in defence of the interests of his own declining mystery, the drapers, who allied his faction with the ascendant grocers and with John of Gaunt, the young king Richard's, uncle, who was then in effective control of royal policy and determined to recover the authority shaken by the Good Parliament. Annual changes of membership greatly diminished the effectiveness of the Court of Aldermen, the Common Council was in the hands of the lesser mysteries, and in the years 1377 to 1381 Londoners had to pay enormous taxes. Civic authority was in disarray, intermittent violence and disorder prevailed, and in 1381 the City Fathers proved unable to hold the City itself during the Peasants' Revolt.[13]

On Thursday 13 June 1381 Kentish rebels (to whom a renegade priest, John Ball, had been preaching at Blackheath) swarmed across London Bridge, where the drawbridge had been let down, while the men of Essex poured into the City through Aldgate, both incursions being evidently the result of aldermanic incompetence and/or the presence of large numbers of sympathizers within the walls. The palaces of the archbishop of Canterbury at Lambeth and of John of Gaunt (hated for his attempts to destroy the City's liberties) at the Savoy were both sacked, while the king and his entourage took refuge in the Tower, where they were besieged by the rebels. On the next day Richard rode out to Mile End to try to appease the men of Essex, but in his absence other rebels swept into the Tower, dragged out the unfortunate archbishop, and beheaded him and four others on Tower Hill. Perhaps 150 people were beheaded in London on that day, including thirty-five Flemings, probably weavers whose presence endangered the livelihood of native craftsmen. Meanwhile the king spent an uncomfortable night at his Great Wardrobe or stores depot near Blackfriars, the Tower being uninhabitable.[14]

The tide turned on the next day. Richard went to Westminster Abbey, made his confession to the anchorite there (probably one of the monks), and then rode back to meet the Kentishmen at Smithfield, where they were drawn up under the leadership of Wat Tyler opposite to St Bartholomew's Hospital (Plate 13). A parley ensued, followed by a fracas in which Tyler was severely wounded (and later executed) by the mayor, William Walworth. At this critical moment Richard commanded the now uncertain rebels, 'Be still, I am your King, your leader and your chief', and was able to lead them away from the City towards Clerkenwell. Meanwhile the mayor and aldermen belatedly drummed up armed men from the wards, and when confronted with effective force the leaderless rebels capitulated.[15]

So far as London was concerned, this was the end of the revolt—the worst breakdown of order until the Gordon Riots four hundred years later (1780)—but civic turbulence continued. In October 1381 John of Northampton was elected mayor, the current bench of aldermen being discredited, and in his two years of power the assault on the civic establishment was resumed, free trade in victuals being reaffirmed and victuallers being prohibited from holding any judicial office, which of course included the offices of mayor, sheriff, and alderman. This aroused the alarm of the leaders of the great non-victualling mysteries, fearful for their own interests, and in the mayoral election of 1383 Northampton was ousted in favour of Sir Nicholas Brembre, a grocer. Some three months later, in February 1384, Northampton raised a disturbance and riot among the lesser folk which ended in his capture, trial by the King's Council, and imprisonment at Tintagel Castle in Cornwall.[*] The populist challenge to the established order of things was over.[17]

In the counter-revolution which now ensued the election of the Common Council was permanently restored to the wards (where the aldermen's influence was strong), apparently because this was now thought to favour the greater guilds. Aldermen became eligible for re-election without any interval in their term of office, in 1394 the old custom of tenure for life was revived (it still prevails today, though nowadays there is a 'gentlemen's, agreement' for retirement at 70 years of age), and virtually none of the innovations made under John of Northampton's leadership survived.[18]

During and after his three-year mayoralty Brembre became actively involved in natonal affairs and was one of the king's confidants whose arrest was demanded in 1387 by the formidable quintet of noble magnates known as the Lords Appellant. After the forces supporting the king had melted away Richard sought refuge in the Tower, where the then mayor (Nicholas Exton, fishmonger) and aldermen ingloriously deserted him and admitted the triumphant Appellants to the City; and at the ensuing meeting of the Merciless Parliament in February 1388 they also abandoned Brembre, now accused on slender evidence of high treason, who was executed at Tyburn.[19]

After these terrible events the ruling oligarchy closed ranks, and internal conflicts faded away in face of the shared external dangers of the times. This was just as well,

---

[*] But for the Queen's intercession Northampton would have been executed. He was released from prison in 1387 but never recovered his former influence. He died in 1397.[16]

for in May 1392 the king, who had never forgotten the City's desertion of him in 1387–8, suddenly arrested the mayor and sheriffs, took the City's liberties into his own hands, and even ordered the removal of the lawcourts to York, thereby depriving the Londoners of an important source of business. Money evidently lay at the root of this quarrel, for Richard had been angered by the Londoners' refusal after 1388 to grant him loans. So after the City had agreed to pay £10,000 for a royal pardon, its liberties were restored (though at first only conditionally), and in October a new mayor was elected and the lawcourts returned. But the City establishment in its turn did not forget or forgive the king's arbitrary behaviour; and when Henry of Lancaster overthrew Richard in 1399 he was readily accepted by the citizens; and as Henry IV he always took care to retain London's goodwill.[20]

For its part the City oligarchy was glad to have survived. By the end of Richard's reign it was in fact more stongly entrenched than ever, and between 1400 and the ructions of the 1640s London was to enjoy nearly two and a half centuries of relatively stable government. The domination by the leading members of the greater guilds, from whom most of the aldermen were drawn, was indeed so complete that within that period all the mayors were members of one of the more powerful guilds such as the Mercers or Grocers.[21]

The Political Capital

In the eleventh and twelfth centuries the centre of gravity of the royal court had gradually shifted from Winchester, the main seat of the old Wessex monarchy, to London. Edward the Confessor had focused attention on Westminster by setting a major royal residence there beside his newly rebuilt abbey, and later on the Exchequer and King's Court of Common Pleas had settled in William Rufus's Great Hall. Thus through the association of royal palace, church, and rudimentary machinery of government the lineaments of an embryonic capital were already emerging by around 1200.[22]

In the later Middle Ages this association grew stronger, the prestige of the abbey being greatly enhanced by Henry III, whose devotion to the cult of Edward the Confessor provided an important motive for him to start the rebuilding of the great church and to have his own tomb there, near to the shrine of his canonized ancestor. For several centuries thereafter most reigning sovereigns were buried in the abbey, which, as both royal mausoleum and cult centre for the royal saint as well as traditional scene of successive coronation ceremonies, also became the physical manifestation of a royal mythology analogous to but different from those of the contemporary Scottish and French monarchies.[23] These processes were continued by Richard II, another royal devotee of Edward the Confessor, through whose gifts to the abbey the rebuilding of the nave was resumed after a pause of about a century.[24] By that time the affairs of royal palace and abbey had also drawn together in other ways. Part of the royal treasury was kept in the abbey, several abbots served as treasurers of the Exchequer, the Council of State met in the monks' refectory, and until its exclusion in c.1380 the nascent lower house of

Parliament, the Commons, met in the chapter house, or in later years in the refectory.[25]

The evolution of Westminster towards the position of a political capital was however, interrupted for over half a century by the Scottish wars of Edwards I, II, and III. So long as the subjugation of the Scots was a main objective of the Crown, York had great advantages over Westminster as the seat of government. Under Edward I the Exchequer and Court of Common Pleas were removed thither for nearly seven years, and the headquarters of even the Chancery was established there. In the 1330s there was another concentration of royal administration at York when the young Edward III revived his grandfather's aggressive Scottish policies, much to the distress of the tradesmen of Westminster, who suffered greatly in consequence. But the North was economically backward compared to the South, and after the outbreak of the Hundred Years War with France in 1338 Westminster became the political centre of the realm once again. The Exchequer and Common Pleas came back from York, by 1345 the Court of Chancery was also sitting in Westminster Hall, and so too from the mid-1360s was the Court of King's Bench. In the later years of Edward III the King's Council frequently met at Westminster, and most important of all, Westminster had become the normal place of meeting of Parliament; for whereas in the first decade of his reign the meetings had more often than not been elsewhere (five at York, for instance), between 1339 and 1377 all thirty-one Parliaments were held at Westminster (Plate 14).[26] This concentration of political and administrative power at the royal suburb had an important spin-off for the City of London when the Great Wardrobe — the royal commissariat for the purchase and storage of all manner of commodities such as cloth, furs, wax, spices, and groceries needed for the king's household, his clerks, and his army and navy — finally settled in 1361 (after moving with the king to the North and even overseas) in a large house near Baynard's Castle and the great convent of the Black Friars.[27]

There was another spin-off too. The permanent presence of government at Westminster meant that the City became the natural place to which successive kings resorted whenever they urgently needed ready cash to supplement their own inelastic resources; and the City's response to these frequent demands accelerated its development as the national centre of the money market. For however much Westminster was becoming the centre of political power, it was the City which provided the economic motor of the realm; and at times of national political crisis this metropolitan power was apparent (as we have already seen in Chapter 5) in several different ways: (1) as shaper of events, (2) as place for the acclamation of a new king, and (3) as supreme political and economic prize.

In the later Middle Ages popular support for the acclamation of a new king with a dubious title to the Crown was essential for his success; and Londoners and their leaders took on the role (sometimes reluctantly) of speaking for the Third Estate of the whole nation, the Estate of the Commons, whose public recognition of a new title to the throne was deemed as necessary as that provided by the Lords spiritual and temporal.

All three elements described above are certainly discernible at the deposition of Edward II in 1326–7, which depended in large measure upon the support of the capital and the active participation of the Londoners, by whom, as Froissart observed in reference to this revolution, 'tout le royaulme d'Angleterre se ordonne et gouverne'. But at the next dynastic crisis, in 1399, at the deposition of Richard II, whose treatment of London had (as we have already seen) evoked such hostility there, the London magnates were much more cautious; for although an official deputation of citizens welcomed Henry of Lancaster when he was still far from the City, and withdrew allegiance to Richard, they did not do so until Henry had been in the country for six weeks and had already made Richard his prisoner. For a usurper the element of acclamation provided soon afterwards largely by Londoners in support of Henry's claim to the Crown was nevertheless of crucial importance.[28]

During the magnates' war games of the 1450s the City's policy was self-interested neutrality and the maintenance of the status quo; so when the insurgent Yorkist lords were advancing towards London in 1460 the civic authorities decided to admit them rather than suffer the City to be sacked for the Lancastrian cause. Thus London had changed sides and was lost to the king, and thereafter the Yorkists possessed the massive financial support of the Londoners, fearful of the revenge which would follow a return of the Lancastrians. In 1461 Margaret of Anjou (queen of the semi-demented Lancastrian Henry VI) made a cardinal error when after routing the Yorkists at the Second Battle of St Albans (17 February) she did not immediately march on to London. Instead she retired northward and so allowed Edward of York to enter the City, where the citizens took a prominent and evidently enthusiastic part in the series of acclamation ceremonies by which his title as King Edward IV was recognized. His title was confirmed on 29 March by his victory over the Lancastrians at Towton in Yorkshire, but it is hard to imagine his ultimate success without the support of London.[29]

At the last medieval crisis of the succession, when Richard of Gloucester successfully usurped the Crown in 1483, the civic authorities had to be jostled into reluctantly supplying the necessary element of popular acclamation.[30] So on each crucial occasion since Magna Charta the formalities of the transfer of power took place at London or at London's royal suburb of Westminster, where every coronation ceremony since that of Harold in 1066 had been held. London had truly become the political capital of the realm, and almost a distinct unit within it.

London and the Economy

We have already seen that by 1300 the population of London stood at between 60,000 and 100,000, still less than half that of Paris. Perhaps one in sixty of all the peoples of England were living in London then.[31] Despite its huge size Paris was nevertheless less demographically dominant within France than was London within England, for in France large provincial cities such as Lille, Rouen, or

Bordeaux were larger and more numerous than their counterparts in England, and the proportion of Frenchmen living in Paris was therefore only one in eighty or ninety of the national total.[32]

The population of London is thought to have reached a peak around 1300, followed by a small decline. But in 1348–9 it was greatly reduced by the first of the periodic visitations of bubonic plague which devastated Europe (the last outbreak in London being the 'Great Plague' of 1665). During the course of about a year and a half it seems that there were upwards of some 18,000 deaths in London as a whole.[33] New cemeteries were formed at West and East Smithfield, and recent archaeological excavations at the latter have uncovered long trenches for mass burials, the bodies (some already partly decomposed at the time of interment) being carefully laid with their feet facing east towards the Holy Land.[34]

No epidemic of comparable suddenness or severity to the Black Death of 1348–9 had ever visited London, and the population did not return to its pre-plague levels until around 1500–50, after the lapse of some 200 years. Nevertheless London recovered more quickly than most provincial towns. The growth of wool exports concentrated trade and mercantile capital there, and London was still able to attract migrants from the rest of the half-empty country — to encourage them, the fine to purchase the City's freedom was reduced in 1381. There was little pressure on space in the City, through shortage of labour real wages rose, and throughout most of the fifteenth century London was a prosperous and stable place. By around 1500 perhaps one in forty of the total national population lived in London, and its relative economic power had also increased.[35]

The Geographical Distribution of Wealth in England

Quantative assessment of London's economic power in relation to that of the rest of the realm becomes possible for the first time (albeit in crude form) through use of the records of the taxes which were levied by the Crown with ever-increasing frequency in the later Middle Ages. In the late twelfth century London was evidently three times as wealthy as the second city, York, but the first detailed picture of the geographical distribution of wealth throughout most of the realm is contained in the records of the lay subsidy levied by Edward III in 1334. Despite their limitations, these show that London's wealth was growing not only in absolute terms, but also relative to all other towns, for its assessment at £11,000 was five times as great as that of Bristol (by then the second city in the urban league), and over six times greater than that of York in third place.[36]

During the ensuing two centuries London's lay wealth seems to have increased fifteen fold — five times as fast as the average three fold increase throughout the rest of England. By the first quarter of the sixteenth century London's share was around 9 per cent of the total assessed lay wealth of the country[37] — an enormous proportion in a still overwhelmingly rural economy and in the 1520s London was paying nearly ten times as much as Norwich (then the second city) and fifteen times as much as Bristol.[38]

Of course some reservations have to be attached to such figures, but it is nevertheless clear that during the preceding two centuries a very substantial geographical redistribution of England's wealth had taken place. Whereas in the 1330s the main concentration of lay wealth (apart from that of London) had been in a belt extending from Gloucestershire and Berkshire through the Midlands to Norfolk and South Lincolnshire, by 1515 it comprised almost the whole of England south of a line from the Wash to the Severn estuary, and eight of the ten wealthiest counties came within what may now be termed the London orbit (in order of magnitude, Middlesex, Essex, Kent, Surrey, Suffolk, Hertfordshire, Huntingdonshire, and Berkshire).[39] London was in fact exerting its economic pull more

Fig. 16. Geographical distribution of assessed lay wealth in 1515; the 17 wealthiest counties

strongly than ever before, and greatly enlarging the differences in wealth between the South-East and most of the rest of the country.*

The Crafts of London

Virtually every medieval English skill except those connected with agriculture, mining, and quarrying was practised in London. An early fifteenth-century list of London crafts shows that all the basic medieval raw materials — wool, skins, metals, wood, and stone — were in widespread use. Many of the manufacturing industries were concerned with dress, but there was also a great miscellany of others such as the tallow-chandlers, cardmakers, fletchers (i.e. arrowmakers), potters, ropers, and soapmakers, etc. There were many crafts, too, engaged in the food and drink trades; and lastly there were the great mercantilists — mercers, grocers, drapers — few in number but great in wealth.[40] Workshops were small in scale, the number of apprentices a master was allowed to take being limited by his guild. But with general economic expansion and growth of demand also came specialization of labour and increased use of unapprenticed semi-skilled employees or journeymen. There was a constant flux in the fortunes of individual mysteries, and always it was the merchant guilds — the suppliers of raw materials and/or the sellers of the finished product — which achieved ascendancy over the manufacturers. The dyers, for instance, upon whom the weavers and fullers came to depend, had to import much of the materials of their trade, and so became merchants rather than manufacturers — capitalists dealing in the finished article, whose guild ranked high in the pecking order of the London livery companies.[41] This ascendancy was reflected in the relative wealth of different parts of the City, where concentrations of industrial workshops were appearing in outlying areas such as Aldgate or across the river in Southwark, while the richest areas were in or near to Cheapside — the centre of the retail and distributive trades — and beside the river.[42]

The Supply of Food, Fuel, and Raw Materials

The existence of the huge human antheap of London exercised a powerful economic influence over much of the rest of the realm, most clearly to be seen in the feeding and fuelling of London. It has recently been calculated that 1,000,000 bushels of grain (the staple foodstuff) were needed each year to sustain the estimated population of London in 1300, and that to provide this quantity would have required some 250,000 acres of ground; 100,000 tons of wood fuel were also needed per annum.[43]

Through this vast demand zones of specialized production were evolving around London. Closest to the City perishable fruit and vegetables were produced, 2 square miles between Holborn and Charing Cross being devoted to horticulture,

* Only lay wealth has been considered here, but the inclusion of clerical wealth makes little difference to the geographical hierarchy.

and intensive cultivation there[44] was assisted by ready supplies of horse manure. Milk, pigs, and poultry were all marketed from not far away, Essex and Suffolk supplied butter and cheese, and meadow and pasture in such places as Tottenham or the fertile Lea Valley provided hay for horses and fattening grounds for cattle, some of which were driven up from the Midlands and even further north.[45]

Grain, the main foodstuff, although bulky could be easily transported, and because the cost of carriage overland was four or five times greater than by water, most of it came to London along the Thames. From down river it was brought to Billingsgate, mainly from those parts of Kent bordering on the Thames estuary, Faversham being the main port there; but sometimes in years of scarcity it was brought from as far as Norfolk and the Wash ports. Upstream, Henley, 35 miles from London as the crow flies, was at the head of the effectively navigable river and was the entrepôt for the collection and storage of corn brought there by cart from beyond Oxford, and bound for Queenhithe, above London Bridge.[46] Henley also had a large trade in firewood from the nearby Chiltern Hills, and in many wooded areas around London which were accessible by water there was substantial commercial production of faggots and charcoal needed for braziers and bakers' ovens. Supplying the demand for fuel probably affected the productive resources of a wide area around London as much as did that for grain, and as early as the thirteenth century coal was already being brought to London by sea from the distant North-East.[47] Without the availability of such coal London's rising demands for fuel might indeed have been impossible to supply, with incalculable consequences for the long-term development of the capital.

What may already be termed an embryonic London economic region was in fact beginning to spread outwards for up to some 60 miles in places where water transport was available. Much of the London cornmongers' trade was done wholesale, especially if the grain was to be delivered by water, and by sample; and some grain did come overland from local markets such as at Uxbridge or High Wycombe.[48] But the ever-extending tentacles of London's economic influence did not depend solely on the demand for food and fuel. Tin was brought from faraway Cornwall for the making of pewter, and the distant origin of this principal raw material did not prevent London's becoming the leading centre of the pewter industry, governed by its own livery company which had powers to regulate the quality of pewtermaking throughout the whole country.[49] Similarly much of the manufacture of alabaster effigies and reredoses was carried on in London, to which John of Gaunt in 1374 ordered the delivery of six cartloads of alabaster from the mines of remotest Derbyshire for the tombs of himself and his first wife at St Paul's.[50] Royal building at Westminster Palace or Westminster Abbey drew up stone from Yorkshire and Portland, as well as marble from Purbeck, where royal officers were stationed to superintend buying and dispatching operations.[51] Much of such traffic was water-borne, but London was still the hub of the road system, just as it had been under the Romans, and carriage of goods by land was evidently widespread, sometimes over quite long distances. In the fifteenth century carts were regularly used for the transport of goods even between London and

Southampton, where carriage by sea would have been possible; and the existence in the twelfth century of a 'Londenestret' at Gamlingay in Cambridgeshire shows that London, all of 50 miles away, was regarded as the natural terminal point of major roads.[52]

Overseas Trade

Much of London's growing economic power in the later Middle Ages was derived from its role as a centre of foreign trade. It is to the large commercial transactions and the banking and credit mechanisms to which this trade gave rise that the origin of the City of London as an international financial and commercial centre may be traced.

Until around the end of the thirteenth century overseas trade was for a long period largely in the hands of aliens, and England's economic position then has been compared to that of a partially developed colony where foreigners exported raw materials and imported wine, cloth, and luxury goods. Until the 1270s the trade in wool — by far the largest single export — was dominated by Flemish merchants from the great cloth-manufacturing towns of the Low Countries, and even after political ructions had dislocated the trade Italians were the main beneficiaries. Perhaps due to lack of capital London merchants were not fully exploiting the advantages of their nodal position within the North European trading region extending from Scandinavia to the mouths of the Rhine, the Thames, and the Seine. This was particularly so in the case of the Baltic trade in such things as furs, herrings, timber, pitch, and ships' chandlery, which was dominated by German merchants. As early as 1157 the men of Cologne had had their own premises in Upper Thames Street at the Steelyard — an association or German Hanse to which successive kings, perenially short of cash, granted valuable commercial privileges.[53]

In the later Middle Ages this pattern of trade changed greatly. As finished cloth replaced raw wool as England's chief export — in the early sixteenth century it amounted to 90 per cent of all exports, the turning point in the importance of the two having been passed around 1450[54] — so London's share in the overseas trade of the nation became ever greater. So too, in general, did that of the denizen (i.e. native) merchants of London in relation to that of their alien competitors, particularly in the case of wool. Between the 1280s and the mid-1330s, for instance, London's share of wool exports rose from 25 to 44 per cent of the national total, while within that same general period denizen merchants' share of that London trade trebled.[55] Throughout these years the wool trade was the object of frequent royal regulation, notably by the establishment of Staple towns, sometimes on the Continent and sometimes in England, through which all wool for export had to pass, and by the fluctuating treatment of alien and denizen wool merchants. In the later fourteenth century the Staple was firmly fixed at Calais (then an English possession), and the greater part of the trade came into the hands of the Fellowship of the Staplers, a group of English merchants itself dominated by rich London capitalists.[56] By the 1490s 58 per cent of English wool exports were being made through London, and all of the City's wool trade was in the hands of denizen merchants.[57]

The wine trade — England's largest single import — was even more affected by political events than the wool business, and London denizen merchants' share of it varied considerably. After the union of Gascony and England in 1152 (by the marriage of the future Henry II with Eleanor of Aquitaine), Gascon wines had gradually come to the fore in the English market. In London the trade was concentrated around Queenhithe in the riverside ward known as the Vintry, and there, in the early fourteenth century, over a quarter of all Gascon exports to England were landed from the capacious ships called cogs, which each carried up to 100 tuns of wine (equivalent to around 100,000 litres).[58] Much of this trade was then still in the hands of alien merchants, but after about 1330 their share declined, and by 1350 denizen merchants handled well over half of London's imports. There, much of the wine was sold in the City's taverns (said in 1309 to be over 350 in number) or to middlemen for distribution outside London, notably in the Home Counties, the Midlands, and even further afield. But this flourishing trade was severely dislocated by the Hundred Years War, the price of wine rose greatly, particularly in relation to that of ale, and not until the end of the fifteenth century was there a substantial measure of recovery. By that time the trade was dominated by Bristol and London, the latter's share of 40 per cent of all imports pointing to the very large distributive network centred on the City.[59]

By far the biggest single item of English overseas trade in the later Middle Ages was the export of cloth. In this field London gradually achieved an overwhelmingly predominant position, focused through the weekly marts held at Blackwell Hall in Basinghall Street (Plate 32). Through their trading connexions both at home and overseas the merchant capitalists of London were able (subject to fluctuations in the supply of bullion earned through overseas trade) to provide the credit which played a key part in the expansion of the domestic cloth industry; and their business methods permeated throughout the mercantile economy.[60]

Yet despite their importance the denizen cloth exporters of London never during the two centuries for which customs records of cloth exist (1347–1547) had more than about half of the City's trade, the rest of which was in the hands of Hanse and other alien merchants. Many of the latter were Italians, whose ships regularly visited the Thames, and who used new methods of business accounting, including arabic numerals, and new ways of organizing foreign credit.[61]

The English denizen merchants of the overseas cloth trade, or Merchant Adventurers, were quite distinct from and suffered less regulation by the Crown than their counterparts in the wool trade, the Fellowship of the Staplers. Of the Adventurers trading in the Low Countries in the early fifteenth century those of London formed the principal group. Within that group the leaders were those belonging to the Mercers' Company, many of whose richest members had long been involved in overseas trade; but similar groups of Merchant Adventurers also existed in the Grocers', Drapers', Haberdashers' and Skinners' Companies. Within this interguild Fellowship of Merchant Adventurers of London each member traded individually, sharing with others the cost of chartering a ship, while the Fellowship organized the fleets which sailed from London to the quarterly cloth marts in the Low Countries and generally directed the Adventurers' mercantile policy overseas.[62]

The sheer scale of the cloth trade was enormous. England became the leading supplier of cloth throughout much of Europe; and in the early fifteenth century London, handling on average some 13,000 cloths* per annum, already had over 40 per cent of the nation's total exports. A century later the volume of London's cloth trade had much more than trebled. By the early 1540s it had almost doubled again to some 97,000 cloths per annum, and more than four-fifths of the nation's cloth exports were then passing through London.[63]

London Loans to the Crown

These very large commercial operations demonstrate the wealth and sophisticated financial techniques which existed in London by the end of the Middle Ages; and successive kings, endemically short of money, exploited this situation to the full. As early as the mid-twelfth century the great City magnate Gervase of Cornhill had lent money to King Stephen's embattled queen, and thereafter the imposition of tallages on the Jews was, until their expulsion in 1290, a useful extra source of royal revenue. But loans to the Crown became much more important after Edward I had in 1275 imposed a customs duty on the export of wool, for this provided greatly improved security for the lenders, to whom the future customs receipts or part of them could be, and often were, assigned for repayment.[64] He and his sucessors, notably Edward III and Richard II, also became adept at manipulating their power over the wool staple in order to pressurize the City into providing loans. And getting loans was not the only way to exploit the City's wealth, for Henry VI sold monopolies of such lucrative offices there as that of wine gauger.[65]

In the thirteenth century the lenders had chiefly been Italian bankers, who alone possessed the techniques and resources required to satisfy royal demands occasioned by frequent wars.[66] After the bankruptcy of the Florentine firms of the Bardi and the Peruzzi in the mid-1340s, however, the London merchants came into their own. One of the first of these was Sir John Pulteney (d. 1349), alderman, mayor, and draper, who frequently lent large sums to Edward III. He was also a backer of William De La Pole (d. 1366), the greatest English royal financier of the mid-fourteenth century. Although the Poles' family power base was in distant Hull, William nevertheless found it convenient to run a large house in the heart of London, in Lombard Street, next door to that of his brother Richard, who also made loans to Edward III and who became enough of a Londoner to be elected an alderman.[67] By 1377 a group of City merchants headed by Nicholas Brembre and William Walworth had lent the enormous sum of £10,000, while the City itself

*The standard English broadcloth was approximately 24 yards long and 1.5 to 2 yards wide.

corporately advanced another £5,000, the principal pledge (soon redeemed) for the repayment of both loans being the receipts from the London wool customs.[68]

Richard II continued to borrow freely throughout his reign, particularly in the earlier years, and London's contributions to these loans amounted to nearly one-third of the total, easily outweighing those of all other cities and boroughs put together. Henry IV borrowed still more freely, London's share of the total being even greater (around 44 per cent), but the City as a unit hung back, perhaps because it regarded a usurper as a bad risk, and certainly demonstrating in its resistance to royal importunities a much stronger position vis-à-vis the Crown than hitherto.[69] So the advances made by individual merchants were correspondingly greater, and the greatest of them was Richard Whittington, three times mayor of London. He had made his fortune as a mercer dealing in luxury goods, his customers including several great men of Richard II's court; and in 1392–4 he was supplying the royal household itself through the Great Wardrobe with goods to the value of over £3,400. Thence he moved naturally into the business of royal finance, and between 1388 and 1422 (the year before his death) he made seven loans to Richard II totalling some £2,000, and fifty-one to Henry IV amounting to some £30,000. In many cases repayment was secured by assignments upon the wool tax at various ports, and this led him into a third field of activity, as collector of the wool tax in London and also as a considerable exporter of wool.[70]

His long career exemplifies the growing interdependence of court and City, and the delicate balance between the needs of State finance and the preservation of civic privilege. Henry VI was even more dependent on loans from London than his predecessor — between 1448 and 1460, for instance, the City corporately gave or lent some £30,000 and the merchants of the Calais staple another £60,000. Edward IV, to whom large loans had also been made in the 1460s and 1470s, summarily paid off his debts to the City by selling various long-disputed rights and privileges to the mayor and citizens. Neither Crown nor City could afford to do without the other.[71]

'The Flower of Cities all'

According to the legend, it was as he was trudging homeward up Highgate Hill that Dick Whittington turned to take a last look at London and heard the bells of St Mary le Bow proclaiming 'Turn again, Whittington, thrice Lord Mayor of London'. Although it seems rather unlikely that he would have taken this road, his family roots being in the West Country, it certainly was from Highgate Hill that thousands of people from many parts of England caught their first glimpse of London. Their first immediate impression must have been of the sheer size of the place, three times as large as Bristol or York, enclosed by landward walls 2 miles in length, and the skyline dominated by St Paul's and a forest of church towers and spires. Here was something totally different from anywhere else in the land.

St Paul's itself was one of the greatest cathedrals in Christendom (Plate 16). The eastern arm, twelve bays in length, was rebuilt in the Gothic style in the second half of the thirteenth century, while the equally immense Norman nave was widely used for business and all manner of other profane purposes. Soaring over the crossing was the great tower and steeple, the latter (first completed in 1221 and finally destroyed by lightning in 1561) some 500 feet in height and dwarfing the spires of the churches closely clustered within the City's walls.[72] Most of these towers and spires were built in the later Middle Ages, when many of the little Saxon or Norman parish churches were enlarged or rebuilt with aisles, porches, and perhaps a chantry chapel, and embellished with peals of bells, all reflecting Londoners' piety and their growing wealth. Hardly any visible traces of this burst of medieval creative energy now survive, but St Sepulchre's Without Newgate, despite much alteration, still retains some fifteenth-century flavour.[73]

Even less survives of the monastic houses founded in the later Middle Ages. During the thirteenth century five friaries were established in London. The Augustinians (or Austins) settled near Broad Street and the Crutched Friars (or Friars of the Holy Cross) near present-day Fenchurch Street Station; but the two largest were those of the Greyfriars in Newgate Street, in the monastic buildings of which Christ's Hospital School was founded after the Dissolution, and of the Dominican Blackfriars, whose monastery near the mouth of the Fleet River took in the sites Baynard's Castle and Montfichet Tower and was palatial enough for Parliament to meet there (in 1311) and for the Emperor Charles V to stay there in 1522. Almost next door, though just outside the walls of the City, were the Carmelite Whitefriars, of whom John of Gaunt was a patron.[74]

Also just outside the walls were the Franciscan Minoresses, from whom the street to the north of the Tower and now known as Minories takes its name; and nearby was the Cistercian Abbey of St Mary Graces, founded in 1349 by Edward III after the Black Death as a plague cemetery. Further north stood the Priory of St Mary Bethlehem, founded in 1247, and which as Bethlehem Royal Hospital (Bedlam) survived the Dissolution and moved, first in 1815 to Lambeth and thence in the 1930s to Beckenham. Probably the last in point of time and certainly the most famous of London's religious houses was the Carthusian monastery at the Charterhouse, founded in 1371 by Sir Walter De Manny, one of Edward III's most redoubtable military commanders, on the site of another plague cemetery. After its dissolution by Henry VIII the Charterhouse eventually became the home of the public school of that name, founded in 1611–14, which remained there until its removal to Godalming in 1872.[75]

Dick Whittington, or any stranger coming from Highgate Hill, would probably have passed close to the Charterhouse and entered the City at Aldersgate — one of the landward gates originally built by the Romans. Several of the gatehouses were now inhabited by City officials, while Geoffrey Chaucer lived 'above the gate at Aldgate' from 1374 to 1386. Ludgate and Newgate were used as prisons, and in 1415 access to the moor to the north of the City, where there were 'divers gardens' or allotments, was improved by the building of Moorgate. The walls themselves, their foundations still Roman, were periodically repaired by the City authorities, and until gunpowder came into use they provided an effective deterrent to all attackers, none of whom ever breached them.[76]

Having passed through Aldersgate the stranger would at once be confronted by the immensity of St Paul's. The cathedral and its precinct were almost a microcosm of London at large, the churchyard enclosed by a high wall within which stood the bishop's palace, the deanery, and the houses of the thirty greater canons, of whom in the mid-fourteenth century about two-thirds were in some way or other in the service of the government. There was also a college and common hall for the lesser clerics concerned with the daily recital of the liturgy, a school, a parish church, and an open-air pulpit at St Paul's Cross, to which the great bell of the cathedral summoned the citizens for meetings of the folkmoot or the proclamation of important public events.[77]

In the narrow crowded streets, many of them only 15 feet wide or less, the traveller would also have been quickly confronted by the butchers' filth in the shambles along Newgate Street, where the slaughtering of animals and the disposal of the offal resulting therefrom frequently exasperated the City authorities.[78] This was the western end of the line of food markets which extended along the City's main east–west streets. By the thirteenth century there were shops — perhaps 400 of them in 1300 — as well as open-air stalls in Cheapside, which was becoming the City's principal retail centre for all manner of high-value manufactured goods. The shops were extremely small (many only some 6 feet by 10 feet), and behind there were alleys lined with 'selds' where traders could store and display their wares in chests or cupboards.[79] Further east were the Stocks market (on the site of the Mansion House) and Leadenhall, both established by the City authorities; and at the end of the long chain of food markets was the ancient East Cheap, not far from the Bridge.

By the end of the Middle Ages London contained a growing variety of secular buildings. In the topmost range were some fifty town houses of bishops and abbots, most of whom were summoned regularly to Parliament, and who therefore tended to have their town base around the Strand, Fleet Street, or Holborn. The bishops of Ely, for instance, had their palace off Holborn, and the church of St Etheldreda's in Ely Place was their private chapel. London's merchant mandarins were also building their own mansions (the great hall and wooden roof of Crosby Hall, originally in Bishopsgate, still survives in re-erected form in Chelsea), and almost all of these palaces were laid out around a courtyard, with the main chamber — the hall — at the back and a range of lesser buildings fronting the street. Livery companies followed much the same lines in the building of their halls, of which by 1475 there were well over a score.[80]

Run-of-the-mill houses might have stone foundations, but above ground they were mostly lined with lathe, loam, and plaster on a timber-frame. In the fifteenth century bricks were being used for chimney stacks, and windows were often embellished with glass. Most houses stood end-on to the street, with gabled frontages, and might have only two or even one room per floor; but, as carpenters' expertise increased, three-storey buildings with overhanging jetties sometimes over 5 feet in length provided more living space for the occupants. In central areas like Cheapside, where land values were high, many houses had five storeys, while in suburbs such as Houndsditch small two-storey cottages predominated. Inns, of which there were some 200 in the 1380s, were chiefly concentrated outside the City gates or in Southwark, where there was room for long narrow stable yards. After the Black Death pressure on space probably declined, and in the early sixteenth century there were gardens and orchards even within the walled area. Privacy, however, was always a rare and expensive commodity in medieval London.[81]

The Commercial Waterfront

The most important topographical change in later medieval London was the advancement of the waterfront southward from Thames Street. Most of this reclamation was done piecemeal by individual property owners, who extended their narrow river frontages further and further out into the river, their quays and wharves and warehouses being protected from tide and current by timber or stone defences. This process was virtually complete by around 1500, when a sliver of land extending from Blackfriars to the Tower and in places up to 350 feet wide had been reclaimed. Wyngaerde's panorama of *c*.1544 shows the irregular but very solid buildings which stood upon it, one of the most solid being the German merchants' privileged enclave of the Steelyard, its site now occupied by Cannon Street Station. Until the early fourteenth century Queenhithe — probably the oldest of London's Saxon harbours — was the principal public landing place for goods, and is still marked by a deep inlet in the line of the rest of the modern waterfront. But as the tonnage of ships grew larger the passage through London Bridge became more difficult, and the centre of gravity of the port moved downstream to Billingsgate, beside which was built the first royal Custom House.[82]

Royal and Civic Undertakings

Despite its overwhelmingly commercial functions the City waterfront was nevertheless dominated by two great public undertakings, one royal and the other civic: the Tower and the Bridge. During the thirteenth century the Tower was enormously enlarged and strengthened: Henry III surrounded the Normans' White Tower with a new curtain wall and eight towers, thereby doubling the enclosed area of the castle, and Edward I constructed an outer curtain wall and moat, plus an elaborate western land entrance and a great watergate (Plate 17). Although there were splendidly appointed royal apartments there, Henry III seldom used them except in times of political crisis, and the Tower became more a place of retreat from rebellious subjects than either a place of residence or a defence from foreign invaders. While it also contained the royal armoury, mint, prison, treasure house for the royal records and Crown jewels, and even the royal menagerie of exotic animals (including leopards, a polar bear, and an elephant), throughout most of its history it was first and foremost 'like a fleet kept in being; its passive presence important for controlling London'.[83]

It was probably with this same purpose in mind that, after the disuse of the private castles of Baynard and Montfichet at the western end of the City water-front, Edward I had the course of the City wall adjusted to take in the newly established precinct of the Black Friars, thereby establishing within the City a royal footing readily accessible from Westminster if need should arise.[84]

The maintenance of the walls, gates, and of course the great stone bridge built between 1176 and 1209 (and described in Chapter 5) was the responsibility of the City authorities; and successive kings, while concerned for the safety of London from external attack, may also have eyed the strength of the City's defences with some foreboding. Londoners' resources were truly immense, and defence was not the only field of construction in which the City Fathers were busy. There were prisons and markets to be managed, and above all there was the provision of an adequate supply of water. Much of the City's need was supplied from the Thames or from wells, but in the mid-thirteenth century water was brought in lead pipes from springs near Tyburn, some 3 miles from the City, to a conduit head in Cheapside, the flow being provided solely by gravity and natural pressure. In the fifteenth century the system was extended eastward up Cornhill, and when the supply was increased by water taken from springs at Paddington, 200 tons of lead had to be purchased for the pipes.[85]

Most of this water eventually drained away in one way or another into the hundreds of cesspits with which the surface of the City was honeycombed, some of them 20 feet deep and large enough for a man to drown in. Privies were often put up directly over these pits, and several of the dozen or more public latrines which existed in the fourteenth century were built over running water, on London Bridge, at Queenhithe and over the Walbrook, for instance.[86] Sanitary regulations were enforced either by the Assize of Nuisance (consisting of twelve aldermen) or by the wardmotes, in which the local alderman presided. Tolls, taxes, and statute labour were levied to pay for street cleaning; there were rakers, scavengers, and surveyors of the pavements to see to the work; and filth and rubbish were removed by teams of horses and carts or by river in dung boats, all either hired or owned by the City's embryonic sanitary department.[87]

Last in this series of civil undertakings was the building of the City's Guildhall. Since at least the thirteenth century civic government had been conducted from a hall on part of the present site. Between 1411 and 1431 (years of comparative calm in the City's affairs) a great new guildhall — the largest in the realm — was built in the Perpendicular style; and around this immense ceremonial chamber there were clustered civic offices, courtrooms, a chapel, and a library. Perhaps the new Guildhall was a response to Richard II's recent embellishment of Westminster Hall; it was certainly (to quote its historian, Caroline Barron) 'an eloquent monument to the civic pride, wealth and administrative skill of the fifteenth-century Londoners'.[88] Despite being twice devastated by fire, in 1666 and 1940, the crypt, porch, and walls still stand unshaken and unshakeable.

Suburbs, Southwark, and Westminster

From time immemorial the City's jurisdiction had extended over a sizeable area outside the walls. The limits of this extramural area were marked by bars across the principal roads — as, for example, at Temple Bar and Holborn Bars — beyond which straggled unorganized but growing suburbs. This outward spread was greatest towards the west, where in 1394 the Ward of Farringdon, which had hitherto straddled the wall, was divided into two: Farringdon Within and Farringdon Without, each with its own alderman.[89] Already these new suburbs were becoming more socially distinct from one another, for as Westminster became more and more the normal seat of royal power so it and the western suburbs became the natural place of residence for court, clerks, and Parliament men. Just as naturally the eastern waterside suburbs became the centre for the repair, fitting out, and victualling of ships, while away from the Thames there was lime-burning, brickmaking, and metalwork. Along the River Lea there were fulling mills, and closer to the City there were clustered the braziers, spurriers, arrowsmiths, and all manner of craftsmen whose skills were needed for the supply of the Tower (Plates 15 and 20).[90]

To the west of the City stood the town houses of bishops, abbots, and growing numbers of lay magnates, the greatest of these being the Palace of the Savoy, built *c.*1345–70 by Henry Duke of Lancaster at vast expense from the proceeds of his campaigns in France. Fleet Street and the Strand were becoming arteries of conspicuous consumption,[91] and through its situation midway between the City and Westminster this neighbourhood also became the natural stamping ground of the nascent legal profession. Gradually there developed the four Inns of Court — Lincoln's Inn, Inner Temple, Middle Temple, and Gray's Inn — wholly independent bodies for the study and practice of the law whose members enjoyed a monopoly of pleading at the Bar (and continued to do so until very recently). At least one of these powerful societies — that of the Inner Temple — has occupied its present site for over 600 years, since the mid-fourteenth-century lease granted to the lawyers by the Order of Knights Hospitallers. Hardly a stone's throw away in what was already the legal quarter of London was the Domus Conversorum in Chancery Lane, originally built by Henry III for converted Jews, but which after the expulsion of the Jews from England in 1290 was used for the accommodation of Chancery clerks and the storage of Chancery records, and on the site of which stands the Public Record Office, now at the time of writing (1997) empty and forlorn, but until a couple of years ago still used as the repository of medieval legal and other archives.[92]

Across the river lay London's oldest suburb: unruly raffish Southwark, sprawling outward from the bridgehead which was its *raison d'être* down the High Street, Tooley Street, and Bermondsey Street. Despite being commonly known as 'the Borough', Southwark had no central civic authority, and public control was exercised by five separate manorial courts. Outside the City yet very close to it, Southwark was therefore a natural refuge for the outcast and the rejected:

craftsmen not free of their guilds (who could practise their trades there without interference), alien immigrants (especially Flemings), prostitutes, and down-and-outs of all kinds; and it was notorious for its evil-smelling tanneries, its numerous prisons, and its general lawlessness. But Southwark was also a travel centre, the natural point of departure or arrival for pilgrims and travellers to or from Canterbury or the Continent; so the main street was lined with great inns such as Chaucer's Tabard, where brewing, victualling, stabling, and carting all provided work. Yet despite its always being the poor relation of the powerful City at the other end of the bridge, Southwark by the time of Henry VIII paid more tax in the subsidy of 1543–4 than the great City and County of Bristol; and it was primarily economic motives which drove the City Fathers to buy (by royal charters granted to them in 1327, 1462 and 1550) a measure of control over this rich but turbulent neighbour.[93]

Lastly there was Westminster. Like Southwark, it was outside the City's jurisdiction and lacked borough status; and the size of their resident populations (each estimated at about 2,000 around 1400) was very similar.[94] But their *raisons d'être*—abbey and royal court (Westminster) and bridgehead (Southwark)— were quite different, and Westminster had only a single manorial court, that of the abbey, which in addition to large expanses of open land also owned two-thirds of the urban area. In 1300 this extended along much of the road from Charing Cross to the palace, skirted round the abbey precinct, and thence along the north side of Tothill Street. The economy was mainly based on supplying the requirements of visitors: pilgrims, lawyers, suitors, courtiers, Parliament men, and great nobles, plus their often numerous attendants. So most of the inhabitants of Westminster were involved in one way or another in the victualling trades, taverns being at least as numerous as in Southwark; as were prostitutes. Upmarket tailors flourished, and there was a virtually continuous demand for building craftsmen.[95] Nearly all of these trades depended in large measure upon the frequent presence of the Parliament men and royal household, which in the later Middle Ages numbered between 200 and 400. Luckily for the fortunes of the tradesmen of Westminster the less frequent meetings of Parliament in the fifteenth century were compensated by the longer residences of the king, and hence by the royal council's more numerous meetings there. Even so, there were marked fluctuations in Westminster's prosperity, not always corresponding with those of the City. Westminster was already a unique urban entity.[96]

Londoners

Written evidence for the later Middle Ages is very much more plentiful than for any previous period. For the first time in the history of London thousands of the people who lived there are known to posterity by name, and by much else too. Who they were, where they came from, their education and learning, their social and religious behaviour — all these are fields which from the thirteenth century onwards can be charted with increasing precision.

Throughout the medieval period London was largely peopled by immigrants, upon whom it depended for its survival — as, indeed, had always been the case since Roman times. Medieval migrants journeyed to London from all parts of England, but until around the mid-thirteenth century most came from the Home Counties and the South-East. Thereafter there was an influx from the Midlands and East Anglia which was large enough (or influential enough, some of these immigrants being well-to-do cloth-traders) to modify the spoken dialect hitherto prevalent in London into the East Midland type of speech from which later evolved the early standard English of the whole nation.[97] However the Scottish wars and the periodic residence of the court in the North stimulated more distant contacts with London, and late fifteenth-century records show that nearly half of all the apprentices enrolled at that time by the tailors' and the skinners' guilds or companies came from the northern counties — in marked contrast with the situation in Paris, where over half the immigrants came from the nearby Île de France.[98]

London's immigrants were drawn from every social class, and their reasons for coming were equally diverse. At the top of the social pyramid, and (unlike all other migrants) not permanently resident in London, were the bishops, abbots, and territorial magnates of England. More numerous were the priests and religious; and Chaucer relates that many of those who served in the City's three hundred chantries had

> . . . run to London to earn easy bread
> By singing Masses for the dead,
> Or find some Brotherhood and get enrolled.

At the Inns of Court students came from all over the country, creating a continuous interplay between capital and provinces well illustrated in the career of William Paston (1378–1444), the son of a lowly Norfolk husbandman who studied law in London before building up a flourishing practice in his native county and ultimately becoming a justice in the Court of Common Pleas at Westminster. At the time of his death he owned lands in Hertfordshire and Suffolk as well as in Norfolk, and a considerable amount of ready money and plate.[99]

For countless other migrants the possibility of accumulating such riches added to London's natural attraction as the principal centre of trade and industry. Many younger sons with no hope of any family inheritance were drawn up, a case in point being Richard (Dick) Whittington (d. 1423), the third son of a small landowner in Gloucestershire. Other migrants, probably very numerous, were recruited from the commercial or industrial sections of villages and small towns, and were often of burgess stock, as was Chaucer's grandfather, a burgess of Ipswich. There were also many migrants of servile origin, who acquired free status if they had lived unchallenged in the City for a year and a day. In the fourteenth century some villeins were still being reclaimed, though with difficulty, even so distinguished a person as a London alderman and sheriff being arrested as a villein while on a visit to his native village in Norfolk, and having a long struggle to disprove the charge.[100]

There was also a small number of alien migrants from overseas, perhaps amounting in the fifteenth century to some 2 to 4 per cent of London's total population.[101] The Jews had been expelled by Edward I in 1290 (they were not allowed to return until the 1650s), and their place as moneylenders was taken intermittently by the Italian merchants, expert in international money dealings as well as in trade. There was also the Hanseatic merchant community in the Steelyard, but both Italians and Germans were very small in number and only transient residents in London. By far the most numerous aliens were the 'Doches': Flemings and Dutch. They settled permanently, mainly in the suburbs or Southwark, where, free from guild and civic interference, they could practise the valuable skills which they brought with them, notably weaving, brewing, and metalwork.[102]

Women and Children

It is likely that in the later fourteenth century women outnumbered men in London, so if children are also included this section of the population must certainly have amounted to well over half the total. The records relating to women were rarely compiled by women, and are often permeated with the circumstances of their husbands, whether living or dead. This was particularly so in the case of the wives or widows of citizen freemen, about whom more is known than about other women. But this group formed only a minority of the total female population, for perhaps only one in three of the adult men were citizens (though the proportion rose in the sixteenth century);[103] and the majority of medieval London's women left no trace of their existence — other, of course, than through the pangs of childbirth.

Most women married, and childbirth was the central reality of perhaps about twenty years of their lives. The mortality rate amongst London mothers and infants is not known, but in Florence in the 1420s the deaths of one in every five married women seem to have been associated with childbearing. There too nearly half of all babies are estimated to have died at or shortly after birth,[104] and in London the rate of childhood mortality may well have been comparable.[105] So for both women and men marriage was often a stony path, the security of the matrimonial state being probably a common reason why women trod it. For *femmes soles* the commonest alternatives were the convent (which offered a different kind of security), domestic servitude, or prostitution. Women had to pay a high price for even such security as matrimony might provide, for on marriage the husband acquired control of his wife's freehold lands for the duration of the marriage, plus absolute possession of her goods and chattels. Nor could women take part in the government of ward or guild or be members of either Common Council or the Court of Aldermen.[106]

Yet despite this subordination the later Middle Ages were in some senses a golden age for women. Shortage of labour after the Black Death opened new opportunities for them, and in the City there were privileges to be enjoyed from 'the custom of London' which were not available elsewhere. A woman married to a freeman could share in the advantages of his status, rent a shop, trade on her own account, and take in her own apprentices; and a widow had the right to a house and income for life (unless she remarried) and a substantial share of her husband's goods and chattels. Many widows of freemen (and there were a great many widows in London, partly because men married women younger than themselves) did continue their husband's business, and could devise lands, money, and movable wealth as they pleased. The main fields in which women have always worked were already apparent, notably clothing (including silk), victualling, drink (including brewing), and laundering; but unusual occupations included those of broker, bookbinder, and even armourer.[107]

By the end of the fifteenth century this supposed golden age for women was coming to an end. Due to growth of population there was no longer a labour shortage, and it became difficult for women to enrol as apprentices or to bind them and run their own businesses. Their historian, Dr Caroline Barron, even thinks that 'In some senses women lost ground in the sixteenth century in the City of London which has still to be recovered.'[108]

But while women's lot fluctuated, childhood was always a precarious pilgrimage. Upbringing and education were as much concerned with the inculcation of respect for authority and the established moral order of things as with instruction in the three Rs, and beating was universally accepted as the best way to enforce obedience. Apprenticeship, which generally began at about the age of 14 and involved leaving the family home, marked the break between childhood and adolescence; and for a child to attain majority was itself an achievement, for something like a third of the orphans of London freemen died between the ages of 7 and 21.[109]

Education and Learning

During the later Middle Ages there was a very large expansion of literacy, and from the later twelfth century, and more particularly from the thirteenth, far more written records of public business, chiefly relating to finance or justice, were produced than ever before, as the lists of archives in the Public Record Office or the Corporation of London's Records Office clearly show. Most of these records were compiled in London or Westminster, and most of them were written in Latin or French, but English was being increasingly used as a literary, legal, and commercial language, and eventually it superseded Latin as the principal written as well as spoken language. To 'get on' in later medieval London — the chief seat of court, government, and the law, as well as a place of immense importance for both the Church and the world of commerce — it was essential for a man or woman to be literate. Ability to read and write was, for instance, a condition of admission to apprenticeship in some City guilds; and it has been calculated that by the 1460s and 1470s 40 per cent of all lay male Londoners could read Latin, while even more could in all probability read English. Nor were women far behind, to judge from the frequency with which they acted as their husbands' executors and ran their own businesses.[110]

Most London children probably learned to read and write either at home or at small informal schools often provided by chantry or other priests without a full-time cure of souls — the forerunners of the 'petty' or 'dame' schools of later centuries. There were also song schools attached to churches, notably at St Paul's, where boys learned to read and sing the liturgy; and several more of these schools were founded in the fifteenth century. At a higher level London's three or four grammar schools, where Latin was almost the only subject taught, were all located at important churches such as St Martin's le Grand, or at Westminster Abbey, where a grammar school was kept in the almonry from the fourteenth century. But from the 1390s the Church's monopoly was being challenged by the establishment of half a dozen 'unlicensed' grammar schools, which the authorities at St Paul's were unable to prevent; and in the 1440s a group of enterprising London rectors secured the foundation at Cambridge of a teacher training college, later to evolve into Christ's College.[111]

London had no university of its own until the nineteenth century but it nevertheless enjoyed considerable intellectual and literary eminence at a much earlier date. St Paul's and the open-air pulpit at Paul's Cross within the cathedral precinct were centres of theological and preaching activities; and at the Inns of Court London was also the national centre for the training of lawyers in the later Middle Ages, when law formed a much larger proportion of the sum of knowledge than in later times and when the English common law was not taught at the two universities of Oxford and Cambridge. There were libraries at St Paul's, Westminster Abbey, and many of the religious houses, and even in some parish churches. The famous 'public' library at Guildhall was first formed in about 1423, financed by the executors of Richard Whittington, who had himself contributed £400 to the building of a library at Grey Friars.[112] Other rich London merchants founded schools not in London but in their own native towns, and entrusted the management of them to their own particular livery company. These pre-Reformation 'company schools' were in widely separated parts of England, and several of them still survive, that set up in 1487 by Sir Edmund Shaa, a goldsmith, in Stockport, Cheshire, being a case in point.[113]

London was also pre-eminent in the field of creative literature. Authors had to support themselves as best they might, and London offered them the widest variety of employment and was the best place to solicit the favour of rich patrons. Geoffrey Chaucer (?1340–1400), who was the son of a London vintner, made his living chiefly in a succession of posts in the royal service. Thomas Hoccleve (?*c*.1370–?*c*.1450) was a clerk in the privy seal office for twenty-four years, and William Langland (late fourteenth century), although a native of the West Midlands, seems to have lived most of his impoverished and sometimes mendicant adult life in London. John Gower (?*c*.1325–1408), though himself not poor, spent his later years in London at the Priory of St Mary Overie (now Southwark

Cathedral), where his tomb may still be seen. It was at Westminster that after his long residence abroad William Caxton chose to set up his printing press, close to the courtly circles where patrons were to be found, and where between 1477 and 1491 he printed nearly eighty separate books. The mounting metropolitan demand for reading matter gave rise to the formation of half a dozen 'bookmaking' craft guilds, such as those of the text writers or the bookbinders.[114]

The Religious and Civic Community

The Christian religion was as real to medieval Londoners as the air they breathed or the ground they trod, for never in the history of the whole Western World, either before or since, was one particular interpretation of the meaning of life so universally and unquestioningly accepted. Salvation could only be gained through the Church and its sacraments; and in London the miracle of the Mass was celebrated daily in a galaxy of parish churches, chantry chapels, and religious houses. The observances of the Church permeated into every corner of life throughout the whole community, enfolding all its members within the confines of their shared faith.

The parish churches, well over a hundred in number including those in the suburbs, were the bedrock of the visible Church. Stained glass and walls heavily painted with religious imagery produced a soft light to which flickering votive candles and devotional sculpture added the sense of mystery later destroyed by the Reformers' whitewash and clear windows. Worshippers stood or knelt upon the stone floors, for there were in general no seats for the laity, and as they listened to the priest's *sotto voce* recital of the Latin liturgy they also made their own private supplications, reaching out for the 'perfyte loue and charitie' with one another which was demanded by the Church. On the other hand, however, it seems that in practice throughout England behaviour in church was often irreverent, some priests ignorant and/or worldly, their preaching spasmodic and perfunctory until the arrival of the friars, and the services performed with little dignity.

Parishioners were of course well known to each other as neighbours, for the parish church was seldom further than just around the corner, and through the bond of shared worship it was often the centre of a small close-knit community. Many churches had perpetual post-obit intercessionary foundations, i.e. chantries with their own stipendiary priests and supporting property endowments, and the presence of chantry priests enriched standards of ceremony and music. The parishes were also the focus of nearly 200 fraternities (some short-lived) which originated as communal chantries for Londoners unable to afford to endow their own private chantry, and which multiplied in the two centuries after the Black Death. Gradually their original activities — the provision of seemly burial and prayers for their members — extended into care for the poor and feasts preceded by the celebration of a fraternity Mass, and served generally as a channel for laymen and laywomen (for many of their members were women) to participate in the affairs of the parish.[115]

It seems that these parish affairs were often managed by a self-perpetuating élite consisting of the parson, the wealthier parishioners, the churchwardens, and the alderman of the local ward; and in the building of a new aisle or the management of the church's chantry endowments quite large sums of money could be involved. While the records show that *multi alii* besides the élite sometimes attended parish meetings, it was the great and the good who often gave money and put in long periods of service to their parish; and this was of course regarded as a way of gaining spiritual merit, to which the commendatory prayers of the generality of the parish for such benefactors were a natural complementary response.[116]

In the century or so before the Reformation many of the City's parishes were, it seems, well-articulated small communities in which everyone had their own vital contribution to make. Much late medieval pious endeavour was motivated by the urge for continual prayer for both the living and for the souls in purgatory, and heavenly reward could also be earned by works of charity. Hence there were frequent doles for the poor: at funerals, at feasts, at church doors after Mass, and through testators' bequests. Medieval giving of this kind has often in more recent times been criticized as indiscriminate and ephemeral in effect, and more concerned with the spiritual welfare of the donor than with the physical well-being of the recipient. So it is worth noting that in the later Middle Ages London possessed over thirty hospitals and almshouses for the care of the sick, aged, and destitute. Most of them followed the Augustinian religious rule and, to quote their recent historian, 'owed their foundation and upkeep to the philanthropy of wealthy merchants'. There were also ten leper hospitals, standing in a ring around the City, the most famous of which was that of St James, in the fields near Westminster.[117]

Several of these hospitals were associated with one of the City's livery companies, and three of those for lepers had been founded by the mayor and aldermen. For an ambitious citizen service in the parish, besides earning spiritual merit, also opened the way to office at ward and guild levels, and even at Guildhall itself. As in the parishes, many of the business activities of the guilds or livery companies were closely associated with prayers for the souls of deceased members, the relief of the poor, and the celebration of the feasts of the Church. It was, for instance, the Skinners' Company which provided splendid processions on the feast of Corpus Christi, which falls in early summer, a suitable time for such outdoor festivities. Civic awareness of London's unique stature was finding varied means of expression: in the use (since the thirteenth century) of London's own coat of arms and its own motto, which naturally took the form of a prayer — 'Domine, Dirige Nos'; in pageants, processions to St Paul's, or the celebration of such great national occasions as a coronation or the return of Henry V after Agincourt; and the splendour of all such events was enhanced by the brilliantly coloured clothes in vogue in the later Middle Ages, shown off by new dyes imported from far afield and (for men) worn in the tightly fitting fashions made possible by the discovery of cutting cloth on the cross.[118]

The most important event in the civic calendar was the annual swearing-in of the new mayor. The charter granted to the City by King John in May 1215 on the eve of the Magna Charta crisis had recognized London's right to the mayoralty but had required all future incumbents to present themselves to the sovereign or in his absence to his justices to swear fealty. At first each mayor, accompanied by the sheriffs, aldermen, and leading guildsmen, had ridden on horseback from the City to the king's palace at Westminster, which was of course the usual seat of the royal courts of justice. From the middle of the fifteenth century until 1856 the mayor and his retinue travelled by water, but since the removal of the lawcourts to the Strand in the 1880s the procession — now known as the Lord Mayor's Show — goes little further than Temple Bar. Use of the grander title 'Lord Mayor' gradually came in during the fifteenth century, and the newly rebuilt Guildhall provided a suitable setting for each Lord Mayor's banquet, an annual event for over four centuries. Such indeed has become the Lord Mayor's state that today he has precedence within the City over every other subject of the sovereign; and even in the fifteenth century he had precedence there over the archbishops and the king's brothers, and was assessed to the poll tax as an earl.[119]

London and Paris

By the end of the Middle Ages London and Paris had emerged as the capital cities of the two principal states of Western Europe. Whereas England had for several centuries been highly centralized, with strong uniform institutions and law, and regionalism was correspondingly weak, the French state had been assembled more recently through the expansion of the Capetian monarchy from its heartland in the Île de France, beyond which it was confronted by powerful regional forces. So the historical structure of the two states differed fundamentally; and so too did that of their capital cities.

Medieval Paris had originated on an island in the Seine, where stood the royal citadel or fortress-palace, and from this tiny nucleus the city had throughout the Middle Ages expanded on both sides of the river. In London, by contrast, the confines of the medieval city had followed largely unchanged the line of the Roman walls; and from the time of Edward the Confessor Westminster had replaced the walled City itself as the principal metropolitan seat of the monarchy. So the French kings' mastery in Paris was much greater than that of their English counterparts in London — even the Louvre, which gradually became the principal place of Parisian royal residence, was originally an integral part of the medieval fortifications of the expanding city, not separate from it, as Westminster was from London. The *prévôt* of Paris was a royal official, and no separate municipal administration emerged there until the mid-thirteenth century, long after that of London.[120]

Royal mastery of Paris is also exemplified in the successive enlargements of the walled area or enceinte of the city by Philip (II) Augustus (1180–1223) and Charles V

(1364–80). In Roman times the walled area of London (133 hectares) was one of the largest in Western Europe, and probably about twice as big as that of contemporary Lutetia (Paris). But after the two medieval enlargements the enclosed area of Paris, comprising ground on both sides of the Seine, was over three times as big as that of medieval London.[121] By the end of the Middle Ages Brussels, Bruges, Ghent, and even faraway Novgorod as well as Paris were all larger in area than London; and in all these cities the original enceinte had been enlarged at least once. In English cities, on the other hand, the building of successive lines of defence was much less common (though enlargements made at Bristol and Northampton are notable exceptions), the generally more secure condition of the island making such expensive investment less necessary than on the Continent.[122]

The reasons why the two cities grew were also very different. Paris grew to be the largest city in Western Europe because it was the seat of a powerful monarchy and because from the time of Philip Augustus it became the permanent seat of royal justice and financial administration — everybody with business of State to transact had to come to Paris, even when the king was not there; and in the thirteenth century the university drew large numbers of students to Paris from all over Christendom. London, by contrast, was above all a centre of manufacturing and particularly of trade, both domestic and overseas — this was the honey pot which had drawn successive monarchs from Saxon times onwards to it. In landlocked Paris, however, trade was pre-eminently concerned either with the provisioning of this 'demographic monster' or with the supply of luxury goods, while as a centre of long-distance commerce Paris was merely an annexe of Bruges.[123]

Just as geographical situation was of course an underlying ingredient in these economic contrasts, so too war, combined with internal factions and social émeutes, was a principal cause of the great fluctuations in the fortunes of medieval Paris. This was much more extreme than in the case of London, and continued to be a periodic feature of the history of Paris. From its apogee in the early fourteenth century, when its population of some 200,000 was at least twice as big as that of London and its intellectual and cultural prestige had spread throughout Europe, Paris declined after the ravages of the Black Death and the wars with England to the haggard city of the 1420s: occupied by the English 1420–36, for nearly a century a capital seldom visited by the king, still a gigantic centre of consumption but supported by only slender resources of production, with thousands of houses deserted and its population halved.[124] No catastrophe of this magnitude has ever (not even the Black Death or the Plague and Great Fire of 1665–6) beset London since the Dark Ages; yet Parisian vitality was such that well before the end of the fifteenth century the city had in large measure recovered, and once more became, like London, the capital of the realm. By then both London and Paris enjoyed incontestible ascendancy within their respective states; but in the turbulent world of the sixteenth and seventeenth centuries the paths of the two cities were to diverge further from each other than they ever had during the Middle Ages.

PART III

The Genesis of Modern London
1530–1700

INTRODUCTION

Towards the end of the sixteenth century London burst out of its ancient confines, and the built-up area began to spread out over the surrounding countryside in all directions — a process that was to continue with varying intensity until well into the twentieth century. By around 1600 London was already by far the largest centre of population, the largest market for consumer goods, and the largest industrial centre in the realm. It was also the chief port and commercial and financial centre as well as the seat of government and the lawcourts; and increasingly it was becoming the national centre of fashion and social intercourse. These differences between London and the provinces had now become so great that they amounted to differences of kind and no longer merely of degree. Through the pervasive influence of its very uniqueness London was beginning to loosen the bonds of time-honoured assumptions and ways of thought and behaviour, and was becoming the harbinger of new social attitudes and motivations. In the world overseas London had by 1700 become the most populous of all Western European towns and cities, poised to become the foremost commercial city in the world, eventually surpassing even Amsterdam and already far surpassing Paris.

These themes are discussed in Chapter 7. But there were other fields of equal importance for both London itself and for the nation. Without London's acquiescence the Henrician Reformation would surely have taken a very different course, and the secularization of much of London life which ensued from the destruction of the religious houses and chantries there marked the end of the compact medieval civic community hitherto knit together by an almost universally accepted religious faith (Chapter 8). Politically, too, London on several occasions played a decisive role in the constitutional struggles of the seventeenth century (Chapter 9). Internally, the suburban expansion of London was impelled under the leasehold system of estate development for some three centuries (c.1600–1900), and at Covent Garden in the 1630s a new and almost as long-lasting mode of residential town planning emerged (Chapter 10). The problem of how to govern the sprawling new metropolis was not successfully solved, however, and the legacy of this seventeenth-century failure still troubles London today (Chapter 11). All in all, the period between around 1530 and 1700 was the most momentous in the whole history of the capital, and by the latter date such social features of modern life in London as its vastness, its anonymity, its precariousness, and its underlying stability despite the prevalence of extremes of wealth and poverty, were already manifest (Chapter 12). London had travelled far towards becoming the prototype for modern metropolitan civilization.

7

The Rise of the Metropolis

Far more is known about this crucial period of the sixteenth and seventeenth centuries than about any earlier times. The growing use of printing, and of paper in place of costly parchment as a writing material, the spread of literacy, and the inauguration of numerous new series of public records such as the State Papers have all provided posterity with deep new mines of information. For London itself there is John Stow's great *Survey of London* (1598), the first full-length printed account of the capital; and above all there are the registers of christenings, marriages, and burials which in 1538 every parish throughout the land was required to keep (though by no means all of them have survived), and through the computerized use of which a flood of new light has in recent years been shed upon the numbers and behavioural patterns of the peoples of the nascent metropolis.[1]

Numbers

Through this new technology we now know that, in round numbers, the population of London (as recently estimated) appears to have risen from perhaps some 75,000 in 1550 to 200,000 in 1600; thence to around 400,000 in 1650; and to some 575,000 in 1700.* This perhaps more than sevenfold increase was in marked contrast with that of the rest of England, the population of which in the same period, according to the best estimates, did not even double. This disparity in the rate of growth was particularly marked between 1550 and 1650, when London's numbers grew by perhaps over 500 per cent, while those of the rest of England increased by possibly around 60 per cent; and in the second half of the seventeenth century the population of England excluding London actually fell, while that of London continued to rise, though at a slower rate than previously. So whereas in 1550 the population of London may have amounted to only some 2.5 per cent of the whole of England, by 1700 the proportion had grown to over 11 per cent; and it

---

* Modern estimates vary greatly, figures as high as 120,000 for 1550 and as low as 490,000 for 1700 having been given by Roger Finlay and Beatrice Shearer.[2]

has even been argued that by around 1700 one in every six of the peoples of England had at some stage of their lives had direct experience of London life.[3]

Whatever the precise figures may really have been (and learned discussions about them will certainly continue), what is not in doubt is that the growth of London's population was unique, and that (as we shall see later) it had immensely important repercussions on the rest of the country, notably in the stimulation of agricultural productivity — the indispensable precondition for economic advance. Why this upsurge of population took place is not, however, clear, and Professor Sir Tony Wrigley, whose writings have shed so much light on the role of the metropolis, has admitted that 'the reasons for the exceptional growth of London from the early sixteenth to the late seventeenth century remain imperfectly understood. Its rise both deserves and demands much more attention than it has received.'[4]

The growth was moreover unique in both its extent and in its persistence. In England provincial towns with over 5,000 inhabitants were until around 1700 growing at little more than the national average rate (excluding London), and certainly nothing like as fast as the capital, the population of which was throughout far greater than that of all other English towns combined. In comparison with continental Europe too, London's growth was greater and more continuous than that of any other metropolis. From about 1650 onwards the population of such large centres as Naples, Madrid, and Venice all began to fall; and even in Paris, where in 1550 the population had been more than double that of London, growth virtually ceased after about 1670. So by about 1700 London became for the first time the largest city in Western Europe, or indeed in the whole of the Western world with perhaps the sole exception of Constantinople, which by around 1750 London had also overtaken. Moreover it was only in Holland that any one city comprised such a large proportion of the total national population as did London. There Amsterdam, with some 200,000 inhabitants in 1650, contained some 8 per cent of the Dutch total, but thereafter its population also began to fall; and in highly centralized France, where the total population was some four times as big as that of England, only 2.5 per cent of the French lived in Paris.[5]

Mortality and Migration

London's unique demographic situation was the product, mainly, of high mortality coupled with very high immigration. Its demographic pattern was therefore different from that of the rest of the country, and indeed from that generally prevalent throughout Western Europe, where late marriage kept down the rate of population growth. Late marriages, giving rise to large numbers of single young adults and a low rate of fertility, were of course also prevalent in London — around 1600 the average age of men in London at first marriage appears to have been no less than 28 years[6] — as well as in the provinces, but outside the metropolis the depletion of the adult population caused by periodic high rates of mortality could only be replaced by increased fertility. This was of course a slow process, whereas in London such shortfalls were quickly made good by increased immigration from the rest of the country, where there was in general a substantial excess of births over deaths until the mid-seventeenth century.[7]

The scale of this immigration was so great that it was able to generate the sevenfold increase in the population of the metropolis despite periodic disastrous outbreaks of disease there. One of the earliest of these outbreaks was the epidemic of influenza in 1558–9, when the rate of mortality in London more than doubled.[8] Bubonic plague was, however, a more frequent visitor. Indeed it was seldom completely absent from London until the late seventeenth century, and in many years its presence was strong enough to have a significant impact on the average rates of mortality. But there were also several terrible epidemics, notably those of 1563, 1603, and 1625, during each of which between a fifth and a quarter of the population of London died from all causes — over six times the normal rate of mortality; and in the final and most famous onslaught in 1665 over 80,000 people died from all causes (over five times the normal rate) — roughly equal to the total contemporary number of inhabitants in the five largest provincial cities. Yet such was the pull of London that even these catastrophic depradations were quickly made good by fresh migrants, an average of some 7,000 of whom, so it has been calculated, were needed every year to maintain London's phenomenal rate of growth of population. Many of these were rootless poor, lured by the hope of London wages — in the seventeenth century over 50 per cent higher than in the provinces.[9] There was also a sizeable body of apprentices, attracted from all parts of the country by metropolitan opportunities for advancement, over 1,100 of whom of provincial origin were, for instance, admitted to the freedom of the City in the single year 1690;[10] and a numerically small but important intake, partly only seasonal, of the nobility and landed gentry. Altogether London's annual requisite of 7,000 migrants was from about 1600 onwards sucking up roughly half of England's total excess of births over deaths.[11]

But migration was also the result of 'push' out of the country. There the slow steady rise of the national population, as a whole still overwhelmingly engaged in agriculture, was beginning to cause land shortages, and surplus numbers were accompanied by falling standards of living. Rural population pressures of this kind tended to result in England not into subdivision of ever-smaller holdings but in the creation of a landless class able to move to the towns.[12] Enclosures and conversions to grassland for sheep-farming, followed by stagnation in the price of wool, and price inflation only partly matched by increased wages, were destabilizing the traditional patterns of rural life. So too were the more efficient uses of land by the introduction of such practices as mixed farming, crop rotation in parts of south-east England, and increasing specializations. Improved agricultural methods produced increased agricultural output per head of the labour force; and this gain was of course both an essential prerequisite of London's growth and a direct response to the vast demand for food there. In such unsettled rural conditions there were always plenty of migrants ready to move up to the capital, the contrasting demographic trends of metropolis and provinces being complementary to each other, with London acting as an electrical 'earth' for the absorption of the dangerous social tensions generated by surplus rural population.[13]

London also recruited a significant number of migrants from abroad. At the beginning of the sixteenth century there were probably some 3,000 foreigners in London, but at the end of Henry VIII's reign in 1547 this number had roughly doubled; and after the Protestant Reformation made under Edward VI (1547–53) the total had probably reached at least 10,000. Nearly all these migrants arrived from the Low Countries or France, particularly the former, many coming in search of work as well as for religious reasons. The volume of migration fluctuated greatly, the rate in the years 1567–72 (when religious strife on the Continent was acute) being particularly high. Dr Pettegree has estimated that between 1550 and 1585 some 40,000 or 50,000 foreign refugees came to London, although there were probably never more than 10,000 there at any one time.[14]

In the last quarter of the seventeenth century there was another great tide of migration from overseas. Nearly all of these newcomers were Huguenots from northern France, the peak in the number of arrivals recorded at the French church in Threadneedle Street being in 1687, two years after Louis XIV's Revocation of the Edict of Nantes.[15] But whereas the sixteenth-century refugees had mainly settled within the City, the extramural suburbs being then still small, the Huguenots' two principal areas of settlement were in Soho and Spitalfields, both of which had the advantage of being outside the area of the City Corporation's authority. By 1700 there some 20,000 to 25,000 Huguenots in and around London.[16]

Continental Comparisons

Despite this sizeable contribution of migration from abroad it was basically the combination of high mortality in London and excess of births in the provinces which enabled the population of London to continue to grow even during the second half of the seventeenth century, when (as previously mentioned) that of England as a whole was falling. Elsewhere in Europe urban and non-urban demographic trends generally both moved in the same direction as one another. In Holland and the Spanish Netherlands, for instance, one of the most urbanized regions of Europe, the population of both town and country fell after about 1650, while in both Paris and the rest of France the population was stagnant in the later seventeenth century. Both the Low Countries and France had, however, suffered grievously from the seemingly endless Continental wars of the seventeenth century, and from the heavy taxation to which war gave rise[17] — burdens from which England (despite the Civil War) was largely free until the 1690s and which were always of a different order of magnitude from those endured in many parts of the Continent. English agriculture was moreover always capable of meeting the constantly rising demands of the capital for food, and even indeed, in good harvest years, of exporting grain to many parts of continental Europe, including France and Holland.[18] In France, on the other hand, cereal yields (in terms of the number of grains harvested from each grain sown) were lower than in England, and the balance between supply and demand for food was still so fine that there were over twenty general famines in the sixteenth and seventeenth centuries, as well as countless local ones.[19] In England there were no such disasters, though there were shortages from time to time; and as more efficient methods of food production required less labour, migrants continued to stream in ever-larger numbers to London. There, in the teeming new suburbs, they were free to ply almost any trade, unrestricted by the City's guilds, which by the mid-seventeenth century had largely ceased trying to regulate the workers in the extramural areas — unlike in Paris and many other Continental cities, where powerful restrictive medieval trade practices still prevailed.[20]

Conditions for large-scale uninterrupted growth were therefore uniquely favourable for London. But the demographic mechanism of high mortality in the capital and excess births in the provinces which underlay the massive migration to the metropolis was itself complemented, as we shall later see, by other forces moving in the same direction towards the ever-increasing concentration at London of many of the most important features of the national life.

The Economic and Financial Metropolis

Growth in population stimulates demand, and hence investment, specialization, the division of labour, and non-local trade. Since that growth of demand was greatest in London its potent economic effects were increasingly exerted through the capital. It was most clearly manifested there through the presence of court, Parliament, and the fashionable beau monde, which made London, in Professor F. J. Fisher's phrase, 'a centre of consumption where men expended the revenues which they had acquired elsewhere'.[21] Stimulated by rising demand, London, despite its geographically eccentric position within the island of Britain, became the centre of the national distributive system, whether for goods transported by land, river, or sea. Metropolitan demand was also of course a powerful stimulant of agricultural specialization and productivity. By the end of the seventeenth century, indeed, it was changing the economic geography of much of the country, each region concentrating increasingly upon its own specialities. In the field of foreign trade the gradual transition from the export-led expansion of the first half of the sixteenth century to the increasingly import-led growth of the seventeenth century transferred the leading role from the manufacturer — in most cases the provincial clothiers — to the merchants in the City, who were able in growing measure to pay for their imports by the development of re-exports from London and by the provision of shipping and financial services there.[22] Through the great fortunes which could be made in this way or by capital gains in the manipulation of money, a new breed of financier had emerged by around 1700, separate from trade and peculiar to London.

Metropolitan Conspicuous Consumption

During the sixteenth and seventeenth centuries the royal court became less peripatetic and more firmly fixed at Westminster. It also became larger, and at times (notably under Henry VIII and the Stuarts) more extravagant. Membership of both Houses of Parliament was also increasing, and after 1640 the sessions were more frequent and longer. Great territorial magnates when in attendance at court needed to live in a palace of their own, such as Northumberland House, which was built in the early seventeenth century on the site of a convent near Charing Cross. More numerous than the score or so of such grandees were the great men of the shires — lesser peers, baronets, and knights whose numbers were much enlarged by the prodigal creations of James I. To them a house in London was becoming a normal appendage — generally a terrace house bought on a long lease and occupied chiefly during the law terms and the sessions of Parliament. Lastly there were the esquires and gentlemen of modest fortune, who, like their titled colleagues, grew very greatly in number during the sixteenth and seventeenth centuries. Their sporadic — though after 1660 increasingly common — visits to London were often made to attend to legal or financial business relating to their country estates, and generally they would be content to rent a furnished house.[23]

It was in this context that in the early seventeenth century there developed a London 'season', beginning in the autumn and continuing until late spring, during which provincial magnates of varying degree came up to London, often accompanied by their families. London was in fact becoming the social as well as the political capital, generating an ever-growing demand for goods and services — most obviously for food, accommodation, and clothing, but also for transport — hackney coaches for hire and sedan chairs were novelties in the 1620s and 1630s — and entertainment of all kinds, notably the Shakespearian theatre.[24]

Au fond this élite was a country-based élite. It was their lands in the country and their castles, palaces, or manor houses which provided their income, power, influence, and homes. In London, by contrast, they were little more than birds of passage, though in their sojourns there they spent a vast amount of income generated in the provinces, and by this creation of demand they further stimulated the growth of the metropolis.

This process was generally regarded as a deplorable drain on the provinces, an attitude expressed in one of Ben Johnson's plays where a young gallant newly arrived in town was told that ' 'twere good you turned four or five acres of your best land into two or three trunks of apparel'.[25] In 1632 Charles I issued a proclamation ordering the gentry to leave London within forty days and 'keepe their Residence at their Mansions in the Country'; and soon afterwards over 200 offenders were prosecuted in the Court of Star Chamber for non-compliance.

It was all to no avail, of course, for the lure of the metropolis was too powerful. London had something to offer to everybody with money to spend: it was the place where 'rich wives, spruce mistresses, pleasant houses, good dyet, rare wines, neat servants, pleasures and profits the best of all sort' could be found.[26] No provincial city or town — not even York, where a handful of the landed magnates of the shire did have town houses — could provide such a range of amusement as London.[27] Metropolitan ascendancy in the cultural and social fields had, indeed, become as unrivalled as it also was in the political, commercial, financial, and legal fields. Nor did even seventeenth-century Paris display such a degree of concentration in the affairs of the nation, for in the 1660s the French monarchy removed to Versailles; Rouen and Lyons could respectively claim to rival Paris as the commercial and financial capitals of France, and the provincial *parlements* and *états* (which had no equivalent in England) still reflected vigorous local feelings.

The Emergence of Metropolitan Markets

For all its importance as a trendsetter, conspicuous consumption by the élite amounted to only a small proportion of the total metropolitan demand for goods and services, the scale of which was so great that Defoe could refer almost as a matter of course to the 'general dependence of the whole country upon the city of London — for the consumption of its produce'.[28] This was written in the 1720s, but the situation had already been pretty much the same for some time. By 1700, with a population of some 575,000, equivalent to 11 per cent of the total population of England, the capital's basic requirements were gigantic — over 1,000,000 quarters of corn per annum (so it has been estimated), around 88,000 beeves, 600,000 sheep, 150,000 hogs, 8,000 tons of cheese, a little over 8,000 tons of butter,[29] and over 500,000 tons of coal. Other mineral requirements included as early as around 1630 94 per cent of the Derbyshire and Yorkshire lead shipped through Hull, most of the iron produced in the Weald of Sussex, and (rather later) most of the tin produced in Cornwall, plus in 1691 over four-fifths of the stone hewed in the Isle of Portland.[30]

This consumption was made possible by the enormous relative wealth of London, which was very widely diffused. The wage rates of both craftsmen and labourers in London were throughout the seventeenth century (as we have previously seen) almost always at least 50 per cent higher than in the rest of Southern England, and although the price of foodstuffs was also higher the difference was not great enough to offset the higher wage rates.[31] The per capita wealth of London in the 1690s was thought by the contemporary political economist Charles Davenant to be at least twice that of the rest of the country, and his estimate is supported by London's disproportionately large share of national taxation. In the 1650s, for instance, London paid nearly 40 per cent of the total yield from the excise duty on beer, and in the 1730s no less than 70 per cent of all the licensed dealers in coffee and tea were to be found in the capital.[32]

By the end of the seventeenth century London's totally distinct pattern of consumption was becoming sufficiently pronounced for it to begin to act as an independent generator of growth throughout much of the rest of the economy. (Other forces were of course working in the same direction, but none as powerfully as London.) This consumption was made possible by important improvements in transport; and these improvements were in turn responses to the demands of

Fig. 17. Turnpike roads in 1720 radiating out from London

metropolitan consumption. By the 1630s there already existed a far-reaching goods
carrier service linking some two hundred country towns with London, based on
regular schedules and recognized connexions with London inns; and a regular
postal service between London and the principal provincial towns was introduced
at about the same time. By around 1700 there were about 400 weekly carrier
services to London from almost all parts of England. At distant Kendal there
were four carriers each with a dozen horses, and one team would set out every
week, the journey taking ten days each way, excluding Sundays. Packhorses were
complemented by four-wheeled wagons, which were five times more efficient. At
Frome in 1710 a carrier who ran a weekly service to London had five wagons and
thirty-nine horses. Woollen cloth and agricultural produce were often the main
items carried up to London, and downward traffic included imported draperies
and groceries, particularly tea, and a wide range of miscellaneous goods. The
volume of this road traffic was constantly growing, and it was no accident that

the first turnpike trust was established (in 1663) for the repair of a stretch of the Great North Road, one of the principal arteries leading out of London; and road improvements led to the growth of stagecoach services catering for passenger traffic.[33]

There were also corresponding advances in transport by water, though carriage by road remained, according to Defoe, 'the very medium of our inland trade'.[34] By the 1580s the Thames was navigable to Burcot (only 7 miles in a straight line below Oxford), and by the later seventeenth century all the way to Lechlade. Its tributaries were also improved. In Elizabethan times the River Lea was spruced up by a special Commission of Sewers, and in 1698 over 3,700 tons of malt were being shipped on it from Ware to London. Similarly the Wey was made navigable after an Act of 1651, and within little more than a decade 4,000 loads of timber were passing down it annually.[35] Much further afield metropolitan influence is apparent in the petition addressed by the London wholesale cheesemongers to the House of Commons in 1695 in support of a Bill for the improvement of the River Derwent in distant Yorkshire and hence (they hoped) the reduction of their carriage costs on the cheese and butter which they bought there and shipped coastwise from Hull for the metropolitan market.[36]

Improvements in transport and communications and the existence of the vast metropolitan market were of course closely linked. They in turn were linked to the growth of regional specialization, particularly in agriculture or in trades closely related to agriculture; and it was in the direction of such specializations that lay economic advancement for the whole nation. In much of the country round London a new breed of market gardeners supplied fruit and vegetables, and there was also extensive production of milk, poultry, and eggs.[37] Further out there flourished a ring of market towns whose prosperity largely depended on supplying the metropolis with a particular commodity. Farnham sent up vast quantities of grain; Hatfield, Hitchen, Luton, and others were, in the later sixteenth century, 'onely upholden and maynteyned by the trade of making Maults and of the cariage thereof up to London by horse and carts'. In the time of Charles I more distant Royston was sending 180 wagonloads of malt every week;[38] and most of Henley's inhabitants were (according to Camden) watermen 'who make their chiefest gaine by carrying downe in their barges wood [mainly beech from the Chilterns] and corne to London'.[39] From the grazing lands of the south Midlands or even further afield thousands of cattle travelled to London on the hoof, often via the great livestock market at Barnet or the fattening grounds of East Anglia and the marshlands of the Thames estuary.[40] Even faraway Newcastle felt the power of London, for (according to modern calculations) some 8,000 miners, coal-heavers, and sailors were by around 1650 engaged in the supply of coal to London. When their families are taken into account the numbers dependent on the London coal trade must have amounted to around 25,000 people.[41]

By the end of the seventeenth century the idea that London might indeed be a source of economic strength rather than a drain upon the nation was being dimly perceived for the first time, and Davenant questioned the hitherto 'common and received notion that the growth of London is pernicious to England; that the kingdom is like a rickety body with a head too big for the other members'. But his contemporary, John Houghton, went further and wondered what the consequences would be if London were to double its size. He thought that

In likelihood, we should spend twice as many coals, which would double the shipping to Newcastle and that double the trade at Newcastle... Whatsoever is said here for Newcastle will likewise serve for Norfolk for stuffs, stockings or fish; for Suffolk and Cambridgeshire for butter; for the counties about London for most sorts of food; for the West for serges, tin, etc.; for Cheshire for cheese; for Derby and Yorkshire for lead, alum and several other; and in short, for all counties and places in them; for there is no county or place in England but directly supplies London, or at one hand or other supplies them that do supply it.[42]

And Defoe was saying much the same a little later. Thus small local markets were drawn into the orbit of regional ones such as Bristol or Norwich, which in their turn were assimilated into the metropolitan influence of London. By the mid-seventeenth century metropolitan markets had been established in most of the principal commodities of life — livestock, corn and malt, dairy produce, wool, cloth, and coal. London merchants, or their agents or factors acting on commission, bought direct from the producer or at the local or regional market, and dispatched the goods, either on the hoof or by wagon or boat, to London for resale (again often by factors on commission), distribution, processing, and ultimate consumption. Livestock farmers, for instance, might sell through markets like those at Ely or Thame to jobbers or drovers who acted for or resold to London dealers. They in turn supplied the grazing butchers who kept the stock in pastures near London until the carcass butchers required it. Similarly the corn trade had its own complex structure, much of the business being done on the basis of samples only.[43]

City, Crown, and National Credit System

The rise of a metropolitan market system in England in the sixteenth and seventeenth centuries was unique — nowhere else was there either a national or such a highly centralized structure; and it depended crucially upon the growth of efficient credit mechanisms. Local commercial transactions were, of course, settled in coin, but in the wholesale trade conducted over longer distances it had long been customary for sellers to allow credit to buyers, and so sellers to London (graziers, dairymen, clothiers, and many others) accumulated credit balances there. These were recorded by the bill obligatory or bond: an acknowledgment of a debt and an undertaking to pay it at a certain date in the future. From the simple IOU there evolved the more flexible bill of exchange: an order signed by A requiring B to pay on demand or at a fixed date a certain sum of money to C, or to the bearer. In the first half of the seventeenth century credit instruments of this kind became common tools of business throughout the country, drawn primarily on London, where the commodity markets were sufficiently large and varied for bills to be bought and sold at a discount in the settlement of all manner of commercial transactions. Merchants or factors or scriveners there were already beginning to act much like later bankers, running current accounts, paying interest on deposits, and disbursing moneys as authorized by their customers, arranging for country landowners' rents to be transferred to London for expenditure there, and paying off debts incurred in London for provincial purchases made there. By around 1650 the primitive foundations of a rudimentary banking network based on London were already being assembled.[44]

These credit mechanisms arose from the needs of commerce. They were based on mutual trust between the participants, and were not geared to the needs of the State. Trust of the Crown in financial matters, on the other hand, was seldom strong, and the Crown's requirements were in any case different from those of the commercial world. Relations between the Crown and the emergent London money market were therefore often discordant, and it was not until the end of the seventeenth century that there was a measure of convergence of interest, much to everybody's advantage.

The Crown needed to borrow very large sums of money, particularly in time of war, for longer periods than was normally available on bonds or bills of exchange, and offered the receipts of future taxes, notably those from the Customs, as security. Under Henry VIII huge loans for his futile wars were raised abroad, particularly at Antwerp, then approaching the zenith of its commercial power; and it was at Antwerp that the first great English financier of modern times, Sir Thomas Gresham (1517–79), learned much of his trade. A Londoner by birth, the son of a mercer and Lord Mayor, and himself a member of the Mercers' Company, Gresham was for some fifteen years the Crown agent at Antwerp for the negotiation of royal loans. He made frequent journeys across the Channel, and altogether spent about six years abroad. He became adept at exploiting the rate of exchange for the advantage of the Crown (and of himself, for he was a wily and hard-headed businessman), he was concerned in the great Elizabethan recoinage of c.1560, and in all financial matters was the Government's chief adviser. In old age he used some of his vast wealth — he was reputedly the richest commoner in England — not only for the foundation of Gresham College but also for the building of a bourse or trading centre for the more convenient transaction of business, his four-storeyed courtyard Royal Exchange (erected 1566–7) in the heart of the City being modelled on that of Antwerp.[45]

By that time Antwerp was already beginning to suffer from the political disruption which culminated in the sack of the city by the Spaniards in 1576 and the destruction of its prosperity. In 1569 Gresham was advising the Queen's Council to raise loans from her own subjects, and this was done more and more, Elizabeth's requirements being relatively small. But with the accession of James I the scale of royal borrowing vastly increased, and it was on the London money market that nearly all Crown loans were raised — and almost as frequently prolonged. Lenders included courtiers and royal favourites, but individual resources were not large enough, and so syndicates of concessionaires were formed to exploit the patent rights and monopolies which the Crown granted in return for loans. The greatest of these concessions was the Great Farm of the Customs, whereby the revenue from the Customs duties was leased to a business syndicate in return for a fixed rent. The first such lease granted by James I was for seven years from Christmas 1604, at an annual rent of £112,400.[46]

In this new milieu of financial 'wheeling and dealing' around the honey pot of the early Stuart court a new brand of entrepreneur evolved in the City: men who through their business connexions and through royal concessions of one kind or another made immense fortunes, and often established themselves or their descendants as landed gentry. Baptist Hickes, for instance, a mercer and a member of a syndicate which lent to James I, set himself up in Gloucestershire as Viscount Camden. Sir William Cockayne, skinner and Lord Mayor, and also a large creditor of James, bought estates in several counties, and all six of his daughters married into the peerage. And the estate of Sir Paul Pindar, who was deeply involved in the farm of the Customs, was valued by his cashier at no less than £236,000.[47]

In the face of the inexorably rising demands of the Crown even larger sources of liquid capital were, however, needed, and much of this was provided through the Corporation of London. Between 1604 and 1626 the Corporation acted (reluctantly) as contractor for the raising of six Crown loans, negotiating with the Privy Council over the size of the sum demanded and then transferring the collection of it to the individual livery companies and/or assessing the inhabitants of each of the wards. After 1617 the Corporation often acted as guarantor of royal loans, and in 1627–8, when the King's debts were rapidly escalating, it even became contractor for the sale of Crown lands for the repayment of long overdue loans.[48]

So in the early seventeenth century 'finance', both private and royal or public, was beginning to bulk more heavily on the economic scene than it ever had hitherto, and the City Corporation, the livery companies, and sometimes even ordinary householders were all being drawn into the world of money dealings. The Corporation itself, by acting as an intermediary between the Crown and the private lender with liquid capital to invest, could tap sources of loanable funds otherwise unavailable; its Chamber (or Treasury), where cash temporarily deposited for payment of royal loans sometimes earned interest for the depositor, was acting much like a bank;[49] and in the case of the Ulster Plantation the Corporation served virtually as the Crown's own agent.[50]

But although the metropolitan money market had been transformed within some three-quarters of a century (c.1565–1640), there was still a fundamental obstacle to its continued evolution towards the establishment of a national bank. This obstacle was the often arbitrary conduct of the Crown in financial matters. Repayment of loans, which were ostensibly made for short terms but which in practice were often renewed, was often years in arrears, royal credit fell to its nadir in 1639, and ultimately the Crown was only able to borrow from persons or syndicates to whom it had granted concessions. By 1640 the Court of Aldermen knew that the numerous creditors whom it or the livery companies had hitherto been able to dragoon into lending would lend no more, and the refusal of the City to help Charles was (as we shall see in Chapter 9) a crucial factor in obliging the king to summon Parliament. Royal threats to coin brass money, or the seizure in 1640 of privately owned bullion deposited for safe keeping in the Tower, did not encourage lenders; and nor did royal immunity from the normal processes of the law available to creditors for the recovery of money. Lending to the Crown was in fact a chancy business, and could only be placed on a stable basis after the achievement of parliamentary control of Government finances.[51]

This took another half-century, i.e. until in the aftermath of the Revolution of 1688 the worlds of commercial (or private) and Crown (or public) finance began to fuse together to lay the foundations of a single national money market in London. The political rift of 1640 between King and Parliament had however, also been a notable landmark in financial history, for new means of raising money had been needed to provide for the sinews of the impending war. Parliament relied heavily on the new excise duty introduced in 1643, but it is also at about this time that the London goldsmiths assumed a new importance. After Charles's seizure of the bullion in the Tower people with cash to spare began to deposit it for safe keeping with the goldsmiths, who paid interest for it (often at 6 per cent) and lent it out at higher rates (often to the Government at 8 or 10 per cent), and ran cash accounts for their customers. They also began to deal in commercial bills of exchange and even to issue banknotes.[52]

Some of the earliest of these new financial middlemen, or bankers, were scriveners, who *inter alia* drew up and organized bonds and mortgages or loans for their customers. One such was (Sir) Robert Clayton, the son of a North-amptonshire joiner, who was apprenticed to his scrivener uncle and in due course amassed a vast fortune and became Lord Mayor. More usually, however, they were goldsmiths, of whom Alderman Edward Backwell (d. 1683) was one of the most prominent. From his shop, well known by its sign of a unicorn, in Change Alley adjoining the Royal Exchange, he was in the early 1650s performing many of the functions of a modern banker, and after the Restoration he and a dozen others like him were advancing enormous sums to the Crown on the security of taxes authorized by Parliament. Gradually entrepreneurs of this kind were ceasing to be primarily goldsmiths or rich merchants for whom finance was only a sideline to their own particular field of business, and becoming specialist financial capitalists, active in all dealings in money. The age of privately owned banks, or banks owned by partnerships (as opposed to modern joint-stock banks), had arrived.[53]

Meanwhile the City Corporation had also made very large loans to Charles II, but its relative importance as a lender was nevertheless declining. Government expenditure, on the other hand, was increasing by leaps and bounds, and when Charles, desperate for money to finance the fleet for the impending Third Dutch War, was refused a loan by the bankers, he ordered the famous Stop of the Exchequer in January 1672.[54]

At that time Charles owed fourteen London goldsmith-bankers a total of well over £1,000,000, repayment of which was now frozen. The largest creditor was Sir Robert Vyner, who was owed £416,000, followed by Alderman Backwell with

£295,000; and both they and half a dozen others were eventually ruined, three being imprisoned for debt. (Survivors included such later famous houses as Hoare's and Child's.) Some 2,500 of the affected banks' customers also suffered severe or even crippling losses.[55]

But despite this disaster the development of English banking was not greatly retarded. Only five years after the Stop there were some forty London goldsmiths keeping 'running cashes' for their customers,[56] and soon afterwards the commercial prosperity of the 1680s was generating fresh capital for investment, much of it in the newly formed joint-stock companies which were proliferating in the later seventeenth century. Moreover the Stop itself was in one respect a valuable harbinger for the future course of Crown finances, for within a few years it was agreed that the Crown should pay the hard-hit bankers interest at 6 per cent on their outstanding loans, which were thus converted from their original comparatively short-term purpose into permanently funded long-term Crown debts. (Ultimately the capital of these debts to the bankers was subsumed into the infant national debt.)[57]

After the Revolution of 1688 the public finances benefited from Dutch influence in government, and parliamentary control of Crown finances created conditions in which much more reliable security for public loans could be offered than ever before. The Government could therefore successfully borrow money on terms which allowed its debts to be left outstanding for many years or even indefinitely. Simultaneously the onset of some twenty-five years of almost uninterrupted and prodigiously expensive war with France raised Government need for money far beyond the capacity of the private partnership banks to supply. In 1693 the first long-term Government loan, of £1,000,000, to be raised under authority of an Act of Parliament, offered subscribers either life annuities or a form of tontine, payment being guaranteed from excise duties placed in a special separate fund at the Exchequer.[58]

This loan marks the inauguration of the national debt. It was followed in 1694 by the establishment of the Bank of England, by means of which a consortium of powerful men of the City undertook to lend the Government £1,200,000 at 8 per cent interest, payment being guaranteed from specified duties allocated by Act of Parliament.[59] This was the first English joint-stock bank. The money was quickly raised, and by its charter of incorporation the Bank was allowed to discount bills of exchange, issue notes, and do other kinds of commercial banking. Thus it embodied under one roof (at first at Mercers' Hall and soon at Grocers' Hall) the fusion of the commercial and the public worlds of finance.

So (despite a hiccup in 1696–7) the Government had managed to construct a financial mechanism which in combination with the growing wealth of the nation gave it seemingly unlimited means of raising money from the population at large. In this initial phase of long-term borrowing, however, the Government relied very largely upon the financial expertise and wealth of the London mercantile community. Of the 1,268 subscribers to the flotation of the Bank of England in 1694 87 per cent were resident in London, Middlesex, Surrey, or Hertfordshire, and they put up nearly 90 per cent of the original capital sum of £1,200,000. It may be noted, too, that 123 of the subscribers were Huguenots, and that Sir John Houblon, the Bank's first governor, was of Huguenot extraction. By 1698 a total of nearly £7,000,000 had been raised on Government long-term loans.[60]

The obverse of this transformation of the techniques of public finance was the contemporaneous metamorphosis of commercial finance. Since the Restoration a primitive market in the shares of half a dozen of the great trading companies like the East India Company had been developing, much like the market already established in Amsterdam some fifty years earlier. By 1685 several of the companies were also issuing bonds redeemable at par and carrying a fixed rate of interest. The market was, however, still very small, for in 1688 there were only fifteen joint-stock companies in existence, and it was not until public confidence in the royal credit had been established that such companies proliferated. By 1694 lists of the prevailing prices of stocks and shares (including that of the Bank of England) were being published, with quotations for a wide range of items.

At first dealings in the share market had taken place either in the Royal Exchange or in one of the coffee houses nearby. During the company promotion mania of 1692–3, which was followed by the deflationary crisis of 1696–7, the stockjobbers (who dealt in shares on their own account) and stockbrokers (intermediaries acting on commission who put would-be buyers and sellers in touch with one another) earned such a bad reputation that they were expelled from the Royal Exchange and their activities subjected by an Act of Parliament of 1697 to a measure of restraint. Jonathan's coffee house in Change Alley (between Cornhill and Lombard Street) now became their principal place of business, and it is from that resort that the modern Stock Exchange is directly descended.[61]

Another of London's great modern service industries was also emerging at about this time: insurance. Of its three main branches — marine, fire, and life — marine was probably the oldest, insurance of both ships and their cargoes having been practised sporadically in the Middle Ages. Throughout most of the seventeenth century much of this business was done in Amsterdam, but London was beginning to get a growing share of it. In the 1680s shipowners, ships' captains, and merchants began to congregate at Edward Lloyd's coffee house in Tower Street (near the Upper Pool of London), which became the recognized centre for shipping news and shipping insurance; and in 1696 Lloyd issued the first *Lloyd's News* dealing with these matters.[62]

The insurance of buildings against fire was much boosted by the Great Fire of 1666, Nicholas Barbon, the famous building speculator, being the virtual founder of this branch of insurance. Between 1686 and 1692 he insured over 5,000 houses, the premiums being at the rate of 2.5 per cent for brick houses and 5 per cent for timber ones. By 1700 there were three fire offices doing business, of which the most long-lived was the Amicable, better known from its distinctive fire-mark as the Hand-in-Hand. But the scale of their business was still small, and was confined to buildings in London. Even smaller was the business of life insurance, which ultimately was to become the most widespread of all forms of insurance, but which depended for its efficiency upon the compilation of accurate tables of mortality. The science of statistics was still in its infancy, and the first life insurance office, the Society for the Assurance of Widows and Orphans, was not established until 1699.[63]

Thus in the closing years of the seventeenth century the City of London was becoming a great financial emporium, and the new institutions of the Financial Revolution were beginning to emerge. But those same years also marked the beginning of the decline of the City Corporation, and just when the London mercantile community was demonstrating its financial power and expertise the Corporation was demonstrating its financial incompetence and virtual bankruptcy. This culminated in the Orphans' Act of 1694, the very same year as the foundation of the Bank of England.

It had long been the custom in the City that when a freeman died leaving children under the age of 21, one-third of his personal estate should be set apart for the future use of his orphans. This money was held in the City's Chamber or Treasury, the common fund into which (from whatever source it came) all the Corporation's income (chiefly from rents, fines, and fees for admission to the freedom) was paid, and from which all its out-payments, including even royal loans, were made. Income was falling, however, particularly in the aftermath of the Great Fire, while expenditure was rising: the Civil War, the Restoration, the expensive Quo Warranto legal proceedings, as well, of course, as the Fire itself, all cost the Corporation a lot of money. Debts rose fivefold between 1660 and 1681, the repayment as each child came of age of the principal of the 'Orphans' Portions' (which by 1684 amounted to over £500,000 pounds), became impossible, and payment of only the interest on the portions amounted to three-quarters of the Corporation's total expenditure in that year.[64] As Professor Carlton has aptly written,

The aldermen of London were rather like the management of a company running at a loss, who dip into their employees' pension trust-fund to balance the books. So long as the company expands, with many young employees and few reaching retirement age, such an expedient buys time. Yet if the company fails to make fundamental reforms, disaster is inevitable. London never made such reforms.[65]

Just as the Corporation failed (as we shall see in Chapter 11) to adapt its structure to meet the problem of the new suburbs, so too it failed to adapt its methods of raising revenue to meet its own needs. By in effect raiding the Orphans' money it merely postponed its inevitable ultimate bankruptcy.

By 1694 the debt amounted to £700,000, and the Corporation was obliged to go cap in hand to Parliament for assistance. The upshot was the Orphans' Act, the main provisions of which were the consolidation of all the Corporation's debts into a single account known as the Orphans' Fund, and the imposition of extra duties on all coal and wine entering London, to be used for the eventual liquidation of the debt.[66] It was not until well into the eighteenth century, when the continuing growth of the capital produced a corresponding rise in the yield of the coal dues, that the Corporation recovered its solvency. But it never recovered in full measure the prestige which it had hitherto possessed for so many centuries.

London and the World Overseas

At the beginning of the sixteenth century London's economic ascendancy over the rest of England was already very marked, but politically and economically England herself was still only a lightweight performer in relation to the outside world, islanded on the periphery of continental Europe. Her role on the international scene was analogous to that of her own colonies in later years, selling primary or unfinished products to more advanced economies and buying manufactured goods in exchange. By far the largest export was of course woollen cloth, but much of it was sold abroad 'white', to be dyed and dressed on the Continent by foreign workers; and foreign merchants — chiefly Hanseatics from Germany, or Italians — also conducted over half of London's overseas trade, both export and import, and used foreign ships to do so.[67] During the next 200 years London's domestic economic ascendancy became even more pronounced, and the wealth of her merchant community became far greater than that of any provincial counterpart. This was a change of degree but, in relation to the world overseas, a change of fundamental order, for by 1700 the capital city of this small offshore island was poised to become the principal commercial metropolis of Europe, rivalled only by Amsterdam.

During the first half of the sixteenth century London had been little more than a satellite of Antwerp, the first great entrepôt of the modern world, into whose orbit each new branch of international trade was drawn. However, London's uniquely favourable geographical position opposite to Antwerp's River Scheldt gave the capital a sharp edge over the provincial ports, and London's share of English cloth exports rose from some two-thirds at the beginning of the sixteenth century to more than four-fifths in some years of the 1540s. During this period the volume of cloth exports through London doubled, and vast fortunes were made by the Merchant Adventurers, whose convoys of little ships sailed across the narrow seas to Antwerp twice yearly in May and November. But in the 1540s foreign merchants still had over half of London's cloth exports, and overseas trade was largely export-led, with London providing the funnel which connected the provincial producers of unfinished cloth with the highly skilled dyers and dressers of the Netherlands.[68]

By 1560 this long period of growth in overseas trade was over, and within less than twenty years political, commercial, and religious turmoils in the Netherlands had brought Antwerp's commercial greatness to an end. Much of London's cloth trade was diverted eastward to the North German and Baltic ports, its volume fell by about 20 per cent from the level of the boom years, and its share of the national total also declined. But in the longer term London gained from the depression of the third quarter of the century, for it compelled her merchants to search for new, more distant markets, and particularly for alternative sources for the luxury goods which they had hitherto purchased in the Antwerp entrepôt. London's overseas trade became increasingly import-led, her merchants became far more active in its promotion than they had needed to be in the years of Antwerp's ascendancy; and their geographical horizons widened immeasurably.[69]

With one exception, London had little direct part in the great voyages of exploration of the sixteenth century. This one exception was the expedition under Sir Hugh Willoughby and Richard Chancellor, which was financed by a group of London merchants and set out from London in 1553 to find a north-eastern passage to the Indies. It ended in disaster for Willoughby, and although Chancellor was eventually received in audience by the Tsar Ivan the Terrible in Moscow, it was not through Russia but through English penetration of the Mediterranean that the insatiable domestic demand for luxury goods was largely met. At the turn of the century London was handling 80 per cent of all imports, and between the mid-1560s and 1620 the quantity passing through London of such items as silks, wines, currants and raisins, spices, and pepper increased prodigiously — this last, for instance, no less than fivefold. Much of this demand came, no doubt, from London itself, already notorious for its conspicuous consumption; and by the early 1630s the mainly luxury products of Spain, Portugal, and the Mediterranean accounted for over half of imports made to London by English merchants.[70]

By that time, too, foreign merchants' share of London's overseas trade had largely dwindled away. In 1598 the Hanseatics had been finally expelled from London after a series of ructions with the Merchant Adventurers, who had been increasingly active in the Baltic after the collapse of Antwerp; and the Italians' role had petered out too.[71] The foreigners' place was taken by the merchants of the score or more of royally chartered companies which were granted monopolies over trade in specified regions overseas, and which between the 1550s and the 1720s had a firm grip on much of English foreign commerce. Some of these companies were of the 'regulated' variety, of which the Merchant Adventurers had provided the proto-type, each member trading individually and sharing the cost of each ship chartered by the company. Others operated more like joint-stock companies, trading as a corporate entity; and some changed from one method to the other, for company organization was then still in its infancy. Nearly all of them originated in London, and were to a large extent dominated by London money and London men.[72]

The first of these companies was the Russia Company (1555), established as a result of Willoughby and Chancellor's expedition. The majority of its two hundred members were London merchants already involved in foreign trade, many of them as Merchant Adventurers.[73] The Eastland Company, chartered in 1579 for trade with the Baltic and Scandinavia, had 'residences' in four of the East Coast ports as well as London, but absolute control of it was nevertheless exercised for many years from London.[74] The two principal progenitors of the Levant Company (1581), trading mainly with Turkey, were both great London merchants already active in foreign trade, as also were many of their associates;[75] and the greatest of all the chartered companies, the East India Company (1600), was closely related to the Levant Company. One-third of those who petitioned for the company's first charter were Levanters, and the charter itself was addressed to 'The Company of Merchants of London trading into the East Indies'. Its early organization was something of a cross between a medieval guild and a modern limited company, but it was from these ungainly origins that there later grew the mightiest commercial body in the nation and which was in India virtually an independent state in its own right. Its Court of Committees (i.e. Directors) was dominated by City men, and from the first all its business was conducted exclusively through the port of London.[76]

In the first three decades of the seventeenth century half a dozen companies were chartered for trade with the New World, but in that vast new field of commerce most business was done by unregulated individuals or partnerships. The two principal import commodities were tobacco, nearly 2,000,000 lb. of which were already coming into London annually from America in the later 1630s, and sugar, which was established in Barbados in the 1640s. Exports throughout the seventeenth century still consisted overwhelmingly of woollens (72 per cent of all London's domestic exports in c.1700),[77] the 'New Draperies' made of lighter textures than the traditional broadcloths having found strong markets in the Mediterranean area. Re-exports — the re-exporting of goods produced abroad and shipped to England before being redispatched elsewhere — were also creating an entirely new sector of commerce in which at the end of the seventeenth century London had almost a monopoly, with over four-fifths of the nation's total re-export trade.[78] Most of the commodities came either from the East or the New World. Even in its early years the East India Company had imported far more pepper than the domestic market could absorb, and in the 1670s some nine-tenths of it was being re-exported, as also in large quantity were light Indian calico fabrics. Around 1700 two-thirds of all imports into England of American tobacco — by then a gigantic trade in which London had a preponderant share — was being re-exported to continental Europe.[79]

Lastly in this great age of expansion of overseas commerce came the triangular trades, in which home-produced goods were exchanged at Port A for other commodities which were sold at Port B, where other products were bought for transport back to England. Much the most important of these new trades was the slave trade, which is generally associated with Bristol and Liverpool, but in which London was at first also heavily involved. The incessant demand for servile black labour in the West Indies arose through the widespread cultivation of sugar there, and in 1672 the Royal African Company was granted a chartered monopoly to trade with West Africa. At least two-thirds of the Company's stock was held by London businessmen, and during the first forty years or so of its existence the Company consigned around 100,000 slaves to the West Indies.[80] London continued to be the leading port in the Atlantic slave trade until about 1720, when Bristol took the lead.[81]

Of all the chartered trading companies of Tudor and Stuart times only one still survives: the Hudson's Bay Company, which was set up in London in 1670 with territorial rights and governing powers over a large part of the northern wilderness which later became Canada. It remains the oldest merchant trading company in the world.[82]

During the seventeenth century the value of English overseas trade rose fivefold, and in 1700 London handled 69 per cent of total exports, 80 per cent of all imports, and 86 per cent of re-exports. So the history of English foreign commerce in the seventeenth century forms an integral part of the history of London. It was mainly in this period, starting in the 1590s soon after the final collapse of the Antwerp enterpôt, that the meteoric rise of Dutch hegemony in world trade, and a series of English challenges to it, took place. The first of these challenges, in which a City syndicate headed by Alderman (Sir) William Cockayne attempted in 1614 to wrench the dyeing and dressing of unfinished English broadcloth away from the Dutch, was promptly defeated by the infant republic's States General, which forbade the importation of all dyed cloth. In the second half of the century Anglo-Dutch commercial rivalry was continuous. The Navigation Act of 1651 (in the framing of which London's pushy new mercantile leaders had an important share) was directed specifically at the Dutch worldwide carrying trade and the Amsterdam entrepôt, and led to the first of the three Anglo-Dutch wars (1652–4, 1665–7, 1672–4), in the second of which the Dutch fleet penetrated up the Medway and might well have attacked London itself. These wars proved largely abortive, for England was not yet able to rival Dutch shipping capacity, the lower Dutch rates of interest, Dutch industrial productivity, or the political efficiency of the loosely federated United Republic in the promotion of Dutch commercial interests.[83] The subsequent French challenge mounted by Louis XIV and his minister Colbert proved for a while more formidable. But the age of worldwide Dutch commercial hegemony was already passing its high noon,[84] and the great advances in financial techniques made in London (partly under Dutch influence) after the Revolution of 1688 set in motion England's take-off towards global primacy, during which from the mid-eighteenth to the late nineteenth century London, as the successor to Antwerp and Amsterdam, was the centre of the world economy.

So London's standing in relation to the world overseas had been transformed during the sixteenth and seventeenth centuries; and it may be briefly noted in parenthesis that this transformation found a reflection in the mounting contrasts between London and Paris. In 1700 the population of each capital was in the region of 500,000 to 575,000, and both cities were, as always, the supreme prize of which the sovereign must at all costs retain possession, as Henri III in 1588 and Charles I in 1642 were to discover too late. But whereas Paris may be viewed as seat of royal absolutism and of Counter-Reformation Catholicism, London may be seen as centre of municipal independence, Protestantism, and the Great Rebellion. London's internal stability was certainly one reason why her people never endured anything comparable with the sufferings of Parisians from blockades, disease, fear, and near starvation in the late 1580s and mid-1590s, or during the Fronde of 1651–2.

In the seventeenth century London's population was increasing much faster than that of Paris, where growth arose more from the needs of the State for a bureaucracy than from those of trade or industry, and where it had virtually ceased by 1670. By that time the medieval guilds of Paris, their monopolies, and the Crown's control over them were all being deliberately strengthened,[85] while in London powerful economic expansion was destroying the authority of the ancient City companies and of many of the newer chartered companies. In Paris the permanent removal of the royal court to Versailles bifurcated the French capital just when in England outward spread was diminishing the centuries-old separateness of London and Westminster.

Finally, we may consider the impact of overseas trade on London and on London's role within the nation. In the seventeenth century foreign commerce began for the first time to cater for growing mass demands, principally for new commodities such as tobacco, sugar, and Indian textiles. By 1700 goods of this kind were probably reaching a large proportion of households throughout the country, and as most of them came through London (nearly 10,000 tons of tobacco, for instance, in that year), the importance of London as national distributive centre was much increased.[86]

Foreign trade also stimulated old industries and propagated new ones. Shipbuilding on the Thames began to grow rapidly in the 1580s,[87] and throughout the seventeenth century the building of the large ships needed for the Levant and Far Eastern trades was heavily concentrated there, the East India Company having its own yards at Deptford and Blackwall (Plate 38). Tobacco processing, sugar-refining, silk-weaving, and the making of hats from the waterproof skins of beavers became important new London industries, centred chiefly in the East End and Southwark; and the export of the 'New Draperies' in dressed form boosted the dyeing and finishing trades. With nearly 250,000 people of English extraction living in the American colonies in 1700, with little industry of their own and virtually dependent for their imports on goods supplied from the mother country, London's manufactures were, indeed, bound to benefit. The port itself generated jobs on a massive scale (not all, of course, through foreign trade, for coastal traffic was also very great), and so contributed to the ceaseless growth of London — seamen, ships' chandlers, watermen, warehousemen, clerks, porters, carters, all of whom in their turn required the services of thousands more people to supply their needs and those of their families. By 1700, so Professor Ralph Davis has suggested, a quarter of the population of the metropolis was dependent in one way or another on the port.[88]

So far as the rest of the economy was concerned, foreign trade was a great generator of liquid capital within a still fundamentally agricultural, non-industrial country in which the fixed assets of wealth were not readily convertible into cash. In the seventeenth century the value of foreign trade was growing much faster than national income, and although great fortunes were made in the City by other means (notably through the wholesaling of food, through Government finance, or latterly through the stock market and dealings in money), a significant proportion of London's accumulated merchant capital nevertheless originated in this foreign trade. It was this reservoir of capital that infused much-needed liquidity into the economy, created new markets overseas for domestic products, and developed the infant service industries of banking and insurance.[89] The new vigour generated by such use of this capital enabled London to act with increasing power as an engine of growth throughout the nation.

8

Religious and Educational Revolution

Until the early sixteenth century the people of England had shared almost unquestioningly an ancient religious faith which embraced the whole nation. But then (to quote the recent words of Susan Brigden), they found themselves under Henry VIII 'caught up in a Reformation, not at first of their making, but in time made by them'.[1] Because the English Reformation began in the capital and seat of royal power, Londoners were suddenly faced with conflicting loyalties and religious choices in matters where at least outward unity had hitherto in large measure prevailed. For Henry VIII and indeed for his successors London's religious conformity was of cardinal importance for the successful enforcement of the royal will throughout the rest of the realm. So London was the stage upon which much of the national drama of the religious upheavals of the sixteenth and seventeenth centuries was enacted.

The Reformation in London 1529–1558

At the beginning of the sixteenth century the Church in London still commanded immense outward prestige. The townscape was dominated at every turning by the towers and steeples of over a hundred churches, St Paul's Cathedral (the spire of which was the highest in the realm) was the focal point of processions and ceremonies, and it was from Paul's Cross — the famous wooden pulpit in the cathedral churchyard — that events of state and royal proclamations were publicly announced. In 1381 there were, so it was thought, nearly 700 secular clergy in London, as well as several hundred monks, friars, and nuns who served in the capital's religious foundations, over thirty in number. Some of the clergy were rich, notably those possessed of City parish benefices, and there was much outward display, exemplified in the gorgeous state kept by Cardinal Wolsey in the 1520s at his palaces at York Place (soon to be Henry VIII's Whitehall) and Hampton Court. But there was also a devout and learned London élite, both lay and clerical, gathered round such figures as Colet, More, and Erasmus, where the new learning of Christian Humanism was studied and its strictly orthodox precepts put into practice. At a more general level the Church was in the early 1520s still held in sufficiently high regard for nearly half of Londoners' wills to contain bequests to the religious houses. Unquestioning faith, conventional but nevertheless deeply felt piety, aspersion of the shortcomings of some clergy and profound respect for the sanctity of others were all part of the seemingly immutable landscape of the Church, *sicut erat in principio, et nunc, et semper, et in saecula saeculorum.*[2]

Within this splendid fabric, however, cells of heresy already existed. In the early sixteenth century Lollardy was reviving in London, and because it manifested itself above all in the study of the Bible in English this was a faith which could be practised privately at home. Fundamental doctrines such as belief in transubstantiation and in purgatory were being impugned, and the Pope was regarded as Antichrist. For copyists of the prohibited vernacular texts, who needed secrecy for their work, London was both a natural refuge and the centre of the growing market for forbidden books. Similarly London was also the natural resort of the evangelical brethren who from 1518 onwards, when Martin Luther's tracts first appeared in the City, were spreading the new messages of justification by faith in Christ alone; and for these active proselytizing preachers London could also provide the largest audiences. In 1526 copies of William Tyndale's New Testament in English, printed in Cologne, were beginning to reach London and provide the tools for more numerous conversions. Under the rule of Bishop Cuthbert Tunstall more heretics were detected in the diocese of London during the 1520s than almost anywhere else in the realm; it was from London that Sir Thomas More's persecution of heresy (1529–32) was directed, and from there that many of the sufferers from it were drawn.[3]

Even so, the number of religious dissidents in London was still only tiny when the Henrician hurricane burst, and it is hard to understand how within only some thirty years Londoners' religious attitudes could be so utterly transformed. At first there was general failure to realize either the permanence of the break with Rome or its full implications, followed by the fear and horror engendered by the execution of More and Bishop John Fisher and the first of the Carthusian monks (1535). There was much uncertainty, too, caused not least by frequent changes in the royal will, as for instance when the injunctions of 1538 requiring curates to buy a vernacular Bible and expound it to their flocks were soon followed by the printing of it being stopped and stringent restrictions being imposed on who might read it, either privately or openly ('no women, nor artificers...' etc); and there was no doubt much complacency and time-serving, many Londoners having perhaps too much to lose to make any response either to the faraway Pilgrimage of Grace (1536) or to the Dissolution of the Monasteries.[4]

Between 1536 and 1542 all of London's thirty or more religious houses were dissolved. They included the great Abbey of Westminster (which was refounded as a short-lived bishopric), half a dozen houses of Augustinian canons and canonesses, half a dozen friaries, the Knights Hospitallers at the Temple and in Clerkenwell, and the Carthusian house near Smithfield, where seventeen of the monks refused to take the Henrician Oath of Supremacy and were executed with great barbarity.[5]

But all the while the new teachings were spreading — in 1540 there were six copies of the new Great Bible in St Paul's Cathedral alone[6] — the popular appetite for preaching was growing, and the burning of heretics drew dramatic attention to the ideas for which the victims suffered. In those early days the new ideas had the searing power which Christianity itself had had in its infancy, or which in more recent times new political ideologies have sometimes had for a while; and in such circumstances the proponents of change always have an influence out of all proportion to their numbers. Above all, religious change advanced with the mere passage of time. Early Protestantism was of course a revolutionary protest movement and in part a defiance of authority; and as such it made a particular appeal to the young, who through incessant immigration congregated in very large numbers in London.[7] In 1550, so Professor Rappaport has calculated, well over half the male population of London was under 30 years of age, and there were over 7,000 apprentices living there.[8] None of these youths had more than childhood memories of the religious faith practised before the break with Rome. Their attitudes had been moulded in the confusion of the 1530s and 1540s, and as time passed it was those ideas that they inculcated into their own children, many of whom became the first generation of 'cradle Protestants' in Elizabethan times.

During the reign of Edward VI the dissolution of the chantries marked the next decisive step in the advance of the Reformation. There were over 300 of them in London, founded (as we have already seen in Chapter 6) for the purpose of offering Masses and prayers and the maintenance of lights for the salvation of the souls of the dead. Most of them were situated within one of the parish churches and were often maintained by the fraternities which formed the religious manifestations of the guilds and livery companies. Their dissolution was perhaps of greater importance for the ordinary layman or laywoman than either the Dissolution of the Monasteries or the Henrician break with Rome had been, for the destruction of the chantries entailed rejection of belief in purgatory, the doctrine about death and judgement around which so many late medieval religious practices had revolved; and, as we shall see later, this rejection also had lasting social consequences. At about the same time — in 1547–8 — parish churches were stripped of images and ornaments and their walls purified with whitewash. At St Paul's itself the great rood, all the chapels and altars, and much 'goodly stonework' were demolished. Everywhere the burning of lights was virtually prohibited, and the use of ashes and palms on Ash Wednesday and Palm Sunday respectively was discontinued.

Meanwhile heresy proliferated, royal authority (so terrifying under Henry VIII) being much impaired by the new king's minority. In 1548 a flood of polemical Protestant tracts permeated London, where no fewer than thirty-nine printers were by then working; and in the following year the new Prayer Book introduced the use of English and transformed the rite of the Mass, thereby incidentally ensuring the discontinuance of traditional religious music.[9]

The godly leaders of reform wanted a far more radical revision, however, and the presence of thousands of newly arrived refugees from the Continent, most of them from the Low Countries or France, provided the context for the inception of a fully reformed and truly Protestant Church in the City. The 'Stranger churches' at Austin Friars (later known as the Dutch church in Old Broad Street) and at St Anthony's in Threadneedle Street for the French and Walloon community were established in 1550 by a royal charter which granted their members licence to practise their own rites and discipline free from all interference by the English authorities — an astonishing concession which may have originated with the Protestant-minded king himself. The mere existence of these radical Protestant communities, modelled chiefly on the example of Zwingli at Zurich, provided a constant stimulant for further change in the still only half-reformed English Church. They also drew over to London yet more Protestant refugees from Continental persecutions, and by the end of Edward VI's reign in 1553 foreigners probably formed a larger proportion of the total population of the capital than at any other time in the sixteenth century.[10]

After the accession of Mary the Strangers' churches dispersed and some of their members returned to the Continent,[11] while at Westminster the Benedictine monks returned to the abbey. But the Marian reaction, although at first widely welcomed, proved too short to take root. The queen's Spanish marriage was much disliked, and fear that it would bring with it the Inquisition seemed about to be realized when under Bishop Bonner's auspices the medieval laws against heresy were revived and accusations were made against over 400 of London's evangelical community. Between February 1555 and June 1558 seventy-five victims were burnt for heresy in or near London, many of them at Smithfield, and their sufferings evoked widespread compassion. However, Londoners chose overwhelmingly to conform, as they had before and as they were soon to do again.[12]

By 1558 they must have become resigned to change, and although nearly half of London's beneficed clergy did not conform to the Elizabethan settlement, the laity once more accepted the new dispensation. Susan Brigden's study of the wording of the preambles of Londoners' wills suggests that even at moments when inmost thoughts were most likely to find written expression, there was throughout those fateful years from around 1530 to around 1560 a very considerable measure of submission to the changes successively imposed by royal authority.[13] Sheer fear, at first engendered by Henry VIII's murderous despotism, and religious indifference — or at any rate uncertainty caused by the spread of the dynamic new teachings — were probably the main ingredients in this submissiveness. But by whatever inscrutable private processes individual Londoners' religious ideas may have been motivated, it is certain that in the middle decades of the sixteenth century the ancient unity of faith was irretrievably lost; and the changes of thought and behaviour which this loss and the ensuing religious plurality represented were perhaps the most fundamental in the whole history of London since the coming of Christianity itself.

More immediately the abandonment of the need for prayers for the souls in purgatory had enduring social repercussions, for money hitherto devoted to the deliverance of the dead could now be used for the benefit of the living. Despite the controversies surrounding Professor Jordan's study of charitable benefactions made by Londoners, there seems to be no doubt that the proportion of benefactions made for religious purposes fell steeply during the course of the sixteenth century, while the proportion given for the benefit of the poor rose greatly, and continued to do so in the first half of the seventeenth century. (Educational benefactions, by contrast, were always substantial and fluctuated much less.) It is also probable that a large proportion of all Londoners' charitable benefactions consisted of capital endowments, for such things as schools, workhouses, almshouses, hospitals, libraries, apprenticeship foundations, or lectureships, and thus represented a permanent enrichment of the social fabric of the metropolis.[14]

Religious Divergence in the Age of Puritanism

In matters of faith Government policy during the first decade after the Elizabethan settlement was comparatively lenient, and for those who favoured the old ways the presence of several foreign embassy chapels in London may have enabled them to hear Mass, just as here and there in the country did the private chapels of Catholic-minded gentry, now served by ageing Marian priests. But after the arrival in 1574 of the first seminary priests trained abroad for the English mission and the fierce enforcement of the penal laws against Catholic practice, London became the natural centre for the concealment of newly arrived priests and for their subsequent dispatch to safe refuges in the provinces. Indeed William Allen, founder of the Catholic seminary at Douai, thought that 'nowhere do men lie more safely than in London'. Much of this covert activity revolved around the Inns of Court, where there were many papists, particularly in Gray's Inn; and there were other centres of recusancy nearby, in Holborn, Covent Garden, Drury Lane, and St Giles — all, it may be noted, in suburban areas outside the vigilant watch of the City authorities. In the early seventeenth century there was still a small but significant Catholic community in London, reinforced no doubt by the strong Catholic presence which despite the Gunpowder Plot of 1605 existed in courtly circles during most of the reigns of James I and Charles I.[15]

It was also in the lenient years of the early 1560s that Puritanism first began to make itself felt. At the time, the Elizabethan settlement must have seemed a makeshift halfway house, anything but permanent. Soon godly men and women were beginning to seek 'further reformation' of both worship and Church government, but still within the Established Church and embracing the whole realm. The long-term failure of all such attempts to impose such a 'further reformation' led during the next hundred years to the fissiparity of English religious attitudes into innumerable sects.[16]

In London the Marian exiles, reinvigorated by their residence in the great Continental centres of Calvinism, were soon occupying positions of power in the Church. Edmund Grindal became bishop, four out of five of the archdeaconries of his diocese and the deanery of St Paul's were all held by former exiles, and the Strangers' churches, newly revived under Calvinist auspices, though now under episcopal authority, were openly providing examples of a fully reformed godly Church polity. By the mid-1560s there was widespread defiance of the royal injunctions on clerical dress, and in the ensuing visitation insisted upon by the queen thirty-seven London ministers were suspended.[17]

After this controversy clerical ascendancy amongst the godly reformers passed from the beneficed parish clergy of London into other less orthodox hands. These were the unbeneficed stipendiary curates and lecturers who were paid by the parish vestries to preach; and in reference *inter alia* to the strength of their influence a distinguished modern historian has stated that 'The Protestant Reformation was more successful in London than in any other part of the kingdom.'[18] Preaching was the central manifestation of reformed religious practice, and in London one of its earliest and most uninhibited platforms was at Holy Trinity in the Liberty of the Minories (formerly the site of a convent). There, immune from episcopal visitation, preached several of the future leaders of Puritanism, and it was from here that the movement probably first took its name, for John Stow, writing in 1567, states that a group 'who called themselves puritans or unspotted lambs of the Lord... kept their church in the Minories without Aldgate'.[19] It was certainly in the heady atmosphere engendered at the Minories that ephemeral separatist congregations emerged (notably in 1567, when 100 of the godly were arrested), the distinguishing feature of their members' faith being their attachment to their preachers and rejection of all forms of Established Church government. In these early separatist or 'gathered churches' of London some historians have indeed seen the origins of Cromwellian Independency and modern Congregationalism.[20]

For about a century, from the Elizabethan settlement to the Restoration, London's religious life was dominated by preaching, and particularly by the parish lectureships. One of the first of these lectureships was established at St Antholin's, Budge Row, where sermons of perhaps an hour in length were soon being preached on five weekday mornings. After 1580 there was active lecturing in a quarter of all the London parishes, and after 1610 in over one-third of them. At least half of the lecturers (and in the 1640s and 1650s over three-quarters of them) have been identified as Puritans. These were the pacemakers in the processes of religious change in London during the period of the secondary reformation which began around 1560, and their influence was far greater than that of the beneficed parish clergy, who were in general not likely to be firebrands because 70 per cent of their livings were in the gift of either the Crown or the Church itself. The mere existence of the lectureships, mostly paid for by parochial levies, provides powerful evidence of the Puritan laity's dissatisfaction with the regime provided by the Church and of their determination to obtain a godly preaching ministry.[21]

It was in this Puritan milieu that in the 1570s and 1580s London became the centre of an organized campaign for 'further reformation'. From the cell formed by John Field, a militant Calvinist and sometime preacher at Holy Trinity, Minories, who has been described as 'the organizing secretary of Elizabethan presbyterianism',[22] conferences of ministers were arranged and a Book of Discipline for the establishment of a theocratic regime wholly separate from all existing secular rule was promulgated. But Presbyterianism was never preponderant in the English Protestant tradition, its leaders were imprisoned, and the last known conference of Elizabethan Presbyterian ministers took place in London in 1590.[23]

Although rigorous Presbyterianism was thereafter in eclipse for some time, moderate Puritanism continued to flourish, and there is evidence that, despite undoubted dissatisfaction with the Established Church, the prescribed communion service was very widely accepted, even in the 1630s in such a large suburban parish as St Saviour's, Southwark.[24] William Laud's attempts as bishop of London (1628–33) to control the parish lecturers failed, although he was more successful in suppressing the Feoffees for Impropriations, a group of rich London Puritan lawyers and merchants set up in the later 1620s to buy up lay impropriations, establish lectureships, and support godly ministers.[25] The general effect of his ascendancy was nevertheless to rekindle hostility to episcopacy, and hence to reinforce the revival of Presbyterianism caused by the political crisis of 1640 and the Scottish intervention in English affairs.[26]

This dramatic resurgence of Presbyterianism in the early 1640s was followed by its political collapse in the City in 1647–8 in face of the Separatism or Independency by then predominant in the Army, the rise of the sectaries and glimmerings of religious toleration, the general reaction against Puritanism, and the final resolution of the Puritan problem by the extrusion, through the Act of Uniformity of 1662, of internal opposition within the Established Church, though at the cost of creating a large permanent faction of Protestant Dissent outside it. In these momentous years London's religious affairs were subsumed into the religious and political affairs of the whole nation, which will be discussed in Chapter 9; but some aspects of them may be briefly distinguished here.

At the outbreak of the English Revolution in 1640–1 most men and women of whatever brand of Puritan sympathy were united in opposition to the Laudian dispensation, and a wave of religious radicalism swept through London. Numerous new lectureships were established in 1641–2, the number of Puritans amongst the lecturers reached its peak, and there was an unprecedented influx of Puritan clergy, particularly during the sessions of the Westminster Assembly of Divines from 1643 to 1648.[27] This had been summoned by the Long Parliament to advise on the new form of Church government to be created after episcopacy had been abolished in 1642. The great majority of its 120 members, carefully selected by Parliament, were Presbyterians, many of them dominated by Scottish influence, and in 1646 a parliamentary ordinance imposed a Presbyterian ecclesiastical system throughout the realm. In London some half a dozen presbyteries or classes were erected, and Presbyterian Church order seems to have been established in over fifty of the City parishes, mostly of the more well-to-do sort. A London Provincial Assembly or Synod met regularly between 1647 and 1660 and as well as supervising the metropolitan classes it also acted as an advisory body for Presbyterians all over England.[28]

But the system did not take lasting root. The Scottish army was no longer so important for the parliamentary cause, and the only enduring legacy of the Westminster Assembly was the Westminster Confession of Faith, which is still revered by British Presbyterians. Very soon the Presbyterian leaders of the City were in inevitably unsuccessful confrontation with the Independents in the Army. Unlike the Presbyterians the Independents subscribed to no closely defined doctrines, they wanted no ordered system of Church government, and in their 'gathered churches' or congregations they separated themselves entirely from the traditional parishes. In the confused and questing conditions of the 1640s— between 1642 and 1646 there was no nationally imposed system of ecclesiastical discipline — Independency had great appeal, particularly in the ranks of the Army, and nearly forty 'gathered churches' are thought to have sprung up in and around the City. After the final triumph of the Army in 1648 and the occupation of the City, Presbyterianism in London began a long slow decay.[29] Under Cromwell and the Independent Army there was a greater measure of religious toleration than there had ever been under the more rigorous rule of the parliamentary Presbyterians; and even the performance of the long-proscribed liturgy of the Prayer Book was connived at by the authorities, as John Evelyn recorded in his Diary when he received Holy Communion at St Gregory by St Paul's on Easter Sunday in 1655.[30]

After the Restoration the Act of Uniformity of 1662 required all clergy to conform to the liturgy of the Church of England. In London and Westminster some fifty ministers refused to do so and were ejected from their livings; and about twenty-five had already been ejected when Anglican clergy who had lost their livings through sequestration during the Interregnum were restored.[31] The ejected ministers commanded a substantial body of lay supporters, variously estimated by modern historians to have been by the early eighteenth century between 10 and 20 per cent of the total population of London.[32]

The ejections thus resulted in the rise of organized Dissent as an enduring feature of London's religious life. The main Dissenting groups, in descending numerical order, were the Presbyterians, Independents, Baptists, Quakers, and Fifth Monarchists. Many of them were of low social status (petty shopkeepers, artisans, and labourers), they were most heavily concentrated in the City parishes without the walls, and during the persecutions of the 1680s they were meeting in several hundred different places, often in private houses used on only one or two occasions. They shared hostility to bishops and to the new Prayer Book, both of which they regarded as revivals of popish practices, and also condemned the moral degeneracy of the royal court and its Catholic undercurrents.[33] When in the 1670s the possibility that the Catholic James, duke of York, might succeed his brother as king became increasingly likely, all strands of opposition, religious and otherwise, found their focus in the Popish Plot of 1678–81, which was enacted in the capital and will be discussed in Chapter 9. In London the often irrational fear of popery which then manifested itself found expression in the addition to the inscription at the base of the Monument commemorating the Great Fire of 1666 of words attributing the cause of the conflagration to 'Popish frenzy' — words not deleted until 1830, after the Catholic Emancipation Act of the previous year. After the Revolution of 1688 the granting of restricted toleration to Dissenters and the resultant erection of permanent meetings in London and elsewhere aroused Anglican trepidation for 'the Church in Danger'. Religious differences were indeed to be a critically important ingredient in the tumultuous politics of the reigns of William and Mary and Anne.[34]

In the 1680s London's religious scene was further diversified by the arrival of large numbers of Huguenot refugees from France. By 1700 there were over twenty Huguenot congregations in the London area. The members of those in the eastern suburbs were mostly weavers or connected with the textile industry and practised chiefly Calvinistic forms of worship, whereas half a dozen of those in West London conformed to the Anglican liturgy.[35]

There was also another aspect of the religious milieu of Restoration London: that presented by Samuel Pepys in his Diary. He welcomed the return of the Prayer Book services, attended his parish church fairly regularly, and said grace at home before and after meals. But in the whole of the Diary he never mentions having received Holy Communion, and the extent of his religious experience is encapsulated in the entry 'A good sermon, a fine church, and a great company of handsome women'.[36] Pepys's orthodox piety was the harbinger of a brand widely prevalent in the Georgian Church of England, far removed from what he regarded as the fanaticism of the extreme sectaries, and even further removed, perhaps, in this now deeply divided city, from the faith which, only a little more than a century before his birth in 1633, had been almost universally professed and which was now almost equally widely regarded as relating to Antichrist.

Literacy, Education, and the Inns of Court

The transformation of religious ideas during and after the Reformation was mirrored in the transformation of English education between about 1560 and 1640. During this period the quasi-monopoly of learning hitherto enjoyed by the clergy was broken, and Puritans began to see literacy and education as instruments to be used against ignorance, superstition, and idleness. By the end of the seventeenth century the level of literacy in England was probably higher than had ever hitherto been attained anywhere else, and was unequalled elsewhere in contemporary Europe.[37]

Recent research by Professor David Cressy has shown that the level of literacy in London was substantially higher than in the rest of the country. Samples of evidence for the 1640s show that whereas in rural England 70 per cent of all men were unable to sign their names, the comparable figure for London was probably only 22 per cent — by far the lowest known rate of illiteracy throughout the nation. During much of the seventeenth century only about 25 per cent of London tradesmen and craftsmen could not sign (in the provinces the rate was almost double), and by the 1690s this figure had fallen to 13 per cent. Amongst London apprentices and servants there was also a very high level of literacy, only 18 and 31 per cent respectively being unable to sign; and amongst the women of London there was towards the end of the seventeenth century a pronounced extension of literacy unmatched elsewhere, for by around 1700 about half of them were able to sign their names.[38]

Protestant religious zeal, always particularly strong in London, placed great emphasis on the importance of education. This was no doubt partly the cause of the high level of literacy there, but there were other reasons too. Many of those enterprising migrants who were drawn in such numbers to London by the lure of opportunity may well have been literate when they arrived, or at least keen to learn; and in the uniquely mercantile environment of the metropolis literacy was certainly a more valuable asset in life than in the less frenzied countryside. It is also reasonable to suppose that the heavy concentration of the printing industry in London and the tremendous expansion of its output in the 1640s had a favourable bearing on the rate of literacy there.[39] In the second half of the sixteenth century printing had been restricted to members of the London Stationers' Company; presses were only allowed in London, Oxford, and Cambridge; and their output was subject to heavy censorship. Even during the 1640s, when censorship disintegrated, almost all printing, particularly of news-sheets, was still being done in the capital. The situation changed little when censorship and control of the master printers was reimposed after the Restoration and the *London Gazette* (started in 1665) became the nation's virtually sole regular source of printed news. Indeed London's dominance of English printing lasted for at least a generation after the final abandonment of government censorship in 1694, for in 1724 there were still only twenty-eight printing houses outside the capital.[40]

This ascendancy helps to explain why literacy flourished in London as nowhere else. So too does the vast wealth of the capital, by means of which schools and educational facilities of all kinds were founded, endowed, and supported on a scale unknown elsewhere. Here, as in other fields of metropolitan endeavour, success bred success.

Instruction in basic literacy to a substantial proportion of the male population of London was, of course, by far the most widespread branch of teaching; but the 'petty schools' where much of this instruction took place, although undoubtedly very numerous, were often short-lived and have not left much trace of their existence. Nor have many of those schools where writing, arithmetic, and simple accounts were taught, often as a preparation for apprenticeship. Even the establishments where instruction at a higher level was provided, chiefly by clergymen, are hard to pin down, despite their importance in London. Here study of grammar and the learned languages equipped pupils for entry to the universities and the

Inns of Court; and because in the late sixteenth and much of the seventeenth centuries there was a surplus of university-trained clergy, for whom London presented the best chances of professional employment, it was there that this form of education flourished.[41]

All the schools so far discussed were privately owned fee-charging businesses, generally conducted in the proprietor's own house. London's principal educational distinction was, however, provided by the dozen or so great schools which were either founded or effectively refounded in the sixteenth century. The first was St Paul's School, refounded in 1509 by Dr John Colet, dean of the cathedral. The boys were taught free of expense and the school was richly endowed with property inherited by Colet from his father, a former master of the Mercers' Company, to which the oversight of the school was committed. In 1560 came the Merchant Taylors' School, founded by members of that Company and providing admission *inter alia* for 100 boys free of charge; and at about the same time the ancient monastic school at Westminster Abbey was reconstituted by Queen Elizabeth. In 1565 the riches gained in the practice of the law provided Sir Roger Cholmeley, formerly Lord Chief Justice and a commissioner for the suppression of the chantries, with the resources for a grammar school at Highgate. Christ's Hospital (1553), an orphanage which evolved into a grammar school, was founded largely through the efforts of leading London citizens; and this catalogue could be continued.[42]

All of these centres of education owed their existence to the great wealth of the capital city, whether manifested in commerce or in the royal courts at Westminster. (The school which Thomas Sutton established at the Charterhouse in 1611 provides a notable exception, for his fortune was largely built upon coal-mining rights in Durham.) At university level, too, Gresham College was set up on the wealth of the greatest mercer and financier of Elizabethan times, Sir Thomas Gresham (d. 1579), at his house in Bishopsgate. The lectures delivered there covered a wide variety of subjects, including astronomy, geometry, music, and medicine;[43] and although the Royal Society can trace some of its roots to the meetings held at Oxford during the Interregnum, the savants of that most prestigious of all learned societies (founded in 1660) soon made London, and Gresham College in particular, their headquarters.

Gresham College did not, however, develop into a metropolitan university, and nor did the Inns of Court, although the prestige of the Inns was so great that they were referred to in the early seventeenth century as England's 'Third Universitie'.[44] During the sixteenth and seventeenth centuries there was an immense increase in the volume of legal business transacted in the ancient courts of King's Bench, Common Pleas, and Chancery; and several new courts were set up, notably those of Requests, Wards and Liveries, Star Chamber, and Augmentations. In this litigious age even quite humble people could and did seek justice through one or other of the royal courts, and most such business was transacted in London, much of it in Westminster Hall itself or in the adjoining chambers. In Chapter 6 we saw that in the later Middle Ages the Inns of Court, conveniently situated between the walled City and Westminster, had become centres for the instruction of lawyers in the common law. Now between 1500 and 1600 the number of entrants to the Inns quadrupled,[45] the vast majority of them coming from the ranks of the gentry, squirarchy, or peerage, who regarded the Inns as 'seminaries and nurseries wherein the gentrie of this Kingdome are bredd and trayned upp', and as 'schools of civility and chivalry, as well as law'. Nine out of ten of these young gentlemen came up to London from the provinces, often more intent on entering the social, political, and intellectual life of London and on forming 'connections' valuable in later life, than on making the law their profession; and after a stay of a couple of years or so, living either within the Inns or in nearby lodgings or tenements, many returned to their country origins, well impregnated at an impressionable age with metropolitan modes of thought and behaviour, and well equipped to become provincial leaders[46]— well over half the members of the Long Parliament of 1640 had, indeed, previously attended one or other of the Inns of Court.[47]

Others, with poorer prospects at home, no doubt stayed on permanently in London, for there was much money to be made there in the law. Hugh Audley, for instance, who was admitted to the Inner Temple in 1603, held a post in the Court of Wards and is said to have died worth £400,000. His principal heir (including the inheritance of the lands in west London later known as the Grosvenor estate) was a scrivener. Scriveners were draftsmen of deeds but they also acted as loan brokers, money matters and land agency being other fields in which London-based lawyers were becoming increasingly active. Even more London-oriented was the leading medical institution, the Royal College of Physicians, founded by royal charter in 1518 and soon afterwards endowed by Act of Parliament with licensing powers extending over the whole of England, though in the early days much of its fellows' work was done at court.

So London was without question the leading teaching and intellectual centre of the realm. During the years between 1560 and 1640 there had been a very great extension of education at all levels. Later in the seventeenth century, however, a period of near-stagnation ensued, when the religious enthusiasm which in the past had often motivated rich benefactors was in decline; and even the importance of the Inns of Court as institutional centres for the teaching, regulation, and lodging of the English Bar diminished sharply.[48]

Nevertheless, London's intellectual pre-eminence was not in doubt, and it also began to manifest itself in a new field: that of science, or as it was then called, natural or experimental philosophy. It was in the City, where he worked as physician to St Bartholomew's Hospital for most of his life, that William Harvey in 1616 first publicly stated his theory of the circulation of the blood, his discovery of which was one of the great landmarks in the scientific revolution of the seventeenth century. In the post-Restoration period — one of the most distinguished periods in the history of English science — London was the natural resort of amateur virtuosi and men of learning concerned with the discussion and promotion of scientific knowledge of all kinds. Nearly half the members of the Royal Society in its early days were aristocrats (such as Robert Boyle, who had his laboratory in Pall Mall for many years), landed gentlemen, or persons connected with court or government, and it was only in London that there existed a leisured and educated community large enough to support such a body. London was also the centre of the publishing and book trades, and the principal place for the manufacture and sale of scientific instruments such as microscopes, telescopes, barometers, and quadrants. The metropolis was, too, the natural home of the Royal Observatory, established at Greenwich in 1675 for the advancement of navigation and nautical astronomy. Through the publication of its *Philosophical Transactions* (started in 1665), and through the extensive correspondence with country-based scholars which was conducted by its officers (of whom the experimental philosopher Robert Hooke was the most distinguished), the Royal Society acted as a focus for the dissemination of 'natural philosophy' nationwide; and in the coffee houses around which so much of post-Restoration social life revolved, there were frequent informal meetings of savants, as Pepys records in his Diary. It was indeed in London that the conscious propagation of scientific knowledge, which was to lead ultimately to the triumph of science throughout the Western world, was first tentatively attempted.[49]

9

Political Revolutions

Many of the contours of the political landscape of sixteenth- and seventeenth-century England can be usefully viewed from a metropolitan vantage point. The extent to which the Tudors' despotism was founded on the power of London is a matter for historians of politics, but it is certain that never did any of those formidable monarchs ever lose control of London; and throughout the whole of the sixteenth century Londoners never backed rebellion (e.g. Wyatt, 1554; Essex, 1601), or usurpation (Northumberland and Lady Jane Grey, 1553), nor ever attempted to exert duress against the Crown. But the tribulations of Charles I, and even perhaps those of James II, may in substantial measure be attributed to failure to retain the support and control of the capital city. Contemporaries certainly had no doubt about the importance of London in determining the course of political events. For the royalist Clarendon, London was 'the sink of all the ill humour of the Kingdom';[1] and in 1643 another royalist thought that 'If...posterity shall ask...who would have pulled the crown from the King's head, taken the government off the hinges, dissolved Monarchy, enslaved the laws, and ruined their country, 'twas the proud, unthankful, schismatical, rebellious, bloody City of London'.[2] Two centuries later Macaulay held that 'it is no exaggeration to say that, but for the hostility of the City, Charles the First would never have been vanquished, and that, without the help of the City, Charles the Second could scarcely have been restored'.[3] Modern historians, while using more circumspect language, have in general agreed.

London's part in shaping the political development of the nation was never more important than in the crucial years of the early 1640s. It was the refusal of the City élite to grant Charles I yet another loan that more than any other single factor precipitated the breakdown of the regime and forced the king to summon Parliament after eleven years of personal rule. It was to the safe haven of the City that the Five Members fled after the king's failure to arrest them in the House of Commons on 4 January 1642; and it was as a result of his loss of authority in the City that only six days later Charles made the fateful mistake of withdrawing from the metropolis, to which he did not return until 1648, and then only as a prisoner. It was London, too, which in the early years of the conflict paid for most of the parliamentary war effort, principally by means of compulsory weekly assessments most efficiently collected; and it was the London Trained Bands, which in 1642, when they were some 8,000 in number, protected Parliament when its own forces were still weak, and which in large measure deterred the king from attacking London in November of that year and thereby prevented his gaining a decisive military victory once and for all.

Modern historians (and in particular Dr Valerie Pearl) have shown that, despite its commanding influence on events in 1640–3, London was a deeply divided city, and its eventual support of the parliamentary cause was far from being a foregone conclusion. Dr Robert Brenner has suggested that the basically conservative merchants of the chartered trading companies — the Merchant Adventurers, the Levant, the East India, and others — were generally royalist in sympathy while those active in the largely unregulated trades with the New World were often Puritan and supporters of Parliament. Often, however, loyalties were in a state of agitated flux, and the high-handed actions of the Crown in the 1630s, notably the forfeiture of the City's Ulster estates in 1635 (into the promotion of which the Corporation and a dozen of the livery companies had been browbeaten by James I in 1612), and the establishment of the New Incorporation of the suburbs in 1636 (to be discussed in Chapter 11), had certainly evoked general resentment. Nevertheless until the crisis of January 1642 neither the Court of Aldermen nor Common Council supported the policies of the opposition led by Pym in Parliament, and as recently as 25 November 1641 they had entertained the king at a magnificent banquet in the City in honour of his return from his seemingly successful expedition to buy off the Scots. They had also presented him with a gold cup containing £20,000; and Charles seems to have thought that he had the City on his side and could therefore mount a counter-attack against the parliamentary opposition and their ever-rising demands.[4]

In reality, however, there were not at that time many royalist sympathizers besides the leaders of the municipality and some of the richest citizens. In the growing confusion and excitement at the end of December caused by frequent street demonstrations (the London apprentices being always liable to riot at such times) and petitions presented by the citizens to the House of Commons (where their support was warmly welcomed by Pym and his followers), municipal authority in the City was collapsing. It was at this crucial moment that the annual elections held on 21 December transformed the political temper of Common Council. Hitherto, existing members seeking re-election had been generally returned again, but now many of the old leaders were excluded in favour of new men actively sympathetic to the parliamentary Puritans.[5]

What this meant in deciding which side the City government would take in the impending clash between king and Parliament was very soon apparent, for on 4 January 1642 — the very day on which Charles had attempted to arrest the Five Members — the new Common Council elected a revolutionary Committee of Safety to preserve the City's security. This was dominated by supporters of Parliament, and in its capacity of Commission of the Militia it very soon obtained control of the Trained Bands (hitherto under the authority of the Lord Mayor), which were called out to defend Parliament as well as the City. On 5 January the king came to Common Council to demand — unsuccessfully — that the Five Members should be handed over to him; and on the following night rumours that a Cavalier onslaught on the City was impending spread panic through the City:

for in the dead of night there was great bouncing at every man's door to be up in their arms presently and to stand on their guard, both in the city and suburbs, for we had heard (as we lay in our beds) a great cry in the streets that there were horses and foot coming against the City. So the gates were shut and the cullisses let down, and the chains put across the corners of our streets, and every man ready on his arms.[6]

But the royalist marauders never appeared, and when the king left Whitehall on 10 January the triumph of the City's supporters of Parliament seemed to be complete, the Five Members being welcomed back to Westminster by a great parade of the Trained Bands. The deposition and imprisonment six months later of the royalist Lord Mayor, Sir Richard Gurney, primarily for having bravely proclaimed the royal Commission of Array for the gathering of forces for the king, marked the end of the first phase of the Puritan Revolution in London. (He remained in the Tower until his death there in 1647.) The full power of the metropolis had been committed to the support of Parliament.[7]

In its early stages the Civil War almost seemed like a conflict of London versus king and provinces; and as always at such times of political disintegration possession of London was the supreme prize. In November 1642 Charles's army captured and pillaged Brentford and advanced as far as Turnham Green, only 6 miles west of the City. There Parliament's newly raised forces were joined by the Trained Bands under their commander, Sergeant-Major-General Skippon, and for some hours the two armies confronted each other until eventually the royalists drew back, never again to get so close. By that time the construction of defensive earthworks around the City had already begun, and was resumed on a huge scale early in 1643, London being entirely enclosed within a line of trenches 11 miles in length and strengthened by over twenty forts. This massive effort commanded almost universal support amongst the Londoners. Portions of the work were allocated to the parishes, trades, and livery companies, whose members marched forth with 'roaring drums, flying colours and girded swords'. Women and little children joined in too.

> From ladies down to oyster wenches
> Labour'd like pioneers in trenches,
> Fell to their pick-axes and tools,
> And help'd the men to dig like moles.

Such was the urgency of affairs that the work was even continued on Sundays.[8]

But this unity of sentiment (comparable only with that which prevailed during the aerial Blitz of 1940) did not last long; and since its inspiration was basically defensive, London's active role in the determination of national affairs began to diminish for a while. In 1642–3 the Trained Bands had proved their mettle in their

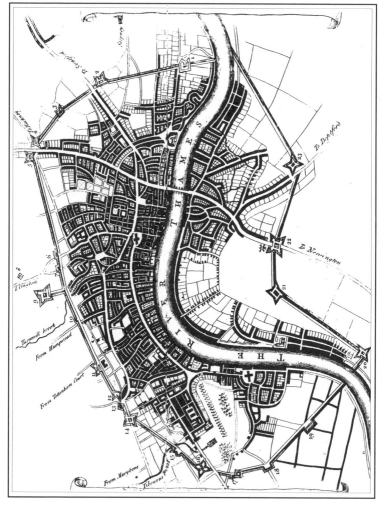

Fig. 18. Civil War defences, 1642

march to the relief of Gloucester and in the two battles of Newbury, but they were not present at either of the two great parliamentary victories of Marston Moor (1644) and Naseby (1645), and militarily London had by the end of the First Civil War in 1646 been overshadowed by Cromwell's New Model Army. Politically the revolutionary fervour of the winter of 1641–2 had subsided, especially after the austere and radical Lord Mayor, Alderman Isaac Penington, (who had succeeded the royalist Gurney) had completed his term of office in October 1643. There was growing resistance to the weekly assessments imposed by Parliament, and to the new excise tax, which even fell on such essential foods as meat and ale. After Naseby there was widespread fear and hatred of the victorious New Model, for the payment of which Londoners were being so mercilessly squeezed and the continued existence of which seemed increasingly unnecessary.[9]

The decline of London's importance in shaping events became more marked after the failure of the attempted counter-revolution of 1647. The leaders of the Puritan Revolution of 1641–2 had begun to find their own position in City government being challenged by the Independent sectaries and socially 'inferior' radicals (many of them non-citizens living in the suburbs), allied to the political and religious Independents in the all-powerful Army. The old leaders wanted a negotiated settlement with the king, a Presbyterian programme for the Church, and above all peace — they were, after all, primarily men of commerce whose prosperity depended on the restoration of favourable conditions of trade. A series of monster petitions was presented to the House of Commons, backed up by organized mob pressure, while inside the Commons the parliamentary peace party led by Denzill Holles attempted to disband the New Model Army and create a counter-force for the defence of Parliament and London, consisting principally of reformadoes (disbanded soldiers from both sides) and the newly reorganized London Trained Bands. For some weeks in the summer of 1647 the immediate point at issue between Parliament, the City, and the Army was concerned with control of the Trained Bands, but when they refused to turn out under the City's orders to face the Army advancing under Sir Thomas Fairfax, their command was vested in a parliamentary committee. The City's Presbyterian leaders did not, however, heed this warning of their own underlying weakness, and for several days at the end of July Parliament was terrorized by Presbyterian-inspired mobs of apprentices and reformadoes, who ultimately obtained the repeal of the obnoxious militia ordinance. After this outrageous violence, probably encouraged from the City, sixty Independent members of the Commons took refuge with the Army, and on 3 August Fairfax, already in the neighbourhood of Hounslow Heath, announced his intention to march on London immediately. So submission was the only course open to the City's rulers. The fugitive members returned to Parliament escorted by the Army, the forts on the western approach roads were surrendered and on 7 August the Army marched through the City and over London Bridge in a great show of strength. The Presbyterian counter-revolution had collapsed.[10]

The Army had thus become the defender of the integrity of Parliament, and a purge of the City's now discredited government at once ensued. The Lord Mayor and three Aldermen were sent to the Tower, a new and strongly Independent Lord Mayor was installed, and the fortifications built only five years before were at Fairfax's insistence demolished, so that London could never be a centre of armed resistance to the revolution.[11]

But although the Army now seemed to be incontestibly in control of the country's destiny, its leaders were very uncertain how to proceed, and under Fairfax's auspices there now took place the famous Putney Debates between representatives of the soldiers and of the London Levellers. The latter were the spokesmen of many people, particularly in London (the main centre of the Leveller movement), whose hopes and ideals the war had failed to fulfil.[12] The discussions took place in Putney church and lasted for some ten days before Fairfax and Cromwell put an end to them. They were never renewed, but through the simple declaration made by Colonel Thomas Rainborow — 'I think that the poorest hee that is in England hath a life to live as the greatest hee' — they nevertheless remain an indelible landmark in the history of English radical thought.

Meanwhile in London the rift between citizens and soldiers continued to widen, for although the Army had politically and militarily compelled the obedience of the City, the City still withheld payment of taxes. It was also becoming the principal centre of royalist conspiracy. In December there was a plot to seize the Tower, in March 1648 there were bonfires in the streets to celebrate the anniversary of the king's coronation, and in April the Lord Mayor and other officials nominated by the Army were assaulted by riotous apprentices. So when the Second Civil War broke out in May 1648 with the insurgence in Wales, followed by risings in Kent, Essex, and the North, the issue of the conflict depended very largely upon whether Parliament and the Army could keep possession of a predominantly hostile capital.[13]

That they did so was largely the work of Major-General Skippon, who from May 1648 until after the execution of the king eight months later was once again commander of the City militia and of such other forces as remained in the London area after the departure of the New Model Army for the wars. He successfully prevented the London royalists from giving armed assistance to the insurgents in Kent and Essex, and although at the height of the conflict the Court of Common Council petitioned Parliament on several occasions to open a treaty with the king, the City Fathers, still smarting from their humiliations in 1647, lacked the strength of will to declare openly for Charles. London's role was in fact a passive one.[14]

After Cromwell's victory over the Scots at Preston and the surrender of Colchester in August 1648 the victorious Army took a much tougher stance towards the City, which it regarded as the centre of royalist disaffections, than it had a year earlier. Half a dozen leading royalists and Presbyterians were imprisoned, and as the City was still proving recalcitrant in paying the assessments, troops were quartered within the walls for the first time in the course of either of the civil wars. The treasuries of several livery companies were looted; St Paul's Cathedral was pillaged; and Pride's Purge of the House of Commons on 6 December was re-echoed in the City, where all the councilmen who had supported the recent proposals for a treaty with the king were banned from standing in the Common Council elections of that month, and two-thirds of the existing incumbents lost their seats. By the time of the king's execution on 30 January 1649 the City's rulers were totally subservient to the will of the Army; and even the arrears of taxes were being paid.[15]

During the Commonwealth there was considerable Government interference in the affairs of the City, where the new men in the ascendant — political Independents and moderate republicans, often drawn from an emerging new radical merchant class — were dependent on the Army and enjoyed little popular backing.[16] In 1649 the Lord Mayor was imprisoned for refusing to proclaim the abolition of the monarchy, and four other Aldermen were deposed. The ancient right of the Court of Aldermen to veto the proceedings of Common Council was formally abolished, and there was much meddling in the City's elections. The Protectorate Government being short of money, troops were sometimes sent into the City to 'assist' in the levying of taxes. Its authority rested solely upon Cromwell's prestige and the power of the Army; but after the Protector's death (1658) the leaders of the Army fell out amongst themselves, and in this power vacuum the City virtually assumed the role of a national authority. 'What does the City?', enquired a member of Charles II's entourage, still in Brussels at about this time. Some Londoners, he thought, 'say, as they helped to drive out the father, they will help to bring in the son'.[17]

The immediate sequence of events leading up to the Restoration was in fact triggered off at the Common Council elections of 21 December 1659, when enemies of the Army and of the Rump (the small remnant of the Long Parliament that had survived Pride's Purge of 1648, now newly recalled) were returned in large numbers. Soon they were telling General George Monk, marching slowly southward from Scotland with a disciplined army, that they desired a 'free and full Parliament', and were refusing to pay any taxes until the members excluded in Pride's Purge (over 150 in number) were readmitted. With crass folly the Rump took up this challenge, declared the Common Council dissolved, and ordered Monk, who had arrived in London a few days earlier, to remove the gates and portcullises of the City and quarter troops there.[18]

At first Monk obeyed, and the distasteful work began. The citizens were not overawed, however, and after conferring with the Court of Aldermen he suddenly addressed a letter to the Rump peremptorily requiring that every seat in the House should be filled up within a week, as a preliminary to the calling of a new parliament. All at once the restoration of the monarchy became inevitable; and Pepys records how on that memorable day (11 February 1660) there was 'common joy ... everywhere to be seen!'. Dozens of street bonfires celebrated the event, 'and all along burning and roasting and drinking for rumps ... Indeed, it was past imagination, both the greatness and the suddenness of it.'[19]

So Macaulay's verdict that 'without the help of the City, Charles the Second could scarcely have been restored' was of course correct. But the almost universal euphoria engendered by the Restoration did not last long, for London was still a deeply divided city, particularly in matters of religion, where many of the expectations of the citizens were mutually incompatible; and the next eruption of metropolitan radicalism upon the course of national events was not long in coming. This manifested itself in a new form; and for almost the only time in their history the City Fathers found themselves for a while on the 'losing side' at the end of a national convulsion.

The Popish Plot and the struggle for the Exclusion Bill (1678–81) were worked out very largely in London. In the mid-1670s the possibility that a Catholic (James, duke of York) might succeed to the throne superimposed a fresh political dimension on the religious divisions which had for so long permeated popular metropolitan culture. A score or more Exclusionist or Whig clubs — of which the Green Ribbon Club, meeting at the King's Head in Chancery Lane, was the most famous — organized demonstrations, preaching, and the printing of tracts, woodcuts, almanacs, and even playing-cards with anti-papist pictures. They managed pope-burning processions which took place on 17 November (the anniversary of Queen Elizabeth's accession),[20] and they produced a mass petition, signed by some 16,000 men, demanding the renewed session of Parliament.[21] Under the direction of the Whig leader Lord Shaftesbury, emissaries were sent out all over the provinces to organize support, and in the general election of 1681 (the third within less than three years) forms of instruction to Members were for the first time widely circulated by party agents.[22] In London Tory crowds had their own different, Anglican-based, manifestations of anti-popery, the Whigs being characterized as republicans and Dissenters who intended to destroy both monarchy and Established Church; and through the fictitious revelations of Jesuit conspiracies made by Titus Oates and others all London was gripped with paranoic fear. It was in these tumultuous years, when Shaftesbury and the other Whig leaders were from the security of their London base pioneering the development of mass propaganda and nationwide political machinery, that ancient religious divisions, aggravated by the problems left unsolved at the time of the Restoration, were transmuted into permanent political parties, the rivalries of which were to dominate the English political scene for the next two centuries or so. Even the very names Whig and Tory first came into general use at about the time of the Exclusion Bill crisis, both being terms of abuse. So too did the word 'mob', a shortened form of the Latin *mobile vulgus*.[23]

But this early attempt to pressurize the Crown through the force of carefully organized public opinion failed. Charles II (unlike his father and his brother) never forgot the paramount importance of retaining possession of the capital. Throughout the whole crisis public order in London was maintained by the Trained Bands or citizens' militia, appointment of the officers of which since the Militia Act of 1662 were made by the Crown. Gradually the lieutenancy began to see the Whigs rather than the papists as the real troublemakers;[24] and by the political master stroke of summoning his fourth and last Parliament to Oxford instead of Westminster the king deprived the Whigs of the support of their metropolitan power base. It sat for little more than a week, for when the Commons resolved to bring in yet another Bill to exclude the duke of York, Charles ordered its dissolution and thereafter ruled without a parliament.

There now ensued a systematic and successful campaign to ensure that at future general elections royalist or Tory members would be returned in large numbers. Three-quarters of the members of the House of Commons were elected by the parliamentary boroughs, where much of the Whigs' support was concentrated; so if the Crown could successfully challenge the legal basis of the boroughs' rights and privileges, the municipal corporations could then be remodelled to give the Crown control of the appointment of the officers in them and hence of the electors. Out of over 240 boroughs and other chartered corporations (including many of the City livery companies) which by means of the legal device of a royal writ of Quo Warranto either forfeited or surrendered their charters between 1680 and October 1688, only London — the greatest prize of all — defended its case up to the final (adverse) legal judgement. Between October 1683 and October 1688 the City had no charter and was governed by a Royal Commission, all its officers being appointed by the king to act only during his pleasure. The Lord Mayor, sheriffs, and recorder were all nominated by the Crown, eight Whig aldermen were dismissed, and Common Council was dispensed with altogether. In this extra-ordinary throwback to the times of Henry III, Edward I, or Richard II, when London had on occasion been 'taken into the King's hands', the great capital city was reduced to total submission. The extent of the triumph of the Crown was demonstrated when the Parliament summoned by James II in 1685 proved com-pletely subservient to him; and the implacable Whigs who had represented the City during the Exclusion Crisis were replaced by four Tory aldermen.[25]

The Exclusion Crisis and its aftermath was the last occasion when City radical-ism fused with national politics with such devastating power and crushing results. In 1685 London played no part in Monmouth's rebellion, and it had a less active share in the Revolution of 1688 than in any other of the convulsions of the seventeenth century. (The Corporation was by then almost bankrupt, as we saw in Chapter 7.) In October 1688 James II restored the City's ancient rights in an unsuccessful attempt to regain support there. On 11–12 December there were violent anti-popery riots during the power vacuum created by the king's flight, and London was crazed with fear by rumours that thousands of disbanded Irish soldiers were marching on the capital; but these tumults had little effect on the course of events and were more akin to the Gordon Riots of 1780 than to previous disorders.[26] When William and Mary summoned a representative assembly to consider the political way forward, they were careful to include the Lord Mayor, the entire Court of Aldermen, and fifty representatives of the Common Council as well as all the MPs who had sat in Parliament under Charles II. But despite this recognition of the weight of the capital almost as a separate estate of the realm, the relative importance of the City Corporation, although still enormous, was in the national context beginning to ebb from the levels of the great tides of the 1640s or of 1660. With the rapid growth of the suburbs, particularly after the Great Fire of 1666, the great majority of Londoners now lived outside the Corporation's jurisdiction. London's vast unwieldy size, coupled with the corresponding diversity of opinions (religious, social, or political) of its inhabitants, was already beginning to be an obstacle in bringing metropolitan political influence to bear on national events — as it was still to be a century and a half later.

10

The Processes of Growth

So far, we have been primarily concerned with London's relationship with the rest of the realm. We must now turn to the internal workings of the metropolis and examine the mechanics of the huge expansion of the built-up area during Elizabethan and Stuart times.

Overall growth of the Elizabethan and Stuart capital was particularly fast between around 1560 and 1640, but its scale and timing varied greatly from one part of London to another. In terms of numbers the largest area of growth was always in the eastern suburbs, where most of the inhabitants were poor migrants: a recent study of the population of Whitechapel and Stepney has shown that between 1560 and 1640 only 14 per cent of the inhabitants were native-born Londoners.[1] In the northern and southern suburbs expansion was particularly rapid between 1560 and 1600, but in the west the main period of growth was in the seventeenth century. By about 1630 the combined population total of the suburbs north of the river is thought to have been as large as that of the City itself (within and without the walls). There the population actually began to decline in the middle decades of the century, until by 1700 it was probably little greater than it had been in 1560. So within a period of only about eighty years (1560–1640) the fundamental nature of London had been transformed. By the outbreak of the Civil War it was already a burgeoning metropolis; and by 1700 something like four times as many of its people lived in the suburbs on either side of the river as in the ancient City itself (within and without the walls), which was now islanded in the surrounding seas of bricks and mortar.[2]

It was also in the sixteenth and seventeenth centuries that the social diversification of the various *quartiers* of London began to set irreversibly in the outlines of their modern mould. This process had of course begun when Edward the Confessor had built a royal palace beside his great abbey at Westminster, thereby ensuring that the rich and fashionable quarters would always be on the western side of town, clustered round the seat of royal power. From the sixteenth century onwards the results of this royal impulse were reinforced by more powerful demographic, geographical, and economic pressures. In general, migrants from the provinces tended to settle in the suburbs, where they were less subject to the control of the

guilds or of any effective municipal authority. The peripheral parishes just outside
the walls and those along the river were therefore the poorest parts of London in
Tudor and Stuart times, whilst the rich still lived in the central parts of the City,
particularly along the line of Cheapside, or in parts of Westminster.[3] (In Paris, by
contrast, where the commercial influence of the river was not so great, the poor
crammed into the old central *quartiers*, which were largely abandoned by the rich.)[4]
When the volume of London's seaborne trade became so big that the handling of
shipping could no longer be confined to the waterfront within the City — as began
to happen in the seventeenth century — the unchanging facts of geography dictated that the port would spread downriver. In the string of hamlets at Wapping,
Shadwell, Limehouse, and Poplar which sprang up along the riverside about half of
the workforce were mariners, and there was also an insatiable demand for unskilled
labour, much of it needed for the loading and unloading and cartage of ships'
cargoes, and for all the other multifarious ancillary activities of the port. Away from
the river John Stow, writing in the 1590s, could already refer to the 'continual
building of small and base tenements, for the most part lately erected' between
Bishopsgate and Shoreditch, and to the road from Aldgate to Whitechapel being
'pestered with Cottages and Alleys'.[5] By 1700 the open fields and nursery gardens of
Spitalfields had been transformed into streets of houses, mainly for the accommodation of silk-weavers, and the teeming population of the East End, as we may now
begin to refer to these parts of London, amounted to around 150,000.[6]

   To the north and south of the City there was no outward 'pull' comparable in
strength to that of the royal court westward or to that of the growing port
eastward. So London has never had its North or South End, and the social profiles
of these quarters have never been as sharply defined as those of the West and East
Ends. Nevertheless some enduring features were beginning to emerge. After the
Dissolution of the Monasteries several of the religious houses which had ringed the
northern outskirts of the City had been converted to lay use as private mansions,
but in the mid-seventeenth century their owners and other aristocratic residents of
the locality began to drift westward towards more fashionable Westminster. This
exodus was soon followed by building development, and from the domestic
workshops established in post-Fire Clerkenwell there gradually spread the industrial belt which circumscribed much of the northern outskirts of eighteenth- and
nineteenth-century London.[7] Over on the south side of the river, too, Southwark
was also industrializing itself, brewing and victualling for the numerous inns, as
well as for the theatres and public gardens there, being the principal trades of what
amounted to a market town busy in the supply of foodstuffs and manufactured
goods to the gigantic metropolitan centre of consumption situated at the other
end of London Bridge.[8] After about 1630 Southwark's most distinguished residents, the bishops of Winchester, ceased to live in their episcopal palace there,
moving westward like their noble counterparts in Clerkenwell, though the bishops
in due course went as far as Chelsea for their new abode.[9]

   But it was at this western end of the built-up area that the social articulation of
the capital became most clearly manifest. As the seat of the royal court and of

Parliament, Westminster was the natural point around which the landed élite tended to concentrate more and more. Westminster and the western suburbs also had the fortuitous advantage of being (at least in the most commonly prevailing weather conditions) upwind of the City which, so John Evelyn writing in 1661 relates, was frequently darkened by a 'hellish and dismall Cloud of ... pernicious Smoake' caused by the enormous consumption of sea coal.[10] Westward gravitation was moreover strengthened by the nearby presence of the Inns of Court, conveniently situated between Westminster and the City. Here lived or lodged the lawyers and the students of the law, many of them of 'gentle' origin, and together forming London's oldest, most enduring, and most distinctive professional *quartier*. The West End was never, however, the exclusive preserve of this social and professional élite, for the concentration there of so many of its members generated a colossal demand for services of all kinds (notably for food, clothes, transport, entertainment, and domestic service). Much of this demand was supplied locally, and even the great nobleman lived cheek-by-jowl with those who provided for his needs or requirements and who always formed the vast majority of the inhabitants in even the most exclusive areas of the West End.

Landownership

Through the Dissolution of the Monasteries the Crown had obtained possession of a very substantial amount of the land around the City upon which the streets and houses of the new suburbs were soon to be built. Henry VIII had actually started to acquire some of these lands before the Dissolution, for between 1531 and 1536 he had got hold of several hundred acres of land in the great parishes of St Margaret, Westminster, and St Martin-in-the-Fields and in Holborn and even Chelsea, in order to preserve the purity of the springs by which his new Palace of Whitehall (confiscated from Cardinal Wolsey) was supplied with water. Further east more lands formerly belonging to the ring of religious houses which had surrounded the City had also come into his possession.

Some of these lands acquired by Henry VIII in the 1530s still belong to the Crown, notably London's 'royal' parks — St James's Park, Green Park, Hyde Park, and Regent's Park. So too does much of Piccadilly and Jermyn Street, as well as Carlton House Terrace and the whole of the south side of Pall Mall (except for the site of No. 79, given by Charles II to Nell Gwynne),[11] all of which are today administered by the Crown Estate Commissioners. But most of the properties acquired by the Crown in the sixteenth century have been dispersed, and in many cases this was done quickly. The Russell family, earls and later dukes of Bedford, acquired Covent Garden, which had formerly belonged to Westminster Abbey, by royal grants of 1541 and 1552; and by the time of his death in 1550 Thomas Wriothesley, first earl of Southampton, Lord Chancellor under Henry VIII, had obtained lands in Bloomsbury. These two great families retained at least part of their estates for very many years (the Russells kept Covent Garden until 1914), but it was more usual for lands newly alienated by the Crown to change hands several times before building development began, and for these changes to split up large blocks into ever-smaller holdings — a process often spread over a century or more. Down at the grass-roots level the agencies by which London's enormous growth was achieved were in general extremely small in scale.[12]

Within the City itself it has been estimated that at the eve of the Dissolution some two-thirds of London were in the hands of religious persons of one kind or another.[13] Not all the properties belonged to the monastic houses, but their holdings were nevertheless substantial, as in the case of the nuns of St Helen's, Bishopsgate, who owned nearly the whole of the parish of St Helen's as well as properties in numerous other parishes. After the dissolution the main immediate beneficiaries of grants from the Crown were often men with connexions at court. Amongst the recipients of London lands between 1532 and 1547 over 150 held some position there, about a third of them of some importance, such as Sir Thomas Audley, recipient of the Priory of Holy Trinity, Aldgate. The short-term effects of the change of ownership of so much property within the City were, however, often mitigated by the fact that much of it was held on long leases, and the change from religious to secular landlords made little immediate difference to the tenants.[14] A near contemporary annalist said of the early 1560s that 'faire houses in London' were still 'plenteous, and very easie to be had at low and small rents, and by reason of the late dissolution of Religious houses many houses in London stood vacant, and not any man desirous to take them'.[15]

Attempts to prevent Growth

This situation must have changed very soon afterwards, for in the 1560s and 1570s the population of London grew very rapidly. Much of this growth was crammed within the City's jurisdiction within and without the walls, but the population of the adjacent suburbs was also growing by leaps and bounds,[16] and by 1580 the Lord Mayor and aldermen were so alarmed that they sent a letter to the Privy Council drawing attention to 'the vast increase of new buildings and number of inhabitants within the City and suburbs of London, chiefly occasioned by the great resort of people from all parts of the Kingdom to settle here'; which, so the aldermen thought, 'would prove of dangerous consequence, not only to this great metropolis, but likewise to the Nation in general if not timely remedied'.[17]

In July 1580, after an exchange of letters between the Privy Council and the Lord Mayor, the queen issued a proclamation attempting to limit the future growth of the capital. Orderly government and the provision of food 'upon reasonable prices' were perceived to be threatened by the 'great multitudes of people brought to inhabit in small roomes, whereof a great part are seene very poore ... heaped up together, and in a sort smothered with many families of children and servantes in

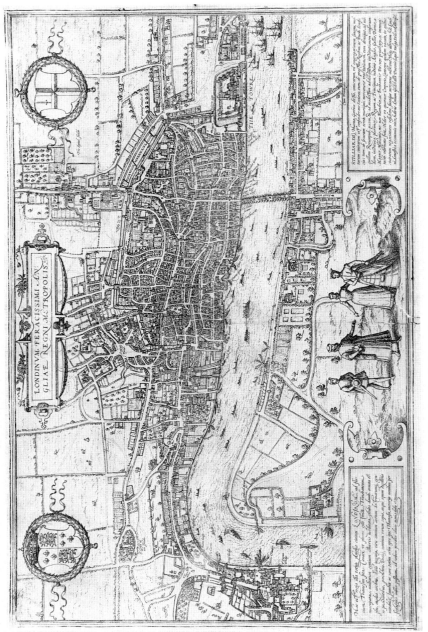

Plate 20. Braun and Hogenberg's map-view of London (2nd edn, 1574)

Plate 21.
London in 1720

Plate 22.
London in 1831,
before the railways

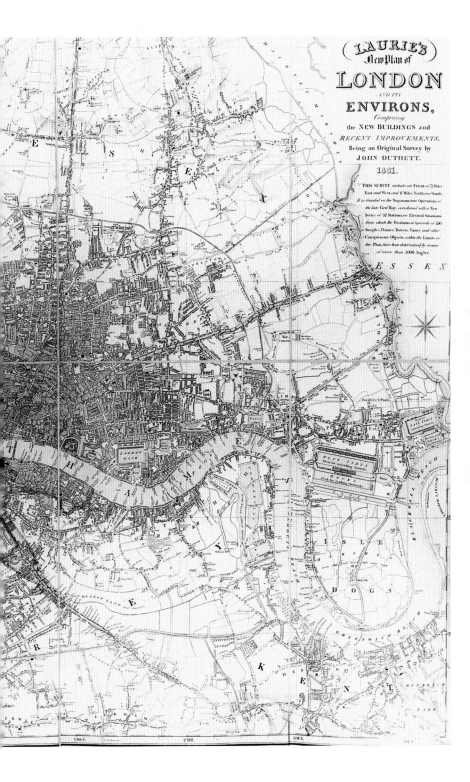

LAURIE'S
New Plan of
LONDON
AND ITS
ENVIRONS,
Comprising
the NEW BUILDINGS and
RECENT IMPROVEMENTS.
Being an Original Survey by
JOHN OUTHETT.
1831.

THIS SURVEY *includes an Extent of* 7 *Miles*
East and West and 6 *Miles North and South.*
It is founded on the Trigonometric Operations of
the late Gen.l Roy, connected with a New
Series of 32 *Stations, on Elevated Situations*
from which the Positions of upwards of 450
Steeples, Domes, Turrets, Vanes, and other
Conspicuous Objects, within the Limits of the
Plan, have been determined by means
of more than 5000 *Angles.*

Plate 23.
Railways and
underground
railways in
1913

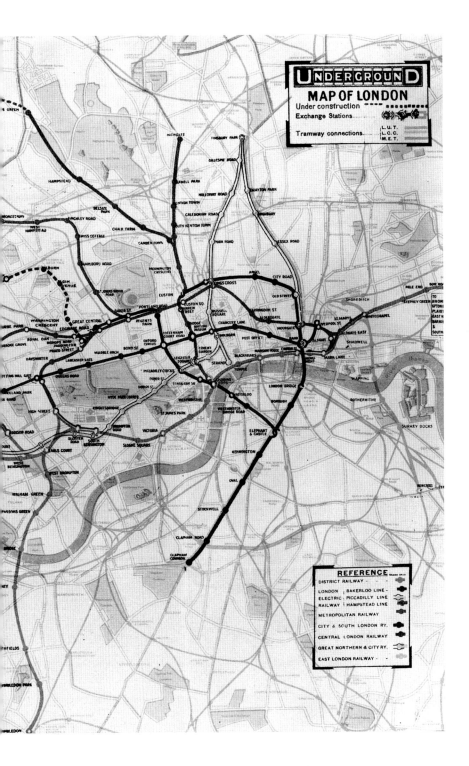

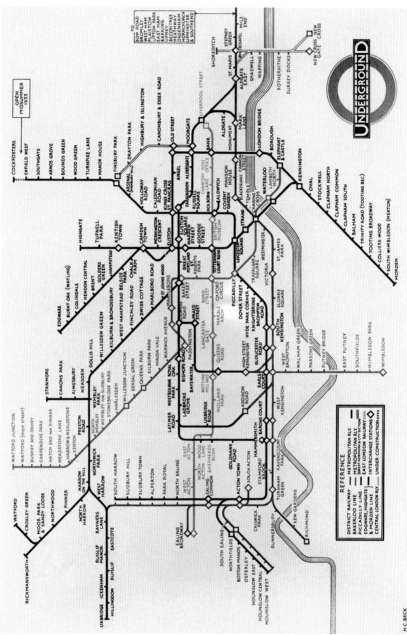

H C BECK

Plate 24. Underground railways in 1933

one house or small tenement, . . . for remedie whereof' Her Majesty forbade all new building within 3 miles of the gates of London, and also prohibited the subdivision of existing houses and the letting of rooms to lodgers.[18]

This was the first of a long series of proclamations (reinforced from time to time by specially appointed building commissioners and even by Acts of Parliament) issued by Elizabeth, James I, Charles I, Cromwell, and Charles II, the purpose of which was to prevent the inexorable expansion of London. But the pressures for that expansion were always stronger than the Government's power to enforce a policy which in any case only aggravated the conditions of overcrowding which it hoped to prevent. The regulations were therefore frequently modified in detail. In 1607, for instance, James I introduced the important proviso that there should be no new building within 2 miles of the gates of London except on old foundations or in the courtyard of an existing house. However, the Crown repeatedly undermined its own authority by the sale of licences to build, and by allowing offenders to compound for the retention of illegal buildings, both of which proved to be valuable sources of revenue to a Government perenially short of money. The policy of limitation was nevertheless not completely abandoned until the 1690s. Thereafter no further attempt was made to hem London in until the inauguration of the Green Belt in the 1920s and 1930s.[19]

The Leasehold System

Between the sixteenth and the early twentieth centuries most of London's suburbs were developed under the leasehold system, the central feature of which was the building lease. An owner of undeveloped land who wanted, without losing possession of his property, to get a larger income from it than he could from its agricultural rent, but who was unable or unwilling to invest capital of his own, would grant what was in the seventeenth century regarded as long-term leases at very low, i.e. ground, rents, with a proviso that the lessee should at his own cost erect a house or houses on the site. At the end of the term the buildings would revert to the ground landlord, who would then be able to charge a much higher rent, known as a rack rent, than he had been able to get for the undeveloped site.

The leasehold system virtually guaranteed that for some three centuries an ample supply of generally cheap building land was always available in the suburbs — until, indeed, the resumption of efforts to restrict the outward growth of London in the mid-twentieth century. Building materials were cheap too, for there were abundant local supplies of brick-earth, and Baltic timber came through the port in huge quantities. The opportunities for financial gain which the leasehold system offered also guaranteed an endless procession of people willing to speculate in the chancy fields of suburban development. They were drawn from almost every walk of life, knowledge of the building trades being no doubt useful but certainly not a necessary qualification, for there was an infinite variety of ways in which an intending speculator could participate. The classic procedure was, however, for the speculator, whether a builder or not, to covenant with the ground landlord to take one or more building leases and sink his capital (often borrowed) into the cost of putting up houses in the expectation of quickly finding purchasers for them when completed, thereby earning himself his profit and enabling him to move on to another similar speculation elsewhere.

Speculative building in the suburbs was of course always a messy as well as a chancy business, and never more so than in its earliest days. Until well into the seventeenth century the usual term for building leases was only thirty-one years. This was, for instance, the earl of Salisbury's practice on his land on the west side of St Martin's Lane, where he was granting building leases in the second decade of the century. By mid-century forty-one years became the norm, by around 1700 it was sixty-one years,[20] and in the eighteenth century it rose again to ninety-nine years. Short-term building leases led inevitably to shoddy building. Stables were often converted into houses; existing houses were divided into tenements; inconspicuous gardens and yards were covered with jerry-built sheds or dark narrow alleys leading nowhere; chimney stacks and sometimes whole houses collapsed; and even prefabrication was not unknown, for (according to one of the royal proclamations) some of 'those that doe make new buildings doe cause the [wooden] frame to be made in other places and suddenly sett upp the same'. It was in this speculator's paradise that some of the clusters of grossly overcrowded and insanitary tenements notorious in Victorian times as 'rookeries' may well have had their origin.[21]

The Origin of Residential Town Planning in London

Paradoxically it was from the incoherent suburbs of the early seventeenth century that there emerged the prototype of what was to become London's distinctive tradition of residential town planning. This was the great nobleman's estate, laid out as a quasi-self-contained and sometimes almost secluded community ranged around a central rectangular open space. Often a church, or the proprietor's own town mansion, provided the principal feature of the buildings lining this open space or square, which was surrounded by subsidiary residential streets; and sometimes there was a market. This concept was first realized on some 20 acres of the earl of Bedford's land at Covent Garden, where in the 1630s a large rectangular piazza was formed, with uniform ranges of arcaded 'portico' houses on the north and east sides and a church to the west. (On the south side already stood Bedford House, the London palace of the Russell family.) This revolutionary design, in the Italian manner still totally unfamiliar in a London accustomed to crockets and jutties and mullioned windows and half-timbered gables, was (almost certainly) the work of Inigo Jones, Surveyor General of the King's Works and the leading executive member of the successive building commissions set up to regulate the suburbs of London by both James I and Charles I. Through his two visits to Italy Jones had acquired first-hand knowledge of formally designed piazzas with churches, such as those at Venice, Florence, and Leghorn; and it therefore seems likely that the promotion of the Covent Garden scheme on classical lines may have been due to the surveyor general or even to his master, the king himself, rather than to the earl of Bedford, whose previous essays in suburban building development on his adjacent lands in Long Acre and St Martin's Lane had been entirely undistinguished. Charles, on the other hand, was contemporaneously employing Jones to finish the Queen's House at Greenwich and to design a great new royal palace at Whitehall, of which only the Banqueting House (1619–22) was ever built; and here was an opportunity both to embellish his architecturally somewhat uncouth metropolis and to demonstrate by example how residential development could and should be done there.[22]

Here too was a useful opportunity to replenish the royal coffers, for the licence to build 'howses and buildings fitt for the habitacons of Gentlemen and men of abillity', granted in 1631, cost the earl of Bedford £2,000, and three years later he had to pay another £2,000 for a pardon for previous infringements of the building regulations on his other lands nearby. At first the building leases granted by Bedford were for the usual term of thirty-one years, but very soon this was increased, generally to forty-one years, and he built three of the seventeen arcaded portico houses himself, by direct labour at his own expense, partly, no doubt, to serve as exemplars for the speculators who took the adjacent plots and were required to build conformably with these models. In conjunction with three neighbouring landowners the earl also supplied running water from springs in Soho, which was piped into the houses; but the builders had to construct brick sewers to carry surface water away to the main sewer (flowing down to the Thames), which was the earl's responsibility. The extent of Bedford's involvement as ground landlord was indeed considerable, for he also paid for the building of the church of St Paul on the west side of the piazza, and by 1635 he had spent over £13,000 (including the cost of the two licences) on the development of his estate. Nevertheless, the realization of the whole 20-acre enterprise depended overwhelmingly on individual speculators, for of the 180 or so houses whose first occupants are known, only 15 were first inhabited by the building lessee; or, to put it the other way round, some 165 were built as speculations and were sold on completion to intending residents.[23]

Jones's idea of arcaded portico houses (probably derived from the Place Royale, now called the Place des Vosges, of c.1605 in Paris) never became popular in London: and Covent Garden's famous fruit and vegetable market grew up spontaneously with no official recognition before 1670, unlike the markets deliberately planted into the development of some later estates. However, the concept of the central square, the church, and the uniform ranges of houses in the surrounding streets became in later Stuart, Georgian, and even in Victorian times the standard dress of very many of London's residential estates, particularly in socially self-conscious West London. Generally the church was not in the main

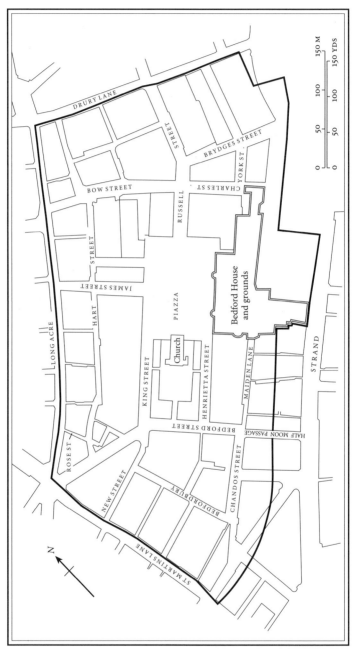

Fig. 19. The Bedford Estate in Covent Garden

square — St James's, Piccadilly, on the earl of St Albans' estate, or St George's, Hanover Square, are cases in point. In Georgian times churches sometimes found no place at all, as on the Berkeley estate in Mayfair, or were merely speculative proprietary chapels, like the Grosvenor Chapel on the Grosvenor estate, also in Mayfair. Later, when more religious times returned, churches made a come-back — at St Paul's, Onslow Square, South Kensington, for instance — or were actually placed within the open space of the square itself, as at St James's on the Norland estate in North Kensington. Even on that distant outpost, where building development took place in the 1840s, more than two centuries after Inigo Jones's heyday, the Covent Garden model plan is still apparent in the square, the church, the rectilinear layout of the surrounding streets, and the uniform façades of many of the terrace houses in them — even, too, in the partial seclusion of the estate created by the limited access originally provided to and from the surrounding slums of Long Acre and the Potteries.[24]

But, as mentioned above, Jones's arcaded portico houses in the piazza never caught on, and the model design for the uniform façades of London's terrace ranges is actually to be found not in Covent Garden itself but in nearby and almost contemporaneous work over which Jones, as the man in day-to-day charge of the work of Charles I's building commissioners, certainly had at least considerable influence. This was in Great Queen Street, Holborn, and the adjacent west side of Lincoln's Inn Fields, where between 1638 and his death five years later William Newton, a speculator from Bedfordshire, was buying land and parcelling it up into individual plots which he either sold or upon which he built houses himself. Drawings of a range in Great Queen Street erected under Newton's auspices — none of it now survives — show that its façade was expressed in terms of a classical order, the ground storey providing the podium and the upper storeys representing the columns, which supported a heavy wooden eaves cornice. With or without columns or pilasters — and although Newton's houses in both Great Queen Street and Lincoln's Inn Fields had pilasters, they were very soon left out elsewhere — this exemplar, with its great emphasis on the first-storey level, remained the basic language of London's terrace-house design for over 200 years, just as Covent Garden did in terms of estate layout. In the eighteenth century Great Queen Street was already being acclaimed as 'the first regular street in London', and Jones's hand in it taken for granted, as it also was round the corner on the west side of Lincoln's Inn Fields. There the classical grammar of the façade of this much grander range was equally apparent, as the sole survivor, Lindsey House, still attests.[25]

The great open space at Lincoln's Inn Fields survived undeveloped largely through the persistent opposition of the nearby lawyers, who frustrated several attempts to build there. This was in fact an early example not of an aristocratically planned estate layout but of successful action by an articulate pressure group; and it was not until after the Restoration, when demand for fashionable houses picked up again after the dour years of the Interregnum, that the Covent Garden exemplar was followed, in Bloomsbury. There the earl of Southampton had in about 1657 built himself a long low south-facing mansion, and in the early 1660s he laid out the land in front of it as a square — Southampton (now Bloomsbury) Square, the first open space in London to be actually called a Square — surrounded on its other three sides by ranges of terraced houses erected under the terms of forty-two-year building leases; and only a few yards away there were stable yards and a market.[26]

Virtually contemporaneously much the same thing was also happening, though on a grander scale, in St James's Field, where the earl of St Albans, a companion in exile of Charles II, was rewarded soon after the Restoration with a sixty-year lease of the Crown lands to the north-east of St James's Palace. But he soon found that on only leasehold tenure there were no takers for the noblemen's palaces which he intended should line his great St James's Square, and in 1665 he managed to get a Crown grant of the freehold of this central area. He then sold off individual plots, mostly to builders, who erected houses before or after finding purchasers. This most fashionable of all London squares was therefore exceptional in that most of the houses in it were usually occupied by the owners of the freehold. Elsewhere on the estate building development advanced rapidly, almost all of it on the usual specu-lative basis of building leases, and by 1676 St Albans' rent roll amounted to some £4,120 per annum. The layout included a church (St James's, by Wren, 1676–84) and a market (closed in 1816), and St Albans himself lived in the biggest of the *palazzi* in the square, the fronts of which exhibited almost complete outward uniformity.[27]

The presence of such noble proprietors as the earls of Southampton and St Albans in the principal house on their respective estates was no doubt good for business and conferred social cachet on the rest of their domains. This was also the case in Leicester Fields, where in the 1670s the earl of Leicester followed Lord South-ampton's example and laid out ranges of leasehold houses grouped to form a square in front of his own mansion, which had been built by his ancestor in the 1630s.[28]

The Building Speculators

In the great housebuilding boom which prevailed throughout West London in the post-Restoration years even squares without an aristocratic promoter and unem-bellished with either a nearby church or market were none the less able to command a large measure of social pretension. This was the case in Red Lion Square, Soho Square, and Golden Square, all laid out by speculative builders, the inhabitants of the last of which, for instance, included in 1707 half a dozen peers, half a dozen army officers, and a similar number of other residents of title.[29]

It was in the 1660s, 1670s, and 1680s that building speculators first began to operate in the suburbs of London on a large scale. The most famous of them was Dr Nicholas Barbon, an unscrupulous financial manipulator of genius whose usual procedure was to get hold of land with potential for development, raise capital on it by loans and mortgages, stake out streets, and let out individual plots on building leases. Rupert Street and Gerrard Street were amongst his earliest speculations (1677).[30] Thence he moved on to the adjacent Newport Ground which he bought for £9,500 and on the security of which he borrowed £30,000, demolished Lord Newport's old mansion there, and let the ground to builders, thereby making himself an income of some £1,000 per annum. He also reserved for himself the valuable market which he established on this messy little development, virtually all trace of which was obliterated in Victorian times by the formation of Charing Cross Road.[31] The early 1680s found him active on the south side of the Strand, knocking down two more ancient palaces and laying out streets lined with his standardized house fronts. In Holborn he was busy organizing the building of Red Lion Square and Bedford Row, and even in distant Spitalfields it was evidently worth his while to build cheap little houses suitable for that unfashionable area.[32]

In Soho, where some 500 houses were built in the last quarter of the seventeenth century, the main entrepreneurs were Richard Frith, a bricklayer from whom Frith Street takes its name, and his three partners, a timber merchant, a City goldsmith, and a 'gentleman' (probably a lawyer of some kind). Their operations were sometimes in direct competition with those of Barbon, but in general there was plenty of ground and plenty of opportunity for everybody, though few participants in this risky business seem to have made much money. Both Barbon and Frith died in debt, as also did two of Frith's associates; and one of the entrepreneurs in Golden Square, having spent time in prison for debt, was eventually murdered in his own house after a dispute at cards.[33]

In East London the mechanics of building were very much the same as in the West End, and by around 1700 there were over 10,000 houses in the parish of Stepney alone.[34] But great men like the earl of Bedford did not buy land there, so Covent Garden had no eastern siblings, and everything was higgledy-piggledy. In the two main areas of growth — to the north-east of the City (in Spitalfields, Whitechapel, and towards Mile End) and in the long narrow riverside strip — the houses were much smaller than in the west, three-storey dwellings being a rarity. In some parts, notably those just outside the City walls in the Minories, East Smithfield, and the Liberty of St Katharine's, houses were densely packed to levels far above those which became so notorious in parts of the East End in the mid-nineteenth century. This high density of housing was not, however, accompanied by multi-occupation, nor does there seem to have been serious overcrowding (except in Whitechapel); and the building speculators may well have roughly kept pace with housing demand in East as well as West London.[35]

Hardly any of the thousands of houses put up in the great post-Restoration building boom still stand. This is not surprising, for rebuilding was already in full swing in the first half of the eighteenth century (notably in St James's and Soho), when the original comparatively short building leases were beginning to expire; and in more recent years steadily rising land values have caused frequent rebuildings. The rare survivors include Nos. 36, 42, and 43 Bedford Row and Nos. 55 and 57 Great Ormond Street, all probably built by Barbon. The original seventeenth-century street layout does, however, still exist in many places, and not just in the great set pieces of estate planning like Covent Garden or Bloomsbury or St James's. It is very apparent, for instance, in a fashionable area like Albemarle, Dover,

Stafford, and Old Bond Streets, off Piccadilly, where development began in the 1680s on the site of Lord Chancellor Clarendon's great house, or in such earlier streets as Panton and Oxenden Streets (east of the Haymarket). The original names of streets also survive in very large numbers, often — as in the case of the half-dozen mentioned above — honouring a former owner such as the duke of Albemarle, or a building speculator such as Sir Thomas Bond or Colonel Thomas Panton. Occasionally the irregular shape of the fields which existed before they were covered with bricks and mortar and the boundaries of which became the boundaries of the developers' properties can still be detected in the line and course of the streets. The disjointed layout of much of the area between Regent Street and Wardour Street, for instance, derives directly from the irregular configuration of the medieval fields there and from their divided ownership at the time of building development.[36]

Water Supply and Drainage

For centuries London's water supply had come either from private wells, local springs, or from the ancient public conduits which under the auspices of the City authorities had provided free water at about a dozen public conduit heads such as the famous Cheapside Standard. In medieval times this piped water, the flow of which relied entirely on gravity and natural pressure, had been brought from springs as far afield as Paddington, St Marylebone, and Islington, but in 1581 the first pumped supply was provided by an enterprising Dutchman who harnessed the rapid flow of the Thames through the arches of London Bridge to turn a huge wooden waterwheel and pump water as high as Cornhill. Between 1608 and 1613 London's supply was further enlarged by the construction of the New River — a channel some 10 feet wide and 4 feet deep and no less than 38 miles in length, along which spring water from Hertfordshire flowed to large reservoirs in Islington. Thence wooden pipes set below ground conveyed it beneath the streets of the City, with small lead pipes branching off to those houses whose owners wished to pay for a supply. The main projector of this great work of engineering was (Sir) Hugh Myddelton, a rich City goldsmith who persuaded James I to provide financial backing for it and in 1619 to incorporate it by royal charter as the New River Company.[37]

Later in the seventeenth century these examples of speculative enterprise were widely followed, notably by the Shadwell Waterworks Company (1669) for East London and for the West End by the York Buildings Waterworks (1675) in Villiers Street off the Strand, where an 'Engine...moving easily and without noise' pumped water up from the river. London's water supply was in general no doubt much improved by the spread of such 'commercial' water, but meanwhile the City's interest in its conduits declined. Several of the public outlets, including the Cheapside conduit, were not rebuilt after the Great Fire, and the poor had to depend either on wells or on a communal handpump connected to a commercial supply which only flowed when the often absentee landlord had paid the company's dues.[38]

Water brought into houses had to be taken out too, and most of it simply soaked away in the cesspits dug under or near to them. In the days before the development of water closets, earth closets were in general use, and from time to time the ordure accumulated in these pits, known as night-soil, was carted away, usually at night (hence the name), to a public laystall — as Samuel Pepys recorded in 1663 when he went to bed late 'leaving the men below in the cellar emptying the turds up' through his neighbour's house, from which they had overflowed (not for the first time).[39] Sewers existed, of course, but until the early nineteenth century, when it acquired its malodorous significance, the word 'sewer' meant a channel for the removal of surface water; and the maintenance of these channels was the sole function of the commissioners of sewers established in the London area by an Act of Parliament of 1532. Until the early nineteenth century the connexion of bog-houses or houses of office with the street sewers (built either by the ground landlord or his building lessee) which drained surface water into the nearest natural sewer or stream was in theory forbidden in London, and sometimes actually prevented. Even in Cheapside there was as late as 1844 no underground drainage: 'its nightsoil is kept in poisonous pools, of which the inhabitants pump out the contents into the open channels of the street in the night, or have them removed by nightmen'.[40]

The Great Fire and the Rebuilding of the City

In September 1666 fire engulfed the City for four days and nights and destroyed four-fifths of the fabric, including St Paul's Cathedral, the Guildhall, the Royal Exchange, 87 churches, 44 livery company halls, and over 13,000 houses (Plate 19). It had started in a bakery in Pudding Lane near the foot of London Bridge, and, fanned by a strong wind, it defied all the efforts of the Lord Mayor, the duke of York, and the king himself to extinguish it. Some 80,000 residents had to leave their homes, and some never returned.[41]

Designs for the rebuilding of the City with a new layout plan were quickly made by Sir Christopher Wren and John Evelyn, but were rejected as impracticable; and in consequence traces of the City's medieval or even Roman street plan can still be seen, despite the depredations made by the massive redevelopments of recent years. The rebuilding took some ten years to complete (not counting St Paul's and the parish churches), the innumerable property disputes which arose from it being expeditiously settled by the specially established Fire Court. A number of improvements were made: a few streets were widened and some steep gradients near the river reduced, Guildhall was given an impressive approach by the construction of King Street and Queen Street, and commercial facilities were improved by the provision of better markets and the formation of a continuous quay along the riverside between the Tower and London Bridge.[42]

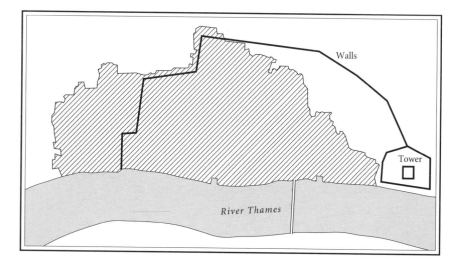

Fig. 20. Extent of destruction by the Great Fire, 1666

The greatest improvements, however, were the compulsory use required by the Rebuilding Act of 1667 of better building materials — brick or stone instead of wood — and the detailed regulations governing the four standardized classes of houses about to be built in the City.[43] Regulations of this kind had been foreshadowed in the proclamations issued some fifty years earlier by James I for the control of building in the suburbs. Now in the aftermath of the Great Fire the rules were given statutory authority, at least within the City; and although their application did not extend to the suburbs they were often used there by ground landlords like Lord Leicester in Leicester Fields in 1670 as a model in the building specifications to which building lessees were required to conform.[44] The Act of 1667 was in fact the forerunner of the great series of London Building Acts of the eighteenth and nineteenth centuries by which the safety of the fabric of the capital was slowly but vastly improved.

The cost of building these thousands of new houses was paid for by their owners, without assistance from public funds and without the benefit of insurance against fire (still a thing of the future) — a remarkable testimony to the wealth of the City. For the rebuilding of the streets, prisons, gates, and the Guildhall itself, however, a tax on the vast quantities of coal entering the Port of London from the distant mines of north-east England was imposed; and part of the proceeds was also used to pay for the rebuilding of St Paul's (completed in 1711) and some fifty of the eighty-seven churches destroyed by the Fire. All of them were designed by Wren, and their towers and steeples clustering round the great dome of St Paul's provided a matchless skyline for the new London.[45]

The most important effect of the Great Fire upon London as a whole was its long-term acceleration of the outward spread of the suburbs, particularly westward. Two years after the disaster a contemporary stated that 'many citizens...are now residing in the Suburbs, and like to continue there'. Nor, he continued, could they 'justly be compelled to plant [i.e. settle] within the walls again...sith [since] many of them have taken long leases of their houses in the suburbs...and know not how to put off [dispose of] the houses they have taken, and to reimburse themselves without insufferable loss, and diminution'.[46] In 1672 a quarter of the pre-Fire residents of the City had still not returned, and although the bulk of private rebuilding had been finished, something like a sixth of all the new houses were empty. In the City there were higher and more numerous taxes, vexatious and outdated guild restrictions on trade and industry, and frequent liability to serve burdensome ward or parish offices. For retail shopkeepers the lure of the fashionable western suburbs was particularly strong, and many of the 'eminent Mercers, Silk-men and Lacemen' who, for instance, had hitherto been in business in Paternoster Row never returned from their new quarters in the streets off Covent Garden Piazza.[47] So the Fire was an important element in the fall of the population of the City which (as previously mentioned) was taking place throughout the second half of the seventeenth century. Whereas around 1550 most of the peoples of London had lived within the tightly knit jurisdiction of the City Corporation, by 1700 most of them lived outside it, in Westminster, Southwark, or the adjacent parishes;[48] and we must now look at the attempts made to devise an appropriate form of government for these new extramural suburbs.

11

The Administration of the Metropolis

Never before in England had there been suburban growth on a scale comparable with that of seventeenth-century London; by around 1700 the population of its eastern suburbs alone was at least four times as great as that of the whole city of Norwich, then the largest urban centre outside the capital.[1] So the social and administrative challenges presented by this huge new area of bricks and mortar were unpreced-ented: how might the suburbs sprouting up all round the ancient jurisdiction of the City Corporation be governed? The royal and municipal responses to this problem must now be examined, for they had a direct bearing on the subsequent development of the government of London, and hence of an important aspect of the very nature of the capital. Indeed they still do so after the lapse of more than three centuries, and appear likely to continue to do so for the foreseeable future.

Au fond the problem for the authorities boiled down to the maintenance of the established social order, or, more specifically, to the preservation of the peace, the relief of the poor and the surveillance of orphans, the suppression of vagrancy, and, in times of food shortage, the maintenance of the supply of grain, plus, in times of plague, the protection of public health. Authority in these matters was exercised on the one hand by the Crown, acting mainly through the Privy Council, the Court of Star Chamber, and the Justices of the Peace of the various commissions of the peace in the metropolitan area (the City, Middlesex, Westminster, and Surrey), and on the other hand either by the innumerable authorities within the City or by the parish vestries in the suburbs. The structure of government in the metropolitan area was in fact much the same as that which prevailed in and around any of the great provincial cities. Only the scale of the matter in hand was different — indeed of a quite different order.

The City, the Corporation, and the Other London

The City was unique in its dense institutional fabric. In the area within the jurisdiction of the Corporation the twenty-six ancient wards (including

Southwark), each with its own alderman, still provided the foundation of communal public life. The wards were divided into 242 precincts, and there were also over 100 parishes, all of these bodies having their own little teams of officers: constables, scavengers, inquest men, beadles, churchwardens. All in all, so Professor Pearl has calculated, perhaps one in ten of all householders held annually some local office or other.[2] In addition there were the guilds and livery companies, over fifty in number in Elizabethan times, which were also active in social matters, and each having its own band of officers. Finally, at the centre of the web lay the City Corporation itself, where except in revolutionary times the Lord Mayor and Court of Aldermen still directed the City's affairs, often acting in close liaison with the Privy Council at Whitehall. By the end of the sixteenth century, however, the Court of Common Council (its 200 or so members elected by the wardmotes) was asserting a growing authority, particularly in matters of economic regulation and municipal taxation. Just as the precincts, wards, parishes, and guilds all had their elected or appointed officers, so too did the powers at Guildhall, where there were nearly 500 paid offices within the City's gift.[3]

Within this tightly knit network of overlapping and often conflicting jurisdictions there developed a system of social administration which although often harsh and brutal by modern standards was probably nevertheless well in advance of those then prevalent elsewhere in England.[4] The weekly doles distributed by the parishes to the impotent poor (the sick, the young, the old, and widows) were the basic form of poor relief. The funds for these doles were provided either from the rents of houses which had been bequeathed to the parishes and which were also sometimes used to house the indigent poor, or from the taxes for the poor which were first raised in the City in 1547, many years before national poor rates were enjoined. There was also a rate equalization scheme, supervised by the Court of Aldermen, by which rich parishes assisted poor ones. Parish efforts were frequently supplemented by pensions and gifts in kind from the guilds and livery companies, from the wardmotes, and from private charity; and relief was not restricted either to freemen of the City or even to householders, although most recipients of the weekly doles were in fact householders.[5]

The City Corporation itself was also active in matters of social control, concerning itself (as we shall see later) in the abatement of successive epidemics of plague, and during times of dearth in the supply of grain. More enduring success attended the five great acquisitions which it made between 1547 and 1553, all but one of them of property previously belonging to monastic houses. These acquisitions consisted of the hospital previously attached to the priory of St Bartholomew's, Smithfield; the originally monastic hospital of St Thomas's, Southwark; the hospital for lunatics attached to the priory of St Mary Bethlehem outside Bishopsgate; the dissolved monastery of the Greyfriars in Newgate Street, which the Corporation converted into Christ's Hospital for orphans and helpless children; and the recently built but already disused royal palace of Bridewell on the banks of the Fleet River.[6] In the 1670s St Bartholomew's and St Thomas's were providing a total of nearly 500 beds for the sick,[7] and both still survive (though the future of

Bart's is in 1997 in doubt) as two of London's greatest hospitals, St Thomas's having in Victorian times removed to Lambeth. Bethlehem Royal Hospital (from which the word 'bedlam' is derived) also survives as one of the leading psychiatric hospitals in the country, having moved in 1675–6 to Moorfields and thence in 1815 to Lambeth; it is now at Beckenham in Kent. Christ's Hospital for children became a famous school and ultimately removed to Horsham in Sussex in 1902; and the Corporation's concern for infants did not end there, for it acted as the public guardian of orphans' property, a job which (as we saw in Chapter 7) provided valuable revenue for the civic coffers.

In addition to caring for the sick, the insane, and the orphaned, the Corporation also attempted to provide for the able-bodied poor. During the Commonwealth and again in 1698 it attempted to establish a central workhouse or Corporation of the Poor for the whole City.[8] Both attempts were unsuccessful; but the penal regime which the Corporation provided at Bridewell proved more enduring. In the later sixteenth and early seventeenth centuries vagrancy in London was growing, but until 1614, when the Justices of the Peace of Middlesex, Surrey, and Westminster began to establish their own 'houses of correction', the Corporation's Bridewell was the only place where wandering immigrants, out-of-work journeymen, apprentices, or servants could be judged, punished, and sent on their way. It was also from Bridewell that large-scale transportation to the American colonies began, in 1618–19, when ninety-nine children were dispatched to Virginia.[9]

There was, however, another London where these municipal foundations either did not exist or only did so in much weaker form. This other London consisted of the Borough of Southwark, the City of Westminster, the liberties, and the out-parishes or suburbs. During the early seventeenth century the total population of this other London began to exceed that within the City's jurisdiction (within and without the walls), and continued to do so by an increasingly wide margin.[10] Here in this mostly new London the social problems confronting the numerous authorities within the City presented themselves in even more acute form.

Southwark had always been regarded with suspicion by the City authorities. During the Middle Ages it had been an unchartered manorial borough over which the City had acquired some control; but although the Corporation had in 1550 purchased a royal charter which opened the way to the complete integration of the Borough into the City, these rights were never fully exercised, and the ward of Bridge Without always remained a token ward without either Common Councilmen or an elected alderman.[11] Westminster too had had manorial government in medieval times, here provided by the court of the abbot, but the City had never meddled in Westminster, and after the dissolution of the abbey the rapidly growing urban nucleus was administered by a new and somewhat ineffective Court of Burgesses established in 1585 and chosen by the dean and chapter of the newly established collegiate church.

Outside the City's jurisdiction the main foundation of order was provided (even in Southwark and Westminster) by the parish vestries (i.e. assemblies) and their unpaid officers: the churchwardens, constables, surveyors of the highways, and overseers of the poor. By 1600 the vestries had statutory power to raise rates for the maintenance of the highways and for poor relief, and their activities were supervised by the Justices of the Peace for Middlesex and Surrey. But such large and rapidly urbanizing parishes as Stepney or Clerkenwell or St Martin-in-the-Fields presented problems quite beyond the vestries' capacity to manage and, to add to the administrative turmoil by which the City was surrounded, there were the numerous exempt areas or 'liberties' which had formerly been monastic precincts. Many of their ancient privileges had survived the Dissolution and still conferred upon them immunity from outside interference. Just outside the City there was a score of them, Whitefriars, the Charterhouse, and St Katharine's by the Tower being the most notable; and even within the City itself there were half a dozen extra-parochial places such as St Martin's le Grand or Holy Trinity, Aldgate. Throughout the seventeenth century many of them were islands of poverty and lawlessness; and some of them survived until much later — St Martin's le Grand, for instance, until 1815, while the independence of St Katharine's was only extinguished when its site was swallowed up in 1825 by a new dock for the inexorably growing port of London.[12]

The 'New Incorporation' of the Suburbs

If the incidence of plague provides any guide to general levels of public health, then there can be no doubt that from around 1600 onwards living conditions were in general worse in the suburbs than within much of the City, nor that the final outbreak in 1665 was much more severe in the fringes of the built-up area than in the centre.[13] Plague in London had always evoked the concern of the Privy Council which since 1518 had been prodding the Corporation to attempt to limit the spread of infection, chiefly by the isolation of victims within their own households. In the 1570s, when large-scale suburban growth was just beginning, the Council's concern intensified, and the discussion of draft plague regulations resulted in 1583 in the issue of a set of printed orders. By that time the Privy Council was also trying to use the City magistrates to enforce royal proclamations and statutes in the liberties and out-parishes as well as within the City itself. The policies thus to be imposed were, however, often repugnant to the City authorities, particularly that introduced under James I of allowing offenders against the proclamations controlling new building to compound with the Crown for money. So the royal and municipal authorities, which should have been natural allies in the maintenance of established order, found themselves increasingly at loggerheads with each other, the Privy Council frequently accusing the Corporation of doing too little too late to control the spread of plague and the Corporation resenting royal interference within either the City or the liberties and out-parishes.[14]

In 1630–1 the times were uniquely favourable for a royal initiative to end this long-standing friction by the provision of a 'political' solution for the problems of the ever-growing suburbs. Charles I's period of personal rule had just begun and he was still full of self-confidence. London was to be controlled and made to provide an ordered setting for the seat of royal power by the imposition of such quasi-royal schemes as that of the earl of Bedford in Covent Garden, the first royal licence for which was granted in 1631. And in the previous year the reappearance of plague in London and the prevalence of economic depression had attracted the attention of the Privy Council once more.[15]

It was in these circumstances that in March 1631 the king's French physician, Sir Theodore de Mayerne, presented Charles with a report on precautions to be taken against plague in the metropolitan area. Food supplies should be controlled, vagrants forcibly expelled, and London generally cleaned up; and with the example of Paris and other Continental cities in mind he called for four new hospitals. But he broke entirely new ground when he proposed a 'chamber, court or office of health' with authority over the whole field of public health (vagrancy, poor relief, and hygiene as well as plague). The new court was to include the Lord Mayor, some of the aldermen, two privy councillors, and two bishops. It was to have absolute power; and most importantly of all its authority was to extend over the whole metropolitan area from Richmond to Greenwich.[16]

These proposals were supported by the king's other physicians and also by the College of Physicians, although when plague went away soon afterwards the urgency of the matter diminished and nothing came of them. With absolutist ideas of this kind for the sanitary administration of London being discussed at court it was not, however, a wise moment for the Court of Aldermen in 1632 to address a petition of complaint to the Privy Council. This rehearsed the deplorable state of the suburbs and lamented that the extraordinary spread of buildings there had drawn up great multitudes of tradesmen and craftsmen who were able to practise their *métiers* there without being freemen of the City, by reason whereof 'the freedom of London which is heretofore of very great esteem is grown to be of little worth'. Discussions ensued, and after a pause of nearly a year they culminated in a request from the Privy Council to the City Corporation to consider whether 'they would accept... part of the suburbs into their jurisdiction and liberty for better government'.[17]

For centuries there had been no outward extension of the administrative area of the City. Several of the wards, such as Cripplegate, included areas outside the line of the ancient defensive walls, and Portsoken was wholly extramural. In 1394 the vast extent of Farringdon Ward had been divided into two, Farringdon Within and Without, each with its own alderman and Common Councilmen, but we have already seen that despite the powers granted to the City by the royal charter of 1550 Southwark had never been integrated administratively. Similarly in the 1630s the Court of Aldermen had no wish to annex the turbulent and ever growing suburbs. What they wanted, purely for the protection of the City's own interests, was a measure of supervisory authority over the out-parishes, but unaccompanied by basic responsibility for the relief of the poor or the maintenance of law and order there; and they were also fearful that the creation in the boisterous suburbs of several fully fledged new wards would upset the time-honoured machinery of the City's existing civic polity. So they prevaricated about the Privy Council's (for them) very drastic proposal.[18]

In the middle years of Charles I's paternal rule the Privy Council did not take kindly to such tactics, and now it moved from proposing to imposing a solution for the suburbs. This was the short-lived New Incorporation or Incorporation of Westminster, as it was called (though it extended to the whole extramural area within 3 miles of the City), which was established in 1636 by royal letters patent. The new body was to have a governor, four wardens, and eighty assistants, and within its extensive area (which was divided into four wards) no one — even a man already free of the City of London — was to trade without seven years' apprenticeship and enrolment within the new incorporation.[19]

This was, of course, a direct challenge to the foundation of all the City's privileges: the freedom, i.e. the status normally acquired by a man on completion of his apprenticeship, when after his admission to his livery company he was sworn and enrolled at Guildhall as a citizen or freeman of London. Within the area of the City's jurisdiction freemen still possessed a monopoly in the practice of their trades, and in the mid-seventeenth century this was still sufficiently valuable for the majority of male householders to pay the fees required for admission to the freedom.[20] But outside the City, in the liberties and out-parishes, was a grey area where on the one hand some livery companies asserted rights of regulation under their own individual royal charters, and where on the other hand large numbers of tradesmen and craftsmen, particularly immigrants, operated unapprenticed and unfettered by any guild. For the City authorities this was bad enough, but the creation of a rival regulatory power all around them was far worse.

In the event the City survived. There was much opposition to taking up the freedom of the new body, frequent lawsuits between the two corporations over freemen and over areas of jurisdiction, and widespread hostility to the Privy Council. Soon after the collapse of Charles's personal rule and the meeting of the Long Parliament in November 1640 the whole project sank into unlamented oblivion. Even during the Civil War the City authorities did not want to annex the suburbs,[21] but when in 1649 the burgesses of Southwark, after a century of existence half in and half out of the City, presented a petition to Parliament asking either for full incorporation within it or for full self-government outside it, the City successfully opposed it;[22] and a petition of 1650 for the incorporation of Westminster also came to nothing. Soon after the Restoration in 1660 the question of the incorporation of the suburbs, now much larger in extent, was discussed again; but the Court of Common Council declared unanimously that 'they conceived the Incorporating the Suburbs of London distinct from the City to be destructive to the interests and trade of the City', and the matter was dropped.[23]

These mid-seventeenth-century events, extending from the early 1630s to the 1660s, are important because their imprint may still be traced in the shape of the modern government of London. It was in those years that the question of whether London should be regarded and treated as a single city or as a loose congeries of *quartiers* first arose. Through the existence of the two cities of London and Westminster this question had already begun to suggest itself, but with the rapid growth of the out-parishes after about 1580 it was first presented in its modern form. The City authorities had made clear that so far as they were concerned the metropolis was not to be a single entity. Their policies, first formulated in the mid-seventeenth century — refusal to enlarge the administrative boundaries of the City and opposition to the creation of any overall authority within the extramural built-up area — became articles of faith with the Corporation. They were supported primarily by economic self-interest but also at first by the unpopularity of the association of proto-unitary ideas of metropolitan government with royal absolutism. So for two centuries the out-parishes were left to manage their own affairs pretty much according to their own devices, and it was not until 1855 that through the establishment of the Metropolitan Board of Works they first acquired the rudiments of any overall administration. Only once, in 1884, and then abortively, has any government ever ventured to propose that the City Corporation should enlarge its domain and embrace the whole of London. So at the very centre of the modern metropolis still presides intact the splendid ancient municipality, its institutional hierarchy as densely structured as ever, but by its mere existence constituting for the rest of London a vacuum instead of the natural focus of metropolitan loyalty and civic pride. The century which has elapsed since 1884 has seen the creation and abolition of two successive directly elected metropolitan-wide authorities (the London County Council 1889–1965 and the Greater London Council 1965–86), and the question first asked in the seventeenth century still has no satisfactory answer. The only certainty about the future government of London is that the present dispensation — no overall authority, either elected or nominated — will not last for very long; and at the time of writing (1997) a quite new idea — an elected mayor on American or Continental lines — is being discussed.

12

Death and Life in London

The most fundamental and all-pervasive ingredient of life in London in the sixteenth and seventeenth centuries was its precariousness. Plague, of course, was never far away, and during the outbreak of 1665 (Plate 18) Pepys records that 'a man cannot depend on living two days to an end'.[1] In two of the worst years of plague — 1603 and 1625 — deaths from all causes exceeded a quarter of the total population. Mortality on this kind of level has never recurred in later years, for even cholera in its worst outbreak in the nineteenth century (in 1848–9) accounted for fewer deaths in the whole of England and Wales (53,000) than had plague in London alone in 1665 (55,797). And even after the effects of epidemics of plague have been discounted, expectation of life at birth in the City in the first half of the seventeenth century ranged between only 25 and 30 years, compared with an average of 46 years for infants born in rural England.[2]

In some of the poorer parishes, notably those just outside the City walls and some of those alongside the river, expectation of life in the early seventeenth century was even lower. At St Mary Somerset it was only 21 years, excluding the effect of plague epidemics.[3] The impact of these epidemics also varied greatly from one part of London to another, the least affected parishes corresponding broadly with those of greatest wealth, mainly in the centre astride Cheapside and in parts of Westminster. Although this differential rate of mortality may be partly accounted for during outbreaks of plague by the flight of substantial numbers of rich residents — during that of 1665 the royal court left London, Parliament was prorogued, and the Inns of Court were deserted — a vital component of it was always, irrespective of the extent of the prevalence of plague, the excessive density of population in the poorest parishes, where life was in Thomas Hobbes's phrase, 'nasty, brutish and short'.[4]

Earning a Living

Making a livelihood was often as precarious as life itself, at least for the great majority of the population dependent on regular earnings for food, fuel, and clothing, and with little or nothing to fall back on in hard times. These earnings were made in an infinite variety of ways. The largest source of employment was provided by the cloth industry and the crafts connected with the export of cloth, for although little actual weaving of cloth took place in London there was a great number of finishing and marketing trades; and if clothes-makers are also included (bodice-makers, hatmakers, milliners, etc.), clothing accounted for between a fifth and a quarter of all employment.[5] Next in terms of numbers came, probably, the workers involved in some way or other with the port, either directly with ships or with the handling of their cargoes, and concentrated largely in the riverside hamlets of Stepney, where in Shadwell, for instance, nearly three-quarters of the working population gained their living by these means.[6] The ceaseless business of supplying food and drink also required thousands of workers; so too did the building, leather, and metal trades. As around one in every twenty houses was used as a tavern, and even more were used as shops, many a living must have been scratched or supplemented by small-scale retailing;[7] and domestic servants, mostly female, may have numbered about one in thirteen of the entire population, if ratios for Georgian and Victorian times are any guide.[8]

Workplace and living quarters were often situated in the same building and were certainly seldom far apart. Workshops were in general still small in scale, but in the new and largely unregulated suburbs they were sometimes larger. In the early seventeenth century Robert Baker, the tailor of Piccadilly Hall, was, for instance, employing some sixty men in the making of his famous piccadills at his shop in the Strand;[9] and riverside industries such as shipbuilding in East London or brewing in Southwark had relatively large workforces. The extramural parishes were in fact becoming the resort of those trades, comprising over half of London's total workforce, which were engaged in some way in the production of goods, while the less numerous workers in exchange-related occupations tended to concentrate within the City.[10] Everywhere in the metropolis, however, earning a living was a chancy business. Demand for labour fluctuated greatly, the labour shortage of the first half of the sixteenth century, caused by the enormous growth of the cloth industry, being followed by depression, unemployment, and (between about 1560 and 1625) increased vagrancy.[11] During the Civil War, too, London's economy suffered severe dislocation, though not so great as that of many provincial towns, and it was not until the early 1650s that wage earners there again enjoyed high wages comparable in real terms to those which had prevailed in the early sixteenth century.[12]

The regulation of the gigantic metropolitan labour force was, at the beginning of the sixteenth century, still largely the concern of the guilds or livery companies, membership of which had in the later Middle Ages become increasingly expensive and exclusive. It has been estimated that in the early sixteenth century only one quarter of all adult men in the City were free citizens and members of a livery company;[13] and the Evil May Day riot of 1517 may well have originated in the pent-up resentments of frustrated journeymen and apprentices with little chance of advancement. During the 1520s and early 1530s, however, the companies' authority to regulate the activities of all Londoners practising trades or crafts in or within

2 miles of the City was greatly enlarged by Act of Parliament, while the fees for enrolling apprentices or admitting new members were greatly reduced. Consequently the number of admissions to the freedom began to rise dramatically. Professor Rappaport has shown that by the 1550s some three-quarters of all adult men within the City were by then citizens, and that at least half the men admitted as citizens at about that time eventually advanced from the status of journeymen to that of householder — i.e. master craftsman or retail shopkeeper.[14] The livery companies had in fact ceased to be the costly and exclusive clubs of late medieval times, while the City in general had become if not exactly a property-owning democracy at least a place where widely diffused ownership contributed a significant measure of social stability.

The companies' control over London's crafts and retail trades started to decline soon after the rapid extension of the built-up area outside the square mile of the old City began in the 1580s. This decline was a long process, not fully completed until the nineteenth century.[15] Indeed many of the royal charters granted to livery companies even after 1660 included areas of up to 10 miles from the City within guild control,[16] and the Tylers' and Bricklayers' Company was still in the 1680s, for instance, conducting searches for defective bricks among the building lots of Soho.[17] But as early as the first decade of the seventeenth century Robert Baker of Piccadilly Hall was making and selling piccadills at his shop in the Strand without having served an apprenticeship and without interference from the guilds.[18] In the large and rapidly expanding extramural suburbs, to which migrants like Baker naturally resorted and which (as we have already seen) were becoming the main centres of manufacturing crafts, the livery companies were unable to exercise effective regulation. And despite the very large increase in the population of the whole metropolis, the number of apprentices was actually falling during the seventeenth century.[19] Apprenticeship was the foundation of the guilds' ancient means of industrial control, and its decline marks, in the words of A. L. Beier, 'a change in the mode of production from the regulated system of the medieval gilds to something like a free-market situation'.[20] This was, of course, a very slow shift, but by the end of the seventeenth century many of the livery companies were beginning to make the long-drawn-out transition from regulative industrial bodies to associations mainly concerned with the management of their often valuable properties and the sponsorship of charitable, educational, or merely clubby interests.

Outside the livery companies' control and excluded from the benefits of membership of them, there was also a substantial minority of rootless men and women who in times of dearth faced impoverishment and destitution, or resorted to crime and/or prostitution. Many of them were subsistence migrants lured to London by the prospect of high wages, or apprentices who had failed to complete the terms to which they had been bound, the 'drop-out' rate in the sixteenth century being nearly 60 per cent.[21] They tended to congregate in narrow self-contained alleys and in the exempt purlieus of the 'liberties' (formerly monastic precincts) — 'no-go areas' which were the harbingers of the 'rookeries' of later times and the denizens of which provided the nucleus of the perennial metropolitan casual labour market. Women without means of subsistence — newly arrived migrants or the wives of absent sailors, for instance — often resorted through necessity rather than choice to prostitution, demand for which came from all social ranks, the average age of men at first marriage around 1600 being apparently 28 years. Some thirty years earlier there were already over 100 recorded bawdy houses in London. Southwark (and Bankside in particular), where social controls were less strict than in the City, was notorious for its 'stews' (brothels) as well as for its playhouses and prisons; and Alsatia (the exempt precinct of the former Whitefriars monastery, between the Temple and Whitefriars Street) was a hotbed of illicit activity of all kinds. In the anonymous conditions prevalent in the rapidly growing suburbs of London crime could flourish almost anywhere, often with plenty of alluring targets available nearby for either casual and opportunistic petty crimes such as pilfering, cut-pursing, and trickery at dicing and gambling, or for highway robbery and house-breaking. And there seems to have been an effective system for the disposal of the swag.[22]

Metropolitan Social Equilibrium

Despite the extremes of personal circumstance experienced by different ranks of the inhabitants of the metropolis, and despite the social problems attendant on the explosion of the capital's population, there was never a complete breakdown of established authority in London in either the sixteenth or seventeenth centuries. The most serious riot of the sixteenth century, 'Evil May Day' in 1517, was an isolated affair in which some 2,000 young men attacked foreigners' premises. It only lasted a few hours, and not a single life was lost, though a dozen of the leaders were subsequently hanged.[23] Even in the 1590s, when there were four consecutive bad harvests (1594–7) and real wages touched their lowest levels, there were only sporadic minor disturbances, the worst of which were in 1595; and never did public order collapse as it did in Paris in 1588 and again at times during the Fronde (1648–52), and in a number of other cities in continental Europe.[24] Nor did Londoners ever experience death by starvation on a large scale.[25] Whereas in Paris stability depended upon the prevailing strength of royal power, in London it was the product of a solid civic infrastructure where personal involvement of some sort was very widespread, and where the oligarchic flavour of much of the City's government, although strong (particularly within the Corporation), never reached a point where alienation from the established order became dangerously prevalent.

The City authorities' involvement in the supply of grain illustrates their responsiveness to social challenges. In normal times the great markets such as those at Smithfield or Leadenhall still met much of the demand for food in the City, while in times of dearth the authorities had for several centuries been purchasing corn for redistribution. In the 1540s, however, the aldermen were finding it necessary to buy grain almost every year and store it in their granaries at the Bridgehouse adjacent to the riverside quays, or at Leadenhall. As the aldermen usually made a loss on these transactions the livery companies also became involved, agreeing in 1578 to take the job over; but they too generally made a loss.[26] In the early seventeenth century the authorities' intention was to provide in times of shortage one-third of the City's estimated consumption, and in the 1650s the price of bread was still being regularly set by the Court of Aldermen.[27] But later in the century the commercial mechanisms for the supply of grain (and of all other forms of food), reinforced by the recent establishment of a dozen new markets such as those at Covent Garden and Spitalfields, were well able to meet demand, and municipal operations ceased.[28]

Nevertheless there were, of course, years of severe shortage and high prices, and of general economic hardship. This was particularly so during such periods of rapid inflation as the 1540s and the closing years of Elizabeth's reign; and during the whole of the sixteenth century the real income of wage earners in London is thought to have fallen by over one-third.[29] The possibility of a bad harvest was a continuous threat hanging over the poor, and when bread prices jumped the number of households needing relief also leaped upwards. But the rate of inflation of food prices in London throughout the whole of the sixteenth century averaged less than 1.50 per cent per annum.[30] Moreover London wage rates throughout both the sixteenth and seventeenth centuries were always substantially higher than elsewhere in southern England (in the seventeenth century over 50 per cent higher), while the price of bread in London was at any rate from the 1590s never more than 25 per cent greater than outside the capital.[31] It is therefore likely that despite the undoubted hardships of life in London, the labouring population there enjoyed greater purchasing power — a differential which no doubt motivated many country dwellers to migrate to London.

The maintenance of social stability cannot, however, be wholly explained in these financial and economic terms, and this was particularly the case in the critical 1590s, the worst decade of either the sixteenth or seventeenth centuries, when the proportion of poor in the population was growing (largely through immigration) and social polarization was becoming more extreme.[32] Fear must also have played its part, for after the near-monthly Newgate gaol deliveries twenty or thirty offenders were sometimes publicly executed in a single day in what has been described as 'probably the bloodiest period in the history of the English criminal law'.[33] In reality, however, the coercive powers of the City authorities were extremely limited, a few days' hard labour in Bridewell and/or a whipping there for such offences as prostitution, vagrancy, or theft being the commonest punishments;[34] and continuing stability seems to have depended primarily on what Dr Ian Archer has termed 'the solidity of the élite' and its capacity to respond in some measure to changing popular pressures.[35]

The nucleus of the élite consisted of the aldermen and their deputies, who were leading Common Councillors. They were a homogeneous group, not internally divided (as the City authorities had so often been in turbulent times in the fourteenth century), even by religious issues, and in Elizabeth's reign they did not feel threatened or molested by the Government, which was well aware of its own exposed situation. Their authority was supported by a closely knit network of social relationships extending far below the ranks of the élite itself and based both on the territorial loyalties and identities of parish, neighbourhood, and ward and on the occupational ties of the livery companies. By these means, on the one hand channels of communication for the redress of grievances were available, while on the other hand the administration of poor relief could be used for purposes of social control. The funds for this relief (which originated from the hospitals, from parish rates and property rents, from the livery companies, and from private charity) increased considerably in the last three decades of the sixteenth century, but the growth was more than cancelled out by rising prices and rising population, and the amount of relief available per capita in real terms therefore seems to have actually fallen. The application of it nevertheless contributed to stability because it endowed those in authority with a measure of charitable intention and repute while simultaneously promoting deference amongst the recipients. Those in such authority at local or livery company level included people well down the City's social pyramid, and the growing alignment of this increasingly homogeneous middling sort with the élite in the enforcement of established order provided a powerful ballast for the maintenance of the City's equilibrium.[36]

This process continued during the seventeenth century, and was not seriously interrupted even during the Civil Wars and the Interregnum. People of the 'middling sort' were probably increasing as a proportion of the total population, and Dr Peter Earle thinks that by around 1700 they amounted to no less than a quarter of it. On the other hand the number of apprentices (who, with runaways, were often perceived to be potential sources of disorder) fell from around 15 per cent of the metropolitan population in 1600 to less than 5 per cent a century later.[37] In the extramural suburbs, where by 1700 most Londoners lived, there was informal mediation by Justices of the Peace in the settlement of interpersonal disputes, and in the field of misdemeanours such as pilfering, bastardy, and master–servant disputes the frequent prosecution of offenders by the victims provided useful safety valves against many potential social explosions.[38] The middling sort were still well spread out across the metropolis, and although there was social diversification between (most obviously) West and East London, there was as yet no tight residential social segregation. By around 1700 these middling people were getting richer and living longer (which gave them more time to accumulate wealth).[39] More Londoners were enjoying comfortable conditions of life than had ever previously been experienced except by a numerically very small élite; and Dr Earle thinks that this enhancement of living standards in London amounted to a qualitative change from which there developed 'a new type of society which has proved to be a model, not just for the developing middle class of provincial England but for Europeans and Americans and indeed for the whole world'.[40]

Leisure Pursuits and the Elizabethan and Restoration Theatres

Changing social conditions of this kind were mirrored in the changing leisure pursuits of the age. The long association of the Church with many of Londoners' recreational activities was brought to an end by the Reformation. Puritan hostility towards many forms of public amusement gave renewed vigour to private recreation at home in the form of games (draughts, chess, and backgammon were all popular), singing and dancing, smoking (which became widespread in the early seventeenth century), and of course eating and drinking. Drinking, whether at home or in the tavern or alehouse, was probably the means of relaxation most widely favoured by Londoners, followed by gambling in every form and nearly every place.[41]

In the new post-Reformation milieu the provision of many 'recreational facilities' became a matter of business enterprise: the modern 'leisure industry' was making its entrance. Some spectacles were of course free — public executions, for instance, or the annual Lord Mayor's Show — and the practice of archery in the fields outside the City walls was actively encouraged by the Crown throughout the sixteenth century. (The Honourable Artillery Company, which claims to be the oldest military body in Britain, and the headquarters of which are still just outside the City, was incorporated by Henry VIII in 1537 as 'The Fraternity or Guild of Artillery of Longbows, Crossbows and Handguns'.) But most amusements had to be paid for. Cock-fighting was universally popular in all walks of life, gambling being its principal *raison d'être*; and so too were bull- and bear-baiting, though Pepys, on a visit to the bear gardens at Bankside, thought that the latter was 'a very rude and nasty pleasure'. Violent encounters like these required, or at any rate could best be presented in, special arenas the building of which required substantial capital outlay. The more peaceful amusements provided by the bowling alleys and pleasure gardens which sprang up around London, particularly after the Restoration — Marylebone Gardens and Vauxhall Gardens, for instance, both visited by Pepys — or the entertainments first put on by Thomas Sadler at his medicinal wells in Finsbury in 1683, were also considerable commercial enterprises. So too were the coffee houses, which first appeared in 1652. The facilities which they provided — newspapers, pipes and tobacco, gossip, and congenial company — soon constituted a formidable challenge to the taverns, for within ten years there were over eighty coffee houses in the City alone; and it was from the coffee — or very similar chocolate — houses that there evolved the proprietary clubs of Augustan London, of which one of the earliest and most famous was White's, still after more than three centuries in St James's Street, and first opened there as a chocolate house by Francis White in 1683.[42]

But the most famous of all the recreations enjoyed by Londoners during much of the period covered by this chapter was of course provided by the theatre; and in this field the predominance of the capital was absolute, there being no comparable provincial counterpart to the London stage. This predominance, which still largely prevails today, originally owed much to the presence of the royal court, where plays and in the early seventeenth century elaborate masques (some designed by Inigo Jones) were often performed. Starting in the mid-1570s there sprang up around the City some half-dozen or more specially designed wooden buildings, or 'public places', as John Stow called them, round or polygonal in form and enclosing an open yard where stood a stage overlooked by tiers of covered galleries. These first English theatres could accommodate an audience of 2,000–3,000 people[43] and were clustered in two small groups, one in the northern outskirts, in Finsbury and Shoreditch, and the other across the river in Bankside, Southwark. Although they were all deliberately sited by their proprietors outside the jurisdiction of the City authorities, the troupes of players who performed in them needed the protection or licence of some powerful patron such as the Lord Chamberlain or even the monarch in order to avoid the charge of being rogues or 'masterless men'. It was in these precarious conditions that the great masterpieces of Elizabethan and Jacobean dramatic art were written and first performed.

It was also then that the London Commercial Theatre made its début, some of its early sponsors then as now being men of business attracted from other fields by the large financial gains to be had. James Burbage, who in 1576–7 built in Shoreditch the very first London theatre, known simply as 'The Theatre', was originally a joiner by trade, and certainly made a great deal of money. So too did Philip Henslowe, dyer, moneylender and property speculator as well as a principal entrepreneur of the Rose Theatre in Southwark and of the Fortune in Finsbury. Both he and his son-in-law and partner, Edward Alleyn, also had lucrative interests in bear-baiting at Paris Gardens, Bankside, and Alleyn became rich enough not only to buy the Manor of Dulwich but also to found and endow Dulwich College. Shakespeare himself owned a one-tenth share in the Globe and was able after only a dozen years' work in London to buy the largest house in his native town of Stratford-on-Avon.[44] 'Show business' in Elizabethan and Jacobean London could be a very profitable field of endeavour.

But it was also very chancy, for the theatres were periodically shut up in times of plague (four times between 1625 and 1637), and they were constantly under attack from the Puritans. In September 1642, after Charles I's withdrawal from London, an ordinance of the Long Parliament decreed their closure, but the habit of theatregoing had become so ingrained amongst Londoners that the order was often ignored, and even destructive raids by posses of soldiers failed to suppress the theatres altogether.[45]

After the Interregnum the London theatre made a fresh start, and the origins of much of its modern form may be found in the early post-Restoration period. In 1662–3 Charles II authorized Sir William Davenant, the dramatist and Poet Laureate, and Thomas Killigrew, also a playwright and according to Pepys 'a merry droll, but a gentleman of great esteem with the King', to build or hire two separate playhouses in London and to maintain two companies to act in them; all other playhouses were to be suppressed. Although frequently evaded in varying degrees, the duopoly of theatrical rights which these two royal patents established nevertheless survived as a powerful element in the history of the metropolitan theatre until the Theatres Act of 1843; and even now the Theatre Royal, Drury Lane, still exercises its rights under the authority of Killigrew's patent.[46]

The site of the present Drury Lane Theatre — or rather, of part of it — has been in continuous use for theatrical purposes since the new playhouse built by Killigrew and the leading members of his troupe, known as the King's Company, first opened there on 7 May 1663. Little is known about this short-lived theatre, which was burnt down in 1672. Its successor was designed by Sir Christopher Wren. The auditorium, no longer open to the sky as in the theatres of Shakespeare's day, contained an amphitheatre and two tiered galleries above, overlooking a pit and forestage flanked by two tiers of boxes. The stage itself was set within an architectural frame or proscenium formed of paired Corinthian pilasters.[47] This new playhouse therefore embodied several features which became standard in many later London theatres; and so too did the contemporaneous and rather grander Dorset Garden Theatre, built for Sir William Davenant's troupe, which was nominally under the protection of the king's brother, James, duke of York, and known as the Duke's Company.

At first both companies were well supported. In the first eight months of 1668, for instance, Pepys visited the theatre no less than seventy-three times, often with his wife. Sometimes she went without him, and the Diary contains no suggestion that the Restoration stage provided lewd entertainment unsuitable for respectable women.[48] Despite many later vicissitudes the London theatre was firmly established.

PART IV

Augustan and Georgian London
1700–1830

INTRODUCTION

After all the alarums and excursions of the previous two hundred years, the eighteenth and early nineteenth centuries were, relatively, a time of outward stability in the history of London. There was no religious reformation, no civil war, no explosion of population comparable to that which had started in the 1580s, no more outbreaks of plague, and no great fire. Changes were, in general, changes of scale and of quality rather than of fundamental nature. The population continued to increase, the suburbs continued to multiply, and the machinery of metropolitan government became ever more complex; the City continued to refine its techniques of banking, insurance, and financial dealings of all kinds, and London's foreign trade and manufacturing production continued to grow — but all on lines whose general direction had already been marked out by around 1700. Unlike before and after, Augustan and Georgian London was not, in fact, the scene of primary alterations of intrinsic form.

This was nevertheless the period (as generally perceived) of England's industrial revolution, which has been described by one of its foremost historians as 'the most important of all historical transformations to have taken place within these shores';[1] and London's role in this process, and the changing position of the capital in relation to both the rest of the country and to the outside world are the main subject of Chapter 14. Here it may briefly be noted that London's position was also deeply affected by the onset of the concomitant process of urbanization elsewhere in England. Between 1700 and 1801 the population of the metropolis increased from some 575,000 to 960,000. By 1831 it had reached 1,655,000, London's proportion of the total population of England remaining stable throughout the period at around 11 or 12 per cent. During the eighteenth century, however, the number of people living in England in towns with over 5,000 inhabitants excluding London grew more than fivefold, and by 1800 had risen from some 5.5 per cent to 16.5 per cent of the total population of England.[2] Most Georgian urban growth was indeed outside London in the rising industrial centres of the Midlands and the North, for by 1801 Manchester and Liverpool had displaced Norwich and Bristol as the second and third largest towns; and Birmingham was not far behind. So although London was still by far the largest single urban centre (in 1831 over eight times as big as Liverpool), its urban uniqueness within the national economy was no longer quite so absolute. Its political influence had also declined; nor (as we shall see) was it the fountainhead of industrial innovation, the structure of production in the metropolis exhibiting comparatively little change. But in the service sectors London's pre-eminence remained unchallenged, its social cachet as the capital city became ever more pronounced, and internally there was after about 1750 a general advance in London's health, cleanliness, public order, sobriety, and education.[3]

13

The Growth and Structure of London

Despite the more rapid growth of many towns in the Midlands and the North, London's own absolute growth was nevertheless still huge, and it was only through the continuous large-scale migration of individual people on a massive scale that this growth was maintained. Throughout most of the eighteenth century the death rate in London stood at some 40 per thousand, far higher than the national average. This was particularly so in the first half of the century, when the number of burials in the metropolitan area greatly exceeded that of baptisms and the death rate was actually rising to a peak of some 45 to 50 per thousand. In 1740 London's share of all the burials in England amounted to over 20 per cent while its share of the baptisms amounted to less than 12 per cent; and it has been estimated that between 1700 and 1750 the total number of migrants entering the London area amounted to over 500,000. After about 1750, however, a long slow fall in London's death rate began, until by 1841 it stood at only 23 per thousand, hardly different from the national figure of 22 per thousand. London had ceased to be the national sump of mortality, for it seems that within the years 1780–1820 the number of births had begun to exceed the number of deaths in the metropolitan area, perhaps for the first time ever in the history of the capital.[1] But even after this important demographic landmark had been passed, migrants still provided the basis for London's continuing growth, and they even increased in absolute numbers.

By around 1700 it seems that more women were migrating to London than men, thus reversing the earlier male immigrant predominance. On arrival in the capital most female migrants probably went into domestic service, where there was a huge demand for cheap labour, much of it in the eighteenth century being for young female labour. Many migrants came from the more distant parts of England, or from Scotland, Ireland, or abroad; London was beginning to become a cosmopolitan city. Most migrants seem to have been readily assimilated into the metropolis, for there were no immigrant ghettos (despite some heavy concentrations of French and Irish); and it is thought that many migrants remained in London for life.[2]

Growth and Fabric

By 1830 the metropolitan built-up area extended from Hyde Park Corner in the west to Limehouse in the east, a distance of some 5 miles (Plates 21, 22). The terraces of houses in Pentonville in the north were only about 3 miles from those of Kennington in the south, but the total area of continuous building nevertheless far exceeded that of any other city in Western Europe, and tentacles of ribbon development spread villas still further outwards towards Hammersmith, Highgate, and Denmark Hill — early exemplars of the ever-popular English ideal of *rus in urbe* (countryside in the town). Development was particularly fast south of the river, which had hitherto divided the built-up area much more sharply than the Seine had divided Paris. In London the building of two new bridges (Westminster, 1750, and Blackfriars, 1769) opened up a large previously inaccessible area close to both Westminster and the City. A framework of wide straight roads was laid out, between 1816 and 1831 three more bridges were opened, and in 1823–31 cumbersome old London Bridge, which until 1729 had provided the only crossing below Kingston, was itself rebuilt.[3]

It was in the great Georgian period of metropolitan expansion that London became, by the standards of continental Europe, a low-density city, consisting largely of houses intended for single-family occupation.[4] This was no doubt in part due to the absence of the constricting rings of fortifications which hemmed in the outward expansion of, for instance, Vienna and even Paris, where there was also an economic barrier wall with customs posts at which duties were levied on food and other country produce;[5] but the main reason was the abundant supply of cheap land continually made available through the leasehold system of development.

The seventeenth-century origins of this system were described in Chapter 10, and in Georgian times there was little basic change in it. For all landowners it had great advantages. For the aristocratic proprietors of large tracts of Mayfair and St Marylebone, such as the Grosvenor, Portman, and Cavendish-Harley dynasties, it provided a good long-term investment at little cost to themselves, and it enabled them to determine the layout of their estates, usually on the general lines adumbrated in the seventeenth century in the earl of Bedford's Covent Garden. The great squares which form the nodal points of the West End street plan still bear witness to this common ancestry, despite the churches being either less prominently placed or altogether absent, and despite most of the original houses having been long since demolished. In the east of London, where the ownership of land was much more fragmented and small blocks belonging to charities, City livery companies, and private individuals were all jumbled together higgledy-piggledy, there were no comparably grand development plans, but profits could nevertheless be made. South of the river the situation was different again, much of the land developed in the Georgian period being within the three great manors of Lambeth, Vauxhall (both owned by the Church), and Kennington (by the Duchy of Cornwall), in parts of all of which the ancient copyhold system of land tenure still prevailed.[6]

For the building craftsmen and speculators of all kinds there were also hand-some fortunes to be made in the housing industry, particularly during such great peaks of building as the 1720s, 1760s, and early 1820s:[7] and, of course, there were correspondingly large disasters to be endured during their aftermaths, notably after the crash of 1825. Subcontracting between the various crafts of the building trade became the norm in the building of run-of-the-mill terrace houses, the master builder (commonly a bricklayer or a carpenter) who had agreed with the ground landlord for a building lease contracting with other tradesmen for the slating, plumbing, glazing, and so on. Longer leases — by 1800 ninety-nine years was the normal term — encouraged a better quality of building, and a series of Building Acts specifically prescribed it. These stemmed from the Act of 1667 for the rebuilding of the City after the Great Fire, but later Acts applied throughout the suburbs and were at first mainly concerned with the prevention of fire. Those of 1707 and 1709 abolished the use of wood for eaves-cornices and restricted its use in window openings. The massive Act of 1774 laid down a comprehensive code for house construction which prevailed with little alteration for some seventy years; and it also provided for the first time paid and qualified district surveyors to enforce the regulations.[8]

The Building Acts also influenced the outward appearance of the eighteenth- and early nineteenth-century town house, for although its basic vertical character had been formulated in the days of Inigo Jones at Covent Garden, there were important changes of detail. The baroque exuberance of the wooden hooded doorcases much in vogue around 1700, and the tall narrow windows, both gave place to Palladian symmetry and restraint, and from the 1720s onwards the influence of the leading architects of the day filtered down to the speculating builders through countless illustrated pattern books. Towards the end of the eighteenth century the stringent requirements of the Building Act of 1774 imposed a measure of standardization on the appearance of the suburban street (still to be seen, for example, in Gower Street, Bloomsbury).[9] This monotony was, however, partially relieved by the increasing use of Coade's artificial stone (made by Mrs Eleanor Coade at her factory on the South Bank in Lambeth) and stucco orna-mentation. As early as the mid-1770s stucco was being applied to the whole façade of important houses (there are several in Bedford Square, for instance) and by Regency times it was in widespread use in this way, following the example of John Nash's new Regent Street and of his villas in Regent's Park.

Stucco provided the most important innovation in the external appearance of the Georgian town house, and although the detached villa and the semi-detached or paired house were after about 1800 beginning (notably on the Eyre estate in St John's Wood) to provide portents of future change in the very nature of suburban living, they were not yet common, and traditional terraces dressed up in stucco continued to go up in many parts of London until after the 1850s. Apart from the introduction of stucco a similar continuity prevailed in the materials used for house-building and in the way in which the houses were built, small-scale master builders and their subcontractors seldom taking on the building of more than a few houses at any one time. But here too there are signs of impending change in the early nineteenth century. James Burton (father of the architect Decimus Burton) built some 900 houses on the Foundling Hospital and Bedford estates in Blooms-bury; and in 1828 Thomas Cubitt was employing 1,000 men on his housebuilding activities, mainly on Lord Grosvenor's estate in Belgravia and Pimlico (Plate 40).[10] Builders operating on this scale were, however, still altogether exceptional.

While suburban London was thus proceeding on its outward march, two internal transformations were also going forward: the building of the London docks and the formation of Regent Street and Regent's Park, the most important improvements to be made to the fabric of the metropolis since the rebuildings after the Great Fire of 1666. The docks were the work of the merchants and financiers of the City, while the adornment of the West End was initiated by the Crown, or rather the Prince Regent — an apt reminder that London has the rare distinction among the great cities of the world of being both a major port and a capital seat.

Ever since Roman times the Port of London had been located between London Bridge and the Tower, where a score of privately owned wharves provided a frontage of some 1,500 feet known as the Legal Quays for the loading and unload-ing of the dutiable goods of overseas trade. These quays were supplemented by 'Sufferance Wharves' on the south side of the river, and by the Howland Wet Dock, built in 1700. Due to the inexorable growth in the volume of trade in the Port of London, most vessels had to load and unload at their moorings in midstream, and the Pool of London — the stretch of river immediately below London Bridge — had become crammed with great ocean-going ships and hundreds of barges and hoys, as well as with the colliers whose sea coal from Tyneside had to be discharged into lighters and taken to upstream wharves for distribution by cart throughout the ever-growing metropolis (Plates 25, 27, and 28). Congestion was particularly acute between July and October, when the prevailing winds brought in the West Indiamen laden with valuable cargoes which in the processes of unloading suffered enormous depredations by theft.

In 1799 an Act of Parliament established the West India Dock Company with power to build docks in the Isle of Dogs between Limehouse and Blackwall. Two parallel wet docks over 50 acres in extent were built, each 0.5 mile long and entered from the river by basins and locks at either end. Here ships could safely discharge their cargoes into the huge quayside warehouses in four days instead of the four weeks that had hitherto been needed, and a ring of security was provided by a high wall which enclosed the whole area. This gigantic undertaking — the greatest work of engineering in London since the building of the Roman wall in the second century — was completed in six years, and the construction of half a dozen similar enclosed wet docks on both sides of the river soon followed. Within thirty years London had acquired the finest com-mercial facilities of any port in the world.[11] And in Victorian times they were greatly enlarged ever further downstream (Plates 29–31).

Meanwhile, something quite different was proceeding at the other end of the town, where the West End was being transmogrified by the only great piece of town planning ever to be executed in London. These 'Metropolitan Improvements' (as

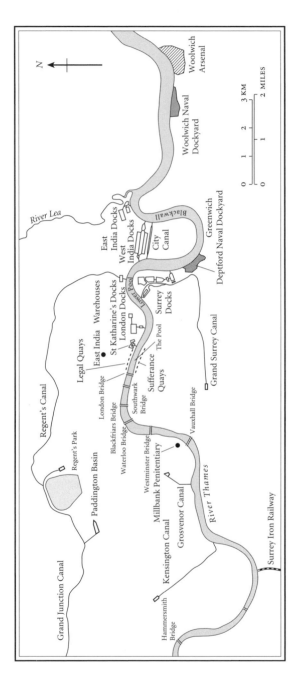

Fig. 21. Bridges, docks, and canals, c.1830

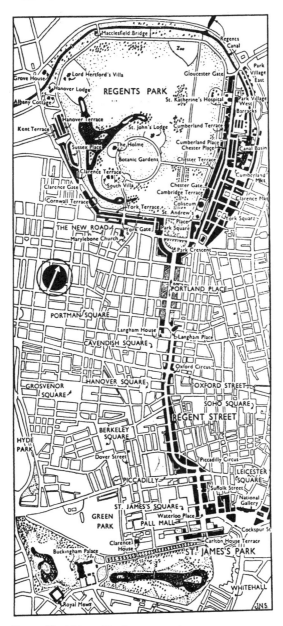

Fig. 22. The Metropolitan Improvements

they were called at the time) extended from Regent's Park in the north to St James's Park in the south, and included a canal (the extension of the Grand Junction from Paddington to the docks), a market, two barracks, and a great new thoroughfare (Regent Street) cut through the existing fabric of narrow crowded streets. To the north of St James's Park, on the site of the Prince Regent's Carlton House, which was demolished soon after his accession as king in 1820, arose the stucco mansions of Carlton House Terrace and the first two of the imposing clutch of gentlemen's clubhouses (the Athenaeum and the United Service, the latter now occupied by the Institute of Directors) which by the 1840s lined the south side of Pall Mall. To the west of St James's Park an all-but-new royal residence — Buckingham Palace — was built at the behest of George IV, who with his architect John Nash were the joint progenitors of all these 'improvements'; and to the east of the park there was a great new *place* — Trafalgar Square, later embellished by the National Gallery and the Nelson Column — and a reconstruction of the neighbouring parts of the Strand.

All these exhilarating events took place either on land which already belonged to the Crown (much of it since its acquisition by Henry VIII) or on land bought by the Crown under the New Street Act of 1813. Building development proceeded in the normal manner of the leasehold system, commercial speculators being granted long Crown leases at low ground rents. In the tract of open country hitherto known as Marylebone (and now as Regent's) Park, the problem was how to lure the nobility and gentry to live so far north of the fashionable West End. Here Nash designed an aristocratic 'garden city' with eight large villas set among groves of new plantations and an artfully contrived lake nearby, all surrounded on three sides by long ranges of stucco-fronted terrace houses. The whole scheme depended heavily on private capital, and in Regent Street when nobody else would do it Nash even undertook the building of the curved Quadrant section himself.[12]

Through the Metropolitan Improvements London became (in Donald Olsen's words) 'an object of pride and a symbol of national greatness'.[13] But this mood did not long survive the death of George IV in 1830 and the dismissal of Nash. Four years later the Palace of Westminster (i.e. the Houses of Parliament) was destroyed by fire in a splendid blaze visible for miles around; and when the rebuilding began, an architectural style entirely alien to the spirit of either Nash's metropolitan improvements or indeed to that of the whole Georgian era was adopted.

The Government of London

After over two centuries of rapid physical expansion London had by around 1800 become a disjointed conglomeration of individually distinct parts. In the centuries-old core the City was the headquarters of banking, insurance, and business of all kinds, internationally as well as domestically. Westminster was the seat of the royal court, Parliament, Government, the lawcourts, and the world of fashion. East

London was dominated by the port and a wide range of industries, while on the south side of the river, beyond the ancient nucleus of Southwark, sprawled rapidly growing new residential suburbs. The whole great mass was surrounded by a ring of 'out-parishes' like St Marylebone or Lambeth, each at its own particular stage of urbanization and absorption into the metropolitan maw.

This diversity was reflected in the generally confused state of the capital's government, or misgovernment. The root cause of the confusion was that after the explosion of the population of the metropolis which had begun in the later sixteenth century, the City Corporation, which had hitherto governed its tight little territory so successfully, became an obstacle to the evolution of any rational arrangements for the whole built-up area. Already by 1700 something like four times as many Londoners lived in Westminster and the suburbs on either side of the river as in the City itself, and by 1831 over nine-tenths of them lived outside the ancient Square Mile. Throughout the Georgian period the City Corporation exercised a baleful influence over the progress of the suburbs — its opposition to the building of Westminster Bridge[14] or to the formation of an unified metropolitan police force are cases in point — and for this and other reasons no structural change in the government of the metropolis took place. How different from the state of affairs in France, where (until 1789) the king in practice governed his capital city despotically and centrally through his intendants, either from Versailles or from the Châtelet in Paris, and there was only one single administration with jurisdiction over all the city.[15]

Paris certainly had nothing remotely like London's seemingly and comparatively almost democratic City Corporation, where in the first half of the eighteenth century the struggle within the Corporation between the mainly Whig Court of Aldermen and the mainly Tory Court of Common Council was compounded by the natural alliance between the Whig grandees of the City and successive Whig ministries at Whitehall. Walpole's London Election Act of 1725 gave statutory authority to the aldermen's traditional power of veto over the Common Council, but after some twenty years the balance shifted in favour of the latter, which gradually took over most of the City's legislative and administrative business. By around 1760 the Corporation's financial situation (previously in dire straits through mismanagement of the Orphans' Fund) had improved, thanks in part to the rise in the yield of the coal tax and also to the Corporation's resort to allowing tenants on its most valuable estates, on payment of a lump sum or fine, to renew their leases many years before their expiry date — a practice which had short-term advantages in the 1750s when many such renewals were made, but which was disastrous in the long term, some tenants on the Corporation's Conduit Mead estate in Mayfair even being given the right to renew their leases in perpetuity.* So with these new resources streets were widened, paved, and lit,

---

* The City's coat of arms displayed on a number of buildings in South Molton Street proclaim the Corporation's ownership, but some tenants hereabouts still pay eighteenth-century rents for their accommodation in this prestigious area of the West End.[16]

and much of the Fleet Ditch was covered over. The City's ancient gates were removed, Newgate gaol was rebuilt, and the Lord Mayor was provided with an imposing official residence at the Mansion House. Within its own little patch the City Corporation managed things quite nicely.

Outside the City there were by around 1800 over ninety administrative parishes or precincts within the built-up area, each with its own local assembly or vestry. Their main functions were the paving, lighting, and cleansing of the streets, the relief of the poor, and the maintenance of the peace. They varied greatly in size, ranging from such oddities as the Liberty of the Old Artllery Ground near Bishopsgate, with a population of less than 1,500 in 1801, to the great parish of St George's, Hanover Square, with over 60,000 residents. The constitutions of the vestries were equally diverse, some being of the 'open' variety, open to all rate-payers wishing to attend, others 'close' or 'select', where all authority was vested in exclusive and self-perpetuating oligarchies; and yet others being mixed. Some degree of supervision over the vestries was exercised by the Justices of the Peace meeting in quarter sessions for each of the three metropolitan counties of Mid-dlesex, Surrey, and Kent; and the Justices also maintained roads, bridges, prisons, and law and order.

These primitive arrangements, still suitable perhaps for the overwhelmingly rural society in which they had evolved over the centuries, were by the early nineteenth century quite inadequate to deal with the problems of an urban area of between 1,000,000–2,000,000 people. Corruption and jobbery were common-place, particularly in rapidly urbanizing parishes with open vestries such as St Pancras, where a furious twenty-year struggle mainly between the defenders of the ancient open vestry and the residents of the new streets and squares in the southern part of the parish ended in 1819 in the establishment by Act of Parliament of a self-perpetuating close vestry. At Bethnal Green the disorderly affairs of the parish were dominated for over thirty years by a Tammany Hall-style boss, Joseph Merceron, who controlled a quarter of the beer-shops and public houses there. Some magistrates (of whom Merceron was one) were equally venal, the 'trading justices' of the metropolitan Benches being notoriously fraudulent.

Yet from the middle of the eighteenth century onwards important improve-ments did take place. Most of them were made by means of the local Acts of Parliament which established trustees or commissioners for such specific purposes as the paving, cleaning, lighting, and watching of the streets in a particular parish or part of a parish or on a particular estate. Authorities of this kind were especially numerous in parishes with unruly open vestries — in Lambeth, for instance, there were nine separate trusts for the lighting of different parts of the parish — and their statutory powers to raise rates (i.e. local property taxes) and pay contractors or salaried employees enabled them to provide passable services. The Westminster Paving Act of 1762, which established commissioners for the paving, cleaning, and lighting of the streets of Westminster, was a landmark in metropolitan street management, and it was soon copied in the local Acts promoted by efficient vestries such as that of St Marylebone. Yet despite this disorderly jumble of local authorities, London was by the end of the eighteenth century famous among the great cities of the world for the quality of the paving and lighting of its streets (or at any rate those of the West End)[17] — the widespread use of paving stone from York and granite sets from Aberdeen being a conspicuous example of the process whereby London demand stimulated the economy hundreds of miles from the metropolis.

There were other changes for the better too. In 1756–61 London's first ring road, circling round the north side of the metropolis from Paddington to the City, was built by two turnpike trusts, thereby greatly diminishing the congestion hitherto caused by the innumerable herds of sheep and cattle wending their way along Oxford Street and Holborn to Smithfield Market (Plate 44).[18] Later other new turnpike roads were built in the approaches to the built-up area on both sides of the river, and in 1826 the fourteen metropolitan turnpike trusts to the north of the Thames were amalgamated under a single body of commissioners. By that time half a dozen gas companies were providing much brighter lighting in many London streets.[19] And the water supply improved, despite the terrible failings of both its quality and quantity which were to be revealed in Victorian times. New companies drew their water direct from the Thames or the Lea, and steam-driven pumps extended their area of service. By 1827 the daily supply of water to each house in West London was 218 gallons; but in East London it was 182 gallons, and south of the river only 93.[20]

Even these (by modern standards) small quantities of piped water helped in the fighting of fires. After 1774 the vestries had a statutory duty to keep engines, pipes (i.e. hoses), and ladders; and the insurance companies also had their own appliances. In the 1790s the St Marylebone Vestry, for instance, kept two engines, nine ladders, and a 30-foot fire escape, and water seems generally to have been available within half an hour of the start of a fire.[21]

The festering problems of London's poor were, however, beyond the capacity of the times to resolve. The parishes were still the usual units of administration and in many cases still depended on the labours of their unpaid and annually appointed overseers of the poor. Corruption was rife; the poor were a 'nuisance' to be if possible shunted elsewhere to prevent their becoming chargeable to the parish under the Act of Settlement; infants were put out to be nursed by pauper women or kept with their mothers in the workhouse; and there were gross abuses of the apprentice system, notably in the late eighteenth century, when cartloads of children sometimes only 6 years old were dispatched from the London workhouses to the cotton mills of the north.[22]

But public awareness of such social pockmarks was mounting. The Foundling Hospital, established by Captain Coram in the 1740s in Lamb's Conduit Fields, provided asylum for many infant poor (though its operations were not always successful). In many parishes workhouses (where life was certainly grim) were built under the powers of local Acts, and in some of these there was an infirmary for the sick. The age and distance at which children might be apprenticed was subjected to parliamentary inquiry and legislation.[23] In practice the poor probably benefited little from these and other innovations, but the mere fact that they were made at all reflects the gradually mounting sense of humanity of the age.

Finally, there was the preservation of civil order. Much of this depended on the family, the Church, and the relationships of employment, but the ultimate sanction was the criminal justice system. This depended for its functioning in great measure on public participation, for most prosecutions, particularly for misdemeanours (about 90 per cent of all crimes) were brought by the victims, many of whom were poor. What have been called 'victimless' offences such as alehouse tippling, prostitution, or vagrancy were the province of the parish constables and paid watchmen, who were perhaps not such an inefficient force as has sometimes been suggested.[24]

All these instruments of law enforcement were reinforced by the justices, through one of whom the first important advance in metropolitan law enforcement in Georgian times was made. This was the novelist Henry Fielding, who in 1748 was appointed a justice for Westminster and took over an office in Bow Street which through bribes and fees had been worth £500 per annum to his predecessor. After his success there in combating the prevailing wave of crime he obtained from the Government a small grant of public money which enabled him to employ half a dozen 'thief takers', or Bow Street Runners, as they soon became known. After his death he was succeeded at Bow Street by his blind half-brother, (Sir) John Fielding. By 1792 seven other Public Offices had been established, at each of which there were three stipendiary (i.e. salaried) magistrates and a small force of paid constables. Then in 1798 Patrick Colquhoun had formed a Marine Police Establishment for the much-needed protection of property in the Port of London. But even after the Gordon Riots of 1780 had convincingly demonstrated the inadequacy of the parochial authorities, there was still no overriding metropolitan authority until the establishment of the Metropolitan Police in 1829 (to be discussed in Chapter 17). Even then the City managed to get itself excepted, and still to this day has its own police force.[25]

Eighteenth-century arrangements for the enforcement of the law were in marked contrast with those in other countries in Europe. England was unique in having neither a professional State police force, the very idea of which aroused atavistic hostility, nor a system of penal servitude; and the problems which arose therefrom manifested themselves particularly acutely in London, which was of course not only the largest city in England but in all Europe as well.

Nevertheless there were certainly plenty of prisons in London, public interest in the condition of which was being aroused by the labours of John Howard and Elizabeth Fry. The City Corporation, with half a dozen of them, was the greatest gaol-master in the whole country; the Justices of the Peace for Middlesex and Surrey each had their own houses of correction and county gaols; and the Royal Courts of Justice at Westminster also had prisons, chiefly for debtors. For better or worse, however, none of them were long-term penal establishments, so the only serious deterrent was the death penalty, supplemented in some degree by transportation to the colonies; and as the chances of catching criminals was small, deterrence, in the opinion of contemporaries, had to be correspondingly strong. Hence the great extension in the eighteenth century of offences punishable by death.[26]

The countless processions of condemned wretches which passed from the Old Bailey and Newgate prison along Holborn and Oxford Street to the gallows tree at Tyburn (near Marble Arch) were familiar sights in Georgian London. (Executions there were discontinued in 1783, and subsequently held outside Newgate.) Some historians have seen in the grim procedures of criminal justice 'a ruling-class conspiracy' conducted against the lower orders for the purpose of keeping them in their place.[27] Others have pointed out that many people concerned in the administration of the criminal law — particularly the prosecutors and the jurors — did not belong to the ruling class, and that the discretion with which the law was often exercised was used in good faith and not arbitrarily.[28] Certainly the percentage of reprieves granted to those condemned to death in London and Middlesex between 1775 and 1818 was steadily rising[29] — in part no doubt a reflection of the growing 'sensibility' of the times; and when a gigantic new 'model' prison was opened at Millbank in 1816 on the site now occupied by the Tate Gallery, penal servitude began to provide an alternative to the rope.

Social Structure: Income and Livelihood

Historians are in general agreement about the shape of the social edifice of Georgian London. At the top there were (in Professor Rudé's estimate) some 200 or 300 noble families and 3,000–4,500 aristocratic and 'gentle' families, all of whom lived in London for some part of the year. In addition there was a rich City mercantile bourgeoisie, perhaps around 1,000 in number, and altogether this upper crust formed about 2 to 3 per cent of the total population in 1801. Dr Earle has suggested that in the early eighteenth century another 20 or 30 per cent of London households — some 20,000 to 25,000 in number — can be regarded as of the middling sort, and the remaining two-thirds or three-quarters of the population were of 'the inferior sort'.[30]

Recent research has shown that the degree of inequality which such figures as these express was greater in London than anywhere else in England. In c.1780 the top 1 per cent of metropolitan households held 21 per cent of all the personal reproducible wealth there, i.e. excluding land and domestically owned investments in the funds; and the top 20 per cent of households held over 75 per cent of it. If non-reproducible wealth, i.e. primarily land, is taken into account, the degree of inequality would probably be greater still. There was unequal distribution of wealth on the national scale too, for in relation to the rest of England London was still the wealthiest part of the country, despite the great advance made during the eighteenth century in the relative position of the north.[31]

Despite these vast differences of wealth and circumstance, death provided a common denominator for all the peoples of Georgian London. In the early seventeenth century the mortality rate in London began to rise and continued to do so for over a century, while that of the rest of the country improved. Typhus and smallpox (particularly virulent in the winter months) may have been partly responsible for this divergence, and an especially potent strain of smallpox which attacked all sectors of society in the first half of the eighteenth century is thought to account for much of the contemporaneous rise in mortality. Infants and young children were especially vulnerable to these two diseases, and nearly half the later decline of mortality was concentrated in those age groups. Other major causes of death included consumption, measles, various forms of fever and convulsions, and conditions arising from excessive consumption of cheap gin in the 1730s and 1740s, when London had over 6,000 dram shops, commonly advertising themselves with the message 'Drunk for a penny, dead drunk for twopence, clean straw for nothing'.

The reasons for the gradual fall of the death rate in the second half of the eighteenth century are, however, less clear. Inoculation (particularly in areas outside London from which migrants were drawn), better medical treatment, or the prevalence of a less potent variety of smallpox, may all provide partial explanations; but better living standards are also thought (by John Landers in his recent book) to have been important. The decades when mortality was particularly high (the 1730s and 1740s) coincided with a period of decline in housebuilding in London, leading to deterioration in both the quality and quantity of accommodation available. The fall in the mortality rate which began in the third quarter of the eighteenth century also coincided with the end of the period of economic stagnation, the recovery of housebuilding, and the rapid geographical expansion of London. Improved hygiene, ventilation, and sanitation all no doubt had something to do with it too, as did the increasing use of cotton clothes. Dr Schwarz has suggested that with ever-growing social and commercial ties between the capital and the adjacent counties, the peoples of the catchment area from which London's migrants were mainly drawn in course of time themselves developed a measure of immunity to metropolitan diseases. What is certain is that by the early nineteenth century London was 'no longer a national reservoir of lethal infections'.[32]

The Wealth-Holders and 'The Middling Sort'

The great and the rich lived at 'the polite end of the town' to the west of the City. Here, mainly in the streets and squares off Piccadilly and Oxford Street, stood the town houses of the peerage and the richer landed gentry, ranging from princely palaces like those of the duke of Norfolk in St James's Square or of Lord Chesterfield in South Audley Street down to outwardly unostentatious terrace houses such as may still be seen in, for instance, parts of Grosvenor Street. Many of them were the work of the leading architects of the day, but none of them (even the Prince Regent's Carlton House) rivalled the splendours of such Parisian counterparts as the Palais Royal or the Luxembourg. Often they were shut up for much of the summer, the social season being mainly a winter affair; but gradually it began later, and by the 1830s the high season extended from April to July.[33] Many families only held their houses on lease, their real homes being on their estates in the country, and so there was little impediment to the slow migration westward of the principal centres of fashionable residence, from Soho and Leicester Square towards Mayfair (though through its proximity to the palace St James's Square retained its unique cachet). There was, however, as yet, little residential social segration: rich and poor often lived close together, for the demands of the former for domestic services of all kinds, and for transport (coachmen, grooms, and sedan-chair carriers), generated local hinterlands of labouring inhabitants, as can still be seen in parts of Mayfair, notably within 200 yards of the north side of Grosvenor Square itself.[34]

Most of the wealth of which this metropolitan world was the product was derived from ownership of land, some of it in London itself, as in the case of the dukes of Bedford (Covent Garden and Bloomsbury) or Lord Burlington (off Piccadilly). Marriage into the mercantile plutocracy or a well-paid sinecure could also be lucrative, and there were many aristocratic holders of Government funds and stocks in the great 'moneyed companies'. Much the same applied to the wealth of the gentry, but that of the City financial bourgeoisie was acquired largely from banking and overseas trade; and it was in commerce and finance, heavily concentrated in London, rather than in manufacturing or industry, that most large non-landed fortunes originated. Many such wealthy merchants still lived in the City rather than in the West End, but like the nobility and gentry they sometimes had a place in the neighbouring countryside, Osterley Park, some 10 miles west of the City, for instance, formerly the property of Sir Thomas Gresham, having been acquired by Sir Francis Child the banker in 1711 and subsequently transmogrified by his descendants to designs by Robert Adam.[35]

Far larger numerically was the substantial and dynamic middling section of the population, whose main characteristics have been defined by Dr Earle as 'accumulation, self-improvement and the employment of capital and labour'.[36] The incomes of this middling sector, which might come from wholesaling, middleman dealings, retailing, manufacturing, or from professional fees or investments in the funds, ranged between £60 and £200 per annum,[37] and by the end of the eighteenth century this was doubtless the largest mass of such people in the whole world. They were scattered throughout all parts of the metropolis, but there were concentrations in the City, North London, and the commercial parts of Westminster.[38] Very roughly, they may be divided into the various categories propounded by Professor Rudé: shopkeepers and trades-men; the men of the manufacturing, carrying, and servicing trades; and the professional men and artists.[39]

'Shopocracy' was a reality in Georgian London, for at the end of the eighteenth century shopkeepers formed between 11 and 14 per cent of London's employed population. Half of them were in the food and drink trades,[40] but there was infinite variety in both the field and scale of their operations, which ranged from the magnificient displays in Wedgwood's West End showrooms down to the meanest dram-shop in Limehouse. In general, shopkeeping was a family affair, the multi-tude of small businesses mirroring the mainly small scale of metropolitan industry (which will be discussed in Chapter 14). Transport requirements also provided limitless scope for small-scale commercial enterprises, many of them centred on the horse; but the needs of the port demanded thousands of lightermen, wharfin-gers, warehousemen, and coal merchants, to mention only a few riverside occupa-tions; and the proprietors of the numerous inns engaged in the carrier and stagecoach trades managed increasingly complex businesses and were the fore-runners of the hotels and goods offices of the railways.[41]

Lastly there were the professional men, some 5,000–7,000 in number at the beginning of the eighteenth century (so Dr Earle has calculated), encompassing between a third and a quarter of all London's middling sort.[42] Their growing numbers reflected the national growth of prosperity and improvement in the quality of life. Most of the best pickings in the Church, the law, and medicine were, of course, in London, where there were numerous rich livings like that of St James, Westminster, ripe plums at the Bar, the Bench, and the bureaucracy of the lawcourts, and large fortunes to be made by such successful physicians as Dr John Radcliffe, the munificent benefactor of Oxford University. The professions also provided important channels of upward social mobility, even the most disreput-able attorneys being generally designated as 'gentlemen'. Standards of practice were improving too: in 1729 there was a Regulating Act for the attorneys, and the Law Society saw the light of day a century later.[43] In medicine the 'inferior' branches of the profession — the apothecaries and surgeons — were the main agents of advancing pharmaceutical and anatomical knowledge, in which the new 'exotic' drugs of the East brought to London by the East India Company and the new London hospitals provided opportunities for the accumulation of enlarged scientific experience.[44]

Other professions — notably the architects, painters, musicians, and men of letters — were also heavily concentrated in London, which as the cultural centre of the nation, provided lucrative opportunities for successful practitioners — Sir Robert Taylor (who left a fortune of £180,000, Oxford being the recipient of most of it), Sir Joshua Reynolds, and George Frideric Handel spring to mind. All of these professions were to a considerable degree dependent on rich patrons, but others relied on the State. The long wars with France generated a new career *métier* of civil service bureaucrat, and Professor Holmes has calculated that by the 1720s there were probably some 2,700 posts open to career officials in the London offices of the Government. There was also a great increase in the number of army and navy officers, for whom half-pay on discharge became the regular practice early in the eighteenth century.[45] All in all the burgeoning professions of Georgian London had an importance out of all proportion to their still relatively small numbers, and the proliferation of their various expertises reflected the growing size of the service sector in the metropolitan economy.

'The Inferior Sort'

Some two-thirds to three-quarters of the population of London were of 'the inferior sort' or 'the mechanic sort', whose annual income did not exceed about £60. Dr L. D. Schwarz has shown that adult working men of this category formed 75 per cent of London's total adult male population. Only about 5 or 6 per cent of these working men were self-employed artisans in the manufacturing trades, and 90 per cent of them were in some form of employment by a third party — a much higher proportion than has often been supposed. Two-thirds of the working population were unskilled or semi-skilled.[46]

Within this large disparate mass four loosely definable groups may be distinguished: master craftsmen, small shopkeepers, and market tradesmen; skilled journeymen and apprentices; unskilled and semi-skilled wage-earning labourers of all kinds; and a large submerged or floating population with, for one reason or another, little or no means of support.[47]

Apart from those craftsmen and shopkeepers who lived and worked under the same roof, 'settled' working men generally rented accommodation. Most Londoners were lodgers, renting a single room for perhaps 1s. or 2s. a week, or even for as little as 1d. a night, and often the room was shared with other tenants. The householders to whom these pittances were paid might themselves live in another part of the same house and pay rent to the ground landlord or more probably an intermediary. There were no specifically 'working-class' districts, but there were tight little islands or 'rookeries' of overcrowded tenements in such places as St Katharine's by the Tower, parts of Southwark, and particularly the neighbourhood of Drury Lane, Long Acre, and St Giles, this last being a notorious resort of thieves and mendicants, as *The Beggar's Opera* of 1728 makes clear.[48]

Recent research has shown that real wage rates in London were comparatively high in the 1720s, 1730s, and 1740s, when the rate of population growth was low, but that they fell during the second half of the century; and that after the confused period of the Napoleonic Wars they rose once more, particularly in the early 1820s.[49] As a guide to living standards this general picture does, however, need to be qualified. Wages were often not the only source of income of a household; there were great wage variations between different trades, some of which might be prospering when others were declining; and the unskilled and semi-skilled majority of the labour force, including women and children, moved frequently from one occupation to another in response to demand, ever willing to learn any new job.[50]

Life for the labouring population was in fact full of uncertainties; and one of the greatest of them was the price of food, particularly of bread. This was the staple fare of the poor, who (so the London bakers calculated) consumed some 8 lb. of it per head per week. Bread accounted for between a quarter and a half of a labourer's weekly budget, so when the price of it rose after bad harvests (as it did in the 1790s, for instance) and was not accompanied by a corresponding increase of earnings, the effect on thousands of households was devastating.[51]

Much of the uncertainty of life was, however, rooted in unemployment or underemployment. This might be caused by long-term movements in the trade cycles, or by wars and financial crises (though wars also increased demand for labour, particularly of women and children), or above all by seasonal fluctuations. The West End luxury trades were greatly affected by the London social Season, while in the port the peak arrival time of ocean-going ships in the autumn was followed by a labour glut caused by large numbers of seamen waiting to be taken on for the next sailings. Easterly winds greatly reduced the movement of shipping on the Thames, and when it froze (seven times in the eighteenth century) all riverside work stopped. The weather was of general importance too, for very many trades were carried on out of doors and were particularly susceptible to rain. In winter the number of admittances to the workhouses always rose, and when a hard winter coincided with high bread prices and/or an economic downturn, there was widespread distress.[52]

This was particularly severe in the large submerged section of the population at the very bottom of the social pile — beggars, vagrants, prostitutes, down-and-outs, petty thieves, and above all the unemployed or underemployed from all walks of life — whom contemporaries were apt to lump indiscriminately together as criminals, but who, if they did resort to crime, generally did so through the compulsion of the direst poverty.[53] Crimes motivated by the need to survive — to enable the perpetrator to feed, clothe, and house him — or herself and his or her family — are thought to have been far more common than either 'acquisitive' crimes committed purely in pursuit of pecuniary gain or crimes of social or political protest. Even in that notoriously violent age most crimes were against property and not against the person, and although the volume of crime increased in proportion to the growth of London, violent crime was diminishing by around 1800. There were no doubt many hardened criminals, and organized gangs no doubt operated sporadically; but the existence of a 'criminal class' with its own recognizable identity seems unlikely.[54]

The question whether the standard of living of labouring people was improving in the eighteenth and early nineteenth centuries has been much discussed, and at any rate so far as London is concerned there can be no simple answer.[55] Francis Place (1771–1854), the Westminster tailor and Radical reformer, who lived in London all his life, wrote in 1829 that 'the people are better dressed, better fed, cleanlier, better educated, in each class respectively, much more frugal, and much happier...' than thirty years previously.[56] The real wage rates of skilled men, particularly those in trades producing costly finished goods such as coaches, scientific instruments or top-quality watches, or in printing, were probably improving throughout much of the first half of the nineteenth century, and particularly in the 1820s.[57] But where mass demand for a product existed or was growing, semi-skilled artisans such as tailors, shoemakers, or cabinetmakers found themselves threatened by unskilled labour (often that of women and children), of which there was nearly always an unlimited supply. This oversupply led to extensive use of casual labour, much of it done at home and paid on piece-rates, the exploitation of which led on through the division of the processes of labour to the sweating so widely practised in nineteenth-century London.[58] For men, or women, or children caught in this trap, living standards meant little more than getting work and earning enough money to buy bread.

As always, women came off worst. Research by Dr Earle suggests that in the early eighteenth century 'a high proportion of women were wholly or partly dependent on their own earnings for their livelihood'. The earnings of a typical working woman amounted to only 5s. a week, and the level of female employment was highest in a woman's childbearing years, when the struggle against acute poverty was at its most intense.[59] Domestic service was by far the commonest form of female labour, particularly for young girls, for whom hard drudgery was almost unending. In the early nineteenth century Mrs Wollaston of Clapham was requiring her housemaid to rise at 5 a.m. and work till 8 p.m., but on Mondays, the weekly washing day, she was to start at 1 a.m.; her board wages were £14 per annum.[60] Conditions of this kind were common, and living-in service did at least confer some security against hunger and homelessness.

Apart from domestic service the range of occupations open to women was extremely narrow, most employment being in the needle trades, in laundering, or in the retail trades, particularly of food and drink. During the eighteenth century demand for ready-made clothes grew enormously, and as virtually all female garments and most men's as well (except tailors' outerwear) were made by women, work was often available. There was much variety of skill in the making of such things as stays, bodices, hooped petticoats, shirts, shifts, gowns, and all manner of headwear. Much of such work could be done at home on piece-rates, so exploitation of the women involved was not difficult, particularly as demand was often seasonal, intermittent, and subject to changes of fashion.[61] Small shops or market stalls, particularly those dealing in food and drink, or the hawking of goods in the streets (fruit and vegetables, fish, meat, milk, even water, or old clothes) all provided precarious opportunities for women to scrape a few shillings, often to supplement their husbands' earnings. In virtually all forms of employment women provided a large part of the casual labour force in London; and in fields in which they found themselves in competition with men, the effect of their presence was to diminish the money value of all labour there.[62]

14

London and the Genesis of the Industrial Economy

The first generation of historians of the industrial revolution in England discussed their subject mainly in terms of coal, steam, mechanical inventions, and the growth of the factory system in the great new manufacturing towns of the North. They compressed the process of industrialization into the half-century between about 1780 and 1830, and metropolitan participation in it was seldom even mentioned. But more recently other factors have been introduced, notably the effects of metropolitan demand and the contribution of the service sector of the economy, and emphases have changed. The time span of the industrial revolution has also been greatly lengthened, to some two centuries or more, extending from around 1650 to 1850, and the whole process is seen as having been much more gradual than had previously been thought. Even the appropriateness of the name 'industrial revolution' has been questioned, and most of those two centuries are now sometimes referred to as a period of proto-industrialization. In this new historiographical landscape London has a more prominent place.

Demography and Demand

From whatever viewpoint it may be regarded it is certain that in the long term the industrial revolution produced a large and lasting increase in real incomes per head.[1] So long as the great mass of the national income was spent on food, and most workers worked on the land, lasting economic advance was bound to be slow and limited. Only when enough 'spare' income existed to stimulate demand for other commodities would it be possible to break out of the vicious circle of rising population and declining returns from the finite quantity of land available for cultivation, and to enter a virtuous circle in which surplus rural labour could be employed to meet demand for manufactured goods, working either in the country or increasingly in the towns, and in either case stimulating further growth of population and the more efficient production of food.

By far the largest concentration of such 'spare' income had of course for centuries been situated in London. We have already seen that throughout the seventeenth-century wage earners there probably had the highest living standards of any in the country and enjoyed greater purchasing power than their fellows outside the capital; and this situation probably continued throughout the first half of the eighteenth century.[2] Many of London's peoples already in a measure enjoyed the high real incomes per capita (high by the standards of the time) which were later to characterize industrial economies throughout the world, and their demands for goods of all kinds as well as for food and fuel inaugurated what has been called the consumer revolution of the eighteenth century. In London the virtuous circle was already in being — surplus rural labour was being drawn up to the capital, where employment was to be had in industrial or increasingly in service occupations, while (as we saw in Chapter 7) by its constantly growing demands, primarily for food, fuel, and clothing but also for hitherto inessential goods, London stimulated specializations and hence productivity per capita, thereby releasing more labour for non-agricultural pursuits.

So metropolitan demand galvanized the economies of even the most distant parts of England; and this influence was constantly enlarged by better means of transport. Turnpike trusts improved the roads, and canals linked the Midlands with London. In the course of the eighteenth century the volume of the London carrying trade by road more than trebled,[3] and by around 1820 Thomas Russell and Co. was running a daily service of wagons drawn by eight horses between Exeter and London, with subsidiary services going on to distant Cornwall (Plate 42).[4] At the opposite end of the country, in Northumberland and Durham, London's demand for coal, by around 1830 over 2,000,000 tons per annum, required the employment of perhaps some 12,000–15,000 people outside the metropolis, as miners, coal-heavers, and sailors. When their families are taken into account the total number of people in the North-East dependent on London's need for coal may have been not far short of 50,000; and they in their turn, by creating local demand for food, stimulated agricultural productivity. To cope with this metropolitan demand, which in 1830 amounted to nearly one-third of the total output of the North-East coalfields, the mines, too, became more productive, and the primitive railway lines which were laid to carry the coal from the pitheads to the riverside loading staithes (Plate 43), and which were the forebears of the national railway system, were at least in part a response to metropolitan demand.[5]

New Financial Mechanisms

This stimulation of demand and of growth of population were the most direct and powerful pressures exerted by the metropolis in the evolution of the industrial economy. But at one remove London made its own other distinctive contributions to this process through the provision of financial and commercial services, which grew ever more important as the economy grew more complex, and through its international pre-eminence as a centre of finance, far ahead of Paris, and rivalled only by Amsterdam. Indeed the City can be regarded as a quasi-independent self-motivated sector of the economy, busy in such crucial fields as the organization of capital resources and of mechanisms for dealings in them, and in the provision of insurance and credit, trading in money as well as in commodities becoming an increasingly important part of its business.

Much of this kind of activity had been going on for centuries, but in the 1690s it received renewed impetus through the foundation of the Bank of England and the gradual acceptance of the concept of a permanently funded public debt. The financial revolution which was thus set in motion took some fifty years of jerky movement to settle down. At first the most urgent problem was the Government's rapidly mounting short-term floating debt; but gradually Exchequer Bills became recognized as interest-bearing negotiable securities, with repayment statutorily guaranteed from the land and malt taxes and cashable at the Bank of England, which thus became the chief agent for the provision of short-term loans to the Government. For the permanent debt the Government began to rely on the Bank and the East India Company, both of which made long-term loans in exchange for trading favours. In 1711 the idea that the State should sell trading monopolies to a company in return for a sum of money to be used for the reduction of the national debt took root in the formation of the South Sea Company, which, in exchange for taking responsibility for nearly £10,000,000 of the debt, was granted a monopoly of British trade with South America and the Pacific Islands, then supposed to be an area of limitless riches. A burst of company promotions ensued, and a mania of speculation in the often worthless stocks of these new companies produced the boom and collapse known as the South Sea Bubble of 1720. The public credit suffered a severe loss of trust, and a skilful restructuring of the debt and of the various company stocks involved by Sir Robert Walpole, followed by two decades of his management of the funds, were needed for full recovery.[6]

By 1750 the national debt amounted to £78,000,000, and serious attempts to pay it off had ceased. During the Seven Years War (1756–63) 37 per cent of Government expenditure was raised by public borrowing, and at the end of the Napoleonic Wars (1815) the total national debt amounted to £670,000,000.[7]

This capital was drawn very largely from London itself and from the Home Counties, as research by Professor P. G. M. Dickson has shown. We have already seen that in 1694 87 per cent of the subscribers to the flotation of the Bank of England lived in London or the adjacent counties, and in the mid-eighteenth century it was still the case that most public creditors (i.e. those holding Government, Bank, East India, or South Sea Company stocks) were residents of London or its environs. Indeed English investors are thought to have become by around 1750 even more strongly metropolitan-based than they had been in the 1690s, though foreign ownership (chiefly Dutch) of Government stock then amounted to around one-sixth of the total. These English investors were mostly drawn from the London mercantile bourgeoisie and *petite bourgeoisie*— merchants, bankers, jobbers, brokers, lawyers, shopkeepers, craftsmen, and even domestic servants; and women formed an important minority of the fundholders — perhaps around one-fifth.[8]

The successful flotation of successive Government loans was heavily dependent on a small number of specialist London financial contractors who subscribed for large sums and quickly resold at a profit to 'permanent' fundholders. Just before the South Sea Bubble crisis the total number of these public creditors is thought by Professor Dickson to have been about 40,000 (irrespective of whether they lived in London or elsewhere); and by 1756 they probably numbered about 60,000. Small investors, with less than £500 each in the Bank of England and East India stock, formed about a fifth of the total number of the fundholders, but between them they owned less than one-tenth of the total stocks, ownership of which was heavily concentrated in blocks of over £1,000.[9] Nevertheless, if we accept Peter Earle's estimate that in the early eighteenth century London contained some 30,000 households of middle or 'gentry' station,[10] and if we assume that three-quarters of Professor Dickson's 40,000 public creditors resided in or near London, it appears that fundholding, albeit often in very small amounts, was becoming widespread throughout the metropolis. An increasingly numerous new urban class of 'town' or 'city' gentlemen whose wealth and social position was not primarily based on ownership of land, was beginning to emerge.

The extraordinary success of the funds depended on public confidence; and this was powerfully reinforced by the knowledge that there was an easily accessible market for all Government and allied stocks: the fundholder knew that he could sell as easily as he could buy. During the eighteenth century the activities at Jonathan's coffee house in Change Alley evolved into a sophisticated market which could rival the much older bourse in Amsterdam. Early attempts by the Government to impose a system of licensed brokerage to be administered by the City Corporation petered out, and in 1773 the brokers acquired their own house, known as the Stock Exchange, just behind the Royal Exchange. This soon proved too small, and in 1801 much larger premises were built in Capel Court on part of the site still occupied by the present Stock Exchange building. By that time the buying and selling of Government stocks had long been a routine matter, some 35,000 transfers being made in a single year in the mid-eighteenth century; and regular settlement days for clearing all bargains were established. The distinction between jobbers acting as suppliers of stock and brokers acting as agents, often in speculative transactions, was becoming clearer. The peculiar vocabulary of the Stock Exchange already included such terms as par and scrip (short for subscription) as well as the familiar menagerie of bears, bulls, and stags; and perhaps even lame ducks (defaulters) were first hatched there. Regular lists of price quotations for stocks were being printed by around 1700 (the lineal forebears of the present Official Lists), but even in the 1750s a typical list only included twenty-one items, almost all of which were Government loans or stocks of the Bank, East India, or South Sea Companies.[11]

Quite distinct from the field of public credit dominated by the three great joint stock companies and the Stock Exchange were the private bankers, who provided private credit. Between the renewal of its charter in 1708 and 1826 the Bank of England enjoyed a monopoly of joint-stock banking, all other banks being business partnerships in which the number of partners was limited to six. The needs of the Government had become far greater than such firms could supply, but for their private customers they could still provide numerous important services.[12]

The 'West End' banks, of which Hoare's in Fleet Street, Coutts' in the Strand, and Drummond's at Charing Cross still exist (in name, anyway), dealt mainly with the landed gentry and aristocracy, for whom they provided short-term loans or mortgages, transfers of cash between country and town, and management of investments in Government stocks; and in the second half of the eighteenth century the wealth of nabobs like Clive and Warren Hastings generated a new and lucrative trade. Bankers of this kind became socially indistinguishable from their customers, Henry Hoare, for instance, having a large estate at Stourhead in Wiltshire, where Colen Campbell designed a magnificent Palladian mansion for him.[13]

The business of the private bankers in the City — some seventy in number by 1800 — was different. Their general trade was in discounting bills of exchange, but they also made short-term loans and even lent on call. Thus they were more concerned in the financing of trade than of fixed investments in buildings, machinery, or land improvement. After about 1770 they found a rapidly growing new field of business as agents for the numerous country banks which were springing up in many provincial towns, sending down cash or notes, providing them with running accounts and sometimes with overdrafts, and handling the floods of bills of exchange which were incessantly being transferred between the provinces and the metropolis, and by means of which much of the nation's business was conducted in the eighteenth century. By 1775 the City bankers' network of dealings had become so large and complex that they set up a central clearing house in Lombard Street.[14] Throughout the land the arrival of the London newspapers and commercial correspondence was indeed so important locally that in 1816, for instance, merchants in distant Dundee, where the London mail coach arrived at eight o'clock in the evening, were often still doing business in the coffee houses at midnight.[15]

Insurance was also developing its own increasingly specialized technical expertise. From the frenetic speculation associated with the South Sea Bubble there emerged two stable new companies specializing mainly in marine insurance: the Royal Exchange Assurance and the London Assurance. Most marine business continued, however, to be transacted through personal contacts made in such City coffee houses as Lloyd's, where lists of ships and up-to-date shipping news were available. By the middle of the eighteenth century London had become the most important centre of marine insurance in Europe; and by 1810 private insurers at Lloyd's were underwriting risks to the value of £140,000,000, with a total premium income of over £10,000,000, most of it no doubt drawn from policyholders within the metropolis, where a large proportion of British foreign trade was still concentrated. In 1773 the underwriters took rooms of their own in the Royal Exchange, and in 1811 they provided themselves with a committee to manage their affairs; but the responsibility for the liabilities accepted by underwriting a policy remained a matter for each individual.[16]

Fire risks provided most of the rest of the metropolitan insurance market. Here half a dozen London companies, of which the Sun (1710), the Royal Exchange Assurance, and the London Assurance (both 1720) were the most important, at first shared the greater part of the business, which was largely confined to London property. Even as late as 1790 over half the premiums of the Sun Fire Office came from the London area,[17] and the insurance of commercial premises and the stocks of merchants and manufacturers had overtaken private houses as the main field of business. Other metropolitan firms included the Phoenix (1782), the County (1807), the Guardian (1821), and the Alliance (1824), most of these being unchartered joint-stock companies in which only a small proportion of the full value of each share was actually paid up, thus providing the shareholders with a safeguard against unlimited liability. By 1832 there were thirty-five fire insurance companies in England and Wales, of which fifteen were in London. These fifteen had over 60 per cent of the whole business.[18]

Life insurance was still, even at the beginning of the nineteenth century, in its infancy, but growing very rapidly. The pioneer in this field was the Equitable (1762), but by 1800 there were six life offices in London, and by 1839 over seventy. The first Income Tax Act of 1799 established the exemption of life-insurance premiums from liability for tax. With-profits policies first appeared in the early nineteenth century, and the payment of bonuses was soon generally prevalent. So too was the payment of commission to agents — often solicitors or brokers — for the introduction of new policyholders. By the 1840s it was thought that there were around 100,000 life policies in being, reflecting both the growing complexity of the economic system and the increased flow of income to the middle ranks of the social hierarchy, whose members provided most of the demand for life insurance.[19]

Metropolitan Industry

In the world of commerce and finance London was the national leader, but in industry the position was different. Throughout the Georgian period, and even to some extent into the 1860s, there were few fundamental changes in methods or scale of production there (though brewing was a notable exception), and the inventions associated with the industrial revolution were in general not made or introduced in London. What distinguished metropolitan industry was its extraordinary size — at the beginning of the eighteenth century London was the largest manufacturing centre in Europe, with perhaps 40 per cent of its labour force engaged in production[20] — and its extraordinary range, almost every trade practised elsewhere in England (apart from those concerned with agriculture or mining) being carried on somewhere in the capital. No single craft (such as cutlery in Sheffield) predominated, but the clothing of the human body provided through its limitless ramifications the numerically largest occupation.

Nor was there any single industrial area in the capital. Some crafts, particularly such as those of the tailors or shoemakers which provided for a basic universal need, or the various branches of the building trades, were to be found in all parts of London in the eighteenth century, while others were concentrated in particular localities: clock- and watchmaking in Clerkenwell, silk-weaving in Spitalfields, hatmaking in Southwark, tanning in Bermondsey, ceramics in Lambeth — where Delftware and Coade stone were made — and at Chelsea and Bow — where London's two most famous porcelain factories were situated. Such local concentrations were growing in number, and in the big trades such as tailoring or furniture-making there was widening differentiation between the upmarket bespoke craftsmen of the West End and the semi-skilled artisans producing ready-made standardized goods in the East End.

During the eighteenth century the traditional controls exercised by the City companies or guilds were in many trades being or already had been largely shaken off. In the ever-growing suburbs there had always been a virtual free-for-all, and the benefits conferred by the freedom of a City company or by serving an apprenticeship were diminishing. The link between each company and its own particular craft was progressively weakened by the admission of recruits from new occupations unconnected with any of the old companies; and in the 1830s the ancient craft monopolies within the City were finally brought to an end.[21]

Despite the decline of guild control many London trades were still organized on traditional lines, with masters employing journeymen and apprentices in small-scale units of production. In most crafts proliferation of small workshops rather than aggregation into larger units of production was the characteristic metropolitan response to market change. The amount of capital needed to set up as a master was often very small, and this was particularly so in those numerous fields where the domestic or putting-out system, in which work was given out to be done at piece-rates in the homes of the workers, was generally prevalent. As we have already seen, this led to the subdivision of labour and hence to the use of cheap sweated labour which could be taken on or put off at a moment's notice to suit the requirements of the employer. Much of this labour was provided by women, and apprenticeship was in some trades little more than exploitation of child labour.[22]

Conditions of this kind were especially common in the important metropolitan luxury or semi-luxury trades, where seasonal fluctuations and changes of fashion often produced sudden changes of demand. The silk-weavers of Spitalfields, for instance, worked at home (Plate 37) and were amongst the poorest of London workpeople, for in times of depression when work was scarce they had no defence (except rioting) against exploitation, the ease with which women and children could be employed in many operations such as silk-winding or filling the weavers' shuttles being an important cause of the endemic suffering of most workers in the industry. In the shoemaking trade, where little capital was needed to set up as a master, piecework done at home was also widespread, and the exploitation of apprenticeship degraded the trade. The journeymen tailors, on the other hand, were through their trade organizations able to insist on work being done at their employers' workshops (Plate 36); but the rise of mass-market demand led gradually to the dilution of their skills and to growing use of cheap labour.[23] In the watchmaking industry, in which nearly 7,000 people were in the 1790s employed in Clerkenwell in the making of about 120,000 watches per annum (over half for export), subdivision of labour had proceeded so far in 1817 that there were over 100 different branches of the trade.[24]

However, the structure of an industry did not always follow these lines in trades associated with the demands of changing fashion. In the bespoke West End furniture-making trade the many different crafts involved (joiners, upholsterers, gilders, carvers, cabinetmakers, etc.) were often drawn together within a single workplace where a master entrepreneur might employ a dozen or more people. In the early nineteenth century the size of these 'comprehensive' firms was growing; Gillow's, for instance, had around 100 people at their workshop in a small yard in aristocratic Mayfair, while Seddon's of Aldersgate Street had stock worth over £100,000.[25] This trend towards larger units of production was also common in trades unconnected with fashions and in which substantial capital was needed.

The most striking example of this was in the brewing industry (Plate 39), where through economies of scale available in the processes of production eleven breweries dominated the metropolitan trade by the end of the eighteenth century, the largest firm — Whitbread's — sometimes producing 200,000 barrels of porter beer (i.e. stout) in a single year; and similarly in the distillery business, which was basically metropolitan, seven large London firms dominated the production of spirits.[26] In the building of warships for the Admiralty the Thames region was the main source of supply, and in the mid-eighteenth century the dozen or so new merchantmen which the East India Company was needing every year were nearly all built on the river itself (Plate 38).[27] Woolwich Arsenal was the principal centre for the manufacture and inspection of cannon and shot, and other trades such as sugar-refining, mainly carried on in East London, or the Southwark glass industry, were also conducted on a substantial scale. Even in the field of building, which was still dominated by small master craftsmen or speculators, there were in the early nineteenth century a few very large entrepreneurs, such as Thomas Cubitt and Alexander Copland.[28] Large units of industrial production were not altogether unknown in Georgian London.

This was also true of the use of water and steam power, two of the great hallmarks of the industrial revolution in the North. The little River Wandle, which entered the Thames at Wandsworth and which although only 10 miles in length had a very strong current, provided power for over fifty waterwheels which drove flour and snuff mills and calico-printing works. The London water companies were among the first metropolitan users of steam pumping engines, which were also set up in mills of all kinds (notably the great Albion flour mill at

Blackfriars) and in the big breweries. By the end of the eighteenth century there were more steam engines with more horsepower in London than in the whole of Lancashire, one of the heartlands of the northern industrial revolution.[29] And for two or three decades in the early nineteenth century London was a leading centre of mechanical engineering, Joseph Bramah, Henry Maudslay, Marc Isambard Brunel, the Rennies, and others having their workshops there, heavily concentrated along the South Bank of the Thames in Southwark and Lambeth.[30]

Lastly, there were several London trades whose importance in the national scheme of things was out of all proportion to the number of workers involved in them. For the first time London became a world leader in the making of precision instruments — *inter alia* mathematical, optical, astronomical (including for the Royal Observatory at Greenwich), and navigational — for all of which there was a growing demand. This field was a natural expansion from the watchmaking industry, London having large reservoirs of skilled labour available; the trade was chiefly concentrated in small workshops along the Strand and Fleet Street.[31] It was towards this same part of the capital around Fleet Street that another essentially metropolitan industry was increasingly gravitating in the eighteenth century — that of printing, and of the closely linked trades of journalism, publishing, and bookselling. It was here that Britain's first regular daily newspaper, the *Daily Courant*, was issued in 1702, here that Dr Johnson lived while compiling his Dictionary, and here in the 1780s in Printing House Square that was first published *The Times* newspaper, which in the first two centuries of its existence exerted a potent influence over the life and thought of the whole nation.[32]

So London's industries were infinitely varied, both in the nature of what they produced and in the way in which they were organized. In general, many of them were extremely stable, few important changes of method or structure being made in the eighteenth and early nineteenth centuries. But although the capital remained as always the largest centre of manufacturing industry, and its aggregate output must have reflected the great increase of London's population throughout the period, some industries were already declining in face of competition from the provinces, where food, fuel, rents, and raw materials were often cheaper, and wages usually so. By around 1750 the once-dominant London framework-knitting or stocking-weaving industry had been eclipsed by competitors in Leicestershire, Derbyshire, and Nottinghamshire; and the shoemaking trade was beginning to migrate to Northampton. The less skilled branches of silk manufacture, notably that of silk-throwing, which was amenable to factory structure based on the use of water power, were already in steep decline in London in the 1760s;[33] and many parts of the watches assembled in Clerkenwell were made in Lancashire.[34]

In the early nineteenth century provincial competition of this kind, fortified by rising mass consumption, became increasingly strong in the clothing and luxury trades. Nevertheless large sections of them remained in London near to the main centre of demand, where the traditional small-scale structure prevalent in these fields was only able to withstand this competition by widespread use of sweated labour. Meanwhile by the mid-nineteenth century London's heavier industries, such as shipbuilding and engineering, were increasingly handicapped by distance from the sources of their principal raw materials, coal and iron. Manufacturing industry was in fact beginning to become a less important element in the metropolitan economy as a whole, while the service sector — particularly the ever-diversifying financial services provided by the City and the commercial business of the Port — continued to grow in relative importance, and ultimately led the world. If, indeed, London may be said to have missed the industrial revolution, the capital had certainly had its own financial revolution, which was propelling the metropolitan economy in directions increasingly different from those of much of the rest of the country. It was in part this divergence that William Cobbett was dimly apprehending in the 1820s in his furious denunciations of the City stock-jobbers and of what he called the great, infernal, stinking Wen — so utterly unlike and (as he thought) so parasitical on the rest of the nation.

The City, the Nation, and the World

Despite the tremendous concentration of financial resources and expertise in the metropolis, the heavy new installations of the industrial revolution, such as factories, iron foundries, and mines, were not, in general, directly financed by London money. The amount of fixed capital needed for buildings and machinery was not often large, and came mainly from ploughing in profits, or from mortgages or the personal resources of the partners in a business. There was little overall shortage of capital; rather, indeed, there was a shortage of opportunity for long-term investment, mortgages on the security of bricks and mortar providing throughout much of the eighteenth century the only important alternative to the Government funds. Even the field of canal building (where sometimes there was a local shortage of capital) did not often attract London investors. There was very little metropolitan money in the construction of either the Grand Junction or the Kennet and Avon Canals (though the Thames and Severn did attract a substantial amount), or in the canals of the Midlands and the North, and canal company shares were not even put on the official lists of the Stock Exchange until 1811.[35] The total investment in canal building down to 1815 was in any case tiny — some £20,000,000 — compared to the £440,000,000 of Government loans floated in the war years between 1793 and 1815;[36] and because they were safe and easily negotiable, the funds still had unrivalled attractions for long-term metropolitan investors.

But although London's direct contribution was not the main source of fixed industrial capital, recent research has shown that it was greater than had hitherto been supposed.[37] Child's Bank and the Sun Fire Office, for instance, both made advances to the duke of Bridgewater for his famous canal in Lancashire.[38] In the same county London money was involved in the early days of Pilkington's glass-works;[39] London coal merchants had capital in the coalfields of the North East, and from at least 1765 London merchants provided business ability as well as capital in the growing South Wales iron industry. (The metal used in the rebuilding of London Bridge in the 1820s was supplied from the Cyfarthfa Ironworks at Merthyr Tydfil, which had been established in 1765 by a London iron merchant.)[40] Even the great Carron Ironworks in Scotland relied extensively and for many years on London banks (notably Glyn's) and London bills of exchange for permanent capital loans.[41] In London itself large-scale industries such as the breweries no doubt used their advantages of situation in raising capital locally; but even here, at Truman, Hanbury and Buxton's brewery in Spitalfields in 1760, for instance, less than a quarter of the firm's total assets were in fixtures (brewhouse, pubs, and utensils), while the remainder was in stocks of raw materials, beer, and trade debts, i.e. working, circulating capital.[42]

It was in this vital matter of the circulation of capital that London played a crucial role in the industrialization of the economy. London was the sluice through which, by means of bills of exchange, savings — often originating as surpluses from agricultural areas — could be channelled to areas — often mainly industrial — where credit and working capital were needed. Taxation, too, drew up the nation's revenues to the metropolis, where much of it was redistributed, particularly in times of war, to industrial centres such as Coalbrookdale or South Wales in the form of massive Government contracts for the equipment of the army and navy.[43] Although England had long ceased to be a congeries of unrelated economic regions, it did not yet enjoy a fully integrated money market, and needed the link provided by London. Banks were still local, and payments from one part of the country to another tended to be made through the capital, where London's acceptance of country bankers' bills of exchange or notes supplied an endorsement of their validity. There were added advantages in dealing through London after Thomas Richardson, a clerk in a City bank which acted as London agent for a number of country banks, had set up in a room off Cornhill in 1802 as a bill broker. In this new form of business he acted as intermediary between country banks wanting bills of exchange to discount (i.e. bankers with surplus cash in search of short-term investment) and other banks looking for short-term capital. This speciality proved so successful that by 1823 his firm, then known as Richardson, Overend and Gurney, had the enormous annual turnover of £20,000,000 (equivalent to over one-third of the total public revenue at that time). London was, indeed, the heart through which the financial lifeblood of the nation was pumped.[44]

Much less clear is the role of foreign trade, and that of London in particular, in the advancement of the industrial economy.[45] Although the value of London's import and export trade more than trebled during the eighteenth century, the metropolitan share of the English total certainly fell — imports from 80 per cent in 1700 to 66 per cent in 1800, and exports (69 per cent in 1700) and re-exports (86 per cent) to 62 per cent taken together.[46] The principal reason for this decline of London's predominance was, of course, the rise of the west coast ports of the industrial north — Liverpool, Whitehaven, and Glasgow — and their favourable geographical position for the rapidly expanding trade with the New World, in which the principal export commodities were textiles and ironwares, with sugar from the West Indies and tobacco and cotton from North America the principal imports. Trade with the East Indies, on the other hand, remained virtually a London monopoly, and as a proportion of the national total this too grew rapidly. The proportion of domestic exports and retained imports to and from continental Europe fell correspondingly, but re-exports to Europe continued to flourish, and in 1800 London still retained well over half this trade.[47] So London too had its perennial advantages of geography, and when the substantial reorientation of England's trade from Europe to the New World, and the changes in commodities which this entailed, are taken into account, the extent of the fall of the metropolitan share of total foreign trade was not all that great.

The significance of this overseas trade in the evolution of the economy has been much discussed by historians. During the eighteenth century it grew more rapidly than did the economy as a whole, and it has been suggested that in the 1780s and 1790s exports accounted for nearly 60 per cent of the national increase in industrial output.[48] But by the early nineteenth century most of these exports were either cotton textiles (which in 1802 replaced woollens as the largest single export commodity) or iron goods — two sectors of the economy in which London had little or no direct share.[49] So the influence which London exerted through its foreign trade was primarily through re-exports and imports, and was largely indirect. Most immediately, foreign trade stimulated the vast early nineteenth-century improvements made in the port itself through the building of wet docks and warehouses. It created jobs on a massive scale — directly through the need for nearly 40,000 seamen to man the ships registered in 1799 at London,[50] and for an army of dock labour (shipwrights, warehousemen, porters, carters, etc.), as well as of tradesmen of all kinds who in turn supplied the everyday needs of the port workers and their families. It also stimulated industry around the port — sugar-refining and tobacco-processing, for instance. Further afield, not only in London itself but increasingly throughout the whole country, it generated consumption, particularly of goods which would not otherwise have been available (tea, sugar, coffee, tobacco, for instance), and by thus widening ranges of choice it enhanced living standards and stimulated other demands, notably for cotton manufactures. Much of the prosperity and rising numbers of London's urban gentry was based on this foreign trade, and without such wealth it is impossible to suppose that London could have continued to provide the crucial metropolitan link in the virtuous circle of the evolving national economy.

Britain's overseas trade, and particularly that of London, was, of course, closely linked to the world of City finance. After the disruption of international commerce during the Napoleonic Wars Amsterdam never recovered its former importance, while London's financial expertise had been sharpened by the great wartime flotations of Government debts and by the remittance of subsidies to Britain's Continental allies. It was also sharpened by the establishment of a new breed of (foreign) family merchant bank specializing in international business, notably those founded in London by Sir Francis Baring and by Johann Schroder (both of German extraction), by Nathan Rothschild (German Jewish), and (later, in the 1830s) by the American George Peabody—all four firms being still today in existence in the City, the house of Morgan Grenfell being lineally descended from George Peabody and Co. and Baring's since 1995 being in Dutch ownership. After the return of peace in 1815 the Government's need to borrow money fell sharply, but foreign governments and companies soon began to resort to London for loans, offering higher rates of interest to investors than those available from the British funds. Baring's organized the payment of reparations by France, and a loan to the Tzar of Russia; Rothschild's managed loans for Prussia and Austria (1818–21); then came half a dozen of the new South American republics, and Greece. Between 1822 and 1825 some twenty loans for foreign states, totalling a nominal figure of about £40,000,000, were chiefly subscribed for by British investors. British capital (and some of foreign origin too), all channelled through the City, had become an export, reversing the net inflow of foreign capital which had prevailed throughout most of the eighteenth century; and sterling was moving towards becoming the world currency of the nineteenth century, centred on London and universally acceptable as a means of payment and exchange.[51]

At first this supremacy was not very firmly based, for it depended largely upon the business confidence engendered by the Bank of England's return in 1821 to payments in gold (which had been suspended since 1797), upon the gradual establishment of free trade, and upon the 'Pax Britannica' of 1815–1914; and all of these were still delicate plants in the 1820s. Speculative mania led inevitably in 1825 to a crash on the Stock Exchange, in which, through the financial links provided by the bill brokers between the provinces and London, the country bankers were also deeply involved, eighty of them being declared bankrupt. The dangerous instability of a banking system still based largely on small privately owned firms had been revealed; and it was only after legislation of 1826 and 1833 had cleared the way for the establishment of joint-stock banks, and the Bank of England itself had gradually assumed a quasi-regulatory role in the money market, that the City began to acquire its Victorian reputation for solidity and reliability, far removed from the turbulent and unsteady times of the earlier years of the previous century.[52]

In the evolution of Britain's economy during the industrial revolution London has not until recently received its due share of attention, but through its stimulation of agricultural and industrial productivity, the migration of surplus rural population, and the development of commercial and financial skills, its influence was crucial. The stimulus of metropolitan demand was in substantial measure responsible for raising levels of agricultural productivity per man in England to at least double those in France, and this enabled a higher proportion of the total population to make its living outside agriculture, mainly in urban industry or services. Except in Holland, where the numbers of town dwellers had passed its peak, this process had by 1800 advanced much further in England than anywhere else in Europe, the proportion of peoples living in towns in France being less than half that of the urban peoples of England; and Paris, with a population of 546,000, contained only some 2 per cent of the national population, while London's 960,000 amounted to over 11 per cent of the peoples of England.[53]

Through the City of London Britain was also able to raise the huge sums of money needed to pay for over a century of almost endemic war with France (1689–1815). With an efficient system of taxation (until the introduction of income tax in 1799 based chiefly on the land tax and customs and excise), the State was able through the expertise of the City to service the massive public debts incurred during these wars. Britain became the most highly taxed country in Europe (with the exception of Holland), and by the late eighteenth century the tax burden was far heavier in England than in France both per capita and as a share of national income. By 1783 the British national debt was greater than that of far more populous France on the eve of the Revolution in 1789.[54] Yet there was in Britain no widespread resistance to the collection of taxes; and this has been attributed to the importance of parliamentary consent in providing a secure foundation for the operation of the nation's fiscal system.[55] The lineaments of the powerful coalition of Westminster, Whitehall, Bank of England, and moneyed men of the City — the 'gentlemanly capitalism' and 'the Establishment' of the future — were beginning to emerge, and to play an increasingly important role in the running of the nation.

The City's capacity to raise money for the State was moreover a vital ingredient in Britain's metamorphosis from the militarily and politically second-rank nation of the sixteenth and seventeenth centuries to the position of leading world power after 1815. In 1680 the population of England was less than a quarter of that of France, and in 1820 less than two-fifths, while that of England, Wales, Scotland, and Ireland as a whole was hardly more than two-thirds of the French figure of 30,500,000. Yet (as Professor Sir Tony Wrigley has emphasized) success in war proceeds as much from the efficient mobilization of national income and wealth as from the absolute extent of total resources available;[56] and Britain, it has been suggested, was 'about a century ahead of France in evolving modern financial institutions'.[57] Through her more efficient system of public borrowing at low rates of interest, England, either directly or through her allies, was able to deploy against France sea and land forces out of all proportion to her relative resources of population, natural wealth, and military structure. Without the financial resources mobilized in the City, existing foreign markets would not have been kept and new ones would not have been won — with immeasurable consequences for the industrializing economy.[58] Final victory over France, Professor Lawrence Stone has unequivocally stated, 'was won not so much by military prowess, technological innovation or diplomatic skill as by overwhelming financial superiority. At bottom, victory in war was a question of money, not men'.[59]

Lastly in this discussion of the City's influence in the national economy, there are the earliest recorded figures (dating from Regency times) for the nation's foreign earnings from the provision of commercial and financial services (shipping, banking, insurance, discounting bills of exchange for foreign trade, the supply of international credit facilities, etc.) and for income from overseas investments. These show that in the 1820s these earnings amounted to no less than

30 per cent of the total value of all exported products; and later in the century the proportion was even larger. It is indeed a remarkable fact that despite the enormous manufacturing output of the new industrial towns of the North, the value of the national imports always throughout the whole of the nineteenth century (when Britain was 'the workshop of the world') exceeded that of exports; and it was only through invisible earnings, substantially generated through the City, that a favourable national balance of payments was ever achieved at all.[60]

15

Religion, Education, and Leisure

The religious earthquake of the Reformation and Counter-Reformation was followed by a number of secondary tremors of lesser but still formidable power. The most notable of these was what Sir John Plumb has termed 'the acceptance of modernity..., the replacement of the Providence-dominated world of early modern and medieval Europe by the world of expanding knowledge and science, of discoverable nature and rational exploration'.[1] This very gradual process was far from complete even at the end of the Georgian era, when evangelicanism was in rising spate and the Victorian religious revival was still to come. There was nevertheless a sharply different intellectual climate between, for instance, the world of the Charity School movement of the 1690s and that of the Benthamites' University College — 'the Godless College in Gower Street' — of the 1820s.

During the twenty-five years or so after the Revolution of 1688 religion continued to be as closely intertwined with politics as it had been at any time since the Reformation. But the continuing importance of religious issues did not mean that many people were particularly devout, and devotion was conspicuously absent as a cause of the Sacheverell Riots of 1710, which were — with only one exception (the Gordon Riots, 1780) — the worst outbreak of mob violence in the metropolis in the whole of the eighteenth century. London was at that time a centre of militant Toryism (reinforced by war-weariness and the association of the war with Whig finance and the Whig ministry) as well as of Whig Dissent, and at the peak of Whig fortunes in the reign of Queen Anne there was widespread fear that the Church of England was threatened by the supposed advance of Dissent as well as by the traditional bogey of popery. So when the Whig Government unwisely impeached a High Anglican parson, Dr Henry Sacheverell, for an inflammatory sermon preached before the Lord Mayor and Corporation in St Paul's, an apparently well-organized Tory 'Church' mob of perhaps 5,000 wrecked half a dozen Dissenting meeting houses around Holborn on the night of 1–2 March 1710, and order was only restored after eight hours by the use of troops.[2]

Soon after this successful exploitation of the war cry of 'the Church in Danger' the Tory victory at the general election of 1710 was celebrated by an Act of

Parliament establishing a commission for the building of fifty new churches in the great new suburbs of London, which were regarded as strongholds of Dissent. The cost of this programme was to be paid for by an additional duty on all coals brought into the Port of London. Only a dozen new churches were in fact built during the course of the twenty-five years or so of the commission's active life, but Nicholas Hawksmoor designed six of them, Thomas Archer two, and James Gibbs and John James one each. The Act had stipulated that the churches were to be built of 'stone and other proper Materials with Towers or Steeples for each of them', and the distinguished architectural presence of such splendid buildings as Christ Church, Spitalfields, or St Anne's, Limehouse, still dominates the surrounding landscape.[3]

A handful of other churches were also built in the 1720s and 1730s, of which Gibbs's St Martin-in-the-Fields was the most famous and soon became the prototype of countless churches in America. But for the rest of the eighteenth century proprietary chapels provided the only important enlargement of Anglican accommodation available in the ever-growing metropolis. These chapels were built, owned, and managed as commercial concerns by private patrons, who charged substantial rents for the use of most of the pews. By 1800 there were, for instance, eight such chapels in the single mainly well-to-do parish of St Marylebone.[4] For half a century, from the 1720s to the 1770s, the Established Church in London sank into a state of comfortable torpor which reflected the relaxed religious attitudes of its mainly leisured congregations. Pluralism and non-residence were widely prevalent among the clergy, but the curates who actually did the work were wretchedly paid and notoriously poor.[5] So there was never any difficulty about getting a clergyman to perform a clandestine marriage.

In the post-Restoration period the two most popular 'privileged' (usually extraparochial) places where such weddings could be had were at St James's, Duke Place and Holy Trinity, Minories; but later, after a change in the law, most clandestine marriages were conducted within the Rules of the Fleet Prison, adjoining the north side of Ludgate Hill. Between 1694 and 1753, when Lord Hardwick's Marriage Act put a stop to these practices throughout England (but not Scotland), something of the order of 250,000 weddings were solemnized there, and by 1740 at least half of all Londoners married at the Fleet. Fees were certainly low there, and an immediate union could always be had on demand, often in a tavern or alehouse. Predilection for private weddings rather than in the parish church of one or other of the parties concerned was uniquely strong in London, and (odd though it may seem) may have reflected an element of social emulation.[6]

Outside the Established Church the old Nonconformist sects (the Presbyterians, Independents, Baptists, and Quakers) also lost much of their vigour, though their members increased in absolute numbers, and they maintained their old strength in the mercantile community of the City, where the halls of a number of livery companies were often let to them for their Sunday meetings. The Roman Catholics, of whom there were some 11,000 in London in 1767, depended heavily on the chapels of foreign embassies for the practice of their faith, and kept a very low

profile throughout the eighteenth century. Deep-seated hatred of popery nevertheless persisted, as the Gordon Riots demonstrated in 1780.[7]

Yet despite the widespread religious laxity prevalent in the middle decades of the
eighteenth century, the seeds of a revived 'vital religion' were already beginning to
sprout. The long ministry of John and Charles Wesley, which effectively began in
1738, was always closely connected with the metropolis; and so too was that of the
Calvinistic George Whitefield, Moorfields at first and then the Wesleyan Methodist
Chapel in City Road being the Wesleys' headquarters, while Whitefield had a large
tabernacle in Tottenham Court Road. Their open-air preaching to huge congregations at such places as Kennington Common brought religion directly to the poor,
and although the impact of Methodism in London was not so great as in some
other parts of the country, it nevertheless conduced directly or indirectly to the
proliferation of new sects in the second half of the century, the countess of
Huntingdon's Connexion and the followers of Joanna Southcott being cases in
point.[8] More importantly, Methodism was also a potent ingredient in the social
evolution of the whole nation, having (so it has been argued) on the one hand a
stabilizing influence — the French historian Elie Halévy even claimed that Methodism prevented revolution in England in the 1790s — while on the other providing through its spiritual egalitarianism and its structural organization models for
working-class political development in the future.[9] Religious Dissent and political
radicalism were indeed often intertwined.

By the 1790s the Church of England was also experiencing another kind of
resuscitation, mainly from a small group of evangelical clergy and laymen, several
of whose leading members lived in the parish on the outskirts of South London
from which the Clapham Sect takes its name. Its members included Zachary
Macaulay (merchant, and father of the historian), Henry Thornton, banker and
MP, and William Wilberforce. Through this formidable circle of wealthy intellectuals strict evangelical codes of morality and behaviour as well as of religious
observance were taken to the rich and powerful, whom the Methodists had not
greatly influenced. The Clapham evangelicals' zeal for good works found early
expression in the establishment of foreign missionary societies, and in the abolition of the slave trade (1807), the long campaign for which was led by Wilberforce.
They also provided themselves with a monthly magazine, the *Christian Observer*,
for the dissemination of their ideas (1802); and by around 1830, on the eve of the
great age of reform, the Clapham Sect was exerting a powerful influence throughout the Church in London and indeed throughout much of the whole country.[10]

This evangelical reforming zeal underlay the long series of philanthropic endeavours which were always active in one form or another in Augustan and Georgian
London. The first of these endeavours — the charity school movement which
began in the 1690s — was based on ideas broadly held later by the evangelicals.
Under the general auspices of the Society for Promoting Christian Knowledge
(founded in London in 1699), the charity schools provided an explicitly Anglican
education free of charge for the children of the poor, much of the teaching being
intended to inculcate social and religious discipline and submission. Some

instruction in the three Rs was also given, and the reading-book recommended for use by the infant scholars was the Anglican catechism. In the mid-1730s there were over 130 charity schools in London, many of them housed in handsome new buildings such as the Westminster Greycoat School in Great Peter Street (which still survives), all the capital and running costs being met by private subscribers. The main motive for this great effort seems to have been to reaffirm the spiritual ascendancy of the Church of England in face of the dangers perceived to be threatening it after the Revolution of 1688, much as the evangelicals wished to reassert the Church's influence in the life of the nation a century later.[11] Just as the Anglican Establishment of the 1690s supplemented religious education by invoking through the London Society for the Reformation of Manners (founded in 1691) the rigours of the law for the suppression of vice and immorality, so too in 1787 did the Clapham evangelicals set up the Proclamation Society to stimulate the practice of their stringent standards of social conduct.[12]

When the Church settled back into its mid-Georgian repose in the 1720s and 1730s the vigour of the charity school movement also declined, and the provision of hospitals became a favoured object of humanitarian concern. One of the earliest of these was Guy's Hospital in Southwark, founded in the 1720s by Thomas Guy, who had made a fortune during the South Sea Bubble. Others instituted at about this time included the Westminster (1720), St George's (1733), the London (1740), Captain Thomas Coram's Foundling Hospital (1742), and the Middlesex (1745), all of which were funded by voluntary subscriptions. This burst of metropolitan activity was followed by the establishment of a score of general hospitals in the provinces, and in London from the 1750s onwards by more specialized institutions, notably for lying-in women and for the treatment of smallpox, venereal disease, and insanity. It was probably humane benevolence (plus a dash of self-interest) rather than religion which prompted well-to-do Londoners to subscribe to these institutions. The treatment provided in them was by later standards primitive, and it may be doubted whether it had any significant effect on the very high death rate prevalent in Georgian London. But the hospitals did at least provide centres of medical education, where medical knowledge could be gradually accumulated.[13]

Knowledge was indeed lacking in many fields. So the early pioneers of social reform were much concerned with the dissemination of facts. Thus Jonas Hanway (1712–86), the champion of pauper children and of the chimney sweeps' climbing boys, visited every workhouse in London and disclosed that the mortality rate of the infant parish poor was at least 80 or 90 per cent;[14] and the investigations by John Howard (1726?–1790) of London gaols, later reinforced by the example of the humanity of the Quaker Elizabeth Fry (1780–1845) in her work for the female prisoners in Newgate, disclosed conditions hitherto either unknown or ignored.

Despite widespread social ignorance and the fact that the eighteenth century was not a distinguished one in the history of metropolitan education, some development did nevertheless occur. There were certainly many dame schools and petty schools, as well as often short-lived private commercial schools (which have left little trace of their existence) where the three Rs and the elements of bookkeeping were taught; and the evidence of signatures suggests that in the early eighteenth century the literacy rate in London was substantially above the national average. In the 1780s numerous Sunday schools, in which children learned to read and recite the catechism, were opened, largely under evangelical guidance and after 1803 supported by the interdenominational Sunday School Union, which was formed by a group of City men.[15]

An altogether new phase began in 1798 when Joseph Lancaster opened a school in Southwark in which the three Rs and the Scriptures (but not the catechism) were taught, use being made of the monitorial system whereby the older children instructed the younger ones. At about the same time much the same methods, previously practised by the Revd Andrew Bell in Madras, were introduced at the parochial school at St Botolph's, Aldgate, and from these two experiments there emerged the (Lancastrian) British and Foreign School Society and the National Society for Promoting the Education of the Poor in the Principles of the Established Church. By 1816 there were over fifty schools in London in union with one or other of these two societies, and although the number of children under instruction in them only amounted to some 12,000, it is not too much to claim that the first lasting foundations of the English elementary day school had been laid. Less auspiciously, the establishment of the two societies also marked the modern origin of the 'religious difficulty' which for so long bedevilled English educational history.[16]

But there was little purpose in providing schools for the inculcation of religious principles if there were no churches to assist the pupils in the practice of those principles in later life. In London alone in about 1815 there were said to be fifty parishes with a total of over 1,000,000 inhabitants where the existing churches were not capable of containing even 10 per cent of the population. Although for the Establishment the wisdom of educating the new urban masses might still be open to question, there could be no doubt, in face of the spread of Dissent, democratic ideas, and economic discontent, about the desirability of providing churches for them. So in 1818 the Church Building Commission was established by Act of Parliament and equipped with £1,000,000 of public money. In London grants were made for the building of thirty-three churches (mostly in growing suburbs such as Lambeth or St Marylebone), but substantial contributions were usually also needed from private subscribers and/or church rates. In this way over 50,000 new seats were provided, of which more than half were subject to the payment of pew rents. But in the 1820s the population of London rose by well over 250,000, so the commission was not able to keep pace with the problem, even after another £500,000 had been voted to it in 1824.[17] Thereafter there were no more parliamentary grants, and by 1830 the relationship of Church and State had been fundamentally changed by the Catholic Emancipation Act and the repeal of the Test and Corporation Acts.

Most of these new London churches were in the Grecian manner — the cheapest available — and the remainder in the Gothic. Although their architects included some of the foremost practitioners of the day (Nash, Soane, Smirke, T. Hardwick,

Barry, and C. R. Cockerell),[18] the financial stringency necessarily imposed by the commission inhibited their designs. Those churches which still survive often convey a sense of puzzled failure and disappointed hopes.

In the early nineteenth century the Church, although not exactly 'in Danger' as it had been a century previously, was none the less being weakened by the advance of religious indifference and the utilitarian radicalism embodied in the copious writings of Jeremy Bentham and in the ceaseless activities of Henry Brougham, Francis Place, and others — the secular counterpart of the evangelical movement. In the 1820s Mechanics' Institutes were formed under Benthamite auspices in many parts of the country for the instruction of working men in scientific, technical, and literary subjects. In London the first of these institutes was opened in 1824 under the presidency of Dr George Birkbeck, and as Birkbeck College it still exists as a constituent part of the University of London. During the course of the next twenty years about sixty Mechanics' Institutes were established in the metropolis, their work being supplemented by the Society for the Diffusion of Useful Knowledge, founded by Brougham in 1826. It was in that same year, too, that the Benthamites founded University College, London, which, to quote the words of Lord Briggs, was 'open to members of all religions or none, to provide a less expensive and more utilitarian education for the sons of the industrial and commercial middle-classes than that provided in Oxford and Cambridge.'[19]

So London at last had its own seat of higher learning, though still not quite yet its own university. During the seventeenth century the Inns of Court had served some of the purposes of a university, but in Georgian times their use as finishing schools for the sons of the gentry had diminished. Public use of the British Museum, in the birth of which in 1753 the Government had assisted almost in a fit of absent-mindedness rather than through any carefully considered act of policy, was until well into the nineteenth century regulated with the utmost stringency. London had, however, become the principal centre of medical education in England, much of it provided by Scottish physicians like Dr William Hunter, who lectured in his own anatomical theatre in Great Windmill Street.[20] The foundation of University College as a centre for the study and teaching of the whole field of modern knowledge had quickly engendered a counterblast from the Church in the establishment of King's College in the Strand (1828), but it was nevertheless 'the Godless College in Gower Street' which later provided the prototype for the red-brick universities established in the provinces during the latter part of the nineteenth century.

Leisure and its Commercialization

London was the intellectual, artistic, and fashionable capital of the nation as well as its centre of government and the economy. This metropolitan culture was largely a reflection of the essentially aristocratic nature of Georgian society in general, but (unlike the cultures of such great Continental capitals as Paris and Vienna) it was also increasingly impregnated by middle-class attitudes and modes of behaviour — by the values of the City as well as of the court. As we have already seen, London through its sheer size and wealth did much to create the mass demands needed to stimulate the formation of a consumer society. Part of this process took place in the field of leisure, where through the advance of commercialization the pleasures of London were enjoyed by greatly widening sections of the population.[21]

This can be seen in one of the jewels of Georgian metropolitan culture: the theatre. This was a wholly commercial affair, for the days when a troupe of actors needed royal or aristocratic protection or patronage were over; nor did the theatre enjoy financial support from the Crown. This lacuna was offset by the virtual duopoly of performance of the spoken word conferred by the royal theatre patents, under which Drury Lane and — after 1732 — John Rich's new Covent Garden theatres operated; while over in the Haymarket Sir John Vanbrugh's Queen's Theatre (1705) opened under a royal licence and soon became the home of opera. Here in these three great houses dawned a golden age illumined by Handel's forty-year association with the Opera House, David Garrick's long reign (1747–76) as actor-manager at Drury Lane, and first performances of classic plays by Goldsmith and Sheridan at Covent Garden.

By the 1770s a contemporary commentator could write that 'the playhouse in London is for all classes of the nation. The peer of the realm, the gentleman, the merchant, the citizen, the clergyman, the tradesman and their wives equally resort thither to take places, and the crowd is great.'[22] This widespread support was of course growing continually as London's population also grew, and it could only be provided for by the enlargement of the theatres. Between 1791 and 1811 Drury Lane and Covent Garden were both rebuilt twice (both of them were destroyed by fire within six months of each other in 1808–9), and the Haymarket Opera House was also rebuilt in 1790–1 after a fire, and remodelled again in 1816–18. After its first rebuilding (which cost £150,000) in 1791–4 Drury Lane had an enormous capacity of over 3,500: theatre had become very big business indeed. With auditoria of this size spectacular scenic effects superseded the more intimate style of acting prevalent in Garrick's day as the main attraction; and the projecting forestage and stage boxes retreated behind the proscenium arch, further separating audience from performers.[23]

But even these huge new theatres could not keep pace with the demands of the ever-expanding metropolis, and a number of small 'minor theatres' such as the Sans Pareil (Strand, 1806) and the Royal Coburg (later the Old Vic, Waterloo Road, 1818) were established, where productions of generally little artistic merit were performed. On the fringes of the thespian world, and often also on the fringes of the metropolis, there sprouted up a miscellany of popular forms of entertainment which included Astley's Amphitheatre in Lambeth, the Aquatic Theatre at Sadler's Wells, the panoramas in Leicester Square and Regent's Park, and the menagerie at Exeter Change in the Strand.

In the world of music Handel's long residence gave London a period of very great distinction. His gigantic oeuvre of operas, oratorios, and other works provided the material continually needed to satisfy the prevailing craze for Italian opera or for performances at the concert rooms or in the semi-professional musical clubs which proliferated. After his death in 1759 many other foreign musicians, of whom the young Mozart and J. C. Bach were the most distinguished, came to London, sometimes for long visits, lured, no doubt, by the fame of London's wealth and the opportunities for making money there; and in the 1790s Haydn came twice for the performance of his last twelve symphonies, which had been specially commissioned for London audiences. But by around 1800 London's halcyon days of music were coming to an end, and the new Romantic music found its greatest expression elsewhere.

Like the theatre, the visual arts were also reaching a wider public. Portraiture dominated painting throughout much of the eighteenth century, and in the hands of such artists as Reynolds and Gainsborough was by its nature largely aristocratic. But the situation had begun to change slowly after William Hogarth (1697–1764) had in 1732 produced *The Harlot's Progress* — the first of his series of engravings of modern moral subjects. Hogarth was born in London and lived there all his life, with a house and workshop in Leicester Square and a country cottage (which still stands) at Chiswick. His engravings — the pictorial equivalents of the novels of Henry Fielding — sold in thousands, and the later development of such reproductive processes as aquatint and mezzotint further enlarged the clientele of the art market and led on to the mass sales of the political and social satires of James Gillray and others. In the field of painting the foundation of the Royal Academy in 1768 and the inauguration of its annual exhibitions emphasized London's position as the national centre of patronage for artists all over the country. The (Royal) Society for the Encouragement of Arts, Manufactures and Commerce was already in being, and other bodies all concerned with the promotion of the fine arts soon followed — Alderman John Boydell's Shakespeare Gallery in Pall Mall (1786), the Society of Painters in Water-Colours [sic] in Lower Brook Street (1804), the British Institute for Promoting the Fine Arts, also in Pall Mall (1805), and the Society of British Artists in Suffolk Street (1823). By the 1820s the visual arts had largely by means of the exhibition rooms of Pall Mall and St James's become big business, like the theatre rather earlier. The widely diffused interest which they now commanded was implicitly recognized in 1824 when Parliament authorized the purchase of the collection of old-master paintings formed by J. J. Angerstein (a retired Lloyd's underwriter), and which formed the nucleus of the National Gallery.[24]

All these new galleries also served as foyers where the arts of conversation and genteel social intercourse, which were so carefully cultivated in Georgian times, could be practised. With the royal court generally either at St James's, or from the 1760s at Buckingham House (later rebuilt by George IV and John Nash as Buckingham Palace), or at any rate not far away at Kensington or Hampton Court, London was very much the social capital of the nation. This was particularly so during the season, when in the winter and early spring the great houses of the West

End (and many not so great ones too) filled up for the metropolitan social round, the commanding heights of which in Regency times were controlled by the *grandes dames* of Almack's Assembly Rooms in King Street, St James's, where even the duke of Wellington was on one occasion refused entry because his dress did not conform to their prescriptions. The metropolis had perhaps reached its optimum size for 'civilized' living, still compact enough for men to be able to get about easily on foot. James Boswell, in the conduct of his extensive social peregrinations, nearly always walked, and only occasionally resorted to a Hackney carriage or a Thames wherry. A friend of his remarked that 'The chief advantage of London ... is, that a man is always so near his burrow.'

In the early eighteenth century much social life revolved around the coffee houses, of which by 1739 there were over 500 in London and which provided middle-class and commercial centres for the exchange of news and the discussion of public events. Soon they divided on functional lines, Lloyd's, for instance, becoming the centre for marine insurance, and Garraway's in Cornhill being the resort of merchant bankers. Further west the division tended to be on political lines, Button's in Convent Garden being favoured by the Whigs, including Steele and Addison, while White's in St James's Street was a Tory stronghold. From a few of these establishments there gradually evolved the 'proprietary' clubs of the mid-eighteenth century, owned and managed by the proprietor from whom they often took their name and who provided food, drink, and the exclusive use of rooms for the subscribers (i.e. members). White's, Boodle's, and Brooks's, whose clubhouses still adorn St James's Street, are cases in point, all of which were centres of heavy drinking and often ruinous gambling in the days of Sheridan and Charles James Fox. A little later, however, 'members' clubs' entirely owned and managed by the members became the norm, and all the great West End clubs which were founded in the generation or so after 1815 were of this kind. The United Service (1815–16), the Travellers' (1819), and the Athenaeum (1824), for instance, all in Pall Mall, provided luxurious rendezvous for groups of gentlemen united by common tastes and social background, while the Carlton (1832) and the Reform (1834) were the private headquarters of the two rival political parties.[25]

The pleasure gardens which also proliferated in Georgian times catered for a far larger public than the clubs. By the later eighteenth century there were scores of them in and around London, the most famous being at Vauxhall, where the wooded avenues, arcaded promenades, supper kiosks, and concert pavilion extended over some 12 acres. The price of admission was only 1s., so Vauxhall's appeal extended far beyond fashionable society—in 1833 some 27,000 people crowded in on a single day; and in the plantations away from the bright lights flirtatious social liberties could be discreetly taken. Much the same sort of entertainment took place at Ranelagh Gardens in Chelsea, which like Vauxhall could be approached by river; but here there was a large rotunda 150 feet in diameter where assemblies were often held. Nearer the centre of things, in Oxford Street, was the magnificent but short-lived Pantheon (by James Wyatt, 1772), famous for its concerts and masquerades.[26]

Many of Georgian London's leisure activities were suffused by gambling and drinking, just as they had been in the seventeenth century. (Gambling was even put to serious use when £300,000 was raised by a lottery in 1753 for the establishment of the British Museum.) This was particularly so in the case of violent pursuits such as prizefighting and cock-fighting; and there was always much drunkenness on such turbulent occasions as St Bartholomew's Fair in Smithfield or on the eight annual hanging days at Tyburn gallows. Ale and porter (nowadays called stout) were consumed in vast quantities in the London beerhouses, of which there were nearly 6,000 in 1740; but in the 1730s and 1740s gin was so cheap that it became the favourite drink of the very poor until heavy taxes were imposed. Better-heeled Londoners drank wine, and particularly port, often on a heroic scale. To be drunk was accepted as a natural and commonplace condition, at any rate for men; and no doubt this was good for business for the women of the town, who could be picked up in the streets all over London, though the main 'red light district' was around Covent Garden, where fashionable disorderly houses disguised themselves under the label of 'bagnios'.[27] Competitive outdoor games, which were later to become so important in English national life, were, however, still unknown apart from cricket, which in 1814 found a permanent metropolitan home at Thomas Lord's ground at St John's Wood, and under the auspices of the Marylebone Cricket Club set London on the way to becoming the national capital of organized sport.

By the end of the Georgian era the enjoyment of many of the pleasures which London had to offer was diffused throughout a substantial section of the population. Foreign visitors were astonished at the extent of the wealth of the place: 7 miles of shops extending almost continuously along the two main east–west thoroughfares from Mile End to Parliament Street and from Shoreditch to Tyburn. Bow windows, plate glass, and bright lights were all used to exploit impulse buying, and in Oxford Street alone there were over 150 shops selling 'the whim-whams and fribble-frabble of fashion.'[28] Elsewhere there were palatial showrooms such as those of Josiah Wedgwood or of the bookseller James Lackington in Finsbury Square, known as 'The Temple of the Muses'. Printing was indeed getting into its stride for the first time, with books on all manner of subjects, and above all through newspapers and magazines. Newspapers, besides disseminating information about the events of the day, also contained advertisements — i.e. they stimulated demand;[29] and the fashion magazines which began to appear in the 1770s contained numerous fashion plates. So fashion too became more widely diffused, and also more ephemeral, for whereas in 1711 Addison thought that in the bucolic West Country 'the fashions of Charles II's reign were still worn', by the end of the eighteenth century London designers and publishers could change them within weeks or months. The metropolitan-led consumer society was coming into being.[30]

Dr Johnson's remark, made in 1777 and perhaps the most famous of all his numerous remarks, that 'when a man is tired of London he is tired of life; for there is in London all that life can afford'[31] will still bear repetition. A survey of the pleasures and *divertissements* of the capital would not be complete without reference to the outward beauty of the place, at least as portrayed in the works of Canaletto (who lived in London for several years), Samuel Scott, Sandby, and other artists, in whose pictures the sun seems always to be shining. But of course there was an obverse to those arcadian scenes. Smoke caused by the ever-growing consumption of coal was as early as 1711 prompting Swift to inveigh against soot-laden showers of rain; the stonework of St Paul's was being corroded even before building had been completed, and in the early nineteenth century visitors frequently commented not only on the smoke but also on the dirt, the damp, and the fog, often so thick that candles were needed even at noon[32] — depressing portents of future conditions in the Victorian metropolis.

16

Metropolitan Politics and Metropolitan Class

After the tremendous ructions of the seventeenth century London's position in the political life of the nation was never as dominant as it had often hitherto been, but its influence was exerted in new ways. Some twenty-five years of almost continuous war with France (1689–1713) brought into being a large new civil bureaucracy, much of it based in London, where by 1725 there were well over 2,000 Government officials, not to mention around a thousand part-time Customs officers in the Port of London.[1] Besides being the headquarters of this enlarged executive arm of Government, London—or to be more precise, the City—provided the driving force behind the financial revolution, which was also in some measure the product of the vast cost of the French wars. The newspaper industry which sprang up after the expiry of the licensing laws in 1694 also had its natural home in the capital. Greatly increased quantities of political and other information quite suddenly became widely available, and it was from London that much of it was disseminated to the provinces, where local newspapers habitually reprinted large chunks of the metropolitan press.

Between 1689 and 1715 there were more general elections than in the whole of the rest of the eighteenth century. Much of the intense party strife which prevailed in those years radiated out from London, where it pervaded social life. Party political clubs like the aristocratic (Whig) Kit-Cat Club proliferated, and coffee houses became the resort of upper and middling sorts of Londoners in search of political news and rumour, some of these establishments such as the (Tory) Cocoa Tree in Pall Mall eventually evolving into the clubs of one or other of the two parties. Even the theatre was impregnated by political antagonisms, most of the best dramatists—Congreve, Addison, Farquhar, and Vanbrugh, for instance—being Whigs.[2] It was from this hothouse metropolitan atmosphere that (as during the Popish Plot, 1678–81) extra-parliamentary agitations and petitions emerged, and nationwide 'instruction' campaigns attempting to pressurize MPs' voting behaviour were organized:[3]

And, of course, the metropolis comprised by far the largest concentration of population within the realm—by 1800 over 1,000,000 people lived within less than 10 miles of Westminster—and its mere size gave it a potential power which could never be wholly ignored by either Government or Parliament. Although it only returned ten MPs and in terms of population was therefore grossly underrepres-

ented in the House of Commons, the electorate of the four 'metropolitan' constituencies (the City, with four Members, and Westminster, Middlesex, and Southwark with two each) were all extremely large—18,000 in the case of Westminster in
1807[4]—and often unmanageable, particularly in the City, where internal divisions
constantly prevailed. Politically the metropolis was, indeed, a largely unassimilated
mass, uniquely distinct from the great landed interests upon which the national
political system was based; and it had a strong and sometimes uncontrollable
clout.

Between 1688 and 1714 there was a realignment of party positions within the
City—to some extent a reversal of their respective pre-1688 roles—and for many
years thereafter this had a direct bearing on the City's impact on national politics.
Within the Corporation the Whigs in 1689 were in the ascendant in both the Court
of Aldermen and of Common Council. The wealthy mercantile grandees heavily
involved in the ensuing financial revolution were also mainly Whigs, and soon they
were drawing back from the populist ideas which had been espoused in Whig
circles during the Popish Plot crisis. Much of this ground was gradually taken over
by the Tories, who by 1705 had the advantage in Common Council. After the
accession of George I the monied City Whig oligarchs, whose fortunes were still
largely being made by providing for the financial needs of the State, became the
natural allies of successive Whig ministries, while the middling people (small
merchants, retailers, and master craftsmen) gravitated towards the Tory or 'Country' opposition, always on the lookout for extra-parliamentary allies.[5]

These battle positions lasted basically unchanged for a long time. From the early
1720s until the mid-1780s the City in the broader sense (Common Council,
Common Hall, and freemen) was almost always in opposition to Government,
so much so that Walpole, by his City Election Act of 1725, even found it necessary to
reduce the parliamentary franchise in the City and to confirm the right of the
(mainly Whig) Court of Aldermen to veto the acts of the (mainly Tory) Common
Council. But in general the City did not make its political power much felt until at
least the mid-1750s. George I's accession evoked only insignificant disorders in
London, and by 1745 Jacobitism there amounted (at any rate in retrospect) to little
more than an inarticulate and orderless dislike of the established authorities. Only
when it spoke with unanimity, as it did in 1733 in successful opposition to Walpole's
Excise Bill, was the City's voice effective; and even then its effectiveness owed much
to the support of a colourful London press campaign, led by such slogans as 'No
Slavery—No Excise—No Wooden Shoes', symbolizing the supposed enslavement
of the people of France, supposedly brought about by the excise duty there.[6]

The Birth of Metropolitan Radicalism

In the mid-1750s and early 1760s there began to flow that current of opinion later
referred to as eighteenth-century radicalism (recently defined as involving 'the

attempt to change the world and to change it for the better'),[7] which led on to the revolutionary radicalism of the 1790s and thence towards the mainstream of the nineteenth-century working-class movement. One of the original and at first most invigorating sources of that great river was in London. Only in London was there a structure (the various courts of the City Corporation, and the livery companies) long experienced in participating in national politics, and itself propelled by a large body of people some at least of whom felt that they got a poor deal in the prevailing social and political world. The symbols of established order—Parliament, law-courts, and prisons in particular—where decisions of national import were made or enforced were, moreover, only too temptingly visible in the capital city and provided natural focuses (or sometimes targets) for direct political action. So in the 1760s London exerted a greater and more enduring influence on national politics than at any other time in the eighteenth century. Extra-parliamentary pressure became open and organized, Opposition MPs had to adapt their policies to suit the demands of the supporters whom they had hitherto made use of, and the influence of the City itself became increasingly submerged in the more power-ful flood of metropolitan-wide political forces.[8]

This new phase in City and national politics may be traced back to the unlikely figure of the slave-owning West Indian nabob William Beckford, MP for the City and twice Lord Mayor, who as early as the election of 1761 was deploring that 'little pitiful boroughs send members to parliament equal to great cities'.[9] The real catalyst was, however, supplied by John Wilkes, a cheerful and unscrupulous demagogue who erupted on the national scene in 1763 after the Ministry had misguidedly had him arrested on a 'general' (or open) warrant for allegedly libelling the king. A week later he was released on grounds of parliamentary privilege (he was MP for Aylesbury) and was already a popular hero, escorted to his house by a vociferous crowd chanting the great war cry of the new radicalism, 'Wilkes and Liberty'. Subsequently general warrants were declared illegal, but after his publication of an obscene poem had landed him in further trouble he fled to France. In January 1764 he was for the first time expelled from the House of Commons, and when he did not appear for his trial for seditious libel he was declared an outlaw.[10]

After four years of self-imposed exile he returned and in the general election of 1768 he stood unsuccessfully for the City, where established interests were too strong for him. But in the more fluid and partly urbanized constituency of Middlesex he found natural supporters in the large and unorganized electorate and was triumphantly returned at the head of the poll, which was held in the county town of Brentford, some 10 miles west of the City. The news was greeted with wild enthusiasm in London, and for several days his victory was celebrated in the streets by 'the inferior set' of his supporters, who roamed about the fashionable parts of town huzzaing and smashing the windows of unpopular grandees or at night peremptorily requiring lights to be immediately displayed at their houses.[11]

Wilkes's outlawry was still in force, however, so soon afterwards he surrendered himself in the Court of King's Bench (April 1768). But as he was being escorted across Westminster Bridge to the King's Bench Prison in St George's Fields, Southwark, his coach was seized by a band of his muscular devotees and dragged all the way along Whitehall and up the Strand to the City, and thence on to Spitalfields, where after receiving suitable acclamation he managed to elude his fans and make good his escape to the prison. During the next fortnight there were more riots, culminating on 10 May, the day of the opening of the new Parliament, when crowds assembled outside the prison, which was defended by a detachment of Foot Guards, vainly hoping to see the new Member come out to take his seat in the Commons. A skirmish ensued, the soldiers opened fire, and several people were killed in what became known as 'the St George's Fields Massacre'.[12]

In the following month Wilkes's outlawry was reversed, but he was sentenced to twenty-two-months' imprisonment for his various offences, and in February 1769 he was expelled from the House of Commons for the second time. Less than two weeks later the sturdy freeholders of Middlesex again returned him as their Member, only for the election to be declared null and void. This process was repeated twice more in quick succession (all in Wilkes's absence, he being still in prison), until eventually, after the fourth poll, the Commons resolved in May 1769 that as Wilkes was ineligible, the defeated candidate, Colonel Luttrell, had been duly elected instead—one of the most extraordinary decisions ever taken in that House.[13]

The Wilkite affair is important in the history of London because it was during the atmosphere of excited outrage which it created that the first approximation to a programme of parliamentary reform was propounded. In February 1769 the Society of Supporters of the Bill of Rights had been founded by a group of Wilkes's rich City friends to pay off his debts; but very soon it and other metropolitan radicals, in association with the Opposition within Parliament, were organizing petitions of protest not just from London itself but from many other parts of the country too. Their main object was the redress of the Middlesex electors' grievances and the reinstatement of Wilkes, but some also addressed themselves to other discontents as well. By January 1770 petitions bearing the signatures of well over 50,000 voters (perhaps something like a quarter of the whole electorate of England and Wales) had been presented. Soon afterwards Alderman Beckford was explicitly advocating shorter parliaments, the restriction of government placemen and pensions, and more equal representation of the people.[14]

The failure of this metropolitan-inspired radical agitation of 1769–70 hardly diminishes its importance as a landmark in the history of extra-parliamentary activity, for it was the first of its kind, antedating by ten years the analogous activities of the Yorkshire and other County Associations in 1779–80. The petitioners' demands were brusquely rejected by the Commons early in 1770,[15] and Beckford died a few months later. Wilkes's ultimately successful campaign soon after he emerged from prison in April 1770 to ensure the publication of parliamentary debates evoked little support in the provinces, though there was a succession of disturbances in the capital. By that time Wilkes had turned his attention to a lucrative career in the City, of which he was chosen Lord Mayor in 1774; and at the general election in that year radicals won seven of the ten parliamentary seats in the metropolitan area. But in the whole House of Commons there were only half a dozen other like-minded members, so in electoral terms radicalism was still a largely metropolitan affair. It was therefore a City alderman who in the Commons proposed the first of a long succession of annual motions pressing for shorter parliaments; and it was a London MP—Wilkes himself, safely back again for Middlesex—who in 1776 first proposed elections by adult male suffrage. London radicalism had indeed moved a long way since, only fifteen years earlier, Beckford's tentative demands for the reform of the rotten boroughs had first been heard.[16]

How had this come about? Amongst the voters, the bulk of radical support came, in the City, from the small merchants, manufacturers, and master craftsmen of Common Hall, and the liverymen of the lesser companies; and, in the urban out-parishes of Middlesex, from the numerous petty tradesmen who owned free-hold property worth as little as 40s. a year. For this 'middling sort' Wilkes's capacity to 'cock a snook' at established authority had great appeal, as it also no doubt had for the voteless crowds who had so frequently demonstrated for 'Wilkes and Liberty'. The *menu peuple* also had economic grievances, the 1760s, and the years 1768 and 1769 in particular, being times of widespread and often violent industrial disputes and primitive strikes; but they needed a focus such as that previously evoked in the long tradition of London street disturbances by such matters as 'the Church in Danger', the Excise, or just plain 'No Popery' to mobilize their full power. Xenophobic and backward-looking attitudes such as these were through force of his own circumstances diverted by Wilkes into more specifically political channels. As a quintessentially 'anti-Establishment' figure (at any rate in the 1760s), Wilkes inspired widespread sympathy as the supposed victim of the tyranny of the great, whose privileges were resented by 'the meaner sort'. So not only did he, by standing for Middlesex, extend the geographical boundaries of metropolitan radicalism far beyond the City, but more importantly he also extended its social boundaries and galvanized into political action a multitude of people who had hitherto been regarded as having no concern in the shaping of the affairs of the nation.[17]

After the failure of the Wilkite metropolitan-inspired radical agitation of 1769–70 there was a pause, until in the crisis of the nation's affairs in 1779–80 during the American War of Independence a new initiative was taken, not in London, but by the Yorkshire Association of freeholders, which petitioned for parliamentary reform and appealed for support throughout the rest of the country. In the metropolis large unwieldy committees were set up in the City and in the parliamentary constituencies of Middlesex and Westminster to discuss and promote reform. The Westminster constituency had now largely taken the lead in metro-politan radical affairs, and it was in the report of a Westminster subcommittee that what were later to become the famous six points of the People's Charter of 1838 were first explicitly formulated: equal electoral districts, annual parliaments, manhood suffrage, vote by ballot, payment of MPs, and the abolition of property qualifications.[18]

This report was dated 27 May 1780,[19] but six days later the metropolitan reform movement was prostrated by the Gordon Riots—the last and greatest outbreak of disorder in the long series of demonstrations and disturbances in eighteenth-century London. The war with the rebellious Americans (for whom there had been some sympathy in London)[20] was going badly, the nation's old (and Catholic) enemies, France and Spain, had joined the struggle, bringing with them a threat of invasion, and the agitation for reform was again in the ascendant. It was in this situation that what began as a relatively orderly demonstration against a recent Act of Parliament for the relief of Roman Catholics from some of the penal laws turned into an orgy of rioting, looting, and drunkenness.

Traditional anti-popery was certainly a powerful ingredient in the affair. On 2 June 1780 some 60,000 supporters of the Protestant Association, of which Lord George Gordon was president, held a rally in St George's Fields and then moved *en masse* across the river to present a petition of protest, bearing over 100,000 signatures, to Parliament. After the Commons had refused to discuss it under duress and a detachment of Guards had had to make a passage for the beleaguered Members to leave, the demonstration, which had hitherto been composed of 'the better sort of tradesmen', seems to have changed character. Late at night, and reinforced by people 'of a different description', groups in the crowd moved away and destroyed the Catholic chapels of the Sardinian ambassador near Lincoln's Inn Fields and of the Bavarian embassy in Warwick Street, St James's. The next targets were the Catholic Mass-houses in Moorfields, the houses of magistrates who had had some of the demonstrators arrested, and soon afterwards that of Lord Chief Justice Mansfield in Bloomsbury Square, where soldiers opened fire for the first time. The reaction of the authorities was, however, so feeble that Newgate Prison (where a few of the rioters had been incarcerated) was successfully attacked, and after the prisoners had been released the buildings were set on fire. Much the same treatment was given to four other gaols, the Bank of England itself was besieged, and the gin distillery of a wealthy Catholic was broken into and set on fire with appalling results. After nearly a week order was finally restored by some 10,000 troops, over 200 people having been killed in the process. Another twenty-five were subsequently hanged, and the very large sum of over £100,000 paid out in compensation from public funds for the destruction of or severe damage to some fifty buildings.[21]

Professor George Rudé's studies of the crowd in London have led him to conclude, in relation to the Gordon Riots, 'that behind the slogan "No Popery" and the other outward forms of religious fanaticism there lay a deeper social purpose: a groping desire to settle accounts with the rich, if only for a day, and to achieve some rough kind of social justice'.[22] In earlier disturbances such as over the Excise in 1733 or in the Middlesex election of 1768 as well as in the Gordon Riots he has seen 'an underlying class hostility of the poor against the rich'.[23] Such attitudes certainly prevailed in later years and may have a very long history.

However this may be, the Gordon Riots do mark a watershed in the evolution of metropolitan radicalism, for when it revived a decade later after the inevitable reaction caused by the riots, it did so in a new and very different form.

Revolution and Class

This new form was of course the product of the French Revolution, which for the next half-century or so cast a long shadow over the course of English and not least metropolitan politics. But London radicalism had deep roots extending back through Wilkes to the constitutional struggles of the seventeenth century for which there was no equivalent in Paris. So even after the Revolution had broken out in 1789 London continued to draw much of its strength from native radical sources, notably those of Dissent and the trade clubs, or from those of America, rather than from France. Popular political behaviour in the two cities therefore differed sharply, for although London working men were never able to emulate the Parisian sansculottes in the exploitation of revolutionary situations, they nevertheless exerted a continuous influence spread over many decades, in striking contrast with the sansculottes, who were suppressed by force in 1795 and hardly heard of again until the 1830s.[24]

But there was one great similarity, for, in the words of Professor Gwyn Williams, 'it was in 1792 that "the people" entered politics' in both countries.[25] In Paris they exerted their power for the first time by storming the Tuileries and proclaiming the Republic, while in London they formed a society—the London Corresponding Society (LCS), founded at the Bell tavern in Exeter Street, off the Strand. (This otherwise unremarkable pub still exists, but is now called the Hogshead Alehouse)

The foundation of the LCS marks the birth of a metropolitan political movement of the 'lower orders' or *menu peuple* wholly independent of any other section or class of society. Hitherto their periodic participation in political affairs had always been under outside auspices—that of Wilkes, for instance, or of the City— and generally in opposition to the Ministry. Now for the first time they were on their own, for Thomas Hardy, the founder of the LCS, was a shoemaker, most of its members were (in Hardy's words) 'tradesmen, mechanics and shopkeepers', and its subscription (unlike those of other more expensive reform groups) was only 1d. a week.[26] Working men's Friendly or Benefit Societies had, of course, been in existence for very many years, as also had numerous London trade societies, which shared many of the features of the old guilds;[27] and in the late eighteenth-century alehouse convivial and/or debating clubs were numerous in London and formed an integral part of plebeian social life;[28] but the LCS was different in being explicitly political in purpose.

Political and economic interests were, however, becoming increasingly closely intertwined, and were to become still more so during the social turmoils soon to come; and it was in the unstable economic relationships which ensued from those turmoils that the pre-industrial hierarchical social structure of the eighteenth century began to evolve into the class society of Victorian times.[29] Although the social conditions to which the new factory system of production in some northern towns gave rise were of course of central importance in this process, it has nevertheless been claimed that 'The working class was born in the workshop, not the factory.'[30] Consciousness of separate class identity was indeed also growing amongst the London artisans, and their role was to be crucial in the evolution of class in England.

The LCS probably never had an active membership of more than around 5,000, organized into forty-eight divisions, but it acted as a national centre for the advancement of such political aims as annual parliaments and universal suffrage, and in March 1794 it attempted to summon a British Convention. By that time the outbreak of war with France (February 1793) and revolutionary events in Paris had evoked a powerful popular reaction in England. The repressive measures taken by the Government included the suspension of habeas corpus and the arrest of Hardy, the veteran reformer Horne Tooke, and a dozen others and their imprisonment in the Tower on charges of high treason. Their acquittal in October 1794 was celebrated by a triumphant procession through the streets of London, and, assisted no doubt by the economic crisis of 1795, the LCS was once again strong enough to organize a huge public meeting in Copenhagen Fields, Islington (said to have been 200,000 in number, and, if so, probably the largest gathering ever hitherto held in London). But repression was already the order of the day again, 'seditious meetings' of this kind were banned, and an Act of 1799 against unlawful Combinations and Confederacies specifically suppressed the LCS and several other reform societies as well as workers' combinations, as the trade societies or embryonic trade unions were then called.[31]

The proscription of both the political and trade clubs at the same time threw them together, heightening their shared sense of opposition to the established order in both the workshop and in national affairs and their awareness of their separate incipient working-class identity. Despite the Combination Laws many trade clubs nevertheless flourished during the war years, when high Government expenditure and the recruitment of thousands of men into the armed services stiffened the labour market.[32] Awareness of the connexion between wage levels and the strength of organized labour grew, and negotiations with employers and (notwithstanding the danger of prosecution) even strikes were openly conducted (use of the word 'strike' in this sense dates from around 1810). Most of this activity took place in the skilled trades—the core of the metropolitan working-class movement—where artisans were as much concerned to protect themselves from competition from the unorganized unskilled as from the oppressiveness of their employers. With the leadership of such men as the shipwright John Gast and the breeches-maker Francis Place (who masterminded the repeal of the Combination Laws in 1824) they increasingly concerned themselves in political affairs.[33]

Yet despite the great advantages which the radical reformers and the early trade unionists of the metropolis possessed—notably their proximity to the seat of national power and the concentration there of by far the largest multitude of working men in the whole country—London did not provide the seemingly natural focal point for the reform movement of the early nineteenth century, and national attention often moved away from the metropolis to events in the provinces. London's population was becoming too large and too diffuse in its social and occupational structures for its full influence to be effectively brought to bear in any sustained effort. And the nascent working-class movement and its leaders were beset by endemic inability to exploit near-revolutionary situations (as the sansculottes did so easily). Having held impressive and generally orderly mass meetings on the outskirts of the built-up area, leaders such as 'Orator' Hunt apparently did not know what to do next; and constitutional means for the translation of extra-parliamentary pressure into political action hardly existed— a problem still evident even in Chartist times.

In reality, of course, the dichotomy between reform and revolution was seldom as simple as this, not least because there were so many strands in the texture of metropolitan politics. After Pitt's accession to power in 1784 the City for some twenty-five years nearly always supported him and/or the Tories, but its import- ance in metropolitan politics was gradually overshadowed by that of the West- minster parliamentary constituency. There Charles James Fox was one of the Members from 1780 until his death in 1806, and the large franchise and several prolonged and rowdy elections provided opportunities for widespread popular political activity. This tradition was continued by a rich aristocrat, Sir Francis Burdett, who, after spending a fortune in contested elections for Middlesex, refused to contribute a farthing to the expenses of his candidature in Westminster in 1807, his success there being entirely due to the assiduous canvassing of a committee of tradesmen organized by Francis Place—a notable innovation in the history of parliamentary elections. Like Wilkes, Burdett got himself impri- soned at Parliament's behest (in the Tower, in his case, in 1810), and during his long representation of Westminster (1807–37) he did much, at least until 1832, to make his constituency a pacesetter for radicalism in London and throughout the country.[34]

London was also in the early nineteenth century a scene of much ideological ferment. This was stimulated by the beginnings of an independent popular radical press, its influence from 1816 demonstrated by the large sales of, for instance, William Cobbett's *Twopenny Trash* and T. J. Wooler's *Black Dwarf*, published every Sunday morning in Finsbury.[35] It was through such publications that the radical activists who supported the weekly meetings (often held in taverns) of the numer- ous London debating societies were kept informed of current national ideas and events.[36] The bookseller Thomas Spence, too, was purveying impractical yet (to the authorities) alarming ideas which were taken up by a small but determined cadre of revolutionary followers.[37] And there often hovered in the shadows of the new working-class landscape of the London political underworld a small group of violent conspirators such as Colonel Despard and his handful of followers (exe- cuted in 1803), whose intended seizure of the Bank and the Tower was to have been the signal for a general insurrection—procedures based on Parisian examples which were never to prove congenial in London.[38]

Fears of violent revolution were nevertheless real—'One insurrection in London and all is lost', exclaimed the Prime Minister, Lord Liverpool, as he looked sombrely out from his town house.[39] This was particularly so in the five years of distress after Waterloo, when postwar economic dislocation evoked unemployment and several popular agitations. The passing of the Corn Laws of 1815 (which prohibited the import of grain until the price reached 80s. per quarter) produced crowd disturbances more in line with eighteenth-century traditions than with current popular radicalism and severe enough for soldiers to be called out.[40] At the end of 1816 two mass meetings—the first in the capital since 1795—were held in Spa Fields to protest against distress and for reform. The first was addressed by 'Orator' Hunt, but a part of the second was hijacked by a handful of Spenceans led by Dr Watson and Arthur Thistlewood, who with a few followers attempted (like Colonel Despard in 1803) to seize the Tower and inaugurate an armed rising. Government repression at once ensued, reinforced after the Peterloo Massacre near Manchester (August 1819) by the Six Acts. In the Cato Street Conspiracy of February 1820 the proponents of violence made what proved to be the last attempt at a revolutionary coup when Thistlewood and his accomplices plotted to assassinate all the Cabinet whilst they dined at a house in Grosvenor Square.[41]

There then unexpectedly supervened the bizarre affair of Queen Caroline, whose return to England in June 1820 presented ribald Londoners for over a year with an exquisite weapon for the ridicule of the King and the Government—an opportunity fully exploited by the artisans' trade societies.[42] The City, the parliamentary Whigs, and the radical press, as well as the London trades and some of the largest crowds ever seen in London all coalesced in support of this ill-treated and ill-behaved woman; and even her funeral was used as an anti-Government demonstration. She had died at her house in Hammersmith, but was to be buried in her native Germany, and her body therefore had to be conveyed to the port of embarkation at Harwich. The authorities had decided that it should proceed around the northern outskirts of London and not pass through the City, from which much of the queen's support had come; but her adherents had other ideas. Barricades of wagons blocked the official route (clear proof of careful organization), shots were fired by the escort of Life Guards, and ultimately there was only one way for the distracted cortège to go—eastward along the Strand, under Temple Bar, and through the City, with the Lord Mayor at its head.[43]

Just as the Cato Street Conspiracy marked the end of metropolitan attempts to overthrow the Government by violence, so the Queen Caroline affair marked the end (to quote John Stevenson) of 'the great agitations in the traditions of Wilkes in which a largely metropolitan-based movement dominated the political scene'.[44] Thereafter radicalism declined steeply, partly no doubt due to improved economic conditions in the early 1820s. When it revived in the 1830s it did so under provincial rather than metropolitan auspices; and London as seat of government, commerce, and press served, for a while, more as the stage where much of the drama of the nation's political evolution was enacted than as the driving force that produced the performance.[45]

PART V

Metropolitan and Imperial London
1830–1914

INTRODUCTION

Between the end of the Georgian era (1830) and the outbreak of World War I (1914) Britain was transformed into what historians have often called the first industrial and urban society. In the procreation of this unprecedented economy London occupied a unique position, apart from and different from that of all other cities and towns; and through its sheer unprecedented immensity it provided the prototype for future metropolitan cities of the world.

Nevertheless the half-century between the 1820s and the 1870s was in some respects a period of apparently diminished metropolitan influence. London had not been in the forefront of the industrial revolution as commonly understood (though it was still the largest centre of manufacturing industry in the country), nor in these mid-nineteenth-century years was it in the forefront of municipal reform or of radical politics, its amorphous hugeness being a source of weakness rather than strength in those fields. Meanwhile Manchester and the other great new industrial centres of the North were so to speak 'grabbing the headlines' because it was primarily there that industrialization and the social problems arising therefrom were mainly concentrated. But this process in no way weakened the centripetal forces which for several centuries had been concentrating population and economic muscle on London. Indeed the magnetic power of London grew throughout the nineteenth century, notably through the steady enlargement of the field of government, the inexorable growth of the City-dominated service sector of the economy, and above all through the development of mass mobility and mass communication on a scale hitherto unknown. By 1897, when Queen Victoria's Diamond Jubilee was celebrated with spectacular pomp and circumstance, London was the capital city of the Empire on which the sun never set and which extended over a quarter of the land surface of the entire globe—the nodal point of the world economy and of the nascent world system of production.

17

Structures of the Modern Metropolis

In Chapter 13 we saw that according to modern estimates over 500,000 migrants entered the London area during the first half of the eighteenth century, and that it was only through such large-scale movement of individual people that London's growth was maintained. In the nineteenth century, however, there was a massive increase in the scale of these movements, almost 500,000 migrants coming to London in the single decade of the 1870s; and there was also a very large outflow, both to the rest of the country and abroad.[1] Ceaseless mobility, made possible by new means of transport, became one of the hallmarks of modern urban civilization.

The Transport Revolution

Although steam power was the main agent of the transport revolution, the horse never throughout the whole of the nineteenth century lost its age-old usefulness in London — it could so often reach parts of the capital which the railways could not — and the first important manifestation of the revolution took the form of a new type of horse-drawn road vehicle — the omnibus. This was in 1829, when George Shillibeer's long trunk-shaped vehicles drawn by three horses and carrying up to twenty passengers began to ply between Paddington Green and the Bank of England in the City. They were an immediate success; fierce competition from imitators ensued, and within ten years over 600 buses were operating in London (Plate 49). Throughout the rest of the nineteenth century they proved able to withstand the competition of the railways, and from the 1870s of the horse-tramways as well, and even to retain the ascendancy in short-distance journeys, particularly in central districts from which the railways were excluded.[2]

Railways and steam locomotives were, however, the principal expressions of the transport revolution, and it was near London that in 1803 the first public railway (apart from those working as feeders to canals), the Surrey Iron Railway from Wandsworth to Croydon, was built.[3] But the wagons there were drawn by horses, and the first use of steam power for public transport took place not on the railways but on the river, where regular steamboat services, mostly to such down-stream suburbs as Greenwich, began in 1815.[4] The first steam-powered passenger-carrying railway in London, the London and Greenwich, was not opened until 1836, eleven years after the Stockton and Darlington and six years after the Liver-pool and Manchester.

Within less than two decades — by the early 1850s — the framework of a national railway system had been built, and London was connected already with Birmingham, the Midlands, and the North; with East Anglia; with the principal South-Coast towns from Dover to Plymouth; and with Bristol and Holyhead for Ireland.[5] The railways had captured the imagination of the travelling and investing public and become the symbol of Victorian power and progress.

London was the hub of this new network of communication, just as it had been of the roads built by the Romans, and for much the same reasons – geographical location, heavily reinforced in Victorian times by its product, the political, eco-nomic, and demographic ascendancy of the metropolis. That London was the focal point of the railways was at all events not the result of Government policy, for it was the companies, motivated solely by commercial considerations, which pro-posed the routes to be taken by new lines, and in the early years the State did little more than impose operating regulations and by innumerable Acts of Parliament confer the compulsory powers of land acquisition needed by the companies.

In London, in fact, Parliament had been confronted with so many rival propo-sals that a Royal Commission set up to consider them had in 1846 recommended that no future railway north of the river should be allowed within a central area bounded by Marylebone Road, City Road, Finsbury Square, and Bishopsgate Street.[6] The two principal termini already in existence – Euston and Paddington – were both outside this area, the companies concerned having been preoccupied with obtaining access to the docks via the Regent's Canal, in expectation that goods rather than passenger traffic would be their main source of profit. So London was surrounded by a multiplicity of termini (ultimately fifteen in number), and no single great central station such as those to be found in many large Continental cities was ever built, largely because it would have led to acute congestion in the streets; and the cost of building such a thing would have been prohibitive.[7]

Insufferable congestion on the principal streets within the central area never-theless ensued, however, for railway termini by their very nature generate road traffic in their environs. In 1865 some 200,000 people were entering the City daily on foot, the buses made over 7,000 daily journeys through the Square Mile, and cumbersome carts delivering goods to and from the railway termini, still relatively far away, obstructed the narrow streets, as yet little improved except by those formed in the late 1820s as approach roads to the newly rebuilt London Bridge. According to Sir Joseph Paxton, architect of the Crystal Palace (built in Hyde Park for the Great Exhibition of 1851), it took longer to travel from London Bridge station to Paddington than from London Bridge to Brighton.[8]

The solution to this crisis was found, with characteristically Victorian resour-cefulness, in the building of the first underground railway in the world, opened in

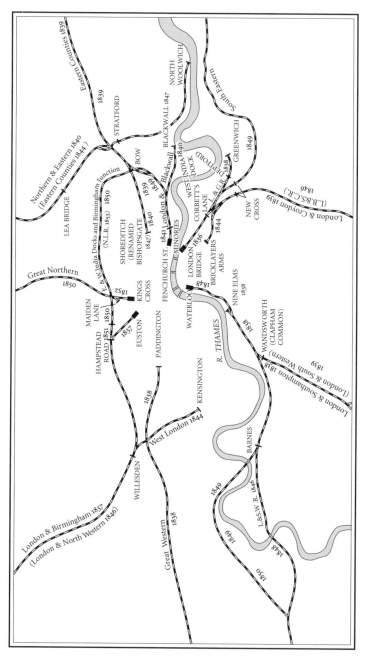

Fig. 23. London railways in 1852

1863 (Plate 51). The Metropolitan was built on 'the cut and cover' principle a few feet below ground level, mostly beneath such existing wide streets as the Marylebone and Euston Roads, and extended from Paddington to Farringdon Street, thus providing passengers arriving at Paddington, Euston, and King's Cross and (from 1867) St Pancras with easy access to the City. Like the early buses, the Underground proved an immediate success, and in 1864 the Metropolitan Railway Company carried nearly 12,000,000 passengers on its 4-mile length. Twenty-five years later it and its rival the Metropolitan District Railway Company had girdled the City, the West End, and much of Bayswater and South Kensington with the Inner Circle line, completed in 1884 and today known as the Circle line, which carried passengers directly to and from nearly all of the ring of railway termini; and from it there also fanned out feeder routes, largely above ground, to such distant suburbs as Hammersmith, Ealing, Richmond, Wimbledon, and even faraway Rickmansworth.

Meanwhile the enforcement of the central railway-free area had been partially abandoned when the main-line companies operating south of the Thames had been allowed to build bridges across the river and site their termini — Victoria, Charing Cross, and Cannon Street (1860–6) — on the edge of the 'exclusion zone', each served by a station on the Inner Circle. Another thrusting new company, the Chatham and Dover, crashed right across not only the river but the City itself, from Blackfriars and Ludgate Hill, to join the Metropolitan at Farringdon Street, thus providing central London with its only direct link from south to north (used mainly for freight traffic until its revival in recent years for passenger through-trains). By the mid-1870s the railway network of central London had to a large extent assumed its modern shape, and over 150,000,000 train journeys per annum were being made from one part of the capital to another.[9]

By that time there had been yet another innovation of cardinal importance — the introduction of horse-drawn trams, running on rails laid along existing main streets. The first line, built by an American, G. F. Train, and opened in 1861, was a failure, largely because its route, westward from Marble Arch beside the mansions of the prosperous Bayswater Road area, did not serve lower middle-class and working-class districts, where the trams soon proved successful. But a tram pulled by two horses and running on a smooth metal track could carry up to fifty passengers, about twice the capacity of a bus, and fares were therefore lower. So the lines authorized by Parliament in 1869 along approach roads mainly in South and East London attracted a huge new clientele which had hitherto not been able to afford to ride. In 1872 Parliament prohibited tramways in a central area consisting roughly of the City and West End — just as it had in earlier years in the case of the railways — but by 1875 trams had extended out to many of the outer suburbs of the built-up area, and were carrying almost as many passengers (over 48,000,000) as the London General Omnibus Company, which then owned most of London's buses.[10]

The next great wave of transport development came around the turn of the century, when the surge of building in the suburbs in the 1890s contributed to

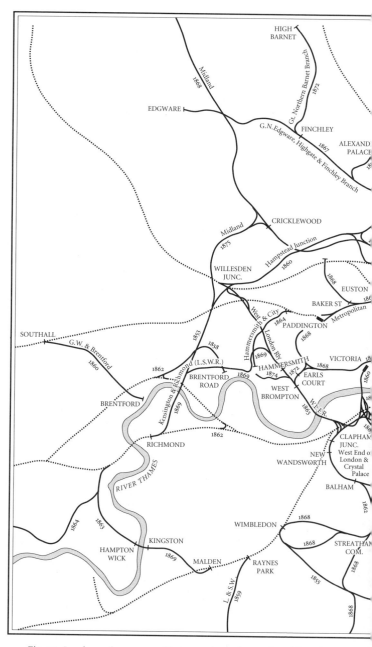

Fig. 24. London railways opened between 1852 and 1875; dotted lines denote railw

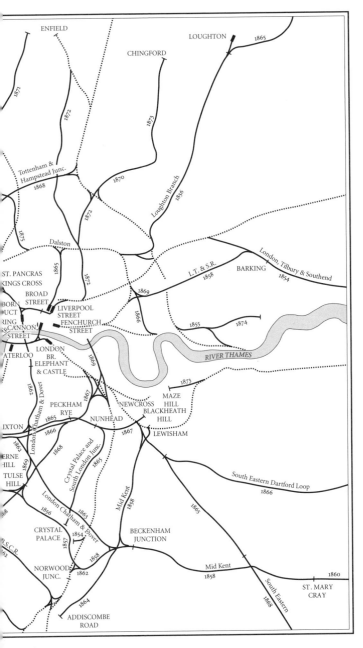

ENFIELD

LOUGHTON
1865

CHINGFORD

1871

1872

1873

Loughton Branch 1856

Tottenham & Hampstead Junc.
1868

1870

1872

1875

Dalston

1865

1872

ST. PANCRAS
KINGS CROSS

L. T. & S. R.
1858

BARKING

London, Tilbury & Southend
1854

BORN
UCT
RING
S CANNON
STREET

BROAD
STREET

LIVERPOOL
STREET
FENCHURCH
STREET

1869

1866

WATERLOO

LONDON
BR.
ELEPHANT
& CASTLE

1855

1874

RIVER THAMES

1869

1862

1873

PECKHAM
RYE

1867

NEWCROSS

MAZE
HILL
BLACKHEATH
HILL

IXTON

1865

NUNHEAD

1867

1866

LEWISHAM

ERNE
HILL

1862
1869

TULSE
HILL

1868

Crystal Palace and South London Junc.

1868

1865

Mid Kent
1858

South Eastern Dartford Loop
1866

S.C.R.

52

London Chatham & Dover

1856

1863

1865

CRYSTAL
PALACE

1857

1854

1858

BECKENHAM
JUNCTION

NORWOOD
JUNC.

1862

Mid Kent
1858

1860

ST. MARY
CRAY

1864

South Eastern
1868

ADDISCOMBE
ROAD

ned before 1852

renewed traffic congestion in the City, where 690 horse-drawn buses were said at times to pass the Bank in a single hour. Just as underground railways had for a while relieved this problem in the 1860s, so the development of deep-level tube railways and of electric and motorized forms of traction had much the same effect forty years later. The City and South London Railway, opened in 1890 and extending from King William Street in the City to suburban Stockwell some 3 miles away, was the world's first electric tube line.[11] This pioneer venture suffered from technical mistakes in its design and construction, and electrically driven trains did not really get under way until the opening in 1900 of the Central line, from Liverpool Street to Shepherd's Bush. Thereafter deep-level tube railway construction was rapid, the central stretches of the lines now known as the Bakerloo, Northern, and Piccadilly being all opened by 1907,[12] much of the necessary business drive and expertise coming from foreign, chiefly American, entrepreneurs, notably C. T. Yerkes. By that time both the Metropolitan and District railways were using electric instead of steam traction; the trams too, now increasingly owned and managed by the London County Council, were going over to electricity, and from about 1905 motor buses were beginning to replace the old horse-drawn vehicles.[13]

Its extraordinary versatility had enabled the horse to withstand and even to gain from the competition of the railways in London, for by around 1900 there were over 300,000 horses at work there – over three times as many as in the 1850s; but that was at or very near the peak of the metropolitan horse population, and it was the internal combustion engine, not steam power, which finally put horses out of the traction business.[14]

In 1875 the number of journeys per annum by train, tram, and bus in the London area had been about 275,000,000 m. Twenty years later it had more than trebled to 1,000,000,000, although the population had risen by less than 50 per cent in the same period. Put in another way, the number of journeys per head of the London population rose from 65 to 165 per annum; and by 1911 this figure had risen to 250 journeys on all public services.[15] Incessant mobility on this scale was something new in the history of London, or indeed of anywhere else, and we must now examine the effect which the transport revolution made on the life and fabric of the capital.

The Social Consequences of the Railways

The railways engendered more far-reaching change for the physical anatomy of Victorian London than any other single factor. Everywhere a powerful immediate impact was felt at the time of their construction, which Dickens, in reference to the building in the 1830s of the London and Birmingham Railway a little north of its terminus at Euston, compared in *Dombey and Son* to 'The first shock of an earthquake, [which] rent the whole neighbourhood to its centre' (Plate 50). In

Plate 25. Looking west, 1804

Plate 26. Looking east, 1930

Plate 27. Unloading near the Custom House, 1757

Plate 28. Fresh Wharf, beside the north end of London Bridge, 1762

Plate 29. Building Canada Dock, Rotherhithe, 1875–6

Plate 30. London Docks, North Quay, 1865

Plate 31.
Royal Albert Dock, c.1964, on the eve of
the collapse of the London docks

Plate 32. Blackwell Hall, Basinghall Street, for centuries the hub of the cloth market

Plate 33. A cloth-merchant's shop, 1690: foreground, the merchant (seated) and his porter; background right, the customer and his servant, with measuring rod; outside, left, a vintner tasting wine

Plate 34. The Royal Exchange, 1777

Plate 35. Payment of dividends on Dividend Day at the Bank of England, 1850

Plate 36. A tailor's shop, *c*.1750

Plate 37. A Spitalfields weaver at his loom, 1895

Plate 38. Shipbuilding at Blackwall Yard, Poplar, 1784

Plate 39. Golden Lane Brewery, 1807

Plate 40. Thomas Cubitt's yard and works, Pimlico, looking west, c.1845–50

Plate 41. Park Royal in the 1930s, with (foreground) Guinness Brewery

such still predominantly green field areas near the urban frontier the railway companies liked to plan their routes through the holdings of a few large land-owners with whom it was easy to come to terms. In more central built-up inner districts, however, their incursions were cataclysmic. There they tried whenever possible to proceed through working-class areas, for the price of the land there would be cheaper and the landowners less likely to object. The railway's agents would then work their way round the densely packed courts and alleys of the tenements to be demolished, offering to pay off the tenants' arrears of rent, or 'a sovereign or two to go out', or sometimes as little as 18d., the rickety insanitary buildings would come crashing down, and their evicted occupants were left to fend for themselves. Between 1859 and 1867, when railway building arising from the partial abrogation of the central exclusion zone was at its height, nearly 37,000 of the labouring classes were displaced from their homes by enforced demolitions for new railways.[16]

The railways were not, however, the only agents of this mass destruction. The building of the West India and St Katharine Docks, the formation of Regent Street, and the street improvements carried out by the City Corporation (notably King William Street and Moorgate Street) and by the Commissioners of Woods and Forests (New Oxford Street, Victoria Street, and Commercial Street) in the 1830s and 1840s had also taken their toll. In all, it has been estimated that between 1853 and 1901 the number of people evicted for docks or new streets amounted to over 28,000,[17] and by the railways to upwards of 120,000.[18]

At first there was wide public welcome for the clearance of areas where crime, disease, and overcrowding were most prevalent. The pockets of insanitary impov-erishment in the central areas would be swept away and the evicted poor could go and live in the more healthy surroundings of the suburbs. But most of the poor depended on casual daily or even hourly employment, and in the 1860s there were said to be 680,000 such workers in central London. They had to live near such sources of work as were available to them, and in any case a man with an average wage of £1 a week or less could not afford a daily fare of even 6d. When they were evicted they simply moved, of necessity, into the nearest lodgings available else-where. The demand for cheap accommodation was thereby increased in relation to the diminished supply, rents rose, aggravated by the general rise in land values created in the central areas by the railways, and the pockets of overcrowding were merely transplanted from one place to another, more intense than ever. 'Where are they all gone, sir?', said one observer in answer to a newspaper reporter's enquiry in 1866; 'Why some's gone down Whitechapel way; some's gone in the Dials [Seven Dials, near Covent Garden]; some's gone to Kentish Town; and some's gone to the Workus.'[19]

In the 1850s and 1860s these unwelcome social consequences of the railways were denounced with increasing frequency, but until 1874 their promoters were not required to provide alternative accommodation, and the investigations made by the Royal Commissioners on the Housing of the Working Classes in 1884–5 showed that no rehousing scheme had yet been carried out by any railway company in London. Even thereafter the alternative accommodation which some companies did provide was not often available at the time of demolition and was therefore used, not by those displaced, but by other families able to afford the higher rents demanded. A substantial part of the real cost of the railways in nineteenth-century London was, in fact, passed on by the companies to the poor.[20]

The railways were, of course, always reluctant housebuilders – it was not their line of business – but they could be compelled to provide special cheap fares for the class which suffered most from their incursions. This was first done in 1860, when the Chatham and Dover's Metropolitan Extensions Act compelled the company to introduce workmen's trains, which began to run in 1865. There were two trains daily in each direction between Victoria and Ludgate Hill via Brixton, Camberwell, and Walworth; and the price of a return ticket was 2d. One train left each terminus at 4.55 a.m., stopped at every station and arrived at the other end shortly before 6 a.m. (Plate 52). From Monday to Friday the evening trains left at 6.15 p.m., and on Saturdays at 2.30 p.m.[21]

In 1861 the North London Railway's Act for its extension through the thickly populated area between Dalston and Broad Street (on the edge of the City) at an estimated cost of 5,000 displacements[22] required one workmen's train to be run each way for a fare of 1d. Three years later it became the normal practice for Parliament to require the promoters of all new lines through the built-up area of London to run workmen's trains.[23] By the early 1880s over 25,000 workmen were travelling daily throughout London on these trains; and in the 1880s and 1890s and later, when the population of central London was falling rapidly, a ring of predominantly working-class suburbs was springing up in such outer areas as Stoke Newington, Walthamstow, West Ham, and Lewisham. By 1912 workmen's tickets represented about 40 per cent of all suburban railway journeys within 6 to 8 miles of the centre of London.[24] The use of this instrument of social policy in the alleviation of the housing problems of the congested central areas was, indeed, and despite its limited effect, a notable landmark in the history of the Victorian metropolis.

Until the early twentieth century daily commuting to work by rail was, however, still small in scale in relation to the size of the total population of the metropolis, or in relation to the scale of late twentieth-century travel. In the 1850s the 27,000 daily commuters who arrived by rail in London were well-heeled middle-class men, often with sizeable domestic establishments to keep up in the suburbs. This generated local employment there, often round pre-existing villages or towns such as Croydon, and especially in the 1870s and 1880s stimulated the potentialities for building development in still largely rural adjacent areas. By around 1900 there were perhaps 250,000 commuters, drawn from a much wider segment of the middle classes, arriving daily by rail in central London, and it has been estimated that if travellers by tram or bus are included, perhaps one man in four of the working population was by 1906 using some form of public transport between home in the inner or outer suburbs and work in the City and West End.[25]

This represents a formidable movement of population, but mass suburban travel was not the result of deliberate policy on the part of the railway companies, even in the case of the Great Eastern, in whose catchment area one in two of the working population were regular travellers. On the contrary, the railway companies were more likely just to respond, in varying degrees, to mounting demand — slowly to the west and north-west, more livelily in South London — than to promote it. In general they emphasized and accelerated social tendencies already in operation or inherent in the topographical situation of a suburb, and seldom dictated the course of its development.[26]

In the central and inner areas the railways' influence was more immediate. By the 1860s they had become the chief agents in the transformation of land uses and in the upward surge of land values. In the City and its environs they attracted storage warehouses and offices, repelled high-quality shops, and repelled or displaced private residents (particularly the poor); while at the outer termini such as Paddington, Victoria, and King's Cross they created zones of boarding houses and hotels. (This was the age of the great railway hotels, notably at Paddington and St Pancras.) Immediately outside their termini the railways attracted coal-yards, gasworks, and industries needing their own sidings; they ruptured the existing street patterns, even (or perhaps especially) if they were built high up on arches, and they created 'twilight' residential areas where housing was seldom renewed and sometimes degenerated into slums. Everywhere, but particularly in the centre, they generated more road traffic, both vehicular and pedestrian.[27] Inner London became a place where few people lived if they had any choice in the matter. If they had choice, they went to the suburbs, or settled there if they came from outside London.

The Urban Fabric

Since at least the sixteenth century London — the ancient nucleus of the capital city — had been surrounded by ever-growing suburbs, but the scale of their growth and the area which they occupied vastly increased in the nineteenth century (Plates 22–3). By 1900 the suburban ring extending from Ealing in the west round to Hornsey in the north, West Ham in the east, and Streatham in the south measured over 12 miles from east to west, and was the largest built-up area in the world. Within Greater London lived one-fifth of all the peoples of England and Wales, a rapidly increasing proportion of them in the outer suburbs.

In more recent times the Victoran suburbs have had a bad press, their supposed shapeless sprawl, monotony, and general dullness being held up to derision. They did, nevertheless, provide a way of living for which large numbers of people craved (and still crave), notably privacy and 'a place to do your own thing'.[28] In the later nineteenth century the cost of living was falling, for many people real incomes were rising rapidly and hours of work shortening. The central areas were being constantly compressed by the railways, street improvements, and the expansion of business premises. Retreat to the suburbs on a massive scale, by many of the more prosperous working classes as well as the middle classes, was the inevitable consequence, greatly facilitated by the new forms of transport.

The suburbs were, of course, inherently dependent, sub-urban places where only some of the functions of the whole city took place; and separation of home and work was a conspicuous feature of all of them. But the extent of their dependence, like that of their supposed anonymity and sameness, can be overstated, for there was infinite variety in London's suburbs, arising from topographical situation, communications, the patterns of landownership, the timing of development, and the element of chance imposed by bankruptcy or death. Many late Victorian suburbs, moreover, clustered round an ancient village such as Hammersmith or Hampstead, where numerous services had always been provided locally and where increasing demand naturally generated more local employment, regular travel between home and work for the suburban workforce being nowhere anything like universal and probably seldom if ever even predominant.[29] From such ancient nuclei many new suburbs probably inherited a measure of the traditional sense of identity of the place.

Despite their great variety the Victorian suburbs of London did, however, share important common features. Everyone who participated in building the houses, whether as ground landlord, developer, builder, or investor, did so in the hope of financial gain; and at any rate until the creation of the London County Council in 1889 there was little public regulation of their activities.[30] Until around 1900, when there was a growing tendency for houses to be built for sale freehold rather than for renting,[31] the leasehold system still prevailed almost everywhere, much as it had in Georgian and even earlier times; and it still produced the plentiful supply of land through which much of suburban London was developed at low housing densities. The long-term building lease at a low ground rent with ultimate reversion to the ground landlord remained the basic legal foundation of the new suburbs, but the lessee often had to accept tighter restrictive covenants than hitherto as to repair and occupancy, particularly on large well-run estates.[32]

Building was in fact London's biggest single industry, over 66,000 people being engaged in it in 1851. There was a handful of large firms, notably that of Thomas Cubitt, builder of many of the tall stucco-fronted houses which still stand in Belgravia and Pimlico. The housebuilding part of the industry was still, however, dominated by small firms, in 1851 80 per cent of them employing fewer than fifty men each; and subcontracting between the different trades of bricklayer, joiner, plasterer, etc. was still common. The great building booms of the later 1870s and 1890s did, however, produce a number of medium-sized firms (building between six and sixty houses per annum) and a few even larger ones,[33] but even at the end of the century most firms were only building six or fewer houses per annum. As to the quality of their work, sometimes cursorily dismissed as jerry-building, generalization is impossible. Much depended on the vigilance of the ground landlord — there was a world of difference between the well-managed estates of, for instance, the dukes of Bedford in Bloomsbury and Covent Garden or of Lord Holland in Kensington and the shanty town run up on William Agar's land in St Pancras. Many houses built in Victorian times have, however, survived far beyond the term of the ground leases under which they were originally built, and their solidity compares favourably with the quality of much of more modern work.

Speculative builders were generally able in one way or another to raise enough capital for the gigantic Victorian investment in suburban bricks and mortar. Ground landlords, or land speculators who bought up land outside the urban frontier in expectation of impending development (and who probably made the biggest profits in the whole process), often made advances to builders in order to 'get things going'. A case in point is Charles Blake, who had made money from indigo in India and who in North Kensington in the 1850s and 1860s combined the roles of landowner, speculator, financier, and builder and ultimately made a large fortune in Notting Hill and Notting Dale. Banks, building societies, and insurance companies all also made substantial loans for suburban development, but generally to the larger speculative builders. For the smaller firms the main source of supply was from solicitors, who were able to tap the steadily growing resources of middle-class savers in search of a safe investment ('safe as houses') yielding around 5 per cent per annum — the very kind of people, indeed, for whom the houses were being built. The whole process was in some measure self-financing.[34]

There were of course periodic hiccups, for both the supply of money and the volume of building in London fluctuated, and were closely interrelated. The speculative boom of the early 1820s, followed by the financial crash of 1825, for instance, put London housebuilding into the doldrums until the mid-1830s; and the financial crisis of 1847 caused numerous bankruptcies in the metropolitan building world. But from around 1860, when the transport innovations of the second half of the nineteenth century were beginning to make themselves felt throughout London, the cycles of metropolitan building diverged from those of the nation as a whole, with peaks in 1868, 1880–1, and 1898, after each of which overbuilding produced an excess supply of houses and was followed by troughs in output. Of course, like all the rest of the country, the volume of housebuilding in London was also greatly affected by the new dimension of mass emigration, the first wave of which took place during the depression of the 1840s. Rising emigration stimulated demand in the countries of destination (chiefly the USA), and hence opportunities for British investment there, while at home it was followed by a fall in the volume of internal migration from country to town and hence in the volume of demand for building. But when the American booms collapsed internal migration in Britain and home investment there became more attractive alternatives than emigration and foreign investment, and the volume of building at home began to rise again.[35]

In general, however, the growth of suburban London throughout the whole of the three-century period between 1600 and 1914 showed a high degree of continuity. There was little fundamental change in the underlying processes of growth, despite its fluctuating pace and volume, and there was never any radical reorientation like that brought about in Edinburgh in the late eighteenth century by the development of the New Town or in Vienna in the later nineteenth century by the creation of the Ringstrasse. The principles of 'Georgian' estate development, planning and design, first adumbrated by Inigo Jones in the 1630s, were still being widely practised throughout the greater part of the nineteenth century. The terraced houses, too, in such places as Bayswater, Belgravia, Pimlico, and large parts of Kensington, huge and coarsely detailed though they often were, nevertheless displayed their Joneseian origins. Nor had the speculators changed greatly: Nicholas Barbon and Charles Blake had much in common. In numerous suburbs of Victorian London a church — usually Gothic in style and often of great beauty — still formed the focal point of new estates and helped to provide them with the valuable cachet of social respectability.

The long dominance of the London terrace house was, however, coming to an end, and a new suburban type, the villa, or the semi-detached villa, was after about 1840 becoming increasingly popular. The first use of pairs of semi-detached houses on a large scale was on the Eyre estate at St John's Wood, where they were going up in the early nineteenth century. By the 1850s villas and semis were all the rage along the suburban frontiers, each with its own front and back garden and representing the city dweller's dream of *rus in urbe* (countryside in the town) within daily reach of Town; and also, perhaps, reflecting the emphasis placed by the prevalent evangelical code of morality on family privacy and closely regulated domesticity.[36] For thirty years or more they went up in all shapes and sizes, their highly eclectic styles exuberantly embellished with ornamental brickwork, steep Gothic gables, and window openings surmounted by flat-sided arches. The building booms of the late 1870s and the 1890s produced a rash of lower middle-class rows of small two-storey houses so arranged as to give a semi-detached impression and intended, in for instance Fulham or Lewisham, for the clerks and superior artisans to whom mid-Victorian prosperity had brought increased spending power. Only at London's first garden suburb, Bedford Park, Turnham Green, where Norman Shaw designed the layout and many of the houses, was there much claim to architectural distinction. Most of the building there, between 1875 and 1881, was in the 'Old English' vernacular idiom and the forerunner of countless thousands of semis later put up in new suburbs like Harrow or Morden in the 1920s.[37]

In all these suburbs of such different kinds there were until about 1900 no blocks of flats (except in Battersea) — buildings designed from the outset for multiple occupancy, and already for many years accepted as the norm in Paris or Vienna. Inside the built-up area, however, blocks of flats had begun to go up in the 1850s, the first, in 1853, being in Victoria Street (newly formed under Government aegis by the Commissioners of Woods and Forests). Others had followed in the Victoria area, at Albert Hall Mansions in Kensington (by Norman Shaw, 1880–7), and in the 1890s in several of the West End squares, where Georgian houses were torn down to make more intensive use of valuable sites. But flats were not numerous, and in the middle-class world flat-dwelling was slow to 'catch on'.[38]

Nevertheless it was widely hoped throughout the second half of the nineteenth century that flats would provide the answer to the intractable problems of housing the working classes. From the 1840s onwards a number of philanthropic or semi-philanthropic trusts and companies built blocks of model dwellings in various overcrowded central districts (Spitalfields and Drury Lane, for instance); but by 1875 the total number of people housed during the previous thirty years (26,000) amounted to only half the regular annual increase in the population of London,[39] and the main value of these 'private' agencies lay in the stimulus which they gave to the need for public action. But the Metropolitan Board of Works (MBW) — London's municipal authority between 1855 and 1889 — had inadequate statutory powers for rehousing, and (unless subsidized by the ratepayers) the high cost of land in the central areas precluded the building of dwellings at rents which the really poor could afford. So the 250 or more blocks of improved dwellings which were erected under the auspices of the MBW were of no direct benefit to the poorest class;[40] and at first the efforts of its successor, the London County Council (LCC), at rehousing by slum clearance were no more successful, notably at the great barrack-like Boundary Street project at Bethnal Green, 1893–1900. By that time, however, rehousing by dispersal had come into favour (just as the middle classes had discovered a long time earlier), and four chunks of land, two inside and two outside the County of London, were bought for the building of large cottage estates, the travel fares of the tenants being subsidized either through the LCC's own tramway network or by workmen's train-fare concessions (this at all events was what was intended). By 1914 nearly 3,000 small mostly two-storey cottages with gardens had been built; and after World War I these LCC suburban estates became the prototype for many council housebuilding programmes throughout the nation.[41]

So far, we have only been considering the kind of buildings in which people lived; but inside the urban frontier, within the existing Georgian nucleus of London, there simmered a cauldron of building activity of unprecedented variety, which was never far from the boil. Here too, besides a multiplicity of architectural styles, there was also a multiplicity of new types of building. Whereas it is hardly an exaggeration to say that hitherto most buildings in London were either houses or churches, the Victorians put up purpose-designed banks, offices, warehouses, market buildings, shops, schools, hotels, restaurants, libraries and museums, and public baths and wash-houses, etc. The equipment provided in many such buildings became more and more elaborate too: gas, electricity, hot-water heating, baths and water-closets, lifts, and better protection against fire.[42]

Most of this sort of work was done by (often large) firms of building contractors who employed a permanent labour force and depended for work on their success in competitive tendering for contracts. This process can be seen at its most intense in the rebuilding of the City between about 1840 and 1870, when the invisible world authority of the financial institutions there generated conspicuous architectural display. The post-Great Fire and Georgian rows of houses which still lined most of the streets were replaced by large showy insurance offices, by banks in more sober dress, by purpose-built office blocks containing the maximum possible letting space, or (away from the main streets) by hundreds of warehouses. At much the same time as this commercial transmogrification was going on, the railways, both above and below ground, were slashing their way through the City, new streets (notably Queen Victoria Street) were being cut across the old fabric, and extensive works being conducted by the City Corporation included the rebuilding of the ancient food markets (Smithfield, Billingsgate, and Leadenhall), the bridging of the Fleet River by Holborn Viaduct, and, lastly and most famously, the building of Tower Bridge (1881–94). Some of these buildings were designed by leading architects of the day: the Hardwicks, C. R. Cockerell, and John Gibson for the insurance companies and the banks, James Bunning and Sir Horace Jones for the Corporation.[43]

Besides these functional or commercial buildings there were also some spectacular feats of engineering, notably the Victoria Embankment, which extended beside the Thames from Westminster to Blackfriars and beneath which was built the underground railway as well as one of the principal sewers in London's new drainage system. Further downstream the Port of London was greatly extended by the construction of the Victoria (1855) and Albert (1880) Docks (the first to make full use of the railway system), and by 1886 Tilbury Docks for the large new steamers of worldwide commerce, 26 miles downriver from the City.

Architecturally the new monumentality of the mid-Victorian City was not widely paralleled elsewhere in London, though the impassive façades of the club houses in and around Pall Mall and St James's Street (several now demolished) provide notable exceptions; and half a dozen great new aristocratic town houses were built (Dorchester House and Brook House, for example, both in Park Lane), while others got magnificent facelifts (i.e. Bridgewater House, Cleveland Row). But the new streets formed by the MBW (such as Charing Cross Road and Shaftesbury Avenue in the 1880s) have a slovenly downmarket air about them. The sizes of the building sites formed by the MBW there were in the interests of economy wholly inadequate, and so were the architects. The theatres thereabouts made little impact on the urban scene (apart from T. E. Collcutt's Opera House, now the Palace Theatre, in Cambridge Circus), and nor did the great restaurants of the 1880s and 1890s (the Holborn or the Trocadero), although nowadays the surviving interiors of that period command nostalgic admiration, as do those of the contemporaneous pubs. London had little to compare with the outward splendour of Paris or Vienna.[44] Still, London was not without its own distinctions: the Palace of Westminster, the British Museum, at South Kensington the Albert Hall and the Albert Memorial, the Natural History Museum, and the Imperial Institute — all except the Albert Hall built under Government auspices and several when the mid-Victorian antipathy for 'official' architecture was at its most intense. At the more prosaic municipal level the schools built by the London School Board after 1870 in the red brick 'Queen Anne' style, or the LCC's staid classicism at County Hall (1908–22) and at the Aldwych and Kingsway, possessed appropriately unpretentious and serviceable everyday qualities. Much the same could be said of the new Government offices in Whitehall, the Admiralty Arch, the Mall, and the new face of Buckingham Palace itself—embellishments made to the processional way in the heart of Imperial London at the height of British power—nothing very bombastic or grandiloquent there.

The Management of London

The term 'metropolis', in explicit reference to the whole of London, began to be widely used in the 1820s and 1830s, and the name of the new Metropolitan Police, set up in 1829, first brought it into common parlance.[45] London was the prototype of this new form of polity, examples of which have since sprung up all over the world; and because through its unprecedented hugeness nobody quite knew how to fit it into the existing scheme of things, it engendered alarm. Fear that London could be seized from established authority, as had happened in Paris in the days of the Revolution, and the need to prevent such an event, explains why the first of the great nineteenth-century reforms of London was in the field of public order.

Sir Robert Peel's Metropolitan Police Act of 1829 was a turning point in the elimination of the riot and disorder which had so often been prevalent in Georgian London. It established a new police office with authority over the whole of the metropolitan area except the City within a radius (as defined a few years later) of some 15 miles of Charing Cross, and presided over by two magistrates or commissioners. These commissioners were appointed by the Home Secretary, to whom they were responsible for their actions; and it was under the direction of the Home Office that in the period 1870–1914 the Metropolitan Police became a recognizably modern professional force. (The Criminal Investigation Department was established in 1878, and fingerprinting was introduced in 1901.) The Act of 1829 in effect transferred one of the principal functions hitherto discharged by the local authorities—the vestries, with their constables and watchmen—to the central government. It was also an important early example of one of the great sea changes of the nineteenth century—the inexorable advance of the power of the State—and it provided a precedent for the removal, by the Poor Law Amendment Act of 1834, of another of the principal functions of the parish vestries to the new centrally controlled Poor Law Unions.

But the City was not included in the Act of 1829 and to this day has its own separate police force, Peel having privately confessed that he would 'be afraid to meddle' with the Corporation.[46] The unreformed and ever-formidable City Corporation was indeed an increasingly notable anomaly on the London scene, in its own narrow interests successfully impeding or manipulating every attempt at metropolitan reform, and the only one of the larger municipal corporations throughout the land to escape reform by the Municipal Corporations Act of 1835. The administrative problems of London were in fact always different from those elsewhere, for in addition to the perennial difficulties caused by the existence of the City Corporation there was also of course the equally perennial problem of the sheer size of the metropolis. This 'province covered with houses' (as one of several abortive Royal Commissions set up to inquire into the state of the City Corporation described the metropolis)[47] was by now too large and disparate for a single unitary municipality to manage, yet despite its diversities (particularly social and topographical) it nevertheless required overall metropolitan direction in such fields as public health and drainage. The ancient structure of local administration had become quite inadequate for the constantly growing problems of urbanization, and the ensuing struggles for the reforms which were so essential for London's well-being revolved around two connected but separate matters — the relationship between the Government and the metropolis which burgeoned all around it, and, within the metropolis itself, the struggle between the centralizers and the anti-centralizers, the latter often led by the City Corporation. Even at the end of the twentieth century much of the more recent history of London's government could still be written around these two themes.

The 1830s and 1840s were the golden age of decentralized localism in London. There were still no metropolitan-wide governmental institutions, apart from the Office of Metropolitan Buildings, a short-lived and somewhat ineffective body set up in 1844 to administer the Building Regulation Acts. The problems of the gross overcrowding of the graveyards in many inner London parishes were handed over to private enterprise, with seven commercial cemetery companies establishing themselves in a ring round the residential suburbs under Acts of Parliament of 1837–41; and such improvements to the fabric of London as the formation of New Oxford Street (1847) and Victoria Park, Hackney (1845) were made under Government auspices. Parish-pump localism had actually been strengthened by John Cam Hobhouse's Vestries Act of 1831, through which five of the largest suburban parishes had replaced their select vestries with assemblies elected by the ratepayers;[48] and there and elsewhere a radical reign of the most rigorous and bigoted economy had been practised for some years. By 1855 the administration of the metropolis was, according to *The Times*, being carried on by no fewer than 300 different bodies, deriving their powers from some 250 different local Acts.[49]

The central issue in the long campaign for the reform of this bizarre situation (so strikingly different from that in Paris, dominated by its powerful prefects) was public health — a matter seldom alluded to in Georgian times. In 1832 over 5,000 Londoners had died in the first of four outbreaks of cholera, which when it infected the water supply attacked whole areas with terrifying violence, its victims sometimes dying within a couple of hours of its first onset. The means by which it was transmitted (by swallowing the tiny bacillus of the cholera *vibrio*) was not, however, fully understood until the 1880s, and in the furious debates about how best to prevent it and other diseases such as typhus, the central figure until the early 1850s was Edwin Chadwick (1800–90), the Benthamite mastermind and arch-centralizer at the new national Poor Law Commission.[50]

In 1838 an inquiry which Chadwick had instigated during an epidemic of typhus in East London suggested that many of the 'Causes of Fever in the Metropolis...

might be removed by proper sanatory [*sic*] Measures', the chief of which were
to be the construction of drains or sewers to all houses and the provision of a
plentiful supply of water to carry away the sewage. This blueprint for the mid-
nineteenth-century sanitary movement was followed in the mid-1840s by other
reports on the sanitary condition of large towns throughout the whole country;
and their evidence challenged every vested interest: landlords, vestries, paving
boards, commissioners of sewers, and above all, the water companies, water
being a key element in any arterial system of drainage.[51]

Most of London's water was now provided by a dozen companies which drew
their supplies unfiltered from the Thames; drainage was mainly by means of
cesspits. These primitive arrangements broke down when the development of
water closets, the use of iron instead of leaky wooden pipes, and the great increase
of population caused vastly larger consumption of water. Much of this soiled water
found its way into the ancient sewers or open watercourses, which discharged into
the same stretches of the river as those from which the water companies drew their
supplies. The Thames became grossly polluted (salmon, formerly plentiful, disappeared altogether), and, as a contemporary observed, many Londoners were
'made to consume, in some form or other, a portion of their own excrement'.[52]

So Chadwick's proposal to replace the seven Crown-appointed Commissioners
of Sewers within the London area by a single huge commission which would
manage water, drainage, paving, and street cleaning for the whole of London,
made good theoretical sense, but of course it stirred up vociferous and widespread
opposition; and the commission for the construction of a metropolitan system of
drainage which was indeed hastily set up under his auspices in 1848, when the
return of cholera was imminent, was a complete failure. When cholera did arrive in
the following year, it killed some 14,000 people in London; and in the third
outbreak, in 1854, there were over 10,000 victims. By that time Chadwick and his
centralizing ideas were totally discredited, and he disappeared from the London
scene.[53]

Meanwhile in the City the Corporation's own commission had survived because
(unlike the other commissions) it was not a Crown appointment which could be
revoked at will by the Government; and in 1848 it appointed a newfangled person
called a Medical Officer of Health. This was Dr John Simon (1816–1904), the
leading figure in the second generation of sanitary reformers, who built the
framework of an entirely new medico-sanitary administration, enforcing for
example the cleaning of privies, the suppression of cesspools (over 5,000 within
the Square Mile), the removal of dung and excrement, and the systematic inspection of common lodging houses. By 1854 his arduous campaign proved its value
when, of the 10,000 fatal cases of cholera in London, hardly more than 200 were in
the City.[54]

So the decentralizers and the champions of local autonomy had triumphed, and
the Metropolis Management Act of 1855 reflected this ascendancy. This created
what has been called 'the world's first two-tier metropolitan system' of government,[55] and so far as London was concerned this was the first legislative attempt to

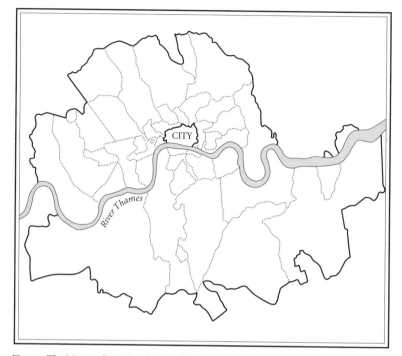

Fig. 25. The Metropolitan Board of Works, vestries, and district boards

tackle the problem of metropolitan administration as a whole — or at any rate, almost as a whole, for the City was still virtually exempt. It swept away all the select and open vestries and the innumerable local paving and lighting trusts and commissions, and gave London a sanitary code roughly similar to that which already existed in much of the rest of the country. But the metropolis was still fragmented into thirty-eight units of administration — elected vestries and indirectly elected district boards — and the members of the new central body, the Metropolitan Board of Works, were elected by these thirty-eight bodies and by the Common Council of the City Corporation, which chose three of the members. With such a system of indirect election, coupled with the continuing existence of the Corporation, the new MBW never commanded any feelings of municipal pride analogous to that prevalent in numerous provincial cities and towns, such as in Birmingham under Joseph Chamberlain.

The MBW powers were, moreover, extremely limited. It had no power to appoint a Medical Officer of Health of its own to advise on matters affecting the health of London as a whole, and it was unable to compel negligent vestries and district boards to execute their statutory duties or to enforce the MBW's own

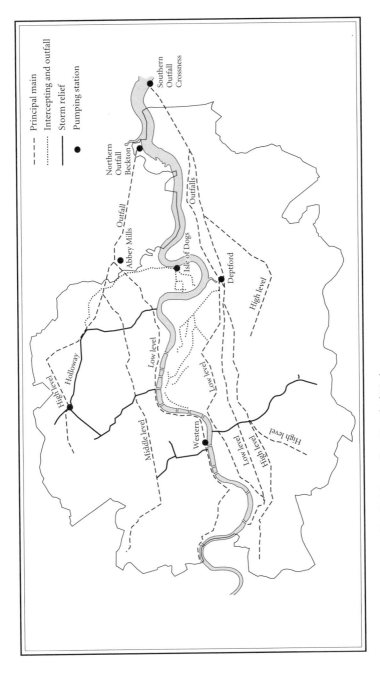

Fig. 26. Sewers constructed by the Metropolitan Board of Works

by-laws. In the course of time it did acquire additional powers for slum clearance, the formation of parks and open spaces, and the abolition of tolls on many of the bridges across the river; and in 1866 it took over control of firefighting. But throughout its whole career the MBW was often handicapped by inadequate power, especially in the field of slum clearance, where it could only sell or lease ground for the erection of labouring-class accommodation but had no power to spend money itself for this purpose, and where until 1884 it was obliged to sell all surplus lands acquired for street improvements within ten years of the completion of the works.[56]

The MBW did, however, achieve the principal purpose of its existence: the building of a main drainage system. After three years of Government meddling in the MBW proposals, the 'Great Stink' emanating from the Thames in the hot summer of 1858 at last persuaded the Government to let the MBW get on with the job on its own, and by 1865 most of the new system was in place. The MBW's engineer, Sir Joseph Bazalgette, built main sewers extending from west to east across London, which intercepted the contents of the old sewers and allowed them to flow into the Thames far below the built-up area. By making use of the natural configuration of the land the flow within the interceptor sewers was mostly by gravitation, but some pumping was necessary, particularly on the south side of the river. On the north side the building of one of the main sewers was combined with the formation of the Victoria Embankment extending from Westminster to Black-friars. This entailed the reclamation of 37 acres of ground from the river and the construction of not only the sewer but also the Metropolitan District Railway beneath the wide new road on the surface — one of the great feats of engineering of a great engineering age.[57]

In general, the record of the reformed vestries and the MBW was like the curate's egg: good in parts. On the one hand, for instance, the vestries never got to grips with the problems of housing, few of them used their optional powers to provide libraries or public baths and wash-houses; and the MBW hestitated to compel the water companies to provide a constant supply[58] — even ten years after the fourth and last epidemic of cholera in 1866, half the houses in London still only had an intermittent supply. All this amounts to what has been described by a distinguished modern historian as 'the scandalous under-administration and under-equipment of the world's largest town'.[59] Yet although the establishment of even the most rudimentary standards of sanitation had proved a far more formidable task than had been expected, some things had nevertheless improved — cesspools, the use of well-water, or the keeping of pigs, for instance, had by 1889 been largely abolished; the streets were less dirty, refuse more efficiently removed, the adulteration of food reduced. Numerous parks or open spaces had been provided or preserved — Hampstead Heath by the MBW, Epping Forest by the City Corporation, besides many other smaller ones; and the vestries and the City Corporation had provided publicly owned cemeteries beyond the built-up area. By 1905 the metropolitan death rate had fallen from 25 per thousand in the 1840s to 15 per thousand.[60]

Little progress had yet, however, been made in the abatement of smoke and other forms of air pollution. Victorian London was notorious for its fogginess and for the gloom which often enveloped it in the winter, the latter mainly due to dense palls of smoke which from a high level obscured the sun. The City Sewers Act of 1851, promoted by the Corporation under the tutelage of its medical officer, Dr John Simon, contained a clause for the abatement of smoke, and in 1853 Lord Palmerston (then Home Secretary) pushed through a Smoke Nuisance Abatement measure which applied to the whole of London. But neither had much effect because they only applied to industrial chimneys and not to domestic ones. So fogs continued to increase in frequency until the 1890s, when they began to decrease, largely, it is thought, because Londoners' coal-burning activities were through the explosion of the suburbs spread over a much wider area than hitherto.[61]

With the passage of time, specialized mechanisms were devised to meet the ever more complex requirements of the metropolis. In 1867 the Metropolitan Asylums Board was set up to provide for the care of the sick poor, and in due course its functions expanded to the provision of a public hospital service for all Londoners. New 'model' prisons — after 1877 all under Home Office management — proliferated (Pentonville, Wandsworth, and Wormwood Scrubs, for instance), though the cellular isolation and absolute silence imposed on prisoners merely replaced the brutish Georgian penal regime with a new one hardly, if any, less grim. In 1870 the State, through the agency of locally elected school boards, at last took the leading role in the provision of elementary education.

Since 1833 the State had made annual grants for the building of schools for the poor, and these grants had been made either through the Church of England's National Society, the main provider of elementary education throughout the land, or the Nonconformists' British and Foreign Society. There were also numerous 'private adventure' schools run for profit, often in squalid and grossly crowded conditions, and ragged schools which under Lord Shaftesbury's auspices catered without charge for 'street Arabs' and children of the poorest class. In the 1840s the average length of children's attendance at schools in London was less than eighteen months, their daily attendance even during that brief period was often intermittent, and due to the frequent migrations of their parents in search of work they often attended half a dozen different schools. Perhaps a third of them did not attend any school at all. Nor was the state of secondary education any better, for in the 1860s there were in the whole of London only forty grammar and proprietary schools for boys, containing just over 6,000 pupils, while for girls there were only twelve such schools, containing less than 1,000 pupils.[62]

The London School Board established in 1870 consisted of some fifty members directly elected by all ratepayers, including women, who were also eligible for election. Under its aegis compulsory elementary education for all children between the ages of 5 and 14 was eventually achieved, despite many difficulties. There was constant rivalry between the board and the denominational voluntary schools; costs — paid for out of Government grants, the rates levied by the board, and out of the 'school pence' (average 2d. per week) payable by parents until

1891 — rose inexorably; and middle-class attitudes towards the very idea of the education of the working classes were still ambivalent. Above all there was the problem of enforcing attendance upon families where the children's wages, often earned in sweated trades like matchbox-making at pitifully low rates, were needed to avoid destitution. In 1891 Charles Booth calculated that 350,000 Londoners lived 'in a state of chronic want', and to many such people education was irrelevant. It was therefore a remarkable achievement for the board to have raised the attendance level of pupils enrolled from 65 per cent in 1872 to 88 per cent in 1904 — a level hardly exceeded in later years, and above the national average despite London's peculiar problems of widespread poverty and huge size.[63]

In 1889 London's first tentative experiment in two-tier metropolitan government came to an end with the abolition of the unloved MBWs by that time discredited by revelations of financial corruption. In 1884 the Liberal Home Secretary, Sir William Harcourt, had attempted to make a reformed City Corporation the foundation for a single municipal authority for the whole of London, but his Bill — the first attempt by any Government since the seventeenth century to tackle the Corporation head-on — got entangled in the parliamentary timetable. This abortive attempt had, however, put metropolitan municipal reform — usually a subject of limited public interest and one likely to arouse much opposition from the interests affected — back on the national agenda. In the more intense political strife which followed the parliamentary reform Acts of 1884–5 the future of London government became to some extent a party matter (though blurred by other factors), the Conservatives identifying with second-tier local autonomy and the Liberals with first-tier centralization. So when Lord Salisbury's Government was reforming local government throughout England and Wales in 1888–9 it created a single London county authority, the London County Council (LCC), directly elected and based on the same area as the MBW, but without police, public utility, or second-tier powers, 'hardly the municipal juggernaut that it was constantly alleged to be, and ... weaker, in fact, than all the county boroughs' in the provinces.[64]

Nevertheless in the early years of this second phase of metropolitan two-tier government the LCC did generate a broader view of London and how its problems might be tackled — what Sidney Webb described as a genuine 'self-governing community'.[65] For the first eighteen years of its existence the Progressives (i.e. Liberals) held power, and party politics injected vigour into the Council's activities, particularly in the closely related fields of transport and housing, where (as we have previously seen) cheap tram fares and working-class dispersal soon became the order of the day. Meanwhile the poorer second-tier authorities were shored up by grants from a London-wide rate equalization fund set up in 1894, paid for by the richer vestries and by the City Corporation (by far the largest single contributor), which tacitly accepted this levy and payment of the rate precepts of the LCC in return for the continuance of its age-old unreformed autonomy.[66]

In 1899 the balance between the first — and second-tier authorities was hardly changed when the areas of the vestries and district boards were reorganized to

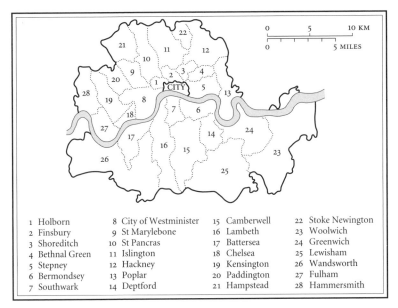

1 Holborn	8 City of Westminister	15 Camberwell	22 Stoke Newington
2 Finsbury	9 St Marylebone	16 Lambeth	23 Woolwich
3 Shoreditch	10 St Pancras	17 Battersea	24 Greenwich
4 Bethnal Green	11 Islington	18 Chelsea	25 Lewisham
5 Stepney	12 Hackney	19 Kensington	26 Wandsworth
6 Bermondsey	13 Poplar	20 Paddington	27 Fulham
7 Southwark	14 Deptford	21 Hampstead	28 Hammersmith

Fig. 27. LCC and Metropolitan Borough areas

produce twenty-eight Metropolitan Boroughs (including the City), each graced with its own mayor, aldermen, and councillors.[67] But the LCC's attempts to practise municipal socialism in the fields of water (from 1902 managed by a centralized quango, the Metropolitan Water Board), the docks (from 1909 taken over by another quango, the Port of London Authority), gas, electricity, or market management all failed, principally through financial constraints or central government obstruction; and on this frame of reference London still did not match many of the larger provincial cities.[68]

In 1904, however, the LCC was allowed to take over control of elementary education from the London School Board. The LCC had in fact been concerning itself with technical education since 1893, when growing realization that Britain was falling far behind her trading rivals, particularly Germany, in the level of industrial training, had prompted the LCC to set up a Technical Training Board on which it was itself, under the chairmanship of Sidney Webb, the senior partner. This new board created a 'scholarship ladder' to enable the brightest children from the board schools to go on to grammar or 'continuation' schools (the days of a publicly financed secondary school system being still far away). It also helped with funds to create polytechnics and technical institutes (eighteen in number), as well as 'monotechnics' for the teaching of individual trades. Soon it moved into support for commercial education — the need for clerks was growing rapidly in the 1890s — and (very soon after its foundation in 1895) for the London School of

Economics; and shortly before its absorption by the LCC in 1904 the Technical Education Board was preparing the way for the long partnership between the LCC and the University of London. Support for education at all levels was indeed to be a distinctive hallmark of the LCC throughout the rest of its existence.[69]

18

The People of London

In Chapter 17 we began to discern some of the physical and administrative lineaments of the metropolis still familiar in the late twentieth century. We must now look at the demographic and economic structures of London, and at the evolution of the social classes and their ways of living.

The Demographic Labyrinth

In 1801 only about one-fifth of the people of Britain lived in cities or towns with 10,000 or more inhabitants, but by 1901 over three-quarters of them did so. This urbanization of the greater part of an entire nation — the first of its kind in modern times, and described by C. F. G. Masterman, writing in 1909, as 'the largest secular change of a thousand years', the change 'from the life of the fields to the life of the city'[1] — was made possible by internal migration, by the high level of the urban marriage rate and hence of the urban birth rate, and at the end of the nineteenth century by the rapid fall in the death rate there. In London in 1891 the marriage rate was much higher than in many rural areas, while the metropolitan death rate had fallen from 25 per thousand in the 1840s to 15 by 1905. This mortality rate was only marginally higher than that of the whole of England and Wales and lower than in any of the industrial cities of the North or in any of the other great capitals of Europe except Brussels, the main ingredient in this advance being the striking fall in infant mortality which took place around 1900. So the peoples of the cities of England and Wales no longer needed migrants for their numerical growth or survival, and through this urban demographic transition 'the growth of the total population became largely dependent on the natural increase of the urbanized population itself'.[2]

Throughout most of the nineteenth century migration was, however, as it had always hitherto been, the main component in the growth of the population of the capital. In the 1840s it drew in about 330,000 people from outside its borders, and in 1851 nearly half of all the people of London had been born elsewhere. In the 1870s immigration reached its peak, but thereafter it began to decline, and natural increase, which in turn peaked in the later 1890s, became the principal element in the continuing rise of the overall population.[3]

These figures relate to the Registrar-General's London Census Division, the area of which, with modifications, became the Administrative County of London in 1888. Within this area the population rose from 960,000 in 1801 (the year of the first of the decennial censuses) to its peak of 4,500,000 in 1901. The rate of increase never fell below 16 per cent per decade until after 1881, and the percentage of the total population of England and Wales living within this area actually rose from some 11 per cent in 1801 to around 14 per cent a century later (see Appendix 2).

By the 1860s, however, the metropolis was spreading far beyond the bounds of the London Census Division, and the statistical concept of a Greater London coterminous with the Metropolitan Police District, which had a radius of roughly 15 miles from Charing Cross, came into being. In the outer suburban ring of this new area the population grew by 50 per cent in each of of the three intercensal decades between 1861 and 1891, and by 45 per cent in the 1890s — a much faster rate than in the inner area. By 1891 almost 20 per cent of the entire population of England and Wales were living in Greater London.[4]

This vast outward expansion of the metropolitan built-up area greatly changed and complicated the patterns of migration. Whereas London had hitherto been overwhelmingly an area of population concentration to which people were drawn from all over the country, the area of the London Census Division or County of London (as we may now call it) became, in terms of migration, an area of population dispersal. The balance between the inward and outward movements of the peoples of the late Victorian metropolis shows that the County of London sustained a net loss of 200,000 migrants to the Home Counties (Middlesex, Kent, Surrey, Hertfordshire, and Essex) in both the 1880s and 1890s, the continued growth of its overall population in these years being, of course, due to natural increase. In the early decades of the twentieth century the net loss was even greater, several of the factors facilitating population dispersal having by then had time to make their full impact, notably improvements in transport which made daily commuting between home and work possible, and the expansion of economic activity outside the County of London. Just as in the earlier phase of urbanization in which (chiefly through migration) large concentrations of population had accumulated, London had been the prototype, so too in this later phase, when through population dispersal urbanization was succeeded by suburbanization, London provided the exemplar.[5]

Most migrants to London came from south and east England, and particularly from the Home Counties, but the pull of the capital exerted itself in some degree all over the country, especially in the later nineteenth century when the impact of the railways was being more fully felt. Most in-migrants therefore came to London from short distances; the majority of them were young — between the ages of 15 and 30 — women outnumbered men, and they tended to settle in the inner suburbs.[6] They came mainly in search of work, prospects (including matrimonial prospects), and in hope of escape from the endless drudgery of much provincial town or village life — hoping, indeed, according to one observer writing in the 1890s, to enjoy 'the difference between the Mile End fair on a Saturday night and a dark muddy lane, with no glimpse of gas and with nothing to do'.[7]

There were also substantial numbers of migrants from overseas, the two largest groups being the Irish and the Jews, the latter escaping from the pogroms in Eastern Europe. In the 1840s 46,000 of the new migrants to London came from Ireland, and by 1851, shortly after the years of the great famine there, some 109,000 Irish-born were living in London, equivalent to 4.6 per cent of the whole metropolitan population (excluding nearly 50,000 children born in England of Irish parents). Their principal areas of settlement were in the dilapidated St Giles and Seven Dials areas of Holborn, along the south side of the river east of London Bridge, and in a few densely packed pockets in North Camberwell and Kensington, in all of which, for different reasons, there were markets for unskilled labour. The Jews did not come in large numbers until the 1880s, when many of them settled in the East End — 20,000 between 1880 and 1886 alone — where there were by that time many Irish-born migrants. Competition there was greatly intensified by the arrival of so many destitute Jews, and distress was especially severe in the footwear and clothing trades. Whitechapel in particular became their stamping ground, and by 1901 nearly a third of the population of this cosmopolitan part of the metropolis was of alien origin.[8]

Migration was not all inward, however, for a substantial number of Londoners, i.e. of those born in London, left the capital for destinations (mostly in the surrounding counties) elsewhere in England and Wales — some 250,000, for instance, in the 1870s.[9] An unknown number emigrated overseas; but as over 1,000,000 citizens left the United Kingdom in that same decade, those from the capital may well have added up to a six-figure number.

In the decade 1901–11 over 600,000 migrants moved into or out of the County of London, and this amounted to over a quarter of all migrations from one county to another throughout the whole of England and Wales.[10] But there was also incessant internal movement within the metropolitan antheap, from one part of the capital to another. Amidst the illimitably complex pattern of internal migration revealed by the census books, two main social gradients, to quote Professor H. J. Dyos's phrase, may be discerned, 'one leading upwards and outwards; the other leading downwards, if not inwards'.[11] Neither type of journey was new, as witness the Georgian suburbs and the City merchants' villas of St John's Wood and Herne Hill on the one hand, and the rookeries of St Giles's and Bermondsey on the other. The causes, too, were much the same as formerly — mounting social aspirations, the grinding exigencies of poverty, the labour markets, and destitution — and so also was the principal result — ever-mounting social differentiation between the various parts of the capital, notably between West and East, and between rundown inner areas and 'green field' suburbs. Only the sheer scale of metropolitan mobility in all its various forms was new, particularly in the second half of the nineteenth century.

The Mid-Victorian Social and Economic Framework

In 1851 the sixth decennial census of population provided a detailed picture of the social and economic structure of London, and of the nation at large. According to calculations made by M. François Bédarida, one-fifth of the London labour force can be classified as of the ruling class or middle class (including the petite bourgeoisie), and four-fifths of the labour force, amounting to some 900,000 people, as working class. This latter category comprised an immense variety of circumstance, ranging from the skilled artisans or 'aristocrats of labour' and mostly male, through the armies of semi-skilled, in which women preponderated, down to what M. Bédarida calls the sub-proletariat of the unskilled and the underworld.[12] Some two-thirds of the metropolitan labour force were engaged in service industries (distribution, exchange, banking and insurance, the professions, and above all domestic service) and one-third in manufacturing. With over 300,000 persons employed in manufacturing (greater than the entire population of Manchester at that time), London was thus still the largest centre of production in the country; and though greatly outnumbered by the workers in the service sector, manufacturing nevertheless comprised a nucleus of employment which had an enormous influence on the social structure of the metropolis.

This general situation had not changed fundamentally during the previous century and a half, though the importance of the service sector had increased. The 'shopocracy' or distribution element was as large as ever, and by 1851 the demands of the railways, the Port, and the vast cartage industry were using nearly a quarter of all men employed in transport in the whole of England and Wales. Commercial clerks were already one of the larger occupational categories in London, and the public services and professions there took 28 per cent of all men employed therein throughout the nation. Women were still seldom found outside their age-old occupations of domestic service, needlework, laundering, and retailing, and provided much of the casual labour always readily available in London. More than 200,000 women worked in domestic service, equivalent to over half the female labour force in London and to one-fifth of all the domestic servants in the whole nation — a striking testimony, incidentally, to the wide extent of middle-class metropolitan wealth.[13]

Nor had metropolitan industry greatly changed. It was still wide in range, mainly handicraft in its structure, and for the most part based on small workshops and much domestic outwork; but large firms were important in such fields as printing, shipbuilding, or brewing. Effective union organization of the labour force had only existed in the skilled trades, the members of which were the natural leaders of the nascent working class, despite their concern to preserve the exclusiveness of their skills from invasion from below. Many trades had been feeling the pressures exerted by provincial competition, the rise of mass markets, and the dilution of skills through the subdivision and consequent sweating of labour.

In the 1860s these pressures greatly intensified. When Thames-side shipbuilding collapsed in 1866, no longer able to compete with the yards on the Tyne and the Clyde which were so much closer to the sources of iron and coal, 27,000 workers were thrown out of work;[14] and with the triumph of free trade the silk-weavers were wiped out by foreign competition. In the prosperous 1850s, when a larger proportion of people had more money to spend than ever before, mass demand for goods such as clothing and furniture had greatly increased. But in London many trades, particularly those concerned with the finishing processes of manufacture, suffered from seasonal fluctuations of demand which precluded long-run factory methods of production — high-class dressmaking and millinery of all kinds are cases in point — and the high value of land and hence of rents in the central areas also made large factories uneconomic. So London industries could only survive by 'sweating': the fragmentation of production amongst home workers (which saved rent and capital), with wages and conditions screwed down to starvation and slum levels (Plate 37).

In two important fields this dilution of skills was accelerated by mechanical invention: the sewing machine and the bandsaw, which came in in the 1840s to 1860s. More generally, however, it was engendered by the presence of thousands of casual workers in the docks and seasonal trades always ready to do any kind of work for any wage, however low; by the wives and children of these casual workers and of workers in declining trades, chained to the district near to their husbands' or fathers' place of work, and constrained to slave for a pittance to supplement the family budget; and by a ceaseless stream of poor, unskilled migrants from Ireland and the Continent as well as from England, also ready to work at anything available. Jews from Eastern Europe, for instance, thousands of whom arrived in the East End in the early 1880s, soon dominated the cheap tailoring and slop-clothing industries there, and pushed skilled native workers into the casual labour market of the docks, markets, and transport, where there was always a surplus of labour, and where (as in the sweated trades) wages were forced down to subsistence levels or even less.[15] By 1889, according to Charles Booth, over 40 per cent of the entire population of the East End were living in poverty.[16]

The principal social effect of these processes was to break down the cohesion of the old artisan culture of the late eighteenth and early nineteenth centuries:[17] the London artisan class was becoming a proletariat. This was a long and never wholly completed transition, stimulated in the mid-1860s by the trade slump and financial crisis, and by the collapse of shipbuilding. Above all there were the massive displacements of the poor in the central districts, engendered by railway incursions (amounting to nearly 37,000 of the 'labouring classes' between 1859 and 1867),[18] street improvements, the building of offices and warehouses, and slum clearances. With their skills diminished and their livelihoods threatened by mounting competitive pressures, thousands of pauperized workers were unable to move from the ever more tightly packed remaining pockets of accommodation in the central districts where most of the demand for casual labour was situated. Slums and the casual labour markets of Victorian London were, indeed, opposite sides of the same coin.

The Coming of Age of the Metropolitan Working Class

We have already seen in Chapter 16 that the long tradition of political radicalism in London extended back at least to the days of Wilkes; and that in the early 1790s there began to emerge a metropolitan political movement of the 'lower orders' or *menu peuple* independent of any other section or class of society, the skilled trades providing the core of this incipient metropolitan working-class movement. In continuing this examination of the evolution of class society through Victorian times we must now turn to the processes of political convergence and social divergence which culminated in the critical years of the 1880s.

The first stage of political convergence began in 1832 when by the extension of the parliamentary franchise thousands of middle-class men were brought within the pale of the constitution; and the capital's representation in the House of Commons was increased from ten to twenty-two—equivalent to only 3.3 per cent of the membership of the whole House, and still far below its 'true' share, whether calculated in terms of wealth or population. But in the reform campaign of 1830–2 there was in London no general agitation corresponding to that prevalent in parts of the provinces, notably Birmingham; and it was not until after the terms of the first Bill were published in March 1831 that London bestirred itself with the formation of the National Union of the Working Classes (NUWC) and the middle-class National Political Union (NPU), the latter set up in November 1831 (nearly two years after Birmingham had given the lead), following the defeat of the second Bill in the Lords.[19]

Nevertheless there was widespread support for reform throughout London, which remained the focus of national attention if only because Parliament itself—the objective of the campaign—was situated there. But this support was not brought to bear effectively until the final phase of the struggle in May 1832, when the huge potential power of the presence of the metropolis was a decisive factor. London had proved too large and too complex, its industries too diverse and too small in scale to be harnessed for successful political action; and there had been divisions not only between the supporters of the NUWC and the NPU, but amongst the activists within each body. For the veteran radical Francis Place, writing in 1840 with half a century's experience behind him, London had 'never moved' politically.

London differs very widely from Manchester, and, indeed, from every other place on the face of the earth. It has no local or particular interest as a town, not even as to politics. Its several boroughs in this respect are like so many very populous places at a distance from one another, and the inhabitants of any one of them know nothing, or next to nothing, of the proceedings in any other, and not much indeed of those of their own.[20]

The passing of the Reform Bill left the working men of London, and indeed of the whole country, in a state of profound disillusionment; and those who had supported the Bill felt that they had been betrayed. After their failure to obtain the parliamentary franchise by political means there was widespread support for industrial action independent of the middle classes; and in 1833–4 an explosion of trade union activity ensued. London was the centre of this activity, where the millenarian expectations of industrial emancipation which were provided for a few months in 1834 by a general union of the trades known as the Grand National Consolidated Trades Union ended in the collapse of a strike by the tailors and in the building trades in the success of an employers' lockout.[21]

After this failure of the London artisans' attempt at national leadership they were for some time unlikely to repeat such an effort *en masse*. So when the Chartist movement got under way in the provinces in 1838 there was at first little enthusiasm for it in London, despite (as previously mentioned) the metropolitan origin of the Chartists' Six Points in 1780, and their rearticulation there in 1837–8 by the London Working Men's Association. For London artisans, with their long radical record, the Chartist programme contained nothing new; and this lack of any general metropolitan support for Chartism when it reached its first climax in 1839 with the meeting of its first general convention in London was to prove fatal for the long-term future of the movement.[22]

This was because, first, Chartism could by its very nature never succeed without a very large amount of metropolitan support; and secondly, because the strength of the first climax was never repeated. During the 1840s Chartism in London did nevertheless gather widespread support (both the national executive of the movement and its newspaper, the *Northern Star*, being transferred to the capital in 1843–4) and it reached a dangerous final climax in March to June 1848. But it was only in those few months that metropolitan and national Chartism moved in sufficiently close phase with each other to present a serious challenge to the State. By that time the new police were able to handle the situation without direct active recourse to troops or firearms.[23]

The sources of and reasons for metropolitan Chartism have been much debated by historians. Most Chartists were artisans, i.e. manual workers practising a specialist trade, drawn mainly (so it has been claimed) not from the best-paid and best-organized trades but from middling ones such as shoemakers, tailors, cabinet makers, silk-weavers, and carpenters.[24] But people drifted in and out of Chartism, and the strength of the movement was always closely linked to the state of the metropolitan economy and of particular trades within it at any one time. In the 1830s and 1840s many long-practised metropolitan trades were being destabilized by the extension of technical or capitalistic innovations; subcontractors and garret-masters reorganized work to reduce the need for skilled labour, and there were cyclical trade slumps, seasonal fluctuations of demand, and endemic unemployment or underemployment. So years of distress, i.e. 1842 and 1848, coincided with peaks of Chartist support, and produced short-lived political unity amongst large numbers of London artisans.[25]

Thus from 1841 onwards London Chartism was certainly a mass movement – even a lowly street scavenger told Henry Mayhew that 'I cares nothing about politics neither; but I'm a chartist.'[26] During the 1840s it also became a more explicitly class-conscious movement, with predominantly working-class activists and leaders, and nourished by its own working-class press, which frequently voiced itself in terms of Owenite socialism or class antagonism, particularly in reference to the middle class.[27]

It was in this context that another national petition (the third) to Parliament was organized, but this time its impact was greatly increased by the news of the revolution in Paris in February 1848, followed by other revolutionary outbreaks elsewhere in Europe. Still more alarming for the Government was the new alliance between the Chartists and the Irish Confederates, for after three years of famine Ireland was, or was thought to be, on the verge of insurrection. To assist the police some 85,000 special constables were enrolled in London in what has been described as a middle-class *levée en masse*;[28] and on 10 April, when there was a mass rally on Kennington Common for the formation of a procession to Parliament for the presentation of the gigantic petition (Plate 53), large bodies of troops were discreetly stationed at strategic points. Once assembled south of the river, however, the Chartists' leaders were told that they would not be allowed to cross back to Westminster. Violent confrontation with established authority was rejected (as it had so often been in the history of Chartism), the meeting dispersed peaceably, and in due course the petition (which had been conveyed to Parliament in three hired cabs) was rejected.[29] Turbulent demonstrations in London, particularly around Clerkenwell Green, continued for several weeks, however, largely inspired by alarming events in Ireland, and in June Ernest Jones and several other Chartist leaders were arrested. By August Jones and others on both sides of the Irish Sea were in prison, and the Chartist challenge had been finally broken by relentless coercion.[30]

So ended a long era of popular agitation. Chartism, with its mass demonstrations and mass petitions and popular orators, had become outmoded, as well as latterly being much discredited by its association with insurrectionary Irish politics. The power of established authority, maintained through the new police, the new penitentiary prisons, and the new workhouses, was far greater than it had been in the eighteenth century; and just as the strength of metropolitan radicalism had declined during the improved economic conditions of the 1820s, so now in the early 1850s, for much the same reason, a period of social peace supervened. Working-class advancement began to come through autonomous working-class organizations and through negotiation on specific issues rather than through unsustainable head-on political challenges to the State.[31]

These new institutions had more durable foundations than those of the 1830s and 1840s. In some skilled trades there emerged a new brand of moderate unionism, small and exclusive in its membership and well organized from London on a national basis. Despite the defeat of a strike by the Amalgamated Society of Engineers in 1852 and the compromise of the long and bitter builders' strikes of 1859–61 (from which there emerged the Amalgamated Society of Carpenters and Joiners), stable unions with limited objectives had come to stay; and in 1860 a permanent multi-trade organization, the London Trades Council, was set up to guide and coordinate the individual London trade societies. Thus during the 'crisis' of 1866–7 which led up to the Second Reform Act, London working men were able by a series of massive and well-managed demonstrations to maintain the momentum of the demand for reform and ensure that at last something was placed on the statute book.[32]

The Act of 1867 increased the number of MPs for the whole metropolitan area from twenty-two to twenty-eight and the total metropolitan electorate by some 30 or 40 per cent. So London was still grossly underrepresented in terms of its population.[33] In 1884–5, however, the franchise was again enlarged, though women were still excluded, and Greater London (despite the reduction of the representation of the City from four to two seats) now returned no less than sixty members, equivalent to 9 per cent of the whole House of Commons. The idea that metropolitan representation there should be proportionate to population was at last being accepted; and with it came an increase in the power of London's political muscle in the nation's affairs.

By bringing most working men within the pale of the constitution a substantial degree of political inclusiveness within the nation had thus been achieved by the mid-1880s. But at the same time social divergence was widening, and the climate of political opinion was changing. In the early 1880s the dogmatically Marxian Social Democratic Federation and the Fabian Society were both founded in London, the former by H. M. Hyndman (a City man converted to socialism after reading Marx's *Das Kapital*) and based on working men's clubs, and the latter soon to be impregnated with the ideas of two of its early leaders, Bernard Shaw and Sidney Webb. The unions too were extending their influence amongst the less skilled sections of the workforce and amongst those difficult to organize, such as the gasworkers, builders' labourers, and railwaymen; and working men's clubs, of which by 1875 there were nearly eighty in the metropolitan area, provided social attractions for their members as well as acting for some years as centres of political commitment to advanced radicalism.[34] But although the working class itself was becoming more aware of its own separate identity (despite its own internal divisions, notably between the 'respectable' and the 'roughs'), the social divide between even the aristocrats of labour and the lowliest white-collar clerk in the City (i.e. the petite bourgeoisie) was steadily widening – hardened in the later 1880s by the mass demonstrations which took place in Trafalgar Square on several winter evenings in February 1886 and again in November 1887, when thousands of the unemployed spread frenzied alarm amongst the middle classes of the West End, breaking club windows in St James's Street and looting in Piccadilly.[35]

Events of this kind were perceived by the middle classes as symptoms of wide-spread social tensions, and were much more frightening than well-ordered union strikes such as those of the women matchworkers of Messrs Bryant and May, successful (against all the odds) in a strike against miserable conditions, or that at the huge Beckton gasworks at East Ham, where a twelve-hour two-shift system of working was replaced by a three-shift schedule. The great Dockers' Strike in 1889 of comparatively unskilled men employed, mostly on a casual basis, in the Port, who demanded an advance of pay from 4*d*. or 5*d*. to 6*d*. an hour — 'the dockers' tanner' — evoked considerable public sympathy. It lasted five weeks, and after their daily mass meetings on Tower Hill the dockers marched in good order past the very citadels of capitalism in the astonished City.[36]

This new mass unionism of the less skilled which came into being in the 1880s and 1890s was in some degree influenced by nascent socialism, but neither it nor the older unionism was either Marxist or revolutionary. Still less so were the working men's clubs, where in the 1880s and 1890s recreation was becoming more important than political activity. Most unions, were, however, becoming increasingly aware that a separate political expression of the distinct identity of their membership was required. The working class, in fact, needed its own political party; and at a conference held in London under the auspices of the Trades Union Congress (which although it had been formed in Manchester in 1868 was soon doing most of its work in London) the Labour Representation Committee was set up in 1900 to establish 'a distinct Labour Group in Parliament'.[37]

The perceived need for the representation of the working class through its own distinct Labour Party can be viewed either as an important step towards the political convergence of the nation or as a step towards social divergence. Either way, by the end of the nineteenth century society had set firm within a class-structured mould. This was the high noon of British capitalism, when social and financial inequality were probably at their most extreme, as was soon to be manifested in the rising tide of national unrest and menacing strikes during the years 1910–14. Although these strikes were not primarily of metropolitan origin, class divisions were nevertheless stark enough in London, aggravated by geographical segregation, particularly of course between the East and West Ends. In Victorian times this segregation had been greatly intensified by the middle-class flight to the suburbs, and personal contact with and personal knowledge of people in other layers of the social pyramid had thereby been much reduced. East London had become a *terra incognita* outside the pale of the civilized metropolis, where the well-to-do ventured as rarely as possible, and where in 1891 90 per cent of the adult population were working class.[38] Ignorance had begotten fear, and although the social explorations of Henry Mayhew in the 1850s and of Charles Booth in the 1880s and 1890s, and the revelations of parliamentary inquiries, notably those of the Royal Commission of 1884–5 on the Housing of the Working Classes, had done much to reduce such ignorance about the condition of the poor, fear and latterly feelings of guilt were nevertheless powerful ingredients in middle-class attempts at social control of the masses.

During the nineteenth century the London working classes had been subjected to increasing interference and discipline from the State, to a degree hitherto unknown. The Metropolitan Police was widely perceived as a hostile force buttressing the existing social order, the growing authority of 'the policeman State' backed by the thirteen stipendiary magistrates' police courts (to which, however, the labouring poor themselves frequently resorted for the settlement of disputes).[39] Even the London School Board was often resented for the formalized disciplines which it imposed on the children of working-class parents.[40]

Housing was, however, the main means used for the attempted improvement of the labouring classes. In the second half of the nineteenth century the slums were the object of a prolonged moral crusade, but they could never be eradicated so long as demand for casual labour persisted, particularly in the central districts. 'The residuum' – the casual poor whose existence so alarmed the well-to-do in the 1880s – survived all the efforts of philanthropic or semi-philanthropic agencies and those of the public authorities to do away with them by rehousing, which without massive public subsidies or the payment of much higher wages was impossible in the central areas where enormous land values prevailed.[41] Indeed, slum clearances, which became more extensive in the 1870s, by reducing the stock of houses actually increased overcrowding; and in 1911 over 750,000 Londoners — more than the entire population of Liverpool — were still living in overcrowded conditions.[42]

What this meant for the people of the East End in the 1880s has been graphically evoked in Professor W. J. Fishman's chronicle of the dark, cold, filthy slums there, the grinding poverty, the deprivation and misery, and the constant nearness of death. Women were the principal victims, uncomplainingly accepting the pains and dangers of childbirth, their subordination to men (from whom they endured frequent violence), and the exploitation of their sweated labour, their wages often being only half those paid to men. Yet all this was generally regarded as preferable to the grim barracks of the workhouse, of which there were six in the East End. In 1851 one in every six Londoners was dying in the workhouse or in hospitals or madhouses; and in the 1870s the Charity Organization Society had led the way in the stricter application of the poor law: the workhouse was to to be made an effective deterrent for the able-bodied pauper, and outdoor relief was to be abolished, or at any rate greatly diminished. Fear and hatred of the workhouse, where families were parted and incarcerated in separate wards, and of the casual ward, where a night of draconian lodging could be had in exchange for stone-breaking or picking oakum, was widely prevalent among the poor, and particularly among the victims of chronic unemployment or underemployment.[43]

Beside the workhouse there were, however, numerous other means by which middle-class values of thrift, independence, temperance, and self-discipline might be inculcated into the labouring masses. After a religious census taken in 1851 had shown that some two-thirds of the population of London did not attend any form of public religious worship on the Sunday when the count was made, efforts to implant Christian principles among the poor were redoubled. Education was always seen as an important means to this end, and Church elementary schools, ragged schools for the destitute, and colleges for the training of teachers were provided.[44] Prompted, perhaps, by a sense of guilt, all Christian denominations sought to foster personal relations between the different social classes, and missionary zeal of this kind led to the establishment of 'settlement' houses in East and South London, notably the Universities' Settlement at Toynbee Hall in Whitechapel, opened in 1884 by Canon Samuel Barnett to 'educate citizens in the knowledge of one another'. It was in the East End, too, that William Booth founded what was to become a worldwide engine of revivalism — the Salvation Army — and that Dr Barnado opened his first home for destitute children.[45]

Official efforts to spread middle-class attitudes and modes of behaviour included the removal of dens of crime and disease like Jacob's Island in Bermondsey, and the dispersal of their inhabitants. Drinking was regulated and the villainous gin palaces of the past were superseded by large brightly lit pubs lavishly embellished with engraved plate glass and polished mahogany. Cock-fighting and ratting were much reduced; and public executions outside Newgate were discontinued (in 1868). Many of the ancient and often disorderly fairs around London were abolished (St Bartholomew's in 1866), and four regular bank holidays were inaugurated in 1871. Parks, public libraries, museums (notably those that sprouted up at South Kensington after the Great Exhibition of 1851), and art galleries such as the Whitechapel Art Gallery and the South London Art Gallery in Peckham provided uplifting new means of recreation — though the British Museum did not open on Sundays until 1896.

Prostitution survived all attempts to suppress it. Most prostitutes were of working-class origin, most were the unskilled daughters of unskilled parents, and most of them catered for a working-class clientele. Often they entered the trade gradually, as a supplementary means of support or to fend off destitution, their charges ranging from around 3s. in poor districts to upwards of £1 in the West End. Generally they obtained customers by walking the streets or resorting to pubs or railway termini, and lived in low-class lodging houses rather than in brothels.[46] In the East End the areas near the Port were the main centres of business, while in the West End there were fashionable marts like the Argyll Rooms near Oxford Circus as well as the streets, where a less expensive girl could always be picked up. It was after a walk down the Haymarket and the Strand in the 1860s that the French historian Hippolyte Taine wrote, 'Every hundred steps one jostles twenty harlots...This is not debauchery which flaunts itself, but destitution...That is the real plague-spot of English society.'[47]

By around 1900 a distinctive working-class culture of its own had come into being, impermeable in many respects to evangelical or utilitarian efforts to mould its nature. Charles Booth thought that after half a century of attempts to Christianize them, the poor generally regarded the churches 'as the resorts of the well-to-do, and of those who are willing to accept the charity and the patronage of people better off than themselves'. Booth also thought that drinking was more prevalent than ever, the temperance movement having made more headway in provincial cities than in London, where its association with Sabbatarianism and the Nonconformist conscience repelled many radically minded artisans with their long tradition of secularism. Betting, which also evoked much middle-class disapproval, was likewise increasing,[48] particularly in the 1880s on horse racing after the advent of the railway telegraph and the popular press, the chance of a windfall providing a ray of hope for lives almost incapable of substantial improvement by saving.[49]

As hours of work began to fall in many trades, and a Saturday half-holiday became usual, the work-centredness of labouring culture, epitomized in the masculine world of the 'house of call', began to decline in favour of family and home, the importance of which were enhanced by the geographical separation of home and work. Middle-class virtues were no doubt fostered thereby, but for the working class much leisure activity still took place in the pub and the street. Hawkers, costers, itinerant brass bands, hurdy-gurdy and Punch and Judy men, and a host of other traders all made the mid-Victorian streets places of entertainment and often of conviviality as well as of the quasi-nomadic economic life so lovingly described by Henry Mayhew. At a more organized level, football, which in London developed as a mass sport later than in the North, came into its own in late Victorian times and provided a powerful generator of masculine cohesion. In 1901 there was wild enthusiasm when Tottenham Hotspur won the Football Association Cup in a replay against Sheffield; and by 1914 there were nearly a dozen professional clubs in London, each one with its own well-defined area such as Fulham or West Ham United.[50]

The most distinctive feature of this new working-class culture was the music hall (to be discussed again later), of which in the 1880s there were some 500 in London. Many of them had begun as adjuncts to pubs, and drink was always an important element in both their appeal and their profitability. Apart from the handful of great theatrical palaces in the West End, the music halls — a peculiarly London phenomenon — were mainly working class in the nature of their audiences, their performers, and the content of the songs and sketches presented in them. These were never just vulgar commentaries on working-class life. To quote W. MacQueen-Pope,

The music hall ... was a club of the clubless. It gave the people what they wanted, in a way they understood. It sang and it pattered on of the unpaid rent, the mother-in-law, the lodger, kippers, erring wives and husbands. It joked about physical violence, seaside holidays and beer. It jeered at foreigners, it glorified this country. It gave the people their patriotism in doses hot and strong.

There was also something more, however, as no less a person than Lenin perceived in 1907 when he wrote that

In the London music halls there is a certain satirical or sceptical attitude towards the common-place, there is an attempt to turn it inside-out, to distrust it somewhat, to point up the illogicality of the everyday.[51]

Music hall was, to quote a modern authority, 'both escapist and yet strongly rooted in the realities of working-class life'; and as the largest halls alone were in the early 1890s entertaining some 45,000 people nightly, their influence was immense. Many of the features of working-class culture were reflected there: its orderliness, its uncomplaining acceptance of the trials and injustices of life, its uninhibited enjoyment of such pleasures as might be available, its indifference to religion and even in some measure to politics, and above all its sense of defensive separatism, impregnated with limited objectives of social welfare rather than with impossible schemes for remodelling the form of the State.[52]

The *Classe Dirigeante* and the *Petite Bourgeoisie*

Working-class Londoners were the rank and file of the metropolitan demographic army, and the upper and middle classes — what the French would call the *classe dirigeante* and the *bourgeoisie* — were its officers and non-commissioned officers. These two cadres amounted, in the mid-nineteenth century, to around one-fifth of the London labour force; and in 1891 Charles Booth thought that the middle classes 'and above' totalled 17.8 per cent of the whole population of the capital — i.e. around 750,000 persons.[53] We must now examine the extent of the wealth of these classes, and their ways of life.

The immense extent of middle-class Victorian metropolitan wealth in relation to the rest of the country can be measured through the records of the income tax. Professor W. D. Rubinstein has shown that in 1879–80 the assessments of business and professional incomes for the City of London were double those of the combined total for the two largest provincial towns, Liverpool and Manchester. For London as a whole (i.e. the area roughly coterminous with that of the future County of London) the assessments exceeded the total for those of the twenty-eight largest provincial towns, despite their combined population being 65 per cent greater than that of London. The assessments for London, indeed, amounted to over 40 per cent of the total for the whole of England and Wales. From figures of this kind Professor Rubinstein has inferred 'not merely that London possessed a larger total business income than all of the chief provincial towns combined but that its middle class was richer *per capita* and almost certainly more numerous than in the provincial towns ... Standing above everything else there was London, the fixed point around which the Victorian middle classes revolved'.[54] Indeed, the metropolis formed probably the greatest concentration of wealth in the world, either then or in any previous age.

Within these middle and upper classes there were infinite gradations of circumstance. At the apex was a handful of great landowners, some of whom drew much of their incomes from the rentals of their estates in London itself (£135,000 per annum by the first duke of Westminster in 1891 from his Mayfair estate alone), and all of whom spent prodigiously in the metropolis, especially when living there during the social season.[55] In the second half of the nineteenth century more than a third of all the non-landed fortunes of over £500,000 made in the whole of Britain had their origin in London, mostly in the City in commerce or finance but also more widely in the food, drink, and tobacco industries.[56] There was also a strong or dominant metropolitan element in many of the service industries, notably in banking and insurance, the professions, the armed forces, and the civil service, as well as in innumerable branches of commerce. In 1851 nearly half of all the commercial clerks in England and Wales worked in London,[57] and in the 1890s one such, Mr Pooter, a senior clerk living at The Laurels, Brickfield Terrace, in Holloway in 'a nice six-roomed residence' from which he travelled daily to the City by bus, was able to keep a live-in servant — a reflection of the growing prosperity of the late Victorian middle classes. Finally, at the bottom of the middle-class pile, were impoverished clerks like Dickens's Bob Cratchit, who although Scrooge paid him only 15s. a week — substantialy less than the earnings of a skilled artisan and well below the minimum liability for payment of income tax of £150 per annum — would nevertheless have regarded himself as middle class. He lived with his family in a four-room house in Camden Town and walked (or, in cold weather, ran) to Scrooge's counting house in the City.[58]

Although the ways of life of this top fifth of the population were outwardly no less varied than the extent of their wealth, certain social assumptions were nevertheless widely taken for granted, notably the hierarchical nature of the existing social order, the paramountcy of respectability (or at any rate of outward respectability), the privacy of the home, and the dominance of men. This code was largely regulated by upper- and middle-class women who, being effectively excluded from working careers of their own, were cast (or cast themselves) as guardians of hearth and family against threatened encroachments from the other four-fifths of the population beneath them. There thus evolved the idea of 'society' — defined in the *Shorter Oxford English Dictionary* as the aggregate of 'persons collectively who are recognized as taking part in fashionable life, social functions entertainments, etc,' — which may be traced to the rackety 1820s, when (as we have already seen) a powerful coterie of aristocratic patronesses began to exert control over admissions to subscription dances at Almack's Assembly Rooms in King Street, St James's.[59] In the 1830s to the 1850s society developed highly structured rituals of social control: the comings-out, the morning calls and card-leaving, the 'at homes', and so on. The rules of social intercourse became more formal and more private — public places of resort like Ranelagh and the Pantheon were things of the past, while gentlemen's private clubs proliferated — and all this reflected the more edifying tone of the royal court, around which, and its levees and drawing rooms, the whole system always ultimately revolved. Always, too, society was quintessentially a metropolitan phenomenon, the influence of which rippled out all over upper- and middle-class Britain.

This metropolitan influence was powerfully reinforced through the sessions of Parliament, when hundreds of leading men and their families came up to London from all parts of the country for 'the season', which (as we have previously seen) had its origins in the early seventeenth century. This now extended from April or May to the end of July,[60] and the seasonal migration to London which it entailed was of cardinal importance in the maintenance of the Victorian Establishment. It was during the feverish social round of the London season — in that of 1849, for instance, Lady Dorothy Neville went to fifty balls, sixty parties, thirty dinners, and twenty-five breakfasts — that contacts and introductions were made, and innumerable dynastic alliances resulted therefrom. The season was indeed the principal marriage market place for the upper classes, for a girl of 17 or 18 'coming out' from childhood would only have two or at most three seasons in which to acquire a husband; and thereafter her chances of success in the matrimonial stakes would be greatly reduced.[61]

The expense of 'doing' a season could be enormous. The mere rent of a house (and many houses were rented, for participants in the season were mainly country-based) could amount to some 650 guineas for a property in, for instance, Wilton Crescent; and the cost of entertaining and dressing a family were huge too. Although this conspicuous consumption did, of course, generate greatly needed employment, much of it was only temporary (in dressmaking and domestic service, for instance), and after the season was over thousands returned to unemployment or at best underemployment. By the 1880s costs were straining the resources of some landed families, and after obtaining admission to society the amount of a man's wealth became as important as its origin. Partly for this reason and partly also through the influence of the Prince of Wales and his pleasure-loving friends known as the Marlborough House Set, London society widened to include manufacturers and men of commerce and latterly the owners of South African, Jewish, or American fortunes. Plutocratic values prevailed, there was a return to large semi-public events such as garden parties, and a measure of liberation for women began through such innovations as the spread of tearooms, telephones, bicycles, motor cars, and travel by public transport, and even at the turn of the century through the widespread popularity of bridge-playing. Despite all this, and its great numerical enlargement, society and its hierarchical foundation survived to a large extent unchanged until World War I in 1914–18.[62]

But although at the turn of the century there were still only about 4,000 families which took an active part in London society, the influence of that society was nevertheless immense. The vastly increased mobility brought about by the railways had extended the grip of metropolitan mores over much of the country, and by the 1860s those concerned with etiquette and decorum had been generally accepted by the middle classes as the foundations of correct social behaviour.[63] In the suburbs respectability, embodying such qualities as industry, sobriety, and self-restraint, was what mattered, and its importance there may be traced back to the Clapham Sect and the Evangelical Revival.

In the High Victorian decades much of middle-class social life revolved around religious observances. The solid suburban gentry or established middle-class men of business who occupied the tall stuccoed mansions of South Kensington or Bayswater or the three-storey villas of Highbury or Norwood, and who often employed upwards of three of four servants, would on Sundays attend their local Anglican church, to the building of which in such large numbers throughout Victorian London they may well have subscribed, and where the sermon was often the main component of the services. On weekdays there would be morning prayers at home, for the assembled family and domestic staff. Lower down the social ladder, what has been termed 'the black-coated proletariat' of clerks, shop assistants, commercial travellers, and teachers were more likely to be chapel-goers, who were strong in the newer suburbs like Lewisham or Ilford, and for whom, like their Anglican contemporaries, the preacher was all-important and sometimes attracted very large congregations. Religion was, indeed, a powerful social cement bonding the respectable classes together in a code of outward decorum.[64] It also no doubt provided the impulse for much of the philanthropic concern for suffering of all kinds, manifested in the 1860s in some 640 charitable agencies whose incomes reflected the enormous scale of mid-Victorian charitable activities in London.[65]

In the 1880s, however, the façade of this religious concensus was beginning to break down. A census conducted by the *Daily News* in 1902–3 showed that throughout the whole of London less than one-fifth of the adult population attended any Christian church — a very large fall since an earlier count made in 1886. Attendances did of course vary greatly from one district to another — those at the Church of England, for instance, from 34 per cent in South Kensington down to less than 5 per cent in the East End; and everywhere women outnumbered men, though not greatly.[66] Although religious observance was still an outward sign of a family's respectability, respectability itself was becoming less important. In the 'Naughty Nineties' the moral earnestness and puritanism of evangelical Christianity were no longer congenial; and with the Prince of Wales setting a new social tone, the pursuit of pleasure became the open objective of many within those classes able to afford to indulge themselves.

For a start, the home itself was more comfortable than hitherto. By the end of the century many suburban houses built during the previous two generations were equipped with gas (for lighting only), mains water (though the supply was often still intermittent and running hot water was a rarity), and water closets. Cheap domestic service was still plentiful — in the 1890s a live-in servant was only paid between £15 and £20 per annum, or sometimes less[67] — so middle-class families had the time and means for amusements within the home. Here the piano was often the focal point, with ballads and music-hall songs on weekdays and hymns on Sunday evenings. Charades and all manner of family games were popular, while beyond the confines of the home there were walks in the parks, and the new craze of bicycling. In many places local clubs for tennis, croquet, or badminton flourished, and within doors, perhaps at the church hall, there were amateur dramatic and literary and debating societies.[68]

For the majority of middle-class families who did not keep a carriage, all activities further afield were largely dependent on buses, trams, and the district and metropolitan and main-line railways. Shopping was a constant preoccupation, and although most of the everyday kind was done locally, with tradesmen in attendance to take orders, the existence of London's unique public transport network made possible the rapid success of large new department stores. William Whiteley of Bayswater can claim to have invented the genre in the 1870s, but most of them were clustered in adjacent parts of Oxford Street and Regent Street, with outcrops near Marble Arch (Selfridge's), Knightsbridge (Harrods), and Kensington High Street.

Greater mobility within London which was such an important feature of late Victorian times was also a sine qua non for the success of the new museums and galleries (heavily concentrated on the estate of the Great Exhibition Commissioners at South Kensington), which must have so greatly enriched the lives of their millions of visitors, as also did the Regent's Park zoo. The golf clubs which proliferated in the outer suburbs in the 1890s, when motor cars were still a rarity, must have depended on the railways for the safe arrival of their clientele; and so too did the line of seaside towns along the South Coast to which middle-class Londoners resorted for day trips and annual holidays.[69]

Likewise the nature of metropolitan theatrical entertainment was much affected by advances in transport, for the rise of the modern 'respectable' West End theatre from the 1860s coincided roughly with the building of the early metropolitan railway lines and the multiplication of suburban train services. For around a generation after about 1830 many of the respectable middle classes had stayed away from the theatre: the sometimes rowdy behaviour of the vast audiences at the two royal patent theatres or at the quasi-licit minor theatres was distasteful, as was any form of mixing with the lower orders. But in 1843 (when free trade was in the ascendant) the monopoly on the presentation of spoken drama hitherto enjoyed by Drury Lane and Covent Garden was abolished. Henceforth the Lord Chamberlain granted licences for theatres where drama was presented, and also examined and if necessary censored the plays there, while the Justices of the Peace continued (as they had since 1737) to license and regulate places where music and dancing were provided.[70]

After the Act of 1843 music halls and theatres developed separately under these two regulatory codes. The halls operated under magistrates' licences and evolved out of pubs and singing saloons such as Evans's Supper Rooms in Covent Garden, where men ate and drank at long tables to an accompaniment of singing and comic turns performed on a stage. From this developed purpose-built music halls (of which the Canterbury of 1848 in Lambeth, formerly a pub, was the prototype), the tables and chairs of the dining area being gradually superseded by fixed seats. Drinking was always an important ingredient in their popularity, but takings at the door eventually became the main source of revenue, particularly in the great West End variety theatres like the Palace or the Coliseum (now the home of English National Opera).[71]

Meanwhile theatres in the West End presented 'legitimate' drama (much of it ever-popular melodrama) under licences from the Lord Chamberlain; and Covent Garden (rebuilt in 1858 after a fire) gradually superseded Her Majesty's (previously the Queen's or King's Theatre) in the Haymarket as the headquarters of grand opera in London. These theatres catered primarily for middle-class audiences whose 'respectable' behaviour was very different from that of the music halls' clientele: eating and drinking in the auditorium was not permitted. Marie and Squire Bancroft were the pioneers in this 'gentrification' of the West End theatres,[72] the process being much assisted by the formation of Shaftesbury Avenue and Charing Cross Road in the 1880s and the building within twenty years of nearly a dozen new theatres there. The audiences were mainly drawn from the fashionable or the respectable suburban middle classes and from visitors to the metropolis, and the West End became synonymous with refined and sophisticated shows, many of them presented by great actor-managers such as Beerbohm Tree or Sir Henry Irving.

It was now acceptable for women (appropriately escorted) to dine out, and often an evening in town was completed by dinner at one of the new restaurants like the Criterion in Piccadilly Circus or the Café Royal in Regent Street. The latter was first opened in the 1860s, and in the 1890s became the favourite meeting place of artists and writers such as Whistler, Sickert, Augustus John, Beardsley, Oscar Wilde, and Max Beerbohm, who (with many others) gave London its famous *fin-de-siècle* cultural reputation.[73]

By that time, however, a formidable challenger to the prosperity of both the music halls and the theatres had appeared: moving films. The first short movies were exhibited in the halls and variety theatres, and the first purpose-built cinema in Britain was opened near Victoria in 1905. By 1911 there were ninety-four cinemas containing 55,000 seats in the whole of London, and a few music halls were already converting to cinema use. At about the same time Joe Lyons was providing appropriately cheap refreshments at his teashops, the first of which was opened in Piccadilly in 1894.[74]

All these new modes of middle-class life resulted in a gradual loosening of the social constraints previously imposed by respectable codes of behaviour; and during the last quarter of the nineteenth century Victorian women began to make their distinctive voices heard. There was a very slow erosion of the idea that their horizons should be limited to the home, important changes in their legal status were made, and educational opportunities (notably the foundation of Queen's College in Harley Street and of what became Bedford College) led on in 1880 to the admission of the first women to degrees at London University.[75] In the field of politics women did not have the right to vote in parliamentary elections, although they could do so at the local government level. Peaceful but ineffective agitation for the vote led in 1903 to the establishment of the Women's Social and Political Union by Mrs Emmeline Pankhurst. This was in Manchester, but much of the increasingly violent and perhaps counter-productive activities of the WSPU were necessarily conducted in London, outside Downing Street, Buckingham Palace, and even within the Houses of Parliament. After the outbreak of war in 1914 the suffragette campaign was called off for the duration, and in 1918 women over the age of 30 were finally and without opposition given the vote.

The advantages gained thereby did not, perhaps, prove as great or as immediate as many women had hoped; and notable among the many surviving bastions of masculine defence were the gentlemen's clubs of Pall Mall and St James's. Many of these clubs had been founded between about 1815 and 1835, but between the early 1880s and 1914 there was another great proliferation of them, and their numbers virtually doubled.[76] In these luxurious rendezvous for groups of well-heeled gentlemen united by common tastes and social background, the comfortable amenities of home could be enjoyed without the patterns of behaviour often imposed there by women, and at much less expense. In their Edwardian heyday the total membership of such clubs may have amounted to around 100,000. These aristocrats, statesmen, service officers, clergy, gentlemen, professional men, and men of business and finance of all kinds were amongst the most influential people in the whole nation. It is now necessary to look at the mechanics of this influence.

19

The Imperial and Global Metropolis

In 1851 London's position in the nation and in the world at large manifested itself at the Great Exhibition of the Works of All Nations, which was held in Joseph Paxton's glass and iron Crystal Palace in Hyde Park — the first-ever international exhibition, implicitly proclaiming British pre-eminence as the workshop of the world, and probably unique amongst its many successors in that it actually made a profit. It was visited by some 6,000,000 people (equivalent to over a third of the total population of England), many of whom travelled to the capital by special excursion trains from all over the country. Some thirty years later London's pride of place was likewise tacitly acknowledged in a different way when an international conference accepted the meridian passing through the Royal Observatory at Greenwich as the prime meridian whence all longitudes were measured, and on which Standard Time throughout the world became based. Later still the celebration of Queen Victoria's Golden and Diamond Jubilees (1887 and 1897) drew attention far and wide to London as the hub and capital of the British Empire — an idea first consciously expressed in 1867 at the time of the highly successful State visit of the Sultan of Turkey and the Viceroy of Egypt.[1]

The members of the élite who ran this metropolitan civilization belonged overwhelmingly to the service sector of the national economy:* it can, indeed, be safely conjectured that in such citadels of the élite as the clubs of Pall Mall there were very few industrialists amongst the members. In mid-Victorian and Edwardian times much of the general growth of service employment which took place throughout the nation was concentrated in the South East Region, where by 1911 over half of all the employment was in services of one kind or another. (In London itself the proportion was of course already much higher.) Although much of this employment was in domestic service, and in transport and distribution, almost a quarter of the increased service employment in the region nevertheless accrued from the professions, Government and defence, and banking and commerce. So by 1911 the South East Region contained well over a third (38 per cent) of all employment

---

* i.e. transport, distribution, banking, commerce, insurance, professions, Government and defence, and miscellaneous (including domestic service)—everything except manufacturing, mining, and agriculture.

throughout Great Britain in those fields. And London, and above all the City, was the heart through which powerful impulses circulated not only throughout the region but throughout many parts of the entire globe.[2]

Although London's share of British visible exports began to falter in the second half of the nineteenth century, the macroeconomic tide was nevertheless in other respects flowing strongly in favour of the metropolis. Just as rising agricultural productivity and industrialization had in earlier times enabled a larger proportion of the population to work and live in towns and had in the long run greatly raised living standards, so now the same underlying principle of the division of labour from which much industrial change had already been derived led naturally on to growing specialization and expertise in the service sector of the economy. The rise of what Professor Harold Perkin has called 'professional society', based on the human capital of specialized expertise rather than on entrepreneurial and competitive capitalism, was the continuation and culmination of the processes of industrialization.[3] Much of this expertise was London-based, where the service sector was so heavily concentrated.

A concomitant of this growth of service-sector expertise was the development of large-scale organizations. Things got bigger, and also more complicated: railways, for instance, replaced stagecoaches, the bits of paper called bills on London became an international currency, and from its headquarters in St Martin's le Grand the Post Office — Britain's first giant bureaucracy — managed the conveyance of mail around the Empire and the world. Communications were revolutionized not only by the railways but by the introduction of the penny post in 1840, and by the electric telegraph line and the telephone (all by 1914 part of the Post Office's domain). The centralizing effects of these new systems of communication find expression in the success of the 'New Journalism' of the 1890s, epitomized in Alfred Harmondsworth's *Daily Mail*, founded in 1896. News and information collected by electrical and wireless telegraphy and printed by mass-production methods was regurgitated out from London all over the country by the nightly newspaper-trains; and when in 1902 the *Daily Mail*, already having a circulation of over 1,000,000 copies, invaded the heartland of the provinces and started to print in Manchester as well as London, the whole contents of each issue being telegraphed thither nightly, Fleet Street virtually dominated what people read about the world around them.[4]

In the ever-shifting balance between metropolis and provinces there was above all the influence of Government itself, the operations of which were enormously extended in the nineteenth century. Even in the heyday of Victorian liberalism the range of Government action in such fields as education or public health was constantly being enlarged, and most of the administrative action which arose therefrom was directed from London. Between 1881 and 1901 the number of officers, clerks, and messengers employed by the Government in London more than doubled; and even after massive Edwardian social legislation had laid the foundations of the Welfare State by establishing old age pensions, health and unemployment insurance, and Labour Exchanges, most civil servants were still employed in London.[5]

The metropolis was also the natural home for the professions and the intellectuals. Between 1800 and 1914 some sixty collective organizations, each in some way regulating its own particular expertise, were established — of solicitors, architects, pharmacists, actuaries, and numerous sorts of engineer, to name only a few[6] — and nearly all of them had their headquarters in London. 'The importance of the professions and the professional classes can hardly be overrated,' wrote a mid-Victorian lawyer, 'they form the head of the great English middle class, maintain its tone of independence, keep up to the mark its standard of morality, and direct its intelligence.'[7] Their numbers were growing proportionately faster than that of the population as a whole, their respective skills becoming more complex and specialized, and their national influence ever greater. In the field of science University College (1828) provided the prototype for the red-brick universities established in many provincial towns during the second half of the nineteenth century, and its hospital (1834) quickly achieved distinction in medicine. The University of London itself, established in 1836 as an examining and degree-conferring body, had by 1914 evolved into the largest centre of higher learning in Britain, exerting an influence on the intellectual life of the nation almost comparable with that of Oxford and Cambridge, several of its constituent institutions and colleges — notably the London School of Economics (1895) and Imperial College of Science, Technology and Medicine (1907) — having quickly gained formidable authority in their respective fields. Later in the twentieth century Bloomsbury became the permanent home of the university, as also of the famous Bloomsbury Group of writers and artists, while the St James's and Pall Mall area maintained its hold on the picture dealers, much strengthened after 1868 by the residence of the Royal Academy at Burlington House in Piccadilly. For the middle-class intelligentsia in general, London was indeed the intellectual and cultural capital of the nation.

It was, however, above all from the City — that 'world within itself centred in the heart of the metropolis', as a contemporary referred to it in the 1850s[8] — that metropolitan influences exerted themselves most strongly. In the Victorian years its centuries of commercial knowledge and experience evolved into their most 'perfect' form, its money market being described by Walter Bagehot in 1873 as 'by far the greatest combination of economical power and economical delicacy that the world has ever seen'.[9]

In essence the City comprised (to borrow the words of its recent historian, R. C. Michie) a series of interrelated markets providing for the requirements of producers and consumers, lenders and borrowers, experts and inexperts — a national and international clearing house for goods, finance, and expertise. Like everything else there, the City's two oldest economic activities — manufacture and commerce — were changing rapidly in Victorian times. In 1881 a third of all firms in the City were still in manufacturing (many in printing and clothes-making), but they were already declining in number, while another third were in commercial services (merchants, dealers, brokers, importers and exporters, and agents of all kinds). Due to the development of the railways and of telegraphic and telephonic communications, London's physical trade, in which goods actually passed through the innumerable warehouses in the City and/or the Port, was becoming relatively less important (despite the more than tenfold increase in the tonnage of foreign trade entering the Port between 1820 and 1901), and by 1913 London handled only 19 per cent of British exports and 33 per cent of imports. For the same reason, however, office trade — the organization of trade worldwide and of the shipping of goods — was growing, and the City was establishing itself as the centre of the world's communications network.[10]

Credit being the lifeblood of commerce, the City by the early nineteenth century had made itself the nation's short-term money market for the mobilization of unused liquid funds, mainly through the circulation of bills of exchange. After about 1850 London-based joint-stock national banking groups such as Barclays began to dominate the movement of short-term funds within Britain, particularly after the spectacular collapse of the discount house of Overend, Gurney and Company in 1866. Although growing use of cheques began to supersede inland bills of exchange as the general means of trade payment, the London bill was nevertheless becoming the principal means for the finance and settlement of international trade. At first bills were used only in connexion with Britain's own overseas dealings, but by 1914 well over half the commercial bills outstanding in London were of foreign origin and drawn in respect of trade otherwise unconnected with Britain. New merchant banks of overseas origin and numerous colonial and foreign banks, each with their own specialities of financing trade by country or commodity, had offices or often their headquarters in the City, for in 1914 the bill on London was, according to a Canadian banker, 'a better currency than gold itself, more economical, more readily transmissible, more efficient, ... by means of the bill on London not only the vast commerce of Britain herself, but also a substantial share of the purely foreign traffic of the world is financed and liquidated'.[11]

The financing of the Government's need for capital was another long-standing City activity, and as with the provision of commercial credit, so here too the field of operations began to spread all over the world. Until the mid-nineteenth century the Stock Exchange had been primarily a market in Government stocks, but between 1850 and 1913 the Government financed itself without long-term borrowing, and the national debt actually fell. So jobbers and brokers turned elsewhere for business, mainly in the development of those complex new infrastructures which required large amounts of fixed capital: railways, gas, water, electricity, telegraphs, and telephones. Meanwhile loans to foreign governments by means of stocks and bonds had burgeoned in the 1820s, and this led naturally on to investment in foreign infrastructure enterprises, particularly in such 'new' developing countries as the United States, Australia, or those of South America. Foreign companies like North American railroad corporations frequently raised loans by stocks and bonds issued in London, or British companies were set up (usually in the City) to own and run operations abroad such as South African gold mines or Argentinian railways or Indian tea.[12] Between 1815 and the mid-1850s capital exports had amounted to some £8,000,000 to £10,000,000 per annum, but thereafter they grew rapidly (though irregularly) to some £200,000,000 per annum by 1914. By that time foreign assets amounted to 33 per cent of all British wealth,[13] and the London capital market was by far the most important in the world for international borrowing (and, incidentally, better organized than its nearest rival in New York).[14]

By providing a market for securities, where assets could always be quickly bought or sold, the Stock Exchange formed the crucial link between the City's other markets operating in the fields of commerce, credit, and capital. In these fields the men of the City earned their bread by acting as intermediaries between buyer and seller or between lender and borrower. Other City men made their living by selling their expertise, which became increasingly important as the national and international economy grew ever more complex. One of the oldest such skills was the management of the shipping on which so much commerce depended. By 1914 about half the world total of merchant shipping was British-owned and -managed, and although many of these ships never entered British ports, much of the fleet was managed from the City, with its advantages of access to worldwide communications and closeness to numerous customers for its marine services.[15]

Shipping had long ago generated another City skill: marine insurance, which was still mainly done by the independent underwriters of Lloyd's. Faced with competition from new joint-stock insurance companies, however, they had taken on one-off or unusual risks and reinsurance (mainly against fire); but marine insurance still provided their main business, and by around 1900 Lloyd's and British companies still handled some two-thirds of the world total of it, mostly from the City. In the early nineteenth century London also dominated fire and life insurance through joint-stock companies or mutual societies, but under the challenge of such other insurance centres as Edinburgh and Norwich many British insurance men took on business all over the world. By 1900, for instance, British companies provided nearly a quarter of all fire insurance in the United States. Although the domination of the City in insurance was not as great as in banking or trading in stocks and shares, many of the ever-larger companies nevertheless found it necessary to locate there for much the same reasons as also motivated the shipping companies, plus the advantages of propinquity for the efficient management of the enormous investment portfolios which accrued from their premium income.[16]

Insurance itself generated other specialized skills, notably those of shipping surveyors and loss adjusters; and many other City activities had much the same effect. Accountants, liquidators, company lawyers, and armies of clerks and book-keepers of every description, all had their place in the City and found a market for the sale of their expertise.[17]

By 1914 the City was the colossus of commerce and credit throughout the Empire (and also of much of the rest of the world) — the nodal point of a colonial urban system in which the economies of the metropolis and of such distant cities as Calcutta or Sydney and their respective hinterlands complemented one another and were heavily interdependent. In parts of London the status of imperial capital was very apparent in the building fabric. Gentlemen's clubhouses such as the East India United Service, the Oriental, and numerous others now defunct; Whitehall's Colonial Office and India Office, and the offices of the 'colonial agencies', heavily concentrated in the Strand; stores like the Army and Navy or the Home and Colonial; even the Tate Gallery (built on Henry Tate's sugar fortune); and above all the Imperial Institute, with its conference hall and displays of Empire products and its 280-foot high tower dominating the landscape of South Kensington — all these were monuments to the mightiness of the imperial metropolis.[18]

This formidable structure was built upon the rock of the pound sterling, in which almost all London's transactions were conducted, irrespective of their amount or of whether they related to business within or outside the imperial orbit. In the City itself, at the very heart of the system, there were at the turn of the century no less than 40,000 firms, wherein worked over 350,000 people, around four-fifths of them in the service sector;[19] This service sector which London so dominated was an active and dynamic, not a passive or dependent, part of the national economy, constantly improving its performance by specialization, improved productivity, and the development of new markets overseas; and one result of this was that in the evolution of its all-important financial institutions Britain (so it is now thought) had a lead of around a century over France, her principal commercial competitor.[20]

In no other country in the world was the service sector of the economy so important as it was in Britain. If Britain in Victorian times was the workshop of the world, the City was its clearing house, without which the economic development of the nation, and of many places overseas too, would have been very different. Throughout the whole of the nineteenth century, and indeed right down to the present day, the value of United Kingdom visible exports did not exceed that of imports, and hence there was always an adverse balance of commodity trade. In the same period, however, earnings from business services of all kinds, in which the City was pre-eminent, and income from overseas investments, grew prodigiously, particularly from the 1870s.[21] By the 1880s total invisible earnings amounted to the equivalent of over half the value of all UK imports, or to three-quarters of the value of exports; and it was only through contributions of this order of magnitude that an increasingly favourable balance of payments was achieved.[22] In the words of Mr Geoffrey Ingham, 'The City's commercial capitalism gradually became a prop for the economy as a whole.'[23]

But the City's influence extended far beyond its contribution to commercial and financial balances, increasingly important as these were when manufacturing exports began to falter after about 1870 and the bills for imported food were rising inexorably in parallel with the growth of population. From its headquarters in the City, service-sector capitalism provided the vital link between the economy at large and the decision-making political and administrative processes of Westminster and Whitehall. From the later seventeenth century the landed interest which formed the traditional basis of power and what P. J. Cain and A. G. Hopkins have called the 'gentlemanly capitalists' of the City had become increasingly closely associated with each other. In the higher reaches of the City the interests of merchants trading overseas or of bankers such as the Hoares or the Barings or the Rothschilds, or of rich nabobs returning from the Indies, gradually merged with those of the landed gentry and aristocracy. Power belonged to the élites of the City, the Bank of England, and the Treasury, with the gentlemanly capitalists of the City gradually exercising more and more influence over national economic policy. In the long run the men of the City were the main beneficiaries of the return to the gold standard (1819), the establishment of free trade, and strict Gladstonian budgets; and 'What was good for the City was good for the nation' became a widely accepted axiom.[24]

With sterling, backed by the Bank and the Treasury, becoming the principal currency of world trade, much of the impulse behind the growth of British foreign investment, commerce, and migration, and of the imperialist expansion associated therewith, emanated from the City and London in general, particularly after 1850. Just as they had in the early eighteenth century provided most of the capital needed for the Government funds, so between 1865 and 1914 residents of London and its environs subscribed over half the shares of British companies trading overseas, as well as continuing to invest heavily in Government Securities (Plate 35). 'Most of the direct investment overseas of the late Victorian age', we are authoritatively told by Cain and Hopkins, 'flowed from the metropolis.'[25]

When the power of the landed interest began to decline in the 1870s and 1880s and exports faced mounting foreign competition, the balance of strength in the partnership of power tilted further towards the City, where the number of gentlemen active in the prosperous service sector was growing rapidly in Victorian times. The continuing strength of the City-Bank-Treasury connection was demonstrated by the Baring crisis of 1890, when, after this most prestigious firm had got itself into difficulties through excessive loans to Argentina, strong action by the Bank of England backed by the Government prevented a world liquidity crisis.[26] Some of the lineaments of the modern Establishment were beginning to emerge.

Yet despite — or perhaps because of — its crucial role in the nation's economic development, the City has been much criticized for its performance in the Victorian and Edwardian years. Specifically, it has been claimed that through the magnitude of capital exports after about 1850 Britain's home industry was starved of investment.[27] Local and family connections and retained profits were, however, the main sources for 'start up' and small-scale industry, which was often labour- rather than capital-intensive;[28] and the handful of provincial stock exchanges which grew up in the nineteenth century provided capital locally, particularly for their own local specialities, such as Glasgow for mining securities.[29] Despite the relative weakness of the links between the City and industry compared with those between City and Government, there is little evidence of unsatisfied domestic demand for industrial capital; on the contrary there is reason to think that through the strict management of Government finances and the declining profitability of investment in either agriculture or in domestic infrastructures such as railways there was even a shortage of opportunities for the use of surplus capital at home.

Moreover, foreign investments, particularly in the infrastructures of undeveloped parts of the world, did often benefit domestic industry ultimately by opening up new markets for British manufactured goods.[30] On the other hand, however, it is the case that whereas in the years 1870–1914 Britain's two main industrial competitors, Germany and the USA, invested around 12 per cent of their annual income at home, Britain invested only 7 per cent domestically, with another 4 or 5 per cent going abroad. This high rate of foreign investment was unfavourable to domestic industrial growth because the British free trade system without which foreign borrowers would have been unable to repay their debts also laid the country open to the competition of foreign manufactured goods and thus reduced domestic demand and growth.[31]

More generally, the close relationship between the Treasury, the Bank of England, and other important components of the City has been associated by some writers with the allegedly conservative and non-industrial attitudes of the gentlemanly British Establishment, which is held responsible for the nation's supposed long-term economic decline since around 1870.[32] In recent years, however, these ideas have been severely buffeted by, amongst others, Professor W. D. Rubinstein.[33] This 'culture critique', as he calls it, is based on the assumption that Britain was fundamentally an industrial economy which began to decline after about 1870, mainly as a result of the 'anti-industrial cultural spirit' prevalent in such places as the public schools and the corridors of gentlemanly power in Whitehall and the City. Rubinstein claims that, on the contrary, Britain's 'was *never* fundamentally an industrial and manufacturing economy; rather it was *always*, even at the height of the industrial revolution, essentially a commercial, financial, and service-based economy whose comparative advantage always lay with commerce and finance'.[34] And he has demolished the idea that the public schools turned manufacturers' sons against going into manufacturing: inherited family tradition and background, whether industrial, commercial, or professional, was always more important in the choice of career than classy attitudes picked up at school.[35]

London was of course the heart of this commercial, financial, and service-based economy. In around 1900 the capital was the seat of the most dynamic and successful element of the national economy, and the place where a large proportion of the national wealth was concentrated. Nor was this concentration new. We have already seen that as long ago as the early sixteenth century London was paying nearly ten times as much in taxation as the second city (Norwich), and the difference in wealth between the South-East and most of the rest of the country was even then already growing. London's centrality in the national economy antedates the industrial revolution (as commonly understood) by several centuries, was not challenged even while Britain was emerging as the world's first industrial power, and in the years thereafter has remained undiminished. The phenomenal growth of the capital in the second half of the nineteenth century — by 1901 20 per cent of the population of England and Wales lived in Greater London — reflected this ancient dominance. In the words of Professor Dyos, 'the shift of resources into the exploitation of the northern provinces, and others, in the eighteenth and nineteenth centuries might be represented simply as an interlude in a much larger historical trend'.[36] London had reasserted her long-standing pre-eminence, and was still the sun in the solar system of the nation — or, as is sometimes also claimed, its black hole sucking all things into its ever-voracious maw.

PART VI

The Uncertain Metropolis
1914–1997

INTRODUCTION

In 1914 Britain and its Empire stood at the height of their power. Sterling, controlled from Whitehall and the City, provided the global currency of international commerce, and economic and political forces generated in London diffused themselves to the furthest extremities of the world. Yet eighty years later — within the span of only a single long life — the Empire had sunk almost without trace, and Britain herself was often regarded as little more than an offshore island of continental Europe. The hitherto outward flow of economic and political impulses radiating out from Britain, and from London in particular, had largely reversed its direction — even the continued existence of sterling itself is now (1997) in doubt — and social cohesion was under severe strain in England. This transformation provides the background against which to view London's recent history. But the story of the metropolis is not loaded only with foreboding, for although the place and purpose of Britain (and therefore of London) in the world may be uncertain, the City has nevertheless maintained a leading (though much changed) position as a global financial market. In the vast new field of international mass air travel London has made itself the largest centre in the world, tourism has become a major new service industry, and most of its peoples enjoy standards of living unimaginable in 1914.

The World War of 1914–18 marked the onset of the twentieth-century transformation of British fortunes. The air attacks made on London by night by the German Zeppelins (gas-filled airships which cruised at a height of some 10,000–15,000 feet and at a speed of around 50 miles an hour) and the raids made by aeroplanes killed some 600 to 800 people in the capital and injured between 1,000 and 2,000 more. Although their military impact was negligible, these attacks nevertheless symbolized a new realization that the security of the nation, and of London in particular — less than 100 miles from the Front — was no longer inviolable. Both at home and in the trenches Victorian attitudes as well as civilians and soldiers were dying, and after that cataclysmic upheaval the social order resettled in a new mould.[1]

20

The Inter-war Years 1919–1939

The decades of truce between the two World Wars provided a transitional stage between solid and (by modern standards) slow-moving Victorian England and the rise of the restless Welfare State of the post-1945 years. They witnessed a great increase in the scope and scale of Government action, notably in the fields of housing, health, social services, and transport, but full-blown nationalization was still a thing of the future; and in industry and commerce there was a corresponding growth in the size of many companies. London and its peoples continued their massive outward spread, for between 1921 and 1939 the population of Greater London grew from 7,300,000 to 8,600,000. This increase, already by 1927 equivalent to a brand-new city the size of Manchester,[1] was concentrated in the outer suburbs, where the population of numerous such places as Bexley, Harrow, or Chingford grew by over 50 per cent in both the 1920s and 1930s.[2] Many of the residents there had moved out from the County of London, where the population continued to fall (as it had since 1901–11) by around 500,000 between 1921 and 1939. Others were inward migrants, some from such distant areas as Northumberland or Glamorgan, while the remainder accrued from natural increase. Similar movements of population were also taking place in the Home Counties (Middlesex, Kent, Surrey, Hertfordshire, and Essex) which surrounded Greater London.[3] By 1937 the national drift to the South-East had prompted the Government to set up the Barlow Commission to review the distribution of population and industry in Britain — an inquiry which, according to *The Economist*, was really 'a Royal Commission on the Enormity of London'.[4]

With 8,000,000 people living in Greater London in 1931 — equivalent to one-fifth of the population of England and Wales — the metropolis provided a huge market for consumer goods. Between 1870 and 1935 real wages in London doubled, far more women were in paid employment in the inter-war years than hitherto — family incomes being correspondingly increased — and the average number of children per family in all social classes was falling. More people had more money to spend than ever before. New industries in such fields as electrical engineering and motor vehicle production sprang up around the capital, but in 1921 half the total employment in Greater London was in the service sector, which is generally less affected by cyclical economic fluctuations than manufacturing. So even at the depth of the Depression in 1932 the unemployment rate in London (13.1 per cent) was far below that of the country as a whole (22 per cent), and in the words of one authority the capital and its surrounding territories 'appeared as an island of growth amidst a general sea of industrial gloom'.[5] The population was still ethnically and culturally homogeneous, and apart from the General Strike of 1926 relatively peaceful industrial relations usually prevailed (thanks in part, no doubt, to the high level of unemployment in the provinces). Stability and vitality were still the hallmarks of the metropolitan economy, as they had been for so long.[6]

New Ingredients

The Great War was a powerful solvent of traditional social attitudes and mores. Women did all sorts of hitherto unfeminine things, such as working in munition and light engineering factories, or 'manning' the buses, the ministries, and the banks — by 1918 nearly a third of Lloyd's Bank staff were women; and their long campaign (which had been suspended during the war) for the parliamentary vote was at last successful — also in 1918 — though only for women over 30 years of age. Office typing, shorthand, and clerical work began to rival domestic service as the main field of women's paid work, and between 1901 and 1921 the number of female servants in the County of London fell by over a third.[7]

In the inter-war years American mass-consumption culture began to pervade much of British life, and particularly that of London. Ever since Gordon Selfridge of Chicago had opened his new store in Oxford Street in 1909, followed in 1910 by F. W. Woolworth, American influence had percolated through the West End, the postwar rebuilding of Regent Street, for instance, reflecting shop managers' insistence on large windows and open-plan display areas. In Park Lane the great aristocratic mansions of Grosvenor House and Dorchester House had been replaced by American-style hotels, and large chunks of mainly Georgian Grosvenor and Berkeley Squares had been rebuilt with blocks of service apartments. The cinema, too, both in the exotic architectural styles of the picture palaces which sprang up in the West End and throughout the suburbs, and in the predominantly Hollywood-made films which they showed, brought American mass culture to the people of the largest centre of consumption in the world outside America itself. Much of the commercial advertising which proliferated in the 1920s and 1930s displayed its transAtlantic origins, J. Walter Thompson, for instance, having come to London in 1919. And most of the predominantly American-owned foreign companies which established themselves in Britain did so in and around London. The factories of Hoover, Gillette, and Firestone along the Great West Road were cases in point; and the Ford Motor Company started production at its gigantic assembly-line plant at Dagenham.[8]

Many of these inter-war innovations were based on electric light and power. In 1883 Thomas Edison had built the world's first power station near Holborn

Viaduct, but the early generators could only supply very small areas, and a multiplicity of undertakings (seventy in 1917), publicly or privately owned, had sprung up throughout London. Electricity had, however, been successfully used to power the new tube railways and for the District line, for the last of which the massive Lots Road Power Station beside the Thames at Chelsea had been built in 1902–4. The war of 1914–18 greatly enlarged the use of electricity, most of the new small arms and munition factories which sprouted up around London being powered by it, and with the building of more big power stations (notably at Battersea) and the establishment of the national grid in the early 1930s, consumption of electricity both industrially and domestically grew enormously in the inter-war years.[9]

With the almost unlimited flexibility provided by this new form of energy, industry could settle wherever it wanted. As London and its environs provided the largest centre of demand many new consumer industries started up there rather than in the impoverished North, and between 1924 and 1935 Greater London's share of national industrial output rose substantially. Besides the factories which strung themselves along the Great West Road, the semi-derelict 200-acre site of the British Empire Exhibition of 1924–5 at Wembley was quickly colonized by dozens of small new industrial units. A little later much the same thing happened at nearby Park Royal, where, as well as many small manufacturing enterprises, there were motorcar makers and a gigantic new Guinness brewery (Plate 41). Film studios found a natural home around the metropolis, making the ring of them at Elstree, Denham, Pinewood, Ealing, and elsewhere synonymous with British cinema production. Inevitably, too, the infant broadcasting industry made its headquarters in the centre of the capital. Such, indeed, was London's prosperity in relation to that of the rest of the nation that between 1923 and 1939 something like two-thirds of all the new jobs created in Great Britain were in Greater London.[10]

Homes and lives fit for heroes?

Not all of London prospered, however, and in the inner areas there was widespread unemployment and poverty, particularly in the East End concentrations of casual and sweated labour, where the late Victorian structure of the labour market survived with little change. This was also the stronghold of metropolitan support for the Labour party, the organization of which in the capital had been greatly improved by the formation of the London Labour Party in 1914; and in the local government elections of 1919 Labour was able to win control of the East End borough councils and boards of guardians of the poor law there. For the first time within the capital Labour now had power, and under the leadership of its first socialist mayor, George Lansbury (1859–1940), Poplar began to put socialism into practice at local level. But in 1920 the postwar boom collapsed and the worst depression for decades had a devastating effect in the borough, where casual labour in the docks and along the riverside dominated employment. The depression was of course a national, not a local, problem, however unevenly its impact was felt in different parts of the country or of the metropolis. But the Government did nothing to help poor areas meet their much-increased costs of relief, so (after a year of abortive discussions with Whitehall) the Poplar borough councillors refused to be constrained any longer within the established local government system. In order to mitigate the effect of the soaring local rate demands caused by the cost of poor relief for the unemployed, they refused to continue to collect rates on behalf of central authorities like the LCC, whose funds came from London as a whole. And in the fullness of time thirty Poplar councillors were imprisoned for contempt of court at the instigation of the LCC (Plate 54).[11]

There (in Brixton and Holloway gaols) they remained for six weeks, attracting nationwide attention and embarrassment for the Government, until they were unconditionally released in October 1921. By that time mass unemployment had compelled the Minister of Health to allow the grant of out-relief to the able-bodied unemployed without their having to undergo either a workhouse or labour test, by the end of the year an Act for pooling the costs of metropolitan outrelief had been passed, and for twenty months the Poplar Guardians defied the Government over the levels of relief which they paid. But throughout 1922–3 the Government avoided taking on Poplar again, and the dispute over relief was ultimately settled in Poplar's favour by the Labour Government of 1924.[12]

'Poplarism' — defined in the addenda to the *Shorter Oxford English Dictionary* as 'the policy of giving generous or (as was alleged) extravagant outdoor relief, like that practised by the Board of Guardians of Poplar in 1919 or later', and by another authority as 'the use of local government by the labour movement as a base to defend working-class standards of living...'[13] — was also practised in some measure in other East End boroughs (sometimes referred to in the press as 'Little Moscows') such as Bethnal Green and Stepney. Like Chartism in the 1830s and 1840s its strength depended on mass support and its successes or failures on defiance of established authority; and although both movements were at the time widely denounced as revolutionary, most of the aims of both of them came in later years to be almost universally accepted. For better or worse, however, direct action was not to prove the most effective vehicle for the advancement of working-class interests. Although the nine-day General Strike in May 1926 commanded substantial support in London, particularly amongst transport, printing, and electricity workers, determined action by the Government withstood the challenge; and the strike proved to be the last massive organized protest for some years.[14]

By 1936, however, the rise of the Nazis to power in Germany had been echoed, albeit faintly, in England by Sir Oswald Mosley's blackshirted British Union of Fascists, whose provocative marches through the East End with its large Jewish population led to huge counter-demonstrations organized by the Communist party. Alarming riots, barricades, and street fighting ensued, but the blackshirts never commanded mass support, and the disorders had no lasting results.[15]

Any repetition of Poplarism had been made much more difficult in 1929, when the Government abolished the boards of guardians and their unions and transferred poor law functions to the county councils. Despite much work by charitable and voluntary social agencies and by some of the borough councils, widespread poverty persisted in many inner London working-class areas, notably Poplar, Bethnal Green, Bermondsey, Stepney, and Notting Dale in North Kensington. In 1934 an independent report recorded that 500,000 people in London were still living below the poverty line as Charles Booth had defined it in the survey which he had made forty years previously in late Victorian times. So despite generally rising standards of life and labour, great contrasts in material circumstance still abounded between different parts of London in the inter-war years.[16]

In 1934 Labour gained control of the LCC for the first time, and retained possession of it until its abolition in 1965; and Labour also won over half of the twenty-eight metropolitan boroughs.[17] The leader of the Labour members of the LCC was Herbert Morrison, a Londoner born and bred and sometime mayor of Hackney, who since 1915 had been secretary of the London Labour Party — an arch-pragmatist ('a Fabian of Fabians', thought Beatrice Webb),[18] well aware that Labour could only win or retain power through the ballot box, and only with substantial support from middle-class voters — a very different kind of socialist from George Lansbury. Overbearing, not always popular even within his own party, and often disliked outside it, Morrison yet has some claim to the very rare (and perhaps unique) distinction of having for a few years (until 1940, when he entered the wartime Coalition Government) provided London with effective political leadership.

Under Labour the LCC's housing effort was switched from the cottage estates outside the County to slum clearance in the inner areas, and the number of people rehoused rose nearly fivefold. Four- to six-storey blocks of flats became the norm, nearly half of them situated in four boroughs: Camberwell, Lambeth, Lewisham, and Wandsworth. After the abolition of the poor law unions and the Metropolitan Asylums Board in 1930 the LCC took over more than sixty hospitals, which were re-equipped and modernized. More money was spent on education, health, and welfare; there were more and better parks and open spaces, brightened up with facilities such as cafés and tennis courts[19] — local government with a human face.

Much of this may seem rather small beer, but in a number of crucial fields the LCC's scope for action was either nil or severely limited. The major utilities of the docks, water, and electricity were all already in public control, not, however, of the elected metropolitan council but of ad hoc authorities (later known as quangos). More importantly, by the early 1920s not far short of half the people of Greater London lived outside the County of London (the area administered by the LCC), within which the population continued to fall. Enlargement of the County boundaries was therefore a sine qua non for the effective management of the whole metropolitan built-up area. In 1923, however, the Ullswater Royal Commission on London Government had recommended against any such change.[20] Conservatives were opposed to any Greater London Authority, and as Labour was never during the inter-war years in control of both the Government and the LCC at the same time, there was no chance of such a thing in the foreseeable future. So Morrison himself had had to abandon the idea of a wide-ranging metropolitan municipality when, as Minister of Transport in the second Labour Government (1929–31), he had been the architect of the most important quango of all: the London Passenger Transport Board.[21]

Hitherto there had been half a dozen often wastefully competing elements in London's transport system. The largest was the Combine, presided over by Lord Ashfield and Frank Pick, which managed most of the deep-level electric underground railways, the largest bus company, and several tramways.[22] There were also the Metropolitan Railway, the main-line railways' suburban services, the tramways, mostly owned by the LCC and other local authorities, and some sixty privately owned bus companies.[23] By 1933 the underground and Metropolitan railways had extended out far and wide (Plate 24), to Edgware (1924), Watford (1925), Morden (1926, the only important extension south of the Thames), Stanmore (1932), and Cockfosters (1933). Some of these extensions — notably those to Edgware and Cockfosters — were financed with the help of Government money made available to alleviate unemployment. South of the river the Southern Railway (formed in 1923 by the amalgamation of the Victorian companies) had by 1930 electrified all its suburban services, bringing nearly 250,000 passengers into central London every weekday morning.[24]

Thus the tentacles of metropolitan transport extended far beyond the County of London, and the unified control of it which all political parties agreed was necessary could not be provided by the LCC without an extension of its boundaries. Hence Morrison's London Passenger Transport Board (LPTB) of 1933: an independent and unsubsidized public authority with a monopoly of public transport throughout London, the services provided by the main-line railways being the only exception.[25]

Throughout the whole of the inter-war period there was no effective territorial planning of Greater London as a whole: within the LPTB area well over 100 different bodies were in 1938 exercising such exiguous planning powers as existed. The moguls of the Underground and Metropolitan companies had been able to generate new business by building railways beyond the existing urban frontier ('run the trains and they will come', LCC officers had realized as early as 1893), and great seas of suburbia had spread around the island of the County of London in such places as Morden, and in the Metroland areas of Neasden, Pinner, and Harrow.[26] Moreover the LCC had itself contributed to this dispersal of population by building its vast Out-County estate at Becontree in Essex, where between 1920 and 1938 over 25,000 dwellings, most of them cottages, provided accommodation for some 116,000 people; but for some years there were inadequate public transport and educational facilities (which the LCC had no power to provide outside its own boundaries) and little local employment until Ford's settled at nearby Dagenham in the early 1930s.[27] Elsewhere, however, the LCC encountered hostility in its search for Out-County housing sites, and so in frustration turned in on itself to its own beleaguered and demographically declining fieffdom, where it concentrated on slum clearance. But it was still aware of the implications of London's huge expansion, and in 1935 Morrison gave concrete expression to the idea of a green girdle around London by offering financial contributions to assist local authorities outside the County to buy or preserve open space for public access. By 1939 some 14,000 acres of Green Belt land had been acquired, and an important first step taken towards the physical control of the metropolis.[28]

Yet despite all the messy haphazard limitations of the inter-war metropolis, and in particular the problems for the future engendered by the social polarization which the outward movement of population greatly augmented, life for hosts of Londoners changed greatly for the better during the 1920s and 1930s. This, in retrospect, was the heyday of London's transport system, when the underground railways were equipped with fine new suburban stations (designed by Charles Holden), the famous 'bull's eye' station name-boards became as much a feature of the London scene below ground as the double-decker red motor buses were on the streets.[29] Trolleybuses were beginning to supersede trams, and the difficulties caused by private motor-car travel had hardly begun. More fundamentally, homes were more widely available to a large and growing section of the population than ever before or since. In the 1930s the average price of a freehold house in the outer suburbs of London was about £650–£750, but there were others as low as £350–£550. House ownership thus became a possibility for better-paid manual workers as well as clerical staff; and the houses or bungalows which they bought probably had water and electricity laid on and a patch of garden. In the words of Alan Jackson, the historian of what he calls 'Semi-Detached London', 'Finding a new home within their financial reach, many thousands had their living standards transformed; in a few short years, the sum of human happiness was immeasurably increased.'[30]

London and the World

In 1924–5 Britain's imperial greatness was celebrated by the British Empire Exhibition at Wembley. Its main purpose was to promote Empire trade, and some 27,000,000 visitors came to see it. Today Wembley Stadium, the annual venue for the Football Association's Cup Final match and for a miscellany of other large-scale events, provides almost the only visible trace of this forgotten piece of imperial history.[31]

At that time the Empire was still getting bigger (and continued to do so until 1937), but the real position of the mother country had changed fundamentally since the heyday of Victorian and Edwardian times. The war of 1914–18 had disrupted the international economy, and from being the world's creditor Britain had become a debtor heavily in hock to the ascendant power of the USA and the dollar. Many foreign investments acquired over the years through the City had been sold to help finance the war,[32] and invisible income, which had hitherto made good the deficit on the balance of commodity trade, fell dramatically. With the onset of the world depression in 1929 a chronic balance of payments problem emerged. The wealth needed to build up a new portfolio of foreign assets no longer existed in Britain, so the volume of overseas loans also fell.[33] To some extent, therefore, the City became more inward looking, and by 1938 UK Government loan stocks, i.e. the national debt, amounted to not far short of half the total value of all securities quoted on the Stock Exchange.[34]

But although Britain's place in the world was very different in the inter-war years, the institutional links of power between the élites of the City, the Bank of England, and the Treasury remained unchanged;[35] and so too did the pre-war Establishment of London-based gentlemanly service-sector capitalism, bureaucrats, and professional men. It was therefore natural that the overriding object of economic policy after the war was to restore the pre-war system,[36] based on global trust in the stability of the pound. Hence in 1925 the return to the gold standard (suspended since 1914) — that potent symbol of British supremacy — regardless of the consequences for industry and labour.[37]

The failure of this return to financial orthodoxy which, in the depth of the world slump, the final abandonment of the gold standard in 1931 represented, was a severe setback for the City and the Establishment in general. In 1932 free trade was abandoned in favour of tariffs on manufactured imports and preferential arrangements within the Empire. From this there emerged the Sterling Area, consisting of those countries, mostly within the Empire, which did most of their overseas trade in sterling, fixed their currencies in relation to the pound, and kept their reserves in sterling.[38] Although this new structure of world trade and finance did certainly amount to a considerable retreat for the City, and the gradual emergence of the dollar and New York as the dominant forces in the world's banking and commercial system was becoming clear, the Sterling Area was nevertheless the largest economic bloc in the world,[39] London was its headquarters, and British power within it was still strong — for many countries there was indeed no alternative to membership of it. Furthermore, the underlying criteria and priorities of Whitehall, the Bank, and the City financial Establishment — notably balanced budgets and a stable pound — still prevailed much as before.[40]

Within Britain itself London's power continued to grow, and the North–South balance to tilt towards London and the South. Between 1921 and 1937 the population of Britain as a whole grew by only 7 per cent while that of London and the Home Counties rose by 18 per cent, 1,000,000 of the latter growth being accounted for by internal migration.[41] By 1938 it was being said that there were

two nations within one. On the one hand a successful and expanding market; on the other a depressed and contracting one. The attraction of the one for the other grows accumulatively. Each new industry in the South requires a host of smaller satellite industries, and each new immigrant from the North or Wales represents increased purchasing power, and so the process gathers momentum.[42]

Moreover the metropolitan Establishment retained its domestic control of economic life, and despite the fall of invisible earnings was not submerged by manufacturing's rising share of national output. More of this industrial output was of course concentrated in the South-East, particularly in the new consumer-goods-oriented factory ring within a 20-mile or so radius of Central London.[43] The City was getting more effective in the financing of industry, mergers were producing larger companies, many with head offices in London,[44] — ICI and Vickers are cases in point — and in the 1920s and 1930s the number of companies in manufacturing and distribution quoted on the Stock Exchange more than doubled.[45]

The ability of the gentlemanly capitalists of London to adapt and survive was indeed remarkable. In the first stages of the emancipation of women in the 1920s and 1930s the social importance of the season as a marriage market had declined, and through high taxation and falling real incomes impoverished aristocrats could no longer afford to keep up a great town house.[46] But there was little change in the inter-war years in the geographical distribution of non-landed large fortunes, London (i.e. the County of London) maintaining its share of about two-fifths of the UK total number[47] despite the more challenging conditions of the 1920s and 1930s and despite the growth without the advantage of inherited capital of a new managerial class within the giant corporations based in London.[48] In the Port, London's share of total UK foreign trade actually rose, from 29 per cent in 1913 to 38 per cent in 1938 (Plate 26).[49]

Other equally powerful forces were also contributing towards mounting metropolitan centralization. There was of course the vast growth of Government action, engendered primarily by the social legislation which foreshadowed the post-World War II Welfare State. Politics, too, were more and more concentrated upon London, which in the inter-war years became a major centre of strength for the Labour party: after the general election of 1929 it held fifty-four of the metropolitan parliamentary seats. Provincial political life, on the other hand, was losing its élan — there were no more Thomas Attwoods or Joseph Chamberlains — and pressure groups like the Federation of British Industries and nationwide trade unions such as the National Union of Railwaymen or the Transport and General Workers' Union needed to have their headquarters in London.[50] Moreover centralization usually brought standardization, and the rise of mass circulation daily newspapers, notably the *Mail*, *Express*, and *Mirror*, spread London ideas and attitudes throughout the whole nation, while many provincial dailies went out of business.[51] In the immensely powerful new communications dimension of radio broadcasting in the 1920s the BBC did develop a network of regional stations, but the officials in them had little independence from head office, control of most programme material broadcast from all stations being centralized in London, and the 'Oxford accent' used by all BBC newsreaders and commentators belittled regional modes of speech.[52]

Thus the BBC (at any rate in its early days) was a standardizer as well as a centralizer, and it was evidently these processes, propelled from many quarters besides the BBC, that George Orwell had in mind when in 1941 he wrote that in the inter-war years

there began to appear something that had never existed in England before: people of indeterminate social class. In 1910 every human being in these islands could be 'placed' in an instant by his clothes, manners and accent. That is no longer the case. Above all it is not the case in the new townships that have developed as a result of cheap motor cars and the southward shift of industry. The place to look for the germs of the future England is in the light-industry areas and along the arterial roads. In Slough, Dagenham, Barnet, Letchworth, Hayes [all in or within a few miles of Greater London] — everywhere, indeed, on the outskirts of great towns — the old pattern is gradually changing into something new. In those vast new wildernesses of glass and brick the sharp distinctions of the older kind of town, with its slums and mansions, or of the country, with its manor-houses and squalid cottages, no longer exist. There are wide gradations of income, but it is the same kind of life that is being lived at different levels, in labour-saving flats or Council houses, along the concrete roads and in the naked democracy of the swimming-pools. It is a rather restless, cultureless life, centring round tinned food, *Picture Post*, the radio and the internal combustion engine. It is a civilization in which children grow up with an intimate knowledge of magnetos and in complete ignorance of the Bible. To that civilization belong the people who are most at home in and most definitely *of* the modern world, the technicians and the higher-paid skilled workers, the airmen and their mechanics, the radio experts, film producers, popular journalists and industrial chemists. They are the indeterminate stratum at which the older class distinctions are beginning to break down.[53]

Here, indeed, was 'the future England', in the formation of which in the 1920s and 30s, London had had such a potent influence.

21

World War II 1939–1945

The years 1939–45 are *sui generis* in the history of London: wholly unprecedented and never — surely — to be repeated, even vaguely. But they were not insulated from past or future, and the influence of events in the capital in those years was to be profound and long-lasting. Of course the whole of the nation, including London, shared in the breakdown of what Orwell called 'the older class distinctions', and in people's changed perceptions and expectations brought about by military service, war work, and hardships of all kinds, and by mass movements of population. London's role was nevertheless unique. The capital was the first city in Britain to receive the full onslaught of German air power, which only a few months earlier had produced spectacular and terrifying victories in Poland, the Low Countries, and France; and in the end 30,000 civilians died in the capital through air attacks — very nearly half of all such casualties sustained throughout the whole of Britain. But London proved able to 'take it' — to borrow the title of the film *London can take it* made in September–October 1940 only a few weeks after the start of the Blitz (i.e. the bombing of 1940–1) — and despite the sometimes unpalatable myths and legends in which the Blitz has become enshrouded, metropolitan defiance and tenacity were fundamental to the ultimate outcome of the war, and hence to the survival intact of basic national institutions, notably Crown and Parliament, and even of the nation itself. Beyond doubt, this was London's finest hour.[1]

During the later 1930s forecasts as to the vulnerability of London to aerial attack had been gloomy in the extreme. The Air Ministry thought that on the outbreak of war there would be a sustained aerial bombardment of Britain, and of London in particular, which would last for some sixty days and in which, on the assumption that each ton of high explosive dropped would cause fifty casualties, killed or wounded, there would be over 18,000 casualties in London alone after a single week of bombing. In 1936 Bertrand Russell thought that London 'will be one vast raving bedlam, the hospitals will be stormed, traffic will cease, the homeless will shriek for help, the city will be a pandemonium', and government itself would collapse.[2]

In the event the casualties were less severe than had been expected, — although the damage to buildings, especially housing, was much greater — and there was no mass panic or outbreak of hysterical neurosis. The storm did not break until a whole year after the start of the war, on the sunny afternoon of Saturday, 7 September 1940, eleven weeks after the Fall of France, when some 320 German bombers escorted by over 600 fighters flew up the Thames and bombed *inter alia* Woolwich Arsenal, Beckton Gasworks, the docks on both sides of the river, and West Ham power station (Plate 55). Conflagrations enveloped large areas of Docklands, and the population of Silvertown was surrounded by fires and had to be evacuated by water. At eight o'clock the attack was resumed by 250 bombers, and lasted until dawn on Sunday; and in the evening there was another assault, by 200 bombers. During those two days nearly 850 people were killed.[3]

This was the start of what the official history of the war later called the Battle of London. Thereafter London was bombed for seventy-six consecutive nights (with only one respite), and over 27,000 high explosive bombs plus uncounted incendiaries were dropped. At first the East End received the main attacks — by 11 November some 40 per cent of all the houses in Stepney had been destroyed or damaged — but later Central London became the principal target, and Buckingham Palace was the object of a deliberate daylight attack. By mid-October about 16,000 houses had been destroyed, 60,000 seriously damaged, and 130,000 slightly damaged. Some 250,000 people had been made homeless, and by early November over 11,000 had been killed.[4]

Soon afterwards the *Luftwaffe* turned its main attention to provincial cities (notably Coventry on 14–15 November, and Liverpool, Birmingham, and Plymouth, to mention only a few), but on many occasions it returned to attack the capital with varying strength for another six months. On 29–30 December the City was 'fired' in a spectacular raid, in which six conflagrations raged within the Square Mile. When the attack was at its most intense the Thames was at low tide, full use could not be made of the fire barges there, and many fires had to be left to rage unchecked. The Guildhall and eight Wren churches were destroyed, Guy's Hospital in Southwark was evacuated. And (to mention only two of the worst raids during this period) on 10–11 May 1941 550 bombers kept up a ferocious onslaught for five hours, destroying *inter alia* the Chamber of the House of Commons and killing over 1,400 people — the largest number in a single night.[5]

This proved to be the last severe raid by piloted aircraft, for on 22 June Hitler invaded Russia; and for two and a half years London experienced a relative intermission from air attack.

That there would be this breathing space was of course not known at the time. During the year after the Fall of France in June 1940 when Britain fought alone, there was no expectation that the air raids would abate within the foreseeable future, but there were real fears of gas attacks and (particularly at first) of invasion (neither fulfilled) as well as of new aerial weapons (to be only too grimly fulfilled in 1944–5). The acceptance and mastery of all these potential hazards, and the Blitz itself, reflects the total transformation of the national mood between the 'palmy' days of the later 1930s, when few people accepted that there would be a war, and the heroic resolution of the early 1940s.

The first mass uprooting of families from their homes, in September 1939, when nearly 1,500,000 people, mostly women and children under the Government's evacuation scheme, had left Greater London, had been followed by bewilderment. The expected air attacks had not materialized, but there was the blackout of all external lighting, the first phase of food rationing, and all the social problems of children separated from parents, of misery in often unwelcoming billets in the 'reception areas', of boredom and loneliness in the country. For over six months the Phoney War period bred little but uncertainty, apathy, and low morale. By Christmas 1939 one half of the people who had left the capital had returned, the highest rate of return being amongst mothers with homes in the impoverished East End.[6]

All this changed dramatically with the appointment of Winston Churchill as Prime Minister, the evacuation from Dunkirk and the collapse of France (May–June 1940). The likelihood of invasion suddenly became a terrible reality. Road signs and directions were removed in order to confuse German soldiers when they arrived, the Home Guard (as yet often without weapons) was formed to fight them, and 15,000 foreigners living in London were interned. Three concentric lines of defence were hurriedly constructed around the capital. These consisted of anti-tank trenches, concrete pill-boxes, and road blocks, the outermost ring (to be manned largely by the Home Guard) encompassing roughly the whole area of Greater London. In the very centre a last stand was to be made around Whitehall by the élite troops of the Guards and the Marines.[7]

However amateurish and largely useless these frantic improvisations may in retrospect appear, they nevertheless engendered a new mood of self-confidence and even of exhilaration. And so it was that 'fewer people left London during the nine months of air attack than the number who went away either just before or just after the declaration of war'.[8]

Nevertheless Mr Churchill later admitted that in the early days of the bombardment the Government had felt some concern about Londoners' morale. Five thousand East Enders had plodded out to Epping and encamped in the Forest; the public soon defied official attempts to prevent sheltering in the tube stations, where by the end of September over 175,000 people were taking nightly refuge; and, at first, the relief services were overwhelmed.[9]

Although unemployment relief had since the 1920s been accepted as a national responsibility, health, education, and welfare services were still largely the province of local government. The function of local bodies was to provide services for their own particular district, and there was great variation in the quality of the service provided. This system assumed that the population would be relatively immobile, and worked passably in peacetime. But when there were mass movements of people across local borders, and costs had to be divided between those attributable to conditions of war or of peace and between the evacuating and the receiving areas, the system was unworkable — particularly in the London Civil Defence Region (i.e. the Counties of London and Middlesex and parts of Hertfordshire, Essex, Kent, and Surrey), where there were ninety-six authorities concerned with billeting and housing, and nine for the emergency rest centres.[10]

Plate 42. One of Russell and Co's Cornish wagons heading towards London near Bodmin in the 1820s (p. 225)

Plate 43. Loading coal for London at Sunderland, County Durham, c.1844. Note the rail tracks (p. 225)

Plate 44. Smithfield Market, *c.*1811

Plate 45. Covent Garden Market, early 19th century

Plate 46.
Unloading a Tyneside collier into a
lighter, probably at Wapping, 1808

Plate 47. Unloading coal from a
lighter to a cart at Adelphi Terrace
and wharf, c.1810

Plate 48. Backing a coal cart to the coal hole of a house, c.1810

Plate 49. London omnibuses, probably at Chelsea, 1845

Plate 50. Building the London and Birmingham Railway at Camden Town, 1836

Plate 51. Construction work at Praed Street near Paddington Station for the Metropolitan, c.1866

Plate 52. Workmen's Train arriving at the London, Chatham and Dover Station at Victoria, 1865

Plate 53. The Chartist meeting at Kennington Common, 1848

Plate 54. Poplar Borough Council marching to obey the summons of the High Court, March 1921; note the Mayor of Poplar, wearing his chain of office

Plate 55. The Blitz: Docklands ablaze during the first mass daylight attack, 7 September 1940

Plate 56. The Blitz: Shelterers at Aldwych Underground Station, 8 October 1940

Plate 57. The Lord Mayor's Show, 1888

Plate 58. Newspaper advertisement of 1986 for sale of County Hall, home of London government 1922–86

The central problem created by the Blitz was not so much the casualty work as the remedying of general disorder and, above all, the relief of social distress. Communications were constantly being disrupted: streets blocked; railway lines and termini damaged; gas, electricity, and water supplies cut off; telephone lines interrupted; and even main sewers burst open — all the machinery of communication upon which any great city depends.[11] Still more exacting, however, was the provision of shelter and food for the homeless, the 'bombed out', who in September 1940 began to arrive in the rest centres in thousands, often in shock, in their nightclothes and having lost all their possessions.

By the end of the month there were some 25,000 people in the grossly overcrowded rest centres, many of them run by the LCC in schools and church halls. Often washing and sanitation facilities were primitive, there was little bedding, few chairs, and food and cooking equipment was totally inadequate. The centres were intended to provide refuge for only a few hours, but soon the outward flow was dammed up by the slow rate of repair of damaged houses and by the victims of unexploded bombs, who had been compulsorily evacuated from their homes until the bombs could be defused or removed. Repair work was primarily the responsibility of the borough councils, but after six weeks of bombardment the authorities had only rehoused some 7,000 people. Moreover, the problem was aggravated by the reluctance of families to move far — installing East Enders in requisitioned houses in the West End was not successful — and there were also the intensely personal difficulties caused by loss of clothes and furniture.[12]

Gradually things did improve, however. In September 1940 the Government gave the LCC a free hand for expenditure on post-raid services, and the rest centres (eventually 780 of them) were improved and adequately equipped.[13] The Council also set up communal feeding centres, which started as mobile field kitchens in the East End and gradually evolved into over 200 British Restaurants, plus, later, a Meals-on-Wheels delivery service.[14] Numerous voluntary agencies, notably the Women's Voluntary Service, supplemented officially provided services and thereby propagated new more personal attitudes between public servants and the public whom they served. With the help of 5,000 men from the Army the repair of damaged dwellings was greatly accelerated, and by August 1941 over 1,000,000 houses had been patched up and made weatherproof.[15] Everywhere there was a new spirit of self-reliance, stoicism, and adaptability.

'Business as Usual' became a popular slogan of the early 1940s, encapsulating attitudes which enabled people to cope with the often daily challenges of the air-raid siren, of fire-watching and civil defence duties, of broken sleep, the blackout, shortage of food, and the rationing even of clothes. People were continually busy — Digging for Victory on allotments in parks or the gardens of London's numerous squares, keeping chickens in back yards, or on duties with the voluntary organizations which had helped to hold the line in 1940–1 and upon which by 1944–5 the post-raid services and many others largely depended. Everywhere people were encouraged by the example of others: by the firemen of London's 25,000-strong force, whose endurance made them popular heroes, by the girls in uniform who attended to the barrage balloons moored in any available open space and floating high in the sky to prevent low-level bombing, and by the crews of the anti-aircraft batteries stationed in the parks, which frequently blazed away at night and made a reassuringly deafening din.

Sheltering, mostly from night raids, engendered quite a new way of life. For domestic use, thousands of Anderson shelters had been issued. These were made of corrugated steel and had to be sunk 3 feet into the ground. They proved effective against practically anything except a direct hit, but they were cramped and often leaked, and many people had no gardens in which to put them. So they were superseded by the Morrison shelter: a steel-framed box for indoor use, which could also be used as a table. Outside the home there were public shelters, erected in the streets or under railway arches, the largest, known as the Tilbury, being in a massive underground goods yard in Stepney, where in October 1940 some 16,000 people were passing the night in filthy and grossly overcrowded conditions. Other East Enders, many of them homeless, took up residence in a vast network of caverns at Chislehurst, where electric light, lavatories, bunk beds, canteens, and even an old piano for sing-songs were installed — in due course.[16] Lastly there were the tube stations, where, by the end of the war, there had been some 53,000,000 attendances (Plate 56).[17] There too, after a shaky start, bunk beds were set up along the platforms and tickets were issued for the 'regulars'. But even there safety was never complete. On 15 October 1940, after a direct hit on Balham Tube Station, a torrent of sludge and water cascaded down on to the platform and buried sixty-five people alive; and three months later over 100 shelterers were killed after a direct hit at the Bank Station in the heart of the City.[18] Sudden death was never far away anywhere in London, but the possibility of it was commonly ignored; and perhaps this explains why even in November 1940 well over half the people of London preferred to take their chance and sleep at home.[19]

There was, of course, another less heroic side to the wartime capital. Doubtless for good reasons, information about the extent of death and destruction caused by the Blitz was severely restricted; and in January 1941 Herbert Morrison as Home Secretary banned the Communist newspaper *The Daily Worker*, which (until the German attack on the Soviet Union in June) was conducting an anti-war campaign. The looting of bomb-damaged buildings was common, and the black market flourished, particularly for rationed goods like clothing and food. Despite the feelings of shared purpose engendered by the war there was also some class hostility, fuelled partly by the contrast between the appalling sufferings in the East End and the high life which in some measure still continued in the less heavily bombed West End. And towards the end of the war the number of industrial stoppages and strikes (although declared illegal by the Government) was growing.[20]

Industry and employment of all kinds had of course been severely dislocated. The Port of London — the largest single source of employment in the metropolis — had by the end of 1940 been reduced by air attacks to a quarter of its capacity, and the number of ships entering and departing for foreign destinations fell from over 50,000 in 1939 to some 16,000 in 1942.[21] By 1943–4, however, several of the largest docks were being used for the construction of the huge concrete caissions up to 60 feet high and 200 feet long needed for the Mulberry artificial harbours during the impending invasion of France.[22] Manufacturing output of many consumer goods had soon after the beginning of the war been severely restricted, but for fear of heavy bombing the Government had at first placed no orders for armaments in London. In late 1940, however, this policy was reversed, and within a year war production was in full swing. Ford's at Dagenham, for instance, made army trucks, and the new factories on the western outskirts of London turned out a wide range of war equipment in large quantity. But, as had always been the case in London, there was also a great deal of small-scale production, much of the furniture industry of north-east London being converted to the making of wooden Mosquito light bombers. And everywhere it was women who provided much of the labour force.[23]

From the start of the war women had volunteered in large numbers for the uniformed services, and very many had worked in civil defence and welfare as well as in the traditional role of nursing. But as the men left for the armed forces women moved into industry, just as they had in World War I. In December 1941 conscription for women was introduced for the only time in British history, and in due course all women under the age of 50 were required to register for work. More nurseries were provided in order to enable mothers with young children to work outside the home, and eventually four-fifths of London's married women were employed to 'do their bit' in one way or another.[24]

London was therefore a well-organized and disciplined place when the final trial began to beset the capital in June 1944. On 13 June, just over a week after the Allied landings in Normandy, the first of the flying bombs (or V-1s or 'doodlebugs'), launched from German bases in Northern France, began to explode in the London area. These were small pilotless aircraft which, when their engines cut out, crashed to the ground and produced explosions of such power that they damaged houses and shattered glass up to a quarter of a mile away. Soon they were falling on London at the rate of 100 per day, the worst hit areas being Croydon (where over 1,000 houses were completely destroyed), Lewisham, and Wandsworth.[25]

During the whole period between mid-June and early September, when the launching sites were overrun by advancing Allied troops, RAF fighters, guns, and balloons destroyed over half the V-1s directed at London. But during these eighty days of the main attack Londoners' morale had been tested almost to breaking point. The bombs might arrive at any time of the day or night, and some people began to live in the tube shelters all the time, now supplemented by eight newly built deep shelters, each containing 8,000 bunks. There was virtually no warning of imminent catastrophe, for there were only twelve seconds in which to fling oneself to the floor or into a doorway between the moment when the engine cut out and the moment of the explosion; and the robotic nature of these new weapons was peculiarly unnerving, fuelling fears of worse things to come. So by the end of August it was estimated that a million people had left London.[26]

By early September the 2,350 V-1s which had fallen on London had killed 5,000 people and injured 15,000 others. But there was still one final challenge to withstand: the rocket attacks by V-2s, the first of which arrived on 8 September while the end of the V-1s was still being celebrated. These monstrous objects, 45 feet in length and weighing 14 tons, were launched from mobile bases in Holland, travelled at twice the speed of sound and reached London in four minutes. They made craters 15 feet wide and 10 feet deep and razed whole rows of houses. By the end of October they were arriving at the rate of four a day, the eastern and north-eastern suburbs being the main victims (Ilford suffered most, receiving thirty-five rockets), but for two whole months all news of the colossal explosions which suddenly reverberated throughout the capital was blacked out. There was no defence of any kind, and because there was no warning either — not even twelve seconds — people felt vulnerable all the time, day and night. During the worst period, January 1945, there were five V-2 explosions somewhere in London every day. By the end of March, when the rocket launchers were withdrawn from Holland, 518 had hit London and killed 2,724 people.[27]

So London withstood this last assault, but it was 'a damned close-run thing', for morale had become fragile and war-weariness was widely prevalent. By as early as the end of June 1941 one in six of the population of the London Civil Defence Region had been made homeless at least once, and in 1944–5 the flying bombs and rockets damaged or destroyed between 1,000,000 and 1,500,000 houses there. Throughout the whole war the London Region, containing one-sixth of all the houses in the whole country, suffered over half of the total damage and destruction to them.[28] It is true that the sheer immensity of London, upon which attack by even several hundred bombers could make little total impact, and the availability of almost complete safety in the tube shelters when pressures above ground became insufferable, were anodynes not to be had in heavily raided and relatively much smaller cities like Coventry or Bristol. London had nevertheless borne the brunt of the assault, thereby earning new respect throughout the rest of the nation (though this was perhaps soon forgotten); and through the greatly increased scope of Government in wartime, the capital's influence over the whole country became even more pervasive than hitherto. The novelist Elizabeth Bowen, watching traffic diverted by a bomb incident stream smoothly down a side street, was struck by 'an overpowering sense of London's organic power', the source for which constantly 'forced for itself new channels'.[29] And the author of one of the volumes of the official history of the war thought that

London, that is, the people of London, symbolised to many onlookers the spirit and strength of resistance. It may not have merited greatness, it may not have borne its trials with greater fortitude than any other bombed city of Western civilisation, but greatness, an uncomfortable greatness, was thrust upon it during the winter of 1940–1. Most Londoners were probably quite unaware of the fact.[30]

22

Disruptions 1945–1997

Britain and its Commonwealth and Empire and its capital city emerged from
World War II severely battered but still intact. The Union Jack still flew over about
a quarter of the world's land surface, and in June 1953 British imperial greatness
found its last and largest celebration in the Coronation of Queen Elizabeth II. The
religious ceremony itself was televised live from Westminster Abbey (a sensational
event in the history of 'the box', watched by millions), contingents from over forty
Commonwealth and Empire countries participated in the procession, which was
held in pouring rain and took forty-five minutes to pass any given point on the
route; and the numerous street parties held throughout London reflected a
national mood of well-being and hope. There was even talk of an impending
'Second Elizabethan Age'.

Yet only three years later the Suez débâcle marked externally the birth of a very
different mood of uncertainty and self-doubt which soon manifested itself in 'the
permissive society': consumerism and the widespread repudiation of traditional
moral standards. In Greater London the population began to fall with increasing
speed. The Port, since Roman times a cornerstone of London's prosperity, collapsed between 1967 and 1981, with the loss of some 25,000 jobs and the closure of
all the docks.[1] In the 1960s and 1970s employment in manufacturing industry in
Greater London fell precipitously, a trend continued in the 1980s. So in the face of
all these and other disturbing developments it is indeed notable that the post-
imperial capital has (all things considered) adapted so adroitly, and within the
space of little more than a single generation, to a new posture as metropolitan
megalopolis of a small densely populated island within the new and highly
competitive world economy of the later 1990s.

Postwar Resurgence

At first there was, it seems, widespread confidence about the future amongst the
great mass of people. Despite the continuance of wartime austerities such as food

rationing — even bread was rationed, for the first time, in 1946 — the creation of the Welfare State under the Labour Government of 1945–51 engendered a hitherto unknown sense of security; and as prosperity gradually replaced austerity popular expectations were revolutionized. By around 1960 working Londoners' real incomes were almost double their pre-war levels, in the new consumer society of the 1960s labour-saving electrical equipment like washing machines, refrigerators, and vacuum cleaners (and of course the soon all-but-ubiquitous television set) came for the first time within the means of the great majority of people, often with the help of 'never never' hire purchase;[2] and in 1959 Mr Harold Macmillan was able to say with much truth that 'Most of our people have never had it so good.' There was also a large measure of social convergence, contrasts between the extremes of wealth and poverty became less pronounced, and political concensus ('Butskellism') prevailed. Race had hardly yet begun to replace class as a major source of antagonism.

Unemployment was almost unknown, and widespread shortage of labour generated much of the upward pressure of wages. By the mid-1950s facilities in the Port — still the largest single employer of manpower in London — had been patched up, and, with Commonwealth trade booming, an average of 1,000 ships docked there each week.[3] Down at Dagenham Ford's was mass-producing 250,000 vehicles a year, and postwar demand, both at home and abroad, still far outstripped supply. Over at Southall and Park Royal double-decker buses were being turned out in large numbers not only for London itself but for many Commonwealth countries; and in the early 1950s London's aircraft industry enjoyed its golden age, with Vickers at Weybridge building the famous Viscount aeroplane and at Colindale and Hatfield De Haviland producing in the Comet the world's first jet airliner. Further out, Heathrow became London's principal airport in 1946, and the first direct services to the United States were started. The first permanent buildings there were opened in 1955, followed three years later by inauguration of a second airport for London at Gatwick. Meanwhile the prosperity of the City and of some inner areas found concrete and glass expression in the office blocks and towers which sprouted up on bomb sites after the removal of most wartime controls over office building. The Shell Centre on the South Bank and the Vickers Tower on Millbank are cases in point.[4]

But although the pre-war problem of unemployment had been solved (at any rate for some twenty years), that of housing had become infinitely more acute. Some 222,000 dwellings in the metropolis had been destroyed or damaged beyond repair,[5] and for six years no new ones had been built. In 1946 desperation drove several thousand people, mostly young and from the East End and known as squatters, to take possession of empty blocks of West London mansion flats awaiting renovation, those in Duchess of Bedford's Walk off Kensington High Street being the most famous case. Thousands of 'pre-fabs' — small prefabricated bungalows, each equipped with modern conveniences and a tiny patch of garden, and therefore very popular — were put up on bomb sites, and provided a small measure of relief. But the main impetus of the postwar housing effort was exerted by the Labour-controlled LCC and the borough councils, which by 1949 had built some 50,000 new dwellings. Most of these were four- to six-storey brick blocks of flats, and on the Lansbury Estate in Poplar — a mixture of houses and low-rise flats — there were to be schools, churches, and shops, very different from the pre-war deserts of Becontree. For a brief while postwar council building had a sensitive human face.[6]

The private building of houses for sale, on the other hand, virtually ceased until the early 1950s, due to shortage of money, materials, and labour, plus the continuance of wartime controls. So the largely unregulated pre-war outward sprawl of suburbia was superseded by State and local authority planning. The two plans drawn up in 1943–4 for the County of London and for Greater London by Professor Patrick Abercrombie were with some modification adopted by the Government and became the basis of London's planning for over twenty-five years; and in 1947 the Town and Country Planning Act gave the Ministry of that name and local councils extensive powers over change of land use and building development. Under these powerful new auspices decentralization provided the principal thrust of metropolitan planning, and by 1947–8 sites for eight new satellite towns had been designated in a ring some 20 to 30 miles from central London. Each was to provide a self-contained and socially mixed community of between 30,000 and 60,000 people. Contemporaneously a Green Belt was instituted around London in which building development was to be tightly constrained — the idea first propounded before the war by Herbert Morrison's LCC and which in the 1950s matured into a statutory metropolitan girdle some 5 to 10 miles in width.[7]

The metropolitan Green Belt has proved to be perhaps the most enduring element in the postwar planning of London, and (now greatly enlarged) it still for a variety of reasons commands strong public support. The new towns, after a slow and shaky start under the paternalistic development corporations, had by around 1960 provided standards of housing far higher than those previously experienced by many of the Londoners who had moved out to them; and in the field of jobs they did succeed in attracting numerous successful industries.[8]

There were other achievements too. The Festival of Britain, held in 1951 in the centenary year of the Great Exhibition, had its national centrepiece in the exhibition mounted on derelict land on the South Bank near Waterloo. After all the deprivations and austerities of the previous twelve years, it provided morale-boosting prospects of things to come, and in the Royal Festival Hall, built by the LCC, it bequeathed to London the nucleus of what was to become the South Bank Arts Centre. Even London's notorious climate was improved, for after the great 'smog' of December 1952 (to which 4,000 premature deaths were attributed) Clean Air Acts greatly reduced pollution from smoke and sulphur dioxide: pea-soup fog became a thing of the past.[9] And in the mid-1960s London became the international capital for the fashion, design, and music of postwar youth — the Swinging London of Carnaby Street, jeans, and mini-skirts, where teenagers had plenty of money to spend. In this new affluent, permissive, and still largely racially

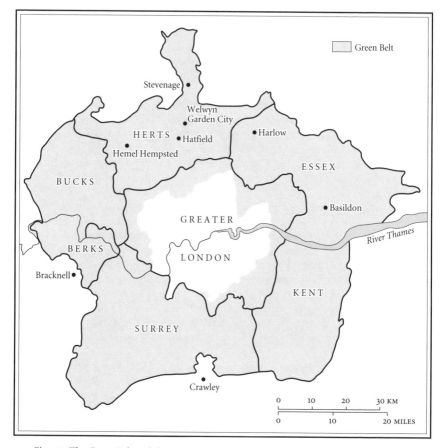

Fig. 28. The Green Belt and the new towns

homogeneous metropolis, its residents secure within the infant Welfare State, the future could still look bright — and certainly very much better than the past.

Alarm Signals

But warning lights were beginning to flash. At national level there was Suez (1956), relative economic decline, the disintegration of the Empire, the onset of seemingly endless wrangling with new 'partners' in continental Europe, and the world oil crisis of 1973. Less noticeably, there was also a gradual debilitation of national concensus (social as well as political), of hitherto generally accepted moral stand-ards, and of national pride. London ceased to be the imperial capital city without becoming anything else in particular; and her economy began to wilt.

This decline was of course primarily a reflection of the national fortunes, but London also had its own peculiar problems. In the 1960s the trade of the Port with the Commonwealth, many members of which were gaining their independence, fell by 50 per cent, and in 1967 the docks began to close, the first being the East India Dock, soon followed by St Katharine's and the London. There were also other causes of this rapid collapse—poor management, bad industrial relations, and failure to modernize to meet the competition of Continental rivals like Rotterdam or Dunkirk, or even of East Coast ports like Dover and Felixstowe—but by 1981 this devastating process was completed with the closure of the Royal group of docks, and the whole port, which as recently as 1956 had been handling record amounts of goods (Plate 31), was concentrated 26 miles downriver at containerized Tilbury, Essex.[10]

The loss of some 25,000 jobs in the docks had 'knock-on' effects in associated activities such as transport, warehousing, and food processing (notably sugar-refining). Manufacturing industry throughout Greater London as a whole was also declining: between 1959 and 1975 it lost over a third of its total manufacturing employment. Similar decline was of course also taking place in other large con-urbations of Britain, and after 1978 throughout the whole of South-East England (where between 1979 and 1992 manufacturing employment fell by 41 per cent), but it was peculiarly intense in London, especially in such fields as clothing and footwear, food and drink, tobacco, timber and furniture, and electrical engineer-ing. Between 1971 and 1981 the rate of unemployment in Greater London almost doubled, from 4.6 per cent to 9.0 per cent of the economically active population; and after falling back during the boom of the mid-1980s it rose again to 11.7 per cent in 1993—well above the average for the nation as a whole. Even in hitherto prosperous outer London and its outskirts large engineering and electrical firms such as British Aerospace (Kingston-upon-Thames), GEC (Willesden), or Thorn-EMI (Hayes and Ilford) shed jobs, while AEC in Southall (where London's double-decker buses were built) closed altogether, and Westland's helicopters flew away from Hayes to a new home at Yeovil in Somerset.[11]

Meanwhile in the old industrial belt of inner London—Docklands, Hackney, Islington, Lambeth and Southwark—the unemployment rate in 1981 was over 14 per cent. Between 1986 and 1989 central London's last great centre of manufac-ture—the newspaper industry—dispersed itself away from Fleet Street. Bad labour relations had fossilized production into out-of-date Victorian methods, but the revolution in information technology made the use of fundamentally new means of production inevitable; and with them came the move to new purpose-built premises in cheaper and more accessible places. By 1989 most of the national press had moved east to Docklands, while other titles went out to Battersea and Pimlico. Fleet Street itself and its environs were quickly colonized by the banks and finance houses of the burgeoning City.[12]

Manufacturing of course only accounted for a small proportion of Greater London's jobs, three-quarters of which in 1981 were in the service sector (compared with about half in 1921), and in that sector the total level of employment did not change greatly in the 1970s. But business office employment was drifting away from the centre, driven by high rents (over five times as great in the City as in such outlying places as Bedford or Basildon), the extra costs in time and money of commuting, and parking problems — the Sun Alliance insurance company, for instance, moved almost all its London staff out to Horsham in 1964. Likewise, the Government was moving thousands of civil servants out to faraway provincial centres; and with advances in telecommunications and information technology a place in the centre was becoming less important, particularly in respect of clerical and junior administrative staff.[13]

These metropolitan job-losses have, however, been partly offset by the huge growth of tourism. In 1990 foreign visitors, some 25,000,000 in number, spent some £4.5 billion in London (far in excess of Londoners' expenditure abroad).[14] Some 300,000 or 400,000 jobs in London are associated with tourism, but many (particularly in hotels, shops, and restaurants) are low paid, seasonal, and liable to severe fluctuation from one year to another. So while tourism is a most valuable source of earning, it has its dangers as a foundation for metropolitan prosperity.[15]

So too does the considerable dependence of both London and the country as a whole upon the great financial centre of the City. We have already seen that since at least 1796 a favourable balance of payments on the nation's foreign account had only been achieved through the contribution of invisible earnings and income from investments abroad. But the City's prosperity is fragile. Britain's national institutions and the London-based gentlemanly Establishment which to a large extent ran them had survived World War II, and (even after the Labour Government's attempt in 1964–7 to restructure the traditional hegemony of Bank, City, and Treasury) a central aim of national policy was still the preservation of sterling as a leading currency in international trade and investment. For some years this had some success — in 1950 half of all international transactions in world trade were still made in sterling — and in 1958 full convertibility with the dollar (suspended since 1939) was resumed. But with the dissolution of the Empire and the decline of Britain's own economy, the relative importance of the Sterling Area and international confidence in it also declined. As a leading world currency the pound was displaced by the dollar, and later by the yen and the mark as well. The now fully convertible sterling balances ceased to be an asset and were gradually run down, and changing national interests led first to the formation of the European Free Trade Association in 1959 and ultimately in 1973 to membership of the European Economic Community.[16]

In adapting to these fundamentally new circumstances the City displayed all its customary agility. In the 1960s and 1970s the big institutional investors (insurance companies, pension funds, and unit trusts) began to exert a greater influence in the money markets, and to be more involved in raising capital for large-scale industry and in company mergers and takeovers. But although a new breed of financial manager was emerging, and top business positions became more professionalized, the old order of gentlemanly directors, still in close alliance with the Bank of England and the mandarins in Whitehall, was by no means entirely displaced.[17] Whoever the decision-makers were, from the 1960s onwards they successfully established for the City a dominant world position in the rapidly expanding market of international securities, both in Eurodollars* and in foreign equities, and after the deregulating Big Bang of 1986 the Stock Exchange became much more internationally orientated. The City, as the one-time credit capital of the world, was able to supply the world economy's need for a financial centre which could provide short- and long-term funds and act as a channel for international lending; and in this new global role it also had the incalculable advantage of conducting its affairs in the world's business lingua franca of English and in being midway in the global time clock between the other two great centres of New York and Tokyo.[18]

However, there was also a downside to the City's impressive postwar record. Its reputation for integrity and reliability has been tarnished by the recurrent crises at Lloyd's and in 1995 by the sudden and spectacular collapse of Baring's, the City's oldest merchant bank; nor has IRA terrorism helped. Although the City still deals worldwide in huge amounts of money, most of this money is now foreign-owned. Whereas in the early 1960s there were some eighty foreign banks represented in London, in 1993 there were some 524 (far more than in either France or Germany or Japan or even in New York, where there were about 340), attracted by the relative lack of regulatory restrictions there.[19] Because of this huge inflow of foreign capital the City has thus become a multinational business entrepôt rather than a British-owned and -managed financial centre.

Despite the precariousness of its prosperity the City has nevertheless retained its vigour and adaptability, in contrast with much of the rest of London's economy; and this overall economic decline has been reflected in a fall in the number of London's people. Just as the population of the ancient City had begun to decline in the 1850s, and that of the County of London had done likewise between 1901 and 1911, so that of Greater London had peaked in 1939 and begun to fall with increasing rapidity thereafter, from 8,600,000, or around 21 per cent of the whole of that of England and Wales, to 6,300,000, or 13 per cent, in 1991.

These figures reflect the continuing outward dispersal of London, which is still the hub of national migration patterns, thousands of mainly young people coming up to the capital chiefly for employment reasons, but leaving later in life chiefly for the improvement of their housing position. This continued outward migration has been a contributory cause of the abandonment of many inner areas to the poor, and the creation therefrom of 'inner city' social problems.[20]

These inner-city problems have been made peculiarly intractable through their association with mass immigration from the Commonwealth and with race relations. The first sizeable group of West Indians, some 500 in number, arrived at

---

* 'Offshore' American dollars which for various reasons could be traded more profitably outside the USA, and which were used much as sterling had been in previous years as a vehicle for the transaction of international trade and long-term loans.

Tilbury in 1948 on board an old troopship, encouraged by the grant of British citizenship by the recent Nationality Act and by the postwar shortage of labour which still prevailed in Britain. Many of them found their first home in London in the Clapham South deep air-raid shelter (one of the eight built in the latter part of the war), which was specially reopened for them. The nearby Labour Exchange at Brixton found them all work within a few weeks (London Transport soon became heavily dependent on immigrant labour), and the nucleus of the Afro-Caribbean settlement at Brixton had been formed.[21]

In the 1950s there was a tremendous influx from the Commonwealth and Pakistan, and by 1961 there were 78,000 West Indian-born migrants in London (including 10,000 in Brixton alone), 64,000 Asians chiefly from India and Pakistan, and 17,000 Africans. West Indian settlements were formed mainly in ageing rundown inner suburbs: Brent, Notting Dale, Hackney, and Haringey north of the river, and south of the river in Lewisham, Southwark, and Lambeth (Brixton). These were deteriorating inner-city areas from which upwardly mobile sections of the indigenous population were moving out, leaving behind the less thriving native-born whites. Here newly arrived West Indians could take over obsolescent privately rented accommodation (not being eligible for public sector housing until qualified by a period of residence in London). Many of them later became buyers and owners, often cramming in numerous tenants in squalid overcrowded conditions in order to pay their mortgages; and in course of time others filled the high-rise council flats which were sometimes shunned by whites. Asian immigrants, on the other hand, were somewhat more widely dispersed, but large settlements of Sikhs and Hindus grew up around Southall, near to their point of entry at Heathrow Airport, and of Bangladeshis around Brick Lane in the East End. In general the Indian and Pakistani populations have settled further out than the Afro-Caribbeans, notably in Newham, Waltham Forest, Merton, and Greenwich, most concentrations being in some way related to local employment opportunities — service-work at Heathrow, for instance, or clothing sweatshops in Spitalfields.[22]

By 1971 6.4 per cent of the population of Greater London had been born in the Commonwealth or Pakistan, and by 1981 this figure had risen to 9.5 per cent. The British-born children of these immigrant groups are not included in these figures, and soon Britain's black or Asian peoples were becoming increasingly indigenous, though still widely regarding themselves as belonging culturally to ethnic minorities. In August 1958 widespread racial tension exploded in Notting Hill, where blacks were beaten up in the streets and their homes besieged by crowds of whites. In the late 1960s and late 1970s racial conflict smouldered in Southall, in Brick Lane frequent racist attacks resulted in several deaths, and the three separate outbreaks of rioting by black youths which took place in Brixton in the summer of 1981 were the most violent street disorders seen in London for at least a century. In the ensuing inquiry police methods were heavily criticized, while high levels of unemployment (particularly among black youths) and bad housing were held to create 'a predisposition towards violent protest'.[23] Thus within little more than a single generation an ethnic underclass had emerged, caught (in the words of

Professor Emrys Jones) 'in a circle of poverty, deprivation and semi- or complete unemployment from which it has proved extremely difficult to escape'.[24] In 1985 the downward spiral continued at Broadwater Farm, Tottenham, where during a riot a policeman was murdered in peculiarly revolting circumstances.

The changed ethnic composition of its population has been perhaps the most important single new departure in London since World War II, and has certainly engendered the most formidable problems. In the early days of mass immigration assimilation of the newcomers and their gradual geographical dispersion had been the ideal, but the sociocultural vitality of the ethnic minorities and the antipathy of many whites towards them proved to be too strong. The continued visibility of coloured groups and the prejudices which this excites has militated against integration on the model of the Jewish community; pluralism based on the acceptance and toleration of differences now has considerable support, and offers more hope than the confrontation implicit in separatism. By international standards the degree of geographical segregation in London is relatively small,[25] but the census of 1991 revealed that nearly 45 per cent of the population of the Borough of Brent described themselves as belonging to a non-white ethnic group, as did over a third in Newham and Tower Hamlets.[26] In 1994 Lord Deedes, a very experienced observer of these matters, thought that through intermarriage between immigrants' children or grandchildren and the 'host' population 'there is taking place a slow merging by descendants of the original migrants into our white society... this slow but accelerating process of assimilation represents the direction in which we are moving'.[27]

These and other recent problems of the metropolis have not been addressed with much distinction by either the Government of the day or by the public authorities created by Government. London has not been and is not amongst the best managed of the world's great cities.

In 1965 the LCC was abolished. The Labour party had ruled at County Hall for over thirty years, and although the metropolitan built-up area now extended far beyond that of the County of London set up in 1889, Labour, secure there in its impregnable electoral majority, had no wish to enlarge its fiefdom to include the mainly Conservative outer suburbs. (Like the City Corporation from the 1630s onwards, the LCC did not wish to widen its horizons to take in the whole of the ever-changing metropolitan townscape.) The new Greater London Council (GLC)'s principality was over four times bigger than that of the LCC and contained more than double its population. The new GLC was to provide the strategic planning overview for some 17 per cent of the whole population of England and Wales, and was to manage such services as main sewers and flood prevention, main roads and traffic planning, refuse disposal, and some housing. This last was shared with the thirty-two London boroughs, which were much bigger ('Big is Beautiful' was fashionable in the 1960s) than the twenty-eight metropolitan boroughs set up for the County of London in 1900, all of which suffered the indignity of either a forced marriage (St Marylebone with Westminster, for instance) or absorption (Battersea, gobbled up by Wandsworth). In the historic core of the metropolis still

Fig. 29. GLC and constituent borough areas

reigned the City Corporation, a well-managed, well-endowed, and exclusive club
for successful businessmen but the mere existence of which obstructed for London
as a whole the development of the municipal pride and loyalty prevalent in many
provincial cities such as Leeds or Manchester, or in other great world cities such as
Paris or New York.

The establishment of a Greater London authority in 1965 marked the final
triumph of the idea first adumbrated in the mid-nineteenth century and first
tentatively manifested in the creation of the Metropolitan Board of Works (MBW)
in 1855, that London was a single urban entity like Manchester or Leeds, capable of
and indeed requiring some form of overall public policy and administration for
certain important fields. But the existence of the thirty-two boroughs — the
powerful lineal descendants of the Victorian vestries — nevertheless showed that
a two-tier system, also first pioneered in the days of the MBW, was still very much
alive in London. Moreover, within little more than a single generation the pace of
economic and technological change and of increased personal mobility has been
so great that new administrative boundaries are out of date almost before they are
established. Even in 1965 Greater London was not great enough for the strategic

planning of land, houses, or jobs, or of population trends — its population (as previously mentioned) was already falling in the 1950s — and for the consideration of such matters it became necessary to take in the whole of South-East England, and more recently even of a Greater South-East. This fringe area extends in a belt around London from Bournemouth in the south-west through Swindon, Milton Keynes, and Peterborough to Ipswich in the north-east, and contains some of the fastest-growing places in the whole country, particularly westward of London along the Golden Corridor of the Thames Valley, where Heathrow provides a powerful magnet. Although not linked to the centre by continuous bricks and mortar, the whole region is in terms of culture, mobility, and employment in varying degrees becoming more interdependent not only locally with adjacent urban sub-centres but centrally too with London itself.[28] With the advent of the personal computer, the mobile telephone, the fax machine, and the Internet, a reverse process of 'de-urbanization' has set in; and the modern business executive can either run his or her affairs from home deep in the country, or commute by car or train from 100 miles or more from the central hub.

So the GLC's administrative area became increasingly obsolete for planning purposes, and after only twenty-one years the council was abolished by another Conservative Government, headed by Mrs Thatcher. Its geographical area had never corresponded with the realities of the metropolis, and its powers were steadily diminished by the (usually hostile) central government by the removal of its functions in drainage and flood prevention, the ambulance service, and housing (the latter to the burgeoning boroughs). In public transport, where in 1970 the Labour Government gave the GLC supervisory control of London Transport Executive, it did have some success with the opening of the first stage of the Jubilee tube line in 1978 and in 1981–3 with a new fares policy ('Fares Fair'); but in 1984 the Conservative Government took public transport away again. At every four-yearly election throughout its history the change of political control at County Hall from one party to the other obstructed the pursuit of consistent long-term policies — a striking contrast with the record in Paris, where the Schema Directeur of 1965 was followed by all subsequent administrations irrespective of their political complexion.[29]

The GLC's main failure was in the field of strategic planning: the principal purpose for which it had been established. By the mid-1960s Professor Abercrombie's proposals of 1943–4 for the decentralization from London of 1,000,000 people and their jobs to new and expanded towns outside the Green Belt had succeeded largely because they were working with the flow of the prevailing social and economic tides: with rising mobility and standards of living, people wanted to move out. But to the surprise of the demographers and hence of the planners the national birth rate rose between 1955 and 1964, and half of this net gain was in the South-East Region, mostly in the outer areas of the ever-outwardly widening ring around London.[30] This whole region, not just its GLC core, was the entity with which strategic planners now had to concern themselves, and the five plans and reports for South-East England prepared between 1964 and 1978 were largely the

work of central government planners, sometimes in association with those of the
local authorities. Their main proposal was to channel continuing outward movement of people into a dozen growth areas (Crawley-Gatwick or Milton Keynes-
Northampton, for example), thereby, it was hoped, creating a polycentric instead
instead of a unicentric city region.[31]

Meanwhile the GLC took four years to prepare its Greater London Development
Plan, followed by another three years for the ensuing public inquiry; and four
more elapsed before the Secretary of State approved the plan in modified form
(1976). Throughout this elephantine process there was frequent conflict between
the GLC and the boroughs, and in 1973 the plan's principal and most controversial
feature, the construction of an 800-mile 'Motorway Box' system, was abandoned.[32]

By that time, however, the decline of manufacturing industry was converting the
planners' postwar obsession with metropolitan overgrowth into concern with the
problems of inner-city decline — a fundamental shift of attitude. By 1975 the GLC
was trying to promote industrial expansion in declining areas. The golden days of
postwar strategic planning were over, and the crisis of the inner city was becoming
the principal item on the metropolitan agenda.[33] Soon after the election of Mrs
Thatcher's Conservative Government in 1979 all forms of planning were firmly
scaled down. The GLC itself was summarily killed off (a quango, the London
Planning Advisory Committee, was to provide planning guidance for the Secretary
of State instead), and attempts made by all governments since 1945 to channel
growth away from the South-East to the North were abandoned. Meanwhile the
population of the erstwhile GLC's Greater London area continued to fall throughout the 1980s. The London Docklands Development Corporation, another
quango, set up in 1981 outside the existing framework of local government (on
the lines of the postwar Labour Government's New Town Corporations) to
redevelop over 8 square miles of derelict dockland vacated by the Port of London
Authority, and the Enterprise Zones contained therein, was soon providing a
spectacular example of an altogether new planning mechanism at work.[34]

The macro-planning of the metropolis has in fact had only limited success; and
this was also the case with planning at more local levels. When the Conservative
Government removed the wartime controls on building in the early 1950s, new
office blocks and towers mushroomed up on bomb sites throughout the City and
inner London. There was an insatiable demand for office space, vast fortunes were
made by property developers, and between 1954 and 1964 (when a Labour Government banned all office building in London without a licence) much of the townscape of central London was transformed by new structures which ignored human
scale and all traditional architectural forms. Planning consent for ugly tall office
blocks was often given in exchange for costly adjacent land owned by the developer
and needed by the LCC for road improvements — a process known as 'planning
gain' — and as 'comprehensive redevelopment' was then the prevailing nostrum
amongst planners, they often gave a sympathetic response to developers' schemes.
In this first postwar building boom most of the vacant sites in the City were
redeveloped, and further afield London acquired Centre Point (at the intersection

of Oxford Street and Tottenham Court Road), the Euston Centre (which enabled the LCC to build an underpass), Stag Place at Victoria, Bowater's at Knightsbridge, the bleak brutalism of the Elephant and Castle redevelopment, and a dozen other concrete jungles of mega-roundabouts, pedestrian tunnels, and elevated walkways.

Elsewhere, however, there was planning paralysis and considerable public hostility to planners' dreams. The developer Jack Cotton's scheme for the redevelopment of Piccadilly Circus in 1959 evoked such an outcry that over twenty years elapsed before it was ultimately decided that this tawdry but ever-popular metropolitan *place* should be left almost unaltered. The Covent Garden saga, caused by the removal of the market to Nine Elms, Battersea, in the early 1970s, did not last so long, but in face of highly articulate local and national opposition, the GLC's schemes for reconstruction had to be abandoned, and the previous fabric (including the fine market buildings, now adapted as a shopping precinct for tourists) remained largely intact.

Just getting a decision and then getting things done often took half a lifetime or more. At strategic level there was the long quest for the site for a third airport for London (ultimately Stansted in Essex was decided upon), and at a more local level there has been an equally perplexing list of problems to be mulled over. In 1958 Peter Palumbo started to acquire the sites needed for his Mansion House Square project in the heart of the City, a 290-feet high office block to be designed by Mies van der Rohe; but after an epic struggle which was at last ended in the House of Lords, the final result (in 1997 at last nearing completion) was something quite different, and by a different architect.[35] More than fifty years were needed to get the National Gallery Extension in Trafalgar Square built (1991), one abortive design being famously described by the Prince of Wales as 'a monstrous carbuncle on the face of a much-loved and elegant friend'; and the new British Library at St Pancras, first mooted in 1971 after years of discussion about other sites, did not open until 1997; its costs will be more than four times greater than the original estimate.[36] In Paris, by contrast, President Mitterand spoke in 1988 of the need for a new national library. Work began in 1992, and the building was opened in 1996.

The planning and building of *grands projets* has not been much practised in London (except in the case of the Regent Street Improvements) since the palmy Georgian days of such great metropolitan landowners as the Grosvenors, the Bedfords, and the Portmans, all of whose descendants have in postwar years been selling off parts of their estates to meet tax bills. Still, there have in recent years been two exceptions. In the 1950s the City Corporation, prompted by the Conservative Government, began to build the Barbican mainly residential estate on a large bomb-devastated area off Aldersgate Street, followed by the Barbican Centre for the Arts, opened in 1982 and sometimes compared with the Pompidou Centre in Paris or the Lincoln Centre in New York. There has also been the regeneration of Docklands by the London Docklands Development Corporation (LDDC), which may prove to be either a unique managerial experiment or an exemplar for future metropolitan structures; and it could even stimulate a renewal of downstream outer East London—a counterpart to the westward Golden

Corridor along the Thames Valley. With public money the Corporation was to provide new roads, sewers, and public transport in order to attract private investment, and by 1988 £441,000,000 of State money had brought in over ten times as much private capital. There were new jobs and expensive new houses for incoming professionals and executives, the Docklands Light Railway provided access to the City, London City Airport took them on business flights to continental Europe, and for the benefit of local residents' needs there was some provision of less costly housing. The pièce de résistance was, however, the huge Canary Wharf office development and its fifty-storey tower, at 824 feet the tallest building in Britain, promoted by the Canadian-based property company Olympia and York. Building work began in 1987, but with the onset of the property slump in 1990 financial difficulties ensued, and when administrators were appointed in 1992 by the banks backing the scheme, only 60 per cent of Canary Wharf had been let.[37]

The ultimate success or failure of Canary Wharf and the whole LDDC way of doing things still remains to be seen; and the Millennium Dome at Greenwich will also have an impact on problems hereabouts. The Docklands Light Railway (DLR) and the first roads built by the LDDC proved quite inadequate for the traffic generated by new developments. Train and platform lengths had to be doubled, but construction of the long-promised extension of the Jubilee tube line from Charing Cross to Canary Wharf and beyond, which will have a far larger capacity than the DLR, did not even begin until 1993; and it was only in that year that adequate road access to the Isle of Dogs from the direction of the City was provided by the hideously expensive tunnel of the Limehouse Link.[38]

Inadequate transport facilities have indeed been endemic throughout postwar London, the fundamental problem (experienced by all large Western cities) being the vast growth of car ownership. In the 1960s London became the hub of the nation's emergent new motorway system (just as it had been of the Romans' roads and the Victorians' railways), and motor traffic poured in and out of the capital daily or (after the completion of the M25 ringway in 1986) circled unceasingly round it, causing mounting congestion and pollution. In central London the removal of bottlenecks to improve traffic circulation had at first been favoured—hence the LCC's Hammersmith flyover and the Hyde Park Corner underpass in 1961–2. But the impact of schemes like these was very limited, the cost of bringing the motorways into the heart of London was financially prohibitive and socially unacceptable, and divided responsibility for roads and traffic management, shared between the Government, the GLC (prior to its demise in 1986), and the boroughs did not help matters. Traffic stagnation and environmental degradation got worse and worse.

Nor has public transport been used to the best advantage in London. Travel to work by bus has greatly declined, many erstwhile passengers preferring to use their cars instead; and on the railways Government reduction of rail subsidies since the mid-1980s has led to much higher fares and reduced services.[39] More travel by underground or tube would seem to offer the best hope for relief of congestion in the central areas, and some new lines have been built. These are the Victoria, from

Walthamstow to Brixton (1968–9), and the Jubilee, from Baker Street to Charing Cross (1979); and the Piccadilly has been extended (partly above ground) to Heathrow (1977) — though Heathrow was until 1998 the only major European airport without a high-speed link into either its capital city or the national rail network. These improvements, however, compare poorly with Paris's high-speed RER which, running on modernized rail and metro lines, carries passengers (sometimes in double-decker trains) direct from the suburbs to the city centre at up to 60 miles an hour. London's equivalent, a crossrail joining Paddington and Liverpool stations, is still under discussion; and in 1991 rail fares in London were nearly double those in Paris or Frankfurt — by far the highest, in fact, in any major European city.[40]

Nevertheless travel on the underground at peak hours grew by 28 per cent between 1983 and 1989, while the number of trains grew by only 6 per cent. So London was an uncomfortable place in which to travel to work, and for many people it was also an uncomfortable place in which to live. The housing problem in the 1980s and 1990s was much the same as it had been a century earlier: shortage of accommodation for the poor. The war had caused huge damage and destruction, much of the surviving stock of dwellings was old, deteriorating, and in need of improvement, and social expectations were rising — households without a fixed bath and indoor lavatory were no longer acceptable. In the early 1980s there was still a shortfall of over 600,000 satisfactory dwellings in Greater London, and although there were over 250,000 applicants on the boroughs' housing lists, the boroughs and the GLC (prior to its demise) were only building some 3,300 new dwellings per annum.[41]

Pressure was strongest in some of the inner boroughs, where in 1981 nearly half (43 per cent) of all households were in rented local authority accommodation. There the high cost of land and councils' lack of funds precluded large-scale new housing projects, while the more prosperous outer boroughs virtually ceased building; and after the demise of the GLC (which had had a redistributive role in the allocation of housing) outward movement for council tenants became more difficult. Pressure was intensified, too, by the sale of council dwellings in conformity with Conservative Government policy, and by the continuing fall in the amount of accommodation available for rent from private landlords: whereas prior to 1914 90 per cent of all London households were privately rented, by 1981 the proportion was only 20 per cent. Finally there was 'gentrification'.[42]

By around 1960, when the outward migration of population from inner London had gathered momentum (either through Abercrombie's planned 'decanting' or through economic and social forces), large decrepit and at first mostly Georgian houses in inner areas could be bought cheaply and regenerated. Young and up-and-coming middle-class couples, fed up with the cost and fatigue of commuting from distant suburbs, began to move into such areas as Canonbury or Barnsbury, and 'do up' the spacious houses available there for their own occupation. Soon gentrification by relatively affluent 'yuppies' was spreading outwards to rundown areas of Victorian or Edwardian housing in Camden, Clapham, and Fulham; and in places like Islington, where the process had advanced furthest, there emerged three distinct groups of residents: the gentrifying owner-occupier newcomers, the tenants of the council flats, and the tenants of the diminishing stock of privately rented accommodation, an increasingly large proportion of this last category being old, poor, unskilled, or of Commonwealth origin.[43]

This state of affairs had first been publicly revealed when the Profumo sex scandal (1963) led on to the exposure of Peter Rachman, a slum landlord who had built a property empire, chiefly in rundown Notting Hill, by the intimidation and eviction of existing unprofitable white tenants and the replacement of them with newly arrived West Indians willing to accept gross overcrowding as the price for a roof over their heads. In 1964 the housing conditions still prevalent in parts of inner London were disclosed in the ensuing Milner Holland inquiry and report.[44]

Just at that time the new GLC was coming into existence (1965), with Labour in power both at County Hall and Westminster, and a determined new housing drive began. But the mainly middle-class boroughs of outer London refused to participate in schemes for the outward movement of population from the inner slums, and the designation of new 'overspill' towns at Milton Keynes, Peterborough, and Northampton could only have long-term effects. So high-rise tower blocks, which had been pioneered by the LCC in the 1950s on the Council's Roehampton estate, became the order of the day, and street after street of slum or sub-standard housing was flattened to provide sites for the new streets in the sky. Within little more than a decade nearly 400 high-rise blocks had been built in Greater London, over a quarter of them in Newham.[45]

This was a powerful rejection of London's tradition of terraced or semi-detached houses, so often admired by perceptive foreigners such as Steen Rasmussen or Donald Olsen. After World War II the first phase of the LCC's Lansbury estate in Stepney (1948–51), consisting of low-rise brick houses or flats with pitched roofs, had adhered to the old language, but there and elsewhere (the Loughborough Road estate in Brixton, for instance) the LCC was by the later 1950s building eleven-storey concrete blocks or tall thin point blocks on the Roehampton model.[46] Very soon, however, it was found that (in the words of Nicholas Taylor) if people are 'hoisted off the ground . . . certain vital links that are normally taken for granted disappear abruptly from their relationships with their neighbours, and indeed with the very earth itself.'[47] To inadequate lifts, often out of order, dark corridors and tunnels, inadequate security and maintenance, absence of outdoor playing space near at hand for small children, were added the structural defects of some system-building, discovered in 1968 when part of Newham's Ronan Point tower block collapsed, killing five residents. Soon afterwards local authorities began to phase out their high-rise housing programmes and started to rehabilitate the existing fabric instead.[48]

The quasi-Messianic belief, widely prevalent in the 1960s, that tower blocks would provide better living conditions than previous forms of dense publicly provided urban housing, seems in retrospect to have been an extraordinary aberration, for which local councillors, architects and planners, and successive governments of both political complexions and their officials were all in part responsible.[49] Tower blocks and the concrete jungles of comprehensive redevelopment areas misfitted the lives of many of the people forced by lack of any affordable alternative to live therein, and were potent ingredients in the destruction of the old networks of family and community that previously enmeshed working-class areas like Bethnal Green, Finsbury, or Southwark. To borrow Mrs Thatcher's famous phrase (irrespective of what she may have actually meant by it), there was no such thing as society any more; and crime, vandalism, and violence flourished as never previously in London in the present century, fuelled by high unemployment and racial antagonisms. The homeless sleeping in doorways along the Strand or in the cardboard shanty towns in Lincoln's Inn Fields or at the sunken roundabout at the south end of Waterloo Bridge are the outward manifestations of social disintegration, social polarization, and the declining 'livability' of London.[50]

So there are plenty of problems, and with better municipal management perhaps some of them might have been avoided or at least mitigated. Since 1986 London has shambled on much as before without the GLC, whose demise has been little regretted. But the capital city deserves something better than the incomprehensible mishmash of quangos, boards, agencies, and Government committes which it has at present.[51] Proposals now (1997) under discussion for a powerful directly elected executive mayor of the whole of Greater London, accountable to an elected assembly, would if implemented move London government in a new and hopeful direction. Quite how the City Corporation and its Lord Mayor would be fitted into such a regime remains to be seen.

London in the Nation and the World

Yet despite the problems and traumas which beset it, London continues, for good or ill, to command a dominant position in the life of the nation. It is still the seat of court, government, and the law, as well as the hub of the commercial, financial, and cultural activity of the nation; and in recent years the influence of London-based institutions and activities has increased. The abolition of the GLC (leaving London with the dubious distinction of being the only world city without its own elected government) and of the metropolitan councils in the provinces, and Government control of local authorities' expenditure by rate-capping, represented important shifts of power to the centre. The great majority of top-rank civil servants are moreover based in London, decisions taken in London may have a (perhaps unconscious) London bias — the decision to provide London with a third major airport, Stansted, rather than to enlarge and upgrade the airports at either Manchester or Glasgow's Prestwick (both vigourously supported locally) may be a case in point. The media too, are dominated by London. Britain lacks regional newspapers corresponding in stature to some of those in France, Germany, or the United States, and although two-thirds of the population of Britain read a daily newspaper, what they read is largely written and produced in London. While in the field of broad-casting efforts have been made to increase regional output, news and current affairs programmes still emanate largely from London.[52] In the words of Professor Ralph Dahrendorf (now Lord Dahrendorf) 'Britain is extraordinarily centralised... not just a unitary state, but one that is run from London in virtually all respects.'[53]

London is also 'the national centre of wealth-making' and of wealth-holders. In the 1960s the main business interests of 42 per cent of all lately deceased non-landed millionaires in Britain were in the City or County of London.[54] At a more general level, incomes per capita in Greater London in 1990 were 27 per cent higher than the national average,[55] while throughout the whole of the South-East Region disposable income per head of population was nearly a third higher than in the North.[56] South-East England, and London in particular, were, in fact, the richest parts of the country, as they had been for centuries.

So the dominance of London is a central element in the North–South divide of Britain. The existence of this divide was officially recognized during the depression of the 1930s, when the economic contrasts between the impoverished North and the relatively prosperous South were particularly acute, and the Report (published in 1940) of the Barlow Commission on the Geographical Distribution of the Industrial Population was (it has been said) in effect a report on the Enormity of London. The establishment of special areas for industrial development in the North, and of financial and other incentives to induce industry to go there, became the staples of successive governments' regional policies, but despite some success they were largely discontinued in the Thatcher years.[57] The North–South divide therefore widened, for while manufacturing employment was falling almost everywhere in both the 1970s and 1980s, most of the growth of service sector jobs was in the South-East. Unemployment was always (until the recession of 1990–2) lower in the South-East than in the North, but the boom in the housing market in the South-East was a powerful obstacle to labour mobility, the prices of average houses in Greater London in 1985 being double those in the North, while for council house tenants migration was even more difficult because demand almost always exceeded supply. So con-currently there was unemployment in the North and shortage of skilled labour in the South;[58] and growing congestion became endemic in the South-East, where over a third of all the people of England and Wales now live and where population density is already far above the national average. The result was an unbalanced and therefore inefficient economy, exacerbating inflation, and balance of payment problems.

These processes were, it is true, to some extent reversed during the recession of 1990–2 which hit the service industries so heavily concentrated in and around London; and nearly half of the rise in unemployment which took place throughout England and Wales in 1990–2 was in the South-East.[59] It seems likely, however, that this reversal will prove to be only a short-term aberration from the powerful long-term trend towards the South, which in recent years has been reinforced by the increased importance of close proximity to continental Europe and by the building of the Channel Tunnel; and figures for 1994 suggest that the North–South divide is in fact beginning to widen again.[60]

23

Valediction

Throughout its whole history London has benefited, as it still does though in new ways, from its advantageous geographical position — this was, after all, the fundamental reason for the founding Romans' choice of site in the first place — which has enabled it since medieval times to be the motor impelling the ascendancy of the South. This London domination has been commented upon, generally with resentment or worse, for a very long time. In 1604 an official at the Port of Sandwich thought that 'All our Creeks seek to one River, all our Rivers run to one Port, all our Ports join to one Town, all our Towns make but one City, and all our Cities and Suburbs to one vast, unwieldy and disorderly Babel of buildings, which the world calls London.'[1] In the 1820s William Cobbett was inveighing against the 'infernal Wen...a smoking and stinking W E N'; and a modern academic has recently declared that, in reference to the 1920s and 1930s, 'The North and its cities reverted [after the interlude of the Industrial Revolution] to the sullen desolation and the impotent hostility which had marked their relations with London and central government since William the Conqueror first laid large areas of the region waste in order to ensure its obedience.'[2]

So discussion about whether London within the nation is a voracious monster or a beacon of light in the surrounding gloom is not new and will certainly continue. Usually, of course, London gets a bad press in these matters, but recent work by the Centre for Economics and Business Research Ltd. shows that there is another side to the story. The economy of Greater London, with a gross domestic product equivalent in 1996 to 19 per cent of that of the whole of the United Kingdom, and bigger than that of Sweden or Austria or Belgium — does in fact pay its way handsomely, and during the last five years it has grown faster than has the rest of Britain. Throughout the 1990s Greater London has been running a large trade surplus with the rest of the UK and the world, amounting in 1995 to over £16 billion; and over 4,000,000 employees in the rest of the UK depend on demand generated in London. But in 1993–4 workers in London paid £6.2 billion more in taxes than was spent by central and local government in London; and without this metropolitan contribution people in the rest of the country would have to pay an increase in the basic rate of income tax of 8.5 pence in the pound in order to maintain the level of services which they currently receive. (Scotland, Wales and the English regions, please note.) So London is subsidizing the rest of the UK, while itself suffering from under-investment in the metropolitan infrastructure, notably in the field of public transport and the underground railway system — something about which the postulated mayor of London might well have something to say. Nor do the substantially higher wage and salary levels prevalent in London necessarily reflect higher living standards. According to the same source job-for-job comparisons show that living standards are only some 9 per cent higher in Greater London than the UK average; and this takes no account of unfavourable differences in the quality of life caused by metropolitan congestion and the great length of time spent by millions of Londoners in travelling.[3]

On the world scene, Britain depends to a greater extent for its livelihood on foreign trade than almost any other country in the world, for (as we have already seen) throughout the past two centuries there has always been a deficit on the nation's visible trade (i.e. on the sale of physical goods), and it has only been possible to balance the nation's books through the contribution of invisible services. The United Kingdom is, moreover, unique amongst major industrial countries in the extent to which its economic prosperity depends on such invisible earnings. From all sources (transport, tourism, income from foreign investments, and professional, financial, and business services, etc.) these amounted in 1992 to 18.2 per cent of gross domestic product — a substantially higher proportion than in any other G7 country — of which the financial sector, including foreign investment income, contributed £18.82 billion.[4] Many of these invisible services had their historical origins (so far as the British economy is concerned) in the City of London — banking, insurance, foreign investment, and brokerage of innumerable kinds — and although they are now provided all over the country and such cities as Manchester, Leeds, Edinburgh, and others are important financial centres in their own right, London is nevertheless still the headquarters of these activities, and the place where a large proportion of the nation's invisible foreign earnings is generated.

The exact amount of these invisible earnings made in the City, as opposed to those made elsewhere in the nation, cannot easily be quantified, but according to calculations made by Mr William Clarke for the year 1963 the City's foreign activities in insurance, merchanting, brokerage, and banking amounted to more than double the national deficit on visible trade, thereby turning what would otherwise have been a trading deficit on the balance of payments into an overall surplus. Similar calculations for other years would doubtless tell much the same sort of story.[5]

The City's contribution to the national balance sheet is in fact of crucial importance to the nation's well-being. In 1992 London was the world's largest foreign exchange centre, the primary centre for ecu and Eurodollar business, its turnover in foreign equities exceeded that of even New York or Tokyo, and it had the largest international insurance market. On the global scene the total volume of invisible trade has been growing faster than that of visible trade[6] — in the new world of information technology invisibles are becoming more and more important; and it is hard to envisage a prosperous British economy without a flourishing City of London.

But it is also hard to envisage a prosperous City without a prosperous world economy, for although London and its adjacent South-Eastern territories may be getting more and more dominant within the nation, London is also becoming more and more dependent on international economic and political forces beyond its control. During the last half-century London has ceased to be an imperial capital, and in the new international division of labour within the global economy which has emerged in the post-colonial era, the City has evolved new functions (previously described) as a specialized world business and financial centre. Social repurcussions have ensued, for at one extreme of the labour market a new highly paid and mostly young City élite has sprouted up, while at the other end are the far more numerous unskilled and semi-skilled workers, many of them of recent Commonwealth origin, trapped in the dilapidated inner areas through the precipitous decline of manufacturing industry and of demand for manual or blue-collar labour. Aggravation of social polarization has resulted, for which the building on American lines of privately guarded residential enclaves for the rich provides concrete evidence.[7]

All other world cities have of course had to adapt to the internationalization of the world economy — Paris and New York, for instance; but what distinguishes London is the degree of its former imperial dominance, and the extent to which internationalization has brought foreign ownership, and hence dependence.[8]

As recently as 1931 the population of Greater London was over five times larger than that of the second city within the Empire (Calcutta), and the transition from being the hub of an advantageous imperial trading system, with secondary cities such as Singapore, Bombay, or Johannesburg dotted around the globe, to a competitor with other primary cities in the world economy has presented London, and the City in particular, with more far-reaching problems than those faced by any of its rivals. Its undoubted success in adapting to the new world economic system has, however, been achieved through acceptance of a substantial measure of internationalization. Forty per cent of all the people who work in the City's banks and stockbroking houses do so for foreign-owned companies and decision-makers;[9] and in the modern global capitalist system the vast sums of money which have come to London so comparatively recently could as quickly be taken out again. London is a location within the world economy where particular services in the business and financial fields are provided, with great efficiency. In the declining manufacturing sector, almost all the factories in London with over 500 employees were by 1982 owned by multinational companies. Much real property in London now belongs to foreigners, led (after the oil price rise of 1973) by Arab buyers (Crewe House in Curzon Street, London Bridge City, the Dorchester Hotel, Harrods, to mention only a very few among many examples), American hotel interests, and more recently followed by the Japanese, whose possessions include Bush House, Bracken House, 55 Bishopsgate, and, of course,

County Hall, for over sixty years the home of London government, for conversion into a hotel and conference centre. The upper echelons of the art market, too, have become largely international, with Sotheby's itself in American ownership since 1983; and large parts of the newspaper and television industries, both heavily concentrated in London, are owned by Rupert Murdoch's News International.[10]

Although this internationalization of London has in the short or medium term brought great benefits, the loss of a substantial measure of economic and financial independence also entails the possibility of conflict between national and international interests; and this diminished authority in the economic and financial fields is of course mirrored in the nation's loss of political autonomy to the European Union. London does in fact in 1997 face fearsome threats of impending change — the birth of the Information Age; de-urbanization (according to one American mayor, the twenty-first-century city 'won't be a city at all but a loose agglomeration of little "people-places", self-contained activity centers where people live, work and recreate');[11] the likely demise of the pound sterling; devolution for Scotland and Wales and of regionalism for England (perhaps London would do better on its own as an independent city state on the lines of Singapore); even the revolution in its own internal management which a directly elected mayor of London would engender — all these present challenges of an importance unsurpassed at any other time in London's history.

Fortunately, ability to adapt to changing circumstances has always been one of London's greatest strengths (and particularly that of the City); and that is still so. Moreover London is not alone, for the nature of great cities everywhere has in recent years been changing with unprecedented speed. In many of them, not only in Britain, population and long-established manufacturing industries have declined, while service employment has grown; de-urbanization — the concomitant of the decline of a city's population and economic base — to smaller regional centres has been gathering momentum, closely linked to the revolution in electronic communication. Even that source of so much British heart-searching, the regional imbalance of the North–South Divide, turns out to have its counterparts elsewhere — in the USA, and in several countries of continental Europe, except that sometimes it is the South that is poverty-stricken (Italy) or the divide is East–West (France or Germany).[12]

So great cities share many problems, and to that extent are in danger of becoming quasi-homogenized. *Capital* cities, in their central historic heartlands, do nevertheless reflect salient aspects of their respective nations, and important messages can be expressed there visually. The grandeur of the Louvre, the Champs-Elysées, and the Arc de Triomphe, and the adjacent Pharaonic embellishments of recent years, are splendid in Paris and provide a wonderful expression of the power and magnificence of the French State. But almost overbearing statements of that kind would be very out of place in London, as would the interminably straight streets of Berlin. In Moscow during the Soviet era the avowed objective of the planners was to reflect the superiority of Marxist-Leninist ideology. In Washington too an ideology is presented, for the whole *mise-en-scène* (based on a layout by a

French architect) of the Mall, Capitol Hill, the White House, and the monuments to Washington, Jefferson, and Lincoln, conveys the uplifting idea that this really is the impregnable citadel of the Land of the Free. But London is different, for there have been no efforts on the grand scale to convey a message (even such Edwardian attempts at imperial grandeur as Admiralty Arch and the Mall hardly stand comparison with Parisian or Washingtonian counterparts), or to overawe or even to impress either the citizen or the visitor. Perhaps this reflects lack of civic pride — it is hard to imagine the Hôtel de Ville in Paris or City Hall in New York being treated like London's County Hall and summarily sold off to a foreign property company (Plate 58). Or perhaps it has something to do with there being two historic centres, the Cities of London and Westminster, rather than a single core. London does nevertheless have an elusive quality of unpompous, unobtrusive restraint and understatement, all the more remarkable for its presence in this erstwhile Imperial Capital; and nowhere can this be more clearly seen than in the royal parks, or in the gently curving thoroughfare of Whitehall, where stand the little statue of Charles I on his horse, the Banqueting House, the Horse Guards and the Cenotaph, and Downing Street nearby; and in the distance the Abbey and the home of the Mother of Parliaments — surely 'A sight so touching in its majesty' that it can stand comparison with any townscape in the world.

APPENDIX 1

Estimates of the Population of London 1550–1801

Prior to the first national census, taken in 1801, the sources for the population of London are discontinuous both in time and/or in the geographical areas to which they apply. Modern scholars have interpreted the substantial quantity of data available in different ways, and produced widely varying results. The published evidence has been reviewed in an article by Vanessa Harding (1990) ('The Population of London, 1550–1700: A Review of the Published Evidence', *London Journal*, 15: 111–28), to which Table 1 is heavily indebted.

Table 1

Date	Population (000)		Total London population as % of England[a]
	City	Total London	
c.1550	56–69[b]	61–75[b]	2.5
1600	131–52[b]	200[c]	5.0
1650	132[d]	400[e]	7.5
1700	93.5[d]	575[f]	11.5
1750	—	675[f]	11.5
1801	129[g]	958[h]	11.0

Notes: The terms 'City' and 'Total London' each denote slightly different areas at different dates. These differences are explained in Harding (1990), 111–28.

All figures are necessarily tentative.

[a] The author has calculated figures in this column from E. A. Wrigley and R. S. Schofield (1989 edn.), *The Population History of England 1541–1871: A Reconstruction* (Cambridge), 531–4.

[b] Harding (1990), 112, 114, 116–17.

[c] Ibid. 112; R. Finlay and B. Shearer (1986), 'Population Growth and Suburban Expansion', in A. L. Beier and R. Finlay (eds.), *London 1500–1700: The Making of the Metropolis* (London), 39–49; E. A. Wrigley (1967b), 'A Simple Model of London's Importance in Changing English Society and Economy 1650–1750', *Past and Present*, 37: 44.

[d] Harding (1990), 112; Finlay and Shearer (1986), 42, 48.

[e] Harding (1990), 112, 128 n. 61; Wrigley (1967b), 44.

[f] Wrigley (1967b), 44.

[g] R. Price-Williams (1885), 'The Population of London, 1801–1881', *Journal of the Statistical Society*, 48: 365–6.

[h] Ibid. 380.

APPENDIX 2

The Population of London and the South-East Region
1801–1991

Date	City	LCC area		Greater London area		South-East Region	
		population (000)	as % of Eng. & Wales	population (000)	as % of Eng. & Wales	population (000)	as % of Eng. & Wales
1801	129	959	10.8	1,097	12.3	2,493	28
1811	121	1,139	11.2	1,304	12.8	2,879	28.3
1821	125	1,380	11.5	1,573	13.1	3,398	28.3
1831	124	1,656	11.9	1,878	13.5	3,915	28.1
1841	125	1,949	12.2	2,208	13.8	4,457	28
1851	129	2,363	13.1	2,652	14.8	5,094	28
1861	113	2,808	14	3,188	15.9	5,850	29.1
1871	76	3,261	14.3	3,841	16.9	6,804	29.9
1881	51	3,830	14.7	4,713	18.1	7,936	30.5
1891	37	4,228	14.6	5,572	19.2	9,096	31.3
1901	27	4,536	13.9	6,507	20	10,497	32.2
1911	19	4,522	12.5	7,160	19.8	11,612	32.2
1921	14	4,485	11.8	7,387	19.5	12,276	32.4
1931	11	4,397	11	8,110	20.3	13,184	33
1939[a]	9	4,013	9.7	8,615	20.8		
1951	5	3,348	7.6	8,194	18.7	15,046	34.3
1961	5	3,200	6.9	7,992	17.3	16,071	34.8
1971	4	3,031	6.2	7,452	15.3	16,931	34.7
1981	4	2,497	5.1	6,713	13.7	16,731	34.1
1991	4	2,504	5.1	6,394	13	16,793	34.1

Note: the figures of population are in some cases approximations due to minor changes in the definition area.

Source: Registrar General's Reports: Office of Population Census and Surveys.

[a] The figures for this year are estimated.

ENDNOTES

PART I. LONDINIUM

Introduction (pp. 7–8)

1. Caesar (1911), 133; Salway (1981), 24–39; Webster, (1980), 31–40.
2. Stow (1908), i. 1–3.
3. Rivet and Smith (1979), 396–8; Gelling (1978), 37; Milne, (1995), 41.
4. Merriman (1990), 25, 34; Milne (1995), 41; Parnell (1993), 12.

1. Urban Origins (pp. 9–18)

1. Salway (1981), 57–9; Strabo (1917–23), ii. 255, 259.
2. Salway (1981), 82–4; Webster (1980), chs. 4 and 5; Dio (1961), 415.
3. Milne (1995), 39–40; Marsden (1980), 12; Hobley (1986), 4–6.
4. Dio (1961), 419.
5. Salway (1981), 84 n.
6. Dio (1961), 421; Webster (1980), ch. 5.
7. Marsden (1980), 14; Milne (1985), 85; Perring (1991), 3–5; MoLAS (1996), 10.
8. Merrifield (1983), 36–40; Milne (1995), 43.
9. Dio (1961), 421–5; Webster (1980), ch. 5.
10. Merrifield (1969), 61–5.
11. Marsden (1980), 13–14; Merrifield (1983), 28–31; Perring (1991), 5. But see also Milne (1995), 42.
12. Marsden (1980), 17; Millet (1996), 34; Wilkes (1996), 27. For Scapula see also Webster (1978), 58–61, 84.
13. Sherlock (1947), 38–40; Merriman (1990), 4–7.
14. Sherlock (1947), 57; Merriman (1990), 2–17.
15. Merriman (1990), 10–29; Merrifield (1983), 2–3.
16. Merriman (1990), 9–18.
17. Fleury (1994), 9–21.

2. Early Londinium (pp. 19–33)

1. Milne (1995), 20–31, 35.
2. Ibid. 43; Hall and Merrifield (1993), 5.
3. Milne (1995), 39–40; (1985), 80–6; Hall and Merrifield (1993), 5–6.
4. Merrifield (1983), 31.
5. Milne (1995), 42; (1985), 44.
6. Milne (1995), 46–7.
7. Marsden (1980), 20; (1987), 21; Merrifield (1983), 42–3; Milne (1995), 44.
8. MoLAS (1996), 23.

9. Marsden (1980), 24–5, 33; Marsden (1987), 3–4; Merrifield (1983), 43–51; Milne (1995), 43–4; Tacitus (1872–4), i. 374–5.
10. Webster (1978), ch. 5.
11. Ibid.; Salway (1981), 113–23; Tacitus (1872–4), i. 372–7.
12. Marsden (1980), 31–4. 13.
13. Tacitus, (1872–4), i. 378; Marsden (1980), 31–6; Merrifield (1983), 52–8; Webster (1978), ch. 5.
14. MoLAS (1996), 18.
15. Marsden (1987), 32–3, 73; Milne (1995), 48–50, 70, 96; (1996), 53–4.
16. Marsden (1980), 32–3; Milne (1985), 37, 44–54; (1995), 65; Perring (1991), 37.
17. Milne (1985), 18–19, 38–9, 44–54; Hobley (1986), 10.
18. Milne (1985), 18, 27, 127–43; Merrifield (1990), 5–6.
19. Tacitus, Agricola, xxi, quoting translation in Salway (1981), 142; Marsden (1980), 41; (1987), 4, 73.
20. Marsden (1987), 38, 76; Milne (1995), 56–7; (1996), 53–4.
21. For the supposed palace see Marsden (1980), 88–96; Merrifield (1983), 72–7. For different views, see Milne (1995), 91–3; (1996), 49–54; Perring (1991), 30–4; and Hassall (1996), 20–3.
22. Marsden (1980), 92; Merrifield (1983), 75, 77.
23. Marsden (1980), 88–96.
24. Marsden (1980), 88–97; Merrifield (1983), 72–7. See also Perring (1991), 34.
25. Grimes (1968), 15–46; Marsden (1980), 80–7; Merrifield (1983), 77–83.
26. Maloney (1988), passim; Merrifield, (1990), 5; Milne (1995), 53, 59–60; MoLAS (1996), 17.
27. Marsden (1980), 48–56, 93; (1987), 24–5, 32–3; Merrifield, (1983), 83–7, 130–2.
28. Carlin (1996); Milne (1995), 69–70.
29. Fleury (1994), 9–21.
30. Merrifield (1983), 57–60; Tacitus (1872–4), i. 378.
31. Ibid.; Marsden, (1980), 25, 36–7; Wacher (1976 edn.), 17, 79–80; see also Hassall (1996), 20.
32. Tacitus, Agricola, xxi, quoting translation in Salway (1981), 142.
33. Marsden (1980), 39–42; Merrifield (1983), 71–2; see also Wilkes (1996), 27–30, and Millett (1996), 34.
34. Merrifield (1983), 51, 102, 109–14; Milne (1995), 60–4; (1985), 103, 118.
35. Marsden (1980), 41, 52.
36. Ibid. 50, 60–1; Perring (1991), 73–5.
37. Merrifield (1983), 93, 96; Milne (1995), 117–18; (1985), 87–91, 106, 114, 117.

3. Change and Decay (pp. 34–47)

1. Marsden (1980), 107–10; Merrifield (1983), 106–9; Milne (1995), 33.
2. Marsden (1980), 109–17; Merrifield (1983), 140–6; Milne (1995), 81–2.
3. The 'dark earth' problem is discussed in Marsden (1980), 167, 178; Merrifield (1983), 140–4; Milne (1995), 71–3; Perring (1991), 78–81; and Yule (1990), passim.
4. Frere (1987), 253, 302; Salway (1981), 544.
5. Marsden (1980), 110–11; Merrifield (1983), 145, 194–5; Perring (1991), 87.
6. Marsden (1980), 115, 148; Merrifield (1983), 144–8; Armitage, West, and Steedman (1984), passim.
7. Marsden (1980), 156–7; Merrifield (1983), 149–53; Milne (1985), 18, 29–32, 143.

8. Marsden (1980), 119–30; Merrifield (1983), 154–67.

9. Salway (1981), 217–30; Perring (1991), 99.

10. Merrifield (1983), 167–83; Perring (1991), 95, 98–9; Salway (1981), 233–4. See also Blagg (1996), 45–7.

11. Merrifield (1983), 171; Hassall (1996), 23; Salway (1981), 231.

12. Marsden (1980), 148–55; Merrifield (1983), 183–92; Perring (1991), 102–4.

13. Frere (1987), 329; Salway (1981), 273–6, 299–300, 320.

14. Perring (1991), 106–9; Sheldon and Tyers (1983), 355–60; Merrifield (1983), 216–27, and revision in (1990), 7–8.

15. Merrifield (1983), 192–4.

16. Ibid. 197–200; Blagg (1996), 45–6; Salway (1981), 288–312.

17. Merrifield (1983), 205; Salway (1981), 290, 315–17.

18. Salway (1981), 339, 342, 345–6; Hassall (1996), 25–6.

19. Merrifield (1983), 209–10; Salway (1981), 324–5, 342, 345.

20. Salway (1981), 341, 344, 356.

21. Mann (1961), 316–20; Merrifield (1983), 210; Salway (1981), 340.

22. Marsden (1980), 146–8; Merrifield (1983), 211–12.

23. Salway (1981), 348, 354–8, 368.

24. Ibid. 360–1, 374–82; Merrifield (1983), 214.

25. Royal Commission on Historical Monuments (1928), 5–6.

26. Merrifield (1983), 214–15.

27. Ibid., 222, 227; Hill, Millett, and Blagg (1980), 2, 62, 69; Sheldon and Tyers (1983), 359–60.

28. Marsden (1980), 82–3, 171–3, 193; Merrifield (1983), 228–35; Hill, Millett, and Blagg (1980), 69; Milne (1995), 85.

29. Salway (1981), 402–4, 426–8.

30. Merrifield (1983), 224–7, 239–45; Parnell (1993), 13–16.

31. Salway (1981), 420–1, 428–9, 433–4 (Zosimus quotation); Frere (1987), 353, 357.

32. Salway (1981), 434, 442–3.

33. Cleere (1978), 36–40; Milne (1985), 104–6.

34. Milne (1985), 112, 115, 118, 124–5; Frere (1987), 284.

35. Frere (1987), 272; Merrifield (1983), 213; Salway (1981), 359–60.

36. Merrifield (1983), 194–7.

37. Milne (1985), 84–6, 142–8; Bateman and Milne (1983), 224–5.

38. Milne (1995), 79.

39. Ibid., 81; Perring (1991), 120.

40. Fulford (1978), 59–69.

41. Merrifield (1983), 199, 206; Perring (1991), 110; Salway (1981), 424–5, 454–5.

42. Marsden (1980), 180–6.

PART II. FROM LONDINIUM TO THE CHARTERED CITY OF LONDON c.400–c.1530

4. Londinium and Lundenwic c.400–c.886 (pp. 53–63)

1. C. Thomas (1981), 240, 250–1.

2. For discussion of this, see Jackson (1953), 229–31; C. Thomas (1971), 22–4; (1986), 48; Alcock (1966–7), 239–40; Wheeler (1935), 56–7; Myres (1986), 31 and n.; Merrifield (1983), 215.

3. Myres (1986) 86–92 and ch. 5 generally, esp. p. 128; Wheeler (1935), 39–40.
4. C. Thomas (1971), 24–6; (1981), 241.
5. Jackson (1953), 198; Myres (1986), 128.
6. Merrifield (1983), 240–5, 250–1, 256–7; Parnell (1993), 13.
7. Myres (1936), 90; (1986), 138–9; Merrifield (1983), 259; Clark (1989 edn.), 5.
8. Merrifield (1983), 238–9, 245, 259; Myres (1986), 131–2.
9. Wheeler (1935), *passim*, esp, 81, 83.
10. C. Thomas, (1981), ch. 10, *passim*.
11. Wheeler (1935), 59–74; Merrifield (1983), 260–2.
12. Brooke and Keir (1975), 87, 207–9, see also Hollister (1990), 289–306.
13. Wheeler (1935), 59–62; Stenton (1934), 6; (1987 edn.), 57–8. See also Brooke and Keir (1975), 207–9.
14. Clark (1989 edn.), 9–11.
15. Merrifield (1983), 263–5; Myres (1986), 130.
16. Myres (1936), 92; Jackson (1953), 230.
17. Vince (1990), 61.
18. Biddle (1989), 21–2.
19. Myres (1986), 129 and n.
20. Alcock (1966–7), 235.
21. Dyson and Schofield (1984), 290–1; Brooke and Keir (1975), 17–19.
22. Dyson and Schofield (1984), 290–5; Brooke and Keir (1975), 18, 198.
23. Dyson and Schofield (1984), 294, 307–8; Vince (1990), 54–5; Brooke and Keir (1975), 137; Lobel (1989), 85.
24. Dyson and Schofield (1984), 306–7; Brooke and Keir (1975), 154–5; Vince (1990), 54–6.
25. Biddle (1989), 22–4; Lobel (1989), 76.
26. Dyson and Schofield (1984), 292; Brooke and Keir (1975), 137; Vince (1990), 69–70.
27. Dyson (1980), 83–95; Blair (1989), 97–8.
28. Dyson and Schofield (1984), 292–3; Biddle (1989), 25–6 quoting Bede; Wheeler (1935), 97 n.
29. Biddle (1989), 24–5.
30. Biddle (1984), and Vince (1984), *passim*.
31. Tatton-Brown (1986), 24.
32. *Daily Telegraph*, 1 Aug. 1988.
33. Biddle (1984), 26; Vince (1990), 17; Hobley (1986), 16.
34. Vince (1994), 116; Rackham (1994), 134.
35. Hobley (1986), 16; Whipp (1986), 148–50; Keene (1994), 24.
36. Biddle (1984), 27.
37. Clark (1989 edn.), 16–17; Brooke and Keir (1975), 15, 19–20, quoting Bede; Wheeler (1927), 11.
38. Vince (1984), 310–12; Biddle (1984), 26.

5. Lundenburg to Municipal Commune *c.*886–1215 (pp. 64–91)

1. Stenton (1987 edn.), 259–60; Brooke and Keir (1975), 19–20.
2. Stenton (1987 edn.), 260, 263–9; Wheeler (1927), 11–12.
3. Brooke and Keir (1975), 96–8; Stenton (1934), 13–14.

4. Quoted in Wheeler (1927), 14; Stenton (1987 edn.), 378, 383–5.
5. Wheeler (1927), 14–15; Brooke and Keir (1975), 21–2.
6. Stenton (1987 edn.), 388–90; Brooke and Keir (1975), 22.
7. Stenton (1987 edn.), 390; Brooke and Keir (1975), 23.
8. Stenton (1987 edn.), 390–2; Wheeler (1927), 16.
9. Stenton (1987 edn.), 392–3; Brooke and Keir (1975), 23–4.
10. Brooke and Keir (1975), 24; Wheeler (1927), 16.
11. Stenton (1987 edn.), 423, 564–5; Brooke and Keir (1975), 25.
12. Stenton (1987 edn.), 565–9; Brooke and Keir (1975), 25–6.
13. Stenton (1987 edn.), 561, 580; Brooke and Keir (1975), 295–6; Harvey (1977), 20–5; Rosser (1989), 12–16.
14. Quoted in *Carmen* (1972), 39–53.
15. Ibid. 43; Stenton (1987 edn.), 596–7.
16. *Carmen* (1972), 45–9; Stenton (1987 edn.), 596–8. See also Brooke and Keir (1975), 26–9.
17. Biddle and Hudson, with Heighway (1973), 21; Wheeler (1935), 104–6; Jackson (1953), 227–8; Tatton-Brown (1986), 22–3. For St Peter's see also Vince (1990), 59–60.
18. Stenton (1987 edn.), 258; Biddle and Hill (1971), 83; Dyson (1978), 210; *Daily Telegraph*, 21 Aug. 1997, 10.
19. Brooke and Keir (1975), 60–1; Biddle and Hill (1971), 83; Dyson (1990), *passim.*
20. Bentley (1985), 124–9.
21. Brooke (1989), 33; Lobel (1989), map of Roman London.
22. There is a large literature on the development near Queenhithe. See Dyson (1978); (1990); Dyson and Schofield (1984); Steedman, Dyson, and Schofield (1992).
23. Merrifield (1990), 12–13; Dyson and Schofield (1984), 293, 299, 302; Steedman, Dyson, and Schofield (1992), 135; MoLAS 96 (1996), 41.
24. Brooke and Keir (1975), 171–7.
25. Biddle and Hudson, with Heighway (1973), 23; Tatton-Brown (1986), 25.
26. Steedman, Dyson, and Schofield (1992), 99–101, 131, 138.
27. Brooke and Keir (1975), 131–3; but see also Keene (1984), 15.
28. Brooke and Keir (1975), 127, 130; Lobel (1989), map of London, *c.*1270.
29. Brooke and Keir (1975), 14–15, 310–12, 330–1; Myers (1972), 77.
30. Brooke and Keir (1975), 231–2, 331–2; Myers (1972), 35.
31. Weinreb and Hibbert (1993), *passim.*
32. Rosser (1989), 12–16; Brooke and Keir (1975), 295–6; Harvey, (1977), 20–5.
33. Quoted in Stenton (1934), 26; Gem (1990), 51–9; Lobel (1989), 91.
34. Parnell (1993), 17–22.
35. Myers (1972), 68–9, 127–31; Brooke and Keir (1975), 110; Corporation of London (1950), 130–1; MoLAS 96 (1996), 41. See also Harding and Wright (1995), *passim.*
36. Stenton (1934), 27, 30; J. Schofield (1994), 34.
37. Biddle (1989), 24; Nightingale (1987), 563.
38. Brooke and Keir (1975), 185–98; Nightingale (1987), 563.
39. Brooke and Keir (1975), 155, 162–70; Reynolds (1977), 94.
40. Brooke and Keir (1975), 151–3, 168.
41. Nightingale (1987), 559, 562–5.
42. Brooke and Keir (1975), 28–9.
43. Reynolds (1972), 339.

44. Brooke and Keir (1975), 192–3, 215–17; Stenton (1934), 8–9.
45. For this whole paragraph see Brooke and Keir (1975), 185–222; Reynolds (1972), 337–41; Corporation of London (1950), 25.
46. Brooke, Keir, and Reynolds (1973), *passim*; Hollister (1990), 289–306.
47. Brooke and Keir (1975), 87, 207–9; Poole (1987 edn.), 69.
48. Brooke and Keir (1975), 35–40, 191.
49. Ibid. 45; Poole (1987 edn.), 70, 352.
50. Brooke and Keir (1975), 45–6; Poole (1987 edn.), 357–8; Reynolds (1972), 348.
51. Brooke and Keir (1975), 46–7, 239.
52. Ibid. 57, 236, 243; Reynolds (1972), 349; Williams (1963), 1–8.
53. Brooke and Keir (1975), 47; Poole (1987 edn.), 70.
54. Brooke and Keir (1975), 49–56; Holt (1965), 48, 221; Williams (1963), 6.
55. Williams (1963), 6–8.
56. Nightingale (1987), 566.
57. Clark (1989 edn.), 30; Keene (1994), 25–6; Nightingale (1996), 96. See also Keene (1989), 107, and Donkin (1973), 132–5.
58. Nightingale (1987), 567.
59. Brooke and Keir (1975), 29, 145–6; Lobel (1989), 86.
60. Brooke and Keir (1975), 31–2, 342; Stenton (1934), 16.
61. Brooke and Keir (1975), 179, 265–70; Nightingale (1995), 87; Reynolds (1977), 73–4.
62. Brooke and Keir (1975), 276–8.
63. Brooke and Keir (1975), 278–9; Reynolds (1977), 123–5.
64. Brooke and Keir (1975), 281–2; Nightingale (1995), 43.
65. Nightingale (1995), 1–2, 13.
66. Ibid. 17–23.
67. Ibid. 25; Biddle and Hudson, with Heighway (1973), 24; Dyson and Schofield (1984), 303.
68. Nightingale (1995), 9–10; Brooke and Keir (1975), 285–8.
69. Brooke and Keir (1975), 261–70; Sawyer (1965), *passim*.
70. Nightingale (1995), 17–21, 34–5.
71. Ibid. 56–8.
72. Quoted in P. Bailey (1989), 3–4.
73. J. Schofield (1994), 27, 32, 86–7, 113.
74. Ibid. 32–4, 95.
75. Stenton (1934), 26–32.
76. Quoted ibid. 30; Keene (1985), 8.
77. Quoted in Brooke and Keir (1975), 23, 25.
78. Nightingale (1987), 577–8.
79. Ibid. 578; Keene (1994), 29; Tout (1923), 3–4.
80. Brooke and Keir (1975), 231–3.
81. Tout (1923), 8–9; Myers (1972), 30–1; Brooke (1989), 37–8.
82. For this whole subject see McKisack (1948), *passim*.
83. Ibid. 78–80; Brooke and Keir (1975), 33–9.
84. Holt (1965), 48, 153, 172; Brooke and Keir (1975), 53, 216; Sharpe (1894–5), 77.
85. Brooke and Keir (1975), 56; Poole (1987 edn.), 479.
86. Holt (1965), 48–9; Brooke and Keir (1975), 52.

6. The Emergence of the Medieval Capital *c.*1216–*c.*1530 (pp. 92–122)

1. Keene (1994), 26; Nightingale (1996), *passim*; Favier (1994), 51.
2. Williams (1963), chs. vii–ix; Reynolds (1977), 110, 131–2; Powicke (1987 edn.), 626–8.
3. Williams (1963), 282–4, 287, 299; Bird (1949), 30.
4. Reynolds (1997), 113–14.
5. Myers (1972), 126; Corporation of London (1950), 52–3; Bird (1949), pp. xxiii–iv.
6. A. H. Thomas (1929), p. xxvii.
7. Bolton (1985 edn.), 263–4.
8. Williams (1963), chs. x, xi; Bolton (1985 edn.), 205.
9. Williams (1963), 41; A. H. Thomas (1929), p. lviii.
10. Corporation of London (1950), 6, 51–2; Myers (1972), 88.
11. Corporation of London (1950), 9–10, 13–15; A. H. Thomas (1929), pp. lviii–lix.
12. Nightingale (1989), *passim*, esp. 8–11, 34.
13. Barron (1981*a*), *passim*; Nightingale (1989), *passim*.
14. Barron (1981*a*), 1–7.
15. Ibid. 7–8; information kindly supplied by an anonymous reader for Oxford University Press.
16. Sharpe (1894–5), i. 225–40; Bird (1949), p. xxiii.
17. Myers (1972), 95–6.
18. Bird (1949), 36, 86 and n.; Corporation of London (1950), 38–9.
19. Bird (1949), p. xxii; McKisack (1987 edn.), 448–59.
20. Barron (1971), *passim*.
21. Myers (1972), 90.
22. Rosser (1989), 16–17, 35–41.
23. Binski (1995), 1–7.
24. Saul (1996), *passim*.
25. Tout (1923), 10; Rosser (1989), 39; Rowse (1972), 45–6; information kindly supplied by an anonymous reader for Oxford University Press.
26. Rosser (1989), 35–43; Tout (1923), 10–11, 14–17; Myers (1972), 30–4.
27. Tout (1923), 22–3; Myers (1972), 40–1; Lobel (1989), 78.
28. McKisack (1948), *passim*; McKisack (1987 edn.), 83–95, 494–6; Barron (1971), *passim*.
29. Barron (1981*b*), *passim*.
30. McKisack (1948), *passim*.
31. Keene (1989), 101; (1994), 25–6. Estimates of the population of later medieval London are based on the work of Dr Derek Keene, whose figures were first put forward in *Urban History Yearbook* (1984), 20, and on the more recent work of Pamela Nightingale (1996: 89–106).
32. Favier (1994), 32–51; Morris (1990), 74–5; Lobel (1989), 91.
33. Hawkins (1990), *passim*; Nightingale (1996), 98, but see also Britnell (1994), 199.
34. Britnell (1994), 198–9, 203–4; Hawkins (1990), *passim*. For the Black Death in general see also Platt (1996) and Harvey (1993), *passim*.
35. Keene (1989), 101; Nightingale (1996), 105–6; Barron, (1994*b*), 53, 56–7.
36. A. R. H. Baker (1973), 245–7; Donkin (1973), 132–5; Glasscock (1973), 184–5.
37. R. S. Schofield (1965), 508.
38. Hoskins (1956), 4.
39. R. S. Schofield (1965), 482–510, *passim*. See also Darby *et al.* (1979), 257.
40. Unwin (1908), 370–1.

41. Thrupp (1948), 9; Carus-Wilson (1967), 222–8; Williams (1963), 175–81.
42. Myers (1972), 40–1; Carlin (1996), 169–77; Keene (1985), 16–18.
43. Galloway and Murphy (1991), 3, 11.
44. Rosser (1989), 133–8.
45. Galloway and Murphy (1991), 9–11; Keene (1989), 104–5.
46. Galloway and Murphy (1991), 6–7, 11; Campbell *et al.* (1993), 175, 179, 180–1.
47. Campbell *et al.* (1993), 174; Galloway and Murphy (1991), 8; Keene (1993–4), 8–10; Bolton (1985 edn.), 165. See also Galloway, Keene, and Murphy (1996), *passim*.
48. Campbell *et al.* (1993), 108, 173–5.
49. Hornsby, Weinstein, and Homer (1989), *passim*; Myers (1972), 22; Bolton (1985 edn.), 192.
50. Myers (1972), 22, 84.
51. Glasscock (1973), 173; V.C.H. Dorset (1908), ii. 332–4, 339.
52. Bolton (1985 edn.), 301–2; Stenton (1934), 21.
53. Bolton (1985 edn.), 174–9; Nightingale (1995), 87.
54. Carus-Wilson and Coleman (1963), 2; A.R.H. Baker (1973), 219–20.
55. Williams (1963), 110, 114. See also tables of wool exports in Carus-Wilson and Coleman (1963).
56. Carus-Wilson and Coleman (1963), 12; Bolton (1985 edn.), 294–6.
57. Calculated from Carus-Wilson and Coleman (1963), 69. See also generally, Harding (1995), *passim*.
58. James (1971), 96; calculation based on Bolton (1985 edn.), 152, and James (1971), p. xvi.
59. James (1971), 94–7, 116; Carus-Wilson (1967), 278; Bolton (1985 edn.), 290.
60. Bolton (1985 edn.), 272; Nightingale (1990), *passim*.
61. Donkin (1973), 121; Bolton (1985 edn.), 311–12.
62. Carus-Wilson (1967), 150–66.
63. Carus-Wilson and Coleman (1963), 88–91, 112–14, 118–19.
64. Coleman (1969), 184–5.
65. Barron (1981*b*) 90–1.
66. Bolton (1985 edn.), 176–7, 340–1.
67. Fryde (1988), 21, 113, 153, 208; *Dictionary of National Biography.*
68. Coleman (1969), 185.
69. Steel (1936), 29–51, 577–97 *passim*.
70. Barron (1969), *passim*.
71. Barron (1981*b*), 90–4, 99–100. In addition to the sources cited in this section see also Bolton (1986); Guth (1986), McFarlane (1981); Nightingale (1989).
72. Morris (1990), 74–5; Lobel (1989), 91.
73. Barron (1989*a*), 48–9.
74. Brooke (1989), 38; Lobel (1989), gazetteer, 63–99 *passim*.
75. Lobel (1989), gazetteer, 63–99, *passim*.
76. Barron (1989*a*), 45–7.
77. Myers (1972), 81, 138, 141.
78. Sabine (1933), *passim*.
79. Keene (1984), 14–15; Keene (1985), 12–13.
80. J. Schofield (1994), 34–5, 41–50; Barron (1989*a*), 49.
81. J. Schofield (1994), 54–5, 60, 133, 146–7; Lobel (1989), map 2.
82. Barron (1989*a*), 53–5; Hobley (1986), 18–20.

83. Carpenter (1994), 98 and *passim*.
84. Barron (1989*a*), 45–6.
85. Ibid. 45–6.
86. Sabine (1934), 308, 317.
87. Sabine (1937), 21–4.
88. Barron (1989*a*), 45; (1974), *passim*.
89. Corporation of London (1950), 27; Barron (1989*a*), 51.
90. McDonnell (1978), *passim*.
91. Barron (1995*a*), *passim*.
92. Myers (1972), 37–8.
93. Carlin (1996), 253–5; Corporation of London (1950), 79; A.R.H. Baker (1973), 246.
94. Rosser (1989), 168; Carlin (1996), 142.
95. Rosser (1989), ch. 5, *passim*.
96. Ibid. 38–40, 145, 158.
97. Ekwall (1956), xvi–xx, pp. lviii–lxiii.
98. Thrupp (1948), 209–10; Autrand and Le Maresquier (1994), 82.
99. *Dictionary of National Biography*.
100. Thrupp (1948), 213, 216; Ekwall (1956), pp. xi, xli; Reynolds (1977), 101.
101. Thrupp (1969), 251.
102. Barron (1994*b*), 55; (1989*a*), 54.
103. Barron (1994*a*), pp. xiii, xxii; Rappaport (1989), 47–53; but see also A.H. Thomas (1929), p. lxii.
104. Hanawalt (1993), 234, 238, quoting David Herlihy and Christiane Klapisch-Zuber, *Tuscans and their Families: A Study of the Florentine Catasto of 1427* (New Haven, 1985), 277–8.
105. Hatcher (1977), 26–30.
106. Barron (1989*b*), 35–6, 48–9.
107. Ibid. 39–40, 43–7; Lacey (1985), 48–57.
108. Barron (1989*b*), 49; (1994*a*), p. xxxiv.
109. Hanawalt (1993), 57, 72, 85–6, 237–8; Thrupp (1948), 203.
110. This section is heavily indebted to Barron (1996), *passim*. See also Thrupp (1948), 156–8.
111. Barron (1996), 225–31; Rosser (1989), 209.
112. Barron (1974), 33; (1969), 232.
113. Barron (1996), 236–7; Jordan (1960), 220–3.
114. *Dictionary of National Biography*.
115. Burgess (1996), *passim*; Barron (1985), *passim*.
116. Burgess (1996), *passim*.
117. Rawcliffe (1984), *passim*.
118. Ibid. 6, 19, 21; Myers (1972), 49–51, 165–71.
119. Sharpe (1894–5), i. 217; Corporation of London (1950), 15–18; Myers (1972), 167–8.
120. Lavedan (1975), 83–4, 118.
121. Ibid. 81–2, 104.
122. Biddle and Hudson, with Heighway (1973), 10–15.
123. Favier (1994), 41–7.
124. Favier (1974), 59–61.

PART III. THE GENESIS OF MODERN LONDON 1530–1700

7. The Rise of the Metropolis (pp. 126–47)

1. See esp. Beier and Finlay (1986a), to which this chapter is heavily indebted.
2. Finlay and Shearer (1986), 38–9, 49.
3. Harding (1990), 111–28; Wrigley and Schofield (1989 edn.), 208–9; Wrigley (1967b), 44, 48–50.
4. Wrigley (1986), 'Urban Growth', 164.
5. Beier and Finlay (1986b), 2–4; Finlay and Shearer (1986), 38–9; Wrigley (1967b), 44–5.
6. Rappaport (1983–4), 9: 118.
7. Beier and Finlay (1986a), 9, 10; Finlay and Shearer (1986), 37, 49; Wrigley and Schofield (1989 edn.), 176.
8. Rappaport (1989), 71.
9. Finlay (1981), 118; Beier and Finlay (1986b), 9; Slack (1986), 61–2; Chartres (1986), 171.
10. Glass (1969), 385, 387.
11. Beier and Finlay (1986b), 9, 10; Wrigley (1967b), 46–7.
12. Fisher (1990), 192. All references to Professor Fisher's seminal writings on London's economic role in the sixteenth and seventeenth centuries are to this collection of his articles.
13. Beier and Finlay (1986b), 10; Finlay and Shearer (1986), 52–3; Wrigley (1986), *passim*.
14. Pettegree (1986), 2, 6, 16–17, 78, 299; Scouloudi (1937–41), 31. See also Finlay (1981), 67–9.
15. Gwynn (1965–70), 371–3.
16. *The Quiet Conquest* (1985), 111; Gwynn (1985), 36.
17. Houtte (1977), 227–9; Finlay and Shearer (1986), 52.
18. Beier and Finlay (1986b), 26; Baker (1936), 402–3; Gras (1915), 281–96.
19. Braudel (1985 edn.), 73–4, 117–18, 122–3.
20. Beier and Finlay (1986b), 26–7; Chartres (1986), 177.
21. Fisher (1990), 106.
22. Fisher (1990), 185–98.
23. Stone (1980), 173–6.
24. Fisher (1990), 111, 114.
25. Quoted ibid. 114.
26. Quoted in Stone (1979 edn.), 388.
27. Stone (1980), 184–5.
28. Quoted in Fisher (1990), 66.
29. Chartres (1986), 178, 181, 183.
30. Willan (1938), 61, 71–2, 74, 76.
31. Chartres (1986), 171–2.
32. Ibid. 174–6.
33. Willan (1976), 12; Clay (1984), ii. 182; Barker and Gerhold (1993), 19–26.
34. Quoted in Chartres (1977a), 73.
35. Willan (1976), 18–19, 123; (1936), 122, 125, 149.
36. Willan (1936), 137. See also Stern (1979), 231, 237.
37. Fisher (1990), 65–72.
38. Quoted ibid. 75.
39. Quoted in Willan (1976), 19.
40. Fisher (1990), 72, 77–8; Chartres (1977b), 21–2.

41. Wrigley (1967*b*), 59–60.
42. Quotations from Fisher (1990), 139–40. London's influence on the economies of provincial towns is also discussed in Corfield (1990), 35–62.
43. Kerridge (1988), 5–6, 29–30.
44. Ibid. 33–6.
45. Ramsay (1975), *passim*; Doolittle (1994), 27–35.
46. Ashton (1960), 17, 23, 79, 87.
47. *Dictionary of National Biography.*
48. Ashton (1960), 27–8, 131–2, 185.
49. Ibid. 27–9.
50. Sharpe (1894–5), ii. 28–45.
51. Ashton (1960), 10, 46, 132, 153, 184, 191; Pearl (1961), 98–103.
52. Wilson (1965), 208.
53. Ibid. 155–6, 213.
54. Clay (1984), ii. 272; Horsefield (1982), 512.
55. Horsefield (1982), *passim*.
56. Melton (1986), 236–42.
57. Horsefield (1982), *passim*; Wilson (1965), 215.
58. Wilson (1965), 218.
59. Ibid. 218–19.
60. Clay (1984), ii. 279–80; Dickson (1967), 254–7.
61. Wilson (1965), 221–4; Clay ii. 276 and n.
62. Wilson (1965), 333–5.
63. Ibid.; Supple (1970), 7–9; Brett-James (1935), 343–4.
64. Kellett (1960–8), *passim*.
65. Carlton (1974), 90–3.
66. Sharpe (1894–5), ii. 579–83.
67. Clay (1984), ii. 103–8.
68. Ibid. 107–12; Ramsay (1975), 22–3, 41, 61; Fisher (1990), 188–9.
69. Fisher (1990), 83, 189; Dietz (1986), 126.
70. Willan (1956), 1–5; Clay (1984), ii. 123–4; Dietz (1986), 122.
71. Clay (1984), ii. 182–4.
72. Coleman (1977), 58–60.
73. Willan (1956), 21.
74. Hinton (1959), 56, 73.
75. Wood (1935), 7, 11, 16–17.
76. Keay (1991), 24–8; Clay (1984), ii. 164.
77. Clay (1984), ii. 138, 144.
78. Dietz (1986), 130–1.
79. Clay (1984), ii. 165–8.
80. K. G. Davies (1957), 66–70, 97–8, 345.
81. French (1992), 30.
82. Gough (1991), 49–56.
83. Israel (1989), 410–15; Brenner (1993), 625–8.
84. Israel (1989), 282–358.
85. Ranum (1968), 35–42, 46, 179–80, 219–28.
86. Clay (1984), ii. 168.

87. Dietz (1986), 127–9.
88. R. Davis (1962), 55, 68, 98, 390; Zahedieh (1994), 239–61.
89. Grassby (1970), *passim*.

8. Religious and Educational Revolution (pp. 148–60)

1. Brigden (1989), 2. I am much indebted to this monumental work.
2. Ibid. 47 and n., 68–9, 73.
3. Ibid. 86–7, 91–2, 106–18, 158–60, 179–87.
4. Ibid. 286–8, 339, 346–7.
5. *Victoria County History of Middlesex* (1969), i. 167 n. 17.
6. Brigden (1989), 332.
7. Ibid. 120–1. See also Brigden (1982), *passim*.
8. Rappaport (1989), 232, 392.
9. Brigden (1989), 438, 444–5; Duffy (1992), 5, 451–9, 465; Snell (1978), 216–23; Kitching (1980), *passim*.
10. Pettegree (1986), 26, 35, 69–70, 78, 292–3.
11. Ibid. 118–19.
12. Brigden (1989), 557–8, 606–12, 619, 625, 628.
13. Ibid. 383, 485, 577, 593, 629.
14. Jordan (1960), 20–6; but see also Archer (1991), 163–5.
15. Prest (1972), 174–86; Dures (1983), 10, 22–6, 56, 83; Stone (1979 edn.), 729–33.
16. Collinson (1990 edn.), 13–14, 28.
17. Ibid. 45–6, 63–4, 68–9, 73, 76, 113–14.
18. Archer (1991), 88.
19. Quoted in Collinson (1990 edn.), 86.
20. Ibid. 84–91.
21. Seaver (1970), 9, 54, 123, 128, 143, 151, 310.
22. Collinson (1990 edn.), 84–6.
23. Ibid. 401, 411–12.
24. Boulton (1984), *passim*. See also Seaver (1985), *passim*, for the ethos of mid-seventeenth-century Puritanism.
25. Seaver (1970), 9, 254.
26. Collinson (1990 edn.), 432–3.
27. Seaver (1970), 268–9, 272–3.
28. Cross (1972), 108–10; Liu (1986), 88, 197.
29. Liu (1986), 88, 105.
30. Seaver (1970), 277.
31. Matthews (1959), 5–6.
32. Harris (1987), 66; Earle (1989), 383; De Krey (1985), 75.
33. Harris (1987), 62–9.
34. De Krey (1985), 74–85, 112–20.
35. Gwynn (1985), 35–8, 101–5.
36. Pepys (1979–83), iii. 54 n., x. 350–3.
37. Cressy (1980), 176; Stone (1964), 68.
38. Cressy (1980), 72, 115, 121, 128–9, 145–54.
39. Ibid. 45–8.

40. Earle (1989), 345.
41. Stone (1964), 42, 44, 75; Earle (1989), 63, 66.
42. Jordan (1960), 210–17.
43. Ibid. 151–3, 253–4; Doolittle (1994), 32–40.
44. Prest (1972), 115.
45. Ibid. 5–7.
46. Quotations, ibid. 11, 13, 23–40. See also Larminie (1990), *passim*.
47. Stone (1964), 79.
48. Ibid. 68–9, 73; Lemmings (1990), 258–9.
49. Hunter (1981), chs. 2 and 3.

9. Political Revolutions (pp. 161–70)

1. Clarendon (1888), i. 264.
2. Quoted in Pearl (1961), 1.
3. Macaulay (1896 edn.), i. 278.
4. Pearl (1961), 113, 126–30; Brenner (1993), 374–89, 633; Ashton (1996), 45–53.
5. Pearl (1961), 119, 130–2.
6. Quoted ibid. 139–47. See also Nagel (1996), 65–86.
7. Ibid. 145, 155–7.
8. Ibid. 263–5; Firth (1926–7), 28–9; V. Smith and Kelsey (1996), 117–48.
9. Pearl (1961), 209–10, 250–5, 261, 274–5; (1972), 37–40. For the changed position of the Trained Bands see Roberts (1996), *passim*.
10. Pearl (1972), 29–56; Gentles (1983), 277–82; Sharpe (1894–5), ii. 240–61; Ashton (1996), 53–8.
11. Gentles (1983), 284; Ashton (1996), 53–8.
12. Gregg (1961), 125.
13. Gentles (1983), 284–9.
14. Sharpe (1894–5), ii. 281–3; Ashton (1996), 53–8.
15. Sharpe (1894–5), ii. 262–302; Gentles (1983), 282–305; Brenner (1993), 543; Ashton (1996), 53–8.
16. Brenner (1993), 541–7.
17. Sharpe (1894–5), ii. 305–8, 319, 345–6, 361.
18. Ibid. 366–7; Pepys (1979–83), i. 1 and unnumbered facing page.
19. Davies (1937), 252–3; Sharpe (1894–5), ii. 368; Pepys (1979–83), i. 50–2.
20. Harris (1987), 92–108.
21. Knights (1993a), 39–67.
22. G. N. Clark (1944 edn.), 97 and n.; see also Harris (1993), 102–9.
23. Harris (1987), 3.
24. Allen (1972), 287–303.
25. Levin (1969), 2, 18, 55–7, 90; Doolittle (1982), 18–19.
26. Sachse (1964), 23–40; Beddard (1988), 36–9.

10. The Processes of Growth (pp. 171–85)

1. Stone (1980), 171–2.
2. Finlay and Shearer (1986), 42–9. See also Harding (1990), 123.

3. Finlay and Shearer (1986), 52–3; Slack (1986), 62–3.
4. Ranum (1968), 98, 101–2, 284–5.
5. Stow (1908), ii. 72, 74; Power (1990), 116.
6. *Survey of London* (1957), 1; Finlay and Shearer (1986), 45, 49.
7. Brett-James (1935), 214–22.
8. Johnson (1969), 304.
9. Brett-James (1935), 408.
10. Quoted in Jennings (1987 edn.), 8–9.
11. *Survey of London* (1960), 29: 377.
12. Stone (1973), 209–11; *Survey of London* (1970b), 19, 50–1.
13. Honeybourne (1931–2), 57.
14. Rosenfield (1961), 86–90, 311, 348–50.
15. Stow (1908), ii. 367.
16. Finlay and Shearer (1986), 42.
17. Quoted in Brett-James (1935), 67–8.
18. Quoted ibid., 69–70.
19. *Survey of London* (1963), 31: 34–5; Sheppard (1982), 19.
20. Stone (1973), 110; (1980), 199, 202.
21. Sheppard (1982), 19–22.
22. *Survey of London* (1970b), 1–98 passim.
23. Ibid. 2–4, 31–2, 73; Summerson (1965), *passim.*
24. *Survey of London* (1973), 276–97.
25. *Survey of London* (1912), 9–11, 96–9; (1914), 42–9; Summerson (1945 edn.), 17–19.
26. Brett-James (1935), 152–60; Summerson (1945 edn.), 23; Stone (1973), 238.
27. *Survey of London* (1960), 29: 3–4, 57–8, 218.
28. *Survey of London* (1966), 33: 4–5; 34: 424–5.
29. *Survey of London* (1963), 31: 143.
30. Ibid. 111; *Survey of London* (1966), 34: 383.
31. *Survey of London* (1966), 34: 363–4.
32. *Survey of London* (1957), 2.
33. *Survey of London* (1963), 31: 139; (1966), 33: 29–30, 37.
34. Brett-James (1935), 418.
35. Power (1972), 238–44, 258; (1978a), 170, 182.
36. *Survey of London* (1963), 31: 1–3; (1966), 33: 1–3.
37. Weinreb and Hibbert (rev. edn. 1993), 470, 541–3.
38. Ibid., 780, 927–9, 974–5.
39. Pepys (1979–83), i. 269; iv. 220.
40. Quoted in Sheppard (1971), 27–8.
41. Reddaway (1940), 26; Pepys (1979–83), 138–40.
42. Reddaway (1940), 221–43, 284, 297–8; Milne (1986), 116–17.
43. Milne (1986), 116–19.
44. *Survey of London* (1963), 31: 8–9; (1966), 34: 424–5.
45. Milne (1986), 83, 120.
46. S. Rolle, *London's Resurrection*, 1668, quoted in Reddaway (1940), 278 n.
47. Quoted in Reddaway (1940), 300–2; see also *Survey of London* (1970b), 8.
48. Finlay and Shearer (1986), 42, 49.

11. The Administration of the Metropolis (pp. 186–92)

1. Finlay and Shearer (1986), 45; Corfield (1982), 11–15.
2. Pearl (1981), 116.
3. Foster (1977), 54, 86, 173–9. See also Archer (1991), 18–20.
4. Pearl (1979), 4.
5. Pearl (1981), 121–31.
6. Sharpe (1894–5), ii. 417, 449–51.
7. Macfarlane (1986), 257.
8. Pearl (1976), *passim*; Macfarlane (1986), *passim*.
9. Beier (1978), *passim*. See also Rappaport (1989), 4–6.
10. Finlay and Shearer (1986), 42, 45.
11. Johnson (1969), 114, 174.
12. Jeffries Davis (1924), 298–300.
13. Slack (1986), 63.
14. Ibid. 65–7; Pearl (1961), 20–1, 30–1.
15. Slack (1986), *passim*; (1980), *passim*.
16. Slack (1986), 71; (1980), 8–9.
17. Quoted in Brett-James (1935), 223–47; see also Pearl (1961), 31–7; Slack (1980), 8–9.
18. Brett-James (1935), 226; Pearl (1961), 33.
19. Brett-James (1935), 230–1; Pearl (1961), 34.
20. Pearl (1979), 13; Rappaport (1989), 53.
21. Pearl (1961), 32 n., 35–7, 268–9.
22. Johnson (1969), 165.
23. Quoted in Brett-James (1935), 241–5.

12. Death and Life in London (pp. 193–201)

1. Pepys (1979–83), vi. 187.
2. Finlay (1981), 91–2, 100, 108, 118; Slack (1985), 151, 308.
3. Finlay (1981), 108.
4. Slack (1985), 154–68.
5. Beier (1986), 147–8; Rappaport (1983–4), 9: 122.
6. Power (1978*b*), 36.
7. Power (1978*a*), 175–7.
8. Earle (1989), 357.
9. Sheppard (1982), 14.
10. Beier (1986), 149–51; Power (1990), 116–17.
11. Rappaport (1983–4), 9: 121–4; Beier (1978), 204, 210–14. See also Rappaport (1989), 5.
12. Pearl (1979), 25; Porter (1996), 18–20, 175–204.
13. A. H. Thomas (ed.), *Calendar of Plea and Memoranda Rolls, 1364–1381* (Cambridge, 1929), p. lxii.
14. Rappaport (1989), 43–9, 334–40, 366.
15. Kellett (1957–8), *passim*.
16. Pearl (1979), 13.
17. *Survey of London* (1966), 33: 107.
18. Sheppard (1982), 13–14.
19. Finlay (1981), 66–7.

20. Beier (1986), 159.
21. Rappaport (1989), 311–12.
22. Archer (1991), 204–15; see also Griffiths (1993), 39–63; Rappaport (1983–4), 9: 118.
23. Rappaport (1989), 15–17.
24. Ibid. 6–7.
25. Power (1986a), 141–2.
26. Gras (1915), 77–85.
27. Pearl (1979), 25, 34; (1981), 119–20.
28. Gras (1915), 87–94.
29. Rappaport (1983–4) 9: 129; (1989), 150.
30. Rappaport (1983–4), 9: 126.
31. Rappaport (1989), 85; Chartres (1986), 171.
32. Archer (1991), 11–13, 92, 154, 241–2.
33. Ibid. 237.
34. Ibid. 237–41.
35. Ibid. 17, 57.
36. Ibid. *passim*, and esp. 96–8, 181–2, 257–8.
37. Earle (1989), 335, 360.
38. Shoemaker (1991), *passim.*
39. Earle (1989), 307–10.
40. Ibid. 337.
41. Ibid. 56, 235.
42. Ibid. 54, 57; Weinreb and Hibbert (1993), 23, 47, 392, 687, 961.
43. Holmes (1960), 2; Pepys (1979–83), x. 444.
44. *Dictionary of National Biography.*
45. G. Davies (1937), 392–6.
46. *Survey of London* (1970a), 35: 1–2.
47. Ibid. 10, 43–4.
48. Pepys (1979–83), x. 443–4.

PART IV. AUGUSTAN AND GEORGIAN LONDON
1700–1830

Introduction (pp. 205)

1. Wrigley (1988), 132.
2. Wrigley (1986), 126–30.
3. George (1985), 33.

13. The Growth and Structure of London (pp. 206–23)

1. Deane and Cole (1967), 111, 127–8, 287; Wrigley and Schofield (1989 edn.), 77–9; Schwarz (1992), 130–1, 236.
2. Earle (1994), 38–54.
3. Croad (1983), *passim.*
4. Olsen (1982), 4.
5. Rudé (1970), 39.

6. Sheppard (1971), 84–93.
7. Sheppard, Belcher and Cottrell (1979), *passim*.
8. Summerson (1988 rev. edn.), 46, 53–4, 105–7.
9. Ibid. 49–51, 106.
10. Sheppard (1971), 98, 100.
11. Ibid. 109–12; Hadfield and Skempton (1979), 184–221.
12. Summerson (rev. edn. 1988), ch. 13; (1935), passim.
13. Olsen (1982), 9.
14. Walker (1979), 33, 37, 45–9, 58–9.
15. Rudé (1970), 39, 46.
16. Rudé (1971), 118–27; Doolittle (1981), *passim*; (1982*b*), 12–14.
17. Rudé (1971), 126–39; Sheppard (1971), 22–9.
18. Sheppard (1958), 94–101.
19. Sheppard (1971), 108–9, 183–5.
20. Spate (1936), 539–41.
21. Sheppard (1958), 72–4, 149–51.
22. Rudé (1971), 138–41; Sheppard (1958), 230–5.
23. Sheppard (1958), 176–80, 235.
24. Shoemaker (1991), *passim*; Rudé (1988), 258–60; Langbein (1983), 101.
25. Rudé (1971), 141–2; Sheppard (1971), 31–2.
26. Langbein (1983), 115–16.
27. Hay *et al.* (1975), 52.
28. Langbein (1983), 120.
29. Emsley (1987), 212.
30. Rudé (1971), 37–8, 48, 52–3; Earle (1989), 80–1; Schwarz (1992), 51–7.
31. James (1988), 543–65, *passim*.
32. Landers (1993), 53–7, 351–7; Schwarz (1992), 128–55, 235–7.
33. Schwarz (1992), 105.
34. Schwarz (1990), *passim*; see also Port (1995), *passim*.
35. Rudé (1971), 38–40, 52–6; Rubinstein (1981), 56–110.
36. Earle (1989), 17.
37. Schwarz (1990), 318; (1979), 258; (1992), 57.
38. Schwarz (1990), 319–28; Earle (1989), 205.
39. Rudé (1971), 58.
40. Schwarz (1979), 257; (1992), 29, 60.
41. Chartres (1977), *passim*.
42. Earle (1989), 60, 354.
43. Holmes (1982), 16, 152, 183; (1986), 152, 333.
44. Holmes (1982), 184–5, 200–3.
45. Ibid. 256, 262–82.
46. Schwarz (1979), *passim*; (1992), 51–7. This section is heavily indebted to Dr L. D. Schwarz's recent works, which continue the classic researches of George (1985) (1st pub. 1925).
47. Rudé (1971), 83.
48. Ibid. 86–8; Earle (1994), 168–9; but see Rudé (1988), 263, 265 for the later decline of the criminal element in St Giles's.
49. Schwarz (1992), 157, 172–4.

50. Ibid. 49, 158, 167.
51. Rudé (1971), 88–90.
52. Schwarz (1992), 95, 104–16.
53. Rudé (1971), 97–8; Linebaugh (1991), p. xxi; Emsley (1987), 209–12, 245–7.
54. Rudé (1988), 243, 262–4.
55. See Schwarz (1985), *passim*.
56. British Museum, Add. MS 27828, fo. 60, quoted in George (1985), 18.
57. Schwarz (1992), 228, 232.
58. Ibid. 121, 182–3, 228.
59. Earle (1994), 114–15, 155.
60. Sheppard (1971), 369–70.
61. Earle (1994), 139–42.
62. Schwarz (1992), 14–22, 45–8, 192; Earle (1994), 144–50.

14. London and the Genesis of the Industrial Economy (pp. 224–38)

1. This section is heavily indebted to the writings of Professor Sir Tony Wrigley and Professor T. C. Barker. See esp. Wrigley, (1967b); (1986); (1988); and Barker (1967). See also, more generally, Crafts (1985); Mendels (1972); and O'Brien (1985).
2. Gilboy (1975), 10–15; Chartres (1968), 171; but see also Tucker (1975), 34.
3. Barker and Gerhold (1993), 22.
4. Gerhold (1993), *passim*.
5. Wrigley (1967b) 60. Figures can also be calculated using Flinn (1984), 217, 274, and Hair and Ross (1844), 5–6.
6. Wilson (1965), 313–17.
7. Dickson (1967), 8–12.
8. Ibid. 281–2, 297–302, 322; see also Brezis (1995), *passim*.
9. Dickson (1967), 273, 285–91.
10. Earle (1989), 80–1.
11. Dickson (1967), 486–520 *passim*.
12. Wilson (1965), 328–9.
13. Ibid. 328–30; Mathias (1969), 167.
14. Mathias (1969), 167–9; Corfield (1982), 73.
15. Michie (1981), 253–4.
16. Rudé (1971), 32–3; Sheppard (1971), 196–7.
17. Dickson (1960), 77.
18. Supple (1970), 11, 82; Dickson (1960), 77; Sheppard (1971), 197.
19. Supple (1970), 110–17, 132–4; Dickson (1960), 103.
20. Earle (1989), 18–19.
21. Kellett (1957–8), *passim*.
22. George (1985), 174–5. See also Green (1996), 16–20.
23. George (1985), 167, 178–201; Schwarz (1992), 186–94, 201–6.
24. George (1985), 175–8; Ellmers (1978), 389.
25. Kirkham (1988), 72, 78; McKendrick (1982), 28.
26. Mathias (1979), 253.
27. Banbury (1971), 41–3.
28. Mathias (1969), 154; Sheppard (1971), 97–8.

383

29. Schwarz (1992), 1.
30. Spate (1938), *passim*; Sheppard (1971), 174–7.
31. Porter (1994), 2–8, 19–23; see also McConnell (1994), *passim*.
32. Barson and Saint (1992), 11–19.
33. Rudé (1971), 28; George (1985), 186, 188, 194, 199.
34. Ellmers (1978), 389–90.
35. Ward (1974), 44–5, 64–5, 68–9, 81–2, 170.
36. Crouzet (1972), 40–1.
37. Ibid. 46–7; Mathias (1969), 177.
38. Ward (1974), 28.
39. Barker (1960), *passim*.
40. John (1950), 24–5, 33–4, 99–101.
41. Campbell (1958), 21–34.
42. Mathias (1969), 148; (1959), 557.
43. Wilson (1965), 327–8.
44. Mathias (1969), 170–5; Black (1996), 121–7.
45. See O'Brien (1985), 773–99; Thomas and McCloskey (1981), 87–102.
46. French (1992), *passim*; Schumpeter (1960), 9–10.
47. Schumpeter (1960), 9–10; Thomas and McCloskey (1981), 90–2.
48. Crafts (1983), 197–9; Crouzet, (1980), *passim*; Thomas and McCloskey (1981), 87–90.
49. Schumpeter (1960), 12; Deane and Cole (1967), 31.
50. Jarvis (1969), 407.
51. Cottrell (1975), 17–19; Mathias (1969), 321–2; Sheppard (1971), 55–6; see also Brezis (1995), 51, 59–60.
52. Mathias (1969), 169, 350–1; Sheppard (1971), 58–62.
53. Wrigley (1986), 123–68; (1994), 71.
54. Stone (1994), 7–8; Cain and Hopkins (1993), 74; see also Mathias and O'Brien (1976), *passim*.
55. Brewer (1989), 130–3.
56. Wrigley (1994), 72–3.
57. Cain and Hopkins (1993), 64.
58. Wilson (1965), 313–17.
59. Stone (1994), 5–6.
60. Mathias (1969), 303–15, esp. 305.

15. Religion, Education, and Leisure (pp. 239–49)

1. Plumb (1982), 333.
2. Holmes (1973), *passim*; (1976), *passim*.
3. Port (1986), pp. ix–xi; Rudé (1971), 101–4.
4. Sheppard (1958), 253.
5. Rudé (1971), 100–6, 112.
6. Brown (1981), *passim*; Boulton (1993), *passim*. See also Earle (1994), 156–65.
7. Rudé (1971), 109–13; Langford (1989), 549–52.
8. Rudé (1971), 106–15.
9. Thompson (1968), 44–8.
10. Rudé (1971), 108; Sheppard (1971), 202–7.

11. Rose (1991), *passim.*
12. Briggs (1979), 72–3.
13. Langford (1989), 134–41.
14. George (1985), 55–8.
15. Sheppard (1971), 208; Rudé (1971), 117; Earle (1994), 36–7.
16. Sheppard (1971), 208–11, 218.
17. Port (1961), 9, 134–9.
18. Ibid. 134–9.
19. Briggs (1979), 223.
20. Langford (1989), 88–9.
21. Rudé (1971), 64; McKendrick (1982), 21–2. See also Borsay (1994), *passim,* for the vitality of provincial culture.
22. Quoted in Mackintosh (1992), 199.
23. Plumb, (1982), 275; Mackintosh, (1992), *passim.*
24. Funnel (1992), *passim;* Wilton (1992), *passim.*
25. Rudé (1971), 77–8; Sheppard (1971), 351–2.
26. Rudé (1971), 73–4; Sheppard (1971), 356–7.
27. Rudé (1971), 70–2, 91–4.
28. McKendrick (1982), 78–80.
29. Plumb (1982), 266–7, 273.
30. McKendrick (1982), 47–9, 96.
31. Boswell's *Life of Johnson,* 20 September 1777.
32. Brimblecombe (1987), 63–4, 72; Fox (1992), 12.

16. Metropolitan Politics and Metropolitan Class (pp. 250–60)

1. Holmes (1982), 239–42.
2. Holmes (1967), 20–4.
3. Dickinson (1987), 78–81.
4. Sheppard (1971), 298.
5. De Krey (1985), 177–212; Horwitz (1987), 181–6; Sutherland (1956), 55–6. See also Doolittle (1982a), 171–6.
6. Rudé (1971), 143–5, 149–51; Sutherland (1956), 54, 64.
7. Hone (1982), 1.
8. Sutherland (1956), 66–7; (1959), 5.
9. Quoted in Sutherland (1959), 10–11.
10. Rudé (1971), 77–8; Sharpe (1894–5), iii. 77–8.
11. Rudé (1971), 164–5, 212–14.
12. Rudé (1971), 164–5, 214–15; Sharpe (1894–5), iii. 82–3. See also P. D. G. Thomas (1978), 221–4.
13. Rudé (1971), 166.
14. Rudé (1971), 166–7; (1962), ch. 7 *passim;* Sutherland (1959), 23.
15. Rudé (1971), 167.
16. Ibid. 168–72; Sutherland (1959), 32.
17. Rudé (1971), 172–4, 191–2, 201; Sutherland (1959), 16–18.
18. Rudé (1971), 175–7; Butterfield (1949), 280, 283, 341–4.
19. Butterfield (1949), 342.

20. Langford (1977), *passim.*
21. Rudé (1971), 178–80, 220–4. See also Stevenson (1992), 94–102.
22. Rudé (1970), 289.
23. Rudé (1971), 226.
24. Rudé (1970), 59; Williams (1968), p. vi.
25. Williams (1968), 4.
26. Rudé (1971), 248.
27. Prothero (1979), 28–40.
28. McCalman (1987), *passim.*
29. Morris (1979), 12, 48.
30. R. J. Bezucha, quoted by Prothero (1979), 3, 345.
31. Rudé (1971), 248; Williams (1968), 78, 80.
32. Schwarz (1992), 174.
33. Stevenson (1992), 189–90, 280; (1977), p. xx; Williams (1968), 110. See also Green (1996), 20–4.
34. Rudé (1971), 242–7, 250; Sheppard (1971), 298.
35. Sheppard (1971), 307–8.
36. Dickinson (1992), 217–19.
37. Stevenson (1992), 239–42; Thompson (1968), 176–9.
38. Stevenson (1992), 223–4.
39. Quoted in Sheppard (1971), p. xix.
40. Stevenson (1992), 235–8.
41. Sheppard (1971), 303–4.
42. Prothero (1979), ch. 7 *passim.*
43. Stevenson (1992), 245–51; Sheppard (1971), 304–7.
44. Stevenson (1992), 251.
45. Dickinson (1992), 223. See also Green (1996), 20–4.

PART V. METROPOLITAN AND IMPERIAL LONDON 1830–1914

17. Structures of the Modern Metropolis (pp. 264–88)

1. Shannon (1934–5), 86; Friedlander (1974), 132; Thomas (1973), 52.
2. Barker and Robbins (1963–74), vol. i. chs. 1 and 2.
3. Sheppard (1971), 123, and information from Dr R. M. Robbins.
4. Barker and Robbins (1963–74), i. 40–3.
5. Robbins (1962), 28–9.
6. Barker and Robbins (1963–74), i. 50.
7. Simmons (1973), 280–1.
8. Barker and Robbins (1963–74), i. 65–6; Sheppard (1971), 138–9.
9. Barker and Robbins (1963–74), i. 163–5.
10. Ibid. 178–97.
11. Ibid. 312, and ii. 15–16.
12. Ibid. ii. 244–5.
13. Ibid. 14–34, 61–84, 116, 118–36.
14. Thompson, F. M. L. (1983), 189 n.; Barker (1983), 103.
15. Barker and Robbins (1963–74), i. 208, and ii. 12.

16. Dyos (1982), 101–18. All references to Professor Dyos's seminal articles on nineteenth-century London are to this collection.
17. Ibid. 238.
18. Kellett (1969), 327–8.
19. Quoted in Dyos (1982), 105–6.
20. Ibid. 101–18.
21. Barker and Robbins (1963–74), i. 173–4.
22. Dyos (1982), 122.
23. Barker and Robbins (1963–74), i. 173–4.
24. Dyos (1982), 91, 98.
25. Kellett (1969), 365–70, 379.
26. Ibid. 376–80.
27. Ibid. 311–24, 337–46.
28. Taylor (1973), passim.
29. Kellett (1969), 367–70.
30. Owen (1982), 116–17.
31. Jackson (1973), 34–5.
32. Olsen (1986), 27–8.
33. Dyos (1982), 161, 164.
34. Ibid. 157–8, 165, 169; *Survey of London* (1973), *passim*.
35. Sheppard, Belcher, and Cottrell (1979), *passim*; Thomas (1973), ch. 13.
36. Thompson, F. M. L. (1982), 13.
37. Summerson (1990), ch. 12.
38. Olsen (1986), 90–8; Summerson (1973*b*), 317, 323–4.
39. Owen (1965), 385.
40. Owen (1982), 109–13.
41. Saint (1989*c*), 215–24; Thorne (1986), 80–8.
42. Summerson (1973*b*), 321–2.
43. Summerson (1990), 193–216.
44. Summerson (1973*b*), 317–19, 325; F. M. L. Thompson (1995), 67–8.
45. Young and Garside (1982), 333; Dyos (1982), 40.
46. Quoted in Sheppard (1971), 35.
47. Quoted in John Davis (1988), 5.
48. Sheppard (1982), 23–30.
49. *The Times* (20 Mar. 1855) quoted in Young and Garside (1982), 21.
50. Sheppard (1982), 26–30.
51. Ibid. 26–7.
52. Quoted in Weinreb and Hibbert (1992 edn.), 957.
53. Sheppard (1982), 23–30.
54. Sheppard (1971), ch. 7.
55. John Davis (1988), 9.
56. Sheppard (1971), ch. 7.
57. Ibid. 283, 286.
58. Ibid. 289; Owen (1982), 136–40, 273, 316.
59. Bédarida (1991), 23.
60. Owen (1982), 149–52, 316. See also Clifton (1992), *passim*.
61. Brimblecombe (1987), 102–3, 111–12, 117.

62. D. Rubinstein (1969), 7–9, 21; Sheppard (1971), 236–7.
63. D. Rubinstein (1969), 2, 20, 35–7, 56–9, 83–9, 112–17.
64. John Davis (1988), 94, 103, 249–52.
65. Quoted by Briggs (1989), 265.
66. John Davis (1988), 168, 172, 250.
67. Ibid. 246–7.
68. John Davis (1989a), 48.
69. Saint, (1989b), passim.

18. The People of London (pp. 289–308)

1. Masterman (1909), 96.
2. Quotation in Lampard (1973), passim. See also Williams and Mooney (1994), passim.
3. Shannon (1934–5), 81–6 (these figures relate to the Registrar-General's London Division 1851–91); Thomas (1973), 452.
4. Waller (1991 edn.), 25; Dyos (1966), 19–20.
5. Friedlander (1974), 128–41.
6. Waller (1991 edn.), 26–7.
7. Quoted in Sheppard (1985), 55.
8. Sheppard (1971), 5–6; Jones (1971), 109, 282; Waller (1991 edn.), 26–7.
9. Shannon (1934–5), 85.
10. Friedlander (1974), 138–9.
11. Dyos (1982), 145.
12. Bédarida (1968), passim.
13. Schwarz (1992), 11–30, 258.
14. Sheppard (1971), 178–80.
15. Jones (1971), passim; Perkin (1972), 525–7.
16. Quoted in Marks (1993), 521.
17. Jones (1974), 484.
18. Dyos (1982), 104.
19. For this and the next paragraph see Read (1964), 83–94; Rowe (1970), pp. xv–xvii; Stevenson (1977), pp. xxi–xxiv; Rowe (1977), 149–76.
20. Quoted in Wallas (1925 edn.), 393–4.
21. Goodway (1982), 9–11.
22. Prothero (1969), 85; Goodway (1982), 12, 221.
23. Goodway (1982), 221–3.
24. Prothero (1969), 83, 103.
25. Ibid. 80–1, 90; Goodway (1982), 18.
26. Quoted in Prothero (1969), 82.
27. Ibid. 94–5.
28. Belchem (1991), 132.
29. Sheppard (1971), 328–30.
30. Belchem (1991), 126–38; Saville (1987), 130–9.
31. Belchem (1991), 138–41.
32. Sheppard (1971), 331–43; Pelling (1972), 41–57.
33. John Davis (1988), 68; Sheppard (1971), 343.

34. Pelling (1972), 72–7, 89; John Davis (1989*b*), *passim.*
35. Jones (1971), 291–6.
36. Ibid. 315–16; Pelling (1972), 93–7.
37. Belchem (1991), 238; John Davis (1989*b*), *passim.*
38. Jones (1971), 355, 389–90.
39. Jennifer Davis (1984), *passim*; Petrow (1994), *passim*
40. Jones (1974), 488–9.
41. Wohl (1977), 316, 340; Gaskell (1990), 5.
42. Wohl (1977), pp. xv, 301–2.
43. Fishman (1988), *passim*, esp. ch. 4; Bédarida (1968), 295; (1991), 120. See also Davin (1994), *passim.*
44. Sheppard (1971), 229–33.
45. Weinreb and Hibbert (1992 edn.), *passim.*
46. Walkowitz (1980), 15, 23–4.
47. Taine (1957), 36. See also F. M. L. Thompson (1988), 257–8.
48. Jones (1974), *passim* (Booth quotation, 471).
49. Holt (1989), 179.
50. Ibid. 166–75.
51. Both quotations from Weightman (1992), 63.
52. Jones (1974), 478, 491, 498–9.
53. Bédarida (1968), *passim*; Booth, quoted in Green (1991), 23.
54. W. D. Rubinstein (1981), 108–10; (1977*b*), 615–19; Lee (1986), 130–1.
55. *Survey of London* (1977), 48.
56. Figures in Rubinstein (1981), 103–4, reworked in Cain and Hopkins (1993*a*), 119.
57. Schwarz (1992), 41–2.
58. Grossmith, George and Weedon, *The Diary of a Nobody* (1894), *passim*; Dickens, Charles, *A Christmas Carol* (1843), *passim.*
59. Davidoff (1973), 16, 23.
60. Horn (1992), 12.
61. Davidoff (1973), 21, 52, 109. See also F. M. L. Thompson (1995).
62. Horn (1992), 9; Davidoff (1973), 59, 67.
63. Davidoff (1973), 57–8, 61.
64. McLeod (1974), *passim*, esp. ch. 5, pp. 132–58; also F. M. L. Thompson (1988), 251.
65. Sheppard (1971), 384–5.
66. McLeod (1974), pp. x, xi, 25, 27, 30, 232, 301.
67. Horn (1975), 125.
68. For a happy childhood in Canonbury in the 1870s, see Hughes (1980 edn.), *passim.*
69. Farrant (1987), *passim.*
70. Weightman (1992), 25, 53, 117.
71. Ibid. 29–31, 34–7.
72. Ibid. 109–13.
73. Weinreb and Hibbert (1992 edn.), 116.
74. Weightman (1992), 40–3, 137. See also Atwell (1980), 5, 23, who quotes the *Evening News* that there were some 500 cinemas in London and its suburbs in 1912.
75. Harte (1986), 112–16, 126–7.
76. Horn (1992), 24.

19. The Imperial and Global Metropolis (pp. 309–17)

1. Harcourt (1979), *passim.*
2. Lee (1984), *passim.*
3. Perkin (1989), pp. xiii, 17–22.
4. Sheppard (1985), 66–7.
5. Garside (1984), 256; Perkin (1989), 21.
6. Perkin (1989), 85–6.
7. Quoted by Reader (1966), 1.
8. Quoted in Michie (1992), 12.
9. Bagehot (1931), 3.
10. Michie (1992) (to which this account of the City is heavily indebted), 16, 33–4, 39; see also Garside (1984), 229.
11. Quoted in Michie (1992), 71–4; see Cain and Hopkins (1993a), 171–2.
12. Michie (1992), 104, 107, 109.
13. Ingham (1984), 63; Dintenfass (1992), 40.
14. Michie (1987), 249–76.
15. Michie (1992), 132–3, 148–9.
16. Ibid. 151, 154, 159–60.
17. Ibid. 174–7, 182.
18. King (1990a), 75–81.
19. Cain and Hopkins (1993a), 130.
20. Ibid. 19, 21, 37, 39, 64.
21. Ibid. 170, 185; Mathias (1969), 305. See also Clarke (1967), 16–21.
22. Figures calculated from Mathias (1969), 305.
23. Ingham (1984), 97.
24. This para. is much indebted to Cain and Hopkins (1993a), esp. 12–13, 26. See also Ingham (1984), 127–34, and Rubinstein (1993), 140–9. For an alternative view of gentlemanly capitalism, see Daunton (1994b), 11–16.
25. Quoted in Cain and Hopkins (1993a), 44–5, 185; see Davis and Huttenback (1986), 209–11, 313–14.
26. Cain and Hopkins (1993a), 31–4, 153–8.
27. These ideas are discussed in Daunton (1994a) and in Michie (1997).
28. Cain and Hopkins (1993a), 192; Michie (1992), 101.
29. Michie (1981), 253–63.
30. Michie (1992), 111–12; Ingham (1984), 64; Cain and Hopkins (1993a), 187, 192.
31. Cain and Hopkins (1993a), 190, 195, 198.
32. These ideas are summarized in Ingham (1984), 22–30 and in Rubinstein (1993), 14–23.
33. Rubinstein (1981), and (1993), *passim.* See also Rubinstein (1986), Lee (1986), and Cain and Hopkins (1993a).
34. Rubinstein (1993), 23–4.
35. Ibid., ch. 3 *passim* esp. pp. 119–21.
36. Dyos (1982), 39.

PART VI. THE UNCERTAIN METROPOLIS 1914–1997

Introduction (p. 321)

1. Weightman and Humphries (1984), 21; Clout (1991), 118.

20. The Inter-war Years 1919–1939 (pp. 322–31)

1. Young and Garside (1982), 201.
2. A. A. Jackson (1973), 326.
3. Friedlander and Roshier (1965–6), *passim*.
4. Young and Garside (1982), 217–19.
5. Hoggart (1992), 4.
6. Green (1992), 8–33.
7. Weightman and Humphries (1984), 23, 123–7.
8. Ibid. 8–9, 23–9, 66–7; Green (1991), 30–1.
9. Weightman and Humphries (1984), 52–5; Barker and Robbins (1974), 106–7.
10. Weightman and Humphries (1984), 46–55, 67; Robbins (1953), 56–7; Michie (1997), 78–82. See also Armstrong (1996), *passim*.
11. Gillespie (1989*b*), 164–5; Branson (1979), chs. 1–5, *passim*.
12. Branson (1979), 100, 107, 111–12, 116–17, 157, 203–4.
13. Gillespie (1989*b*), 163.
14. Branson (1979), 79, 227–30; Weightman and Humphries (1984), 152–4.
15. Weightman and Humphries (1984), 168–9.
16. Ibid. 158; Garside (1984), 249.
17. Young and Garside (1982), 308.
18. Quoted in Mason, (1989), 255.
19. Clapson (1989), 136; Garside, (1984), 249; Sheldrake (1989), 197; Weightman and Humphries (1984), 165–6.
20. Young and Garside (1982), 132–5.
21. Gillespie (1989*a*), 116–25.
22. Barker and Robbins (1974), 164.
23. Gillespie (1989*a*), 116.
24. Barker and Robbins (1974), 258–9.
25. Ibid. 270–82; Gillespie (1989*a*), 119.
26. Quotation in A. A. Jackson (1973), 212, 221–8, 322–3.
27. Ibid. 291–9.
28. Young and Garside (1982), 212–16; Garside (1984), 250–2.
29. Barker and Robbins (1974), 179, pl. 87.
30. A. A. Jackson (1973), 190–1, 323.
31. Weightman and Humphries (1984), 46–7.
32. Michie (1992), 112–13.
33. Cain and Hopkins (1993), 40–6, 93–4; Ingham (1984), 174–6.
34. Michie (1992), 79–80, 83, 135–6, 143; (1997), 81.
35. Ingham (1984), 171–2.
36. Cain and Hopkins (1993), 4–6, 23–5.
37. Ingham (1984), 178–9, 183–7.
38. Cain and Hopkins (1993), 75–80.

39. Ibid. 31–2.
40. Ibid. (1964), 82, 84, 90, 93.
41. Read (1964), 272–4; Lee (1986), 255–6.
42. R. M. Titmuss, *Poverty and Population*, ch. 13, quoted in Read, (1964), 274.
43. Cain and Hopkins (1993), 5, 11–14.
44. Michie (1992), 116, 121–2, 162; Smith (1994 edn.), 294.
45. Ingham (1984), 195–6.
46. Thompson (1995), 76–7.
47. Cain and Hopkins (1993), 22, citing Rubinstein (1981), 103, 104, 115.
48. Perkin (1989), 257–8.
49. Michie (1992), 35.
50. Read (1964), 211, 214–15, 232.
51. Ibid. 207, 248–50.
52. Ibid. 252–3; Robson (1986), 223.
53. Orwell (1941), 53–4.

21. World War II 1939–1945 (pp. 332–8)

1. Titmuss (1950), 559–60; Calder (1991), 224–5, 231–2. See also Ziegler (1995), for a general account.
2. Quoted in Young and Garside (1982), 222–3; Calder (1969), 21–2; Titmuss (1950), 13.
3. O'Brien (1955), 388.
4. Ibid. 386, 389, 402; Titmuss (1950), 257, 276–7, 295.
5. O'Brien (1955), 402, 406, 419.
6. Titmuss (1950), 174, 355, 543.
7. Mack and Humphries (1985), 28, 31.
8. Titmuss (1950), 286.
9. Ibid. 255–9; O'Brien (1955), 392.
10. Titmuss (1950), 52, 204–7, 268 n., 269.
11. Ibid. 239–40.
12. Ibid. 260, 274–85.
13. Ibid. 263–6, 300.
14. Leopold (1989), 202–4.
15. Titmuss (1950), 266–7, 293–5.
16. Mack and Humphries (1985), 59–60, 80–1, 87, 92–3.
17. Titmuss (1950), 331.
18. Mack and Humphries (1985), 70–2, 81, 87, 90–2.
19. Titmuss (1950), 343.
20. Mack and Humphries (1985), 50, 52, 62, 84–5, 139, 151.
21. O'Brien (1955), 409; Young and Garside (1982), 226.
22. Mack and Humphries (1985), 121–2, 124.
23. Ibid. 100–4.
24. Ibid. 56–7, 105–9.
25. Ibid. 128–43; Calder (1969), 560.
26. Mack and Humphries (1985), 140–1.
27. Mack and Humphries (1985), 143–53; Calder (1969), 562.
28. Titmuss (1950), 301, 330, 430.

29. Quoted in O'Brien (1955), 406, from Elizabeth Bowen, *The Heat of The Day* (1949), 86.
30. Titmuss (1950), 268.

22. Disruptions 1945–1997 (pp. 339–56)

1. Clout (1991), 126, 158.
2. Humphries and Taylor (1986), 13.
3. Ibid. 5.
4. Ibid. 57–64.
5. Titmuss (1950), 430.
6. Humphries and Taylor (1986), 140–6.
7. Ibid. 80–92; Munton (1986), 128–30.
8. Humphries and Taylor (1986), 80–91.
9. Agnew and Cooke (1986), 92–4; Brimblecombe (1987), 165–9.
10. Humphries and Taylor (1986), 14–15, 19–20.
11. Wood (1986), 61–5; Smith (1994 edn.), 177, 182; Humphries and Taylor (1986), 21–2.
12. Barson and Saint (1988), *passim*; *Daily Telegraph* (27 Mar. 1989).
13. Manners (1986*b*), 113; Wood (1986), 67; Humphries and Taylor (1986), 74.
14. McWilliams (1993), 12.
15. Manners (1986*b*), 115–17.
16. Cain and Hopkins (1993), 265–91.
17. Ibid. 267–8.
18. Michie (1992), 141, 145–6.
19. Rose (1994*a*), 39, 42.
20. Salt (1986), 52–9.
21. *Daily Telegraph* (17 June 1988), 21.
22. P. Jackson (1986), 152–9; Jones (1992), 179–90; Humphries and Taylor (1986), 110–37.
23. P. Jackson (1986), 152–9.
24. Jones (1991), 186.
25. Ibid 182, 187–90.
26. HMSO (1994), 31.
27. *Daily Telegraph* (28 Dec. 1994), 13.
28. P. Hall (1989), 1–9; Young and Garside (1982), 331–9.
29. P. Hall (1984), 439–41; (1989), 170–2.
30. P. Hall (1989), 35–8.
31. Ibid. 38–44.
32. Ibid. 18.
33. Young and Garside (1982), 327.
34. P. Hall (1989), 14–15, 46–7.
35. *Radio Times* (11–17 May 1985), 12–13.
36. *Daily Telegraph* (30 June, 30 Nov. 1994).
37. *Survey of London* (1994), ch. 24.
38. Ibid. pp. 687–91.
39. Pharoah (1991), 149.
40. *Daily Telegraph* (21 Apr. 1989; 14 Mar. 1992).
41. Dennis (1986), 84–7.
42. Ibid.

43. Humphries and Taylor (1986), 149–54.
44. Ibid. 154–5.
45. Ibid. 155–7.
46. *Survey of London* (1994), ch. 9.
47. Taylor (1973), 80.
48. Humphries and Taylor (1986), 157–60.
49. Glendinning and Muthesius (1994), *passim.*
50. Green and Hoggart (1992), 225–8.
51. J. Hall (1994), 90.
52. Smith (1994 edn.), chs. 11 and 12.
53. Dahrendorf (1982), 104–5.
54. Rubinstein (1981), 115, 238–9.
55. McWilliams (1993), 3, 25.
56. Smith (1994 edn.), 130; see also Rubinstein (1993), 28–9.
57. Smith (1994 edn.), ch. 4.
58. Ibid., chs. 7–9.
59. Ibid. ch. 6; *Daily Telegraph* (14 Aug., 13 Sept. 1994).
60. *Daily Telegraph* (22 June 1995).

23. Valediction (pp. 357–61)

1. Quoted in E. G. R. Taylor, *Late Tudor and Early Stuart Geography 1583–1650* (London, 1934), 106–7.
2. Quotations in Cobbett (1912), ii. 18, 119 and Robson (1986), 222.
3. McWilliams (1996), *passim*, esp. 6–7, 10, 24–31. See also London Chamber of Commerce Press Release, 18 Nov. 1996, and McWilliams (1993), esp. 3–8, 18, 28, 32–3.
4. *Invisibles: Facts and Figures* (1993), 4.
5. Clarke (1965), 137, 140–2.
6. *Invisibles: Facts and Figures*, (1993), 2.
7. King (1990*b*), 71, 120–3, 143.
8. Ibid. 26–30, 42; (1990*a*), 143–9.
9. *Daily Telegraph* (21 Apr. 1989).
10. King (1990*b*), 104–13, 117, 120, 137; *Evening Standard* (21 Aug. 1995).
11. *Wall Street Journal* (2 Apr. 1987), 6. I am grateful to Professor George Napier for this reference.
12. P. Hall (1987*a* and *b*).

BIBLIOGRAPHY

PART I. LONDINIUM (Chapters 1–3)

ARMITAGE, PHILIP, WEST, BARBARA, and STEEDMAN, KEN (1984), 'New Evidence of Black Rat in Roman London', *London Archaeologist*, 4: 375–82.

BATEMAN, NICK (1986), 'Bridgehead Revisited', *London Archaeologist*, 5: 233–41.

—— and MILNE, GUSTAV (1983), 'A Roman Harbour in London: Excavations and Observations near Pudding Lane, City of London, 1979–1982', *Britannia*, 14: 207–26.

BENTLEY, DAVID (1985), 'Roman London: A First Century Boundary', *London Archaeologist*, 5: 124–9.

BIRD, JOANNA, HASSALL, MARK, and SHELDON, HARVEY (1996) (eds.), *Interpreting Roman London: Paper in Memory of Hugh Chapman* (Oxford Monograph, 58; Oxford).

BLAGG, T. F. C. (1996), 'Monumental Architecture in Roman London', in Bird, Hassall, and Sheldon (1996), 43–7.

CAESAR (1911), *Caesar's Gallic War*, trans. Revd F. P. Long (Oxford).

CARLIN, MARTHA (1996), *Medieval Southwark* (London).

CASTLE, STEPHEN A. (1975), 'Excavations in Pear Wood, Brockley Hill, Middlesex, 1948–1973', *Transactions of the London and Middlesex Archaeological Society*, 26: 267–77.

CLEERE, HENRY (1978), 'Roman Harbours in Britain South of Hadrian's Wall', in Joan du Plat Taylor and Henry Cleere (eds.), *Council for British Archaeology Research Report*, 24 (London), 36–40.

DIO (1961), *Dio's Roman History*, trans. Earnest Cary, vii (London).

FLEURY, MICHEL (1994), 'Paris: Epoque Romaine et Post-Romaine', *Franco-British Studies*, 17 (London), 9–21.

FRERE, SHEPPARD (1987), *Britannia: A History of Roman Britain* (3rd edn. London).

FULFORD, MICHAEL (1978), 'The Interpretation of Britain's Late Roman Trade: The Scope of Medieval Historical and Archaeological Analogy', in Joan du Plat and Henry Cleere (eds.), *Council for British Archaeology Research Report*, 24 (London), 59–69.

GELLING, MARGARET (1978), *Signposts to the Past: Place Names and the History of England* (London).

GRIMES, W. F. (1968), *The Excavation of Roman and Medieval London* (London).

—— (1989) 'The Prehistoric Background', in Mary D. Lobel (ed.), *The City of London from Prehistoric Times to c.1520* (*British Atlas of Historic Towns*, iii; Oxford), 6–9.

HALL, JENNY, and MERRIFIELD, RALPH (1993), *Roman London* (Museum of London, 2nd impression).

HASSALL, MARK (1996), 'London as a Provincial Capital', in Bird, Hassall, and Sheldon (1996), 19–26.

HILL, CHARLES, MILLETT, MARTIN, and BLAGG, THOMAS (1980), *The Roman Riverside Wall and Monumental Arch in London* (Tony Dyson (ed.), *London and Middlesex Archaeological Society Special Paper*, 3).

HOBLEY, BRIAN (1986), *Roman and Saxon London: A Reappraisal* (Museum of London Annual Archaeology Lecture, 1985).

JONES, LLEWELLYN RODWELL (1931), *The Geography of London River* (London).

MALONEY, JOHN (1988), *The Guildhall Amphitheatre*, Museum of London leaflet (repr. from *Illustrated London News* (May)).

MANN, J. C. (1961), 'The Administration of Roman Britain', *Antiquity*, 35: 316–20.

MARSDEN, PETER (1980), *Roman London* (London).

—— (1987), *The Roman Forum Site in London* (London).

MERRIFIELD, RALPH, (1965), *The Roman City of London* (London).

—— (1969), *Roman London* (London).

—— (1983), *London: City of the Romans* (London).

—— (1989), 'Roman London', in Mary D. Lobel (ed.), *The City of London from Prehistoric Times to c.1520*, (*British Atlas of Historic Towns*, iii; Oxford), 10–19.

—— (1990), 'The Contribution of Archaeology to Our Understanding of Pre-Norman London, 1973–1988', *British Archaeological Association Conference Transactions*, 10. *Medieval Art, Architecture and Archaeology in London*, 1–15.

MERRIMAN, NICK (1990), *Prehistoric London* (Museum of London).

MILLETT, MARTIN (1996), 'Characterizing Roman London', in Bird, Hassall, and Sheldon (1996), 33–7.

MILNE, GUSTAV (1985), *The Port of Roman London* (London).

—— (1995), *English Heritage Book of Roman London* (London).

—— (1996), 'A Palace Disproved: Reassessing the Provincial Governor's Presence in 1st-century London', in Bird, Hassall, and Sheldon (1996), 49–55.

—— BATTARBEE, R. W., STRAKER, V. and YULE, B. (1983), 'The River Thames in London in the Mid 1st Century AD', *London and Middlesex Archaeological Society Transactions*, 34: 19–30.

MoLAS 96 (1996), *Annual Review for 1995* (London).

MORRIS, JOHN (1982), *Londinium: London in the Roman Empire* (London).

PARNELL, GEOFFREY (1993), *English Heritage Book of the Tower of London* (London).

PERRING, DOMINIC (1991), *Roman London* (London).

PRINCE, HUGH (1989), 'The Situation of London', in Mary D. Lobel (ed.), *The City of London from Prehistoric Times to c.1520* (*British Atlas of Historic Towns*, iii; Oxford), 1–5.

RIVET, A. L. F., and SMITH, COLIN (1979), *The Place-Names of Roman Britain* (London).

Royal Commission on Historical Monuments (England) (1928), *Roman London* (London).

SALWAY, PETER (1981), *Roman Britain* (Oxford).

SHELDON, HARVEY, and TYERS, IAN (1983), 'Recent Dendrochronological Work in Southwark and its Implications', *London Archaeologist*, 4: 355–60.

SHERLOCK, R. L. (1947), *British Regional Geology: London and the Thames Valley* (2nd edn., Geological Survey, London).

STOW, JOHN (1908), *A Survey of London*, ed. C. L. Kingsford, 2 vols. (Oxford).

STRABO (1917–23), *The Geography of Strabo*, trans. Horace Leonard Jones, i and ii (London).

SUETONIUS (1903), *The Lives of the Twelve Caesars*, trans. Alexander Thomson (London).

TACITUS (1872–4), *The Works of Tacitus*, Oxford trans., 2 vols. (London).

WACHER, JOHN (1976 edn.), *The Towns of Roman Britain* (London).

WEBSTER, GRAHAM (1978), *Boudica: The British Revolt against Rome AD 60* (London).

—— (1980), *The Roman Invasion of Britain* (London).

WILKES, JOHN (1996), 'The Status of Londinium', in Bird, Hassall, and Sheldon (1996), 27–31.

YULE, BRIAN (1990), 'The "Dark Earth" and Late Roman London', *Antiquity*, 64: 620–8.

PART II. FROM LONDINIUM TO THE CHARTERED CITY OF LONDON, c.400–c.1530 (Chapters 4–6)

ALCOCK, LESLIE (1966–7), 'Roman Britons and Pagan Saxons: An Archaeological Appraisal', *Welsh History Review*, 3: 229–48.

AUTRAND, FRANÇOISE, and LE MARESQUIER, YVONNE-HÉLÈNE (1994), 'Vie sociale et municipale de Paris aux xive et xve siècle', *London and Paris from the Beginnings to the year 2000, Part 1: From Roman Times to 1800 (Franco-British Studies: Journal of the British Institute in Paris*, 17), 65–83.

BAILEY, KEITH (1989), 'The Middle Saxons', in Stephen Bassett (ed.), *The Origins of Anglo-Saxon Kingdoms* (Leicester), 108–22.

BAILEY, PAUL (1989), *The Oxford Book of London* (Oxford).

BAKER, ALAN R. H. (1973), 'Changes in the Later Middle Ages', in Darby (1973), 186–247.

BAKER, TIMOTHY (1970), *Medieval London* (London).

BARLOW, FRANK (1988), *The Feudal Kingdom of England 1042–1216* (4th edn., London).

BARRON, CAROLINE M. (1969), 'Richard Whittington: The Man behind the Myth', in Hollaender and Kellaway (1969), 197–248.

—— (1971), 'The Quarrel of Richard II with London 1392–1397', in F. R. H. Du Boulay and Caroline M. Barron (eds.), *The Reign of Richard II: Essays in Honour of Mary McKisack* (London).

—— (1974), *The Medieval Guildhall of London* (London).

—— (1981a), *Revolt in London: 11th to 15th June 1381* (London).

—— (1981b), 'London and the Crown 1451–1461', in J. R. L. Highfield and Robin Jeffs (eds.), *The Crown and Local Communities in England and France in the Fifteenth Century* (Gloucester), 88–109.

—— (1985), 'The Parish Fraternities of Medieval London', in Barron and Christopher Harper-Bill (eds.), *The Church in Pre-Reformation Society: Essays in Honour of F. R. H. Du Boulay* (Woodbridge), 13–37.

—— (1989a), 'The Later Middle Ages: 1270–1520', in Lobel (1989), 42–56.

—— (1989b), 'The "Golden Age" of Women in Medieval London', *Reading Medieval Studies*, 15: 35–58.

—— (1990), 'London and Parliament in the Lancastrian Period', *Parliamentary History*, 9/2: 343–67.

—— (1994a), 'Introduction: The Widow's World in Later Medieval London', in Barron and Anne F. Sutton (eds.), *Medieval London Widows 1300–1500* (London), pp. xiii–xxxiv.

—— (1994b), 'The Social and Administrative Development of London 1300–1550', *London and Paris from the Beginnings to the Year 2000, Part 1: From Roman Times to 1800 (Franco-British Studies, Journal of the British Institute in Paris* 17), 53–64.

—— (1995a), 'Centres of Conspicuous Consumption: The Aristocratic Town House in London 1200–1550', *London Journal*, 20: 1–16.

—— (1995b), 'London in the Later Middle Ages 1300–1550', *London Journal*, 20: 22–33.

—— (1996), 'The Expansion of Education in Fifteenth Century London', in J. Blair and B. Golding (eds.), *The Cloister and the World* (Oxford), 219–45.

BENNETT, MICHAEL J. (1983), *Community, Class and Careerism: Cheshire and Lancashire Society in the Age of Sir Gawain and the Green Knight* (Cambridge).

BENTLEY, DAVID (1985), 'Roman London: A First Century Boundary', *London Archaeologist*, 5: 124–9.

BIDDLE, MARTIN (1984), 'London on The Strand', *Popular Archaelogy*, 6: 23–7.

—— (1989), 'A City in Transition: 400–800', in Lobel (1989), 20–9.

—— and HILL, DAVID (1971), 'Late Saxon Planned Towns', *Antiquaries Journal*, 51: 70–85.

—— and HUDSON, DAPHNE M., with HEIGHWAY, CAROLYN M. (1973), *The Future of London's Past* (Worcester).

BINSKI, PAUL (1995), *Westminster Abbey and the Plantagenets: Kingship and the Representation of Power 1200–1400* (New Haven).

BIRD, RUTH (1949), *The Turbulent London of Richard II* (London).

BLAIR, JOHN (1989), 'Frithuwold's Kingdom and the Origins of Surrey', in Steven Bassett (ed.), *The Origins of Anglo-Saxon Kingdoms* (Leicester), 97–107.

BOLTON, J. L., (1985 edn.), *The Medieval English Economy 1150–1500* (London).

—— (1986), 'The City and the Crown, 1456–1461', *London Journal*, 12: 3–10.

BRAUDEL, FERNAND (1988), The Identity of France, i. *History and Environment*, trans. Sian Reynolds (London).

BRIDBURY, A. R. (1962), *Economic Growth: England in the Later Middle Ages* (London).

BRIGDEN, SUSAN (1984), 'Religion and Social Obligation in Early Sixteenth-Century London', *Past and Present*, 103: 67–112.

—— (1989), *London and the Reformation* (Oxford).

BRITNELL, RICHARD (1994), 'The Black Death in English Towns', *Urban History*, 21: 195–210.

BROOKE, C. N. L. (1972), 'Lambeth and London in the Eleventh and Twelfth Centuries', *Report of the Friends of Lambeth Palace Library* (London).

—— (1989), 'The Central Middle Ages: 800–1270', in Lobel (1989), 30–41.

—— KEIR, G., and REYNOLDS, S. (1973), 'Henry I's Charter for the City of London', *Journal of the Society of Archivists*, 4: 558–78.

—— —— (1975), *London 800–1216: The Shaping of a City* (London).

BROWN, THOMAS (1988), 'The Transformation of the Roman Mediterranean, 400–900', in Holmes (1988).

BUCKATEZSCH, E. J. (1950–1), 'The Geographical Distribution of Wealth in England, 1086–1843', *Economic History Review*, 2nd ser., 3: 180–202.

BURGESS, CLIVE (1996), 'Shaping the Parish: St. Mary at Hill, London, in the Fifteenth Century', in John Blair and Brian Golding (eds.), *The Cloister and the World: Essays in Medieval History in Honour of Barbara Harvey* (Oxford), 246–86.

CAMPBELL, BRUCE M. S., GALLOWAY, JAMES A., KEENE, DEREK, and MURPHY, MARGARET (1993), *A Medieval Capital and its Grain Supply: Agrarian Production and Distribution in the London Region c.1300* (Historical Geography Research Series, No. 30, London).

CARLIN, MARTHA (1996), *Medieval Southwark* (London).

CARMEN (1972), *The Carmen De Hastingae Proelio of Guy Bishop of Amiens* ed. Catherine Morton and Hope Muntz (Oxford).

CARPENTER, DAVID (1994), 'King Henry III and the Tower of London', *London Journal*, 19: 95–107.

CARUS-WILSON, E. M. (1967), *Medieval Merchant Venturers: Collected Studies* (London).

—— and COLEMAN, OLIVE (1963), *England's Export Trade 1275–1547* (Oxford).

CHAPMAN, HUGH (1986), (ed.), *Discoveries* (Museum of London Exhibition booklet, London).

CLANCHY, M. T. (1979), *From Memory to Written Record: England 1066–1307* (London).

CLARK, JOHN (1989 edn.), *Saxon and Norman London* (Museum of London Handbook, London).

COLEMAN, OLIVE (1969), 'The Collectors of Customs in London under Richard II', in Hollaender and Kellaway (1969), 181–94.

Corporation of London (1950), *The Corporation of London: Its Origin, Constitution, Powers and Duties* (London).

CREATON, HEATHER (1989), 'The Centre for Metropolitan History: A Progress Report', *London Journal* 14: 68–70.

CURTIS, MARGARET (1918), 'The London Lay Subsidy of 1332', in Unwin (1918), 35–92.

DARBY, H. C. (1936*a*), (ed.), *An Historical Geography of England before A. D. 1800* (Cambridge).

—— (1936*b*), 'The Economic Geography of England, A.D. 1000–1250', in Darby (1936*a*), 165–229.

—— (ed.), (1973), *A New Historical Geography of England* (Cambridge).

—— GLASSCOCK, R. E., SHEAIL, J., and VERSEY, G. R. (1979), 'The Changing Geographical Distribution of Wealth in England: 1086–1334–1525', *Journal of Historical Geography*, 5: 247–62.

DONKIN, R. A. (1973), 'Changes in the Early Middle Ages', in Darby (1973), 75–135.

DYER, CHRISTOPHER (1989), 'The Consumer and the Market in the later Middle Ages', *Economic History Review*, 2nd ser., 42: 305–27.

DYSON, TONY (1978), 'Two Saxon Land Grants for Queenhithe', in Joanna Bird, Hugh Chapman, and John Clark (eds.), *Collectanea Londiniensia: Studies in London Archaeology and History presented to Ralph Merrifield* (London), 200–15.

—— (1980), 'London and Southwark in the Seventh Century and Later: A Neglected Reference', *London and Middlesex Archaeological Society Transactions*, NS 31: 83–95.

—— (1990), 'King Alfred and the Restoration of London', *London Journal*, 15: 99–110.

—— and SCHOFIELD, JOHN (1984), 'Saxon London', in Jeremy Haslam (ed.), *Anglo-Saxon Towns in Southern England*, (Chichester), 285–313.

EKWALL, EILERT (1956), *Studies on the Population of Medieval London* (Stockholm).

FAVIER, JEAN (1974), *Histoire de Paris au xve siècle 1380–1500* (Nouvelle Histoire de Paris; Paris).

—— (1994), 'Paris, Capitale', *London and Paris from the Beginnings to the Year 2000, Part 1: From Roman Times to 1800* (*Franco-British Studies: Journal of the British Institute in Paris*, 17), 32–51.

FITZSTEPHEN, WILLIAM. *See Stenton, F. M.*

FRYDE, E. B. (1988), *William De La Pole: Merchant and King's Banker* (London).

GALLOWAY, JAMES A., KEENE, DEREK, and MURPHY, MARGARET (1996), 'Fuelling the City: Production and Distribution of Firewood and Fuel in London's Region, 1290–1400', *Economic History Review*, 49: 447–72.

—— and MURPHY, MARGARET (1991), 'Feeding the City: Medieval London and its Agrarian Hinterland', *London Journal*, 16: 3–14.

GELLING, MARGARET (1978), *Signposts to the Past: Place-Names and the History of England* (London).

GEM, RICHARD (1990), 'The Romanesque Architecture of Old St. Paul's Cathedral and its Late Eleventh-Century Context', *British Archaeological Association Conference Transactions*, 10. *Medieval Art, Architecture and Archaeology in London*, 47–63.

GLASSCOCK, R. E. (1973), 'England *circa* 1334', in Darby (1973), 136–85.

—— (1975), (ed.), *The Lay Subsidy of 1334* (British Academy, Records of Social and Economic History, NS 2, London).

GRAS, NORMAN SCOTT BRIEN (1915), *The Evolution of the English Corn Market from the Twelfth to the Eighteenth Century* (Cambridge, Mass).

GUTH, DeLLOYD, J. [*sic*] (1986), 'Richard III, Henry VII and the City: London Politics and the "Dun Cowe" ', in Ralph A. Griffiths and James Sherborne (eds.), *Kings and Nobles in the Later Middle Ages: A Tribute to Charles Ross* (Gloucester), 185–204.

HANAWALT, BARBARA A. (1993), *Growing up in Medieval London: The Experience of Childhood in History* (New York).

HARDING, VANESSA (1995), 'Cross-Channel Trade and Cultural Contacts: London and the Low Countries in the later Fourteenth Century', in Caroline M. Barron and Nigel Saul (eds.), *England and the Low Countries in the Late Middle Ages* (Stroud), 153–65.

—— and WRIGHT, LAURA (1995), (eds.), *London Bridge: Selected Accounts and Rentals, 1381–1538* (London Record Society, 31; London).

HARVEY, BARBARA (1977), *Westminster Abbey and its Estates in the Middle Ages* (Oxford).

—— (1993), *Living and Dying in England 1100–1540: The Monastic Experience* (Oxford).

HATCHER, JOHN (1977), *Plague, Population and the English Economy 1348–1530* (London).

HAWKES, S. C. (1961), 'Soldiers and Settlers in Britain, Fourth to Fifth Century' *Medieval Archaeology*, 5: 1–41.

HAWKINS, DUNCAN (1990), 'The Black Death and the New London Cemeteries of 1348', *Antiquity*, 64: 637–42.

HOBLEY, BRIAN (1986), *Roman and Saxon London: A Reappraisal* (Museum of London Annual Archaeology Lecture, London).

HODGES, RICHARD, and WHITEHOUSE, DAVID (1983), *Mohammed, Charlemagne and the Origins of Europe* (London).

HOLLAENDER, A. E. J., and KELLAWAY, WILLIAM (1969), (eds.), *Studies in London History presented to Philip Edmund Jones* (London).

HOLLISTER, C. WARREN (1990), 'London's First Charter of liberties: Is It Genuine?', *Journal of Medieval History*, 6: 289–306.

HOLMES, GEORGE (1988), (ed.), *The Oxford Illustrated History of Medieval Europe* (Oxford).

HOLT, J. C. (1965), *Magna Carta* (Cambridge, 1965).

HORNSBY, PETER R. G., WEINSTEIN, ROSEMARY, and HOMER, RONALD F. (1989), *Pewter: A Celebration of the Craft 1200–1700* (Museum of London).

HOSKINS, W. G. (1956), 'English Provincial Towns in the Early Sixteenth Century', *Transactions of the Royal Historical Society*, 5th ser., 6: 1–19.

HOUTTE, J. A. VAN (1977), *An Economic History of the Low Countries 800–1800* (London).

HUNT, R. W., PANTIN, W. A., and SOUTHERN, R. W. (1948), (eds.), *Studies in Medieval History presented to F. M. Powicke* (Oxford).

IMRAY, JEAN M. (1969), ' "Les Bones Gentes De La Mercerye De Londres": A Study of the Membership of the Medieval Mercers' Company', in Hollaender and Kellaway (1969), 155–78.

IVES, E. W. (1968), 'The Common Lawyers in Pre-Reformation England', *Transactions of the Royal Historical Society*, 5th ser., 18: 145–73.

JACKSON, KENNETH (1953), *Language and History in Early Britain* (Edinburgh).

JACOB, E. F. (1987 edn.) *The Fifteenth Century 1399–1485* (Oxford).

JAMES, MARGERY KIRKBRIDE (1971), *Studies in the Medieval Wine Trade*, ed. Elspeth M. Veale (Oxford).

JOHNSON, DAVID J. (1969), *Southwark and the City* (London).

Johnson, Douglas, Crouzet, François, and Bédarida François (eds.), (1980), *Britain and France* (Folkestone).

Jordan, W. K. (1960), *The Charities of London 1480–1660: The Aspirations and the Achievements of the Urban Society* (London).

Keene, Derek (1984), 'A New Study of London before the Great Fire', *Urban History Yearbook*, 11–21.

—— (1985), *Cheapside before the Great Fire* (Economic and Social Research Council Booklet; London).

—— (1989), 'Medieval London and its Region', *London Journal*, 14: 99–111.

—— (1990), 'Shops and Shopping in Medieval London', British Archaeological Association Conference Transactions, 10. *Medieval Art, Architecture and Archaeology in London*, 29–46.

—— (1993–4), *Centre for Metropolitan History Annual Report* (London).

—— (1994), 'London circa 600–1300: The Growth of a Capital', *London and Paris from the Beginnings to the Year 2000, Part I: From Roman Times to 1800* (*Franco-British Studies: Journal of the British Institute in Paris*, 17), 23–31.

—— (1995), 'London in the Early Middle Ages 600–1300', *London Journal*, 20: 9–21.

Lacey, Kay E. (1985), 'Women and Work in Fourteenth and Fifteenth Century London', in L. Charles and L. Duffin (eds.), *Women and Work in Pre-Industrial England* (London), 24–82.

Lavedan, Pierre (1975), *Histoire de l'urbanisme à Paris* (Nouvelle Histoire de Paris; Paris).

Le Goff, Jacques (1988), *Medieval Civilization 400–1500*, trans. Julia Barrow (Oxford).

Levison, Wilhelm (1946), *England and the Continent in the Eighth Century* (Oxford).

Lobel, Mary D. (1989) (ed.), *The City of London from Prehistoric Times to c.1520*, British Atlas of Historic Towns, iii, (Oxford).

London and Middlesex Archaeological Society Papers. *See Steedman, Ken, Dyson, Tony, and Schofield, John.*

London Assize (1973), *London Assize of Nuisance 1301–1431: A Calendar*, ed. Helena M. Chew and William Kellaway (London Record Society, 10; London).

McDonnell, K. G. T. (1978), *Medieval London Suburbs* (Chichester).

McFarlane, K. B. (1981), *England in the Fifteenth Century: Collected Essays* (London).

McKisack, May (1948), 'London and the Succession to the Crown during the Middle Ages', in Hunt, Pantin, and Southern (1948), Oxford, 76–89.

—— (1987 edn.), *The Fourteenth Century 1307–1399* (Oxford).

Merrifield, Ralph (1983), *London: City of the Romans* (London).

—— (1990), 'The Contribution of Archaeology to Our Understanding of Pre-Norman London, 1973–1988', *British Archaeological Association Conference Transactions*, 10. *Medieval Art, Architecture and Archaeology in London*, 1–15.

Molas (1996), *Annual Review for 1995* (London).

Moorman, John R. H. (1945), *Church Life in England in the Thirteenth Century* (Cambridge).

Morris, Richard K. (1990), 'The New Work at Old St Paul's Cathedral and its Place in English Thirteenth-Century Architecture', *British Archaeological Association Conference Transactions*, 10. *Medieval Art, Architecture and Archaeology in London*, 74–100.

Myers, A. R. (1972), *London in the Age of Chaucer* (Norman, Okla).

—— (1985 edn.), *England in the Late Middle Ages* (Harmondsworth).

Myres, J. N. L. (1934), 'Some Thoughts on the Topography of Saxon London', *Antiquity*, 8: 437–42.

—— (1936), Review of R. E. M. Wheeler's 'London and the Saxons', *Journal of Roman Studies*, 26: 87–92.

—— (1986), *The English Settlements* (Oxford).

NIGHTINGALE, PAMELA (1987), 'The Origin of the Court of Husting and Danish Influence on London's Development into a Capital City', *English Historical Review*, 102: 559–78.

—— (1989), 'Capitalists, Crafts and Constitutional Change in Late Fourteenth-Century London', *Past and Present*, 124: 3–35.

—— (1990), 'Monetary Contraction and Mercantile Credit in later Medieval England', *Economic History Review*, 2nd ser., 43: 560–75.

—— (1995), *A Medieval Mercantile Community: The Grocers' Company and the Politics and Trade of London 1000–1485* (New Haven).

—— (1996), 'The Growth of London in the Medieval Economy', in Richard Britnell and John Hatcher (eds.), *Progress and Problems in Medieval England: Essays in Honour of Edward Miller* (Cambridge), 89–106.

PARNELL, GEOFFREY (1993), *English Heritage Book of the Tower of London* (London).

PELHAM, R. A., 'Fourteenth-Century England', in Darby (1936a), 230–65.

PIRENNE, HENRI (1939), *A History of Europe from the Invasions to the XVI Century* (London).

PLATT, COLIN (1996), *King Death: The Black Death and its Aftermath in Late Medieval England* (London).

POOLE, AUSTIN LANE (1987 edn.), *From Domesday Book to Magna Carta 1087–1216* (Oxford).

POWICKE, MAURICE (1987 edn.), *The Thirteenth Century 1216–1307* (Oxford).

PRESCOTT, A. J. (1981), 'London in the Peasants' Revolt: A Portrait Gallery', *London Journal*, 7: 125–43.

RACKHAM, JAMES (1994), 'Economy and Environment in Saxon London', in Rackham (ed.), *Environment and Economy in Anglo-Saxon England* (CBA Research Report, No. 89; London), 126–35.

RAPPAPORT, STEVE (1989), *Worlds within Worlds: The Structure of Life in Sixteenth-Century London* (Cambridge).

RAWCLIFFE, CAROLE (1984), 'The Hospitals of Later Medieval London', *Medical History*, 28: 1–21.

REYNOLDS, SUSAN (1972), 'The Rulers of London in the Twelfth Century', *History*, 57: 337–53.

—— (1975), 'The Farm and Taxation of London 1154–1216', *Guildhall Studies in London History*, 1: 211–17.

—— (1977), *An Introduction to the History of English Medieval Towns* (Oxford).

ROSSER, A. G. (1984), 'The Essence of Medieval Urban Communities: The Vill of Westminster 1200–1540', *Transactions of the Royal Historical Society*, 5th ser., 34: 91–112.

—— (1989), *Medieval Westminster 1200–1540* (Oxford).

ROWSE, A. L. (1972), 'The Abbey in the History of the Nation', *Westminster Abbey*, (Radnor, Pa).

SABINE, ERNEST L. (1933), 'Butchery in Mediaeval [*sic*] London', *Speculum*, 8: 335–53.

—— (1934), 'Latrines and Cesspools of Mediaeval [*sic*] London', *Speculum*, 9: 303–21.

—— (1937), 'City Cleaning in Mediaeval [*sic*] London', *Speculum*, 12: 19–43.

SAUL, NIGEL (1996), 'Richard II and Westminster Abbey', in John Blair and Brian Golding (eds.), *The Cloister and the World: Essays in Medieval History in Honour of Barbara Harvey* (Oxford), 196–218.

SAWYER, P. H. (1965), 'The Wealth of England in the Eleventh Century', *Transactions of the Royal Historical Society*, 5th ser., 15: 145–64.

SCHOFIELD, JOHN (1984), *The Building of London from the Conquest to the Great Fire* (London).

——(1990), 'Medieval and Tudor Domestic Buildings in the City of London', *British Archaeological Association Conference Transactions*, 10. *Medieval Art, Architecture and Archaeology in London*, 16–28.

——(1994), *Medieval London Houses* (New Haven).

SCHOFIELD, R. S. (1965), 'The Geographical Distribution of Wealth in England, 1334–1649', *Economic History Review*, 2nd ser., 18: 483–510.

SHARPE, REGINALD R. (1894–5), *London and the Kingdom*, 3 vols. (London).

——(1905), *Calendar of Letter Books of the Corporation of the City of London: Letter Book G* (London).

SMYTH, ALFRED P. (1995), *Alfred the Great* (Oxford).

SNELL, LAWRENCE S. (1978), 'London Chantries and Chantry Chapels', in Joanna Bird, Hugh Chapman, and John Clare (eds.), *Collectanea Londiniensia: Studies in London Archaeology and History presented to Ralph Merrifield* (London), 216–23.

STEEDMAN, KEN, DYSON, TONY, and SCHOFIELD, JOHN (1992), *Aspects of Saxo-Norman London*, iii. *The Bridgehead and Billingsgate to 1200* (London and Middlesex Archaeology Society Paper, 14; London).

STEEL, ANTHONY (1936), 'English Government Finance 1377–1413', *English Historical Review*, 51: 29–51, 577–97.

STENTON, F. M. (1934), *Norman London, with a Translation of William Fitz Stephen's Description* (Historical Association, London).

——(1987 edn.), *Anglo-Saxon England* (Oxford).

STOW, JOHN (1908), *A Survey of London*, ed. C. L. Kingsford (2 vols., Oxford).

TAIT, JAMES (1927), 'The Firma Burgi and the Commune in England, 1066–1191', *English Historical Review*, 42: 321–60.

TALBOT RICE, DAVID (1965), (ed.), *The Dark Ages: The Making of European Civilization* (London).

TATTON-BROWN, TIM (1986), 'The Topography of Anglo-Saxon London', *Antiquity*, 60: 21–8.

THOMAS, A. H. (1929), (ed.), *Corporation of London: Calendar of Plea and Memoranda Rolls, 1364–1381* (Cambridge).

THOMAS, CHARLES (1971), *Britain and Ireland in Early Christian Times* AD 400–800 (London).

——(1981), *Christianity in Roman Britain to* AD 500 (London).

——(1986), *Celtic Britain* (London).

THOMPSON, J. A. F. (1965), 'Piety and Charity in Late Medieval London', *Journal of Ecclesiastical History*, 16: 178–95.

THRUPP, SYLVIA L. (1948), *The Merchant Class of Medieval London* (Chicago).

——(1969), 'Aliens in and around London in the Fifteenth Century', in Hollaender and Kellaway (1969), 251–72.

TOUT, T. F. (1923), 'The Beginnings of a Modern Capital: London and Westminster in the Fourteenth Century', *Proceedings of the British Academy*, 11: 487–511.

UNWIN, GEORGE (1908), *The Gilds and Companies of London* (London).

——(1918), (ed.), *Finance and Trade under Edward III* (Manchester).

VEALE, ELSPETH M. (1966), *The English Fur Trade in the Later Middle Ages* (Oxford).

——(1969), 'Craftsmen and the Economy of London in the Fourteenth Century', in Hollaender and Kellaway (1969), 133–51.

Victoria County History of Dorset (1908), ii (London).

VINCE, ALAN (1984), 'The Aldwych: Mid-Saxon London Discovered', *Current Archaeology*, 8: 310–12.

——(1990), *Saxon London: An Archaeological Investigation* (London, 1990).

——(1994), 'Saxon Urban Economies: An Archaeological Perspective', in James Rackham (ed.), *Environment and Economy in Anglo-Saxon England* (CBA Research Report, 89; London), 108–19.

WACHER, JOHN (1974), *The Towns of Roman Britain* (London).

WEINREB, BEN, and HIBBERT, CHRISTOPHER (rev. edn. 1993), *The London Encyclopaedia* (London).

WHEELER, R. E. M. (1927), *London and the Vikings* (London Museum Catalogue, 1; London).

——(1934), 'The Topography of Saxon London', *Antiquity*, 8: 290–302.

——(1934), 'London and the Grim's Ditches', *Antiquaries Journal*, 14: 254–63.

——(1934), 'Mr Myres on Saxon London: A Reply', *Antiquity*, 8: 443–7.

——(1935), *London and the Saxons* (London Museum Catalogue, 6: London).

WHIPP, DAVID (1986), 'Thoughts on Saxon London', *London Archaeologist*, 5: 148–50.

WILLIAMS, GWYN A. (1963), *Medieval London from Commune to Capital* (London).

PART III. THE GENESIS OF MODERN LONDON 1530–1700
(Chapters 7–12)

ALEXANDER, JAMES (1989), 'The Economic Structure of the City of London at the End of the Seventeenth Century', *Urban History Yearbook 1989* (Leicester), 47–62.

ALLEN, DAVID (1972), 'The Role of the London Trained Bands in the Exclusion Crisis, 1678–1681', *English Historical Review*, 87: 287–303.

ARCHER, IAN W. (1991), *The Pursuit of Stability: Social Relations in Elizabethan London* (Cambridge).

ASHTON, ROBERT (1960), *The Crown and the Money Market 1603–1640* (Oxford).

——(1979), *The City and the Court 1603–1643* (Cambridge).

——(1983), 'Popular Entertainment and Social Control in Later Elizabethan and Early Stuart London', *London Journal*, 9: 3–19.

——(1985), 'Samuel Pepys's London', *London Journal*, 11: 75–87.

BAKER, J. N. L. (1936), 'England in the Seventeenth Century', in H. C. Darby (ed.), *An Historical Geography of England before A.D. 1800* (Cambridge), 387–443.

BARKER, THEODORE (1967), 'London and the Great Leap Forward', *Listener* (29 June), 845–7.

——and GERHOLD, DORIAN (1993), *The Rise and Rise of Road Transport 1700–1990* (Basingstoke).

BEDDARD, ROBERT (1988), 'Anti-Popery and the London Mob, 1688', *History Today*, 38 (July), 36–9.

BEIER, A. L. (1978), 'Social Problems in Elizabethan London', *Journal of Interdisciplinary History*, 9: 203–21.

——(1986), 'Engine of Manufacture: the Trades of London', in Beier and Firlay (1986a), 141–67.

——and FINLAY, ROGER (1986a), (eds.), *London 1500–1700: The Making of the Metropolis* (London).

—— —— (1986*b*), 'Introduction: The Significance of the Metropolis', in Beier and Finlay (1986*a*), 1–33.

BINDOFF, S. T. (1973), *The Fame of Sir Thomas Gresham* (Neale Lecture in English History, London).

BOSSY, JOHN (1962), 'The Character of Elizabethan Catholicism', *Past and Present*, 21: 39–59.

—— (1976), *The English Catholic Community 1570–1850* (New York).

BOULTON, J. P. (1984), 'The Limits of Formal Religion: The Administration of Holy Communion in Late Elizabethan and Early Stuart London', *London Journal*, 10: 135–54.

—— (1987), *Neighbourhood and Society: A London Suburb in the Seventeenth Century* (Cambridge).

BRAUDEL, FERNAND (1985 edn.), *Civilization and Capitalism: 15th to 18th Century*, i. *The Structures of Everyday Life*, trans. Sian Reynolds (London).

BRENNER, ROBERT (1973), 'The Civil War Politics of London's Merchant Community', *Past and Present*, 58: 53–107.

—— (1993), *Merchants and Revolution: Commercial Change, Political Conflict, and London's Overseas Trades 1550–1653* (Cambridge).

BRETT-JAMES, N. G. (1935), *The Growth of Stuart London* (London).

BRIGDEN, SUSAN (1982), 'Youth and the English Reformation', *Past and Present*, no. 95: 37–67.

—— (1989), *London and the Reformation* (Oxford).

BURKE, PETER (1977), 'Popular Culture in Seventeenth-Century London', *London Journal*, 3: 143–62.

CARLTON, CHARLES (1974), *The Court of Orphans* (Leicester).

—— (1987), *Archbishop William Laud* (London).

CHAMPION, J. A. I. (1993), *Epidemic Disease in London* (Centre for Metropolitan History, London).

CHARTRES, JOHN (1977*a*), 'Road Carrying in the Seventeenth Century: Myth and Reality', *Economic History Review*, 2nd ser., 30: 73–94.

—— (1977*b*), *Internal Trade in England 1500–1700* (London).

—— (1986), 'Food Consumption and Internal Trade', in Beier and Finlay (1986*a*), 168–96.

CLARENDON (1888), *History of the Rebellion and Civil Wars in England*, ed. W. D. Macray (6 vols., Oxford).

CLARK, G. N. (1944 edn.), *The Later Stuarts 1660–1714* (Oxford).

CLARK, PETER, and SLACK, PAUL (1972), (eds.), *Crisis and Order in English Towns 1500–1700: Essays in Urban History* (London).

—— —— (1976), *English Towns in Transition 1500–1700* (London).

CLAY, C. G. A. (1984), *Economic Expansion and Social Change: England 1500–1700* (2 vols., Cambridge).

COLEMAN, D. C., (1977), *The Economy of England 1450–1750* (Oxford).

COLLINSON, PATRICK (1990 edn.), *The Elizabethan Puritan Movement* (Oxford).

Corporation of London (1950), *The Corporation of London: Its Origin, Constitution, Powers and Duties* (London).

CORFIELD, P. J. (1982), *The Impact of English Towns 1700–1800* (Oxford).

—— (1990), 'Urban Development in England and Wales in the Sixteenth and Seventeenth Centuries', in Jonathan Barry (eds.), *The Tudor and Stuart Town: A Reader in English Urban History 1530–1688* (London), 35–62.

CRESSY, DAVID (1980), *Literacy and the Social Order: Reading and Writing in Tudor and Stuart England* (Cambridge).

CROSS, CLAIRE, (1972), 'The Church in England 1646–1660', in G. E. Aylmer (ed.), *The Interregnum: The Quest for Settlement 1646–1660* (London), 99–120.

DAVIES, GODFREY (1937), *The Early Stuarts 1603–1660* (Oxford).

DAVIES, K. G., (1957), *The Royal African Company* (London).

DAVIES, MARGARET GAY (1971), 'Country Gentry and Payments to London, 1650–1714', *Economic History Review*, 2nd ser., 25: 15–36.

DAVIS, J. (1983), *Heresy and Reformation in the South-East of England, 1520–1559* (Royal Historical Society, London).

DAVIS, RALPH (1962), *The Rise of the English Shipping Industry in the Seventeenth and Eighteenth Centuries* (London).

—— (1973), *English Overseas Trade 1500–1700* (London).

DE KREY, GARY STUART (1985), *A Fractured Society: The Politics of London in the First Age of Party 1688–1715* (Oxford).

DICKSON, P. G. M. (1967), *The Financial Revolution in England: A Study in the Development of Public Credit 1688–1756* (London).

DIETZ, BRIAN (1972), (ed.), *The Port and Trade of Early Elizabethan London: Documents* (London Record Society, 8; London)

—— (1978), 'Antwerp and London: The Structure and Balance of Trade in the 1560s', in E. W. Ives, R. J. Knecht, and J. J. Scarisbrick (eds.), *Wealth and Power in Tudor England: Essays presented to S. T. Bindoff* (London), 186–203.

—— (1986), 'Overseas Trade and Metropolitan Growth', in Beier and Finlay (1986a), 115–40.

DOOLITTLE, I. G., (1982), *The City of London and its Livery Companies* (Dorchester).

—— (1983), 'The City of London's Debt to its Orphans, 1694–1767', *Bulletin of the Institute of Historical Research*, 56: 46–57.

—— (1994), *The Mercers' Company 1579–1959* (Mercers' Company, London).

DUFFY, EAMON (1992), *The Stripping of the Altars: Traditional Religion in England c. 1400– c. 1580* (New Haven).

DURES, ALAN (1983), *English Catholicism 1558–1642: Continuity and Change* (London).

EARLE, PETER (1989), *The Making of the English Middle Classes: Business, Society and Family Life in London, 1660–1730* (London).

FAIRCLOUGH, KEITH (1979), 'A Tudor Canal Scheme for the River Lea', *London Journal*, 5: 218–27.

—— (1982), 'A Tudor Canal Scheme for the River Lea: A Note', *London Journal*, 8: 90–1.

FINLAY, ROGER (1981), *Population and Metropolis: The Demography of London 1580–1650* (Cambridge).

—— and SHEARER, BEATRICE (1986), 'Population Growth and Suburban Expansion', in Beier and Finlay (1986a), 37–59.

FIRTH, C. H. (1926–7), 'London during the Civil War', *History*, NS 11: 25–36.

FISHER, F. J. (1990), *London and the English Economy, 1500–1700*, ed. P. J. Corfield and N. B. Harte (London). This contains *inter alia* the following writings by Fisher: 'The Development of the London Food Market, 1540–1640' (1st pub. *Economic History Review*, 5 (1935), 46–64); 'The Development of London as a Centre of Conspicuous Consumption in the Sixteenth and Seventeenth Centuries' (1st pub. *Transactions of the Royal Historical Society*, 4th ser., 30 (1948), 37–50); 'London's Export Trade in the Early Seventeenth Century' (1st pub. *Economic History Review*, 2nd ser., 3 (1950), 151–61). 'The Growth of London' (1st pub.

in E. W. Ives (ed.), *The English Revolution, 1600–1660* (London, 1968), 76–86); 'London as an "Engine of Economic Growth"' (1st pub. in J. S. Bromley and E. H. Kossman (eds.) *Britain and the Netherlands, Metropolis, Dominion and Province* (The Hague, 1971), 3–16).

FOSTER, FRANK FREEMAN (1977), *The Politics of Stability: A Portrait of the Rulers in Elizabethan London* (Royal Historical Society, London).

FRENCH, CHRISTOPHER J. (1992), '"Crowded with Traders and a Great Commerce": London's Domination of English Overseas Trade, 1700–1775', *London Journal*, 17: 27–35.

GENTLES, IAN (1983), 'The Struggle for London in the Second Civil War', *Historical Journal*, 26: 277–305.

GERHOLD, DORIAN (1993), *Road Transport before the Railways: Russell's London Flying Waggons* (Cambridge).

GLASS, D. V. (1966) (introd.), *London Inhabitants within the Walls 1695* (London Record Society, 2; London).

—— (1969), 'Socio-Economic Status and Occupations in the City of London at the End of the Seventeenth Century', in Hollaender and Kellaway (eds.), *Studies in London History, presented to Philip Jones*, (London), 373–89.

GOUGH, BARRY (1991), 'Lords of the Northern Forest', *History Today*, 41 (Sept.), 49–56.

GRAS, N. S. B. (1915), *The Evolution of the English Corn Market* (Harvard, Mass.).

GRASSBY, RICHARD (1970), 'English Merchant Capitalism in the Late Seventeenth Century: The Composition of Business Fortunes', *Past and Present*, 46: 87–107.

—— (1970), 'The Personal Wealth of the Business Community in Seventeenth-Century England', *Economic History Review*, 2nd ser., 23: 220–34.

GREGG, PAULINE (1961), *Free-Born John: A Biography of John Lilburne* (London).

GRIFFTHS, PAUL (1993), 'The Structure of Prostitution in Elizabethan London', *Continuity and Change*, 8: 39–63.

GWYNN, ROBIN D., (1965–70), 'The Arrival of Huguenot Refugees in England', *Proceedings of the Huguenot Society*, 21: 366–73.

—— (1970–6), 'The Distribution of Huguenot Refugees in England, ii. London and its Environs', *Proceedings of the Huguenot Society*, 22: 509–68.

—— (1985), *Huguenot Heritage: The History and Contribution of the Huguenots in Britain* (London).

HABAKKUK, H. J. (1957–8), 'The Market for Monastic Property, 1539–1603', *Economic History Review*, 2nd ser., 10: 362–80.

HANDOVER, P. M. (1960), *Printing in London from 1476 to Modern Times* (London).

HARDING, VANESSA (1990), 'The Population of London, 1550–1700: A Review of the Published Evidence', *London Journal*, 15: 111–28.

HARRIS, TIM (1987), *London Crowds in the Reign of Charles II: Propaganda and Politics from the Restoration until the Exclusion Crisis* (Cambridge).

—— (1987–8), 'Was the Tory Reaction Popular?: Attitudes of Londoners towards the Persecution of Dissent, 1681–1686', *London Journal*, 13: 106–20.

—— (1993), *Politics under the Later Stuarts: Party Conflict in a Divided Society 1660–1715* (London).

HILL, CHRISTOPHER (1956), *Economic Problems of the Church from Archbishop Whitgift to the Long Parliament* (London).

—— (1961), *The Century of Revolution 1603–1714* (Edinburgh).

—— (1972), *The World turned Upside Down: Radical Ideas during the English Revolution* (London).

—— (1985), *The Collected Essays of Christopher Hill*, i. *Writing and Revolution in 17th Century England* (Brighton).

HINTON, R. W. K. (1959), *The Eastland Trade and the Common Weal in the Seventeenth Century* (Cambridge).

HOLMES, MARTIN (1960), *Shakespeare's Public: The Touchstone of his Genius* (London).

HONEYBOURNE, MARJORIE B. (1931–2), 'The Extent and Value of the Property in London and Southwark occupied by the Religious Houses, the Inns of the Bishops and Abbots, and the Churches and Churchyards, before the Dissolution of the Monasteries', summary in *Bulletin of the Institute of Historical Research*, 9: 52–7 (complete work in M. A. Thesis (London, 1930)).

HORSEFIELD, J. KEITH (1982), 'The "Stop of the Exchequer" Revisited', *Economic History Review*, 2nd ser., 35: 511–28.

HOTSON, LESLIE (1928), *The Commonwealth and Restoration Stage* (Harvard, Mass.).

HOUTTE, J. A. van (1977), *An Economic History of the Low Countries 800–1800* (London).

HUNTER, MICHAEL (1981), *Science and Society in Restoration England* (Cambridge).

—— (1982), *The Royal Society and its Fellows 1660–1700: The Morphology of an Early Scientific Institution* (British Society for the History of Science, Chalfont St Giles).

ISRAEL, JONATHAN (1989), *Dutch Primacy in World Trade, 1585–1740* (Oxford).

JEFFRIES DAVIS, E. (1924), 'The Transformation of London', in R. W. Seton-Watson (ed.), *Tudor Studies presented to A. F. Pollard* (London), 287–311.

—— (1925), 'The Beginning of the Dissolution: Christchurch, Aldgate, 1532', *Transactions of the Royal Historical Society*, 4th ser., 8: 127–50.

JENNINGS, HUMPHREY (1987 edn.), *Pandaemonium 1660–1886: The Coming of the Machine as seen by Contemporary Observers* (London).

JOHNSON, DAVID J. (1969), *Southwark and the City* (Oxford).

JONES, D. W. (1976), 'London Merchants and the Crisis of the 1690s', in Clark and Slack (1976), 311–55.

—— (1972), 'The "Hallage" Receipts of the London Cloth Markets, 1562–c.1720', *Economic History Review*, 2nd ser., 25: 567–87.

JONES, EMRYS (1980), 'London in the Early Seventeenth Century: An Ecological Approach', *London Journal*, 6: 123–33.

JORDAN, W. K. (1959), *Philanthropy in England 1480–1660* (London).

—— (1960), *The Charities of London 1480–1660* (London).

KEARNEY, H. F. (1964), 'Puritanism, Capitalism and the Scientific Revolution', *Past and Present*, no. 28: 81–101.

KEAY, JOHN (1991), *The Honourable Company* (London).

KELLETT, J. R. (1957–8), 'The Breakdown of Gild and Corporation Control over the Handicraft and Retail Trade in London', *Economic History Review*, 2nd ser., 10: 381–94.

—— (1960–8), 'The Financial Crisis of the Corporation of London and the Orphans' Act, 1694', *Guildhall Miscellany*, 2: 220–7.

KENYON, JOHN (1972), *The Popish Plot* (London).

KERRIDGE, ERIC (1988), *Trade and Banking in Early Modern England* (Manchester).

KITCH, M. J. (1986), 'Capital and Kingdom: Migration to Later Stuart London', in Beier and Finlay (1986a), 224–51.

KITCHING, C. J. (1980), (ed.), *London and Middlesex Chantry Certificates 1548* (London Record Society, 16; London).

KNIGHTS, MARK (1993a), 'London's "Monster" Petition of 1680', *Historical Journal*, 36: 39–67.

—— (1993*b*), 'London Petitions and Parliamentary Politics in 1679', *Parliamentary History*, 12: 29–46.

KNOWLES, DOM DAVID, (1959), *The Religious Orders in England*, iii. *The Tudor Age* (Cambridge).

—— and HADCOCK, R. NEVILLE (1971 edn.), *Medieval Religious Houses: England and Wales* (London).

LANG, R. G. (1974), 'Social Origins and Social Aspirations of Jacobean London Merchants', *Economic History Review*, 2nd ser., 27: 28–47.

LARMINIE, VIVIENNE (1990), (ed.), 'The Undergraduate Account Book of John and Richard Newdigate, 1618–1621', *Camden Miscellany*, 30 (Camden 4th ser., 39; London), 149–269.

LEMMINGS, DAVID (1990), *Gentlemen and Barristers: The Inns of Court and the English Bar 1680–1730* (Oxford).

LEVIN, JENNIFER (1969), *The Charter Controversy in the City of London, 1660–1688, and its Consequences* (London).

LIU, TAI (1986), *Puritan London: A Study of Religion and Society in the City Parishes* (Newark, Del.).

MACAULAY (1896 edn.), *The Life and Works of Lord Macaulay*, 10 vols. (London).

MACFARLANE, STEPHEN (1986), 'Social Policy and the Poor in the Later Seventeenth Century', in BEIER and FINLAY (1986*a*), 252–77.

MACLURE, MILLAR (1958), *The Paul's Cross Sermons 1534–1642* (Toronto).

MATTHEWS, A. G. (1959), *Introduction to Calamy Revised: A Revision of the Original Introduction* (London).

MELTON, FRANK T. (1986), *Sir Robert Clayton and the Origins of English Deposit Banking 1658–1685* (Cambridge).

MILNE, GUSTAV (1986), *The Great Fire of London* (New Barnet).

MOODY, T. W. (1939), *The Londonderry Plantation 1609–1641: The City of London and the Plantation in Ulster* (Belfast).

NAGEL, LAWSON (1996), '"A Great Bouncing at Every Man's Door": The Struggle for London's, Militia in 1642', in Porter (1996), 65–88.

PAWSON, ERIC (1977), *Transport and Economy. The Turnpike Roads of Eighteenth Century Britain* (London).

PEARL, VALERIE (1961), *London and the Outbreak of the Puritan Revolution: City Government and National Politics, 1625–1643* (Oxford).

—— (1972), 'London's Counter-Revolution', in G. E. Aylmer (ed.), *The Interregnum: The Quest for Settlement 1646–1660* (London), 29–56.

—— (1976), 'Puritans and Poor Relief: The London Workhouse 1649–1660', in D. Pennington and K. Thomas (eds.), *Puritans and Revolutionaries: Essays in Seventeenth-Century History Presented to Christopher Hill* (Oxford), 206–32.

—— (1979), 'Change and Stability in Seventeenth-Century London', *London Journal*, 5: 3–34.

—— (1981), 'Social Policy in Early Modern London', in Hugh Lloyd-Jones, Valerie Pearl, and Blair Worden (eds.), *History and Imagination: Essays in Honour of H. R. Trevor-Roper* (London), 115–31.

PELLING, MARGARET, (1986), 'Appearance and Reality: Barber-Surgeons, the Body and Disease', in Beier and Finlay (1986*a*), 82–112.

PEPYS, SAMUEL (1979–83), *The Diary of Samuel Pepys*, ed. Robert Latham and William Matthews, William (11 vols., London).

PETTEGREE, ANDREW (1986), *Foreign Protestant Communities in Sixteenth-Century London* (Oxford).

PLUMB, J. H. (1967), *The Growth of Political Stability in England 1675–1725* (London).

PORTER, STEPHEN (1996), (ed. and introd.), *London and the Civil War* (London).

POWER, M. J., 'East London Housing in the Seventeenth Century', in Clark and Slack (1972), 237–62.

—— (1978a), 'The East and West in Early-Modern London', in E. W. Ives, R. J. Knecht, and J. J. Scarisbrook (eds.), *Wealth and Power in Tudor England: Essays presented to S. T. Bindoff* (London), 167–85.

—— (1978b), 'Shadwell: the Development of a London Suburban Community in the Seventeenth Century', *London Journal*, 4: 29–46.

—— (1985). 'London and the Control of the Crisis of the 1590s', *History*, 70: 371–85.

—— (1986a), 'A "Crisis" Reconsidered: Social and Demographic Dislocation in London in the 1590s', *London Journal*, 12: 134–45.

—— (1986b), 'The Social Topography of Restoration London', in Beier and Finlay (1986a), 199–223.

—— (1990), 'The East London Working Community in the Seventeenth Century', in Penelope J. Corfield and Derek Keene (eds.), *Work in Towns 850–1850* (Leicester), 103–20.

PREST, WILFRID R., (1972), *The Inns of Court under Elizabeth I and the Early Stuarts 1590–1640* (London).

—— (1981), *Lawyers in Early Modern Europe and America* (London).

—— (1987), (ed.), *The Professions in Early Modern England* (London).

—— (1991), *The Rise of the Barristers: A Social History of the English Bar 1590–1640* (Oxford).

PRICE-WILLIAMS, R. (1885), 'The Population of London, 1801–81', *Journal of the Statistical Society*, 48: 349–441.

The Quiet Conquest: The Huguenots 1685 to 1985 (Museum of London Exhibition Catalogue, London, 1985).

RAMSAY, G. D. (1975), *The City of London in International Politics at the Accession of Elizabeth Tudor* (Manchester).

—— (1975), 'Industrial Discontent in Early Elizabethan London: Clothworkers and Merchant Adventurers in Conflict', *London Journal*, 1: 227–39.

—— (1978), 'The Recruitment and Fortunes of Some London Freemen in the Mid-Sixteenth Century', *Economic History Review*, 2nd ser., 31: 526–40.

RANUM, OREST (1968), *Paris in the Age of Absolutism* (New York).

RAPPAPORT, STEVE (1983–4), 'Social Structure and Mobility in Sixteenth-Century London', *London Journal*, 9: 107–35, and 10: 107–34.

—— (1989), *Worlds within Worlds: Structures of Life in Sixteenth-Century London* (Cambridge).

REDDAWAY, T. F. (1940), *The Rebuilding of London after the Great Fire* (London).

—— (1966), 'The Livery Companies of Tudor London', *History*, 21: 287–99.

ROBERTS, KEITH (1987), *London and Liberty: Ensigns of the London Trained Bands* (London).

—— (1996), 'Citizen Soldiers: The Military Power of the City of London', in Porter (1996), 89–116.

ROSENFIELD, M. C. (1961), 'The Disposal of the Property of London Monastic Houses, with a Special Study of Holy Trinity, Aldgate', Ph.D. thesis (London).

ROSEVEARE, HENRY (1987), (ed.), *Markets and Merchants of the Late Seventeenth Century: The Marescoe–David Letters 1668–1680* (British Academy, *Records of Social and Economic History*, NS 12; Oxford).

SACHSE, WILLIAM L. (1964), 'The Mob and the Revolution of 1688', *Journal of British Studies*, 4: 23–40.

SALGADO, GAMINI (1984 edn.), *The Elizabethan Underworld* (Gloucester).

SAUNDERS, ANN (1991), *The Royal Exchange* (London).

SCHOFIELD, JOHN (1984), *The Building of London from the Conquest to the Great Fire* (London).

SCOULOUDI, IRENE, (1937–41), 'Alien Immigration into and Alien Communities in London, 1558–1640', *Proceedings of the Huguenot Society*, 16: 27–49.

—— (1985) 'Returns of Strangers in the Metropolis 1593, 1627, 1635, 1639: A Study of an Active Minority'; *Huguenot Society of London Quarto Series*, 57.

—— (1987), *Huguenots in Britain and their French Background, 1550–1800* (London).

SEAVER, PAUL S. (1970), *The Puritan Lectureships: The Politics of Religious Dissent 1560–1662* (Stanford, Calif.).

—— (1985), *Wallington's World: A Puritan Artisan in Seventeenth Century London* (London).

SHARPE, REGINALD R. (1894–5), *London and the Kingdom* (3 vols., London).

SHEPPARD, FRANCIS (1965–70), 'The Huguenots in Spitalfields and Soho', *Proceedings of the Huguenot Society*, 21: 355–65.

—— (1971), *London 1808–1870: The Infernal Wen* (London).

—— (1982), *Robert Baker of Piccadilly Hall and his Heirs* (London Topographical Society Publication, No. 127; (London).

SHOEMAKER, ROBERT B. (1991), *Prosecution and Punishment: Petty Crime and the Law in London and Rural Middlesex, c.1660–1725* (Cambridge).

SLACK, PAUL (1980), 'Books of Orders: The Making of English Social Policy, 1577–1631', *Transactions of the Royal Historical Society*, 5th ser., 30: 1–22.

—— (1984), (ed.), *Rebellion, Popular Protest and the Social Order in Early Modern England* (Cambridge).

—— (1985), *The Impact of Plague in Tudor and Stuart England* (London).

—— (1986), 'Metropolitan Government in Crisis: The Response to Plague', in Beier and Finlay (1986*a*), 60–81.

SMITH, STEVEN R. (1984), 'The London Apprentices as Seventeenth-Century Adolescents', in Slack (1984), 219–31.

—— (1978–9), 'Almost Revolutionaries: The London Apprentices during the Civil Wars', *Huntington Library Quarterly*, 42: 313–28.

SMITH, VICTOR, and KELSEY, PETER, 'The Lines of Communication: The Civil War Defence of London', in Porter (1996), 117–48.

SNELL, L. S. (1978), 'London Chantries and Chantry Chapels', in Joanna Bird, Hugh Chapman, and John Clark (eds.), *Collectanea Londiniensia: Studies in London Archaeology and History presented to Ralph Merrifield* (London) 216–23.

STATT, DAVID, (1990), 'The City of London and the Controversy over Immigration, 1660–1722', *Historical Journal*, 33: 45–61.

STERN, WALTER M. (1979), 'Where, oh where, are the cheesemongers of London?', *London Journal*, 5: 228–48.

STONE, LAWRENCE (1956), *An Elizabethan: Sir Horatio Palavicino* (Oxford).

——(1964), 'The Educational Revolution in England, 1560–1640', *Past and Present*, 28: 41–80.

——(1966), 'Social Mobility in England 1500–1700', *Past and Present*, 33: 16–55

——(1973), *Family and Fortune: Studies in Aristocratic Finance in the Sixteenth and Seventeenth Centuries* (Oxford).

——(1979 edn.), *The Crisis of the Aristocracy 1558–1641* (Oxford).

——(1980), 'The Residential Development of the West End of London in the Seventeenth Century', in Barbara C. Malament (ed.), *After the Reformation: Essays in Honour of J. H. Hexter* (Manchester), 167–212.

——(1986 edn.), *The Causes of the English Revolution 1529–1642* (London).

——(1987), *The Past and the Present Revisited* (London).

STOW, JOHN (1968), *A Survey of London*, ed. C. L. Kingsford (2 vols., Oxford).

SUMMERSON, JOHN (1945 edn.), *Georgian London* (London).

——(1965), 'Inigo Jones', *Proceedings of the British Academy*, 50: 169–92.

SUPPLE, BARRY (1959), *Commercial Crisis and Change in England 1600–1642* (Cambridge).

——(1970), *The Royal Exchange Assurance: A History of British Insurance 1720–1970* (Cambridge).

Survey of London (1912) *St. Giles-in-the-Fields Part I* (*Survey of London*, 3; London).

——(1914), *St. Giles-in-the-Fields Part II* (*Survey of London*, 5; London).

——(1957), *Christchurch, Spitalfields, and Mile End New Town* (*Survey of London*, 27; London).

——(1960), *St. James's, Westminster, South of Piccadilly* (*Survey of London*, 29–30; London).

——(1963), *St. James's, Westminster, North of Piccadilly* (*Survey of London*, 31–2; London).

——(1966), *St. Anne, Soho* (*Survey of London*, 33–4; London).

——(1970a), *The Theatre Royal, Drury Lane, and the Royal Opera House, Covent Garden* (*Survey of London*, 35; London).

——(1970b), *St. Paul, Covent Garden* (*Survey of London*, 36; London).

——(1973), *Northern Kensington* (*Survey of London*, 37; London).

TOLMIE, MURRAY (1977), *The Triumph of the Saints: The Separate Churches of London, 1616–1649* (Cambridge).

UNWIN, GEORGE (1908), *The Gilds and Companies of London* (London).

Victoria County History of Middlesex (1969), i (Oxford).

WATTS, MICHAEL R. (1978), *The Dissenters, from the Reformation to the French Revolution* (Oxford).

WEINREB, BEN, and HIBBERT, CHRISTOPHER (rev. edn. 1993), *The London Encyclopaedia* (London).

WILLAN, T. S. (1936), *River Navigation in England 1600–1750* (Oxford).

——(1938), *The English Coasting Trade 1600–1750* (Manchester).

——(1953), *The Muscovy Merchants of 1555* (Manchester).

——(1956), *The Early History of the Russia Company 1553–1603* (Manchester).

——(1976), *The Inland Trade: Studies in English Internal Trade in the Sixteenth and Seventeenth Centuries* (Manchester).

WILSON, CHARLES (1965), *England's Apprenticeship 1603–1763* (London).

WOOD, ALFRED C. (1935), *A History of the Levant Company* (Oxford).

WOODHEAD, J. R. (1965), *The Rulers of London 1660–1689: A Biographical Record of the Aldermen and Common Councilmen of the City of London* (London).

WRIGLEY, E. A. (1967a), 'London and the Great Leap Forward', *Listener* (6 July), 7–8.

—— (1967*b*), 'A Simple Model of London's Importance in Changing English Society and Economy 1650–1750', *Past and Present*, 37: 44–70.

—— (1986), 'Urban Growth and Agricultural Change: England and the Continent in the Early Modern Period', in Robert I. Rotberg and Theodore K. Rabb (eds.), *Population and History from the Traditional to the Modern World* (Cambridge), 123–68.

—— and SCHOFIELD, R. S. (1989 edn.), *The Population History of England 1541–1871: A Reconstruction* (Cambridge).

YOUINGS, JOYCE (1984), *Sixteenth-Century England* (London).

ZAHEDIEH, NUALA, (1994), 'London and the Colonial Consumer in the Late Seventeenth Century', *Economic History Review*, 47: 239–61.

PART IV. AUGUSTAN AND GEORGIAN LONDON 1700–1830
(Chapters 13–16)

ASHTON, T. S. (1948), *The Industrial Revolution 1760–1830* (London).

BANBURY, PHILIP (1971), *Shipbuilders of the Thames and Medway* (Newton Abbott).

BARKER, T. C. (1960), *Pilkington Brothers and the Glass Industry* (London).

—— (1967), 'London and the Great Leap Forward', *Listener*, (29 June), 845–7.

BARKER, THEO (1993), 'London: A Unique Megalopolis', in Barker and Anthony Sutcliffe (eds.), *Metropolis: The Giant City in History* (Basingstoke), 43–60.

—— and GERHOLD, DORIAN (1993), *The Rise and Rise of Road Transport 1700–1990* (Basingstoke).

BARSON, SUSIE, and SAINT, ANDREW (1992), *A Farewell to Fleet Street* (London, 1988).

BERG, MAXINE, and HUDSON, PAT (1992), 'Rehabilitating the Industrial Revolution', *Economic History Review*, 2nd ser., 45: 24–50.

BETTLEY, JAMES, (1984), '*Post Voluptatem Miscericordia*: The Rise and Fall of the London Lock Hospitals', *London Journal*, 10: 167–75.

BLACK, IAIN S. (1996), 'The London Agency System in English Banking, 1780–1825', *London Journal*, 21: 112–30.

BORSAY, PETER (1994), 'The London Connection: Cultural Diffusion and the Eighteenth-Century Provincial Town', *London Journal*, 19: 21–31.

BOULTON, JEREMY (1993), 'Clandestine Marriages in London: An Examination of a Neglected Urban Variable', *Urban History*, 20: 191–210.

BREWER, JOHN (1989), *The Sinews of Power: War, Money and the English State, 1688–1783* (London).

BREZIS, ELISE S. (1995), 'Foreign Capital Flows in the Century of Britain's Industrial Revolution: New Estimates, Controlled Conjectures', *Economic History Review*, 48: 46–67.

BRIGGS, ASA (1979), *The Age of Improvement* (London, paperback edn.).

BRIMBLECOMBE, PETER (1987), *The Big Smoke: A History of Air Pollution in London since Medieval Times* (London).

BROODBANK, SIR JOSEPH G. (1921), *History of the Port of London* (2 vols, London).

BROWN, ROGER LEE (1981), 'The Rise and Fall of the Fleet Marriages', in R. B. Outhwaite (ed.), *Marriage and Society: Studies in the Social History of Marriage* (London), 117–36.

BUTTERFIELD, H. (1949), *George III, Lord North and the People 1779–1780* (London).

CAIN, P. J., and HOPKINS, A. G. (1993), *British Imperialism: Innovation and Expansion 1688–1914* (London).

CAMPBELL, R. H. (1958), 'The Financing of Carron Company', *Business History*, 1: 21–34.

CHARTRES, J. A. (1977), 'The Capital's Provincial Eyes: London's Inns in the Early Eighteenth Century', *London Journal*, 3: 24–39.

—— (1968), 'Food Consumption and Internal Trade', in A. L. Beier and Roger Finlay (eds.), *London 1500–1700: The Making of the Metropolis*, (London), 168–96.

CHRISTIE, IAN R. (1962), *Wilkes, Wyvill and Reform: The Parliamentary Reform Movement in British Politics 1760–1785* (London).

CLARK, PETER (1987), 'Migrants in the city: The Process of Social Adaptation in English Towns 1500–1800', in Clark and Souden (1987), 267–91.

—— and SOUDEN, DAVID (eds.), *Migration and Society in Early Modern England* (London).

CLARKSON, L. A., (1985), *Proto-Industrialization: The First Phase of Industrialization* (London).

COLEMAN, D. C. (1977), *The Economy of England 1450–1750* (Oxford).

COPPOCK, J. T. and PRINCE, HUGH C., (1964), *Greater London* (London).

CORFIELD, P. J. (1982), *The Impact of English Towns 1700–1800* (Oxford).

COTTRELL, P. L. (1975), *British Overseas Investment in the Nineteenth Century* (London).

CRAFTS, N. F. R. (1977), 'Industrial Revolution in England and France: Some Thoughts on the Question "Why was England First?"', *Economic History Review*, 2nd ser., 30: 429–41.

—— (1983), 'British Economic Growth, 1700–1831: A Review of the Evidence', *Economic History Review*, 2nd ser., 36: 177–99.

—— (1985), *British Economic Growth during the Industrial Revolution* (Oxford).

CROAD, STEPHEN, (1983), *London's Bridges* (London).

CROUZET, FRANÇOIS (1970), 'England and France in the Eighteenth Century: A Comparative Analysis of Two Economic Growths', in R. M. Hartwell (ed.), *The Causes of the Industrial Revolution in England* (London), 139–74.

—— (1972), (ed. and introd.), *Capital Formation in the Industrial Revolution* (London).

—— (1980), 'Towards an Export Economy: British Exports during the Industrial Revolution', *Explorations in Economic History*, 17: 48–93.

CRUICKSHANK, DAN, and BURTON, NEIL (1990), *Life in the Georgian City* (London).

DAVIS, DOROTHY, (1966), *A History of Shopping* (London).

DAVIS, RALPH (1969), 'English Foreign Trade, 1700–1774', in Minchinton (1969), 99–121.

—— (1979), *The Industrial Revolution and British Overseas Trade* (Leicester, 1979).

DEANE, PHYLLIS, and COLE, W. A. (1967), *British Economic Growth 1688–1959: Trends and Structure* (Cambridge).

DE KREY, GARY S. (1985), *A Fractured Society: The Politics of London in the First Age of Party 1688–1715 (Oxford)*.

DE VRIES, JAN (1984), *European Urbanization 1500–1800* (London).

DICKINSON, H. T. (1985), *British Radicalism and the French Revolution 1789–1815* (Oxford).

—— (1987), 'Precursors of Political Radicalism in Augustan Britain', in C. Jones (1987), 63–84.

—— (1992), 'Radical Culture', in Fox (1992), 209–24.

DICKSON, P. G. M. (1960), *The Sun Insurance Office 1710–1960* (Oxford).

—— (1967), *The Financial Revolution in England: A Study in the Development of Public Credit 1688–1756* (London).

DOOLITTLE, IAN (1981), 'The City's West End Estate: A "Remarkable Omission"', *London Journal*, 7: 15–27.

—— (1982a), 'Government Interference in City Politics in the Early Eighteenth Century: The Work of Two Agents', *London Journal*, 8: 171–6.

—— (1982b), *The City of London and its Livery Companies* (Dorchester).

DOWDELL, E. G. (1932), *A Hundred Years of Quarter Sessions: The Government of Middlesex from 1660 to 1760* (London).

DOWNIE, J. A. (1987), 'The Development of the Political Press', in C. Jones (1987), 111–27.

EARLE, PETER (1989), *The Making of the English Middle Class: Business, Society and Family Life in London, 1660–1730* (London).

—— (1994), *A City Full of People: Men and Women of London 1650–1750* (London, 1994).

ELLMERS, CHRIS (1978), 'The Impact of the 1797 Tax on Clocks and Watches on the London Trade', in Joanna Bird, Hugh Chapman, and John Clark (eds.), *Collectanea Londiniensia: Studies in London Archaeology and History presented to Ralph Merrifield* (London), 388–400.

EMSLEY, CLIVE (1987), *Crime and Society in England 1750–1900* (London).

FLINN, MICHAEL W. (1984), *The History of the British Coal Industry*, ii. *1700–1830: The Industrial Revolution* (Oxford).

FLOUD, RODERICK, and MCCLOSKEY, DONALD (1981), (eds.), *The Economic History of Britain since 1700*, i. *1700–1860* (Cambridge).

FOX, CELINA (1992), (ed.), *London: World City 1800–1840* (Yale).

FRENCH, CHRISTOPHER J. (1992), ' "Crowded with Traders and a Great Commerce": London's Domination of English Overseas Trade, 1700–1775', *London Journal*, 17: 27–35.

FUNNELL, PETER, (1992), 'The London Art World and Its Institutions', in Fox (1992), 155–66.

GEORGE, M. DOROTHY (1985), *London Life in the Eighteenth Century* (London, paperback edn.).

GERHOLD, DORIAN (1993), *Road Transport before the Railways: Russell's London Flying Waggons* (Cambridge).

GILBOY, E. W. (1975), 'The Cost of Living and Real Wages in Eighteenth-Century England', repr. in Taylor (1975), 1–20.

GILMOUR, IAN (1992), *Riot, Risings and Revolution: Governance and Violence in Eighteenth-Century England* (London).

GREEN, DAVID R. (1991), 'The Metropolitan Economy: Continuity and Change 1800–1939', in Keith Hoggart and David Green (eds.), *London: A New Metropolitan Geography* (London), 1–33.

—— (1996), 'The Nineteenth-Century Metropolitan Economy: A Revisionist Interpretation', *London Journal*, 21: 9–26.

HADFIELD, CHARLES, and SKEMPTON, A. W., (1979), *William Jessop, Engineer* (Newton Abbot).

HAIR, T. H., and ROSS, M. (1844), *A Series of Views of the Collieries in the Counties of Northumberland and Durham, with Descriptive Sketches and a Preliminary Essay on Coal and the Coal Trade* (London).

HALL, P. G., (1962), *The Industries of London Since 1861* (London).

HAY, DOUGLAS, LINEBAUGH, PETER, RULE, J. R., THOMPSON, E. P., WINSLOW, C., (1975), *Albion's Fatal Tree: Crime and Society in Eighteenth-Century England* (London).

HOLLIS, PATRICIA, (1973), *Class and Conflict in Nineteenth-Century England 1815–1850* (London).

HOLMES, GEOFFREY (1967), *British Politics in the Age of Anne* (London).

—— (1973), *The Trial of Doctor Sacheverell* (London).

—— (1976), 'The Sacheverell Riots: The Crowd and the Church in Early Eighteenth-Century London', *Past and Present*, 72: 55–85.

—— (1982), *Augustan England: Professions, State and Society 1680–1730* (London).

—— (1986), *Politics, Religion and Society in England, 1679–1742* (London).

HONE, J. ANNE (1982), *For the Cause of Truth: Radicalism in London 1796–1821* (Oxford).

HORWITZ, HENRY (1987), 'Party in a Civic Context: London from the Exclusion Crisis to the Fall of Walpole', in C. Jones (1987), 173–94.

INGHAM, GEOFFREY (1984), *Capitalism Divided? The City and Industry in British Social Development* (London).

JAMES, JOHN A., (1988), 'Personal Wealth Distribution in Late Eighteenth-Century Britain', *Economic History Review*, 2nd ser., 41: 543–65.

JARVIS, RUPERT, C. (1969), 'Eighteenth-Century London Shipping', in A. E. J. Hollaender and William Kellaway (eds.), *Studies in London History presented to Philip Edmund Jones* (London), 403–25.

JENKS, L. H. (1963), *Migration of British Capital to 1875* (London, 1927: reissued London).

JOHN, A. H. (1950), *The Industrial Development of South Wales 1750–1850* (Cardiff).

JONES, CLYVE (1987), (ed.), *Britain in the First Age of Party 1680–1750: Essays Presented to Geoffrey Holmes* (London).

JONES, M. G. (1938), *The Charity School Movement: A Study of Eighteenth-Century Puritanism in Action* (Cambridge).

KELLETT, J. R. (1957–8), 'The Breakdown of Gild and Corporate Control over the Handicraft and Retail Trade in London', *Economic History Review*, 2nd ser., 10: 381–94.

KELSALL, FRANK (1989), 'Stucco', *Good and Proper Materials: The Fabric of London since the Great Fire* (London Topographical Society Publication, 140; London), 18–24.

KIRKHAM, PAT (1988), 'The London Furniture Trade 1700–1870', *Journal of the Furniture History Society*, 24: 1–219.

LAMPARD, ERIC E. (1973), 'The Urbanizing World', in H. J. Dyos and Michael Wolff (eds.), *The Victorian City: Images and Realities*, i. (London), 3–57.

LANDERS, JOHN (1993), *Death and the Metropolis: Studies in the Demographic History of London 1670–1830* (Cambridge).

LANDES, DAVID S. (1969), *The Unbound Prometheus: Technological Change and Industrial Development in Western Europe from 1750 to the Present* (Cambridge).

LANGBEIN, JOHN H. (1983), 'Albion's Fatal Flaws', *Past and Present*, 98: 96–120.

LANGFORD, PAUL (1977), 'London and the American Revolution', in Stevenson (1977), 55–78.

—— (1989), *A Polite and Commercial People: England 1727–1783* (London).

LINEBAUGH, PETER (1991), *The London Hanged: Crime and Civil Society in the Eighteenth Century* (London).

MCCALMAN, IAIN (1987), 'Ultra-Radicalism and Convivial Debating Clubs in London, 1795–1838', *English Historical Review*, 102: 309–33.

—— (1988), *Radical Underworld: Prophets, Revolutionaries and Pornographers in London, 1795–1840* (Cambridge).

MACCOBY, S. (1955a), *English Radicalism 1762–1785* (London).

—— (1955b), *English Radicalism 1786–1832: From Paine to Cobbett* (London).

MCCONNELL, ANITA, (1994), 'From Craft Workshop to Big Business: The London Scientific Instrument Trade's Response to Increasing Demand, 1750–1820', *London Journal*, 19: 36–53.

MACKINTOSH, IAIN (1992), 'Departing Glories of the British Theatre: Setting Suns over a Neo-Classical Landscape', in Fox (1992), 199–208.

McKENDRICK, NEIL (1982), 'Commercialization and the Economy', in McKendrick, John Brewer, and J. H. Plumb (ed.), *The Birth of a Consumer Society: The Commercialization of Eighteenth-Century England* (London), 9–194.

MARSHALL, DOROTHY (1969), *The English Poor Law in the Eighteenth Century: A Study in Social and Administrative History* (London).

MARTIN, J. E. (1966), *Greater London: An Industrial Geography* (London).

MATHIAS, PETER (1959), *The Brewing Industry in England 1700–1830* (Cambridge).

—— (1969), *The First Industrial Nation: An Economic History of Britain 1700–1914* (London).

—— (1979), *The Transformation of England: Essays in the Economic and Social History of England in the Eighteenth Century* (London).

—— and O'BRIEN, PATRICK (1976), 'Taxation in Britain and France, 1715–1810: A Comparison of the Social and Economic Incidence of Taxes Collected for the Central Governments', *Journal of European Economic History*, 5: 601–50.

—— and POSTAN, M. M. (1978), *The Cambridge Economic History of Europe*, viii, *The Industrial Economies: Capital, Labour, and Enterprise, Part I: Britain, France, Germany, and Scandinavia* (Cambridge).

MENDELS, FRANKLIN F. (1972), 'Proto-Industrialization: The First Phase of the Industrialization Process', *Journal of Economic History*, 32: 241–61.

MICHIE, R. C. (1981), *Money, Mania and Markets: Investment, Company Formation and the Stock Exchange in Nineteenth-Century Scotland* (Edinburgh).

MINCHINTON, W. E. (1969) (ed.), *The Growth of Overseas Trade in the Seventeenth and Eighteenth Centuries* (London).

MORGAN, E. VICTOR, and THOMAS, W. A. (1962), *The Stock Exchange: Its History and Functions* (London).

MORRIS, R. J. (1979), *Class and Class Consciousness in the Industrial Revolution 1780–1850* (London).

MUTHESIUS, STEFAN, (1982), *The English Terraced House* (New Haven).

NEF, J. U. (1932), *The Rise of the British Coal Industry*, 2 vols. (London).

NEWBERY, CHRISTOPHER (1978), 'Coade Artificial Stone: Finds from the Site of the Coade Manufactory at Lambeth', in Joanna Bird, Hugh Chapman, and John Clark. (eds.), *Collectanea Londiniensia: Studies in London Archaeology and History presented to Ralph Merrifield* (London), 376–87.

O'BRIEN, PATRICK (1985), 'Agriculture and the Home Market for English Industry, 1660–1820', *English Historical Review*, 100: 773–99.

OLSEN, DONALD, J. (1964), *Town Planning in London: The Eighteenth and Nineteenth Centuries* (New Haven).

—— (1982), 'Introduction: Victorian London', in David Owen, *The Government of Victorian London 1855–1889* (Cambridge, Mass.).

—— (1986), *The City as a Work of Art: London, Paris, Vienna* (New Haven).

PLUMB, J. H. (1982), 'Commercialization and Society', in Neil McKendrick, John Brewer, and J. H. Plumb (eds.), *The Birth of a Consumer Society: The Commercialization of Eighteenth-Century England* (London), 265–334.

PORT, M. H. (1961), *Six Hundred New Churches: A Study of the Church Building Commission 1818–1856, and its Church Building Activities* (London).

—— (1986), *The Commissions for Building Fifty New Churches: The Minute Books 1711–1727. A Calendar* (London Record Society, 23; London).

—— (1995), 'West End Palaces: The Aristocratic Town House in London, 1730–1830', *London Journal*, 20: 17–46.

PORTER, ROY (1994), *London: A Social History* (London).

—— SCHAFFER, SIMON, BENNETT, JIM, and BROWN, OLIVIA (1985), *Science and Profit in 18th-Century London* (Whipple Museum of the History of Science, Cambridge, Catalogue).

PRESSNELL, L. S. (1956), *Country Banking in the Industrial Revolution* (Oxford).

PRICE-WILLIAMS, R. (1885), 'The Population of London, 1801–1881', *Journal of the Statistical Society*, 48: 349–441.

PRINCE, H. C. (1973), 'England circa 1800', in H. C. Darby (ed.), *A New Historical Geography of England* (Cambridge), 389–464.

PROTHERO, IORWERTH, (1979), *Artisans and Politics in Early Nineteenth-Century London* (Folkestone).

RADZINOWICZ, LEON, (1948), *A History of the English Criminal Law and its Administration from 1750*, i. *The Movement for Reform* (London).

READ, DONALD (1964), *The English Provinces* c. *1760–1900: A Study in Influence* (London).

RILEY, JAMES C. (1980) *International Government Finance and the Amsterdam Capital Market 1740–1815* (Cambridge).

—— (1986), *The Seven Years War and the Old Regime in France. The Economic and Financial Toll* (Princeton).

ROBBINS, MICHAEL (1953), *Middlesex* (London).

ROGERS, NICHOLAS (1973), 'Aristocratic Clientage, Trade and Independency: Popular Politics in Pre-Radical Westminster', *Past and Present*, 61: 70–106.

—— (1975), 'Popular Disaffection in London during the Forty-Five', *London Journal*, 1: 5–27.

—— (1978), 'Popular Protest in Early Hanoverian London', *Past and Present*, 79: 70–100.

—— (1985), 'Clubs and Politics in Eighteenth-Century London: The Centenary Club of Cheapside', *London Journal*, 11: 51–8.

ROSE, CRAIG (1991), 'Evangelical Philanthropy and Anglican Revival: The Charity Schools of Augustan London 1698–1740', *London Journal*, 16: 35–65.

ROSEVEARE, HENRY, (1991), *The Financial Revolution 1660–1760* (London).

ROTBERG, ROBERT, and RABB, THEODORE K. (1986), (eds.), *Population and History from the Traditional to the Modern World* (Cambridge).

RUBINSTEIN, W. D. (1981), *Men of Property: The Wealthy in Britain since the Industrial Revolution* (London).

RUDÉ, GEORGE (1962), *Wilkes and Liberty: A Social Study of 1763 to 1774* (Oxford).

—— (1970), *Paris and London in the Eighteenth Century: Studies in Popular Protest* (London).

—— (1971), *Hanoverian London 1714–1808* (London).

—— (1988), *The Face of the Crowd: Studies in Revolution, Ideology and Popular Protest, Selected Essays of George Rudé*, ed. Harvey J. Kaye (Hemel Hempstead).

SCHUMPETER, ELIZABETH B. (1960), *English Overseas Trade Statistics 1697–1808* (Oxford).

SCHWARZ, L. D. (1979), 'Income Distribution and Social Structure in London in the late Eighteenth Century', *Economic History Review*, 2nd ser., 32: 250–9.

—— (1990), 'Social Class and Social Geography: The Middle Classes in London at the End of the Eighteenth Century', in Peter Borsay (ed.), *The Eighteenth Century Town: A Reader in English Urban History 1688–1820* (London), 315–37 (1st pub. *Social History*, 7 2 (1982)).

—— (1985), 'The Standard of Living in the Long Run: London, 1700–1860', *Economic History Review*, 2nd ser., 38, 24–41.

—— (1992), *London in the Age of Industrialisation: Entrepreneurs, Labour Force and Living Conditions, 1700–1850* (Cambridge).

—— and JONES, L. J, (1983), 'Wealth, Occupations and Insurance in the Late Eighteenth Century: The Policy Registers of the Sun Fire Office', *Economic History Review*, 2nd ser., 37: 365–73.

SHARPE, REGINALD R. (1894–5), *London and the Kingdom*, 3 vols. (London).

SHEPPARD, FRANCIS (1958), *Local Government in St Marylebone 1688–1835: A Study of the Vestry and the Turnpike Trust* (London).

—— (1971), *London 1808–1870: The Infernal Wen* (London).

—— BELCHER, VICTOR, and COTTRELL, PHILIP (1979), 'The Middlesex and Yorkshire Deeds Registries and the Study of Building Fluctuations', *London Journal*, 5: 176–217.

SHOEMAKER, ROBERT B. (1991), *Prosecution and Punishment: Petty Crime and the Law in London and Rural Middlesex, c. 1660–1725* (Cambridge).

SMITH, RAYMOND (1961), *Sea-Coal for London: History of the Coal Factors in the London Market* (London).

SOUDEN, DAVID (1987), '"East, West—Home's Best?" Regional Patterns in Migration in Early Modern England', in Clark and Souden (1987), 292–332.

SPATE, O. H. K. (1936), 'The Growth of London, A.D. 1660–1800', in H. C. Darby (ed.), *An Historical Geography of England before 1800* (Cambridge), 529–47.

—— (1938), 'Geographical Aspects of the Industrial Evolution of London till 1850', *Geographical Journal*, 92: 422–32.

STERN, W. M. (1952), 'The First London Dock Boom and the Growth of the West India Docks', *Economica*, 19.

STEVENSON, JOHN (1977), (ed.), *London in the Age of Reform* (Oxford).

—— (1992), *Popular Disturbances in England, 1700–1832* (London).

STONE, LAWRENCE (1994), (ed.), *An Imperial State at War: Britain from 1689 to 1815* (London).

SUMMERSON, JOHN (1935), *John Nash, Architect to King George IV* (London).

—— (rev. edn. 1988), *Georgian London* (London).

SUPPLE, BARRY (1970), *The Royal Exchange Assurance: A History of British Insurance 1720–1970* (Cambridge).

SUTHERLAND, LUCY (1956), 'The City of London in Eighteenth-Century Politics', in Richard Pares and A. J. P. Taylor, *Essays Presented to Sir Lewis Namier* (London), 49–74.

—— (1959), *The City of London and the Opposition to Government, 1768–1774: A Study in the Rise of Metropolitan Radicalism* (Creighton Lecture, London).

TAYLOR, ARTHUR J. (1975) (ed.), *The Standard of Living in Britain in the Industrial Revolution* (London).

THOMAS, P. D. G. (1978), 'The St. George's Fields "Massacre" of 10 May 1768: an Eye Witness Report', *London Journal*, 4: 221–4.

THOMAS, R. P., and McCLOSKEY, D. N. (1981), 'Overseas Trade and Empire 1700–1860', in Floud and McCloskey (1981), 87–102.

THOMPSON, E. P. (1968), *The Making of the English Working Class* (London, paperback edn.).

TUCKER, RUFUS S. (1975), 'Real Wages of Artisans in London, 1729–1935', in Taylor (1975), 21–35.

TURBERVILLE, A. S. (1933), *Johnson's England*, 2 vols. (Oxford).

WALKER, R. J. B. (1979), *Old Westminster Bridge: The Bridge of Fools* (Newton Abbot).

WARD, J. R. (1974), *The Finance of Canal Building in Eighteenth-Century England* (Oxford).

WILLIAMS, GWYN A. (1968), *Artisans and Sans-Culottes: Popular Movements in France and Britain during the French Revolution* (London).

WILSON, CHARLES (1965), *England's Apprenticeship 1603–1763* (London).

WILTON, ANDREW (1992), 'Painting in London in the Early Nineteenth Century', in Fox (1992), 167–86.

WRIGLEY, E. A. (1967a), 'London and the Great Leap Forward', *Listener* (6 July), 7–9.

—— (1967b), 'A Simple Model of London's Importance in Changing English Society and Economy 1650–1750', *Past and Present*, 37: 45–70.

—— (1972), 'The Process of Modernization and the Industrial Revolution', *Journal of Interdisciplinary History*, 3: 225–59.

—— (1981), 'Marriage, Fertility and Population Growth in Eighteenth-Century England', in R. B. Outhwaite (ed.), *Marriage and Society: Studies in the Social History of Marriage* (London), 137–85.

—— (1983), 'The Growth of Population in Eighteenth-Century England: A Conundrum Resolved', *Past and Present*, 98: 121–50.

—— (1986), 'Urban Growth and Agricultural Change: England and the Continent in the Early Modern Period', in Rotberg and Rabb (1986), 123–68.

—— (1987), *People, Cities and Wealth: The Transformation of Traditional* Society (Oxford).

—— (1988), *Continuity, Chance and Change: The Character of the Industrial Revolution in England* (Cambridge, paperback edn.).

—— (1994), 'Society and the Economy in the Eighteenth Century', in Stone (1994), 72–95.

—— and Schofield, R. S. (1989 edn.), *The Population of England 1541–1871: A Reconstruction* (Cambridge).

PART V. METROPOLITAN AND IMPERIAL LONDON 1830–1914
(Chapters 17–19)

ALTICK, RICHARD D., (1978), *The Shows of London* (Cambridge, Mass.).

ANNAN, N. G. (1955), 'The Intellectual Aristocracy', in J. H. Plumb (ed.), *Studies in Social History: A Tribute to G. M. Trevelyan* (London), 243–87.

ATWELL, DAVID (1980), *Cathedrals of the Movies: A History of British Cinemas and their Audiences* (London).

BAGEHOT, WALTER (1931 edn.), *Lombard Street: A Description of the Money Market* (London).

BARKER, T. C. (1983), 'The Delayed Decline of the Horse in the Twentieth Century', in F. M. L. Thompson (ed.), *Horses in European Economic History: A Preliminary Canter* (British Agricultural History Society, Reading), 101–12.

—— (1989), 'Business as Usual? London and the Industrial Revolution', *History Today* (Feb.), 45–50.

—— and ROBBINS, MICHAEL (1963–74), *A History of London Transport: Passenger Travel and the Development of the Metropolis*, 2 vols. (London).

BECKSON, KARL (1992), *London in the 1890s: A Cultural History* (New York).

BÉDARIDA, François (1968), 'Londres au milieu du xxme siècle: Une analyse de structure sociale', *Annales, Économies, Sociétés, Civilisations*, 23: 268–95.

—— (1991), *A Social History of England 1851–1990*, trans. A. S. Foster and Jeffrey Hodgkinson (2nd edn., London).

BELCHEM, JOHN (1991), *Industrialization and the Working Class: The English Experience 1750–1900* (paperback edn., Aldershot).

BOOTH, CHARLES (1891–1903), *Life and Labour of the People in London*, 17 vols. (London).

BRIGGS, ASA (1989), Excerpt from Evidence to the Royal Commission on Local Government in London, 1959, repr. in Saint (1989*a*), 265–8.

—— (1982), *Victorian Cities* (paperback edn.).

BRIMBLECOMBE, PETER (1987), *The Big Smoke: A History of Air Pollution in London since Medieval Times* (London).

BYRNE, ANDREW (1986), *London's Georgian Houses* (London).

CAIN, P. J., and HOPKINS, A. G. (1986), 'Gentlemanly Capitalism and British Expansion Overseas, I: The Old Colonial System, 1688–1850', *Economic History Review*, 2nd ser., 39: 501–75.

—— —— (1987), 'Gentlemanly Capitalism and British Expansion Overseas, II: New Imperialism, 1850–1945', *Economic History Review*, 2nd ser., 40: 1–26.

—— —— (1993*a*), *British Imperialism: Innovation and Expansion 1688–1914* (London).

—— (1993*b*), *British Imperialism: Crisis and Deconstruction 1914–1990* (London).

CLARKE, WILLIAM M. (1967), *Britain's Invisible Earnings: The Report of the Committee on Invisible Exports* (Financial Advisory Panel on Exports, London).

CLIFTON, GLORIA C. (1992), *Professionalism, Patronage and Public Service in Victorian London: The Staff of the Metropolitan Board of Works 1856–1889* (London).

COLLINS, PHILIP (1973), 'Dickens and London', in Dyos and Wolff (1973), i. 536–57.

DAUNTON, MARTIN (1983), *House and Home in the Victorian City: Working-Class Housing 1850–1914* (London).

—— (1994*a*) 'London and Industrialisation: Parasite or Stimulus?', *Franco-British Studies: Journal of the British Institute in Paris*, 18: 31–8.

—— (1994*b*), 'The Entrepreneurial State 1700–1911', *History Today* (June), 11–16.

DAVIDOFF, LEONORE (1973), *The Best Circles: Society, Etiquette and The Season* (London).

DAVIN, ANNA (1994), *Growing Up Poor: Home, School and Street in London 1870–1914* (London).

DAVIS, JENNIFER (1984), 'A Poor Man's System of Justice: The London Police Courts in the Second Half of the Nineteenth Century', *Historical Journal*, 27/2: 309–35.

DAVIS, JOHN (1988), *Reforming London: The London Government Problem 1855–1900* (Oxford).

—— (1989*a*), 'The Progressive Council, 1889–1907', in Saint (1989*a*), London, 27–48.

—— (1989*b*), 'Radical Clubs and London Politics, 1870–1900', in David Feldman and Gareth Stedman Jones (eds.), *Metropolis London: Histories and Representations since 1800* (London), 103–28.

DAVIS, LANCE, E., and HUTTENBACK, ROBERT A. (1986), *Mammon and the Pursuit of Empire: The Political Economy of British Imperialism 1860–1912* (Cambridge).

DINTENFASS, MICHAEL (1992), *The Decline of Industrial Britain 1870–1980* (London).

DOOLITTLE, I. G. (1982), *The City of London and its Livery Companies* (Dorchester).

DYOS, H. J. (1966), *Victorian Suburb: A Study of the Growth of Camberwell* (Leicester).

—— (1973), (introd.) *Collins' Illustrated Atlas of London* (Leicester).

—— (1982) *Exploring the Urban Past: Essays in Urban History*, ed. David Cannadine and David Reeder (Cambridge). This contains *inter alia* the following writings by Dyos:

'Railways and Housing in Victorian London' (from *Journal of Transport History*, 2 (1955); 'Some Social Costs of Railway Building in London' (from *Journal of Transport History*, 3 (1957)); 'The Speculative Builders and Developers of Victorian London' (from *Victorian Studies*, 11 (1968)); 'Greater and Greater London: Metropolis and Provinces in the Nineteenth and Twentieth Centuries' (from J. S. Bromley and E. H. Kossman (eds.), *Britain and the Netherlands* (The Hague, 1971)).

—— and REEDER, D. A. (1973), 'Slums and Suburbs', in Dyos and Wolff (1973), i. 359–86.

—— and WOLFF, MICHAEL (1973), (eds.), *The Victorian City: Images and Realities* (2 vols., London).

FARRANT, SUE (1987), 'London by the Sea: Resort Development on the South Coast of England 1880–1939', *Journal of Contemporary History*, 22: 137–61.

FINER, S. E. (1952), *The Life and Times of Sir Edwin Chadwick* (London).

FISHMAN, W. J. (1975), *East End Jewish Radicals 1875–1914* (London, 1975).

—— (1988), *East End 1888: A Year in a London Borough among the Labouring Poor* (London).

FRIEDLANDER, D. (1974), 'London's Urban Transition 1851–1951', *Urban Studies*, 11: 127–41.

—— and ROSHIER, R. J. (1965–6), 'A Study of Internal Migration in England and Wales: Part I', *Population Studies*, 19: 239–79.

GARSIDE, PATRICIA L. (1984), 'West End, East End: London, 1890–1914', in Anthony Sutcliffe (ed.), *Metropolis 1890–1914* (London), 221–58.

—— (1990), 'London and the Home Counties', in F. M. L. Thompson (1990), 471–539.

GASKELL, S. MARTIN (1990), *Slums* (Leicester).

GIROUARD, MARK (1975), *Victorian Pubs* (London).

GOODWAY, DAVID (1982) *London Chartism 1838–1848* (Cambridge).

GREEN, DAVID R. (1985), 'A Map for Mayhew's London: The Geography of Poverty in the Mid-Nineteenth Century', *London Journal*, 11: 115–26.

—— (1991), 'The Metropolitan Economy: Continuity and Change', in Keith Hoggart and David R. Green (eds.), *London: A New Metropolitan Geography* (London), 8–33.

—— (1996), 'The Nineteenth-Century Metropolitan Economy: A Revisionist Interpretation', *London Journal*, 21: 9–26.

GRIFFITH, G. TALBOT (1967), *Population Problems in the Age of Malthus* (2nd edn., London).

GRYTZELL, KARL GUSTAV (1969), *County of London Population Changes 1801–1901 (Lund Studies in Geography, Series B Human Geography*, 33; Lund University, Sweden).

HALL, P. G. (1962), *The Industries of London since 1861* (London).

HARTE, NEGLEY (1986), *The University of London 1836–1986: An Illustrated History* (London).

HARCOURT, FREDA (1979), 'The Queen, the Sultan and the Viceroy: A Victorian State Occasion', *London Journal*, 5: 35–56.

HOLT, RICHARD (1989), *Sport and the British: A Modern History* (Oxford).

HORN, PAMELA (1975), *The Rise and Fall of the Victorian Servant* (Dublin).

—— (1992), *High Society: The English Social Elite, 1880–1914* (Stroud, Glouc).

HUGHES, M. V. (1980 edn.), *A London Child of the 1870s* (Oxford, paperback edn.) (1st pub. 1934).

INGHAM, GEOFFREY (1984), *Capitalism Divided? The City and Industry in British Social Development* (London).

INKSTER, IAN (1991), *Science and Technology in History: An Approach to Industrial Development* (London).

JACKSON, ALAN A. (1973), *Semi-Detached London: Suburban Development, Life and Transport, 1900–1939* (London).

JAMES, HENRY (1905), *English Hours* (London).

JEPHSON, HENRY (1907), *The Sanitary Evolution of London* (London).

JONES, GARETH STEDMAN (1971), *Outcast London: A Study in the Relationship between Classes in Victorian Society* (Oxford).

—— (1974), 'Working-Class Culture and Working-Class Politics in London, 1870–1900: Notes on the Remaking of a Working Class', *Journal of Social History*, 7: 460–508.

KELLETT, JOHN (1969), *The Impact of Railways on Victorian Cities* (London).

KING, ANTHONY D. (1990*a*), *Global Cities and the Internationalization of London* (London).

—— (1990*b*) *Urbanism, Colonialism and the World Economy: Cultural and Spatial Foundations of the World Urban System* (London).

KYNASTON, DAVID (1994), *The City of London, A World Of its Own 1815–1890* (London).

—— (1995), *The City of London, Golden Years 1890–1914* (London).

LAMBERT, ROYSTON (1963), *Sir John Simon 1816–1904 and English Social Administration* (London).

LAMPARD, ERIC E. (1973), 'The Urbanizing World', in Dyos and Wolff (1973), i. 3–57.

LARGE, DAVID (1977), 'London in the Year of Revolutions, 1848', in Stevenson (1977), 177–211.

LEE, C. H. (1981), 'Regional Growth and Structural Change in Victorian Britain', *Economic History Review*, 2nd ser., 34: 438–52.

—— (1984), 'The Service Sector, Regional Specialization, and Economic Growth in the Victorian Economy', *Journal of Historical Geography*, 10: 139–55.

—— (1986), *The British Economy since 1700: A Macro-Economic Perspective* (Cambridge).

LEES, LYNN HOLLEN (1979) *Exiles of Errin: Irish Migrants in Victorian London* (Manchester).

LEWIS, R. A. (1952), *Edwin Chadwick and the Public Health Movement 1832–1854* (London).

MCCALMAN, IAIN (1993), *Radical Underworld: Prophets, Revolutionaries and Pornographers in London, 1795–1840* (paperback edn., Oxford).

MCLEOD, HUGH (1974), *Class and Religion in the Late Victorian City* (London).

MARKS, LARA, (1993), 'Medical Care for Pauper Mothers and their Infants: Poor Law Provision and Local Demand in East London, 1870–1929', *Economic History Review*, 46: 518–42.

MASTERMAN, C. F. G. (1909), *The Condition of England* (London).

MATHIAS, PETER (1969), *The First Industrial Nation: An Economic History of Britain 1700–1914* (London).

MICHIE, R. C. (1981), *Money, Mania and Markets: Investment, Company Formation and the Stock Exchange in Nineteenth Century Scotland* (Edinburgh).

—— (1987), *The London and New York Stock Exchanges 1850–1914* (London).

—— (1992), *The City of London: Continuity and Change, 1850–1990* (London).

—— (1997), 'London and the Process of Economic Growth since 1750', *London Journal*, 22: 63–90.

MORRIS, R. J. (1979), *Class and Class Consciousness in the Industrial Revolution 1780–1850* (London).

—— and RODGER, RICHARD (1993), (eds.), *The Victorian City: A Reader in British Urban History 1820–1914* (London).

MUTHESIUS, STEFAN (1981), *The English Terraced House* (New Haven 1982).

OFFER, AVNER (1981), *Property and Politics 1870–1914: Landownership, Law, Ideology and Urban Development in England* (Cambridge).

OLSEN, DONALD J. (1979), *The Growth of Victorian London* (paperback edn., London).

—— 'Introduction: Victorian London', in Owen (1982), 1–19.

—— (1986), *The City as a Work of Art: London, Paris, Vienna* (Yale).

OWEN, DAVID (1965), *English Philanthropy 1660–1960* (Cambridge, Mass.).

—— (1982), *The Government of Victorian London 1855–1889: The Metropolitan Board of Works, the Vestries, and the City Corporation* (Harvard, Mass.).

PELLING, HENRY (1972), *A History of British Trade Unionism* (London, 2nd edn).

PERKIN, HAROLD (1969), *The Origins of Modern English Society* (London).

—— (1972), Review of G. Stedman Jones, *Outcast London*, in *Economic History Review*, 2nd ser. 25: 525–7.

—— (1989), *The Rise of Professional Society: England since 1880* (London).

PETROW, STEFAN, (1994), *Policing Morals: The Metropolitan Police and the Home Office 1870–1914* (Oxford).

PRICE-WILLIAMS, R. (1885), 'The Population of London, 1801–1881', *Journal of the Statistical Society*, 48: 349–441.

PROTHERO, I. W. (1967), 'The London Working Men's Association and the "People's Charter"', *Past and Present*, 38: 169–73.

—— (1969), 'Chartism in London', *Past and Present*, 44: 76–105.

—— (1979), *Artisans and Politics in Early Nineteenth-Century London: John Gast and his Times* (Folkestone).

READ, DONALD (1964), *The English Provinces c. 1760–1960: A Study in Influence* (London).

READER, W. J. (1966), *Professional Men: The Rise of the Professional Classes in Nineteenth-Century England* (London).

REDFORD, ARTHUR (1926), *Labour Migration in England, 1800–1850* (Manchester).

REEDER, D. A. (1968), 'A Theatre of Suburbs: Some Patterns of Development in West London, 1801–1911', in H. J. Dyos (ed.), *The Study of Urban History* (London), 253–71.

ROBBINS, MICHAEL, (1962), *The Railway Age* (London).

—— (1978), 'Transport and Suburban Development in Middlesex Down to 1914', *Transactions of the London and Middlesex Archaeological Society*, 29: 129–36.

ROBSON, WILLIAM A. (1939), *The Government and Misgovernment of London* (London).

ROEBUCK, JANET (1979), *Urban Development in 19th-Century London: Lambeth, Battersea and Wandsworth 1838–1888* (London).

ROWE, D. J. (1967), 'The London Working Men's Association and "The People's Charter"', *Past and Present*, 36: 73–86.

—— (1968), 'The Failure of London Chartism', *Historical Journal*, 11: 472–87.

—— (1970), (ed.), 'London Radicalism 1830–1843: A Selection from the Papers of Francis Place', *London Record Society*, 5: 1–266.

—— (1977), 'London Radicalism in the Era of the Great Reform Bill', in Stevenson (1977), 149–76.

RUBINSTEIN, DAVID (1969), *School Attendance in London, 1870–1914: A Social History* (New York).

RUBINSTEIN, W. D. (1977*a*), 'Wealth, Elites and the Class Structure of Modern Britain', *Past and Present*, 76: 99–126.

—— (1977*b*), 'The Victorian Middle Classes: Wealth, Occupation and Geography', *Economic History Review*, 2nd ser. 30: 602–23.

—— (1981), *Men of Property: The Very Wealthy in Britain since the Industrial Revolution* (London).

—— (1986), 'Education and the Social Origins of British Elites 1880–1970', *Past and Present*, 112: 163–207.

—— (1993), *Capitalism, Culture and Decline in Britain 1750–1990* (London).

RUDÉ, GEORGE (1964), *The Crowd in History: A Study of Popular Disturbances in France and England 1730–1848* (New York).

SAINT, ANDREW (1989a) (ed.), *Politics and the People of London: The London County Council 1889–1965* (London).

—— (1989b), 'Technical Education and the Early LCC', in Saint (1989a), 71–91.

—— (1989c), ' "Spread the People": The LCC's Dispersal Policy, 1889–1965', in Saint (1989a), 215–35.

SAVILLE, JOHN (1987), *1848: The British State and the Chartist Movement* (Cambridge).

SCHWARZ, L. D. (1992), *London in the Age of Industrialisation: Entrepreneurs, Labour Force and Living Conditions 1700–1850* (Cambridge).

SHANNON, H. A. (1934–5), 'Migration and the Growth of London, 1841–1891', *Economic History Review*, 5: 79–86.

SHEPPARD, FRANCIS (1971), *London 1808–1870: The Infernal Wen* (London).

—— (1982), 'The Crisis of London's Government', in Owen, 23–30.

—— (1985), 'London and the Nation in the Nineteenth Century', *Transactions of the Royal Historical Society*, 5th ser., 35: 51–74.

—— BELCHER, VICTOR, and COTTRELL, PHILIP (1979), 'The Middlesex and Yorkshire Deeds Registries and the Study of Building Fluctuations', *London Journal*, 5: 176–217.

SIMMONS, JACK (1973), 'The Power of the Railway', in Dyos and Wolff (1973), i. 277–310.

STEVENSON, JOHN (1977) (ed.), London in the Age of Reform (Oxford).

—— (1979), *Popular Disturbances in England 1700–1870* (London).

SUMMERSON, JOHN (1973a), *The London Building World of the Eighteen-Sixties* (London).

—— (1973b), 'London, The Artifact', in Dyos and Wolff (1973), i. 311–32.

—— (1990), *The Unromantic Castle and Other Essays* (London), including 'Charting the Victorian World', 157–74; 'The London Building World of the 1860s', 175–92; 'The Victorian Rebuilding of the City of London, 1840–1870', 193–216; 'The London Suburban Villa, 1850–1880', 217–34.

—— (1991), *Georgian London* (illustrated edn., London).

Survey of London (1956), *Southern Lambeth* (*Survey of London*, 26; London).

—— (1973), *Northern Kensington* (*Survey of London*, 37; London).

—— (1977), *Grosvenor Estate in Mayfair* (*Survey of London*, 39; London).

—— (1983), *Southern Kensington: Brompton* (*Survey of London*, 41; London).

—— (1986), *Southern Kensington: Kensington Square to Earl's Court* (*Survey of London*, 42; London).

TAINE, HIPPOLYTE (1957), *Taine's Notes on England*, trans. and introd. Edward Hyams (London), (1st pub. 1872).

TAYLOR, NICHOLAS (1973), *The Village in the City* (London).

THOMAS, BRINLEY (1973), *Migration and Economic Growth: A Study of Great Britain and the Atlantic Economy* (2nd edn., Cambridge).

THOMPSON, E. P. (1968), *The Making of the English Working Class* (Pelican paperback edn., London).

THOMPSON, F. M. L. (1974), *Hampstead: Building a Borough, 1650–1964* (London).

—— (1976), 'Nineteenth-Century Horse Sense', *Economic History Review*, 2nd ser., 29: 60–81.

—— (1982), (ed.), *The Rise of Suburbia* (Leicester).

—— (1983), 'Horses and Hay in Britain 1830–1918', in Thompson (ed.), *Horses in European Economic History: A Preliminary Canter* (British Agricultural History Society, Reading), 50–72.

—— (1988), *The Rise of Respectable Society: A Social History of Victorian Britain 1830–1900* (London).

—— (1990) (ed.), *The Cambridge Social History of Britain 1750–1950*, i. *Regions and Communities* (Cambridge).

—— (1993) (ed.), *The University of London and the World of Learning, 1836–1986* (London).

—— (1995), 'Moving Frontiers and the Fortunes of the Aristocratic Town House 1830–1930', *London Journal*, 20: 67–78.

THOMPSON, PAUL (1967), *Socialists, Liberals and Labour: The Struggle for London 1885–1914* (London).

THORNE, ROBERT (1986), 'The White Hart Lane Estate: An LCC Venture in Suburban Development', *London Journal*, 12: 80–8.

TRISTAN, FLORA (1982), *The London Journal of Flora Tristan 1842*, trans. Jean Hawkes (London).

WALKOWITZ, JUDITH R. (1980), *Prostitution and Victorian Society: Women, Class and the State* (Cambridge).

WALLAS, GRAHAM (1925 edn.), *The Life of Francis Place 1771–1854* (London).

WALLER, P. J. (1991 edn.), *Town, City and Nation: England 1850–1914* (Oxford).

WARD, J. R. (1994), 'The Industrial Revolution and British Imperialism, 1750–1850', *Economic History Review*, 2nd ser., 47: 44–65.

WEIGHTMAN, GAVIN (1992), *Bright Lights, Big City: London Entertained 1830–1950* (London).

—— and HUMPHRIES, STEVE (1983), *The Making of Modern London 1815–1914* (London).

WEINREB, BEN, and HIBBERT, CHRISTOPHER (1992 edn.), *The London Encyclopaedia* (London).

WIENER, MARTIN (1981), *English Culture and the Decline of the Industrial Spirit, 1850–1980* (Cambridge).

WILLIAMS, NAOMI, and MOONEY, GRAHAM (1994), 'Infant Mortality in an "Age of Great Cities": London and the English Provincial Cities compared, c.1840–1910', *Continuity and Change*, 9: 185–212.

WOHL, ANTHONY S. (1977), *The Eternal Slum: Housing and Social Policy in Victorian London* (London).

WRIGLEY, E. A. and SCHOFIELD, R. S. (1981), *The Population History of England 1541–1871: A Reconstruction* (Cambridge).

YOUNG, KEN, and GARSIDE, PATRICIA L. (1982), *Metropolitan London: Politics and Urban Change 1837–1981* (London).

PART VI. THE UNCERTAIN METROPOLIS 1914–1997
(Chapters 20–3)

AGNEW, COLIN, and COOKE, RON (1986), 'Air Pollution Control', in Clout and Wood (1986), 92–100.

ARMSTRONG, JOHN (1996), 'The Development of the Park Royal Industrial Estate in the Inter-War Period: A Re-Examination of the Aldcroft/Richardson Thesis', *London Journal*, 21: 64–79.

BARKER, THEO (1993), 'London: A Unique Megalopolis?', in Theo Barker and Anthony Sutcliffe (eds.), *Megalopolis: The Giant City in History* (Basingstoke), 43–60.

—— (1994), 'Workshop of the World 1870–1914', *History Today*, 44: 30–48.

—— and ROBBINS, MICHAEL (1974), *A History of London Transport: Passenger Travel and the Development of the Metropolis*, ii. *The Twentieth Century to 1970* (London).

BARSON, SUSIE, and SAINT, ANDREW (1988), *A Farewell to Fleet Street* (London).

BATES, L. M. (1985), *The Thames on Fire: The Battle of London River 1939–1945* (Lavenham).

BÉDARIDA, FRANÇOIS (1991), *A Social History of England 1851–1990*, trans. A. S. Forster and Jeffrey Hodgkinson, (2nd edn., London).

BRANSON, NOREEN (1979), *Poplarism, 1919–1925: George Lansbury and the Councillors' Revolt* (London).

BREALEY, R. A., and SORIA, M. (1993), *Revenues from the City's Financial Services* (London Business School City Research Project, Report 1; Corporation of London).

—— and KAPLANIS, E. (1994), *The Growth and Structure of International Banking* (London Business School City Research Project, Report 11; Corporation of London).

BRIMBLECOMBE, PETER (1987), *The Big Smoke: A History of Air Pollution in London since Medieval Times* (London).

CAIN, P. J., and HOPKINS, A. G. (1993), *British Imperialism: Crisis and Deconstruction 1914–1990* (London).

CALDER, ANGUS (1969), *The People's War: Britain 1939–1945* (London).

—— (1991), *The Myth of the Blitz* (London, 1991).

Centre for Economics and Business Research Ltd. *See sub McWilliams.*

City Research Project Reports, *See sub Brealey and Soria; Brealey and Kaplanis; McWilliams; and Rose.*

CLAPSON, MARK (1989), 'Localism, the London Labour Party and the LCC between the Wars', in Saint (1989), 127–45.

CLARKE, W. M. (1965), *The City in the World Economy* (London).

—— (1967), *Britain's Invisible Earnings: The Report of the Committee on Invisible Exports* (Financial Advisory Panel on Exports; London).

—— (1983), *Inside the City: A Guide to London as a Financial Centre* (rev. edn., London).

CLOUT, HUGH (1991) (ed.), *The Times London History Atlas* (London).

—— and Wood, Peter (1986) (eds.), *London: Problems of Change* (London).

COBBETT, WILLIAM (1912 edn.), *Rural Rides*, 2 vols (London).

CROSS, ARTHUR, and TIBBS, FRED (1987), *The London Blitz*, ed. Mike Seaborne (London).

DAHRENDORF, RALF (1982), *On Britain* (London).

DENNIS, RICHARD (1986), 'Housing Problems', in Clout and Wood (1986), 83–91.

FRIEDLANDER, D. (1974), 'London's Urban Transition 1851–1951', *Urban Studies*, 2: 127–41.

—— and ROSHIER, R. J. (1965–6), 'A Study of Internal Migration in England and Wales: Part I', *Population Studies*, 19: 239–79.

GARSIDE, PATRICIA L. (1984), 'West End, East End: 1890–1940', in Anthony Sutcliffe (ed.), *Metropolis 1890–1940* (London), 221–58.

—— (1990), 'London and the Home Counties', in F. M. L. Thompson (ed.), *The Cambridge Social History of Britain 1750–1950*, i. *Regions and Communities* (Cambridge), 471–539.

GILLESPIE, JAMES (1989*a*), 'Municipalism, Monopoly and Management: The Demise of "Socialism in One County", 1918–1933', in Saint (1989), 103–25.

—— (1989b), 'Poplarism and Proletarianism: Unemployment and Labour Politics in London, 1918–34', in David Feldman and Gareth Stedman Jones, *Metropolis London: Histories and Representations since 1800* (London), 163–88.

GLENDINNING, MILES, and MUTHESIUS, STEFAN (1994), *Tower Block: Modern Public Housing in England, Wales and Northern Ireland* (Yale).

GREEN, DAVID R. (1992), 'The Metropolitan Economy: Continuity and Change 1800–1939', in Hoggart and Green (1992), 8–33.

—— and HOGGART, KEITH (1992), 'London: An Uncertain Future', in Hoggart and Green (1992), 220–32.

HALL, JOHN (1994), 'The City and the State: Perspectives from London', *Franco-British Studies: Journal of the British Institute in Paris*, 18: 83–96.

HALL, PETER (1984), 'Postscript: Metropolis 1940–1990', in Anthony Sutcliffe (ed.), *Metropolis 1890–1940* (London), 431–45.

—— (1987a), 'Flight to the Green', *New Society* (9 Jan.)

—— (1987b), 'Europe's Golden Heart', *Sunday Telegraph* (11 Jan.)

—— (1989), *London 2001* (London).

HMSO (1994), *Britain 1995: An Official Handbook* (London).

HOGGART, KEITH (1992), 'London as an Object of Study', in Hoggart and Green (1992), 1–7.

—— and GREEN, DAVID R. (1992) (eds.), *London: A New Metropolitan Geography* (London) (1st pub. 1991).

HUMPHRIES, STEVE, and TAYLOR, JOHN (1986), *The Making of Modern London 1945–1985* (London).

INGHAM, GEOFFREY (1984), *Capitalism Divided? The City and Industry in British Social Development* (London).

Invisibles: Facts and Figures (1993), (British Invisibles, Windsor House, 39 King Street, EC2V 8DQ).

JACKSON, ALAN A. (1973), *Semi-Detached London: Suburban Development, Life and Transport 1900–1939* (London).

JACKSON, PETER (1986), 'Ethnic and Social Conflict', in Clout and Wood (1986), 152–9.

JACKSON, ROBERT (1990), *The London Blitz* (London).

JEWELL, HELEN M. (1994), *The North–South Divide: The Origins of Northern Consciousness in England* (Manchester).

JONES, EMERYS (1992), 'Race and Ethnicity in London', in Hoggart and Green (1992), 176–90.

KING, ANTHONY (1990a), *Urbanism, Colonialism, and the World-Economy: Cultural and Spatial Foundations of the World Urban System* (London).

—— (1990b), *Global Cities: Post-Imperialism and the Internationalization of London* (London).

LEE, C. H. (1986), *The British Economy since 1700: A Macro-Economic Perspective* (Cambridge).

LEOPOLD, ELLEN (1989), 'LCC Restaurants and the Decline of Municipal Enterprise', in Saint (1989), 199–213.

London Economics (1995), *The Role of the City in Company Formation and Growth*, (Report by London Economics; Corporation of London).

LONGMATE, NORMAN (1971), *How We Lived Then: A History of Everyday Life during the Second World War* (London).

—— (1981), *The Doodlebugs: The Story of the Flying Bombs* (London).

MACK, JOANNA, and HUMPHRIES, STEVE (1985), *The Making of Modern London 1939–1945: London at War* (London).

MCWILLIAMS, DOUGLAS (1993), *London's Contribution to the UK Economy* (City Research Project Special Report for the Corporation of London).

—— (1996), *London's Contribution to the UK Economy* (A London Economy Research Programme Special Report prepared by the Centre for Economics and Business Research Ltd.).

MANNERS, GERALD (1986*a*), 'Decentralizing London, 1945–1975', in Clout and Wood (1986), 42–51.

—— (1986*b*), 'Central London', in Clout and Wood (1986), 111–17.

MASON, JOHN (1989), 'Partnership Denied: The London Labour Party on the LCC and the Decline of London Government, 1940–1965', in Saint (1989), 251–64.

MICHIE, RANALD C. (1992), *The City of London: Continuity and Change, 1850–1990* (London).

—— (1997), 'London and the Process of Economic Growth since 1750', *London Journal*, 22: 63–90.

MUNTON, RICHARD (1986), 'The Metropolitan Green Belt', in Clout and Wood (1986), 128–36.

NORTON, ALAN (1983), *The Government and Administration of Metropolitan Areas in Western Democracies* (Birmingham).

O′BRIEN, TERENCE H. (1955), *Civil Defence*, Keith Hancock (ed.), *History of the Second World War*, United Kingdom Civil Series; (London).

OLSEN, DONALD (1964), *Town Planning in London in the Eighteenth and Nineteenth Centuries* (New Haven).

—— (1976), *The Growth of Victorian London* (London).

—— (1986), *The City as a Work of Art: London, Paris, Vienna* (New Haven).

ORWELL, GEORGE (1941), *The Lion and the Unicorn: Socialism and the English Genius* (London).

PERKIN, HAROLD (1989), *The Rise of Professional Society: England since 1880* (London).

PHAROAH, TIM (1992), 'Transport: How Much Can London Take?', in Hoggart and Green (1992), 141–55.

PORTER, ROY (1994), *London: A Social History* (London).

RASMUSSEN, STEEN (1934), *London: The Unique City* (London).

READ, DONALD (1964), *The English Provinces* c. *1760–1960: A Study in Influence* (London).

ROBBINS, MICHAEL (1953), *Middlesex* (London).

ROBSON, BRIAN (1986), 'Coming Full Circle: London versus the Rest 1890–1980', in George Gordon, *Regional Cities in the U.K. 1890–1980* (London), 217–31.

ROSE, HAROLD (1994*a*), *International Banking Developments and London's Position as an International Banking Centre* (London Business School City Research Project Report No. 12; Corporation of London).

—— (1994*b*), *London as an International Financial Centre: A Narrative History* (London Business School City Research Project, Report No. 13; Corporation of London).

RUBINSTEIN, W. D. (1981), *Men of Property: The Very Wealthy in Britain since the Industrial Revolution* (London).

—— (1993), *Capitalism, Culture and Decline in Britain 1750–1990* (London).

SAINT, ANDREW (1989), (ed.), *Politics and the People of London: The London County Council 1889–1965* (London).

SALT, JOHN (1986), 'Population Trends', in Clout and Wood (1986), 52–9.

SHELDRAKE, JOHN (1989), 'The LCC Hospital Service', in Saint (1989), 187–97.

SHEPPARD, DAVID K. (1971), *The Growth and Role of UK Financial Institutions 1880–1962* (London).

SMITH, DAVID (1994 edn.), *North and South: Britain's Economic, Social and Political Divide* (London).

Survey of London (1994), *Popular, Blackwall and the Isle of Dogs* (*Survey of London*, 44; London).

TAYLOR, NICHOLAS (1973), *The Village in the City* (London).

THOMPSON, F. M. L. (1990), *The University of London and the World of Learning 1836–1986* (London).

—— (1995), 'Moving Frontiers and the Fortunes of the Aristocratic Town House 1830–1930', *London Journal*, 20: 67–78.

TITMUSS, RICHARD M. (1950), *Problems of Social Policy* (W. K. Hancock (ed.), *History of the Second World War*, United Kingdom Civil Series; London).

WEIGHTMAN, GAVIN, and HUMPHRIES, STEVE (1984), *The Making of Modern London 1914–1939* (London).

WIENER, MARTIN (1981), *English Culture and the Decline of the Industrial Spirit 1850–1980* (Cambridge).

WOOD, PETER (1986), 'Economic Change', in Clout and Wood (1986), 60–74.

YOUNG, KEN (1975), 'The Conservative Strategy for London, 1855–1975', *London Journal*, 1:56–82

—— and GARSIDE, PATRICIA L. (1982), *Metropolitan London: Politics and Urban Change 1837–1981* (London).

ZIEGLER, PHILIP (1995), *London at War 1939–1945* (London).

INDEX